W9-DBD-391

BLACKS
IN FILM
AND
TELEVISION

Recent Titles in
Bibliographies and Indexes in Afro-American and African Studies

Index to Afro-American Reference Resources
Rosemary M. Stevenson, compiler

A Richard Wright Bibliography: Fifty Years of Criticism and Commentary,
1933-1982
*Keneth Kinnamon, compiler, with the help of Joseph Benson, Michel Fabre,
and Craig Werner*

Index of Subjects, Proverbs, and Themes in the Writings of Wole Soyinka
Greta M. K. Coger, compiler

Southern Black Creative Writers, 1829-1953: Biobibliographies
M. Marie Booth Foster, compiler

The Black Aged in the United States: A Selectively Annotated Bibliography
Lenwood G. Davis, compiler

Àshe, Traditional Religion and Healing in Sub-Saharan Africa and the Diaspora:
A Classified International Bibliography
John Gray, compiler

Black Theatre and Performance: A Pan-African Bibliography
John Gray, compiler

Health of Black Americans from Post Reconstruction to Integration, 1871-1960:
An Annotated Bibliography of Contemporary Sources
Mitchell F. Rice and Woodrow Jones, Jr., compilers

REF.
Z5784
M9
G72
1990

BLACKS
IN FILM
AND
TELEVISION

A Pan-African Bibliography
of Films, Filmmakers,
and Performers

Compiled by
JOHN GRAY

Bibliographies and Indexes in Afro-American
and African Studies, Number 27

GREENWOOD PRESS
New York • Westport, Connecticut • London

NO LONGER THE PROPERTY
OF THE
UNIVERSITY OF R. I. LIBRARY
22108640

Library of Congress Cataloging-in-Publication Data

Gray, John
   Blacks in film and television : a Pan-African bibliography of
films, filmmakers, and performers / compiled by John Gray.
      p.   cm. — (Bibliographies and indexes in Afro-American and
African studies, ISSN 0742-6925 ; no. 27)
   Includes index.
   ISBN 0-313-27486-X (lib. bdg. : alk. paper)
   1. Motion pictures—Africa—Bibliography. 2. Motion picture
industry—Africa—Bibliography. 3. Afro-American motion picture
actors and actresses—Bibliography. 4. Afro-Americans in the motion
picture industry—Bibliography. 5. Afro-Americans in television
broadcasting—Bibliography. 6. Afro-Americans in motion pictures—
Bibliography. I. Title. II. Series.
Z5784.M9G72   1990
[PN1993.5.A35]
016.79143'096—dc20   90-3934

British Library Cataloguing in Publication Data is available.

Copyright © 1990 by John Gray

All rights reserved. No portion of this book may be
reproduced, by any process or technique, without the
express written consent of the publisher.

Library of Congress Catalog Card Number: 90-3934
ISBN: 0-313-27486-X
ISSN: 0742-6925

First published in 1990

Greenwood Press, 88 Post Road West, Westport, CT 06881
An imprint of Greenwood Publishing Group, Inc.

Printed in the United States of America

The paper used in this book complies with the
Permanent Paper Standard issued by the National
Information Standards Organization (Z39.48-1984).

10 9 8 7 6 5 4 3 2 1

Contents

Acknowledgments

In this, my fourth book-length bibliography, I must give thanks once again for the collections of the various Research Divisions of the New York Public Library as well as for the Inter-Library Loan staffs of both the New York Public and Greenwich Libraries. Without the existence of these collections and the help of their ILL staffs a study of this breadth and depth would not be possible. I only hope that New York City's fiscal woes do not serve to further constrict the already limited hours these institutions are now open. To filmmakers William Greaves and St. Clair Bourne I extend an additional note of thanks for their prompt responses to my informational requests. To those who didn't respond - they know who they are...

I realize that acknowledgments to family, friends and loved ones are frowned upon by authors of professional writing guides but I have decided for the fourth time to ignore their advice and pay tribute to my mother. Without her continued assistance in things both related and unrelated to this work I doubt that it would have been completed.

Introduction

Five years ago, when I began the initial research for this
work, I examined a number of the best known books on "black
film" and came up with several key questions. First, where
were the stories of blacks behind the camera, the stories of
the filmmakers, the actors, the technicians, the producers?
Had there been any? If there had been who were they? And,
most importantly, had any written or visual material been done
on them? Also, what about black film traditions or activity
outside of the U.S.? What had been or was being done in
Europe, Africa, the Caribbean and Latin America? Since nobody
seemed ready to provide an answer I decided then to focus my
attention on these areas.

After this my next step was to decide what the criterion
for inclusion and exclusion, both in terms of topics and
individuals as well as types of materials, should be. In the
latter case the answer was simple. As with my previous
bibliographies I opted for the most inclusive policy possible,
stipulating only that the items to be included needed to be
verifiable by myself. Types of materials included range from
books, dissertations, unpublished papers, and periodical and
newspaper articles, to films, videotapes and audiotapes in
most of the major Western languages.

On the issue of topics and individuals my choices have
been somewhat more subjective and selective. In the case of
the Africa section I have decided to include a good deal of
information on both colonial and ethnographic film activity as
well as works on indigenous African films and filmmaking.
This is to provide the researcher with some sense of the
images to which both African and non-African audiences were
exposed prior to the introduction of indigenous African film
activity. In addition I thought it might be useful to include
works which chronicle the types of film activity which led up
to or at least pre-dated the coming of indigenous African
filmmaking. For the U.S., on the other hand, I have chosen to
offer only selective, albeit extensive, coverage of works on
films made by white filmmakers. Materials on seventeen of
these, those judged by the author to have the most historical
importance in terms of their representation of the African
American image from 1915 to 1989, may be found at the end of
the General Works section of the United States chapter.

In this edition I have chosen not to include material on television in the African context but will seek to remedy this in future editions. For the U.S. I have offered only selective coverage due to the large number of recent bibliographies on the subject--# 3182-3183, 3186, 3194, 5988-5992. In the only other editorial choice of note, I have decided to include talk show hosts along with actors and actresses in the individual actors and actresses chapter.   TV journalists have been excluded.

To ensure comprehensiveness I began my research with Anne Powers (5969) and Marshall Hyatt's (5968) African American film bibliographies as well the more recent works on sub-Saharan African film by Francoise Pfaff (748) and Nancy J. Schmidt (5952). Then I set out to do a systematic search of as many and as wide a variety of other finding sources as possible. A few of the works included in this strategy were the Index to Periodical Articles By and About Blacks, Film Literature Index, International Index to Film Periodicals, A Current Bibliography on African Affairs, International African Bibliography, African Book Publishing Record, hundreds of individual clipping files in the Billy Rose Theatre Collection of the New York Public Library's Lincoln Center branch, all relevant vertical files in the NYPL's Schomburg Center for Research in Black Culture, along with the complete runs of some 19 black journals and newspapers. In addition I was also able to search most, if not all, of the currently available CD ROMs--Magazine Index, Academic Index, Reader's Guide to Periodical Literature, MLA International Bibliography, and Biography Index, as well as the 30,000,000 item library database RLIN (Research Libraries Information Network). Supplementing this was material found in my own Black Arts Database, a bibliographic resource containing some 30,000+ entries on arts activity in Africa and the African Diaspora. (For a more complete list of sources consulted see Appendix I)

Accuracy of the book-length citations was achieved by checking each one against the Library of Congress's National Union Catalogue and/or the RLIN and OCLC library databases. When a U.S. location for a work was not listed, the library where it may be found, if known, has been included in brackets after the citation. In addition I have tried to view as many of the journal articles as possible to ensure their accuracy as well.

Whenever possible I have also supplied the birth and death dates and countries of origin of the filmmakers and performers included. Any information on filmmakers or performers for whom I have been unable to locate this information or corrections of inaccurate data will be most appreciated.

For those seeking more general information on some of the countries covered in Blacks in Film and Television, see both the opening section on Cultural History and the Arts and the extensive listing of reference works in Appendix I. Film resources--archives, support organizations, individual production companies, film distributors and film festivals, may be found in Appendix II. Four separate indices--Artist, which includes filmmakers, producers, screenwriters and performers; Title, which lists all film and television titles cited; and Subject and Author Indexes--complete the work.

Organization

Materials in <u>Blacks in Film and Television</u> are broken down
into two basic categories--studies of film/TV in regional
areas and individual countries, and studies of individual
filmmakers and their films. In addition these categories are
further divided into types of materials included: books; book
sections; dissertations, theses and unpublished papers;
journals; articles; and media materials. This system should
become clear after a glance at some of the book's opening
sections.

Availability of Works

Because the bulk of the research for this project was carried
out at two of the New York Public Library's Research Divisions
I can safely say that a majority of the works included here
may be found in those collections:

New York Public Library - Billy Rose Theatre Collection of the
Performing Arts Research Center at Lincoln Center (111
Amsterdam Ave., New York, NY 10023. Tel. 212/870-1639).

New York Public Library - Schomburg Center for Research in
Black Culture (515 Lenox Ave., New York, NY 10037. Tel.
212/862-4000).

For those who don't have access to these collections the best
alternative is the inter library loan department of your
school or local library as well as use of the publishers'
contact addresses in <u>African Books in Print</u>, <u>African Book
Publishing Record</u>, <u>International Literary Market Place</u> and
<u>Books in Print</u>.

I

CULTURAL HISTORY AND THE ARTS

A. ORAL LITERATURE

1. Finnegan, Ruth. <u>Oral Literature in Africa</u>. Oxford: Oxford University Press, 1970. 558p.

2. Okpewho, Isidore. <u>The Epic in Africa: Towards a Poetics of the Oral Performance</u>. New York: Columbia University Press, 1979. 240p.

B. CULTURAL HISTORY AND THE ARTS - AFRICA

3. Asante, Molefi K. <u>The Afrocentric Idea</u>. Philadelphia: Temple University Press, 1987. 232p.

4. _____, and Kariamu Welsh Asante, eds. <u>African Culture: The Rhythms of Unity</u>. Westport, CT: Greenwood Press, 1985. 270p.

5. Balandier, Georges, and Jacques Maquet, general editors. <u>Dictionary of Black African Civilization</u>. New York: L. Amiel, 1974. 350p.

6. Bascom, William R., and Melville J. Herskovits. "The Problem of Stability and Change in African Culture." In <u>Continuity and Change in African Cultures</u>. Chicago: University of Chicago Press, 1959, pp. 1-14.

7. <u>Black Aesthetics: papers from a colloquium held at the University of Nairobi, June, 1971</u>. Edited by Andrew Gurr and Pio Zirimu. Nairobi: East African Literature Bureau, 1973. 216p.

8. Egbujie, Ihemalol I. <u>The Hermeneutics of the African Traditional Culture: An Intrepretive Analysis of African Culture</u>. Roxbury, MA: Omenana, 1985. 175p.

9. Gabel, Creighton, and Norman R. Bennett, eds. <u>Reconstructing African Cultural History</u>. Boston: Boston University Press, 1967. 246p.

10. Maquet, Jean-Noel. _Africanity: The Cultural Unity of Black Africa_. Trans. by Joan Rayfield. New York: Oxford University Press, 1972. 188p.

11. Murdock, George P. _Africa: Its Peoples and Their Culture History_. New York: McGraw-Hill, 1959. 456p.

12. Murray, Jocelyn, ed. _Cultural Atlas of Africa_. New York: Facts on File, 1981. 240p.

13. Okpaku, Joseph, ed. _The Arts and Civilization of Black and African Peoples_. Lagos, Nigeria: Centre for Black and African Arts and Civilization, 1986. 10 vols.

14. _____. _New African Literature and the Arts_. New York: Thomas Crowell, 1969-1973. 3 vols.

15. Sofola, J. A. _African Culture and the African Personality: What Makes an African Person African_. Ibadan, Nigeria: African Resources Publishers Co., 1973. 168p.

Journals

16. _L'Afrique Litteraire et Artistique_, No. 1-52/53 (Octobre 1968-2e/3e trimestre 1979). Continued by _Afrique Litteraire_.

17. _Arts and Africa_ (BBC African Service, British Broadcasting Corporation, PO Box 76, Bush House, Strand, London WC2B 4PH). 1970- . Transcripts of the BBC's "Arts and Africa" show.

18. _Cultural Events in Africa_ (London), No. 1 (December 1964) - No. 117 (December 1975). Ceased publication(?).

Articles

19. "Arts, Human Behavior and Africa." _African Studies Bulletin_, Vol. 5, No. 2 (May 1962). Special issue edited by Alan Merriam.

20. Barber, Karin. "The Popular Arts in Africa." _African Studies Review_, Vol. 30, No. 3 (September 1987). Special issue.

21. Diop, Cheikh Anta. "L'Unite Culturelle Africaine." _Presence Africaine_, No. 24-25 (fevrier-mai 1959): 60-65.

22. Fabian, Johannes. "Popular Culture in Africa: Findings and Conjectures." _Africa_, Vol. 48, No. 4 (1978): 315-334.

23. Harper, Peggy. "The Role of the Arts in Education in Africa." _Teacher Education_, Vol. 8, No. 2 (November 1967): 105-109.

24. Herskovits, Melville J. "The Culture Areas of Africa." _Africa_, Vol. 3 (1930): 59-77.

25. Liyong, Taban Lo. "The Role of the Artist in Contemporary Africa." _East Africa Journal_ (January 1969): 29-39.

26. Moore, Gerald. "The Arts in the New Africa." _African Affairs_, Vol. 66, No. 263 (April 1967): 140-148.

27. Nwoko, Demas. "The Aesthetics of African Art and Culture." _New Culture_, Vol. 1, No. 1 (1978): 3-6.

28. Sieber, Roy. "The Arts and Their Changing Social Function." _Annals of the New York Academy of Sciences_, Vol. 96, No. 2 (January 1962): 653-658.

Festival Culturel Panafricain (Algiers)

29. Festival Culturel Panafricain, 1st, Algiers, 1969. _La Culture Africaine; Le Symposium d'Alger. 21 juillet-1er aout 1969_. Alger: Societe Nationale d'Edition et de Diffusion, 1969. 402p.

30. Festival Culturel Panafricain, 1st, Algiers, 1969. _1er [Premier] Festival Culturel Panafricain, Alger, 1969_. Textes reunis et presentes par Omar Mokhtari. Alger: Editions Actualite Algerie, 1970(?). 310p.

31. Organization of African Unity. _Panafrican Cultural Manifesto. First All-African Cultural Festival, Algiers, 21st July-1st August 1969_. New York: Executive Secretariat of the OAU, 1969. 20p.

Articles

32. Hare, Nathan. "Algiers 1969." _Black Scholar_, Vol. 1 (November 1969): 2-10.

33. "Pan-African Cultural Festival. The first, held in Algeria, in the city of Algiers, during 12 days of July 1969." _Jet_ (August 14 1969): 54-57.

34. "Pan-African Cultural Festival. The first, July 21-August 1, 1969 held in Algeria." _Freedomways_, Vol. 9, 4th Quarter (1969): 355-364.

First World Festival of Negro Arts (Dakar)

35. World Festival of Negro Arts, 1st, Dakar, 1966. _Festival Mondial des Arts Negres. Dakar, 1-24 avril 1966_. Paris: Impressions Andre Rousseau, 1966. 125p.

36. _____. _Premier Festival Mondial des Arts Negres_. Versailles: Editions Delroisse; Paris: Bouchet-Lakara, 1967. 155p.

Articles

37. "The Art of Africa for the Whole World. An account of the first World Festival in Dakar, Senegal, April 1-24, 1966." _Negro History Bulletin_ (Fall 1966): 171-172, 185-186.

38. Eliet, Edouard. "First World Festival of Black Man's Art." _Life_ (April 22 1966): 83-88.

39. "First World Festival of Negro Arts, April 1-24, 1966 (Dakar)." Negro Digest (August 1965): 62-69.

40. Fuller, Hoyt W. "World Festival of Negro Arts: Senegal Fete Illustrates Philosophy of 'Negritude'." Ebony (July 1966): 97-102, 104, 106.

41. Furay, Michael. "Negritude and the Dakar Festival." Bulletin of the Association for African Literature in English, No. 4 (1966): 1-12.

42. Greaves, William. "The First World Festival of Negro Arts: An Afro-American View." The Crisis (June-July 1966): 309-314, 332.

43. Povey, John. "The Dakar Festival of the Arts and the Commonwealth." Journal of Commonwealth Literature, Vol. 3 (July 1967): 103-106.

44. _____. "The First World Festival of Negro Arts at Dakar." Journal of the New African Literature and the Arts, No. 2 (Fall 1966): 24-30.

45. Senghor, Leopold Sedar. "The Function and Meaning of the First World Festival of Negro Arts." African Forum, Vol. 1, No. 4 (Spring 1966): 5-10.

46. World Festival of Negro Arts - Vertical File [Microfiche - Schomburg Center]

Newspaper Articles

47. Garrison, Lloyd. "Debate on 'Negritude' Splits Festival in Dakar." New York Times (April 24 1966).

48. _____. "'The Duke and Those Fabulous Dancers.'" New York Times (April 24 1966).

49. _____. "A Gentle Cold-War Wind Wafts Through Senegal's Festival of Negro Arts." New York Times (April 19 1966).

50. _____. "Real Bursts Through the Unreal at Dakar Festival." New York Times (April 26 1966).

51. Malraux, Andre. "Behind the Mask of Africa; artistic heritage; dancing, music, literature, sculpture." New York Times Magazine (May 15 1966): 30-31+.

52. Shepard, Richard F. "105 U.S. Negro Artists Prepare for Senegal Arts Fete in April." New York Times (February 11 1966).

53. Strongin, Theodore. "Senegal to Hold Negro Arts Fete. International event to begin in Dakar in December 1965." New York Times (June 1964).

Media Materials

54. The First World Festival of Negro Arts (film). Dir.,
William Greaves. 20 minutes. New York, McGraw-Hill, 1968.

55. Nagenda, John. The First World Festival of Negro Arts
(audiotape). London: Transcription Feature Service, 1966.
Duration: 29'09". Tape consisting of personal comments by
various individuals concerning their impressions of The First
World Festival of Negro Arts held in Dakar, Senegal, April 1-
24, 1966. [Held by the Schomburg Center - Sc Audio C-105
(Side 2, no. 1)]

Second World Black and African Festival
of Arts and Culture/FESTAC 77 (Lagos)

56. Festac '77. London: Africa Journal Ltd., 1977. 152p.
Souvenir book of the 2nd World Black and African Festival of
Arts and Culture in Lagos, Nigeria.

57. Moore, Sylvia. The Afro-Black Connection: FESTAC 77.
Amsterdam: Royal Tropical Institute, 1977. 149p. Report for
the Dutch Ministry of Culture on the second World Black and
African Festival of Arts and Culture.

58. Pageants of the African World. Lagos: Nigeria Magazine,
1980. 122p.

59. World Black and African Festival of Arts and Culture, 2d,
Lagos, 1977. Programme General/Deuxieme Festival Mondial des
Arts Negro-Africains ; Festac '77, 15 jan-12 fev 1977, Lagos,
Kaduna. Lagos: Division de la Publicite, International
Secretariat, 1977. 48p.

Articles

60. Donaldson, Jeff. "FESTAC '77: a pan-Afrikan success."
Black Collegian (May-June 1977): 32, 64.

61. Enohoro, Ife. "Second World Black and African Festival
of Arts and Culture: Lagos, Nigeria." Black Scholar
(September 1977): 26-33.

62. "FESTAC: Festival de Arte e Cultura Negro-Africana."
Tempo, No. 335 (Marco 6 1977): 20-26.

63. "FESTAC 77." The Nigerian Year Book 1977-78, pp. 9-46.

64. "Festac '77 in Camera." Africa (London), No. 67 (March
1977): 72-79.

65. Festac '77 - Vertical File [Schomburg Center]

66. "Focus on the 2nd World Black and African Festival of
Arts and Culture." Africa (London), No. 59 (July 1976): 115-
130.

67. Fuller, Hoyt W. "Festac '77: A Footnote." First World
(March/April 1977): 26-27.

6   Cultural History and the Arts

8. Hobbs, Gloria L. "Human Rights Through Cultural
Expression." The Crisis (August-September 1977): 376-377.

69. Johnson, Efe. "Memories of FESTAC: The Afro-American
Experience and Charge." Black Ivory: The Pan-Africanist
Magazine, Vol. 1, No. 1 (1988): 18-20.

70. Jordan, Millicent Dobbs. "Durbar at Kaduna." First
World (March/April 1977): 27.

71. Kay, Iris. "FESTAC 1977." African Arts, Vol. 11, No. 1
(October 1977): 50-51.

72. Monroe, Arthur. "Festac 77 - The Second World Black and
African Festival of Arts and Culture: Lagos, Nigeria." Black
Scholar (September 1977): 34-37.

73. Morgan, Clyde. "International Exchange: the 2nd World
Festival of Black Art and Culture; Lagos." Dance Magazine
(July 1977): 90.

74. Musa, Mamoun B. "The Spirit of FESTAC 77." Sudanow,
Vol. 2, No. 3 (March 1977): 39-41.

75. Opubor, Alfred E. "FESTAC Colloquium: Prolegomena to
Black Though?" Afriscope (March 1977): 7, 9, 11-12, 15, 17.

76. Poinsett, Alex. "Festac '77. Second World Black and
African Festival of Arts and Culture draws 17,000 participants
to Lagos." Ebony (May 1977): 33-36, 38, 40, 44-46.

77. _____. "47 Black Nations Gather for Festac '77 in
Lagos, Nigeria." Jet (February 17 1977): 14-15.

78. Pringle, James. "Searching for Black Roots; World Black
and African Festival of Arts and Culture." Newsweek (February
14 1977): 40+.

79. Said, Abdulkadir N. "Festac '77; More Than Song and
Dance." New Directions: The Howard University Magazine, Vol.
4, No. 2 (April 1977): 4-13.

80. "Spotlight on Festac '77." Africa (London), No. 62
(October 1976): 111-126.

81. "Spotlight on Festac '77." Africa (London), No. 65
(January 1977). Special twenty page section starting after
page 47.

82. "29 days that shook the black world." Ebony (May 1977):
48-49.

83. Waters, Ronald. "Festac Colloquium: A Viewpoint." New
Directions, Vol. 4, No. 2 (April 1977): 14-15.

Newspaper Articles

84. "Cultural Lift for Africa." Christian Science Monitor
(February 15 1977).

85. Darnton, John. "African Woodstock Overshadows Festival."
New York Times (January 29 1977).

86. Ezenekwe, Arthur O. "African Festival: Many Tongues but
One Identity." Christian Science Monitor (February 14 1977).

87. Kuhn, Annette. "Finally...Festac." Village Voice
(December 27 1976).

88. Loercher, Diana. "Black Culture Looks Towards its
Biggest World Festival." Christian Science Monitor (June 30
1975): 23.

Media Materials

89. Festac '77 (1977). Produced and Directed by Regge Life.
12 min. (3/4 inch color video) / 7 min. (16mm color). Brief
chronicle of opening day ceremonies. [Available from the
Black Filmmaker Foundation, 80 Eighth Ave., Suite 1704, New
York, NY 10011. Tel. 212/924-1198]

C. REGIONAL STUDIES

West Africa

BURKINA FASO (Upper Volta)

90. Novicki, Margaret A. "Burkina Faso: A Revolutionary
Culture." Africa Report (July-August 1987): 57-60.

CAMEROON

91. Bahoken, J. C., and Engelbert Atangana. Cultural Policy
in the United Republic of Cameroon. Paris: The Unesco Press,
1976. 91p. (Studies and documents on cultural policies)

GHANA (Gold Coast)

92. Antubam, Kofi. Ghana's Heritage of Culture. Leipzig:
Koehler & Amelang, 1963. 221p.

93. Ghana. Ministry of Education and Culture. Cultural
Division. Cultural Policy in Ghana: A Study. Paris: Unesco
Press, 1975. 50p. (Studies and Documents on Cultural
Policies)

Journals and Newsletters

94. Arts Council of Ghana Newsletter (Accra, P.O. Box 2738).
The Council. Vol. 1, No. 1, March 1975- . Monthly.

95. Ghana Cultural Review, Vol. 1, No. 1, 1965- .

96. Journal of the Performing Arts (School of Performing
Arts, University of Ghana, PO Box 19, Accra, Ghana). Vol. 1,
No. 1 (Jan. 1980-). Semi-annual.

Articles

97. Daniel, Ebow. "Dignity and 'Dondology'." West Africa (June 20 1988): 1112-1113. On the 25th anniversary of the School of Performing Arts.

98. Hammond, Albert. "The Moving Drama of the Arts in Ghana." Sankofa Magazine, Vol. 1, No. 2-3 (1977): 7-10, 13-14.

99. Nketia, J. H. Kwabena. "The Creative Arts and the Community." Proceedings of the Ghana Academy of Arts and Sciences (Accra), Vol. 8 (1970): 71-76.

100. Novicki, Margaret A. "Interview with Mohammed Ben Abdallah Secretary of Education and Culture, Ghana." Africa Report (July-August 1987): 14-18.

GUINEA

101. Guinea. Ministere du domaine de l'education et de la culture. Cultural Policy in the Revolutionary People's Republic of Guinea. Paris: Unesco, 1979. 90p. (Studies and documents on cultural policies)

LIBERIA

102. Best, Kenneth Y. Cultural Policy in Liberia. Paris: UNESCO Press, 1974. 59p. (Studies and Documents on Cultural Policies)

103. Dorsinville, Roger. "Rediscovering Our Cultural Values." In Black People and Their Culture. Washington, D.C.: Smithsonian Institution, 1976, pp. 130-137.

104. Moore, Bai T. "Cultural Involvement and Policy of the Ministry of Information, Cultural Affairs and Tourism." Paper presented at the Seminar on African Studies, July 18-19, 1974, University of Liberia, Monrovia, Liberia. 8p.

NIGERIA

105. Andah, Bassey W. "Cultural Studies and Development." In African Development in Cultural Perspective, with special reference to Nigeria. Ibadan: Dept. of Archaeology and Anthropology, University of Ibadan, 1982, pp. 1-21.

106. Fasuyi, T. A. Cultural Policy in Nigeria. Paris: UNESCO, 1973. 63p. (Studies and Documents on Cultural Policies)

107. Unoh, S. O., ed. Cultural Development and Nation Building: the Nigerian scene as perceived from the Cross River State. Ibadan: Spectrum Books, 1986. 157p.

Journals

108. Abinibi. November 1986-- . Lagos: Lagos State Council for Arts and Culture.

Articles

109. Ajayi-Bembe, Alex. "Lagos State Festival of Arts and Culture Zone Competitions, August 1987." _Abinibi_ (Lagos), Vol. 2, No. 3 (July-September 1987): 13-28.

110. Ali, Z. S. "Centre for Black and African Arts and Civilization." _Nigeria Magazine_, No. 128-129 (1979): 55-61.

111. Barrett, Lindsay. "The Popular Arts in Nigeria in the 1980s." _Positive Review_, Vol. 1, No. 4 (1981): 24-27.

112. Nzekwu, Onuora. "Nigeria, Negritude and the World Festival of the Arts." _Nigeria Magazine_, No. 89 (June 1966): 80-94.

113. Sonuga, Gbenga. "Nigerian Cultural Centres: Government Sponsorship of the Arts." _New Culture_, Vol. 1, No. 10 (1979): 39-52.

114. _____. "The Performing Arts in Contemporary Nigeria." _New Culture_, Vol. 1, No. 1 (November 1978): 35-42; Vol. 1, No. 2 (January 1979): 37-42.

115. Tio, A. "Second Ife Festival of the Arts." _Nigeria Magazine_, No. 102 (September-November 1969): 516-525.

SENEGAMBIA

116. Hoover, Deborah A. "Developing a Cultural Policy in The Gambia: Problems and Progress." _Journal of Arts Management & Law_, Vol. 18, No. 3 (Fall 1988): 31-39.

117. M'Bengue, Mamadou Seyni. _Cultural Policy in Senegal_. Paris: UNESCO, 1973. 61p.

SIERRA LEONE

118. Abraham, Arthur. _Cultural Policy in Sierra Leone_. Paris: Unesco, 1978. 75p. (Studies and documents on cultural policies)

TOGO

119. Aithnard, K. M. _Some Aspects of Cultural Policy in Togo_. Paris: Unesco Press, 1976. 101p. (Studies and documents on cultural policies)

Central and Southern Africa

SOUTH AFRICA (Azania)

120. Campschreur, Willem, and Joost Divendal, eds. _Culture in Another South Africa_. New York: Olive Branch Press, 1989. 288p.

Articles

121. "Botha Shall Be Trampled." West Africa (June 13 1988):
1099. On Amandla, the Cultural Ensemble of the ANC.

122. "Culture Against Apartheid." African Recorder (New
Delhi), Vol. 28, No. 2 (January 15-28 1989): 7743.

123. "Culture and Struggle in Africa." Southern Africa
Report (427 Bloor St. W, Toronto, M55 1X7), Vol. 4, No. 1
(July 1988). Special issue.

124. Dadson, Nanabanyin. "Speaking with one Voice." West
Africa (June 27 1988): 1190. On a tour by the South African
Artistes United in Accra, Ghana.

125. "The Fantastic 'Amandla'." Sechaba (July 1981): 117-122.
On a European tour by the ANC's Cultural Ensemble.

126. Herbstein, Denis. "Reporter's Notebook: The Hazards of
Cultural Deprivation." Africa Report (July-August 1987):
33-35.

127. Masekela, Barbara. "The ANC and the Cultural Boycott."
Africa Report (July-August 1987): 19-21.

128. "Previews and Reviews: Amandla." Westindian Digest, No.
123 (October 1985): 40-42. Review of a London performance by
the ANC's cultural ensemble, Amandla.

ZAIRE (Belgian Congo) and CONGO (Brazzaville)

129. Cultural Policy in the Republic of Zaire: a study.
Prepared under the direction of Bokonga Ekanga Botombele.
Paris: Unesco Press, 1976. 119p. (Studies and documents on
cultural policies)

130. Kangafu-Kutumbagana. Discours sur l'Authenticite; essai
sur la problematique ideologique de "Recours a
l'Authenticite". Kinshasa: Les Presses Africaines, 1973.
58p.

131. Musangi Ntemo. "A la decouverte de la vie culturelle a
Kinshasa." Zaire-Afrique, No. 235 (1989): 237-246.

132. Ndakivangi Mantumba Nimambu. Heritage Culturel Zairois.
Kinshasa: CEDI, 1978(?). 118p.

133. World Black and African Festival of Arts and Culture,
2nd, Lagos, 1977. Le Congo au Festival de Lagos, 1977.
Brazzaville: Republique Populaire du Congo, Ministere de
l'Enseignement Superieur, Charge de la Culture et des Arts,
1977. 43p. Photos.

ZIMBABWE (Southern Rhodesia)

134. Chifunyise, Stephen J. Culture and the Performing Arts
in Zimbabwe. Harare: the Author, 1984. 16p.

135. Index of Arts and Cultural Organizations in Zimbabwe as
at June 1985. Harare: National Arts Foundation of Zimbabwe,
1985. 9p.

East Africa

136. East African Institute of Social and Cultural Affairs.
East Africa's Cultural Heritage. Nairobi: East African
Publishing House, 1966. 128p. (Contemporary African
Monographs, No. 4)

137. p'Bitek, Okot. Africa's Cultural Revolution. Nairobi:
Macmillan Books for Africa, 1973. 109p.

ETHIOPIA (Abyssinia)

138. Eshete, Aleme. The Cultural Situation in Socialist
Ethiopia. Paris: Unesco, 1982. 56p. (Studies and documents
on cultural policies)

KENYA

139. Kipkorir, B. E. Towards a Cultural Policy for Kenya:
Some Views. Nairobi: Institute of African Studies, University
of Nairobi, 1980. 9p. (Paper No. 131)

140. Ndeti, Kivuto. Cultural Policy in Kenya. Paris: UNESCO
Press, 1975. 70p.

MALAWI

141. Baraza: A Journal of the Arts in Malawi. No. 1- ,
1983- . Zomba, Malawi: Dept. of Fine and Performing Arts.
Chancellor College.

MOZAMBIQUE

142. Sachs, Albie. "Mozambican Culture: A Crowded Canvas."
Southern Africa Report (Toronto), Vol. 4, No. 1 (July 1988):
21-24.

SUDAN (Anglo-Egyptian Sudan)

143. Mohamed Abdel Hai. Cultural Policy in the Sudan.
Paris: UNESCO Press, 1982. 43p. (Studies and Documents on
Cultural Policies)

TANZANIA (Tanganyika & Zanzibar)

144. Mbughuni, L. A. The Cultural Policy of the United
Republic of Tanzania. Paris: UNESCO Press, 1974. 72p.

145. Ministry of Arts and Culture. Dar es Salaam:
Sub-Committee on Publications, Committee for the Preparations
for Black and African Festival of Arts and Culture. Dar es
Salaam: Ministry of National Culture and Youth, 1977. 74p.

146. Mlamma, Penina O. "Tanzania's Cultural Policy and its
Implications for the Contribution of the Arts to Socialist
Development." Utafiti, Vol. 7, No. 1 (1985): 9-19. Part of a
special issue on Tanzanian cultural policy.

D. CULTURAL HISTORY AND THE ARTS - AFRICAN DIASPORA

147. Crahan, Margaret E., and Franklin W. Knight, eds.
Africa and the Caribbean: The Legacies of a Link. Baltimore:
Johns Hopkins University Press, 1979. 159p.

148. Fraginals, Manuel Moreno, ed. Africa in Latin America:
Essays on History, Culture and Socialization. Trans. Leonor
Blum. New York: Holmes & Meier, 1984. 342p. [Originally
published as Africa en America Latina. Mexico: Siglo
Veintiuno Editores, 1977].

149. Harris, Joseph E., ed. Global Dimensions of the African
Diaspora. Washington, D.C.: Howard University Press, 1982.
419p.

150. Herskovits, Melville J. The New World Negro; Selected
Papers in Afroamerican Studies. Bloomington: Indiana
University Press, 1966. 370p.

151. Irwin, Graham W. Africans Abroad: A Documentary History
of the Black Diaspora in Asia, Latin America, and the
Caribbean during the age of Slavery. New York: Columbia
University Press, 1977. 408p.

152. Jahn, Jahnheinz. Muntu: An Outline of the New African
Culture. Trans. by Marjorie Grene. New York: Grove Press,
1961. 267p.

153. Kilson, Martin L., and Robert I. Rotberg, eds. The
African Diaspora: Interpretive Essays. Cambridge: Harvard
University Press, 1976. 510p.

154. Knight, Franklin W. The African Dimension in Latin
American Societies. New York: Macmillan, 1974. 148p.

155. Nunez, Benjamin. Dictionary of Afro-Latin American
Civilization. Westport, CT: Greenwood Press, 1980. 525p.

156. Pescatello, Ann M., ed. The African in Latin America.
New York: Alfred A. Knopf, 1975. 270p.

157. Price, Richard. Maroon Societies: Rebel Slave
Communities in the Americas. New York: Doubleday/Anchor,
1973. 429p.

158. Rout, Leslie B. The African Experience in Spanish
America, 1502 to the Present Day. Cambridge: Cambridge
University Press, 1976. 404p.

Newsletters

159. African Diaspora Studies Newsletter (Howard University
Press, 2900 Van Ness St., N.W., Washington, DC 20008). Vol.
1, No. 1, 1984- .

160. Newsletter: Who is Doing What in the Field of
Afroamerican Studies (P.O. Box 70626, Caracas (1070)
Venezuela). Editor: Dr. Angelina Pollak-Eltz. Important
source of information on current research and conference
activities in South, Central and North America with listings
of new books, scholars and research projects.

Articles

161. Chapman, Abraham. "The Black Aesthetic and the African
Continuum." Pan African Journal (Fall 1971): 397-406.

162. Herskovits, Melville J. "On the Provenience of New
World Negroes." Social Forces, Vol. XII, No. 2 (December
1933): 247-262.

163. Songolo, Aliko. "Muntu Reconsidered: From Tempels and
Kagame to Jahnheinz Jahn." Ufahamu, Vol. X, No. 3 (Spring
1981): 92-100.

E. REGIONAL STUDIES - AFRICAN DIASPORA

164. "The Arts." Caribbean Quarterly, Vol. 14, No. 1/2
(1968). Special issue on the arts in the English-speaking
Caribbean.

165. Hill, Errol. "The Emergence of a Caribbean Aesthetic."
Bim, Vol. 17, Nos. 66-67 (June 1983).

166. Symposium on Women in Caribbean Culture (1st: 1981:
Barbados). Journey in the Shaping; report of the First
Symposium on Women in Caribbean Culture--July 24, 1981, ed.
Margaret Hope. n.p.: Women and Development Unit, University
of West Indies, 1981?. 59p.

BARBADOS

167. Just a Few Notes: the Newsletter of the Musicians and
Entertainers Guild of Barbados. Worthing, Barbados: the
Guild, 1977- .

168. Venner, Mary Greaves. "CARIFESTA '81 in Barbados."
Bulletin of Eastern Caribbean Affairs, Vol. 7, No. 2 (May-June
1981): 14-16.

169. Vir, Parminda. "CARIFESTA, Barbados 1981." Frontline
(November-December 1981): 128.

170. Whitman, Kay. "Of Roots, Rhythm and Regional Identity."
Commonwealth (November 1981): 24-25. Review of CARIFESTA '81.

BRAZIL

171. Congresso Afro-Brasileiro (3rd : 1982 : Recife, Brazil).
Os Afro-Brasileiros: anais do III Congresso Afro-Brasileiro,
coordenacao, Roberto Motta. Recife: Fundacao Joaquim Nabuco,
Editora Massangana, 1985. 159p.

172. Freyre, Gilberto. The Masters and the Slaves: A Study
in the Development of Brazilian Civilization. Trans. from the
Portuguese by Samuel Putnam. 2nd ed., rev. Berkeley:
University of California Press, 1986. 537p.

173. Kubik, Gerhard. "Extensionen Afrikanischer Kulturen in
Brasilien." Wiener Ethnohistorische Blatter, Heft 21 (1981):
3-75. Summary in English and Portuguese. Continued in
subsequent issues.

174. Lopes, Helena Theodoro, Jose Jorge Siqueira, e Maria
Beatriz Nascimento. Negro e Cultura no Brasil. Rio:
UNIBRADE/UNESCO, 1987. 136p.

175. Nascimento, Abdias do. Sitiado em Lagos: autodefesa de
um negro acossado pelo racismo. Rio de Janeiro: Editora Nova
Fronteira, 1981. 111p.

176. Nina Rodrigues, Raymundo. Os Africanos no Brasil.
Revisao e pref. de Homero Pires. Sao Paulo: Companhia Editora
Nacional, 1977. 283p. (Orig. 1932)

177. Ramos, Arthur. The Negro in Brazil. Trans. from the
Portuguese by Richard Pattee. Philadelphia: Porcupine Press,
1980. 203p. (Reprint of 1939 ed.)

CUBA

178. Gordils, Yanis. The Presence of Africa in Cuban Culture
(1979?). Typescript. [Held by the Schomburg Center - Sc
Micro F-9754]

179. Otero, Lisandro, with the assistance of Francisco
Martinez Hinojosa. Cultural Policy in Cuba. Paris: Unesco,
1972. 55p. (Studies and documents on cultural policies)

180. Valdes-Cruz, Rosa. "The Black Man's Contribution to
Cuban Culture." Americas, Vol. 34, No. 2 (October 1977): 244-
251.

GREAT BRITAIN

181. Gilroy, Paul. There Ain't No Black in the Union Jack:
the Cultural Politics of Race and Nation. London: Century
Hutchinson Ltd., 1987. 271p.

182. Khan, Naseem. The Arts Britain Ignores: The Arts of
Ethnic Minorities in Britain. London: Commission for Racial
Equality (15-16 Bedford Street, London WC2E), 1976. 175p.

183. Owusu, Kwesi. The Struggle for Black Arts in Britain:
What We Can Consider Better Than Freedom. London: Comedia
Publishing Group, 1986. 172p.

184. _____, ed. Storms of the Heart: an anthology of
black arts & culture. London: Camden Press, 1988. 308p.

Journals

185. Black Arts in London; Listing Guide to Black Theatre,
Film, Dance, Visual Arts and Related Events in London (28,
Shacklewell Lane, Fourth floor, London E8 2EZ. Tel. (01) 254
7295). Editor: Jacob Ross. No. 1- (198-). Bi-weekly.

GUYANA (British Guiana)

186. Cameron, Norman E. Adventures in the Field of Culture.
Georgetown, Guyana: Printed by the Daily Chronicle, 1971.
144p.

187. GUYFESTA: The Guyana National Festival of the Arts '80
National Performances. Georgetown, Guyana: Ministry of
Education, Social Development and Culture, Department of
Culture, 1980. 35p. [Programme]

188. GUYFESTA '80: The Guyana National Festival of the Arts
'80; pictorial review. Georgetown, Guyana: Ministry of
Education, Social Development & Culture, Dept. of Culture,
1980. 56p.

189. GUYFESTA '84: The Guyana National Fesival of the Arts;
1984: pictorial review. Georgetown: Ministry of Education,
Social Development and Culture. Dept. of Culture, 1984. 80p.

190. GUYFESTA '77: The Guyana National Festival of the Arts
'77; pictorial review. Georgetown, Guyana: the Department,
1977. 46p.

191. GUYFESTA '75. Georgetown, Guyana: National History and
Arts Council, 1975. 48p.

192. National History and Arts Council. Guyana Participation
at Carifesta in Jamaica. Georgetown: the Council, 1976. 8p.

193. National History and Arts Council. Guyana Participation
at Second World Black and African Festival of Arts and
Culture, Lagos, Nigeria, Jan. 15-Feb. 12, 1977. Georgetown:
the Council, 1977. 3p.

194. Seymour, Arthur J. Cultural Policy in Guyana. Paris:
UNESCO, 1977. 68p. (Studies and documents on cultural
policies)

Journals and Articles

195. "Carifesta: Georgetown, Guyana, August 25-September 15."
Black World, Vol. 21 (July 1972): 76-78.

196. Cudjoe, Selwyn R. "Carifesta '72: An Historic
Occasion." Shango (Bronx, NY), Vol. 1, No. 1 (1973): 4-6.

197. Institute of Creative Arts. Bulletin. July 1977- .
Irregular.

HAITI

198. Paul, Emmanuel C. Panorama du Folklore Haitien:
Presence Africaine en Haiti. Port au Prince: Editions Fardin,
1978. 323p. (Orig. 1962)

JAMAICA

199. Institute of Jamaica, Kingston. Cultural Policy in
Jamaica: A Study. Paris: UNESCO, 1978. 53p.

200. _____. A Guide to Cultural Policy Development in
the Caribbean. Washington, D.C.: General Secretariat,
Organization of American States, 1984- .

201. Nettleford, Rex. Caribbean Cultural Identity: the case
of Jamaica: An Essay in Cultural Dynamics. Kingston:
Institute of Jamaica, 1978; Los Angeles: Center for Afro-
American Studies and UCLA Latin American Center Publications,
1979. 238p.

Journals

202. Pulse: the heartbeat of Jamaica's entertainment (P.O.
Box 200, Kingston, 5 Jamaica). Vol. 1, no. 1, December
1982- . Quarterly.

UNITED STATES

203. Blauner, Robert. "Black Culture: Myth or Reality?" In
Afro-American Anthropology, eds. Norman E. Whitten and John F.
Szwed. New York: The Free Press, 1970, pp. 347-365.

204. _____. "The Question of Black Culture." In Black
America, ed. John F. Szwed. New York: Basic Books, 1970, pp.
110-120.

205. Gay, Geneva, and Willie L. Baber, eds. Expressively
Black: The Cultural Basis of Ethnic Identity. New York:
Praeger Publishers, 1987. 394p.

206. Gayle, Addison, ed. The Black Aesthetic. Garden City,
NY: Doubleday, 1971. 432p.

207. Herskovits, Melville J. The Myth of the Negro Past.
Boston: Beacon Press, 1958. 368p. (Orig. 1941)

208. Kochman, Thomas, ed. Rappin' and Stylin' Out:
Communication in Urban Black America. Chicago: University of
Chicago Press, 1972. 424p.

209. Pasteur, Alfred B., and Ivory L. Toldson. Roots of
Soul: The Psychology of Black Expressiveness. New York:
Anchor Press/Doubleday, 1982. 324p.

Articles

210. Gayle, Addison. "Blueprint for Black Criticism." First
World (January/February 1977): 41-45.

211. George, Nelson. "Fort to the Future." Village Voice
(January 16 1990): 38. Profile of the Black arts community in
Fort Greene, Brooklyn.

212. Shipp, E. R. "Fort Greene: New Cultural Mecca."
American Visions, Vol. 5, No. 1 (February 1990): 30-34.

213. _____. "Their Muse is Malcolm X; A new generation
of creative artists, based in Brooklyn, is exploring what it
means to be black in the 80's." New York Times (December 4
1988): Sec. 2, pp. 22-23.

214. Tate, Greg. "The Return of the Black Aesthetic: Cult-
Nats Meet Freaky-Deke." Village Voice/Voice Literary
Supplement (December 1986): 5-8.

215. Toldson, Ivory L., and Alfred B. Pasteur. "Therapeutic
Dimensions of the Black Aesthetic." Journal of Non-White
Concerns in Personnel and Guidance, Vol. 4, No. 4 (April
1976).

Media Materials

216. [Black arts criticism conference. Columbia University,
Feb. 23, 1973. Part I] (Audiotape). New York, 1973.
Duration: 59' 56". [Held by the Schomburg Center - Sc Audio
C-157 (Side 1-Side 2)] Discussion of prejudice and criticisms
levelled against black artists, musicians, and writers. Also
discussed are black-created art forms.

217. Contemporary Black Culture (Motion picture) WCBS-TV and
Columbia University. Black Heritage: a history of Afro-
Americans. Section 22: The Cultural Scene: from 1954 to the
current mood. Released by Holt, Rinehart and Winston, 1969.
30 min. b&w. Roundtable discussion with Larry Neal
(moderator), Charlie L. Russell, A. B. Spellman, and Barbara
Ann Teer on the role of the Black artist in the struggle for
self determination for Black people and the current movement
to use art to forward the political aspirations of the Black
community. [Held by the Schomburg Center - Sc Visual MPB-82]

Black Arts Movement

218. Neal, Larry. "The Black Arts Movement." In The Black
Aesthetic, ed. Addison Gayle. New York: Doubleday, 1972, pp.
272-290; Also in The Black American Writer. Volume II: Poetry
and Drama, ed. C. W. E. Bigsby (Baltimore, MD: Penguin Books,
1971), pp. 187-202; and Five Black Writers, ed. Donald B.
Gibson (New York: New York University Press, 1970), pp.
215-221. [Reprinted from The Drama Review (Summer 1968)].

219. _____. "The Social Background of the Black Arts Movement." Black Scholar, Vol. 18, No. 1 (January/February 1987): 11-22.

220. Perkins, Eugene. "The Black Arts Movement: Its Challenge and Responsibity." In The Black Seventies, ed. Floyd B. Barbour. Boston: P. Sargent, 1970, pp. 85-97.

National Black Arts Festival (Atlanta, GA)

221. Flannery, James. "A Black Arts Festival--And More." New York Times (July 31 1988): Sec. 2, pp. 8, 30.

222. Kimmelman, Michael. "Critic's Notebook: Black Arts Festival: Ambition in Pursuit of Vision." New York Times (August 10 1988): C17, C25.

223. National Black Arts Festival - Vertical File [Schomburg Center]

II
AFRICAN FILM

1

General Works

Works in English

224. Ackermann, Jean Marie, ed. <u>Films of a Changing World: a</u>
<u>critical international guide</u>. Washington: Society for
International Development, 1972, 1977. Contents: v. 1 (1963-
1971) -- v.2 (1972-1976). Reprints articles from the
<u>International Development Review</u> on film in the Third World.

225. Diakite, Madubuko. <u>Film, Culture, and the Black</u>
<u>Filmmaker: A Study of Functional Relationships and Parallel</u>
<u>Developments</u>. New York: Arno Press, 1980. 184p.

226. <u>Journey Across Three Continents</u>. New York: Third World
Newsreel (335 W. 38th St., 5th Fl., New York City 10018),
1985. 72p. Program booklet published in conjunction with a
film and lecture series on film of Africa and the African
Diaspora. Includes essays by Mbye Cham, Ferid Boughedir,
Haile Gerima, Clyde Taylor, Lieve Spass, et al.

227. Martin, Angela. <u>African Films: The Context of</u>
<u>Production</u>. London: BFI, 1982. 112p. (Dossier; 6)

228. _____ . <u>Eleventh hour presents Africa on Africa: a</u>
<u>season of African cinema</u>. London: Channel Four Television
(P.O. Box 4000, London W3 6XJ), 1984(?). 19p.

229. Maynard, Richard A., ed. <u>Africa on Film: Myth and</u>
<u>Reality</u>. Rochelle Park, NJ: Hayden, 1974. 84p.

230. Mogadishu Pan-African Film Symposium (1st: 1981). <u>First</u>
<u>Mogadishu Pan-African Film Symposium: Pan-African Cinema--</u>
<u>Which Way Ahead?; Proceedings</u>. Selected and compiled by
Ibrahim M. Awed, Hussein M. Adam, and Lionel Ngakane, comps.
Mogadishu, Somalia: MOGPAFIS Management Committee, 1983.
126p.

231. Oreh, Onuma O. <u>Bringing African Orientation to the</u>
<u>African Cinema</u>. N.p.: n.p., 1975(?). 39p.

232. Rutgers University. Rutgers College. Dept. of Africana
Studies. <u>Film and Africana Politics</u>. New Brunswick: The
University, between 1972 and 1977. [187]p. in various
pagings. [Held by the Museum of Modern Art (# 6009)]

Books with Sections on African Film

233. Armes, Roy. "Black Africa." In <u>Third World Film Making
and the West</u>. Berkeley: University of California Press, 1987,
pp. 214-221.

234. Diawara, Manthia. "Film in Anglophone Africa: A Brief
Survey." In <u>Blackframes: Critical Perspectives on Black
Independent Cinema</u>, eds. Mbye B. Cham and Clair Andrade-
Watkins. Cambridge: The MIT Press, 1988, pp. 37-49.

235. Fuglesang, Andreas, ed. <u>Film-Making in Developing
Countries: the Uppsala Workshop</u>. Motala, Sweden: Dag
Hammarskjold Foundation, 1975, pp. 76-78.

236. Gabriel, Teshome H. "Film and Ideology in Africa." In
<u>Third Cinema in the Third World: The Aesthetics of Liberation</u>.
Ann Arbor, MI: UMI Research Press, 1982, pp. 74-93. Analysis
of films by Jean Rouch, Ousmane Sembene ("Xala" and "Ceddo"),
and Haile Gerima ("Harvest: 3000 Years").

237. Sembene, Ousmane. "Observations." In <u>Symposium on
Cinema in Developing Countries</u>. New Delhi: Publications
Division, Ministry of Information and Broadcasting, Govt. of
India, 1979, pp. 13-16. Brief statement on the state of film
making in sub-Saharan Africa.

238. Slide, Anthony. "Africa." In <u>The International Film
Industry: A Historical Dictionary</u>. Westport, CT: Greenwood
Press, 1989, pp. 3-4.

239. Taylor, Clyde. "Africa." In <u>World Cinema since 1945</u>,
ed. William Luhr. New York: Ungar, 1987, pp. 1-21.

240. Vaughan, J. K. "Africa and the Cinema." In <u>An African
Treasury: Articles, Essays, Stories, Poems by Black Africans</u>,
ed. Langston Hughes. New York: Crown, 1960, pp. 30-35.

241. Vieyra, Paulin Soumanou. "African Cinema: Solidarity
and Difference." In <u>Questions of Third Cinema</u>, eds. Jim Pines
and Paul Willemen. London: BFI, 1989, pp. 195-198.

242. _____. "Cinematographic Art: In Search of Its
African Expression." In <u>Colloquium: Function and Significance
of African Negro Art in the Life of the People and for the
People</u>. Paris: Presence Africaine, 1968, pp. 539-558.

Dissertations and Theses

243. Agbe-Davies, A. A. "Film Activities of African Colonies
under Four European Powers, 1946-51." Thesis (M.A.)
University of Southern California, 1960.

244. Akudinobi, Jude G. "Under the Sign of Darkness: The Africa Film in the 80s." Dissertation (Ph.D.) University of Southern California, 1988.

245. Ayorinde, Adepeju Abimbola. "The Image of Africa in Three Modes of Film Communication." Thesis (M.A.) University of New Orleans, 1987. 49p.

246. Diawara, Manthia. "African Cinema: The Background and the Economic Context of Production." Dissertation (Ph.D.) Indiana University, 1985. 217p.

247. Gabriel, Teshome H. "The Development of the African Film: A Critical Study." Thesis (M.A.) University of California, Los Angeles, 1976. 254p.

248. Ismail, Edward Kaaya. "Africans, Afro-Americans and Narrative Cinema: Aspects of the Evolution of a Visual Literature." Thesis (M.A.) University of Alberta, 1979. 110p.

Journals

249. Black Film Review (110 S St., NW, Washington, DC 20001). Vol. 1, No. 1- . 1985- . Quarterly. Contains frequent articles on African films and filmmakers.

Articles

250. Armes, Roy. "Black African Cinema in the Eighties." Screen, Vol. 26, No. 34 (May-August 1985): 60-73.

251. Bachmann, Gideon. "Film in Black Africa." Variety (May 9 1979): 68, 254, 256.

252. _____. "In Search of Self-Definition." Film Quarterly, Vol. 26, No. 3 (Spring 1973).

253. Bassori, Timite. "Will the African Cinema be Still-Born?" Presence Africaine, Vol. 21, No. 49 (1st Quarter 1964): 108-112.

254. "Cinema in Africa." Africa (February 1975): 54-56.

255. Davis, J. Merle. "The Cinema and Missions in Africa." International Review of Missions (July 1936).

256. Diawara, Manthia. "Popular Culture and Oral Traditions in African Film." Film Quarterly (Spring 1988): 6-14.

257. _____. "Sub-Saharan African Film Production: Technological Paternalism." Jump Cut, No. 32 (April 1986): 61-65.

258. Enahoro, Augustine-Yfua. "Towards a Philosophy of African Cinema." Africa Media Review (Nairobi), Vol. 3, No. 1 (1988): 134-148.

259. Ferenczi, V. "The Film and Some of its Psychosocial
Implications." Presence Africaine, Vols. 6-7, No. 34-35
(1961): 78-99.

260. "Final Communique of the First Colloquy on Film
Production in Africa." Young Cinema, No. 1 (Winter 1983):
16-20.

261. Gabriel, Teshome H. "Images of Black People in Cinema."
Ufahamu, Vol. 6, No. 2 (1976).

262. Gerima, Haile, et al. "Der Afrikanische Film. Part 1."
Filmfaust, No. 39 (May-June 1984): 41-55.

263. Hall, Susan. "African Women on Film." Africa Report,
Vol. 22, No. 1 (January-February 1977): 15-17.

264. Hill, Allen. "African Film and Filmmakers." Essence
(July 1978): 18, 23-24.

265. Hondo, Med. "Africa's Struggling Cinema." World Press
Review, Vol. 29 (April 1982): 60.

266. _____. "Film in Afrika. Part 2." Filmfaust, No.
44 (February-March 1985): 43-47.

267. _____. "What is Cinema For Us?" Jump Cut, No. 31
(March 1986): 47-48.

268. Howard, David. "The Emerging African Cinema: A Quest
for Cultural Identity." The World & I (September 1988): 276-
281.

269. Kamphausen, Hannes. "Cinema in Africa: A Survey."
Cineaste, Vol. V, No. 3 (Summer 1972): 28-41.

270. Kindred, Jack. "Joint Ventures on 'Real' African Pics
by German Outfit." Variety (September 16 1981): 40, 46.

271. Kuryla, Mary. "Black Body: The Potential for a Non-
colonizing Cinema in Africa." Spectator (Fall 1988): 28-37.
Analysis of the African image in films by Jean Rouch, Jean Luc
Godard, Trinh T. Minh-ha and Melissa Llewelyn Davies.

272. Leahy, James. "Tributaries of the Seine. To the
Distant Observer: Problems and Practices of African Cinema."
Monthly Film Bulletin, Vol. 54, No. 639 (April 1987): 106-107.

273. Masilela, Ntongela. "Interconnections: The African and
Afro-American Cinema." The Independent, Vol. 11, No. 1
(January-February 1988): 14-17.

274. Mativo, Kyala. "Cultural Dilemma of the African Film."
Ufahamu, Vol. 1, No. 3 (Winter 1971): 64-68.

275. _____. "Resolving the Cultural Dilemma of the
African Film." Ufahamu, Vol. XIII, No. 1 (1983): 134-146.

276. Minot, Gilbert. "Toward the African Cinema." Ufahamu, Vol. XII, No. 2 (1983): 37-43.

277. Nee-Owoo, Kwate. "Caught in a Cultural Crossfire." West Africa (December 19-25 1988): 2372-2373.

278. Pearson, Lyle. "Four Years of African Film." Film Quarterly, Vol. XXVI, No. 3 (Spring 1973): 42-47.

279. Pfaff, Francoise. "Cinema in Francophone West Africa." African Quarterly, Vol. XXII, No. 3 (1986?): 41-48.

280. _____. "Researching Africa on Film." Jump Cut, No. 31 (March 1986): 50-51.

281. Pike, Charles. "Colonial Africa and Exile Cinema." Afterimage, Vol. 12, No. 5 (December 1985): 14-16. Discussion of the African image in film as portrayed by both the British Colonial Film Unit and contemporary African filmmakers.

282. Poussaint, R. "African Film: The High Price of Division [by geography and theme]." Ufahamu, Vol. 1, No. 3 (Winter 1971): 51-63.

283. Relich, Mario. "From Glitter to Gore in the Film World." West Africa, No. 3358 (December 7 1981): 2907-2911.

284. Roberts, Andrew. "Non-fiction film of Africa before 1940." Historical Journal of Film, Radio and Television, Vol. 8, No. 2 (1988): 203-206.

285. Schmidt, Nancy J. "African Literature on Film." Research in African Literatures, Vol. 13, No. 4 (1982): 518-531.

286. _____. "Focus On: African Filmmaking Country by Country." African Studies Review, Vol. 28, No. 1 (March 1985): 111-114. Review article on the OCIC African film book series.

287. _____. "Recent Films by sub-Saharan Filmmakers." ALA Bulletin (Edmonton, Canada), Vol. 14, No. 2 (1988): 16-25.

288. _____. "Recent Perspectives on sub-Saharan African Film-making." Africa Today, Vol. 36, No. 2 (1989): 17-22. Survey of recent books on African film.

289. Senghor, Blaise. "Prerequisites for a Truly African Cinema." Presence Africaine, Vol. 21, No. 49, 1st Quarter (1964): 101-107.

290. Solanke, Adeola. "Documenting African Film" West Africa (December 19-25 1988): 2373. Preview of documentary "Ouaga, African Cinema Now" (# 399).

291. Sourou Okiole, F. "Problems of African Cinema." Young Cinema, No. 3 (Summer 1982): 24-30.

292. Stam, Robert, and Louise Spence. "Colonialism, Racism and Representation." Screen (London), Vol. 24, No. 2 (March/April 1983): 2-20.

293. Standa, E. M. "The Role of Film in African Development." Busara (Nairobi), Vol. 6, No. 2 (1974): 73-77.

294. Ukadike, Nwachukwu Frank. "Depictions of Africa in Documentary Film." Black Film Review, Vol. 4, No. 1 (Winter 1987/88): 13-15.

295. Vaughan, J. K. "Africa South of the Sahara and the Cinema." Presence Africaine, No. 14-15 (juin-septembre 1957): 210-221.

296. Vieyra, Paulin Soumanou. "Africa: the images that must not fade." UNESCO Courier (August 1984): 7-8.

297. _____. "The Cinema and the African Revolution." Presence Africaine, Vols. 6-7, Nos. 34-35 (1961): 66-77.

298. Wagner, Tereza, and Claude Ondobo. "African Cinema: A Young and Relatively Unknown Art." UNESCO Courier (March 1988): 27-29.

299. Werman, Marco. "African Cinema: A Market in the U.S.?" Africa Report (May-June 1989): 68-70.

300. Wilson, John. "Film Literacy in Africa." Canadian Communications, Vol. 1, No. 4 (Summer 1961): 7-14.

301. Young, Deborah. "See New African Distribution Start via Confabs; Paris Branch Closing." Variety (March 13 1985): 41.

Works in French, Italian, Swedish and Russian

302. Afrique Noire, Quel Cinema?; Actes du Colloque, Universite Paris X Nanterre, decembre 1981. Coordination, Philippe J. Maarek. Nanterre: Association du Cine-Club de l'Universite Paris X, 1983. 97p.

303. Bachy, Victor. Cinema en Afrique Noire: rapport prepare pour le Congres de l'O.C.I.C., Manille, novembre 1980. N.p.: n.p., 1980(?). 62p.

304. Ben el Hadj, Bahri. Une Politique Africaine de Cinema. Paris: Dadci, 1980. 236p.

305. Binet, Jacques, Ferid Boughedir, et Victor Bachy, eds. Cinemas Noirs d'Afrique. Paris: L'Harmattan, 1983. 206p. (Cinemaction; 26)

306. Boughedir, Ferid. Le Cinema Africain de A a Z. Brussels: Editions OCIC, 1987. 206p.

307. Budiak, Liudmila Mikhailovna. Kino stran Azii i Afriki. Moskva: Izdvo "Znanie", 1983. 157p. [Russian text]

308. Camera Nigra: Le Discours du Film Africain. Bruxelles:
OCIC; Paris: L'Harmattan, 1984. 227p.

309. Cheriaa, Tahar. Ecrans d'Abondance, ou Cinemas de
Liberation en Afrique. Tunisie: SATPEC, Organisme Libyen de
Cinema, El Khayala, 1978. 312p.

310. Convents, Guido. Prehistoire du Cinema en Afrique,
1897-1918: a la recherche des images oubliees. Bruxelles:
OCIC, 1986. 235p.

311. Diawara, Manthia. Cinema Africain: politiques de la
production. Paris: Presence Africaine, 1990.

312. Gardies, Andre. Cinema d'Afrique Noire Francophone:
l'espace-miroir. Paris: L'Harmattan, 1989. 191p.

313. _____, et Pierre Haffner. Regards sur le Cinema
Negro-Africain. Bruxelles: OCIC, 1987. 234p.

314. Haffner, Pierre. Essai sur les Fondements du Cinema
Africain. Abidjan: Nouvelles Editions Africaines, 1978.
274p.

315. _____. Palabres sur le Cinematographe: Initiation
au Cinema. Kinshasa: Presses Africaines, 1978. 270p.

316. Hennebelle, Guy, avec la participation de Ola Balogun,
et al. Les Cinemas Africains en 1972. Dakar: Societe
Africaines d'Edition, 1972. 371p.

317. Matanda, Tshishi Bavuala. Litterature et Cinema:
contribution a l'etude de l'adaption dans la culture negro-
africaine. Louvain-la-Neuve: CIACO, 1988. 178p. (Universite
catholique de Louvain. Faculte des sciences economiques,
sociales et politiques; nouv. ser., no. 180). Theoretical
discussion of the adapting of literature into film with
special emphasis on Africa.

318. N'Gosso, Gaston Same, and Catherine Ruelle. Cinema et
Television en Afrique: de la dependance a l'interdependance.
Paris: UNESCO, 1983(?). 84p. (Communication et societe; 8)

319. Nwosu, Joy. Cinema e Africa Nera. Roma: Tindalo, 1968.
154p.

320. Pommier, Pierre. Cinema et Developpement en Afrique
Noire Francophone. Paris: Pedone, 1974. 184p.

321. Sobolev, R. P., and O. V. Teneishvili. Kinematografiia
razvivai ushschikhsia stran Azii i Afriki: bocherki. Moskva:
Izdvo "Nauka", Glav. red. vostochnoi litry, 1986. 246p.
[Russian text. English summary]

322. Sundgren, Nils Petter. Pa Bio Soder om Sahara: En bok
om filmen i det svarta Afrika. Stockholm: PAN/Norstedt, 1972.
111p. [Swedish text]

323. Toffetti, Sergio, ed. Il Cinema dell'Africa Nera, 1963-1987. Milano: Fabbri, 1987. 175p. [Italian text]

324. Traore, Biny. La Problematique du Cinema Africain: son public, ses motivations et ses fonctions. Bobo-Dioulasso, Burkina Faso: Laylee Ouezzin Coulibaly, 1983(?). 47p.

325. Vieyra, Paulin Soumanou. Le Cinema Africain. Paris: Presence Africaine, 1975. 444p.

326. _____. Le Cinema et l'Afrique. Paris: Presence Africaine, 1969. 220p.

Books with Sections on African Film

327. Bassori, Timite. "Le Cinema Commercial en Afrique." In Colloquium: Function and Significance of African Negro Art in the Life of the People and for the People. Paris: Presence Africaine, 1968, pp. 211-217.

328. Rouch, Jean. "Cinema Africain 1966." In Colloquium: Function and Significance of African Negro Art in the Life of the People and for the People. Paris: Presence Africaine, 1968, pp. 223-231.

329. _____. "Situation et Tendances du Cinema en Afrique." In Premier Catalogue Selectif International de Films Ethnographiques sur l'Afrique Noire. Paris: UNESCO, 1967, pp. 374-405.

330. Vieyra, Paulin Soumanou. "Le Concours du Film au Premier Festival Mondial des Arts Negres." In Colloquium: Function and Significance of African Negro Art in the Life of the People and for the People. Paris: Presence Africaine, 1968, pp. 218-222.

Dissertations

331. Amadangoleda, Louis. "Aspects Historiques et Politiques du Cinema dans les Nations Africaines: Etats Francophones d'Afrique Noire." Memoire. Diplome de 'EHESS. 1979-80.

332. Diop, Mohamed. "Mass Media et Culture Traditionelle en Afrique Noire; le Cinema." These, Universite de Droit, d'Economie et de Sciences Sociales, Paris II: Institut francais de presse, 1974.

333. Fray, Delphine. "Le Cinema en Afrique Noire Francophone." These maitrise. Universite de Droit, d'Economie et de Sciences Sociales, Paris II: Institut francais de presse, 1985.

334. Ngando Kingue. "Le Cinema Africain et ses Fonctions Sociales." These de 3e cycle. Science Politique. Paris II. 1979/- .

Journals

335. Adhoua (Cercle d'Etudes et de Recherches Cinematographiques, Palaiseau, France). No. 1-4 (1980-1981).

336. Unir-Cinema: Revue du Cinema Africain (1, rue Neuville, B.P. 160, Saint-Louis, Senegal). Irregular.

Articles

337. Almeida, Ayi-Francisco. "Les Politiques de Communication Sociale au Moyen du Cinema: le cas des pays africains." Tiers-Monde (Paris), Vol. 24, No. 95 (1983): 583-588.

338. Bassori, Timite. "Un Cinema Mort-Ne?" Presence Africaine, No. 49, Ier trim. (1964): 111-115.

339. Bataille. "Cinema et Acteurs Noirs." Presence Africaine, No. 4, 2e trim. (1948): 690-696.

340. Binet, Jacques. "L'Argent dans les Films Africains." L'Afrique Litteraire et Artistique, No. 43 (1977): 90-93.

341. _____. "Classes Sociales et Cinema Africain." Positif, No. 188 (December 1976): 34-42.

342. _____. "Temps et Espace dans le Cinema Africain." Positif, No. 198 (October 1977): 57-62.

343. _____. "Violence et Cinema Africain." L'Afrique Litteraire et Artistique (Paris), No. 44 (1977): 73-80.

344. Bosseno, Christian. "Afrique, Continent des Origines." La Revue du Cinema, No. 424 (February 1987): 62-68.

345. Boughedir, Ferid. "Le Cinema Africain a Quinze Ans." Filmechange, No. 4 (Autumn 1978): 75-80.

346. _____. "Connaissance du Cinema Africain." AGECOP Liaison, No. 7 (mai-juin 1975): 23-24.

347. _____. "Les Films Africains Existent..." Jeune Afrique, No. 635 (1973): 34-37.

348. _____. "Pour une Theorie du Cinema Africain." Ecran, No. 74 (November 30 1974): 47.

349. Caillens, J. "Sur le Cinema." Presence Africaine, No. 12, 4e trim. (1951): 233-234.

350. Cheriaa, Tahar. "Le Cinema en Afrique Noire Francophone." Cinema Quebec, Vol. I, No. 10 (July-August 1972): 22-27.

351. Choupaut, Yves-Marie. "Le Cinema devient un Art Populaire." Balafon, No. 31 (octobre 1975): 40-41.

352. "Les Cineastes d'Afrique Noire et Madagascar." Films et Documents, No. 309 (novembre-decembre 1975): 15-18, 23-26.

353. "Cinema Africain 1972." Eburnea, No. 63 (1972): 34-35.

354. "Le Cinema et les Africains." Esprit, Vol. 9 (1971): 290-292.

355. "Conferencia Africana de Cooperacao Cinematografica." Tempo, No. 334 (Fev. 27 1977): 50-53; No. 335 (Marco 6 1977): 60-64.

356. "La Creation Cinematographique en Afrique." Nations Nouvelles, Vol. 25 (1970): 10-16.

357. Dabla, Amevi. "L'OUA et le Cinema." Afrique Nouvelle (August 7-13 1985): 18.

358. _____. "Pour une Production Africaine Rentable." Filmechange, Vol. 23 (Summer 1983): 45-54.

359. Debrix, Jean-Rene. "Dix Ans de Cooperation Franco-Africaine ont Permis la Naissance du Jeune Cinema d'Afrique Noire." France-Eurafrique (Paris), Vol. 24, No. 235 (1972): 34-36.

360. _____. "Situation du Cinema en Afrique Francophone." Afrique Contemporaine, Vol. 14, No. 81 (septembre-octobre 1975): 2-7.

361. Delmas, Jean. "Situation du Cinema d'Afrique Noire." Jeune Cinema, No. 99 (December 1976-January 1977): 1-2.

362. Dia-Moukouri, Urbain. "Intuition d'un Langage Cinematographique Africain." Presence Africaine, No. 61, Ier trim. (1967): 206-218.

363. Diop, Ababacar. "Comment Concilier le Public Africain et son Cinema." Carrefour Africain, No. 780 (Mai 25 1983): 20-21.

364. Ewande, F. "Causes du Sous-Developpement Africain en Matiere de Cinema." Presence Africaine, No. 61, Ier trim. (1967): 199-205.

365. _____. "Miseres du Cinema Africain." Sentiers (February 1967): 10-12.

366. Ferenczi, V. "Quelques Implications Psycho-Sociales du Film et l'Action Educative." Presence Africains, No. 34-35 (octobre 1960-janvier 1961): 104-123.

367. Haffner, Pierre. "Situation du Cinema Negro-Africain, la decennie 1970/1980." Le Mois en Afrique, No. 184/185 (avril-mai 1981): 127-135.

368. Hennebelle, Guy. "Histoire du Cinema Africain: Entretien avec Jean-Rene Debrix." L'Afrique Litteraire et Artistique, No. 43 (1977): 77-89.

369. _____. "Pour ou Contre un Cinema Africain Engage."
L'Afrique Litteraire et Artistique, Vol. 19 (1971): 87-93.

370. _____, et al. "Ou Vont les Cinemas Africains."
Ecran, No. 30 (Novembre 1974): 36-48.

371. Jeune Cinema, No. 34 (November 1968). African cinema
issue.

372. "Jeune Cinema d'Afrique Noire." L'Afrique Actuelle,
Vol. XV (February 1967). Special African film issue.

373. Kabore, Gaston M. "Qu'est-ce qu'un film Africain?"
Unir Cinema, No. 20-21 (September-December 1985): 35-36.

374. Kieffer, A. "Flashes sur le Cinema Africain: Chartres
sur Afrique Noire." Jeune Cinema, No. 157 (Mars 1984): 7-12.

375. Kodjo, Francois. "Les Cineastes Africains Face a
l'Avenir du Cinema en Afrique." Tiers-Monde, Vol. 20, No. 79
(Juillet-Septembre 1979): 607-614.

376. Lambour, M. C. "Le Cinema Africaine a l'Age de Raison."
Afrique Presse [Paris] (July 1978): 105-109. A look at the
current state and future challenges of African filmmaking.

377. Mangin, M. "L'Afrique sans Fric." Cinema (Paris), No.
386 (February 4 1987): 10-12.

378. _____. "L'Annee Creuse du Cinema d'Afrique."
Cinema (Paris), No. 418 (December 2 1987): 10-11.

379. Medjigbodo, Nicole. "Afrique Cinematographiee, Afrique
Cinematographique." Canadian Journal of African Studies
(Ottawa), Vol. 13, No. 3 (1979): 371-387.

380. N'Sougan, Agbemagnon Ferdinand. "La Condition Socio-
Culturelle Negro-Africaine et le Cinema." Presence
Africaine, Vol. 55, 3e trim. (1965): 32-41.

381. Ouattara, Seydou. "Cinema: Cineastes cherchent
distributeurs desesperement..." Africa International (Dakar),
No. 220 (October 1989): 75-77.

382. Paulhan, Jean. "A la Recherche du Cinema de l'Afrique
Francophone." The French Review, Vol. 55, No. 6 (May 1982):
912-914.

383. Ramirez, I. "El Cine Africano." Cine Cubano, No. 115
(1986): 29-35.

384. Rolot, Christian, and Francis Ramirez. "Problemes et
Perspectives du Cinema en Afrique Noire et a Madagascar."
Africa-Tervuren, Vol. 25, No. 4 (1979): 103-112.

385. Saivre, Denyse de. "Le Cinema de l'Afrique au sud du
Sahara: Quelques Propositions Paradoxales." Franzosisch
Heute, Vol. 2 (June 1982): 157-165.

386. "Seminaire sur le Role du Cineaste Africain dans l'Eveil
d'une Conscience de Civilisation Noire, Ouagadougou, 8-13
avril 1974." Presence Africaine, No. 90 (1974): 3-203.

387. Sissoko, Foussenou. "Les Femmes dans le Cinema
Africain." Afrique Nouvelle (August 21-27 1985): 17.

388. Vencatachellum, I. "Cinema et Developpement Culturel en
Afrique." Filmechange, Vol. 20 (Autumn 1982): 54-61.

389. Vieyra, Paulin S. "Les Arts: Theatre et Cinema: Le
Chant du Madhi--Le Carnaval des Dieux." Presence Africaine,
Vol. XVIII-XIX (1958): 242.

390. _____. "Le Cinema et la Revolution Africaine."
Presence Africaine, Nos. 34-35 (octobre-janvier 1961): 92-103.

391. _____. "La Creation Cinematographique en Afrique."
Presence Africaine, No. 77, Ier trim. (1971): 218-232.

392. _____. "Le Film Africain d'Expression Francaise."
African Arts, Vol. 1, No. 3 (Spring 1968): 60-69.

393. _____. "Ou en Sont le Cinema et le Theatre
Africain?" Presence Africaine, No. 13 (avril-mai 1957):
143-146.

394. _____. "Propos sur le Cinema Africain." Presence
Africaine, No. 22 (Octobre-Novembre 1958): 106-117.

395. _____. "Quand le Cinema Francais Parle au nom de
l'Afrique Noire." Presence Africaine, No. 11 (decembre
1956-janvier 1957): 142-145.

396. _____. "Responsabilites du Cinema dans la Formation
d'une Conscience Nationale Africaine." Presence Africaine,
No. 27-28 (aout-novembre 1959): 303-313.

397. Willane, Oscar. "La Voie Internationale du Cinema
Africain." L'Afrique Actuelle, Vol. XIX (June 1967): 16.

Media Materials

398. Camera d'Afrique, 20 Years of African Cinema (1983).
Director: Ferid Boughedir (Tunisia). 85 min., 16mm, color.
English subtitles. [Available from Mypheduh Films, Inc., 48 Q
St., N.E., Washington, D.C. 20002]. Documentary surveying
filmmaking in Africa with interviews of African filmmakers
on the various dimensions of their craft.

399.   Ouaga: African Cinema Now! (1988).   52 min.   Directed by
Kwate Nee-Owoo and Kwesi Owusu.   Documentary.   Includes
excerpts from major films such as Sarraounia (Hondo), Le Choix
(Ouedraogo), Harvest, 3,000 Years (Gerima), Fad 'Jal (Faye),
and Yeelen (Cisse) along with brief interviews with leading
African and African Diaspora filmmakers--Haile Gerima
(Ethiopia), Safi Faye (Senegal), Louis Massiah (US), John
Akomfrah (Great Britain), Med Hondo (Mauritania), Souleymane
Cisse (Mali).   Shot at the 10th FESPACO festival in
Ouagadougou, Burkina Faso.   [Distributed by Esiri Tete Films,
29 Waltham Drive, Edgeware, Middlesex HA8 5PG, Great Britain.
Tel. 01- 951-3787].

FEPACI (Federation Pan-Africain des Cineastes)

400.   Boughedir, Ferid.   "La FEPACI: pour la liberation du
Cinema en Afrique."   Cinema Quebec, Vol. III, No. 9-10 (August
1974): 49.

401.   "Un Communique de la Federation Panafricaine des
Cineastes."   Ecran, No. 8 (Septembre-Octobre 1972): 20-21.

402.   Hennebelle, Guy.   "Rencontre a Dinard avec des
Responsables de la Federation PanAfricaine des Cineastes."
L'Afrique Litteraires et Artistique, No. 24 (aout 1972):
96-97.

403.   Johnson, Rudy.   "African Film Makers Seek Aid Here."
New York Times (May 21 1973): 42.

404.   Murray, James P.   "African Film-Makers Unable to Get
Results."   New York Amsterdam News (May 5 1973): D-7.   Follow
up to # 397 on the unsuccesful efforts of a FEPACI delegation
to achieve distribution commitments from U.S. companies.

405.   Vieyra, Paulin S.   "Dinard 1971 ou le Cinema, Fait
Politique."   Presence Africaine, No. 80, 4e trim. (1971):
139-142.

FILM FESTIVALS

406.   "African Films at the Cannes Film Festival."   West
Africa, (May 26 1980): 918-919.

407.   "Une Retrospective Historique du Cinema Africain a
Paris."   Afrique, Vol. LXVIII (June 1967): 38-41.

408.   Vieyra, Paulin S.   "Le Cinema au Ier Festival Culturel
Pan-Africain d'Alger."   Presence Africaine, No. 72, 4e trim.
(1969): 190-201.

409.   _____.   "Le Festival Cinematographique de Cannes et
l'Afrique."   Presence Africaine, No. 104 (1977): 143-151.

410.   _____.   "Le 4es Journees Cinematographiques de
Carthage [1972]."   Presence Africaine, No. 86 (1973): 178-187.

411. _____. "Reflexions sur le Premier Concours
International du Film d'Outre Mer." Presence Africaine, No.
17 (decembre 1957-janvier 1958): 118-122.

FESPACO (Festival Panafricain du Cinema de Ouagadougou)

412. Diawara, Manthia. "African Cinema: FESPACO, an
evaluation." In Third World Affairs 1986, ed. Raana Gauhar.
London: Third World Foundation for Social and Economic
Studies, 1986.

Theses

413. Kinda, Theophane. "Le cinema africain: une approche au
travers du FESPACO (Festival panafricain du cinema de
Ouagadougou)." These. Universite de droit, d'economie et de
sciences sociales, Paris II: Institut francais de presse,
1984. 105p.

414. Sanogo, Bassirou. "La Longue Marche du Cinema Africain:
le FESPACO (Festival Panafricain du Cinema de Ouagadougou)
Etape Essentielle de Son Developpement au Plan Socio-Politique
et Culturel." These de 3e cycle. Sociologie. Paris V.
1980.

Journals and Articles

415. Journal du ... FESPACO. Ouagadougou: Impr. nationale,
1983- . Annual.

416. Paquet, Andre. "The 'FESPACO' of Ouagadougou. Towards
Unity in African Cinema." Cineaste, Vol. 6, No. 1 (1973): 36-
38.

1ere Festival (1969)

417. Gerard, Claude. "Festival a Ouagadougou." Jeune
Afrique, No. 425 (1969): 44.

418. Nikiema, R. "Festival en Haute-Volta." Jeune Afrique,
No. 421 (1969): 50.

419. "A Ouagadougou, a lieu le premier Festival de Cinema
Africain." Afrique Nouvelle, No. 1122 (1969): 5.

420. "A propos du Ier festival de cinema Africain tenu en
Haute-Volta." Afrique Nouvelle, No. 1128 (1969): 15.

2eme Festival (1970)

421. Alain, Yves. "Le Festival de Ouagadougou." Jeune
Afrique, No. 478 (1970): 51.

422. Bassori, Timite. "Le Festival du Cinema Africain de
Ouagadougou." Eburnea, No. 35 (1970): 17.

423. "Cinema Africain a Ouagadougou." Afrique Nouvelle, No.
1176 (1970): 15.

424. "Le Deuxieme Festival de Ouagadougou." <u>Carrefour Africain</u>, No. 409 (1969).

425. LeRoy, Marie-Claire. "Africa's Film Festival - Screenings in Upper Volta's Newly Nationalized Cinemas." <u>Africa Report</u>, Vol. 15, No. 4 (1970): 27-28.

426. "A Ouagadougou: Le Cinema Africain." <u>Entente Africaine</u> (Abidjan), No. 4 (mai 1970): 42-47.

427. "Prise en charge pour l'Etat des salles de cinema en Haute-Volta." <u>Afrique Nouvelle</u>, No. 1171 (1970): 5.

3eme Festival (1972)

428. Cluny, Claude Michel. "Cinema Africain: le Festival de Ouagadougou." <u>Cinema</u> (Paris), No. 165 (April 1972): 36-42.

429. Hennebelle, Guy. "Ouagadougou." <u>Ecran</u>, No. 6 (June 1972): 41-43.

430. _____. "Le Troisieme Festival Panafricain du Cinema de Ouagadougou." <u>L'Afrique Litteraire et Artistique</u>, No. 22 (1972): 88-97.

431. Hitchens, Gordon. "Africans Yearn for African Films: Lesson of the Upper Volta Festival." <u>Variety</u> (March 29 1972).

432. _____. "Black Films for African Blacks." <u>Variety</u> (May 3 1972): 199, 206.

433. Vieyra, Paulin S. "Le 3e Festival Panafricaine de Ouagadougou." <u>Presence Africaine</u>, No. 82 (1972): 120-131.

4eme Festival (1973)

434. Choupaut, Yves-Marie. "Festival 1973 a Ouagadougou. Le Cinema Africain etait un Art, Il veut devinir une industrie." <u>France-Eurafrique</u>, Vol. 24, No. 239 (1973): 90-91.

435. Cluny, Claude Michel. "Ouagadougou; Un Cinema Africain Libre s'Affirme." <u>Cinema</u> (Paris), No. 175 (April 1973): 22-25.

436. _____. "4eme Festival de Ouagoudougou. L'Afrique se Delivre de ses Conventions." <u>Afrique-Asie</u>, No. 26 (1973): 45-47.

437. "Festival Panafricain du cinema." <u>Afrique Contemporaine</u>, No. 66 (1973): 17.

438. Paquet, Andre. "The 'FESPACO' of Ouagadougou. Towards Unity in African Cinema." <u>Cineaste</u>, Vol. VI, No. 1 (1973): 36-38.

439. _____. "Ouagadougou." <u>Cinema Quebec</u>, Vol. 3, No. 1 (1973): 38-39.

440. Vieyra, Paulin S. "Le 4e Festival Cinematographique
Panafricain de Ouagadougou." Presence Africaine, No. 88, 4e
trimestre (1973): 218-227.

5eme Festival (1976)

441. Choupaut, Yves Marie. "Deux Generations de Cineastes
Africains au Festival de Ouagadougou." Carrefour Africain,
No. 616 (1976): 4.

442. Gnonlonfoun, Alexis. "Ve FESPACO: qu'en penser?"
Afrique Nouvelle, No. 1390 (1976): 12-15.

443. Hennebelle, Guy. "Le Ve FESPACO grand rendez-vous du
film africain a Ouagadougou." Afrique-Asie, No. 104 (1976):
43-46.

444. Kouassi, Germain. "FESPACO un festival commes les
autres." Eburnea, No. 100 (1976): 28-29.

445. Martin, Marcel. "Ouagadougou." Ecran, No. 45 (March
1976): 16-17.

446. Matchet. "Cameras Roll!" West Africa, No. 3081 (1976):
1017.

447. Salama, Mohand Ben. "Cinquieme FESPACO." Recherche,
Pedagogie et Culture, No. 23-24 (1976): 58-59.

448. Vieyra, Paulin S. "Le cinquieme FESPACO." Presence
Africaine, No. 98 (1976): 87-92

449. Zoungrana, Marc-Andre. "Le 5eme FESPACO: moins qu'hier
et demain?" Carrefour Africain, No. 616 (1976): 1976): 3.

6eme Festival (1979)

450. Festival panafricain du cinema de Ougadougou (6th:
1979). 6eme festival du cinema africain, Ouagadougou du 2 au
10 fevrier 1979. Ouagadougou, Burkina Faso: FESPACO, 1979.
48p.

Articles

451. Aubert, Alain. "Ouagadougou." Ecran, No. 82 (1979):
15-16.

452. Bachmann, Gideon. "Upper Volta Festival Runs Second
Best to Tunisia." Variety (March 7 1979): 24, 28.

453. Bakyono, J. S. "6e FESPACO le festival du compromis."
Ivoire Dimanche, No. 419 (1979): 36.

454. Benon, B. Richard. "VIe Festival Panafricain du Cinema
de Ouagadougou ou la concretisation du Cinema Africain."
Carrefour Africain, No. 688 (1979): 5.

455. Gardies, Andre. "Notes sur un Festival." Annales de l'
Universite d'Abidjan. Serie D, Vol. 12 (1979): 283-298.

456. Gnonlonfoun, Alexis. "FESPACO: rendez-vous a Ouaga en 1979." Afrique Nouvelle, No. 1478 (1977): 22.

457. _____. "FESPACO 79 le rendez-vous du cinema africain." Afrique Nouvelle, No. 1546 (1979): 12-17.

458. _____. "FESPACO 79 que s'est-il passe a Ouaga?" Afrique Nouvelle, No. 1547 (1979): 16-17.

459. Mabrouki, Azzedine. "Le Festival Panafricain de Ouagadougou." Les 2 Ecrans, No. 12 (1979): 8-21.

460. Martin, Angela. "Ouagadougou." Framework, No. 10 (1979): 42-43.

461. _____. "Panafrican Festival." Sight and Sound (Summer 1979).

462. _____. "Panafrican Film Festival." Educational Broadcasting International, Vol. 12, No. 2 (1979): 67-68.

463. Michaud, Paul R. "Upper Volta's 'Favorable' Aspects; Ambition as Black Hollywood." Variety (March 7 1979): 24.

464. "Ouagadougou: VIe Fespaco." Afrique, No. 20 (1979): 52-53.

465. Ruelle, Catherine. "Ouagadougou: dixieme anniversaire." Afrique-Asie, No. 183 (1979): 72-74.

466. "VIe FESPACO: un nouveau prix." Agecop Liaison, No. 45 (1979): 48.

467. Vieyra, Paulin S. "Fespaco 1979." Presence Africaine, No. 111 (1979): 101-106.

7eme Festival (1981)

468. Ahua, B. "Tous les Films du FESPACO." Fraternite Matin, No. 4928 (1981): 81.

469. Ben Idriss, Z. "FESPACO." L'Observateur, No. 2034 (1981): 11.

470. _____. "VIIe FESPACO Visite d'un complexe de production." L'Observateur, No. 2036 (1981): 1, 10-11.

471. Bosseno, Christian. "Ouagadougou 81: le festival des cameras d'Afrique." Afrique-Asie, No. 236 (1981): 57-59.

472. _____. "Ouagadougou: Fete des Cinemas d'Afrique Noire." Image et Son, No. 362 (juin 1981): 119.

473. El Kara, Ki. "VIIe FESPACO C'est parti?" L'Observateur, No. 2035 (1981): 1, 13-14.

474. _____. "VIIe FESPACO. Les Langues et la Fiscalite." L'Observateur, No. 2037 (1981): 1, 10.

475. _____. "VIIe FESPACO. La securite des cineastes."
L'Observateur, No. 2039 (1981): 1, 8.

476. "FESPACO." Observateur, No. 2035 (1981): 8, 12.

477. "FESPACO. Cinq jours apres." Observateur, No. 2038
(1981): 1, 10.

478. Gardies, Andre. "1981: regards sur le VIIe Fespaco de
Ouagadougou." L'Afrique Litteraire, No. 68-69 (1983): 173-
177.

479. Gnonlonfoun, Alexis. "Au rendez-vous du FESPACO 81."
Afrique Nouvelle, No. 1653 (1981): 14-17.

480. _____. "7e FESPACO." Afrique Nouvelle, No. 1650
(1981): 5.

481. _____. "7eme FESPACO en images." Afrique Nouvelle,
No. 1654 (1981): 14-17.

482. Goulli, Sophie el. "Festival panafricain de
Ouagadougou." 7e Art, No. 41 (1981): 23-24.

483. Martin, Angela. "African Cinema: The Young Talent."
Africa Now, Vol. 2 (1981): 86.

484. _____. "Pan-African Festival Shows Great Promise."
New African, No. 163 (1981): 82.

485. Nagbou, Mustapha. "Le FESPACO n'est ni anglophone, ni
francophone, ni arabophone." 7e Art, No. 41 (1981): 6-8.

486. _____. "Yves Diagne: Le FESPACO est un stimulant,
un catalyseur...et un espoir." 7e Art, No. 41 (1981): 9-11.

487. Ngakane, Lionel. "Filmmakers Focus on African
Problems." Africa, No. 116 (1981): 70-71.

488. "Overture du 7eme festival panafricain a Ouagadougou."
Le Soleil, No. 3254 (1981): 13.

489. "VIIe FESPACO Jour J-1." Observateur, No. 2034 (1981):
1, 8.

490. "VIIeme FESPACO: participation record." Carrefour
Africain, No. 710-711 (1981): 1-8.

491. "VIIe Festival Panafricain du Cinema de Ouagadougou."
Agecop Liaison, No. 57-58 (1981): 23-25.

492. Some, Sylvestre. "L'apres FESPACO 1981." Carrefour
Africain, No. 712-713 (1981): 13-14.

493. Traore, Biny. "Les Films Africains." Observateur, No.
2038 (1981): 1, 4-5, 9.

8eme Festival (1983)

494. Festival Panafricain du Cinema de Ouagadougou: FESPACO
1983. Paris: Presence Africaine, 1987. 94p.

Articles

495. Ayari, Farida. "Journal du 8eme FESPACO." Agecop
Liaison, No. 69-70 (janv-avril 1983): 26-33.

496. Bakyono, J. S. "VIIIeme FESPACO: un competition
serree." Ivoire Dimanche, No. 626 (1983): 44-45.

497. Boughedir, Ferid. "Fespaco: le 8e festival panafricain
du cinema de Ouagadougou." Recherche, Pedagogie et Culture,
No. 62 (1983): 89-92.

498. _____. "Le 8 eme Festival Panafricain de Cinema de
Ouagadougou." Septiem Art, No. 48 (1983): 8-10.

499. Gnonlonfoun, Alexis. "Vive FESPACO 83!" Afrique
Nouvelle, No. 1751 (1983): 5.

500. "FESPACO 83." Unir Cinema, No. 5 (1983): 3-12.

501. Martin, Angela. "Popular African Cinema or Art-House
Movies?" Africa Now, No. 24 (1983): 60-61.

502. "Ouagadougou capitale du cinema." Afrique
Contemporaine, No. 126 (1983): 57.

503. Oyekunle, Segun. "Films for the Future." West Africa
(March 21 1983): 725-726.

504. Vieyra, Paulin S. "FESPACO 83, avant premiere."
Afrique Nouvelle, No. 1751 (1983): 18-19.

9eme Festival (1985)

505. Festival panafricain du cinema de Ouagadougou (9th:
1985). Cinema et Liberation des Peuples: du 23 fevrier au 2
mars 1985. Ouagadougou, Burkina Faso: FESPACO, 1985. 63p.

Articles

506. A. D. "Fespaco 85." Unir Cinema, No. 17 (1985): 15-22.

507. Beye, Ben Diogaye. "IXe FESPACO a moins d'une
surprise." Unir Cinema, No. 16 (1985): 10-11.

508. _____. "Pour que vive la FESPACO." Unir Cinema,
No. 16 (1985): 10-11.

509. Borsten, Joan. "Black African Film: The First Small
Steps." Los Angeles Times/Calendar (March 24 1985): 4-5.

510. Daja, Allarabaye. "FEPACI-FESPACO: la fete de la
reconciliation." Unir Cinema, No. 16 (1985): 4.

511.   Ilboudo, Patrick.   "De la Poule Blanche au FESPACO."
Unir Cinema, No. 16 (1985): 13-23.

512.   _____.   "Etude (a Propos du Festival Panafricain du
Cinema de Ouagadougou)."   Peuples Noirs-Peuples Africains,
Vol. 8, No. 44 (mars-avril 1985): 39-51.

513.   Lemaire, Charles.   "9e Festival panafricain du cinema de
Ouagadougou, histoire d'une rencontre."   Afrique Nouvelle, No.
1862 (1985): 14-17.

514.   Ngakane, Lionel.   "Cinema and the Liberation of People."
Africa, No. 164 (April 1985): 88-89.

515.   Peyriere, Marie-Christine.   "Ouagadougou.   Le creux de
la vague."   Cinema, No. 317 (1985): 52.

516.   Young, Deborah.   "High-Spirited Pan-African Fest Falls
Short on Quality Film Fare."   Variety (March 13 1985): 7, 35.

10eme Festival (1987)

See also # 399

517.   Autin, Didier, et Gael Brunet.   "Le FESPACO 1987:
poussier rouge, images noires."   Bulletin des Etudes
Africaines de l'INALCO, Vol. 6, No. 12 (1986): 151-164.

518.   "Burkina Film Festival Host."   West Africa (March 23
1987): 558-559.

519.   "Fespaco 87."   Presence Africaine, No. 143 (1987): 190-
204.

11eme Festival (1989)

520.   Abo, Klevor.   "Cinema/Fespaco '89: Grand Time in Ouaga."
West Africa (March 27-April 2 1989): 480-481.

521.   Gabriel, Teshome H.   "Fespaco after the coup: 1989
Festival of Pan-African Cinema."   The Independent (July 1989):
31-33.

522.   Segal, Aaron.   "Correspondent's Report: The 1989 Pan-
African Film Festival."   Africa Today, Vol. 36, No. 2 (1989):
16.

2

Country and Regional Studies

A. WEST AFRICA

523. Cham, Mbye Baboucar. "Film Production in West Africa."
In Film and Politics in the Third World, ed. John D. H.
Downing. New York: Praeger Publishers, 1988.

524. _____. "Film Production in West Africa: 1979-1981."
Presence Africaine, No. 124 (1982): 168-189.

525. Watts, Stephen. "On the African Movie Menus." New York
Times (April 26 1953). Discussion of the West African film
audience.

Colonial Film Unit

526. Pearson, George. "The Making of Films for Illiterates
in Africa." In The Film in Colonial Development; a Report of
a Conference. London: British Film Institute, 1948, pp. 22-
27. Statement of the aims and goals of the Colonial Film Unit
in making films for the indigenous populations of British West
and East Africa.

527. Slide, Anthony. "The Colonial Film Unit." In The
International Film Industry: A Historical Dictionary.
Westport, CT: Greenwood Press, 1989, p. 93.

528. Smyth, Rosaleen. "Movies and Mandarins: the Official
Film and British Colonial Africa." In British Cinema History,
eds. James Curran and Vincent Porter. London: Weidenfeld &
Nicolson, 1983, pp. 129-143. On colonial filmmaking in
British West and East Africa.

529. Spurr, N. F. "Some Aspects of the Work of the Colonial
Film Unit in West and East Africa." In Visual Aids in
Fundamental Education. Paris: UNESCO, 1952.

Articles

530. Pike, Charles Ben. "Tales of Empire: The Colonial Film
Unit in Africa, 1939-1950." Afterimage, Vol. 17, No. 1
(Summer 1989): 8-9.

531. Sellers, William. "Making Films with the Africans."
The Year's Work in the Film (1950): 37-43. Remarks from the
founder of Britain's Colonial Film Unit on making films for
the rural populations of West and East Africa.

532. _____. "Mobile Cinema Shows in Africa." Colonial
Review (March 1955): 13-14. [Reprinted from Colonial Cinema
(December 1954)]

BENIN (Dahomey)

533. Boughedir, Ferid. "Le Cinema Dahomeen: un cinema qui se
libre." Cinema Quebec, Vol. III, No. 9-10 (August 1974): 38-
39.

534. Cakpo, Barthelemy. "Cinema Dahomeen." Afrique
Nouvelle, No. 1367 (1975): 17.

BURKINA FASO (Upper Volta)

See also FESPACO (# 412-522)

535. Armes, Roy. "Upper Volta." In International Film Guide
1984, ed. Peter Cowie. London: Tantivy Press, 1983, pp. 328-
329.

536. Bachy, Victor. La Haute-Volta et le Cinema. Bruxelles:
OCIC; Paris: L'Harmattan, 1983. 87p. (Collection Cinemedia)

537. Slide, Anthony. "Upper Volta." In The International
Film Industry: A Historical Dictionary. Westport, CT:
Greenwood Press, 1989, p. 373.

Articles

538. Bachy, Victor. "Le Cinema en Haute Volta." Septiem
Art, No. 50 (1984): 15-17.

539. "Death of Burkina prez seen hurting West African pix."
Variety (November 18 1987): 1+.

540. Fisher, William. "Ouagadougou." Sight and Sound
(Summer 1989): 170-173.

541. Gharbi, Neila. "Le Cinema en Haute Volta." Septiem
Art, No. 50 (1984): 14.

542. Hennebelle, Guy. "Cote d'Ivoire, Haute-Volta, Mali,
trois documents sur trois cinemas." Afrique-Asie, No. 271
(1982): 65.

543. Kargougou, Emile. "Le Cinema en Haute Volta.
Comportements et Gouts d'un Public Africain." Bulletin de
Liaison du Centre d'Etudes Economiques et Sociales d'Afrique
Occidentale, No. 6 (1969): 8-12.

544. Michaud, Paul R. "Black Africa's Film School." Variety
(August 1 1979): 47. Discussion of Burkina Faso's film school
INAFEC - Institut Africain d'Education Cinematographique,
founded in 1976.

545. _____. "INAFEC: Major New Force in African Film."
Volta [Newmarket, NH] (December 1979): 1, 5-6. Examines the
trials and successes of the first 3 years of the African
Cinemagraphic Education Institute in Ouagadougou.

546. Taylor, Clyde. "A Tribute to Thomas Sankara: Leader of
Burkina Faso Deposed in Coup." Black Film Review, Vol. 3, No.
2 (Spring 1987): 8.

CAMEROON

547. Barratte-Eno Belinga, Therese. Ecrivains, Cineastes et
Artistes Camerounais: Bio-bibliographie. Yaounde: Ministere
de l'Information et de la Culture, 1978. 217p.

548. Beti, Mongo. "Cameroun." In Le Tiers Monde en Films,
ed. Guy Hennebelle. Paris: Cinemaction Tricontinental, 1982,
pp. 105-107.

549. Ngansop, Guy Jeremie. Le Cinema Camerounais en Crise.
Paris: L'Harmattan, 1987. 145p.

550. Slide, Anthony. "Cameroon." In The International Film
Industry: A Historical Dictionary. Westport, CT: Greenwood
Press, 1989, p. 58.

Articles

551. Aubry, Roger. "Le Cinema au Cameroun." African Arts,
Vol. 2, No. 3 (Spring 1969): 66-69.

552. Bachy, Victor. "Le Cinema au Cameroun." Image et Son,
No. 351 (1980): 87-94.

553. Boughedir, Ferid. "Le Cinema Camerounais: les premiers
pas." Cinema Quebec, Vol. III, No. 9-10 (August 1974): 42-43.

554. "Films Out of Cameroon." West Africa, No. 3212 (1979):
207.

555. Matchet. "Cameroon in Films." West Africa, No. 3141
(1977): 1921.

556. Sango, J. "Pakebo. Ou en est le Cinema Camerounais?"
Bingo, No. 298 (1977): 62, 67.

557. Sumo, Honore. "Genese et Avenir du Cinema Camerounais."
Afrique Litteraire et Artistique, No. 39 (1976): 59-62.

CHAD

558. Bachy, Victor. "Le Cinema au Tchad." La Revue de
Cinema, No. 341 (1979): 341.

GHANA (Gold Coast)

559. Slide, Anthony. "The Ghana Film Unit." In <u>The</u>
<u>International Film Industry: A Historical Dictionary</u>.
Westport, CT: Greenwood Press, 1989, p. 181.

Theses

560. Hyde, Joel Emmanuel. "Film Studios, Accra." Thesis,
Postgraduate Diploma, Kumasi, University of Science and
Technology, Faculty of Architecture, 1973. 65p.

Articles

561. Bachmann, Gideon. "Contact in Ghana." <u>Sight & Sound</u>,
Vol. XLII, No. 4 (Autumn 1973): 203.

562. Collins, John. "Cinema: NAFTI Leads the Way." <u>West</u>
<u>Africa</u> (April 9 1984): 769-770. Interview with Kweku Opoku,
director of Ghana's National Film and Television Institute.

563. _____. "New Blood at Ghana Films." <u>West Africa</u>
(November 14 1983): 2616-2618. On the appointment of Harruna
Attah as director of the Ghana Film Industry Corporation.

564. _____. "A Wealth of Film." <u>West Africa</u> (December
17 1984): 2585-2586. Discussion with Harruna Attah re:
Ghana's film archives.

565. "Ghana Develops Self-Contained Film Studio, 1st African
Nation to Do So." <u>Variety</u> (September 15 1971).

566. Offei-Ansah, Jon. "Film Industry Takes Stock. 40th
anniversary of the Ghana Film Industries Corporation." <u>West</u>
<u>Africa</u> (January 23-29 1989): 101.

567. Redlich, Mario. "Cinema: Ghana's Documentary
Tradition." <u>West Africa</u> (December 3 1984): 2457-2458.

568. Spark, David. "African Cinema: a view from Ghana."
<u>Sight and Sound</u> (Autumn 1988): 224.

GUINEA-BISSAU

569. Durand, Philippe. "Naissance du Cinema en
Guinea-Bissau." <u>Image et Son</u>, No. 338 (Avril 1979): 15-17.

IVORY COAST

570. Bachy, Victor. <u>Le Cinema en Cote d'Ivoire</u>. Bruxelles:
OCIC; Paris: L'Harmattan, 1983. 83p. (Collection Cinemedia)

571. Bonneau, Richard. <u>Ecrivains, Cineastes et Artistes</u>
<u>Ivoiriens: Apercu Bio-bibliographique</u>. Dakar: Nouvelles
Editions Africaines, 1973. 175p.

572. Retord, Georges. <u>Les Premieres Projections</u>
<u>Cinematographiques Cote d'Ivoire</u>. Abidjan: Universite
d'Abidjan, 1986. 27p.

573. Slide, Anthony. "Societe Ivoirienne de Cinema." In The
International Film Industry: A Historical Dictionary.
Westport, CT: Greenwood Press, 1989, p. 323.

Articles

574. Bassole, A. "Cinema Ivoirien Un Marche Anarchique."
Fraternite Matin, No. 5265 (1982): 24.

575. Boughedir, Ferid. "Le Cinema Ivoirien: De Riches
Possibilites." Cinema Quebec, Vol. III, No. 9-10 (August
1974): 30-32.

576. "Le Cinema Ivoirien." L'Afrique Litteraire et
Artistique, No. 20 (1972): 227-234.

577. "Les Debuts Prometteurs du Cinema Ivoirien." Eburnea,
No. 39 (1970): 26-27.

578. Desouches, Dominique. "Le Cinema en Cote d'Ivoire."
Eburnea, No. 48 (1971): 36-39.

579. Hennebelle, Guy. "Cote d'Ivoire, Haute-Volta, Mali,
trois documents sur trois cinemas." Afrique-Asie, No. 271
(1982): 65.

580. Jusu, K. K. Man. "Quel Avenir pour le Cinema Ivoirien?"
Fraternite Matin, No. 6145 (1985): 22.

581. Yao, Djedje. "S.O.S. pour le Cinema Ivoirien."
Fraternite Matin, No. 5282 (1982): 20.

MALI (Soudan Francais)

582. Bachy, Victor. Le Cinema au Mali. Bruxelles: OCIC;
Paris: L'Harmattan, 1983. 85p. (Collection cinemedia)

583. Slide, Anthony. "Mali." In The International Film
Industry: A Historical Dictionary. Westport, CT: Greenwood
Press, 1989, p. 242.

Articles

584. Bachy, Victor. "Un (Relativement) Nouveau Venu au
Cinema: le Mali." Image et Son, No. 341 (juillet 1979):
47-51.

585. Boughedir, Ferid. "Le Cinema Malien; premiers
balbutiements." Cinema Quebec, Vol. III, No. 9-10 (August
1974): 33.

586. Correspondent a Bamako. "Le Premier Film Malien."
Jeune Afrique, No. 433 (1969): 37.

587. Hampate Ba, Amadou. "The African Tale of Cinema."
Discourse, Vol. 11, No. 2 (Spring-Summer 1989): 99-110.
Account of a 1908 European film expedition to Hampate Ba's
village. Translated by Manthia Diawara from an essay
originally appearing in a UNESCO film catalogue (# 5960).

588. Hennebelle, Guy. "Cote d'Ivoire, Haute-Volta, Mali, trois documents sur trois cinemas." _Afrique-Asie_, No. 271 (1982): 65.

589. _____. "Vers un Cinema Malien?" _Afrique-Asie_, No. 30 (1973): 46.

590. "Le Cinema au Mali." _Unir Cinema_, No. 2 (1982): 7-10.

591. Legrand, Georges. "Mali Schoolboys Shoot Their Country's First Film." _UNESCO Features_, No. 554-555 (1969): 26-27.

592. Smart, Christopher. "In Mali, Cultural Life Defies Hardship." _Christian Science Monitor_ (June 17 1986): 34.

593. Tiefing. "Existe-t-il un cinema Malien?" _Esson_, No. 7502 (1976): 4; No. 7507 (1976): 4.

NIGER

594. Benesova, M. "Film in Niger." _Young Cinema and Theatre_, No. 1 (1975): 28-30.

595. Boughedir, Ferid. "Le Cinema Nigerien: l'Authenticite de l'Autodidacte." _Cinema Quebec_, Vol. 3, No. 9-10 (August 1974): 27-29.

596. Ganda, Oumarou. "Menaces sur la Cinema Nigerien." _Bingo_, No. 319 (1979): 29-30.

597. Lemaire, Charles, ed. "Le Cinema au Niger." _Septiem Art_, No. 49 (1984): 5-10.

NIGERIA

598. Balogun, Francoise. _Le Cinema au Nigeria_. Bruxelles: OCIC; Paris: L'Harmattan, 1983. 137p. (Collection cinemedia)

599. _____. _The Cinema in Nigeria_. Enugu: Delta Publications, 1987. 144p. [English trans. of # 598]

600. Ekwuazi, Hyginus. _Film in Nigeria_. Enugu, Nigeria: Moonlight Publishing Ltd., 1987. [For a review see _West Africa_ (May 9 1988): 838-839].

601. Ibadan. University College. Dept. of Extra-Mural Studies. _Report on the Second International Film Festival including comments and critiques by 'Kunle Akinsemoyin and Anne Mobbs_. Ibadan: The Dept., 1962. 24p.

602. Morton-Williams, Peter. _Cinema in Rural Nigeria: A Field Study of the Impact of Fundamental Education Films on Rural Audiences in Nigeria_. Lagos: Federal Information Service, 1957. 207p.

603. Opubor, Alfred E., and Onuora E. Nwuneli, eds. The
Development and Growth of the Film Industry in Nigeria:
Proceedings of a Seminar on the Film Industry and Cultural
Identity in Nigeria. Lagos: Third Press International
Division for National Council for Arts and Culture, 1979.
119p.

Books with Sections on Nigerian Film

604. Armes, Roy. "Nigeria." In International Film Guide
1986, ed. Peter Cowie. London: Tantivy Press, 1985, pp. 259-
261.

605. Oladele, Francis. "Film as an Educational Medium in
Development: The Case of Nigeria." In Films of a Changing
World. Washington, D.C.: Society for International
Development, 1977, Vol. 2, pp. 32-33.

606. Slide, Anthony. "Nigeria." In The International Film
Industry: A Historical Dictionary. Westport, CT: Greenwood
Press, 1989, p. 270.

Dissertations and Theses

607. Ajaga, Mikaila Ishola. "The Content of Films about
Africa: A Study of Nigerian Sociocultural Documentaries."
Dissertation (Ph.D.) University of Iowa, 1985. 138p.

608. Ekwuasi, Hyginus. "Towards a Film Industry: The Film in
Nigeria." Thesis (M.A.) University of Ibadan, 1981.

609. Mgbejume, Onyero. "Film in Nigeria: Development,
Problems and Promise." Dissertation (Ph.D.) University of
Texas at Austin, 1978. 162p.

610. Uchegbu, Benjamin Okechukwu. "The Nature of Colonial
Anti-Nationalist Propaganda in British Africa: The Case of the
Colonial Film Censorship in British Nigeria, 1945-48; a
content analysis of colonial censors' reports on films
considered "suitable" or "unsuitable for African audiences" at
the peak of the nationalist ferment." Dissertation (Ph.D.)
New York University, School of Education, 1978. 284p.

Articles

611. Aig-Imoukhuede, Frank. "The Film and Television in
Nigeria." Presence Africaine, Vol. 30, No. 58, 2nd Quart.
(1966): 89-93.

612. Armes, Roy. "Nigerian Cinema's Unrealised Potential."
New African, No. 209 (1985): 43.

613. Balewa, Saddik. "Nigeria's Film Industry." West
Africa, No. 3513 (December 17 1984): 2584.

614. Ekwuazi, Hyginus O. "The Colonisation of the Nigerian
Film Industry." West Africa, No. 3532 (1985): 883-884.

615. _____. "Films: The Animated Universe." West Africa (June 27 1988): 1162. Discussion of Yoruba-lanuage films.

616. _____. "Sizing Up Differences. On recent developments in Nigerian film industry." West Africa (February 6-12 1989): 180-181.

617. _____. "Towards A Development Scheme for the Nigerian Film Culture." Nigeria Magazine, Vol. 54, No. 2 (1986): 56-67.

618. Fiofori, Tam. "Growth of the Film Industry in Nigeria." Afriscope, Vol. 11, No. 9 (September 1981): 43-46.

619. Ibeabuchi, Aloysius. "Problems of Film Making in Nigeria." Daily Times (Lagos), Vol. 278, No. 169 (1985): 5.

620. Oladele, Francis A. "Film as an Educational Medium in Development: The Case of Nigeria." International Development Review, Vol. 16, No. 4 (1974): 31-32.

621. Ricard, Alain. "Le Cinema Popular Nigerian." Recherche, Pedagogie et Culture, No. 58 (1982): 65-69.

622. _____. "Du Theatre au Cinema Yoruba: le Cas Nigerian." CinemAction, No. 26 (1983): 160-167.

SENEGAL

623. Haffner, Pierre. "Senegal." In Le Tiers Monde en Film, ed. Guy Hennebelle. Paris: CinemAction Tricontinental, 1982, pp. 157-160.

624. Pearson, Lyle. "Senegalese Film." In The International Film Guide 1984. London: Tantivy Press, 1983, p. 286.

625. Sembene, Carrie D. "Cinema in Africa: The Senegalese Experience." In Films of a Changing World. Washington, D.C.: Society for International Development, 1977, pp. 37-39.

626. Slide, Anthony. "Senegal." In The International Film Industry: A Historical Dictionary. Westport, CT: Greenwood Press, 1989, pp. 314-315.

627. Vieyra, Paulin Soumanou. Le Cinema au Senegal. Bruxelles: OCIC; Paris: L'Harmattan, 1983. 172p.

Dissertations

628. Diop, Ababacar. "Cinema et Litterature: Deux Modes de Perception de la Realite Senegalaise." These de 3e cycle. Sciences de l'Information. Bordeaux III. 1979/-.

Articles

629. Ahrold, Kyle. "Senegal's Cinema--Cause for Celebration." Encore American and Worldwide News (February 6 1978): 32-33.

630. "Association des Cineastes Senegalais. Senegal.
Conference de Presse." Unir Cinema, No. 12 (1984): 8-10.

631. Ayari, Farida. "Le Jeune Cinema Senegalais: La Parole a
l'Image." Adhoua, No. 3 (1981): 3-6.

632. Bachy, Victor. "Le Cinema Senegalais." Image et Son,
No. 341 (juillet 1979): 38-43.

633. Boughedir, Ferid. "The Blossoming of the Senegalese
Cinema." Young Cinema and Theater, No. 4 (Winter 1974): 14-
20.

634. _____. "Le Cinema Senegalais: Le Plus Important
d'Afrique Noire." Cinema Quebec, Vol. III, No. 9-10 (August
1974): 24-26.

635. _____. "L'Explosion du Cinema Senegalais." Jeune
Afrique, No. 699 (1974): 46-50.

636. Cham, Mbye B. "Islam in Senegalese Literature and
Film." Africa, Vol. 55, No. 4 (1985): 447-472.

637. Cheikh, Ben. "9 Films Senegalais vont Achetes par
l'Etat." Le Soleil, No. 3227 (1981): 5.

638. "Cinema Senegalais." Cinema Quebec, Vol. II, No. 6-7
(March-April 1973): I-XXIV.

639. "Declaration de l'Association des Cineastes Senegalais."
Afrique Nouvelle, No. 1073 (1968): 14.

640. Diallo, Abdoulaye Bamba. "Cinema Senegalais. Quelque
Chose Cloche." Zone 2 (1981): 23.

641. _____. "Cinema Senegalais. Silence...on ne tourne
plus." Le Soleil Magazine, No. 3305 (1981): 5, 7.

642. Haffner, Pierre. "Le Cinema, l'Argent et les Lois: Une
Situation du Cinema Senegalais en 1981." Le Mois en Afrique,
No. 198-199 (mai-juin 1982): 154-166; No. 203-204 (decembre
1982-janvier 1983): 144-154.

643. Hammer, K. "Senegalesisk Film." Kosmorama, Vol. XXXI,
No. 174 (December 1985): 221-227.

644. Hennebelle, Guy. "Ou en est le Cinema Senegalais?"
Africasia, No. 52 (1971): 47-49.

645. Hoberman, J. "Inside Senegal." Village Voice (February
6 1978): 42, 48.

646. Kumm, B. "African Comedy." Harper's Magazine (December
1976): 96+.

647. Makedonsky, Erik. "Route Etroite pour le Jeune Cinema
Senegalais." L'Afrique Litteraire et Artistique, No. 1
(1968): 54-62.

648. Mortimer, Robert A.   "Engaged Film-Making for a New Society." Africa Report (November 1970): 28-30.

649. Vieyra, Paulin Soumanou.   "Le Cinema au Senegal en 1976." Presence Africaine, No. 107, 3e trim. (1978): 207-216.

650. _____. "The Cinema in Senegal." Benin Review, Vol. 1 (1974): 10-16.

TOGO

651. Akue, Miwonvi. "O.C.T.C. Office Catholique Togolaise du Cinema." Unir Cinema, No. 17 (1985): 27-29.

B. CENTRAL AFRICA

652. Slide, Anthony. "The Central African Film Unit." In
The International Film Industry: A Historical Dictionary.
Westport, CT: Greenwood Press, 1989, p. 72.

653. Smyth, Rosaleen. "The Central African Film Units Images
of Empire, 1948-1963." Historical Journal of Film, Radio and
Television, Vol. 3, No. 2 (1983): 131-147.

654. _____. "The Development of British Colonial Film
Policy, 1927-1939, with Special Reference to East and Central
Africa." Journal of African History, Vol. 20, No. 3 (1979):
437-450.

ANGOLA

655. Abrantes, Jose Mena. Cinema Angolano: Um Passado a
Merecer Melhor Presente. Luanda: Cinemateca Nacional (Caixa
Postal 3512, Largo Luther King 4, Luanda, Angola), 1986.

656. Armes, Roy. "Angola." In International Film Guide
1986, ed. Peter Cowie. London: Tantivy Press, 1985, pp. 39-
40.

657. Carvalho, Ruy Duarte de. O Camarada e a Camera: Cinema
e Antropologia para Alem do Filme Etnografico. Luanda: INALD,
1984. 93p.

658. 10 [dez] Anos Cinema Angolano. Luanda: Cinemateca
Nacional, 1985.

659. Murcia-Capel, Pedro. "Les Cameras de l'Angola."
Afrique-Asie, No. 322 (1984): 56-57.

BURUNDI

660. Otten, R. K. Le Cinema dans les Pays des Grands Lacs:
Zaire, Rwanda, Burundi. Paris: L'Harmattan, 1984. 122p.

661. Ramirez, Francis, and Christian Rolot. <u>Histoire du</u>
<u>Cinema Colonial au Zaire, au Rwanda et au Burundi</u>. Tervuren:
Musee Royal de l'Afrique Centrale, 1985. 525p.

CENTRAL AFRICAN REPUBLIC (Ubangi-Shari)

662. Maillat, Philippe. "Republique Centrafricaine." In <u>Le</u>
<u>Tiers Monde en Films</u>, ed. Guy Hennebelle. Paris: CinemAction
Tricontinental, 1982, p. 154.

GABON

663. Bachy, Victor. <u>Le Cinema au Gabon</u>. Bruxelles: OCIC,
1986. 156p.

664. Boughedir, Ferid. "Le Cinema Gabonais: a la recherche
d'une identite." <u>Cinema Quebec</u>, Vol. III, No. 9-10 (August
1974): 34-35.

665. Slide, Anthony. "Gabon." In <u>The International Film</u>
<u>Industry: A Historical Dictionary</u>. Westport, CT: Greenwood
Press, 1989, p. 173.

RWANDA

666. Otten, R. K. <u>Le Cinema dans les Pays des Grands Lacs:</u>
<u>Zaire, Rwanda, Burundi</u>. Paris: L'Harmattan, 1984. 122p.

667. Ramirez, Francis, and Christian Rolot. <u>Histoire du</u>
<u>Cinema Colonial au Zaire, au Rwanda et au Burundi</u>. Tervuren:
Musee Royal de l'Afrique Centrale, 1985. 525p.

ZAIRE (Belgian Congo) and CONGO (Brazzaville)

668. Mpungu Mulenda Saidi. <u>Un Regard en Marge: le public</u>
<u>populaire du cinema au Zaire</u>. Louvain-la-Neuve: Universite
Catholique de Louvain, 1987. 166p. (Universite catholique de
Louvain. Faculte des sciences economiques, sociales et
politiques; nouv. ser., no. 165)

669. Otten, R. K. <u>Le Cinema dans les Pays des Grands Lacs:</u>
<u>Zaire, Rwanda, Burundi</u>. Paris: L'Harmattan, 1984. 122p.

670. Ramirez, Francis, and Christian Rolot. <u>Histoire du</u>
<u>Cinema Colonial au Zaire, au Rwanda et au Burundi</u>. Tervuren:
Musee Royal de l'Afrique Centrale, 1985. 525p.

671. Slide, Anthony. "Congo, People's Republic of." In <u>The</u>
<u>International Film Industry: A Historical Dictionary</u>.
Westport, CT: Greenwood Press, 1989, p. 94.

Dissertations

672. Mbemba, Albert. "Le Cinema en Republique Populaire du
Congo et son Developpement en Afrique Noire Francophone."
Memoire. Diplome de l'EHESS. 1978-79.

673. Mpungu Mulenda Saidi. "Les Formes de Participation de Zairois au Spectacle Cinematographique." Memoire. Universite Catholique de Louvain (Belgium), 1981.

Articles

674. Bachy, Victor. "Le Cinema en Republique Populaire du Congo." La Revue du Cinema, No. 341 (1979): 44-46.

675. Bondroit, A. "Le Cinema pour Indigenes." Avenir Colonial [Leopoldville] (December 7 1951).

676. Botombele Ekanga Bokkoga. "Le Cinema et la Television au Zaire." Cine-Dossiers, No. 74 (1979): 14-18; No. 75 (1979): 15-18.

677. Buana Kabue. "Le Cinema Zairois: Un Bon Depart." Zaire, No. 195 (1972): 14-17.

678. Cauvin, Andre, and Jean Leyden. "Le Cinema au Congo Belge." Les Veterans Coloniaux (October 1967): 3-12.

679. Haffner, Pierre. "Le Cinema (Zairois) Victime du 'Functionnariat'." Le Monde, No. 10598 (1979): 13.

680. Jadot, Joseph M. "Le Cinema au Congo Belge." Bulletin des Seances a l'I.R.C.B., Vol. XX, No. 2 (1949): 407-437.

681. Kamba, Sebastien. "Les Problemes du Cinema en Republique du Congo." Unir Cinema, No. 12 (1984): 7.

682. Kikassa, Francis. "Cinema Congolais." Congo-Afrique, Vol. 6, No. 7 (1966): 367.

683. Luntadila Luzolo-Mantwila. "Un Apercu du Cinema au Zaire de 1897 a 1972." Zaire-Afrique, No. 73 (1973): 173-183.

684. _____. "Le Cinema Zairois." Zaire-Afrique, No. 74 (avril 1973): 239-250.

685. _____. "Perspectives du Cinema au Zaire." Zaire-Afrique, No. 75 (mai 1973): 311-318.

686. Mulimbi Zaina. "Le Cinema Zairois." Zaire, No. 267 (1973): 40-41.

687. Van Bever, L. "Le Cinema pour Africains." Cahiers Belges et Congolais, No. 14 (1950). 59p. Special issue.

C. SOUTHERN AFRICA

SOUTH AFRICA (Azania)

688. Gutsche, Thelma. <u>The History and Social Significance of Motion Pictures in South Africa 1895-1940</u>. Cape Town: Howard Timins, 1972. 404p.

689. Slide, Anthony. "South Africa." In <u>The International Film Industry: A Historical Dictionary</u>. Westport, CT: Greenwood Press, 1989, pp. 324-325.

690. Tomaselli, Keyan. <u>Cinema of Apartheid: Race and Class in South African Cinema</u>. Chicago, IL: Lake View Press, 1987. 300p.

Dissertation

691. Tomaselli, Keyan. "Ideology and Cultural Production in South African Cinema." Dissertation (Ph.D.) University of Witwatersrand, 1983.

Articles

692. "Le Cinema Sud-Africain est-il Tombe sur la Tete?" <u>L'Afrique Litteraire</u>, No. 78 (1986?). Special issue edited by Keyan Tomaselli.

693. Collinge, Jo-Anne. "Under Fire; as South Africa's Crisis Deepens, Its Independent Filmmakers Document the Pain of Apartheid." <u>American Film</u>, Vol. 11, No. 2 (November 1985): 30-38, 78.

694. Gavshon, Harriet. "Levels of Intervention in Films Made for Black South African Audiences." <u>Critical Arts</u>, Vol. 2, No. 4 (1983): 13-21.

695. Ngakane, Lionel. "The Cinema in South Africa." <u>Presence Africaine</u>, No. 80 (1971): 131-133.

696. O'Meara, Patrick. "Films of South Africa." Jump Cut,
No. 18 (1978): 7-8.

697. Ssali, Ndugu Mike. "Apartheid and Cinema." Ufahamu,
Vol. 13, No. 1 (Fall 1983): 105-133.

698. Tomaselli, Keyan. "Capital and Culture in South African
Cinema: Jingoism, Nationalism and the Historical Epic." Wide
Angle, Vol. 8, No. 2 (1986?): 33-43.

699. _____. "Class and Ideology: Reflections in South
African Cinema." Critical Arts, Vol. 1, No. 1 (1980): 1-13.

700. _____. "Ideological Negotiations in 'Black' South
African Films." Unir Cinema, No. 10/11 (1984): 1-24.

701. _____. "Oppositional Filmmaking in South Africa."
Fuse (Toronto), Vol. 6, No. 4 (November-December 1982): 190-
194.

702. _____. "Racism in South African Cinema." Cineaste,
Vol. 13, No. 1 (1983): 12-15.

703. _____. "Strategies for an Independent Radical
Cinema in South Africa." Marang (Gaborone), No. 4 (1983): 57-
85.

704. _____. "The Teaching of Film and Television
Production in a Third World Context: The Case of South
Africa." Journal of the University Film and Video
Association, Vol. 34, No. 4 (1982): 3-12.

ZAMBIA (Northern Rhodesia)

705. Brelsford, W. V. "Analysis of African Reaction to
Propaganda Film." NADA, No. 24 (1947): 7-22. Discussion of
the reactions of a Zambian film audience to a propaganda film
on venereal disease made by the British Colonial Film Unit.

706. Jules-Rosette, Bennetta. "An Experiment in African
Cinema." In Films of a Changing World. Washington, D.C.:
Society for International Development, 1977, pp. 53-55.
[Reprinted from International Development Review, Vol. 3
(1976): 32-36].

ZIMBABWE (Southern Rhodesia)

707. "A Cinemobile for Zimbabwe." Cineaste, Vol. 9, No. 3
(1979).

D. EAST AFRICA

708. Banfield, Jane. "Film in East Africa." _Transition_ (Kampala), Vol. 3, No. 13 (June 1963): 18-21.

709. Notcutt, L. A., and G. C. Latham, ed. _The African and the Cinema; An Account of the Bantu Educational Cinema Experiment during the period March 1935 to May 1937_. London: Edinburgh House Press, 1937. 256p.

Colonial Film Unit

710. Pearson, George. "The Making of Films for Illiterates in Africa." In _The Film in Colonial Development; a Report of a Conference_. London: British Film Institute, 1948, pp. 22-27. Statement of the aims and goals of the Colonial Film Unit in making films for the indigenous populations of British West and East Africa.

711. Slide, Anthony. "The Colonial Film Unit." In _The International Film Industry: A Historical Dictionary_. Westport, CT: Greenwood Press, 1989, p. 93.

712. Smyth, Rosaleen. "Movies and Mandarins: the Official Film and British Colonial Africa." In _British Cinema History_, eds. James Curran and Vincent Porter. London: Weidenfeld & Nicolson, 1983, pp. 129-143. On colonial filmmaking in British West and East Africa.

713. Spurr, N. F. "Some Aspects of the Work of the Colonial Film Unit in West and East Africa." In _Visual Aids in Fundamental Education_. Paris: UNESCO, 1952.

Articles

714. Pike, Charles Ben. "Tales of Empire: The Colonial Film Unit in Africa, 1939-1950." _Afterimage_, Vol. 17, No. 1 (Summer 1989): 8-9.

715. Sellers, William. "Making Films with the Africans."
The Year's Work in the Film (1950): 37-43. Remarks from the
founder of Britain's Colonial Film Unit on making films for
the rural populations of West and East Africa.

716. _____. "Mobile Cinema Shows in Africa." Colonial
Review (March 1955): 13-14. [Reprinted from Colonial Cinema
(December 1954)]

717. Smyth, Rosaleen. "The Development of British Colonial
Film Policy, 1927-1939, with Special Reference to East and
Central Africa." Journal of African History, Vol. 20, No. 3
(1979): 437-450.

ETHIOPIA (Abyssinia)

718. Potts, Jim. "Film Production Course in Ethiopia."
Educational Broadcasting International, Vol. 6, No. 2 (1979):
102-106.

719. Warren, Herrick and Anita. "The Film Artist in a
Developing Nation: Ethiopia." Horn of Africa, Vol. 1, No. 1
(January/March 1978): 57-58.

KENYA

720. Cinema Leo Survey: (a study of viewer characteristics,
viewing habits, preference and attitudes). Project Director,
Nereah Makau. Nairobi: Daystar University College, Research
Dept., 1988. 2 vols.

721. Kenya. National Archives. Preserving the Images and
Sounds of Kenya's Past: Planning for an Audiovisual Archive.
Nairobi: Kenya National Archives, 1978. 45p.

Articles

722. Champion, A. M. "With a Mobile Cinema Unit in Kenya."
Overseas Education (October 1948): 788-792.

723. Deschler, Hans P. "Film Training in Kenya."
Educational Broadcasting International, Vol. 13, No. 3 (1980):
149-151.

724. Potts, Jim. "Film Training: A Kenyan Perspective."
Educational Broadcasting International, Vol. 9, No. 4 (1976):
171-174.

725. Schideler, Jack. "Kenya Tries Moviemaking." Christian
Science Monitor (January 17 1968): 3.

726. Ukadike, Nwachukwu Frank. "Representing Native Kenya on
Film: Lorang's Way and the Turkana people." Ufahamu, Vol. 17,
No. 2 (1988): 3-14.

MOZAMBIQUE

727. Hochart, Philippe. "Mozambique." In Le Tiers Monde en Films, ed. Guy Hennebelle. Paris: CinemAction Tricontinental, 1982, pp. 145-146.

Articles

728. Besas, Peter. "Black Africa Eyes Own Film Industries. A Typical Case is Mozambique." Variety (August 24 1977): 7, 30.

729. Brossard, Jean-Pierre. "Breve Histoire du Cinema au Mozambique (1975-1980)." Les 2 Ecrans, No. 33 (1981): 21-23.

730. Dagron, Alfonso Gumucio. "Cinema du Mozambique." Afrique-Asie, No. 150 (1977): 61-63.

731. Hallis, Ron. "Movie Magic in Mozambique." Cinema Canada, No. 62 (February 1980): 18-24.

732. Hennebelle, Guy. "Un Message de Lourenco-Marques: Cine-Club au Mozambique." Afrique-Asie, No. 69 (1974): 46-47.

733. Lemaire, Charles. "Le Cinema au Mozambique." Unir Cinema, No. 6 (1983): 3-8.

734. "Mozambique." Unir Cinema, No. 12 (1984): 3-6.

735. Sachs, Albie. "Mozambican Culture: A Crowded Canvas." Southern Africa Report (Toronto), Vol. 4, No. 1 (July 1988): 23-24.

736. Sartor, Freddy. "Filmen in Mozambique." Film en Televisie, No. 288/289 (1981): 60-61.

737. Taylor, Clyde. "Film Reborn in Mozambique: Interview with Pedro Pimente." Jump Cut, No. 28 (1983): 30-31. Discussion of the film scene in Mozambique.

TANZANIA (Tanganyika and Zanzibar)

See also # 248

738. Mahiga, Joseph. "Our Technical and Educational Problems and Needs." In Film-Making in Developing Countries: the Uppsala Workshop, ed. Andreas Fuglesang. Motala, Sweden: Dag Hammarskjold Foundation, 1975, pp. 72-74.

739. Maktaba ya Taifa ya Filamu. Orodha ya Filamu za Kiswahili, 1974. Dar es Salaam: Audio-visual Institute, Wizara ya Habari na Utangazaji, 1974(?). 64p. Filmography. [Swahili text]

740. National Film Library (Tanzania). Film Catalogue, 1971. Dar-es-Salaam: Audio Visual Institute, Ministry of Information and Broadcasting, 1976(?). 130p.

Dissertations and Theses

741. Giltrow, David Roger. "Young Tanzanians and the Cinema: a study of the effects of selected basic motion picture elements and population characteristics on film comprehension of Tanzanian adolescent primary school children." Dissertation (Ph.D.) Syracuse University, 1973. 243p.

742. Leveri, Mark. "Prospects in Developing a Viable Film Industry: a 'close-up' of a decade's production performance of the audio visual institute of Dar es Salaam and the Tanzania Film Company Limited (1973-1983)." Dissertation (M.B.A.) University of Dar es Salaam, 1983.

743. Mponguliana, Joe. "The Development of Film in Tanzania." Thesis (M.A.) University of Dar es Salaam, 1982.

744. Ssali, Mike Hillary. "The Development and Role of an African Film Industry in East Africa, with special reference to Tanzania, 1922-1984." Dissertation (Ph.D.) University of California, Los Angeles, 1988. 183p.

Articles

745. Neville, Alan J. "Tanganyika's Film-making Experiment." New Commonwealth (July 21 1952): 69-71.

746. Smyth, Rosaleen. "The Feature Film in Tanzania." African Affairs, Vol. 88, No. 352 (July 1989): 389-396.

747. Wynne, Donald. "Tanganyika's Film Experiment." Cine-Technician, Vol. 18, No. 96 (1972): 50-52, 56.

3

Individual Filmmakers

748. Pfaff, Francoise. <u>Twenty-Five Black African Filmmakers:</u>
<u>A Critical Study, Filmography, and Bio-Bibliographical</u>
<u>Sourcebook</u>. Westport, CT: Greenwood Press, 1988. 332p.

Articles

749. Haffner, Pierre. "Les Cineastes d'Afrique Noire et
leurs Villes." <u>Film Echange</u>, Vol. 36, No. 4 (1986): 39-46.

750. Trelles, L. "El Cine en el Africa Negra: Ousmane
Sembene y los Cineastas Africanos Posteriores." <u>Imagenes</u>,
Vol. 3, No. 2 (1987): 27-30.

751. Weaver, Harold D. "Black Filmmakers in Africa and
America." <u>Sightlines</u> (Spring 1976): 7-9, 12.

ALASSANE, MOUSTAPHA (1942-   ) (Niger)

752. George, Nelson. "African Cinema Has Promising Future."
New York <u>Amsterdam News</u> (October 15 1977): D-5; (October 22
1977): D-4; (November 26 1977): D-4. Three part bio-
filmography of Alassane.

753. Pfaff, Francoise. <u>Twenty-Five Black African Filmmakers</u>.
Westport, CT: Greenwood Press, 1988, pp. 1-9.

AMPAW, KING (Ghana)

754. Novicki, Margaret A. "Interview with King Ampaw."
<u>Africa Report</u> (July-August 1987): 53-56.

Kukurantumi - The Road to Accra (1983)

755. Ephson, Ben, Jr. "Cinema: 'Kukurantumi - Road to
Acra.'" <u>West Africa</u> (June 25 1984): 1303-1304.

756. "Kukurantumi - The Road to Accra." <u>Variety</u> (December 14
1983): 20.

ANSAH, KWAW (1941-   ) (Ghana)

757. Bentsi-Enchill, Nii K. "Cinema: Fair Deal for Film."
West Africa (November 19 1984): 2319-2220. [Interview]

758. Pfaff, Francoise. Twenty-Five Black African Filmmakers.
Westport, CT: Greenwood Press, 1988, pp. 11-18.

Heritage...Africa

759. Bentsi-Enchill, Nii K. "Black People's Burden." West
Africa (May 30 1988): 956-957. A preview of Ansah's film
"Heritage... Africa" followed by his comments on the
difficulty of making films in Ghana.

Love Brewed...in the African Pot (1981)

760. Canby, Vincent. "Film: Love Brewed...; On Middle-Class
Ghana." New York Times (April 25 1981): 11.

761. "Forbidden Relationship." New African, No. 155 (1980):
70.

762. "Ghanaian Film of Star-Crossed Lovers." Weekly Review,
No. 328 (1981): 59.

763. "Love Brewed in the African Pot." Variety (March 25
1981): 20.

764. "Relevant Love Story Out of Ghana." West Africa (12 May
1980): 824-825.

765. Wilson, Melba. "When Love Triumphed Over Class."
Africa Now, No. 46 (1985): 40.

AREKE, OLANIYI (Nigeria)

766. Diallo, Anthony D. "Howard grad uses film to bridge
cultural gaps." Washington Post (April 13 1989): DC9.

BAKABA, SIDIKI (Ivory Coast)

767. Bailly, D., and J. S. Bakyono. "Sidiki Bakaba le
Deuxieme Age." Ivoire Dimanche, No. 594 (1982): 30-31.

768. Bakyono, J. S. "Sidiki Bakaba le Fou de Theatre."
Ivoire Dimanche, No. 635 (1983): 44-45.

769. _____. "Sidiki Bakaba, Un Comedien Affame de
Liberte." Ivoire Dimanche, No. 544 (1981): 44.

770. Dokoui, Pol. "Sikiki Bakaba au Bout du Tunnel." Ivoire
Dimanche, No. 510 (1980): 36-37.

771. Kokore et Brognan. "Sidiki Bakaba ou la Rage de
Vaincre." Fraternite Matin, No. 5318 (1982): 21.

772. Mathias, Victor L. "Sidiki Bakaba: Un Valeur Sure."
Bingo, No. 361 (1983): 58.

773. Morel Junior, Justin. "Entretien Sidiki Bakaba." Zone
2, No. 164 (1982): 16-17.

774. "Sidiki Bakaba." The Face, No. 75 (July 1986): 57.
[Profile]

Bako

775. Ahua, B. "Le Film 'Bako' en Presence de Sidiki Bakaba."
Fraternite Matin, No. 4934 (1981): 19.

776. "Bako, l'Esclave du 20e Siecle." Bingo, No. 305 (1978):
55-56.

777. Diallo, Abdoulaye Bamba. "Bako ou l'Autre Rive." Zone
2, No. 224 (1983): 18.

778. Gnonlonfoun, Alexis. "Bako a la Recherche d'une
Nationalite." Afrique Nouvelle, No. 1548 (1979): 16-17.

779. Langlois, Gerard. "Bako, L'Autre Rive." Ecran, No. 76
(Janvier 1979): 66-68. [Interview]

780. Thiam, Bebet. "Sidiki Bakaba a Bako." Ivoire Dimanche,
No. 416 (1979): 22-23.

781. Welsh, Henry. "Bako, l'Autre Rive." Jeune Cinema, No.
117 (1979): 46-47.

BALOGUN, OLA (1945-   ) (Nigeria)

782. Pfaff, Francoise. Twenty-Five Black African Filmmakers.
Westport, CT: Greenwood Press, 1988, pp. 19-31.

Articles

783. Boughedir, Ferid. "Le Plus Productif des Cineastes
Africains." Jeune Afrique, Vol. 1065, No. 2 (Juin 1981):
65-67.

784. "Film Art and Monetary Profit." West Africa, Vol.
3277, No. 12 (May 12 1980): 828-829. [Interview]

785. Moore, Carlos. "Le Cinema N'Existe Pas Encore." Jeune
Afrique, No. 1065 (1981): 66-67. [Interview]

786. Sonuga, Gbenga. "'From Alpha to Black Goddess'. Filmmaker in Search of an Idiom." New Culture, Vol. 1, No. 5
(April 1979): 37-42.

787. "Traditional Yoruba Theatre." West Africa (December 3
1979): 2226-2227, 2229. [Interview]

Adjani Ogun

788. Gnonlonfoun, Alexis. "Ola Balogun a Rate le Coche."
Afrique Nouvelle, No. 1438 (1977): 16-17.

Aiye

789.   Osundare, Niyi. "A Grand Escape into Metaphysics."
West Africa, Vol. 3277, No. 12 (May 1980): 826-828.

Alpha

790.   Matchet. "A Nigerian Feature Film." West Africa, No.
2946 (1973): 1657.

Black Goddess (A Deusa Negra)

791.   Afum, Ata. "Black Goddess - A Critique." New Culture,
Vol. 1, No. 5 (1979): 43-44.

792.   "A Deusa Negra" ("Black Goddess"). Variety (April 27
1983): 36-37.

793.   Hoberman, J. "Film: Alien Territories." Village Voice
(April 21 1980): 48-49.

794.   Maslin, Janet. "Film:'Black Goddess." New York Times
(April 18 1980).

795.   "Novos Filmes: A Deusa Negra." Filme Cultura, No. 33
(May 1979): 90.

Cry Freedom

796.   "Cry Freedom!" Variety (July 29 1981): 26.

797.   Mabrouki, Azzedine. "Cry Freedom de O. Balogun." Les 2
Ecrans, No. 4 (1978): 34-35; No. 35 (1981): 34-35.

798.   Peters, C. Geo Leo. "Blood and Beauty." New Nigerian,
No. 172 (1982): 49. .

Ija Ominira (Fight for Freedom)

799.   "Ija Ominira" ("Fight for Freedom"). Variety (September
5 1979): 22. [Review]

800.   Jusu, K. K. Man. "'Pour la Liberte' d'Ola Balogun. Le
Cinema de Liberation." Fraternite Matin, No. 5200 (1982): 15.

801.   Matchet. "Traditional Yoruba Theater." West Africa,
No. 3255 (1979): 2226-2227.

Money Power

802.   Bentsi-Enchill, Nii K. "Money, power and cinema." West
Africa, No. 3393 (1982): 2093-2094.

803.   Boughedir, Ferid. "L'Effet Balogun." Jeune Afrique,
No. 1138 (1982): 65.

804.   "The Return of Money Power." Daily Times [Lagos]
(December 22 1984): 5.

805. Traore, Biny. "Jom et Money Power." Observateur, No.
2525 (1983): 4-5, 10.

BASSORI, TIMITE (1933-   ) (Ivory Coast)

806. Pfaff, Francoise. Twenty-Five Black African Filmmakers.
Westport, CT: Greenwood Press, 1988, pp. 33-42.

Articles

807. Jusu, K. K. Man. "Ecare et Bassori..." Fraternite
Matin, No. 5318 (1982): 19.

808. "To Be Young, Gifted, and Black, and the Founder of a
Nation's Film Industry." Atlas Magazine, Vol. 19, No. 2
(February 1970): 59+.

La Femme au Couteau

809. Thirard, Paul-Louis. "Sur 'La Femme au Couteau.'"
Positif, No. 109 (Octobre 1969): 44-47.

BATHILY, MOUSSA (1946-   ) (Senegal)

810. Pfaff, Francoise. Twenty-Five Black African Filmmakers.
Westport, CT: Greenwood Press, 1988, pp. 43-49.

Le Certificat d'Indigence

811. Leahy, James. "Le Certificat d'Indigence." Monthly
Film Bulletin, Vol. 54 (April 1987): 126-127. [Review]

BEYE, BEN DIOGAYE (Senegal)

Sey Seyeti

812. "Sey Seyeti (A Man, Some Women)." Variety (August 20
1980): 21. [Review]

CARVALHO, RUY DUARTE DE (1941-   ) (Portugal/Angola)

813. Carvalho, Ruy Duarte de. O Camarada e a Camera: Cinema
e Antropologia para alem do Filme Etnografico. Luanda: INALD,
1984. 93p.

Nelisita

814. De Carvalho, Ruy Alberto. "Nelisita: un film Angolais.
De la Tradition Orale a la Copie Standard." Memoire. Diplome
de l'EHESS. 1981-82. [Dissertation]

Articles

815. Gonzalez, Alfredo. "Nelisita uma peca Importante na
Filmografia Angolana." Novembro, No. 74 (1984): 55-56.

816. "Nelesita." Variety (August 10 1983): 22. [Review]

817. "Nelisita." Variety (March 20 1985): 18. [Review]

CISSE, SOULEYMANE (1940-   ) (Mali)

818. Pfaff, Francoise. Twenty-Five Black African Filmmakers.
Westport, CT: Greenwood Press, 1988, pp. 51-67.

Articles

819. Baecque, Antoine de, and Stephane Braunschweig.
"Pionnier et son Pays." Cahiers du Cinema, No. 381 (mars
1986): VI. [Interview]

820. Barrat, Patrice. "Souleymane Cisse: V'la l'bon Vent."
Nouvelles Litteraires, No. 2884 (1983): 46.

821. Conde, Maryse. "Souleymane Cisse le Coup d'Oeil."
Demain l'Afrique, No. 11 (1978): 84-85.

822. Delorme, Christine. "Souleymane Cisse, Cineaste
Malien." Presence Africaine, No. 144 (1987): 133-138.
[Interview]

823. D'Erneville, A. M. "Temoignages: Petit Phrases de
Souleymane Cisse." Unir Cinema, No. 19 (July-August 1985):
22.

824. Drabo, G. "Entretien Souleymane Cisse." Zone 2, No.
175 (1983): 15. [Interview]

825. "Interview with Souleymane Cisse." West Africa
(December 7 1987): 2378.

826. J. R. Z. "Pleins feux sur Cisse Souleymane." Les 2
Ecrans, No. 2 (1978): 18-21.

827. Martin, Angela. "Cisse." Framework, No. 11 (Autumn
1979): 16-17.

828. Minoun, Mouloud, and B. Moulay. "Entretien avec
Souleymane Cisse." Les 2 Ecrans, No. 47-48 (1982): 20-22.

829. Richter, Rolf. "Souleymane Cisse - Gesellschaftsanalyse
als notwendige Selbstverstandigung." Filmwissenschaftliche
Beitrage, Vol. 21, No. 3 (1980): 164-169.

830. Ruelle, Catherine, and Andree Tournes. "Gesprach mit
Souleymane Cisse (Mali)." Filmwissenschaftliche Beitrage,
Vol. 21, No. 3 (1980): 157-163. [Interview]

831. Schissel, Howard. "Cinema: People's Film-maker." West
Africa (May 7 1984): 973-974.

832. Tournes, Andree. "Entretien avec Souleymane Cisse."
Jeune Cinema, No. 119 (June 1979): 16-17. [Interview]

Baara (1978)

833. "Baara." Variety (February 7 1979): 22.

834. Baecque, Antoine de. "Balla le Posseur, Balla l'Ingenieur." Cahiers du Cinema, No. 366 (December 1984): 50-52.

835. "Developing Africa's Cinema." West Africa, No. 3358 (December 7 1981): 2911-2914. Discussion of Baara.

836. Follot, I. "Baara" un film realiste. Bingo, No. 306 (1978): 54

837. Gnonlonfoun, Alexis. "Baara." Afrique Nouvelle, No. 1528 (1978): 16-17.

838. Mabrouki, Azzedine. "Baara de Souleymane Cisse." Les 2 Ecrans, No. 4 (1978): 34-35.

839. Taubin, Amy. "Sympathetic Magic." Village Voice (April 25 1989): 68.

840. Yvoire, J. d'. "Baara." Jeune Cinema, No. 163 (December 1984-January 1985): 31-32.

Finye (The Wind) (1982)

841. Aufderheide, Pat. "Festival Film: Dislocations." Village Voice (October 4 1983): 69.

842. Bassan, Raphael. "Le Vent." La Revue du Cinema, No. 379 (January 1983): 34.

843. Cervoni, Albert. "Le Vent." Cinema, No. 283 (July-August 1982): 42.

844. Coleman, J. "Films: Boy's Own Adventure." New Statesman, No. 110 (November 1 1985): 40-41.

845. Diallo, Abdoulaye Bamba. "Finye, le vent." Zone 2, No. 178 (1983): 18.

846. _____. "Fousseyny Cissokho, L'Amoureux de 'Finye.'" Zone 2, No. 216 (1983): 13.

847. "Finye" (The Wind). Variety (August 25 1982): 15.

848. Gervais, Ginette. "Le Vent." Jeune Cinema, No. 144 (July-August 1982): 41.

849. Gibbal, J.-M. "Le Vent." Positif, No. 264 (February 1983): 81-82.

850. Guerrini, P. "Le Vent." Cinema, No. 293 (mai 1983): 41.

851. Kieffer, A. "Le Vent." Jeune Cinema, No. 150 (April 1983): 42-43.

852. Maslin, Janet. "Wind" from Mali and "Reassemblage" in Senegal." New York Times (September 24 1983): 11.

853. Mimoun, M., and M. Brahimi. "Entretien avec Souleymane Cisse: "Le Vent, cette ouverture sur le monde." Les Deux Ecrans, No. 47-48 (July-August 1982): 20-22.

854. Ruelle, Catherine. "Souleymane Cisse, grand prix du FESPACO 'Finye est une etape'." Ivoire Dimanche, No. 628 (1983): 44-45. [Interview]

855. Stern, Y., et M. Mbaye d'Erneville. "Finye." Unir Cinema (Senegal), No. 23-24 (March-June 1986): 43-45.

856. Taubin, Amy. "Sympathetic Magic." Village Voice (April 25 1989): 68.

Yeelen (Brightness) (1987)

Works in English

857. Astrup, C. B. "Brightness." Film and Kino, No. 5 (1987): 5-6.

858. Diawara, Manthia. "Souleymane Cisse's Light on Africa." Black Film Review, Vol. 4, No. 4 (Fall 1988): 12-16.

859. Hoffman, Rachel. "Film: Yeelen." African Arts, Vol. XXII, No. 2 (February 1989): 100-101.

860. Leahy, James. "Yeelen (The Light)." Monthly Film Bulletin (November 1988): 343-344.

861. Stein, Elliott. "The Bloody and the Brightest." Village Voice (April 18 1989): 71.

Works in French

862. Baecque, Antoine de. "Yeelen - La Lumiere" de Souleymane Cisse: Cela s'appelle l'aurore." Cahiers du Cinema, No. 402 (decembre 1987): 24-27.

863. _____, et Stephane Braunschweig. "Souleymane Cisse: Pionnier en son pays." Cahiers du Cinema, No. 381 (mars 1986): VI.

864. Binet, Jacques. "Souleymane Cisse: Oedipus Negro sur la Lumiere." Positif, No. 322 (Decembre 1987): 4-7.

865. Lajeunesse, J. "La Lumiere." La Revue du Cinema, No. 429 (July-August 1987): 50-51.

866. Lavigne, Nicole. "Yeelen." Sequences, No. 135/136 (September 1988): 91-92.

867. Lequeux, Michel. "La Lumiere." Grand Angle, Vol. 15, No. 103 (Mars 1988): 29-30.

868. Niogret, H. "Yeelen." Positif, No. 317 (July-August 1987): 89.

869. Roy, Andre. "Yeelen." 24 Images, No. 39/40 (Fall 1988): 98-99.

870. Tesson, Charles. "L'Afrique dans la Lumiere: Propos de Cisse." Cahiers du Cinema, No. 402 (decembre 1987): 28-31.

871. _____. "Genese." Cahiers du Cinema, No. 397 (June 1987): 10.

872. Toure, Kitia, et Jacques Binet. "Entretien avec Souleymane Cisse sur 'La Lumiere.'" Positif, No. 322 (Decembre 1987): 8-10.

DIKONGUE-PIPA, JEAN-PIERRE (1940-   ) (Cameroon)

873. Baratte-Eno Belinga, Therese. Ecrivains, Cineastes et Artistes Camerounais: Bio-Bibliographie. Yaounde: C.E.P.E.R., 1978, pp. 41-43.

874. Pfaff, Francoise. Twenty-Five Black African Filmmakers. Westport, CT: Greenwood Press, 1988, pp. 69-78.

Muna Moto

875. Essola Nuck Bidjeck. "Le Cineaste Dikongue Pipa a Cameroon Tribune: 'Je Prepare un Film Historique sur l'Afrique.'" Cameroon Tribune (26 juin 1975): 2.

876. Hennebelle, Guy. "Entretien avec J-P Dikongue-Pipa." Ecran, No. 49 (juillet 1976): 56-57. [Interview]

DONG, PIERRE-MARIE (1945-   ) (Gabon)

877. Pfaff, Francoise. Twenty-Five Black African Filmmakers. Westport, CT: Greenwood Press, 1988, pp. 79-85.

DUPARC, HENRI (1941-   ) (Ivory Coast)

878. Fallet, Pierre. "L'Eclatante Revanche d'Henri Duparc." Eburnea, No. 68 (1973): 13.

879. Pfaff, Francoise. Twenty-Five Black African Filmmakers. Westport, CT: Greenwood Press, 1988, pp. 87-94.

ECARE, DESIRE (1939-   ) (Ivory Coast)

880. Pfaff, Francoise. Twenty-Five Black African Filmmakers. Westport, CT: Greenwood Press, 1988, pp. 95-106.

Articles

881. Ahua, B. "Desire Ecare; Le Cineaste Ivoirien est un Homme Seul." Fraternite Matin, No. 4408 (1979): 20.

882. _____. "Le Retour de Desire Ecare." Fraternite Matin, No. 4390 (1979): 21.

883. Aumont, Jacques. "En Marge de Hyeres: Entretien avec Desire Ecare." Cahiers du Cinema, No. 203 (1968): 21-22.

884. B. A. "Desire Ecare en Greve." Fraternite Matin, No.
5095 (1981): 18.

885. Bachy, Victor. "Dossier." Unir Cinema, No. 19 (July-
August 1985): 11-14.

886. "Le Consecration de Desire Ecare." Eburnea, No. 37
(1970): 26.

887. "Desire Ecare: Encore un Nouveau Film." Fraternite
Matin, No. 1260 (1969): 7.

888. Gerard, Claude. "Desire Ecare s'Explique." Fraternite
Matin, No. 1947 (1971): 3.

889. "Grande Premiere de Gala des Films de Desire Ecare."
Fraternite Matin, No. 1670 (1970): 7.

890. Hennebelle, Guy. "Entretien avec Desire Ecare." Cinema
(Paris), No. 152 (1971): 138-140.

891. _____, and Catherine Ruelle. "Bio-Filmographie."
Unir Cinema (Senegal), No. 18 (May-June 1985): 13.

892. Johnson, Thomas A. "Ivory Coast Lures a Filmmaker."
New York Times (November 9 1972).

893. Jusu, K. K. Man. "Ecare et Bassori..." Fraternite
Matin, No. 5318 (1982): 19.

894. Kokore, Kouassi. "Cinema. Desire Ecare: "faire
confiance aux cineastes ivoiriens." Ivoire Dimanche, No. 204
(janvier 1975): 7-8.

895. "Une Nouvelle Etape dans le Cinema Africain: La Victoire
au Festival d'Hyeres du Realisateur Ivoirien Desire Ecare."
Fraternite Matin, No. 1033 (1968): 7.

896. Predal, Rene. "Deux Cineastes Noirs: Desire Ecare."
Jeune Cinema, No. 34 (November 1968): 4-9. [Interview]

Concerto pour un Exil

897. Ciment, Michel. "Concerto pour un Exil. Entretien avec
Desire Ecare." Positif, No. 97 (1968): 32-36.

898. "'Concerto pour un Exil.' Court Metrage de Desire
Ecare." Avant Scene du Cinema, No. 134 (1973): 40-49.

899. "Desire Ecare Beaucoup de Sympathies et pas d'Argent."
Jeune Afrique, No. 386-387 (1968): 69.

900. Hennebelle, Guy. "Naissance d'un Cinema Ivoirien:
"Concerto pour un Exil" - Opus 1 de Desire Ecare." L'Afrique
Litteraire et Artistique, No. 4 (1969): 75-81.

901. Watrigant, R. "Concerto pour un Exil." Afrique
Nouvelle, No. 1093 (1968): 14.

902. _____. "Concerto pour un Exil." Afrique Nouvelle, No. 1105 (1968): 14.

A Nous Deux, France

903. Amiel, Mireille. "A Nous Deux, France." Cinema (Paris), No. 152 (1971): 138-140.

904. Hennebelle, Guy. "Ecare: "A Nous Deux, France" est l'Analyse Clinique d'un Processus d'Acculturation." L'Afrique Litteraire et Artistique, No. 12 (1979): 197-202.

905. Seguin, Louis. "A Nous Deux, France." Positif, No. 118 (1970): 42-43.

906. Tessier, Max. "A Nous Deux, France." Cinema (Paris), No. 147 (juin 1970): 21-22.

Visages de Femmes (Faces of Women) (1985)

907. Canby, Vincent. "Film: "Faces," two Ivory Coast Tales." New York Times (February 13 1987): C22.

908. Carbonnier, A. "Visages de Femmes." Cinema, No. 318 (June 1985): 30.

909. Ecare, Desire. "Film: "Visages de Femmes." Unir Cinema (Senegal), No. 18 (May-June 1985): 10-12.

910. "Le Football et ... La Femme." Jeune Afrique, No. 692 (13 avril 1974): 13. [Review]

911. Hoberman, J. "It's a Mod, Mod World." Village Voice (February 17 1987). [Review]

912. Lajeunesse, J. "Visages de Femmes." La Revue du Cinema, No. 407 (July-August 1985): 46-47.

913. Pouillaude, J.-L. "Visages de Femmes." Positif, No. 293-294 (July-August 1985): 123.

914. Rinaldi, G. "Visages de Femmes." Cineforum, Vol. 23, No. 245 (June-July 1985): 35.

FADIKA, KRAMO-LANCINE (1948-   ) (Ivory Coast)

915. Pfaff, Francoise. Twenty-Five Black African Filmmakers. Westport, CT: Greenwood Press, 1988, pp. 107-113.

FAYE, SAFI (1943-   ) (Senegal)

916. Pfaff, Francoise. Twenty-Five Black African Filmmakers. Westport, CT: Greenwood Press, 1988, pp. 115-124.

Articles

917. Dia, Oumar. "L'Envers du Decor." Afrique, No. 20 (1979): 53-54. [Interview]

918. Gnonlonfoun, Alexis. "Entretien avec Safi Faye."
Afrique Nouvelle, No. 1562 (1979): 15.

919. Mangin, Marc. "Entretien avec Safi Faye." Droit et
Liberte, No. 389 (1980): 35-36.

920. Martin, Angela. "Faye." Framework, No. 11 (Autumn
1979): 17-19.

921. Maupin, Francoise. "Entretien avec Safi Faye." Image
et Son, No. 303 (February 1976): 75-80.

922. Relich, Mario. "Chronicle of a Student." West Africa,
No. 3393 (1982): 2112.

923. Richter, Erika. "Safi Faye (Senegal) - dem Afrikanischen
Baurern eine Stimme Geben." Filmwissenschaftliche Beitrage,
Vol. 21, No. 3 (1980): 212-221.

924. Traore, Mory. "La Passion selon Safi Faye." Bingo, No.
319 (1979): 28-29. [Interview]

925. Viana, N., et al. "Peliculas." Celuloide, Vol. 25, No.
291 (May 1980): 15-18.

Fad, Jal

926. Courant, Gerard. "Fad, jal." Cinema, No. 247-248
(1979): 27.

927. Paranagua, P. A. "Cannes 1979: 'Fad, jal.'" Positif,
No. 220-221 (July-August 1979): 55.

Kaddut Beykat (Lettre Paysanne)

928. Bosseno, Christian. "Lettre Paysanne." La Revue du
Cinema, No. 320/321 (October 1977): 157-158.

929. Ghali, Noureddine. "Safi Faye. Lettre Paysanne."
Cinema (Paris), No. 205 (1976): 25.

930. Grant, Jacques. "Lettre Paysanne." Cinema, No. 217
(January 1977): 93-94.

931. Kouassi, Guy. "Lettre Paysanne." Fraternite Matin, No.
5372 (1982): 7.

932. Moustapha, Mahama Baba. "Lettre Paysanne de Safi Faye."
Cinemarabe, No. 6 (1977): 36.

933. "Les Pasionarias n'etaient pas au rendez-vous."
Afrique, No. 792 (1976): 56.

934. Pouillaude, J.-L. "Lettre Paysanne." Positif, No. 188
(December 1976): 72.

935. Renaudin, Nicole. "Kaddu Beykat (Lettre Paysanne)."
Films et Documents, No. 309 (1975): 27.

936. Ruelle, Catherine. "'Lettre Paysanne' de Safi Faye." _Afrique-Asie_, No. 171 (1978): 48-49.

937. Schissel, Howard. "Among the Peasants." _New African_, No. 132 (1978): 73.

938. Vaugeois, Gerard. "Lettre Paysanne." _Ecran_, No. 53 (1976): 66.

939. Welsh, Henry. "Safi Faye: 'Lettre Paysanne.'" _Jeune Cinema_, No. 99 (December 1976-January 1977): 8-12.

GANDA, OUMAROU (1935-1981) (Niger)

940. Pfaff, Francoise. _Twenty-Five Black African Filmmakers_. Westport, CT: Greenwood Press, 1988, pp. 125-136.

Articles

941. Boughedir, Ferid. "Les Heritiers d'Oumarou Ganda." _Jeune Afrique_, No. 1053 (1981): 62-63.

942. "Le Cinema Africain Noir a Perdue Oumarou Ganda." _Fraternite Matin_, No. 4880 (1981): 19. [Interview]

943. Diedhiou, Djib. "L'ombre d'Oumarou Ganda." _Le Soleil_, No. 3268 (1981): 8.

944. Gnonlonfoun, Alexis. "Oumarou Ganda dans l'au-dela." _Afrique Nouvelle_, No. 1646 (1981): 21.

945. _____. "Oumarou Ganda: "je prefere le vinaigre des critiques a la pommade des eloges." _Afrique Nouvelle_, No. 1406 (1976): 17.

946. Haffner, Pierre. "Edward G. - Ray Sugar Robinson, alias Oumarou Ganda dit: le conteur." _7e Art_, No. 42 (1981): 16-19; No. 43 (1981): 16-19. [Interview]

947. Hennebelle, Guy. "Un Nouveau Cineaste Nigerien: Oumarou Ganda de 'Moi un noir' a 'Cabascabo.'" _L'Afrique Litteraire et Artistique_, No. 4 (1969): 70-74. [Interview]

948. Malanda, Ange-Severin. "L'Exile et le Lointain: Hommage a Oumarou Ganda." _Presence Africaine_, No. 119 (1981): 170-175.

949. Traore, Biny. "L'Exile d'Oumarou Ganda." _Peuples Noirs- Peuples Africains_, No. 23 (1981): 54-93. [Interview]

950. Vieyra, Paulin Soumanou. "Hommage a Oumarou Ganda: Cineaste Nigerien." _Presence Africaine_, No. 119, 3e trim. (1981): 165-169.

Obituaries

951. "Carnet." _Cinematographe_, No. 65 (February 1981): 77.

952. Goulli, Sophie el. "Oumarou Ganda est Mort." _Septieme Art_, No. 41 (1981): 24.

953. "Il Nous ont Quittes." Cinema, No. 268 (April 1981): 122-123.

954. "Le Grand Sommeil." La Revue du Cinema, No. 359 (March 1981): 8-11.

Cabascabo (1969)

955. Schaaf. "Cabascabo." Afrika Heute, Nr. 9 (1973): 47.

956. Scheifeingel, Maxime. "Cabascabo, un film de Oumarou Ganda." Avant-Scene du Cinema, No. 265 (April 1 1981): 39-50.

957. Watrigant, R. "Cabascabo." Afrique Nouvelle, No. 1142 (1969): 15.

Saitane (1973)

958. Chevassu, F. "Saitane." La Revue du Cinema, No. 276-277 (October 1973): 316-317.

Wazzou Polygame

959. Hennebelle, Guy. "Le Wazzou Polygame un film d'Oumarou Ganda contre le mariage force." Afrique-Asie, No. 4 (1972): 49-50. [Interview]

960. Schaaf. "Wazzou." Afrika Heute, No. 3 (1974): 47.

961. "Le Wazzou Polygame, un film d'Oumarou Ganda." Jeune Afrique, No. 591 (1972): 60-61.

GERIMA, HAILE (1946-) (Ethiopia/US)

962. Gerima, Haile. "Triangular Cinema, Breaking Toys, and Dinknesh vs. Lucy." In Questions of Third Cinema, eds. Jim Pines and Paul Willemen. London: BFI, 1989, pp. 65-89.

963. Pfaff, Francoise. Twenty-Five Black African Filmmakers. Westport, CT: Greenwood Press, 1988, pp. 137-155.

Articles

964. Ahmed, Saleh. "Cinema in Africa is Like Witchcraft." Africa Events, Vol. 1, No. 4 (1985): 64. [Interview]

965. Anderson, Kathy Elaine. "The Filmmaker as Storyteller: An Interview with Haile Gerima." Black Film Review, Vol. 2, No. 1 (Winter 1985): 6-7, 19.

966. Armes, Roy. "Cinema: Haile Gerima: from 'Harvest' to 'Embers.'" London Magazine, Vol. 24 (April-May 1984): 114-118.

967. Cham, Mbye B. "Art and Ideology in the Work of Sembene Ousmane and Haile Gerima." Presence Africaine, No. 129 (1984): 79-91.

968. _____. "Artistic and Ideological Convergence: Ousmane Sembene and Haile Gerima." Ufahamu, Vol. XI, No. 2 (Fall/ Winter 1981-82): 140-152.

969. Edelman, Rob. "Storyteller of Struggles: An Interview with Haile Gerima." The Independent, Vol. 8, No. 8 (October 1985): 16-19.

970. Howard, Steve. "A Cinema of Transformation: The Films of Haile Gerima." Cineaste, Vol. 14, No. 1 (1985): 28-29, 39.

971. Karikari, Kwame. "'Cinema is a Weapon': Ethiopian film-maker Haile Gerima on the cinema and culture." West Africa (July 24-30 1989): 1210.

972. Lardeau, Yann, and Serge LePeron. "Entretien avec Haile Gerima." Les Deux Ecrans, No. 50 (November 1982): 34-36.

973. McMullin, Corine. "Un regard africain sur la sombre Amerique." Afrique-Asie, No. 212 (1980): 53-54. [Interview]

974. Safford, T., and W. Triplett. "Haile Gerima: Radical Departures to a New Black Cinema." Journal of the University Film and Video Association, Vol. XXXV, No. 2 (Spring 1983): 59-65. [Interview]

975. Taylor, Clyde. "Haile Gerima: Firestealer." Africa Now, No. 31 (1983): 81-82.

Ashes and Embers

976. Linfield, Susan. "WNET Breaks the Viet Vet Color Line." Village Voice (May 28 1985): 41.

977. Maslin, Janet. "Screen: 'Ashes and Embers.'" New York Times (November 17 1982): C30.

978. Shepard, Richard F. "TV: PBS's 'Ashes,' About a Black Veteran." New York Times (May 26 1985): 52.

Bush Mama (1976)

979. "Haile Gerima Discusses 'Bush Mama.'" In Tricontinental Film Center: 1977-78. Berkeley, CA: Tricontinental Film Center, 1977, p. 44.

Articles

980. Bassan, Raphael. "Bush Mama." La Revue du Cinema, No. 397 (Septembre 1984): 24-25. Review.

981. Derobert, E. "Bush Mama." Positif, No. 284 (Octobre 1984): 70-71.

982. "Ethiopian Directs." New York Amsterdam News (November 1976): D-15.

983. Ferdinand, Val. "Bush Mama." Black Collegian, Vol. 7 (May-June 1977): 63.

984. Maslin, Janet. "Film: 'Bush Mama' tells the story of a coast ghetto." New York Times (September 25 1979): C8.

985. Monga, Celestin. "Lecon de Courage." Jeune Afrique, No. 1229 (1984): 58-59.

986. Taylor, Clyde. "Film: Bush Mama." First World (May/June 1977): 46-47.

Harvest, 3,000 Years (1975)

See also # 236

987. Daney, Serge. "Rencontre avec Haile Gerima (Une Moisson de 3000 ans)." Cahiers du Cinema, No. 270 (Septembre-Octobre 1976): 63-64. [Interview]

988. Davis, E. "Filming in Ethiopia: The Making of 'Harvest'." Filmmakers' Newsletter, No. 8 (April 1975): 18-19+.

989. Ferent, Catherine. "Le Premier Long Metrage Ethiopien." Jeune Afrique, No. 854 (1977): 60.

990. Hill, Lyndi. "Harvest, 3000 Years." Horn of Africa, Vol. 1, No. 1 (1978): 59.

991. Makarius, Michel I. "Kebebe le fou ou l'Ethiopie Millenaire." Jeune Afrique, No. 807 (1976): 107.

992. Martin, Marcel. "Le Recolte de 3000 ans." Ecran, No. 58 (May 15 1977): 61-62.

993. Pfaff, Francoise. "De Quelle Moisson s'agit-il (dialogue avec Haile Gerima, auteur de "la recolte de 3000 ans"). Positif, No. 198 (Octobre 1977): 53-56. [Interview]

994. Quam, Michael D. "Harvest: 3000 Years. Sowers of Maize and Bullets." Jump Cut, No. 24/25 (March 1981): 5-7.

995. Willemin, Paul. "Interview with Haile Gerima on 3,000 Year Harvest." Framework, No. 7-8 (Spring 1978): 31-35.

HALILU, ADAMU (Nigeria)

996. Balewa, Saddik. "Nigeria's Film Industry." West Africa (December 17 1984): 2583-2584. [Interview]

HONDO, MED (1936-   ) (Mauritania)

Works in English

997. Pfaff, Francoise. Twenty-Five Black African Filmmakers. Westport, CT: Greenwood Press, 1988, pp. 157-172.

Articles

998. Leahy, James. "Cinema Scope South of the Sahara: Med Hondo talks to James Leahy about making a new cinema in Africa." Monthly Film Bulletin, Vol. 55, No. 648 (January 1988): 9-10.

999. "Med Hondo: Film-maker." West Africa (June 6 1983): 1348-1349.

1000. Pfaff, Francoise. "The Films of Med Hondo: An African Filmmaker in Paris." Jump Cut, No. 31 (March 1986): 44-49.

1001. Ranvaud, Don. "Interview with Med Hondo." Framework, No. 7-8 (Spring 1978): 28-30.

1002. Reid, Marc. "Med Hondo Interview: Working Abroad." Jump Cut, No. 31 (March 1986): 48-49.

Works in French

1003. Boughedir, Ferid. "Ancien Cuisinier et Debardeur, l'Emigre Med Hondo Exprime sa Verite de l'Exil." Jeune Afrique, No. 725 (1974): 60-63.

1004. Ciment, Michel, et Paul-Louis Thirard. "Entretien avec Med Hondo." Positif, No. 119 (Septembre 1970): 22-26.

1005. Conde, Maryse. "Med Hondo: Ouvre une Ere Nouvelle." Demain l'Afrique, No. 33-34 (1979): 72-74.

1006. Dura, Madeleine. "Entretien avec Med Hondo." Jeune Cinema, No. 121 (1979): 21-28.

1007. Ghali, Noureddine. "Med Hondo: Je Suis un Immigre." Jeune Cinema, No. 81 (September-October 1974): 29-31.

1008. Hennebelle, Guy. "Entretien avec Med Hondo." Cinema (Paris), No. 147 (1970): 39-50.

1009. Lemaire, Charles. "Accuse, Med Hondo Repond." Afrique Nouvelle, No. 1863 (1985): 16.

1010. Martin, Marcel. "Breve Rencontre...avec Med Hondo." Ecran, No. 81 (June 15 1979): 25-26.

1011. Merzak, M. "Entretien avec Med Hondo." Les 2 Ecrans, No. 13 (1979): 24-26.

1012. "La Pellicule, la Politique et Med Hondo." Jeune Afrique, No. 654 (1973): 29.

1013. Tiao, Luc Adolphe. "Med Hondo: Le Cinema est une Matiere Premiere de Civilisation." Carrefour Africain, No. 710-711 (1984): 5.

Bicots-Negres vos Voisins (1974)

1014. Chevassu, F. "Les 'Bicots-Negres' vos Voisins." La Revue du Cinema, No. 299 (October 1975): 35.

1015. Giraud, T. "Parle de, ou Parler d'Eux...('Bicots-Negres, vos Voisins')." Cahiers du Cinema, No. 254-255 (December 1974-January 1975): 41-43.

1016. Hennebelle, Guy, et A. A. Delati. "Les Bicots-Negres vos Voisins." Ecran, No. 30 (November 1974): 79-81.

1017. Salama, M. Ben. "Les Chants Viendront d'eux Memes ("Les 'Bicots-Negres', Vos Voisins')." Positif, No. 165 (January 1975): 61-62.

Sarraounia

1018. Bakyono, J. S. "Sarraounia, Un Resistante a la Penetration Coloniale." Ivoire Dimanche, No. 666 (1983): 40-43.

1019. Berube, R.-C. "Sarraounia." Sequences, No. 126 (October 1986): 15-16.

1020. Chevallier, J. "Sarraounia." La Revue du Cinema, No. 422 (December 1986): 25-26.

1021. Delmas, Ginette. "Sarraounia." Jeune Cinema, No. 178 (January-February 1987): 46.

1022. "Histoires de Tournage du Film "Sarraounia" de Med Hondo." Presence Africaine, No. 144 (1987): 139-142.

1023. "Sarraounia." Variety (September 10 1986): 19.

1024. Schaar, E. "Sarraounia." Medien, Vol. 31, No. 2 (1987): 95-96.

1025. Silvestri, R. "Sarraounia" Tops Panafrican Fest as Many Records Fall." Variety (March 25 1987): 5-6.

1026. Thirard, Paul-Louis. "Sarraounia." Positif, No. 311 (January 1987): 78.

Soleil O

1027. Cohn, Bernhard. "Soleil O." Positif, No. 119 (1970?): 18-20.

1028. Delmas, Jean. "Med Hondo: Soleil O." Jeune Cinema, No. 48 (1970): 32-38. [Interview]

1029. Hennebelle, Guy. "Med Hondo: 'Soleil O' est un Hurlement de Revolte." L'Afrique Litteraire et Artistique, No. 11 (1970): 62-69.

1030. _____. "Soleil O: entretien avec Med Hondo." Ecran, No. 11 (janvier 1973): 81-84.

Toute la Mort pour Dormir (1977)

1031. Colpart, G. "Nous Aurons Toute la Mort Pour Dormir."
Cinema, No. 223 (July 1977): 103.

1032. Delmas, Jean. "Nous Aurons Toute la Mort Pour Dormir."
Jeune Cinema, No. 102 (April-May 1977): 51.

1033. Grelier, R. "Nous Aurons Toute la Mort Pour Dormir."
La Revue du Cinema, No. 317 (May 1977): 119-120.

1034. Hennebelle, Guy. "Nous Aurons Toute la Mort Pour
Dormir." Ecran, No. 58 (May 15 1977): 50-51.

1035. Lauret, B. "Nous Aurons Toute la Mort Pour Dormir."
Telecine, No. 218 (May 1977): 47.

1036. Thirard, Paul-Louis. "Nous Aurons Toute la Mort Pour
Dormir." Positif, No. 193 (May 1977): 73-74.

West Indies (1979)

1037. Delcroix, Jacqueline. "West Indies." Nigrizia, Vol.
99, No. 4 (1981): 40.

1038. E. J. M. "West Indies, les Negres Marrons de la
Liberte." Demain l'Afrique, No. 33-34 (1979): 70.

1039. Gervais, Ginette, and Madeleine Dura. "West Indies
Story Hier et Aujourd'hui Meme Combat." Jeune Cinema, No. 121
(September-October 1979): 21-28.

1040. Hondo, Med. "A Propos de "West Indies...Les Negres
Marrons de la Liberte"; Critique d'une Critique." La Revue du
Cinema, No. 345 (December 1979): 22-26.

1041. Lambour, M. C. "Les 'Negres Marrons de la Liberte."
Afrique, No. 29 (1979): 65.

1042. Martin, Marcel. "West Indies." Ecran, No. 84 (1979):
63-64.

1043. Maslin, Janet. "Film: 'West Indies,' Musical History."
New York Times (March 8 1985): C10.

1044. Mpoyi-Buatu, Th. "Ceddo" de Sembene Ousmane et "West
Indies" de Med Hondo. Presence Africaine, No. 119 (1981):
152-164. An English translation of this article appears in
John D. H. Downing's Film and Politics in the Third World.
New York: Praeger Publishers, 1988.

1045. Pouillaude, J.-L. "West Indies." Positif, No. 225
(December 1979): 76.

1046. Rivel, Moune de. "Un Mauritanien Tourne l'Histoire des
Antilles." Bingo, No. 319 (1979): 35-37.

ISIAKPERE, FAITH (1955-   ) (Nigeria)

1047. Solanke, Adeola. "A Doer of Deeds." West Africa
(October 3-9 1988): 1838-1839.

KABORE, GASTON J. M. (1951-   ) (Burkina Faso)

1048. Pfaff, Francoise. Twenty-Five Black African
Filmmakers. Westport, CT: Greenwood Press, 1988, pp. 173-182.

1049. "Preserver l'Esprit du Conte - un entretien avec
Kabore." Jeune Cinema, No. 149 (Mars 1983): 15-17.

Wend Kuuni (1982)

1050. Diawara, Manthia. "Oral Literature and African Film:
Narratology in Wend Kuuni." In Questions of Third Cinema,
eds. Jim Pines and Paul Willemen. London: BFI, 1989, pp. 199-
211.

1051. Matanda, Tshishi Bavuala. Litterature et Cinema:
contribution a l'etude de l'adaption dans la culture negro-
africaine. Louvain-la-Neuve: CIACO, 1988, pp. 138-152.

Articles

1052. Ales, D. "Wend Kuuni." Cine Revue, No. 64 (March 8
1984): 8.

1053. Aude, F. "Wend Kuuni le don de Dieu." Positif, No.
277 (March 1984): 70.

1054. Benabdessadok, Cherifa. "Wend Kuuni le don de dieu."
Afrique-Asie, No. 319 (1984): 56-57.

1055. Berube, R.-C. "Wend Kuuni." Sequences, Vol. III
(January 1983): 59.

1056. Bosseno, Christian. "Le Don de Dieu." La Revue du
Cinema, No. 391 (February 1984): 25-26.

1057. Canby, Vincent. "Screen: 'Wend Kuuni.'" New York
Times (March 27 1983). [Review]

1058. Diawara, Manthia. "Oral Literature and African Film:
Narratology in "Wend Kuuni." Presence Africaine, No. 142
(1987): 36-49. [Reprinted in # 1050]

1059. Francia, Luis. "New Directors: From Upper Volta to
Staten Island." Village Voice (March 29 1983): 55.

1060. Taconet, C. "Wend Kuuni." Cinema, No. 304 (April
1984): 57.

1061. Tesson, Charles. "Lorsque l'Enfant Parle." Cahiers du
Cinema, No. 358 (April 1984): 44-45.

1062. "Wend Kuuni." Variety (August 25 1982): 15.

1063. "Wend Kuuni (God's Gift)." Variety (November 17 1982):
26.

KAMBA, SEBASTIEN (Congo)

1064. Hennebelle, Guy. "Un Long Metrage Congolais: "La
Rancon d'une Alliance" de Sebastien Kamba." Afrique-Asie, No.
53 (1974): 50-51.

1065. _____. "Sebastien Kamba, Cineaste Congolais, Nous
Declare." Jeune Afrique, Vol. 6 (October 1970): 43.
[Interview]

KAMWA, DANIEL (1943-   ) (Cameroon)

1066. Baratte-Eno Belinga, Therese. Ecrivains, Cineastes et
Artistes Camerounais: Bio-Bibliographie. Yaounde: C.E.P.E.R,
1978, pp. 80-81.

1067. Pfaff, Francoise. Twenty-Five Black African
Filmmakers. Westport, CT: Greenwood Press, 1988, pp. 185-194.

Articles

1068. Coppola, John. "Cameroonian Film Maker." Topic
(Washington, D.C.), No. 104 (19??): 37-39. [Interview]

1069. "Daniel Kamwa Un Talenteux Camerounais." Bingo, No.
200 (1969): 21.

1070. Hennebelle, Guy. "Daniel Kamwa: Expliquer en Amusant."
Afrique-Asie, No. 124 (1976): 51-53.

1071. Mbounja, Francis Emile. "Daniel Kamwa a Batons
Rompus." Bingo, No. 274 (1975): 16-19, 64. [Interview]

Notre Fille (1980)

1072. Aude, F. "Notre Fille." Positif, No. 250 (January
1982): 85-86.

1073. Bakyono, J. S. "'Notre Fille' de Daniel Kamwa, Les
Moeurs de l'Afrique d'Aujourd'hui." Ivoire Dimanche, No. 527
(1981): 43.

1074. Bosseno, Christian. "Notre Fille." La Revue du
Cinema, No. 367 (December 1981): 54.

1075. Gervais, Ginette. "Notre Fille." Jeune Cinema, No.
139 (December 1981-January 1982): 48-49.

1076. Lardeau, Yann. "Notre Fille." Cahiers du Cinema, No.
331 (January 1982): 57.

Pousse Pousse

1077. Gbegnonvi, Marie-Louise. "Pousse-Pousse." Afrique,
No. 10 (1978): 92-93.

1078. Hennebelle, Monique. "Daniel Kamwa, Laureat du Meilleur Scenario 1974 Decerne par l'Agence de Cooperation Culturelle et Technique: "Dans Pousse-Pousse, Je Denoncerai la Pratique de la Dot au Cameroun." L'Afrique Litteraire et Artistique, No. 33 (1974): 69-73. [Interview]

1079. Lajeunnesse, J. "Pousse Pousse." La Revue du Cinema, No. 307 (June-July 1976): 104-106. [Review]

1080. Sultan, Rene. "Pousse-Pousse" film de Daniel Kamwa. Union, No. 209 (1976): 4.

MAHOMO, NANA (1930-   ) (South Africa)

1081. Pfaff, Francoise. Twenty-Five Black African Filmmakers. Westport, CT: Greenwood Press, 1988, pp. 195-204.

Articles

1082. Anthony, David H. "Black Scholar Interviews: Mahomo." Black Scholar, Vol. 7 (May 1976): 30-35.

1083. _____. "Clandestine Filming in South Africa: An Interview with Nana Mahomo." Cineaste, Vol. 7, No. 3 (1976): 18-19, 50.

1084. _____. "Nana Mahomo un Sud-Africain Contra l'Apartheid." Afrique-Asie, No. 120 (1976): 65-66.

1085. "Nana Mahomo." Film Library Quarterly, Vol. IX, No. 1 (1976): 11-18.

Last Grave at Dimbaza (1974)

1086. Gabriel, Teshome H. Third Cinema in the Third World. Ann Arbor, MI: UMI Research Press, 1982, pp. 45-47.

Articles

1087. Clarke, Robert H., and Cynthia Grant Schoenberger. "Filming the African Revolution." International Development Review, Vol. 18, No. 2 (1976): 28-31.

1088. Duteil, Christian. "La Derniere Tombe au Dimbaza." Jeune Cinema, No. 91 (1975): 31-33.

1089. Fraser, C. Gerald. "'Dimbaza,' Film Smuggled Out of South Africa, Won Aid of Church and Labor." New York Times (October 27 1975): 52.

1090. Gabriel, Teshome H. "Let Their Eyes Testify": An Interview with Nana Mahomo." Ufahamu, Vol. VII, No. 1 (1976): 97-113. Discussion with Mahomo re: "Last Grave at Dimbaza."

1091. Hall, Susan. "Last Grave at Dimbaza." Film Library Quarterly, Vol. 9, No. 1 (1976): 15-18.

1092. Hennebelle, Guy. "Le Derniere Tombe a Dimbaza." Ecran, No. 41 (1975): 62-63.

1093. O'Connor, John J. "TV: On Oppression in South Africa." New York Times (October 27 1975): 52.

1094. Raynor, William. "White Safari That Put Apartheid on Film." The Times [London] (June 24 1974).

1095. "'Secretly' Made Black Labor Pic in Ottawa; So. Africa Protests." Variety (November 13 1974): 39.

1096. Taylor, Clyde. "Last Grave at Dimbaza." Black Collegian, Vol. 11 (February-March 1981): 14+.

1097. Unger, Arthur. "Controversial Look at South Africa." Christian Science Monitor (October 24 1975): 26.

MALDOROR, SARAH (1929-   ) (France/Guadeloupe)

1098. Pfaff, Francoise. Twenty-Five Black African Filmmakers. Westport, CT: Greenwood Press, 1988, pp. 205-216.

Articles

1099. Aufderheide, Pat. "Sarah Maldoror." Black Film Review, Vol. 4, No. 4 (Fall 1988): 7-8.

1100. Boughedir, Ferid. "Paris Decouvre l'Angola et Sarah Maldoror." Jeune Afrique, No. 646 (1973): 76.

1101. Conde, Maryse. "Maldoror Change de Veste." Afrique, No. 47 (1981): 47.

1102. Ferrari, A. "Le Second Souffle du Cinema Africain." Telecine, No. 176 (Janvier 1973): 2-9.

1103. Harvey, Sylvia. "Third World Perspectives: Focus on Sarah Maldoror." Women and Film, Vol. 1, No. 5-6 (1974): 71-75, 110.

1104. Pfaff, Francoise. "Sarah Maldoror." Black Art, Vol. 5, No. 2 (1982): 25-32.

1105. "Sarah Maldoror Nous Declare." Jeune Afrique, No. 469 (1969): 45. [Interview]

1106. Yao, Henri. "Sarah Maldoror le Pionnier." Bingo, No. 301 (1978): 59-61.

Sambizanga

1107. Gomis, Gabriel Jacques. "Sambizanga ou Ballade pour un Militant." Afrique Nouvelle, No. 1309 (1974): 22-23.

1108. Hennebelle, Guy. "Sambizanga." Ecran, No. 15 (May 1973): 69-71.

1109. _____. "'Sambizanga' les Premieres Luttes en Angola." Afrique-Asie, No. 25 (1973): 56-57.

1110. Hennebelle, Monique. "'Sambizanga': un film de Sarah Maldoror sur les Debuts de la Guerre de Liberation en Angola." L'Afrique Litteraire et Artistique, No. 28 (1973): 78-87.

1111. Ralison, Lalao. "Freiheitskampf in Angola 'Sambizanga'." Afrika Heute, Nr. 21/22 (1972): 482-483.

1112. Relich, Mario. "Film Review: Africa's Women Filmmakers." West Africa (21 June 1982): 1650.

1113. "Sambizanga" a repressao colonial. Tempo, No. 217 (1974): 38-43. [Interview]

1114. "Sambizanga" de Sarah Maldoror. Zaire, No. 255 (1973): 34.

1115. Segal, Aaron. "Film review, Sambizanga." Africa Today, Vol. 21, No. 1 (1974): 67.

1116. Siegfried, Shula. "Avec 'Sambizanga' Sarah Maldoror Continue le Combat." Afrique-Asie, No. 11-12 (1972): 118-119.

Velada

1117. Pina, Marie-Paule de. "Sarah Maldoror: apres 'Sambizanga' 'Velada.'" Afrique-Asie, No. 62 (1974): 49.

MAMBETY, DJIBRIL DIOP (1945-   ) (Senegal)

1118. Pfaff, Francoise. Twenty-Five Black African Filmmakers. Westport, CT: Greenwood Press, 1988, pp. 217-225.

Touki-Bouki

1119. Touki-Bouki de Djibril Diop Mambety: Description et Analyse Filmique. Sous la direction d'Andre Gardies ... et al. Abidjan: Universite Nationale de Cote d'Ivoire, Centre d'enseignement et de recherche audio-visuels, 1982. 159p. (Communication Audio-Visuelle; No. 5)

Articles

1120. Allones, F. R. d'. "Touki-Bouki." Cinema (Paris), No. 346 (Mar 19/25 1986): 4.

1121. Bassan, Raphael. "Touki-Bouki." La Revue du Cinema, No. 415 (April 1986): 36-37.

1122. Bernard, Jean. "Un Film Africain: Touki Bouki." Afrique Nouvelle, No. 1347 (1975): 24.

1123. Cervoni, Albert. "Touki Bouki." Cinema (Paris), No. 177 (1973): 39.

1124. Diop, Abdou Aziz. "Lecture de Film: "Touki-Bouki" de Djibril M. Diop." Unir Cinema, No. 16 (1985): 27-29; No. 17 (1985): 25-26.

1125. Le Roux, H. "Touki-Bouki." Cahiers du Cinema, No. 382 (April 1986): 61.

1126. Pouillaude, J.-L. "Touki-Bouki." Positif, No. 304 (June 1986): 79.

1127. Prelle, Francois. "Touki-Bouki de Djibril Diop. Le Rire de l'Hyene." Bingo, No. 247 (1973): 64-65.

1128. Sy, A. A. "Lecture de Film: "Touki-Bouki." Unir Cinema, No. 18 (May-June 1985): 14-15.

1129. Wagner, J. "Touki-Bouki ("Une Autre Logique"). Unir Cinema, No. 23-24 (March-June 1986): 47.

MBALA GNOAN, ROGER (Ivory Coast)

1130. Aizicovici, Francine. "Roger M'Bala: en toute liberte pour Bouka." Cinema (Paris), No. 430 (February 24-March 1 1988): 17.

1131. Daja, Allarabaye. "Entretien avec Mbala." Unir Cinema, No. 20 (September-December 1985): 9-12.

1132. Datche, Simplice. "La Cote d'Ivoire a l'Honneur." Ivoire Dimanche, No. 368 (1978): 36.

1133. Jusu, K. K. Man. "Roger M'Bala: maitre de l'humour." Fraternite Matin, No. 6141 (1985): 12.

1134. Kane, Samba. "Quatre Cineastes Ivoiriens "a l'aussaut" de Ouaga." Fraternite Matin, No. 2469 (1973): 7. [Interview]

1135. Kouassi, Germain. "M'Bala Gnoan realisateur ivoirien le cinema doit repondre aux aspirations du peuple." Bingo, No. 240 (1973): 32-33.

1136. "Roger M'Bala ou le triomphe d'un obscur." Eburnea, No. 63 (1972): 34-35.

Ablakon

1137. Kouame J-B, K. "Ablakon" aux studios. Le film du peuple. Fraternite Matin, No. 6144 (1985): 9; No. 6146 (1985): 8.

Amanie

1138. N. A. P. "Festival de Carthage: la realite et la rigeur. Amanie, de Gnoan M'Bala, de nouveau a l'honneur." Fraternite Matin, No. 2378 (1972): 7.

1139. Yoboue, Koffi. "Gnoan M'Bala (l'auteur d'Amanie): une recompense? Une responsabilite?" Fraternite Matin, No. 2330 (1972): 7.

MWEZE, NGANGURA (Zaire)

1140. Aufderheide, Pat. "Ngangura Mweze." Black Film Review, Vol. 4, No. 4 (Fall 1988): 8-9.

La Vie Est Belle (1987)

1141. Keleko, Yewande. "Rhythm and Laugh." West Africa (July 10-16 1989).

1142. Maslin, Janet. "Film: 'La Vie est Belle.'" New York Times (November 18 1987): C21.

1143. "La Vie est Belle (Life is Rosy)." Variety (May 27 1987): 18.

MWINYIPEMBE, MUSINDE (Tanzania)

See # 1458-1472

N'DIAYE, SAMBA FELIX (Senegal)

1144. Martin, Angela. "N'Diaye." Framework, No. 11 (Autumn 1979): 19-20.

NGAKANE, LIONEL (South Africa)

See # 1473-1475

OUEDRAOGO, IDRISSA (1954-) (Burkina Faso)

1145. Daja, A. "Entretien avec Idrissa Ouedraogo." Unir Cinema (Senegal), No. 18 (May-June 1985): 6-9.

1146. Fiofori, Tam. "Burkina. Film Realities." West Africa (April 27 1987): 820-821. [Profile/Interview]

1147. Pfaff, Francoise. "Interview with Idrissa Ouedraogo." Black Film Review, Vol. 4, No. 1 (Winter 1987/88): 11-12, 15.

Le Choix (The Choice)

1148. James, Caryn. "Review/Film: Universality in Story by African." New York Times (March 24 1988).

Poko

1149. Ayari, Farida. "Poko, la mort au bout du chemin." Adhoua, No. 4-5 (1981): 8.

Yaaba

1150. Brown, Georgia. "Arms and the Man." Village Voice (October 10 1989): 90. [Review]

1151. Enahoro, Carole. "Real-to-reel." West Africa (December 25 1989-January 7 1990): 2152-2153. [Review]

1152. Werman, Marco. "'Yaaba' Comes from Africa to Speak to the World." New York Times (October 22 1989): Sec. 2, p. 20.

OYEKUNLE, OLUSEGUN (Nigeria)

1153. Bonner, Lesley. "Nigeria's Hollywood Hero." New African, No. 186 (1983): 44-45.

1154. Drame, Kandioura. "Oyekunle on the African Film Industry." Afriscope, Vol. 11, No. 2 (1981): 27-30, 33. [Interview]

1155. "Segun Oyekunle." Network Africa, Vol. 2, No. 9 (1985): 18, 20.

1156. "Top Award for Nigerian Filmmaker." Africa, No. 112 (1980): 70-71.

SAMB-MAKHARAM, ABABACAR (1934-1987) (Senegal)

1157. Pfaff, Francoise. Twenty-Five Black African Filmmakers. Westport, CT: Greenwood Press, 1988, pp. 227-236.

Articles

1158. "Ababacar Samb Cineaste Africain." Jeune Afrique, No. 573 (1972): 55.

1159. Konata, Aminata. "Un Jeune Cineaste Senegalais, Samb Ababakar Pose le Probleme 'des anciens et des modernes.'" Bingo, No. 153 (1965): 34-35.

1160. Laude, Andre. "Une Revelation: Ababacar Samb." Jeune Afrique, No. 246 (1965): 30-31.

1161. Paquet, Andre. "Babacar Samb-Makharam: De la Notion d'Universalisme." Cinema Quebec, Vol. II, No. 6-7 (March-April 1973): XVIII-XX.

1162. Saint-Mathieu, D. de. "Breve Rencontre avec Ababacar Samb, secretaire general de La Federation Panafricain des Cineastes." Ecran, No. 33 (Fevrier 1975): 12-14.

Obituaries

1163. "Ababacar Samb-Makharam." Variety (December 30 1987): 46.

1164. Bassori, Timite. "Samb Ababacar: Un Vieux Compagnon de Route." Presence Africaine, No. 145 (1988): 179-180.

1165. Schoenberner, Gerhard. "Umschau: Pionere des Schwarzafrikanischen Films." Film und Fernschen, Vol. 16, No. 5 (1988): 40-41.

Codou

1166. Alain, Yves. "'Codou' d'Ababacar Samb, Un Film que l'on n'Attendant Plus." Soleil, No. 217 (1971): 58-59.

1167. "Codou." Afrique Nouvelle, No. 1237 (1971): 4.

1168. Paquet, Andre. "Ababacar Samb, "Codou" et le Cinema au Senegal." Cinema Quebec, Vol. I, No. 10 (July-August 1972): 28-31. [Interview]

1169. Rouch, Jean. "Codou par Ababakar Samb." Jeune Afrique, No. 565 (1971): 62-63.

Et la Neige N'Etait Plus

1170. Mendy, Justin. "Et la neige n'etait plus." Afrique Nouvelle, No. 967 (1966): 15.

1171. Schaaf. "Et La Neige N'Etait Plus." Afrika Heute, Bd. 10/11 (1973): 52.

Jom

1172. Bassole, A. "'Jom' (de Ababacar Samb), Un Hymne a la Dignite." Fraternite Matin, No. 5300 (1982): 19.

1173. Dia, Alioune Toure. "Jom" ou la dignite. Bingo, No. 333 (1980): 58-59. [Interview]

1174. Diallo, Abdoulaye Bamba. "Jom" de Ababacar Samb Makharam. Zone 2, No. 140 (1982): 18.

1175. Gervais, Ginette. "Jom." Jeune Cinema, No. 144 (1982): 40-41.

1176. "Jom." Variety, Vol. 307, No. 4 (1982): 17.

1177. Lemaire, Charles. "Jom." Unir Cinema, No. 1 (1982): 13-14.

1178. Traore, Biny. "Jom et Money Power." Observateur, No. 2525 (1983): 4-5, 10.

SEMBENE, OUSMANE (1923-   ) (Senegal)

Works in English

1179. Pfaff, Francoise. The Cinema of Ousmane Sembene, A Pioneer of African Film. Westport, CT: Greenwood Press, 1984. 207p.

Books with Sections on Ousmane Sembene

1180. Armes, Roy. "Ousmane Sembene." In Third World Film Making and the West. Berkeley: University of California Press, 1987, pp. 281-292.

1181. Gabriel, Teshome H. "Interview with Ousmane Sembene." In Third Cinema in the Third World. Ann Arbor, MI: UMI Research Press, 1982, pp. 111-116.

1182. Mortimer, Robert. "Ousmane Sembene and the Cinema of Decolonization." In Film and Africana Politics. New Brunswick: Rutgers University, between 1972 and 1977.

1183. Pfaff, Francoise. Twenty-Five Black African Filmmakers. Westport, CT: Greenwood Press, 1988, pp. 237-266.

1184. Rosen, Miriam. "Sembene, Ousmane." In World Film Directors, ed. John Wakeman. New York: H.W. Wilson, 1988, Vol. 2, pp. 1001-1011.

1185. Stone, Les. "Ousmane, Sembene." In Black Writers: A Selection of Sketches from Contemporary Authors. Detroit: Gale Research Inc., 1989, pp. 443-445.

1186. Vieyra, Paulin Soumanou. "Five Major Films by Ousmane Sembene." In Film and Politics in the Third World, ed. John D. H. Downing. New York: Praeger Publishers, 1988. See also Noureddine Ghali's "An Interview with Ousmane Sembene" in this same volume.

1187. Weaver, Harold D., Jr. "A Major Political Filmmaker, Ousmane Sembene: an interview." In Film and Africana Politics. New Brunswick: Rutgers University, between 1972 and 1977. 33p. [Also held by the Schomburg Center as a separate microform - Sc Micro F-9790]

Dissertations and Theses

1188. Kale, McDonald Ndombo. "Social and Political Commitments in the Films of Sembene Ousmane." Thesis (M.A.) University of Illinois at Chicago, 1980. 54p.

1189. Moore, Carrie Dailey. "Evolution of an African Artist: Social Realism in the Works of Ousmane Sembene." Dissertation (Ph.D.) Indiana University, 1973. 318p.

1190. Okore, Ode. "The Film World of Ousmane Sembene." Dissertation (Ph.D.) Columbia University, 1982. 305p.

1191. Tekpetey, Alphonse Kwawisi. "Social and Political Committment in the Works of Ousmane Sembene." Dissertation (Ph.D.) University of Wisconsin-Madison, 1973. 490p.

Articles

1192. "African Cinema Seeks a New Language." Young Cinema, Vol. 3 (Summer 1983): 26-28. [Interview]

1193. Armes, Roy. "Ousmane Sembene: Questions of Change." Cine-Tracts, Vol. IV, No. 2-3 (14-15) (Summer-Fall 1981): 71-77.

1194. Cham, Mbye. "Art and Ideology in the Work of Sembene Ousmane and Haile Gerima." Presence Africaine, No. 129 (1984): 79-91.

1195. _____. "Artistic and Ideological Convergence: Ousmane Sembene and Haile Gerima." Ufahamu, Vol. XI, No. 2 (Fall-Winter 1981-82): 140-152.

1196. _____. "Ousmane Sembene and the Aesthetics of African Oral Traditions." Africana Journal, Vol. 13 (1982): 24-40.

1197. Diallo, Siradiou. "Film: Sembene Ousmane: Africa's Leading Film Maker." Encore (April 1973): 45-48. [Interview]

1198. "Film-Makers and African Culture." Africa, No. 71 (July 1977): 80. [Interview]

1199. Garb, Gill, and Nii K. Bentsi Enchill. "Ousmane Sembene: the medium is the message." Africa Now, Vol. 3 (1981): 75-76. [Interview]

1200. Jensen, M. "The Role of the Filmmaker: Three Views; Interview with Ousmane Sembene." Arts in Society, Vol. 10, No. 2 (1973): 220-225.

1201. McClain, Ruth Rambo. "Ousmane Sembene--Griot of Celluloid." Encore American and Worldwide News (February 6 1978): 34-35.

1202. "Ousmane Sembene at the Olympic Games." American Cinematographer, Vol. 53, No. 11 (1972): 1276, 1322.

1203. Perry, G. M., and P. McGilligan. "Ousmane Sembene: An Interview." Film Quarterly, Vol. 26, No. 3 (Spring 1973): 36-42.

1204. Peterson, Maurice. "Movies: Ousmane Sembene." Essence (March 1973): 8. [Interview]

1205. Relich, Mario. "Ousmane Sembene in London." West Africa (April 20 1981): 3208-3209, 3211-3212.

1206. Schissel, Howard. "Portrait; Sembene Ousmane: film-maker." West Africa (July 18 1983): 1665-1666.

1207. "Sembene." Seven Days [New York] (March 10 1978): 26-27. [Interview]

1208. "Sembene Ousmane and the Censor." Africa [London] (October 1978): 85.

1209. Sevastakis, M. "Neither Gangsters nor Dead Kings." Film Library Quarterly, Vol. 6, No. 3 (1973): 13-15+.

1210. Weaver, Harold D., Jr. "Film-makers Have a Great Responsibility to Our People." Cineaste, Vol. VI, No. 1 (1973): 26-31. [Interview]

Newspaper Articles

1211. Gross, Linda. "'Fellow Feminist': The Father of African Film." Los Angeles Times (August 15 1978): 1, 12-13.

1212. Hoberman, J. "Inside Senegal." Village Voice
(February 6 1978): 42, 48.

1213. Johnson, Thomas A. "A Film Force from Senegal." New
York Times (January 27 1978): C5.

1214. _____. "A Film Maker in Senegal Stresses African
Culture." New York Times (August 31 1974): 12.

Works in French and Spanish

1215. Minyona-Nkodo, Mathieu-Francois. Comprendre les Bouts
de Bois de Dieu de Sembene Ousmane. Issy-les-Moulineaux,
France: Ed. Saint-Paul, 1979. 95p.

1216. Vieyra, Paulin S. Ousmane Sembene Cineaste: Premiere
Periode, 1962-1971. Paris: Presence Africaine, 1972. 244p.

Dissertations

1217. Jacquemain, Jean-Pierre. "Comparaison de l'Ecriture
Litteraire et Cinematographique chez Sembene Ousmane."
Dissertation (Ph.D.) Louvanium University (Zaire), 1970.

1218. Ntahombaye, Philippe. "Sembene Ousmane, Romancier
Senegalais, Poete et Cineaste." Memoire de Licence en
Philologie Romane. Bruxelles: Universite Libre de Bruxelles,
1970.

Articles

1219. Alvarez Diez, I. "El Cine del Africa Actual."
Casablanca, No. 9 (September 1981): 6-7. [Interview]

1220. Artese, Alberto. "Conversazione con Ousmane Sembene e
Thierno Faty Sow." Cineforum, No. 277 (1988): 21-24.

1221. Ayari, Farida, Sylvaine Kamara, Mohamed Maiga and
Francois Soudan. "Jeune Afrique fait parler Sembene Ousmane."
Jeune Afrique, No. 976 (1979): 71-75. [Interview]

1222. B. A. "Sembene Ousmane, les Cineastes ne sont pas les
martyrs." Fraternite Matin, No. 5218 (1982): 16.

1223. _____. "Sembene Ousmane pour la diversite."
Fraternite Matin, No. 5230 (1982): 17. [Interview]

1224. Bakyono, J. S. "Ousmane Sembene parle..." Ivoire
Dimanche, No. 597 (1982): 46.

1225. Bonnet, Jean-Claude. "Ousmane Sembene."
Cinematographe, No. 28 (1977): 43-44. [Interview]

1226. Cheriaa, Tahar, and Ferid Boughedir. "Jeune Afrique
fait parler Sembene Ousmane." Jeune Afrique, No. 795 (1976):
54-56. [Interview]

1227. Diallo, Siradiou. "Jeune Afrique fait parler Sembene
Ousmane." Jeune Afrique, No. 629 (1973): 44-49.

1228. Dupas, Jean. "Ousmane Sembene et sa conception du cinema Africain." Nawadi Cinema (1 aout 1968): 64-68.

1229. Ebony, Noel. "Ousmane Sembene temoigne..." Afrique [London], No. 15 (September 1978): 92-95. [Interview]

1230. Ghali, Noureddine. "Ousmane Sembene. 'Le Cineaste de nos Jours, peut remplacer le conteur traditionnel...'" Cinema, No. 208 (April 1976): 83-95. [Interview]

1231. Grelier, R. "Ousmane Sembene." Image et Son, No. 322 (November 1977): 74-80.

1232. Hennebelle, Guy. "Deux Cineastes Noirs: Ousmane Sembene." Jeune Cinema, No. 34 (Novembre 1968): 4-9. [Interview]

1233. _____, et al. "Le Cinema de Sembene Ousmane." Ecran, No. 43 (January 1976): 41-50.

1234. James, Emile. "Sembene Ousmane." Jeune Afrique, No. 499 (July 28 1970). [Interview]

1235. "Ousmane Sembene a l'Honneur." Afrique Nouvelle, No. 1254 (1971): 11.

1236. "Ousmane Sembene l'affirme: le cinema est la plus grande ecole du soir d'Afrique Noire." Bingo, No. 176 (1967): 24.

1237. "Ousmane Sembene: 'L'Afrique est un marche important qui n'a pas sa propre creation cinematographique." Afrique Nouvelle, No. 1033 (1967): 15. [Interview]

1238. "Sembene Ousmane." Dossier reuni par Daniel Serceau. CinemAction, No. 34 (1985). 96p.

1239. "Sembene Ousmane contra la "generation commerciale" du cinema Africain." Agecop Liaison, No. 43 (1978): 40-41.

1240. Trelles, L. "El Cine en el Africa Negra: Ousmane Sembene y los Cineastas Africanos Posteriores." Imagenes, Vol. 3, No. 2 (1987): 27-30.

Camp Thiayore (1988)

1241. Nee-Owoo, Kwate. "Breathing Life into Film." West Africa (December 19-25 1988): 2374. [Interview]

Ceddo

Works in English

See also # 236, 248

1242. Allen, Tom. "The Third World Oracle." Village Voice (February 20 1978): 40. [Review]

1243. Arman, Ayi Kwei. "Islam and 'Ceddo.'" West Africa,
No. 3503 (1984): 2031.

1244. Coad, M. "Senegal: Ousmane Sembene and 'Ceddo.'"
Censorship, Vol. 10 (August 1981): 32-33.

1245. Gabriel, Teshome H. "Ceddo: A Revolution Reborn
Through the Efforts of Womanhood." Framework, No. 15-17
(1981): 38-39.

1246. Gregor, Ulrich. "Interview with Ousmane Sembene."
Framework, No. 78 (Spring 1978): 35-37.

1247. Gupta, Udyan. "Banned in Senegal." Seven Days [New
York] (March 10 1978): 25.

1248. Iyam, David Uru. "The Silent Revolutionaries: Ousmane
Sembene's Emitai, Xala, and Ceddo." African Studies Review,
Vol. 29, No. 4 (1986): 79-87.

Works in French

1249. Amengual, Barthelemy. "Ceddo." Positif, No. 195-196
(1977): 83.

1250. Amiel, Mireille. "Ceddo." Cinema, No. 249 (1979): 92-
93.

1251. Bassan, Raphael. "Ceddo." Ecran, No. 83 (1979): 62-
63.

1252. Bonnet, Jean-Claude. "Ceddo." Cinematographe, No. 28
(Juin 1977): 43-44.

1253. Bosseno, Christian. "Ceddo." La Revue du Cinema, No.
342 (1979): 114-118. [Interview]

1254. "Ceddo de Sembene Ousmane." Afrique Contemporaine, No.
105 (1979): 36-37.

1255. Daney, Serge. "Ceddo." Cahiers du Cinema, No. 304
(1979): 51-53.

1256. Diallo, Abdoulaye Bamba. "Ceddo pour les Ecrans."
Zone 2, No. 246 (1984): 19.

1257. Lemaire, Charles. "Ceddo." Unir Cinema, No. 13
(1984): 9-10.

1258. Louisy, Louis-Georges. "Ceddo." Afrique, No. 27
(1979): 52.

1259. Mpoyi-Buatu, Th. "'Ceddo' de Sembene Ousmane et 'West
Indies' de Med Hondo." Presence Africaine, No. 119 (1981):
152-164. An English translation of this article appears in
John D. H. Downing's Film and Politics in the Third World.
New York: Praeger Publishers, 1988.

1260. Nave, Bernard. "Ceddo." Jeune Cinema, No. 104 (1977): 43-44.

1261. Pfaff, Francoise. "Entretien avec Ousmane Sembene: a propos de Ceddo." Positif, No. 235 (October 1980): 54-57.

1262. Statt, Bruno. "Ceddo de Sembene Ousmane." Revue Africaine de Communication, No. 1 (1981): 36-42.

Emitai (1971)

Works in English

1263. Peters, Jonathan A. "Aesthetics and Ideology in African Film: Ousmane Sembene's Emitai." In African Literature in Its Social and Political Dimensions, eds. Eileen Julien, Mildred Mortimer and Curtis Schade. Washington, D.C.: Three Continents Press, 1986, pp. 69-75.

Articles

1264. Diack, Moktar. "'Emitai' or Africa Arisen." Young Cinema and Theater, No. 4 (1972): 27-29.

1265. Diop, Magatte, and Michael Popkin. "Film: Drawing the Line at Rice." Village Voice (March 15 1973): 76. [Review]

1266. "Emitai." Independent Film Journal (November 27 1972).

1267. Iyam, David Uru. "The Silent Revolutionaries: Ousmane Sembene's Emitai, Xala, and Ceddo." African Studies Review, Vol. 29, No. 4 (1986): 79-87.

1268. Matchet. "Emitai." West Africa, No. 3020 (1975): 535.

1269. Pfaff, Francoise. "Myths, Traditions and Colonialism in Ousmane Sembene's Emitai." CLA Journal, Vol. 24, No. 3 (March 1981): 336-346.

Works in French

1270. Diatta, Esther. "Emitai ou la Resistance Collective." Jeune Afrique, No. 860 (1977): 90-91.

1271. "Emitai, 'Dieu du Tonnerre.'" Afrique Nouvelle, No. 1129 (1971): 14.

1272. "Emitai, un long metrage Senegalais de Sembene Ousmane." Africasia, No. 44 (1971): 62-63.

1273. James, Emile. "Un Nouveau Film de Sembene Ousmane 'Emitai.'" Jeune Afrique, No. 539 (1971): 52-55. [Interview]

1274. Jouvet, Pierre. "Emitai." Cinematographe, No. 27 (1977): 40.

1275. Nave, Bernard. "Emitai." Jeune Cinema, No. 103 (1977): 34-36.

Mandabi (1968)

Works in English

1276. Harrow, Kenneth. "The Money Order: False Treasure or True Benefice." In Interdisciplinary Dimensions of African Literature, eds. Kofi Anyidoho, Abioseh M. Porter, Daniel Racine and Janice Spleth. Washington, D.C.: Three Continents Press, 1985, pp. 75-87.

1277. Lester, Jules. "Mandabi: Confronting Africa." In Film Festival. New York: Grove Press, n.d. [1970], pp. 23-27, 74-78.

1278. Ousmane, Sembene. The Money-Order; with White Genesis. Translated by Clive Wake. London: Heinemann, 1972. Novel upon which the film is based.

Articles

1279. Coq, Peter de. "Mandabi." Afrika Heute, Nr. 8 (1973): 46.

1280. Devin, Jean. "A Senegalese Film and French-Algerian Cooperation." Young Cinema and Theater, No. 2 (1969): 26-27.

1281. Frazer, John. "Mandabi." Film Quarterly, Vol. 23, No. 4 (Summer 1970): 48-50.

1282. Goldstein, R. N. "Mandabi." Film News, No. 30 (June 1973): 21.

1283. Tarratt, Margaret. "The Money Order." Films and Filming, Vol. 20, No. 4 (1974): 45, 48.

Works in French

1284. Ousmane, Sembene. Vehi-Ciosane ou Blanche-Genese, suivi du Mandat. Paris: Presence Africaine, 1965. 221p.

Articles

1285. Arbois, Janik. "Le Mandat." Avant-Scene-Cinema, No. 90 (1969): 147-150.

1286. Cervoni, Albert. "Le Mandat." Cinema (Paris), No. 134 (1969): 119-121.

1287. Ciment, Michel. "Mandabi (Le Mandat)." Positif, No. 100-101 (1968-69): 45.

1288. "Mandabi: Nouveau Film Tourne par O. Sembene." Afrique Nouvelle, No. 1076 (1968): 14.

1289. "'Le Mandat' de Ousmane Sembene." Zaire, No. 354 (1975): 66-67.

1290. Morellet, Jean-Claude. "La Critique et 'Le Mandat.'" Jeune Afrique, No. 418 (1968): 6-7.

1291. "Un Film dont on parle et dont on parlera longtemps "Le Mandat" d'Ousmane Sembene." <u>Bingo</u>, No. 195 (1969): 41-42.

1292. Watrigant, R. "Le Mandat." <u>Afrique Nouvelle</u>, No. 1150 (1969): 11.

La Noire De... (Black Girl)

1293. Ousmane, Sembene. <u>Voltaique. La Noire De ...</u> <u>Nouvelles</u>. Paris: Presence Africaine, 1971. 215p. (Orig. 1962)

1294. Ropars-Wuilleumier, M. C. "A Propos du Cinema Negro-Africaine: La Problematique Culturelle de La Noire de..." In <u>Colloque sur Litterature et Esthetique Negro-Africaines</u>. Dakar: Nouvelles Editions Africaines, 1979, pp. 291-299. [Reprinted from <u>Recherche, Pedagogie et Culture</u>, No. 17-18 (1975): 10-15].

Articles

1295. Allou. "M'Bissine Diop l'Emouvante Interprete du Film de Sembene Ousmane 'La Noire de'." <u>Bingo</u>, No. 168 (1967): 10-13.

1296. Delmas, Jean. "La Noire de..." <u>Jeune Cinema</u>, No. 22 (1967): 20-22.

1297. Ellovich, Risa. Review of Black Girl. <u>American Anthropologist</u>, Vol. 79, No. 1 (1977): 198-200.

1298. Landy, Marsha. "Politics and Style in Black Girl." <u>Jump Cut</u>, No. 27 (July 1982): 23-25.

1299. Spass, Lieve. "Female Domestic Labor and Third World Politics in La Noire de." <u>Jump Cut</u>, No. 27 (1982): 26-27.

1300. Veysset, Marie-Claude. "La Noire de: un film, deux visions." <u>Jeune Cinema</u>, No. 34 (Novembre 1968): 10-11.

Xala (1974)

Works in English

See also # 236

1301. Ousmane, Sembene. <u>Xala</u>. Translated by Clive Wake. London: Heinemann, 1974. 114p.

Articles

1302. Fischer, Lucy. "Xala: A Study in Black Humor." <u>Millennium Film Journal</u>, No. 7-9 (1980-81): 165-172.

1303. Gabriel, Teshome H. "Xala: A Cinema of Wax and Gold." <u>Jump Cut</u>, No. 27 (1982): 31-33.

1304. _____. "Xala": A Cinema of Wax and Gold." <u>Presence Africaine</u>, No. 116 (1980): 202-214.

1305. Harrow, Kenneth. "Sembene Ousmane's Xala: The Use of Film and Novel as Revolutionary Weapon." Studies in Twentieth Century Literature, Vol. 4, No. 2 (1980): 177-178.

1306. Iyam, David Uru. "The Silent Revolutionaries: Ousmane Sembene's Emitai, Xala, and Ceddo." African Studies Review, Vol. 29, No. 4 (1986): 79-87.

1307. Landy, Marsha. "Political Allegory and Engaged Cinema: Sembene's Xala." Cinema Journal, Vol. 22 (Spring 1984): 31-46.

1308. Lyons, Harriet D. "The Use of Ritual in Sembene's Xala." Canadian Journal of African Studies, Vol. 18, No. 2 (1984): 319-328.

1309. McGuinness, Richard. "Too Many Wives." Soho Weekly News (October 9 1975): 33. [Review]

1310. Ngara, John. "Xala-An Allegory on Celluloid." Africa, No. 64 (December 1976): 51.

1311. Pfaff, Francoise. "Three Faces of Africa: Women in Xala." Jump Cut, No. 27 (July 1982): 27-31.

1312. Siskel, Gene. "'Xala' a potent Senegalese Film." Chicago Tribune (June 11 1976): Sec. 3, p. 3.

1313. Turvey, Gerry. "'Xala' and the Curse of Neo-Colonialism." Screen, Vol. 26, No. 3-4 (May-August 1985): 75-87.

1314. "Xala." Essence, Vol. 6 (January 1976): 28.

1315. "Xala (Impotence)." Variety (August 20 1975): 19.

1316. "Xala, by Sembene Ousmane." West Africa, No. 3099 (1976): 1748.

Works in French

1317. Matanda, Tshishi Bavuala. Litterature et cinema: contribution a l'etude de l'adaption dans la culture negro-africaine. Louvain-la-Neuve: CIACO, 1988, pp. 120-137.

1318. Ousmane, Sembene. Xala; roman. Paris: Presence Africaine, 1973. 171p. Novel upon which the film is based.

Articles

1319. Cheriaa, Tahar. "Problematique du Cineaste Africain: l'Artiste et la Revolution." Cinema Quebec, Vol. III, NO. 9-10 (August 1974): 12-17.

1320. Delmas, Jean. "Xala." Jeune Cinema, No. 93 (1976): 30-32.

1321. _____, et Ginette Delmas. "Ousmane Sembene: 'Un Film est un Debat'." Jeune Cinema, No. 99 (December 1976-January 1977): 13-17.

1322. De Vos, J.-M. "Xala." Film en Televisie, No. 216-217 (May-June 1975): 15.

1323. Hennebelle, Monique. "'Xala' une impuissance sexuelle bien symbolique." Afrique-Asie, No. 79 (1975): 63-64.

1324. Huannou, Adrien. "'Xala': une satire caustique de la societe bourgeoise senegalaise." Presence Africaine, No. 103 (1977): 145-157.

1325. Jouvet, Pierre. "Xala." Cinematographe, No. 18 (1976): 44.

1326. Mulimbi Zaina. "Xala 'Un Requisitoire Contra la Bourgoisie d'Affaires.'" Zaire, No. 355 (1975): 61.

1327. Sane, Julien K. "Xala, l'Afrique par Sembene." Afrique Nouvelle, No. 1341 (1985): 16-17.

1328. Sultan, Rene. "'Xala'...ou les formes de l'impuissance." Union, No. 193 (1976): 4.

SENGHOR, BLAISE (Senegal)

1329. Bhely-Quenum, Olympe. "Jeune Cinema d'Afrique Noir: Une Chimere." L'Afrique Actuelle, Vol. XIX (June 1967): 8-15. [Interview]

SI BITA, ARTHUR (Cameroon)

1330. Aufderheide, Pat. "Arthur Si Bita." Black Film Review, Vol. 4, No. 4 (Fall 1988): 10-11.

SISSOKO, CHEIK OUMAR (1945-) (Mali)

1331. Aufderheide, Pat. "Cheik Oumar Sissoko." Black Film Review, Vol. 3, No. 3 (Summer 1987): 9, 19.

1332. Diawara, Manthia, and Elizabeth Robinson. "New Perspectives in African Cinema: An Interview with Cheick Oumar Sissoko." Film Quarterly (Winter 1987): 43-48.

1333. Wera, Francoise. "Entretien avec Cheick Oumar Sissoko." Cine-Bulles (Montreal), Vol. 6, No. 3 (1987): 39-41.

Finzan

1334. Gnonlonfoun, Alexis. "Cinema: Cri de Femme." Africa International (Dakar), No. 218 (juillet/aout 1989): 65.

Nyamanton

1335. Diawara, Manthia. "Film: Images of Children." West Africa (August 25 1986): 1780-1781. [Review]

1336. "Nyamanton" ("The Garbage Boys"). Variety (December 17 1986): 27-28.

SOKHONA, SIDNEY (1952-   ) (Mauritania)

1337. Daney, Serge, and Jean-Pierre Oudart. "Entretien avec Sidney Sokhona." Cahiers du Cinema, No. 285 (February 1978): 48-57.

1338. Hennebelle, Monique. "Entretien avec Sidney Sokhona." Ecran, No. 44 (fevrier 1976): 53-54.

Nationalite: Immigre

1339. Boughedir, Ferid. "L'emigration vue par emigre." Jeune Afrique, No. 787 (1976): 52.

1340. Daney, Serge, et al. "Nationalite: Immigre" de Sidney Sokhona. Cahiers du Cinema, No. 265 (mars-avril 1976): 25-43.

1341. Hennebelle, Monique. "Un nouveau film nationalite: immigre." Afrique-Asie, No. 102 (1976): 46-48. [Interview]

Safrana

1342. "Film that fights for political consciousness." New African, No. 130 (1978): 64.

1343. Gnonlonfoun, Alexis. "Safrana ou 'le droit a la parole.'" Afrique Nouvelle, No. 1430 (1976): 2.

1344. _____. "Sidney Sokhona, J'aime le 'Flashback'." Afrique Nouvelle, No. 1485 (1977): 16-17. [Interview]

1345. Martin, Marcel, et Guy Hennebelle. "Safrana ou le Droit a la Parole et Voyage en Capital." Ecran, No. 67 (mars 1978): 58-61.

SOW, THIERNO FATY (Senegal)

1346. Artese, Alberto. "Conversazione con Ousmane Sembene e Thierno Faty Sow." Cineforum, No. 277 (1988): 21-24.

TCHISSOUKOU, JEAN-MICHEL (Senegal)

1347. Leahy, James. "La Chapelle" ("The Chapel"). Monthly Film Bulletin, No. 54 (April 1987): 108-109.

THIAM, MOMAR (1929-   ) (Senegal)

1348. Pfaff, Francoise. Twenty-Five Black African Filmmakers. Westport, CT: Greenwood Press, 1988, pp. 267-273.

Sarzan (1963)

1349. Matanda, Tshishi Bavuala. Litterature et Cinema: contribution a l'etude de l'adaption dans la culture negro-africaine. Louvain-la-Neuve: CIACO, 1988, pp. 97-119.

TRAORE, MAHAMA JOHNSON (1942-   ) (Senegal)

1350. Pfaff, Francoise. Twenty-Five Black African
Filmmakers. Westport, CT: Greenwood Press, 1988, pp. 275-287.

Articles

1351. Braucourt, G. "Breve Rencontre avec Mahama Traore."
Ecran, No. 34 (March 1975): 18-20. [Interview]

1352. Broullon, Marvis, and Gary Crowdus. "'Cinema in Africa
Must Be a School': An Interview with Mahama Traore."
Cineaste, Vol. VI, No. 1 (1973): 32-35.

1353. Delati, Abdou Achouba. "Mahama Johnson Traore sur la
voie d'une ethique negro-africaine." Cinema (Paris), No. 194
(janvier 1975): 92-96. [Interview]

1354. Delmas, Jean, and Ginette Delmas. "Mahama Traore...
'Au Service du Peuple.'" Jeune Cinema, No. 99 (Decembre 1976-
January 1977): 3-7. [Interview]

1355. Diallo, Abdoulaye Bamba. "Entretien avec Mahama
Johnson Traore." Zone 2, No. 238 (1984): 15-16. [Interview]

1356. _____. "Mahama Johnson Traore secretaire general
du FEPACI." Le Soleil Magazine, No. 3305 (1981): 7.

1357. Hennebelle, Guy. "Entretien avec Mahama Traore: "Je
suis pour le cinema politique, contre un cinema commercial
contre un cinema d'auteurs." L'Afrique Litteraire et
Artistique, No. 35 (1975): 91-99.

1358. Paquet, Andre. "Mahama Traore; Du Rapport
Film/Public." Cinema Quebec, Vol. II, No. 6-7 (March-April
1973): XIII-XVII.

1359. "Traore ne manque pa de culot." Jeune Afrique, No. 439
(1969): 51.

1360. "Un Prix Pour Johnson Traore." Bingo, No. 304 (1978):
50-51.

Diakhabi

1361. "Diakhabi un film de Johnson Traore ou du Cine-Club a
la Mise en Scene." Bingo, No. 197 (1969): 26-27.

Diegue Bi

1362. Alain, Yves. "Diegue Bi, le Film de Johnson Traore,
Releve la Femme Senegalais." Bingo, No. 213 (1970): 38-39.

Lambaaye (1972)

1363. Chevassu, F. "Lambayo." La Revue du Cinema, No.
276/277 (octobre 1973): 222-223.

Njangaan (1974)

1364. Bernard, Jean. "Un Film de Mahama Traore." Afrique Nouvelle, No. 1350 (1975): 16-17.

1365. Smallwood, Lawrence C. "Njangaan." Freedomways, Vol. 15, No. 4 (1975): 293-296.

Revenant, Le

1366. Alain, Yves. "Johnson Traore 'Le Revenant'." Bingo, No. 330 (1980): 64.

VIEYRA, PAULIN SOUMANOU (1925-1987) (Senegal)

1367. "Cine Util y Conciencia Nacional." Cine Cubano, No. 115 (1986): 58-60. [Interview]

1368. Pfaff, Francoise. Twenty-Five Black African Filmmakers. Westport, CT: Greenwood Press, 1988, pp. 289-303.

Obituaries

1369. Benoist, Joseph Roger de. "Paulin Soumanou Vieyra." Presence Africaine, No. 147 (3eme trim. 1988): 123-126.

1370. "Fondu au Noir: Paulin Soumanou Vieyra." La Revue du Cinema, No. 439 (juin 1988): 78.

1371. Kobe, Werner. "Paulin Soumanou Vieyra." EPD Film (Frankfurt), No. 5 (March 1988): 18.

1372. "Paulin Soumanou Vieyra." Variety (December 30 1987): 46.

1373. Schoenberner, Gerhard. "Umschau: Pionere des Schwarzafrikanischen Films." Film und Fernschen, Vol. 16, No. 5 (1988): 40-41.

En Residence Surveillee (House Arrest)

1374. "En Residence Surveillee (House Arrest)." Variety (November 17 1982): 20.

III

BLACK FILM IN THE DIASPORA: EUROPE, THE CARIBBEAN AND LATIN AMERICA

1

Country and Regional Studies

1375. Chimbonda, Paul. "La Cinematographie, Un Art Economique: Perspectives pour le Developpement du Cinema dans les Petites Antilles et dans la Caraibe." Memoire de Maitrise, Sciences Juridiques et Economiques, Guadeloupe, 1983-1984. 83p.

BRAZIL

1376. Stam, Robert. "Blacks in Brazilian Cinema." In Film and Politics in the Third World, ed. John D. H. Downing. New York: Praeger Publishers, 1987, pp. 257-265.

Articles

1377. "O Negro no Cinema Brasileiro." Film e Cultura, Vol. 40 (agosto-outobro 1982). Special issue.

1378. Stam, Robert. "Samba, Candomble, Quilombo: Black Performance and Brazilian Cinema." Journal of Ethnic Studies, Vol. 13, No. 3 (1985): 54-84.

1379. _____. "Slow Fade to Afro: The Black Presence in Brazilian Cinema." Film Quarterly, Vol. 36, No. 2 (Winter 1982-83): 16-32.

CUBA

1380. Giral, Sergio. "Cuban Cinema and the Afro-Cuban Heritage." In Film and Politics in the Third World, ed. John D. H. Downing. New York: Praeger Publishers, 1987, pp. 267-277. [Reprint of # 1425]

1381. Lopez, Ana. "Images of Blacks in Cuban Cinema." Black Film Review, Vol. 4, No. 3 (Summer 1988): 5, 18-20.

GREAT BRITAIN

1382. Daniels, Therese, and Jane Gerson, eds. The Colour Black: Black Images in British Television. London: BFI, 1989. 160p.

1383. Mercer, Kobena, ed. Black Film/British Cinema. London: Institute of Contemporary Arts (12 Carlton House Terrace, London SW1Y 5AH), 1988. 62p. (ICA Documents; 7)

1384. Third Eye Symposium (1983: London, England). Third Eye: Struggle for Black & Third World Cinema. London: GLC Race Equality Unit, 1986. 69p.

Books with Sections on Black British Filmmaking

1385. Auguiste, Reece/Black Audio Film Collective. "Black Independents and Third Cinema: The British Context." In Questions of Third Cinema, eds. Jim Pines and Paul Willemen. London: BFI, 1989, pp. 212-217.

1386. Mercer, Kobena. "Diaspora Culture and the Dialogic Imagination: The Aesthetics of Black Independent Filmmaking in Britain." In Blackframes: Critical Perspectives on Black Independent Cinema, eds. Mbye B. Cham and Claire Andrade-Watkins. Cambridge, MA: The MIT Press, 1988, pp. 50-61.

1387. Pines, Jim. "The Cultural Context of Black British Cinema." In Blackframes, eds. Mbye B. Cham and Claire Andrade-Watkins. Cambridge, MA: The MIT Press, 1988, pp. 26-36.

1388. Slide, Anthony. "Black Independent Filmmaking in the United Kingdom." In The International Film Industry: A Historical Dictionary. Westport, CT: Greenwood Press, 1989, p. 33.

Articles

1389. Crusz, Robert. "Black Cinemas, Film Theory and Dependent Knowledge." Screen, Vol. 26, No. 3-4 (May-August 1985): 152-156.

1390. Fraser, C. Gerald. "New British Films Made by Blacks." New York Times (May 21 1988): 54.

1391. Fusco, Coco. "Black Filmmaking in Britain's Workshop Sector." Afterimage, Vol. 15, No. 7 (February 1988): 11-13.

1392. "The Last 'Special Issue' on Race?" Screen (London), Vol. 29, No. 4 (Autumn 1988).

1393. Pines, Jim. "Blacks in Films, The British Angle." Multiracial Education, Vol. 9, No. 2 (1981).

Media Materials

1394. <u>Representation and Blacks in British Cinema</u>. 90 min. Includes excerpts from Sapphire (1959), Flame in the Streets (1961), Pressure (1974), Black Joy (1977), Blacks Britannica (1979), Babylon (1980), and Burning an Illusion (1981). [Available from British Film Institute, Education Department, 21 Stephen St., London W1P 1PL. Tel. 01-255 1444].

GUADELOUPE

1395. Chevallier, Jacques. "Martinique-Guadeloupe: les racines et l'exil." <u>La Revue du Cinema</u>, No. 424 (February 1987): 56-61.

1396. Durand, Philippe. "Pour un Cinema Guadeloupeen." <u>Image et Son</u>, No. 338 (avril 1979): 9-12.

HAITI

1397. Slide, Anthony. "Haiti." In <u>The International Film Industry: A Historical Dictionary</u>. Westport, CT: Greenwood Press, 1989, p. 189.

Articles

1398. Antonin, Arnold. "Panorama del Cine en Haiti." <u>Cine Cubano</u>, No. 110 (1984): 50-60.

1399. "Festival du Film Haitien." <u>Haiti Culture</u> (New York), Vol. 5, No. 10 (November 1989): 8. Review of Haitian film and video festival - "Images of Haiti."

1400. Suggs, Donald. "What's Up, Doc?" <u>Village Voice</u> (October 24 1989): 74. Preview of Haitian film and video festival "Images of Haiti: A Film and Video Festival."

JAMAICA

1401. Marshall, Victoria M. "Filmmaking in Jamaica: "Likkle but Tallawah." <u>Black Film Review</u>, Vol. 3, No. 1 (Winter 1986-87): 7, 23.

1402. Slide, Anthony. "Jamaica." In <u>The International Film Industry: A Historical Dictionary</u>. Westport, CT: Greenwood Press, 1989, p. 215.

MARTINIQUE

1403. Chevallier, Jacques. "Martinique-Guadeloupe: les racines et l'exil." <u>La Revue du Cinema</u>, No. 424 (February 1987): 56-61.

1404. Durand, Philippe. "Naissance du Cinema Martiniquais." <u>Image et Son</u>, No. 333 (Novembre 1978): 16.

2

Individual Filmmakers

AKOMFRAH, JOHN (1957-   ) (Ghana/Great Britain)

1405. Rosen, Miriam. "Interview: Gardner and Akomfrah." Black Film Review, Vol. 5, No. 4 (Fall 1989?): 4-5, 30. Discussion with Black Audio Film Collective member John Akomfrah and African American independent Robert Gardner on the challenges facing Black independents in the UK and USA.

ANTONIN, ARNOLD (Haiti)

1406. "Arnold Antonin habla de su Pelicula." Cine Cubano, No. 91-92 (March 1978): 32-34.

1407. Argilagos, V. "Haiti: el camino de la libertad." Cine Cubano, No. 97 (1980): 86-91. Interview with Antonin on his own work and on Haitian filmmaking in general.

1408. Daney, Serge, T. Giraud, R. Sapene. "Entretien avec Arnold Antonin." Cahiers du Cinema, No. 262-263 (January 1976): 109-113. [Interview]

Haiti, le Chemin de la Liberte

1409. "America Latina: Vigencia del Documental Politico. Haiti: Mito y Razon." Cine al Dia, No. 22 (November 1977): 12-17. Interview with Antonin on "Ayiti, min chimin libete," the first film made in Haiti by a Haitian. A summarized translation of this interview appears as "Haiti: Myth and Reason: Interview with Arnold Antonin" in Cinema-TV Digest, No. 40 (Summer 1980).

1410. Hennebelle, Guy. "Haiti, le Chemin de la Liberte." Ecran, No. 49 (Juillet 1976): 75. [Review]

1411. Maupin, Francoise. "Haiti, le Chemin de la Liberte." Image et Son, No. 300 (November 1975): 62-65.

ATTILLE, MARTINA (Great Britain)

1412. Fusco, Coco. "Young, British and Black: The Sankofa Film and Video Collective." Black Film Review, Vol. 3, No. 1 (Winter 1986-87): 12-18. Interview with Martina Attille of the Sankofa Film/Video Collective.

1413. Jackson, Lynne, and Jean Rasenberger. "The Passion of Remembrance: An Interview with Martina Attille and Isaac Julien." Cineaste, Vol. 16, No. 4 (1988): 23.

BLACK AUDIO FILM COLLECTIVE (Great Britain) (formed 1983)

1414. Fusco, Coco. Young British & Black: The Work of Sankofa Film/Video Collective and Black Audio Film Collective. Buffalo, NY: Hallwalls/Contemporary Arts Center (700 Main St., 4th Fl., Buffalo, NY 14202), 1988. 63p.

Articles

1415. "Expedition": extracts from a tape-slide test in two parts by the Black Audio Film Collective. Screen, Vol. 26, No. 3-4 (1985): 157-165.

1416. Kruger, Barbara. "Sankofa Film/Video Collective and Black Audio Film Collective." Artforum (September 1988): 143-144.

1417. White, Armond. "Racing Ahead." Film Comment, Vol. 24, No. 4 (July-August 1988): 2-3. Discussion of a New York symposia on the Black British film collectives Sankofa and Black Audio Film Collective.

Handsworth Songs

1418. Auguiste, Reece. "'Handsworth Songs': some background notes." Framework, No. 35 (1988): 4-8.

1419. Cook, P. "Handsworth Songs." Monthly Film Bulletin, No. 54 (March 1987): 77-78.

1420. Gilroy, Paul, and Jim Pines. "'Handsworth Songs': Audiences/Aesthetics/Independence, An Interview with Black Audio Film Collective." Framework, No. 35 (1988): 9-18.

1421. Rushdie, Salman. "Songs Doesn't Know the Score." The Guardian [London] (January 12 1987): 10. [Review]

1422. Williamson, J. "Cinema: To Haunt Us." New Statesman (January 9 1987): 26-27. [Review]

CEDDO FILM AND VIDEO WORKSHOP (Great Britain)

1423. "Ceddo." In Storms of the Heart: an anthology of black arts & culture, ed. Kwesi Owusu. London: Camden Press, 1988, pp. 93-99. Profile of the Black British film collective.

EXUME, WILLY (Haiti)

1424. "Kouche Pa Bay." Haiti Culture (New York), Vol. 5, No. 9 (October 1989): 7. [Review]

GIRAL, SERGIO (Cuba)

See also # 6068, 6073

1425. Giral, Sergio. "Cuban Cinema and the Afro-Cuban Heritage: An Interview with Sergio Giral." Black Scholar, Vol. 8, No. 8-10 (Summer 1977): 63-72.

1426. Lopez, Ana, and Nicholas Peter Humy. "Sergio Giral on Filmmaking in Cuba." Black Film Review, Vol. 3, No. 1 (Winter 1986-87): 4-6.

1427. Relich, Mario. "Cinema: An Afro-Cuban Film Season." West Africa (November 18 1985): 2423-2424. On films by Giral and Tomas Guttierez Alea.

Maluala (1978)

1428. "Maluala." Variety (July 30 1980): 23.

1429. Westerbeck, C. L., Jr. "The Screen: Hidden History." Commonweal, Vol. 105 (July 21 1978): 470-471.

El Otro Francisco (1975)

1430. Canby, Vincent. "Film: A Cuban "Uncle Tom's Cabin." New York Times (July 1 1977): C8.

1431. Grelier, R. "L'Autre Francisco." La Revue du Cinema, No. 315 (March 1977): 54-57.

1432. Lesage, Julia. "The Other Francisco": Creating History." Jump Cut, No. 30 (March 1985): 53-58.

1433. West, D. "The Other Francisco." Cineaste, Vol. 8, No. 2 (1977): 47.

Rancheador (1977)

1434. Berube, R.-C. "Rancheador." Sequences, No. 90 (October 1977): 32-33.

1435. Galiano, C. "Sobre 'Rancheador' y el Tema de la Esclavitud habla Sergio Giral." Cine Cubano, No. 93 (1977): 98-102.

GOMEZ, SARA (d.1974) (Cuba)

1436. Chanan, Michael. The Cuban Image: Cinema and Cultural Politics in Cuba. Bloomington: Indiana University Press, 1985, pp. 280-292. Analysis of Gomez's film career. Includes an extensive discussion of "De Cierta Manera" (One Way or Another).

One Way or Another (1974)

See also # 1436

1437. Kaplan, E. Ann. "The Woman Director in the Third World: Sara Gomez's One Way or Another (1974)." In Women and Film: Both Sides of the Camera. New York/London: Methuen, 1983, pp. 189-194.

1438. LeSage, Julia. "One Way or Another: dialectical, revolutionary, feminist." Jump Cut, No. 20 (1979): 20-23.

JULIEN, ISAAC (Great Britain)

1439. Fung, Richard. "Eyes on Black Britain: An Interview with Filmmaker Isaac Julien." Fuse (Toronto), Vol. XI, No. 4 (1987-88): 25-28.

1440. Rich, B. Ruby. "Isaac Julien Interviewed." Village Voice (June 28 1988): 32, 36. Interview with a Sankofa Film/Video Collective member.

Looking for Langston (1989)

1441. Brown, Fred, Jr. "Waiting for Langston." Black Film Review (Summer 1989): 12-13.

1442. Hemphill, Essex. "Brother to Brother." Black Film Review (Summer 1989): 14-17. [Interview]

1443. Moore, Suzanne. "Looking for Langston." New Statesman & Society (June 16 1989): 41. [Review]

Newspaper Articles

1444. Hoberman, J. "Young, Gifted, Black." Village Voice (November 7 1989): 67, 70. [Review]

1445. James, Caryn. "Seek and Hide." New York Times (October 1 1989): 61. [Review]

1446. Kennedy, Lisa. "Closeting Langston Hughes." Village Voice (October 10 1989): 39. On the conflict between the Hughes estate and filmmaker Julien on Julien's representation of Hughes.

1447. _____. "Listening for Langston." Village Voice (November 14 1989): 49. On the ongoing conflict between Julien and the Langston Hughes estate.

1448. _____. "Off-Screen: Do It Properly." Village Voice (November 14 1989): 120.

1449. Sterritt, David. "Looking for Langston." Christian Science Monitor (November 24 1989): 10.

1450. Trescott, Jacqueline. "'Langston': poet versus premiere - disputed film to open here." Washington Post (December 9 1989): C1.

Passion of Remembrance (1986)

1451.   Jackson, Lynne, and Jean Rasenberger.   "The Passion of Remembrance: An Interview with Martina Attille and Isaac Julien."   Cineaste, Vol. 16, No. 4 (1988): 23.

Territories

1452.   Pines, Jim.   "Territories."   Framework, No. 26-27 (1985): 3-9.   Interview with Julien on his film "Territories" and on black filmmaking in Britain.

LAOU, JULES AMEDE (France)

1453.   Belanger, Denis.   "Entretien avec Julius-Amede Laou." Cine-Bulles (Montreal), Vol. 7, No. 4 (1988): 22-25. [Interview]

1454.   Reid, Mark.   "The Films and Plays of Jules Amede Laou." Black Film Review, Vol. 3, No. 1 (Winter 1986-87): 8-9.

The Quimboiseuse and the Major-Domo

1455.   Rosen, Miriam.   "Saving the Last Dance: The Quimboiseuse and the Major-Domo."   Black Film Review, Vol. 4, No. 3 (Summer 1988): 4.

LARA, CHRISTIAN (Guadeloupe)

1456.   Tesson, Charles.   "Antilles, Annee Zero."   Cahiers du Cinema, No. 318 (December 1980): IX-X.   [Interview]

LUCIEN, OSCAR (Venezuela)

1457.   Marshall, Victoria.   "Film Clips."   Black Film Review, Vol. 5, No. 4 (Fall 1989?): 2-3.   Profile of the Afro-Venezuelan documentary filmmaker.

MWINYIPEMBE, MUSINDO (Tanzania/G. Britain)

1458.   Giddings, Paula.   "Third World Activists: Two Women Committed to Change the World."   Encore American and Worldwide News (June 4 1979): 20-22.

Blacks Britannica

1459.   Howard, Juanita R.   "Blacks Britannica: A Film Review and Sociological Analysis."   In Journey Across Three Continents.   New York: Third World Newsreel, 1985, pp. 46-49.

Articles

1460.   Ariade, Folami.   "Freedom and the Independents." Essence, Vol. 10 (July 1980): 11, 12, 15.

1461.   Biskind, P.   "WGBH Censors "Blacks Britannica": A Shameful Act by PBS' Showcase Station."   Film Library Quarterly, Vol. 12, No. 1 (1979): 17-19+.   (Reprinted from Seven Days).

1462. "The Black Scholar Interviews: David Koff and Musindo Mwinyipembe." The Black Scholar, Vol. 10 (May-June 1979): 68-80. Discussion of Mwinyipembe's controversial film "Blacks Brittannica."

1463. "Blacks Britannica." Variety (March 28 1979): 22.

1464. "Brutal Censorship." New African, No. 142 (1979): 73-74.

1465. "Court OK's Airing of Docu Edited by Hub's WGBH-TV." Variety (August 16 1978): 51.

1466. Dreyfuss, J. "Blacks Brittanica. Racism in Public TV." Jump Cut, No. 21 (November 1979): 4-5.

1467. Mwinyipembe, Musindo. "Television: The 'Blacks Brittannica' Affair." Encore American and Worldwide News (April 1980): 46.

1468. Pappas, P., and Michelle Wallace. "Blacks Britannica": an interview with David Koff and Musindo Mwinyipembe." Cineaste, Vol. 9, No. 4 (Fall 1979): 26-29.

Newspaper Articles

1469. Brown, Les. "Court to Rule on TV Film on Blacks." New York Times (August 9 1978): C22.

1470. The Observer [London] (July 16 1978): 25. [Review]

1471. O'Connor, John J. "The Case of the Doctored Documentary." New York Times (July 30 1978): Sec. 2, pp. 1, 23.

1472. Unger, Arthur. "'Totally Biased'. British Raciscm 'Documentary' Fans TV Fire." Christian Science Monitor (August 8 1978): 5.

NGAKANE, LIONEL (South Africa/G. Britain)

1473. Lionel Ngakane interviewed by Robert Serumaga (Audiotape). London: Transcription Feature Service, 196?. Duration 8'11". [Held by the Schomburg Center - Sc Audio C-50 (Side 2, no. 4)]

Articles

1474. Crowdus, Gary. "South African Filmmaking in Exile: An Interview with Lionel Ngakane." Cineaste, Vol. 15, No. 2 (1986): 16-17.

1475. Paquet, Andre. Lionel Ngakane: "L'Afrique Anglophone doit Rattraper son Retard." Afrique-Asie, No. 30 (1973): 44-45. [Interview]

OVE, HORACE (1939-   ) (Trinidad/G. Britain)

1476. Hodgson, C. "British Independent Cinema: Horace Ove."
Film, No. 64 (August 1978): 6. [Interview]

1477. Paskin, Sylvia. "Going to Meet the Man." Monthly Film
Bulletin (London), Vol. 54, No. 647 (December 1987): 361 and
back page (filmography). [Interview]

King Carnival

1478. Wilson, D. "King Carnival." Monthly Film Bulletin,
Vol. 44 (July 1977): 149. [Review]

Playing Away

1479. Canby, Vincent. "'Playing Away,' a comedy." New York
Times (March 13 1987): C19.

1480. Coopman, J. "Ove's 'Playing Away' Addresses Britain's
West Indian Communities." Variety (July 23 1986): 33.

1481. Dieckmann, Katherine. "Film: The Shock of the New."
Village Voice (March 17 1987): 58.

1482. Hoberman, J. "Film: Something Wicket This Way Comes."
Village Voice (April 12 1988): 63. [Review]

1483. Kelleher, Ed. "Playing Away." Film Journal (June
1988): 67-68.

1484. "Review/Film: Clash of Cultures in 'Playing Away'."
New York Times (April 1 1988): C4.

Pressure (1976)

1485. Blatchford, R. "Painting it Black in Babylon." Times
Educational Supplement, No. 3217 (January 28 1977): 79.

1486. Coleman, J. "He Stoops." New Statesman, Vol. 95
(February 17 1978): 230-231.

1487. Lermon, S. "Toward Doomsday." Times Educational
Supplement, No. 3273 (March 17 1978): 94.

1488. "Pressure." Films and Filming (April 1978): 49.

1489. Wilson, D. "Pressure." Monthly Film Bulletin, Vol. 45
(April 1978): 68.

Reggae (1970)

1490. Axthelm, K. "Reggae." Film Library Quarterly, Vol. 9,
No. 4 (1977): 50.

1491. Durgnat, Raymond. "Reggae." Films and Filming, Vol.
18, No. 1 (October 1971): 66.

1492. Rugg, Akua. "Reggae." Race Today (March 1978): 70-71.

PALCY, EUZHAN (Martinique)

See also # 2141, 2164, 2188, 6073

1493. Aubenas, J. "Canne a Sucre et Sucrerie." Visions, No. 15 (January 15 1984): 14. [Interview]

1494. Elder, Sean. "Director Euzhan Palcy." Premiere (October 1989): 56-57.

1495. Goldin, Greg. "Moral Messenger." Interview (September 1989): 52. [Interview]

1496. Matousek, M. "Film: The New Directors." Interview (February 1985): 97-98. [Interview]

1497. Micciollo, H. "Propos d'Euzhan Palcy." Cinema, No. 298 (Octobre 1983): 33-34. [Interview]

A Dry White Season

1498. Aufderheide, Pat. "A Different Freedom." Black Film Review, Vol. 5, No. 3 (Summer 1989): 6-10, 31.

1499. "Black Actors Angry Over Dog's Pay in Brando Film." Jet (June 13 1988): 62.

1500. "Brando says studio sold him out on 'Dry White Season.'" Jet (October 23 1989): 63.

1501. Glicksman, Marlaine. "Tempest: Euzhan Palcy's 'Dry White Season'." Film Comment (September-October 1989): 64+. [Interview]

1502. Lacher, Irene, and Jack Kelley. "Euzhan Palcy Has a Face the Camera Loves but Finds the View Better Behind the Lens." People (October 16 1989): 71-72.

1503. McKenna, Kristine. "Tough, Passionate, Persuasive: Euzhan Palcy battled for five years to put her vision of apartheid on screen, and then lured Marlon Brando back to work - for free." American Film (September 1989): 32+.

1504. Rosen, Marjorie. "A woman for all seasons: Euzhan Palcy - director, writer, miracle worker." Ms. (October 1989): 18-19.

1505. Southgate, Martha. "Euzhan Palcy, the director of A Dry White Season, may well be the first Black woman ever to direct a major studio film." Essence (October 1989): 31-32.

Newspaper Articles

1506. "Apartheid pic 'White Season' won't play So. Africa, says producer Weinstein." Variety (October 4 1989): 8, 22.

1507. Baneshik, Percy. "'Dry Season' plays So. Africa after all." Variety (November 1 1989): 12.

1508. Collins, Glenn. "A Black Director Views Apartheid."
New York Times (September 25 1989): C15, C20.

1509. Dry White Season - Clippings [Billy Rose Theatre
Collection]

1510. Flamm, Matthew. "A Quest for Truth; 'A Dry, White
Season' director discusses her mission." New York Post
(September 17 1989): 35, 37.

1511. Freedman, Samuel G. "Black Agony Pierces the Heart of
an Afrikaner." New York Times (September 17 1989): 17-19.

1512. Gold, Richard. "'Dry White Season' makers, stars
praise MGM for making anti-apartheid pic." Variety (September
13 1989): 6.

1513. Maslin, Janet. "Dry White Season." New York Times
(September 20 1989): C19. [Review]

1514. Sinclair, Abiola. "Euzhan Palcy directs." New York
Amsterdam News (September 30 1989).

Rue Cases Negres (Sugar Cane Alley) (1983)

Works in English

1515. Warner, Keith Q. "On Adapting a West Indian Classic to
the Cinema: The Implications of Success." In Journey Across
Three Continents. New York: Third World Newsreel, 1985, pp.
41-45.

1516. Zobel, Joseph. Black Shack Alley = La rue Cases-
Negres. Translated and introduced by Keith Q. Warner.
London: Heinemann; Washington, D.C.: Three Continents Press,
1980. 182p. Martiniquan novel upon which the film is based.

Articles

1517. Benson, Sheila. "Sugar Cane Alley." CoEvolution
Quarterly (Summer 1984): 125.

1518. Coleman, J. "Films: Write Angles." New Statesman (May
18 1984): 28-29.

1519. Denby, David. "Sugar Cane Alley." New York (April 30
1984): 88-89.

1520. De Stefano, G. "Sugar Cane Alley." Cineaste, Vol. 13,
No. 4 (October 1984): 42+.

1521. Forbes, J. "Rue Cases Negres (Black Shack Alley)."
Monthly Film Bulletin (July 1984): 210-211.

1522. Haskell, Molly. "Arts/Media: Some Films Men and Women
Can't Talk About." Ms. (May 1984): 16+.

1523. Irvine, L. "Sugar Cane Alley." Film Journal (June
1984): 26.

1524. Jefferson, Roland S. "Sugar Cane Alley." Black Scholar (March/April 1985): 57-59.

1525. Kanter, Deborah. "Sugar Cane Alley." Caribbean Review (Winter 1985): 32-33.

1526. Karp, A. "Sugar Cane Alley." Boxoffice (August 1984): R100.

1527. Kauffmann, Stanley. "Stanley Kauffmann on Films: Warm Climates." The New Republic (April 30 1984): 26-27.

1528. Linfield, Susan. "Sugar Cane Alley: an interview with Euzhan Palcy." Cineaste, Vol. 13, No. 4 (October 1984): 43-44.

1529. "Rue Cases Negres." Films and Filming, No. 357 (June 1984): 35.

1530. Turan, Kenneth. "Sugar Cane Alley." California (June 1984): 113-114.

Newspaper Articles

1531. Attanasio, Paul. "Movies: Sweet 'Sugar': Euzhan Palcy's Martinique Memoir." Washington Post (March 2 1985): G1, G2.

1532. Canby, Vincent. "Film View: Third World Truths from 'Sugar Cane Alley.'" New York Times (April 22 1984): Sec. 2, pp. 17, 22.

1533. Maslin, Janet. "Sugar Cane Alley, in Martinique." New York Times (April 6 1984): C24.

1534. "Rue Cases Negres (Street of the Black Shacks." Variety (September 21 1983): 20-21.

1535. Sarris, Andrew. "Oscar Hangover, Third-World Crossover." Village Voice (April 24 1984): 49, 59.

1536. Sterritt, David. "Two Films from Foreign Lands with Fresh Insights on Children." Christian Science Monitor (April 26 1984).

1537. "Sugar Cane Alley (Rue Cases Negres)." Variety (April 11 1984): 20.

Works in French

1538. Bassan, Raphael. "Rue Cases Negres." La Revue du Cinema, No. 387 (Octobre 1983): 47.

1539. Beaulieu, J. "Rue Cases Negres." Sequences, No. 117 (Juillet 1984): 33-35.

1540. Curchod, O. "L'Epure d'une Memoire Antillaise." Positif, No. 273 (Novembre 1983): 11-13.

1541. Delmas, Ginette. "Rue Cases Negres." Jeune Cinema, No. 153 (Octobre 1983): 45-46.

1542. Laurent, O. "Rue Cases Negres." Visions, No. 141 (Decembre 15 1983): 13.

1543. Menil, A. "Rue Cases Negres." Cinematographe, No. 93 (Octobre 1983): 34.

1544. Micciollo, H. "Rue Cases Negres." Cinema, No. 298 (Octobre 1983): 31-32.

1545. "Rue Cases Negres." Cine Revue, No. 63 (Septembre 22 1983): 38.

1546. "Rue Cases Negres." Film, No. 130 (November 1984): 12.

1547. Swinnen, W. "Rue Cases Negres." Film en Televisie, No. 320 (January 1984): 29.

1548. Toubiana, S. "Les 'Monstrables.'" Cahiers du Cinema, No. 352 (Octobre 1983): 8-13.

RAMEAU, WILLIE (France)

1549. Reid, Mark. "A Conversation with Willie Rameau." Black Film Review, Vol. 3, No. 1 (Winter 1986-87): 10-11, 24.

Lien de Parente (1982)

1550. Neubourg, M. "Premier Film: Lien de Parente." Cinematographe, No. 118 (April 1986): 66. [Review]

RHONE, TREVOR (Jamaica)

Milk and Honey (1989)

1551. Bekar, Lorena. "A Land of Milk and Honey." Cinema Canada (July-August 1987): 4. Film for which Rhone co-wrote the script.

1552. Kauffman, Stanley. "Milk and Honey." The New Republic (July 31 1989): 25.

1553. McTair, Roger. "Milk and Honey." Cinema Canada (January 1989): 20.

1554. "Milk and Honey." Variety (September 7 1988): 27.

1555. Novak, Ralph. "Milk and Honey." People (July 17 1989): 11-12.

1556. Phillips, Julie. "Dirty Laundry." Village Voice (June 20 1989): 94.

Smile Orange (1976)

1557. Eder, Richard. "Film: 'Smile Orange'; Jamaican Story." New York Times (May 20 1976): 44. Review of the film adaptation of Rhone's play.

1558. Oster, Jerry. "Exotica Enters, Smiling." New York Daily News (May 21 1976): 61.

1559. Rugg, Akua. "Smile Orange." Race Today (March 1978): 69.

1560. Smile Orange - Clippings [Billy Rose Theatre Collection]

SANKOFA FILM/VIDEO COLLECTIVE (Great Britain)

See also # 1412, 1439-1440

1561. Fusco, Coco. Young British & Black; The Work of Sankofa Film/Video Collective and Black Audio Film Collective. Buffalo, NY: Hallwalls/Contemporary Arts Center (700 Main St., 4th Fl., Buffalo, NY 14202), 1988. 63p.

1562. Kruger, Barbara. "Sankofa Film/Video Collective and Black Audio Film Collective." Artforum (September 1988): 143-144.

1563. White, Armond. "Racing Ahead." Film Comment, Vol. 24, No. 4 (July-August 1988): 2-3. Discussion of a New York symposium on the Sankofa and Black Audio Film Collectives.

Passion of Remembrance (1986)

1564. Jackson, Lynne, and Jean Rasenberger. "The Passion of Remembrance: An Interview with Martina Attille and Isaac Julien." Cineaste, Vol. 16, No. 4 (1988): 23.

1565. Paskin, Sylvia. "Without Heroes or Victims." Monthly Film Bulletin, Vol. 53, No. 635 (December 1986): 362-363. Interview with the Sankofa collective on "Remembrance."

1566. "Passion of Remembrance." Films and Filming, No. 386 (November 1986): 42.

1567. "The Passion of Remembrance." Variety (December 10 1986): 10.

1568. Pines, Jim. "The Passion of Remembrance." Framework, No. 32/33 (1986): 92-103. Interview with the Sankofa Collective on the aesthetics behind "Remembrance."

1569. Williamson, J. "Cinema: A World of Difference." New Statesman (December 5 1986): 23.

SHABAZZ, MENELIK (Great Britain)

1570. Forbes, Calvin. "Menelik Shabazz: Changing the Color of English Cinema." Black Film Review, Vol. 2, No. 2 (Spring 1986): 6, 14-15, 23.

1571. Leahy, James. "Bearing Witness and Burning an Illusion: Menelik Shabazz talks to James Leahy about Black film-making in Britain." Monthly Film Bulletin (April 1989): 101-102.

Burning an Illusion (1982)

1572. Auty, M. "Burning an Illusion." Monthly Film Bulletin, Vol. 49 (August 1982): 165-166.

1573. "Burning an Illusion." Film, No. 105 (April-May 1982): 3.

1574. "Burning an Illusion." Variety (July 28 1982): 22.

1575. Coleman, J. "Films: Gaudy Works." New Statesman (July 30 1982): 27-28.

1576. French, Philip. "The Road to Liberation." The Observer [London] (July 25 1982): 28. [Review]

1577. Kirkhope, T. "Burning an Illlusion." Filmnews, Vol. 8, No. 1-2 (January-February 1983): 8. [Interview]

1578. Roddick, N. "Black on Black: Burning an Illusion." Sight and Sound, Vol. 51, No. 4 (Autumn 1982): 299. [Review]

1579. Screen International (August 7 1982): 44. [Review]

1580. Stimpson, M. "Burning An Illusion." Films and Filming, No. 334 (July 1982): 24-25. [Review]

Step Forward Youth (1977)

1581. Badder, D. J. "Step Forward Youth." Monthly Film Bulletin, Vol. 45 (February 1978): 35.

Time and Judgement (1988)

1582. Leahy, James. "Time and Judgement." Monthly Film Bulletin (April 1989): 100-101.

IV

BLACK FILM IN THE DIASPORA: UNITED STATES

1

General Works

1583. Alsina Thevenet, Homero, and Hugo R. Alfaro. El Negro en el Cine. Buenos Aires?: Arte Bella, 1951. 21p.

1584. Black American Films: A Touring Exhibition. New York: Black Filmmaker Foundation, 1983. 32p. [English and French text]

1585. Black Images in Film: A Photographic Exhibition in the Schomburg Center for Research in Black Culture: April 26-July 9, 1984. New York: Schomburg Center for Research in Black Culture, NYPL, 1984. 32p.

1586. Black on Black. St. Louis: Saint Louis Art Museum, 1982. 37p. Catalog of a travelling film exhibition.

1587. Bogle, Donald. Blacks in American Films and Television: An Encyclopedia. New York: Garland, 1988. 510p.

1588. _____. Toms, Coons, Mulattoes, Mammies, and Bucks: An Interpretive History of Blacks in American Films. Rev. and expanded ed. New York: Continuum Publications, 1989. 322p. (Orig. 1973)

1589. Cripps, Thomas. Black Film as Genre. Bloomington: Indiana University Press, 1978. 184p.

1590. _____. Slow Fade to Black: The Negro in American Film, 1900-1942. New York: Oxford University Press, 1977. 447p.

1591. Ellis, Shirley. The Negro in American Film. New York: United States Information Service, 1957. 12p.

1592. Hennebelle, Guy, ed. Le Cinema Noir Americain. Paris: Cerf, 1988. 205p. (CinemAction)

1593. History of Blacks in Film. Los Angeles: William Grant Still Community Arts Center, 1983. 102p. [Exhib. cat.]

1594. Jerome, V. J. The Negro in Hollywood Films. New York: Masses and Mainstream, 1950. 64p.

1595. Leab, Daniel J. From Sambo to Superspade: The Black Experience in Motion Pictures. Boston: Houghton Mifflin, 1975. 301p.

1596. Mapp, Edward. Blacks in American Films: Today and Yesterday. Metuchen, NJ: Scarecrow Press, 1972. 278p.

1597. Maynard, Richard A., ed. The Black Man on Film: Racial Stereotyping. Rochelle Park, NJ: Hayden Book Co., 1974. 134p. High school textbook focusing on the treatment of minorities, particularly blacks, in American films.

1598. Murray, James P. To Find an Image: Black Films from Uncle Tom to Super Fly. Indianapolis: Bobbs-Merrill, 1973. 205p.

1599. Nesteby, James R. Black Images in American Films, 1896-1954: The Interplay Between Civil Rights and Film Culture. Washington, D.C.: University Press of America, 1982. 281p.

1600. Noble, Peter. The Negro in Films. New York: Arno Press, 1970. 288p. (Reprint of 1948 ed.)

1601. Patterson, Lindsay, comp. Black Films and Filmmakers: A Comprehensive Anthology from Stereotype to Superhero. New York: Dodd, Mead, 1975. 298p.

1602. Pines, Jim. Blacks in the Cinema: The Changing Image. London: British Film Institute, Education Dept., 1971. 24p.

1603. _____. Blacks in Films: A Survey of Racial Themes and Images in the American Film. London: Studio Vista, 1975. 143p.

1604. Sampson, Henry T. Blacks in Black and White: A Source Book on Black Films. Metuchen, NJ: Scarecrow Press, 1977. 333p.

1605. Silk, Catherine, and John Silk. Racism and Anti-Racism in American Popular Culture: Portrayals of African-Americans in Fiction and Film. Manchester: Manchester University Press, 1990. 176p.

Books with Sections on the Black Image in Film

1606. Archer, Leonard C. "Black Images on the Silver Screen." In Black Images in the American Theatre: NAACP Protest Campaigns - Stage, Screen, Radio and Television. Brooklyn: Pageant-Poseidon, Ltd., 1973, pp. 183-224.

1607. Bogle, Donald. "Movies." In Black Arts Annual 1987/88. New York: Garland, 1989, pp. 159-184. Survey of Black activity in American film from 1987-1988.

1608. Bonds, Frederick W. "Negro Drama in Moving Pictures
and Radio." In The Negro and the Drama. College Park, MD:
McGrath Publishing Co., 1969.

1609. Campbell, Edward D. C. "Film, Slavery In." In
Dictionary of Afro-American Slavery, eds. Randall M. Miller
and John David Smith. Westport, CT: Greenwood Press, 1989,
pp. 240-243.

1610. Cripps, Thomas R. "The Dark Spot in the Kaleidoscope:
Black Images in American Film." In The Kaleidoscope Lens: How
Hollywood Views Ethnic Groups, ed. Randall M. Miller.
Englewood Cliffs, NJ: Jerome S. Ozer Publishers, 1981, pp.
15-35.

1611. _____. "The Myth of the Southern Box Office: A
Factor in Racial Stereotyping in American Movies, 1910-1940."
In The Black Experience in America: Selected Essays, eds.
James C. Curtis and Louis L. Gould. Austin: University of
Texas Press, 1970, pp. 116-144.

1612. Davis, Ossie. "The Power of Black Movies." In A
Freedomways Reader: Afro-Americans in the Seventies, ed.
Ernest Kaiser. New York: International Publishers, 1977, pp.
217-220. [Reprint of # 1685]

1613. Ellison, Mary. "Blacks in American Film." In Cinema,
Politics, and Society in America, eds. Philip Davies and Brian
Neve. New York: St. Martin's Press, 1985, pp. 176-194.

1614. Killens, John Oliver. "Hollywood in Black and White."
In White Racism: Its History, Pathology and Practice, eds.
Barry N. Schwartz and Robert Disch. New York: Dell, 1970, pp.
398-407.

1615. Macpherson, Kenneth. "A Negro Film Union--Why Not?"
In Negro Anthology, ed. Nancy Cunard. London: Wishart & Co.,
1934, pp. 335-338.

1616. Maynard, Richard. "Everything But a Man: The Black Man
in the Movies." In The Celluloid Curriculum: How to Use
Movies In the Classroom, ed. Richard A. Maynard. Rochelle
Park, NJ: Hayden Book Company, 1971, pp. 148-164.

1617. Monaco, James. "The Black Film (and the Black Image)."
In American Film Now. New York: Oxford University Press,
1979, pp. 185-213. Includes profiles of the work of Ossie
Davis, Gordon Parks, Melvin Van Peebles, Bill Gunn and Michael
Schultz.

1618. Moss, Carlton. "The Negro in American Films." In
Anthology of the Afro-American in the Theatre: A Critical
Approach, ed. Lindsay Patterson. Cornwells Heights, PA:
Publishers Agency, 1967, pp. 229-236. [Reprint of # 1755]

1619. "Motion Pictures." In Encyclopedia of Black America,
eds. W. A. Low and Virgil A. Clift. New York: McGraw-Hill,
1981, pp. 571-582.

1620. Noble, Peter. "The Coming of the Sound Film." In _Anthology of the Afro-American in the Theatre: A Critical Approach_, ed. Lindsay Patterson. Cornwell Heights, PA: Publishers Agency, 1967, pp. 247-266.

1621. Peavy, Charles D. "Black Consciousness and the Contemporary Cinema." In _Popular Culture and the Expanding Consciousness_, ed. Ray B. Browne. New York: Wiley, 1973, pp. 178-200.

1622. Sugy, Catherine. "Black Men or Good Niggers?" In _Film and the Liberal Arts_, ed. T. J. Ross. New York: Holt, Rinehart and Winston, 1970, pp. 293-301. [Repr. of # 1791]

1623. Taylor, Clyde. "Black Cinema in the Post-aesthetic Era." In _Questions of Third Cinema_, eds. Jim Pines and Paul Willemen. London: BFI, 1989, pp. 90-110.

1624. Trumbo, Dalton. "Minorities and the Screen." In _Proceedings of the Writers Congress_. Berkeley: University of California Press, 1944.

1625. Ward, Francis. "Black Male Images in Films." In _A Freedomways Reader: Afro-America in the Seventies_, ed. Ernest Kaiser. New York: International Publishers, 1977, pp. 221-229.

1626. Warren, Nagueyalti. "From Uncle Tom to Cliff Huxtable; Aunt Jemima to Aunt Nell: Images of Blacks in Film and the Television Industry." In _Images of Blacks in American Culture_, ed. Jessie Carney Smith. Westport, CT: Greenwood Press, 1988, pp. 51-117.

1627. Zito, Stephen. "The Black Film Experience." In _The American Film Heritage_, ed. Tom Shales, et al. Washington, D.C.: Acropolis Books, 1972, pp. 61-69.

Dissertations and Theses

1628. Ashton, Charlotte Ruby. "The Changing Image of Blacks in American Film: 1944-1973." Dissertation (Ph.D.) Princeton University, 1981. 318p.

1629. Bloom, Samuel William. "A Social Psychological Study of Motion Picture Audience Behavior: A Case Study of the Negro Image in Mass Communication." Dissertation (Ph.D.) University of Wisconsin-Madison, 1956. 439p.

1630. Burke, William Lee. "The Presentation of the American Negro in Hollywood Films, 1946-1961: Analysis of a Selected Sample of Feature Films." Dissertation (Ph.D.) Northwestern University, 1965. 379p.

1631. Chaudhuri, Arun. "A Study of the Negro Problem in Motion Pictures." Thesis (M.A.) University of Southern California, 1951.

1632.   Ewell, Robbi Linwood.   "The Afro-American Image in U.S. Film, 1900 to 1945."   Thesis (M.P.A.) Cornell University, 1984.   85p.

1633.   Greadington, Barbara A. Gant.   "The Effect of Black Films on the Self-Esteem of Black Adolescents."   Dissertation (Ph.D.) University of Miami, 1977.   172p.

1634.   Hudson, Octavia.   "Audience Racial Composition and Interaction as Determinants of the Appeal of Black Films to Whites."   Dissertation (Ph.D.) Harvard University, 1979. 109p.

1635.   Ismail, Edward Kaaya.   "Africans, Afro-Americans and Narrative Cinema: aspects of the evolution of a visual literature."   Thesis (M.A.) University of Alberta, 1979. 110p.

1636.   Mapp, Edward Charles.   "The Portrayal of the Negro in American Motion Pictures, 1962-1968."   Dissertation (Ph.D.) New York University, 1970.   188p.

1637.   Nesterenko, Genevieve.   "La Representation du Noir dans le Cinema Americain Contemporain (1960-1972)."   These de 3e cycle.   Cinema.   Paris VIII.   1973/1978.

1638.   Shook, Mollie.   "Changing the Racial Attitudes of White Students Toward Blacks Using Commercially Produced Films." Dissertation (Ed.D.) Duke University, 1972.   160p.

1639.   Theodore, Terry.   "The Negro in Hollywood: A Critical Study of Entertainment Films Containing Negro Themes."   Thesis (M.A.) University of Southern California, 1962.

1640.   Wallace, Webster Lively.   "Attitudes of Black College Freshmen Toward Contemporary 'Controversial' Black Films." Dissertation (Ph.D.) Georgia State University, College of Education, 1975.   190p.

Journals and Newsletters

1641.   Black Camera; The Newsletter of The Black Film Center Archive (Afro-American Studies Department, Memorial Hall East #25, Indiana University, Bloomington, IN 47405).   1986-   .

1642.   Black Filmmaker Foundation Newsletter (New York).   Vol. 1,   No. 1 (Summer 1983-   ).   Ceased publication?

1643.   Black Film Review (PO Box 18665, Washington, D.C. 20036).   Vol. 1, No. 1, 1985(?)- .   Co-produced with the Black Film Institute of the University of the District of Columbia.

1644.   Chamba Notes (Brooklyn, NY).   1978- .   Newsletter. Ceased publication?

Articles

1645.   Ajaye, Franklin.   "Hollywood: Fade to White?"   Essence (November 1981): 15+.

1646. Alexander, Francis W. "Stereotyping as a Method of Exploitation in Film." Black Scholar, Vol. 7 (May 1976): 26-29.

1647. Allen, Bonnie. "Blax, Smax Was It Something We Said?" Essence, Vol. 9 (December 1978): 44. Article on the demise of blaxploitation films and the lack of black film projects to fill the gap.

1648. Ansen, David. "A Revival of Black Movies?" Newsweek (January 7 1985): 50.

1649. Asendio, James. "History of Negro Motion Pictures." International Photographer, No. 12 (January 1940): 16-17.

1650. Aughtry, Charles. "Report on the Conference on 'The Image of the Negro in American films.'" Modern Drama, Vol. XII, No. 4 (February 1970): 428.

1651. Black American Literature Forum, Vol. 12, No. 4 (Winter 1978). Special Black film issue.

1652. "The Black Boom." Liberator, Vol. 4 (August 1964): 16+.

1653. "Black Films Still Big Business, 47 Projected." Jet (November 23 1972): 50.

1654. "Black Hollywood: Out of the Movie Kitchen and Into Society and the Money." Life (January 23 1970): M19-M21.

1655. "Black Imagery on the Silver Screen." Essence, Vol. 3 (December 1972): 34.

1656. "Black in Hollywood." Photoplay Movies and Video, Vol. 37 (July 1986): 28-33.

1657. "Black Market." Time (April 10 1972): 53. Commentary on the rise of blaxploitation films.

1658. "The Black Movie Boom." Newsweek (September 6 1971): 66.

1659. "Black Oriented Films Seen Losing Ground." Jet (January 17 1974): 88.

1660. "Blacks blast movie and TV industries' perpetuation of old stereotyped images." Jet (November 28 1988): 64.

1661. "Blaxploitationers of 1972." Variety (January 3 1973).

1662. Bogle, Donald. "Blacks in Film, Part I: Color Comes to Hollywood." Dollars & Sense, Vol. 7 (August-September 1981): 14-18.

1663. _____. "Blacks in Film, Part II: Breakthroughs in the 1940s and 1950s." Dollars & Sense, Vol. 7 (October-November 1981): 14-18.

1664. _____. "Blacks in Film, Part III: The Black Movie Boom of the 1960s and 1970s." Dollars & Sense, Vol. 7 (December 1981-January 1982): 40-45.

1665. _____. "Blacks in Film, Part IV: Back to Square One--Almost." Dollars & Sense, Vol. 7 (February-March 1982): 54-57.

1666. _____. "A Familiar Plot; A Look at the History of Blacks in American Movies." The Crisis, Vol. 90 (January 1983): 14-19.

1667. Bowser, Pearl. "The Boom is Really an Echo." Black Creation, No. 4 (Winter 1973): 32-34.

1668. Brown, Cecil. "Blues for Blacks in Hollywood." Mother Jones, Vol. 6 (January 1981): 20-28, 59.

1669. Brown, Roscoe C. "Film as a Tool for Liberation?" Black Creation, No. 4 (Winter 1973): 36-37.

1670. Brownfeld, Allan C. "New Films Degrade Blacks, Stimulate Violence." Human Events, Vol. 34 (March 2 1974): 17.

1671. Burrell, Walter. "Black Screen Image: Where is It Going in the Seventies?" Soul Illustrated (February 1970): 19-20.

1672. Cameron, Earl. "The Negro in Cinema." Films and Filming, Vol. 3, No. 8 (May 1957): 9-11.

1673. Canby, Vincent. "Race to Film Race Issues: Indies React to Negro News." Variety (July 17 1963).

1674. "Civil Rights Groups Attack Films." Jet (September 14 1972): 50. On blaxploitation films.

1675. Coleman, Willette. "Crying at the Movies." Black Collegian, Vol. 5 (January-February 1975): 30-32.

1676. Collier, Aldore. "Why Hollywood Ignores Black Love and Intimacy. Black stars challenge race and market fears that limit on-screen romance." Ebony (April 1989): 39+.

1677. Cope, D. "Anatomy of a Blaxploitation Theatre." Jump Cut, No. 9 (October-December 1975): 22-23.

1678. Couch, William, Jr. "The Problem of Negro Character and Dramatic Incident." Phylon, Vol. 11 (1950): 127-133.

1679. Cripps, Thomas R. "Black Films and Film Makers: Movies in the Ghetto, B. P. (Before Poitier)." Negro Digest, Vol. 18 (February 1969): 21-48.

1680. _____. "The Death of Rastus: Negroes in American Films Since 1945." Phylon (Fall 1967): 267-275.

1681. _____. "Encore Essay: Down and Out in Hollywood." Encore American and Worldwide News (October 1981): 37-38.

1682. _____. "Movies, Race, and World War II: Tennessee Johnson as an Anticipation of the Strategies of the Civil Rights Movement." Prologue, Vol. 14 (Summer 1982).

1683. Daney, Serge. "For a Black Positive Image." Cahiers du Cinema, No. 308 (fevrier 1980): 10-13.

1684. Darrach, Brad. "Hollywood's Second Coming." Playboy (June 1972). Report on the black movie boom of the 1970s.

1685. Davis, Ossie. "The Power of Black Movies." Freedomways, Vol. 14, No. 3 (1974): 230-232. [Reprinted in # 1612]

1686. Dempsey, Michael, and Udayan Gupta. "Hollywood's Color Problem; Charging a Decline in Minority Hiring, Angry Black Leaders are Threatening a Boycott at the Movies." American Film, Vol. 7, No. 6 (April 1982): 66-70.

1687. Denby, David. "Getting Whitey." Atlantic (August 1972): 86-89.

1688. "Do Negroes Have a Future in Hollywood?" Ebony, Vol. 11 (December 1955): 24-30.

1689. Draper, Arthur. "Uncle Tom Will You Never Die?" New Theatre (January 1936).

1690. Dupree, Adolph. "Pearl Bowser: A Flickering Light at the End of the Lens." About Time, Vol. 13, No. 12 (December 1985): 8-11.

1691. Dworkin, Martin S. "The New Negro on Screen." The Progressive (October 1960): 39-41; (November 1960): 33-36; (December 1960): 34-36; (January 1961): 36-38; (February 1961): 38-41.

1692. "The Expanding World of the Black Film." Black Creation, Vol. 4, No. 2 (Winter 1973): 25-43. Special Black film section including essays by James P. Murray, Pearl Bowser, Roscoe C. Brown, Jr., and Michael Mattox.

1693. Fay, Stephen. "Era of Dummies and Darkies." Commonweal (October 30 1970): 125-128.

1694. "51 Black-oriented Films Produced Since Mid-1970." Jet (September 21 1972): 58-59.

1695. "Filmmakers Design Plan to Boost Minority Input." Jet (October 22 1984): 59.

1696. Franklin, Oliver. "Building a Black Film Audience." Sightlines (Spring 1976): 10-12.

1697. Freedomways, Vol. 14 (3rd Quarter, 1974). Special Black film issue.

1698. Gabriel, Teshome H. "Images of Black People in Cinema: A Historical Overview." Ufahamu, Vol. VI, No. 2 (1976): 133-167.

1699. Garfield, John. "How Hollywood Can Better Race Relations." Negro Digest, Vol. 6 (November 1947): 4-8.

1700. Gauthier, Guy. "Survivre a la Traite et au Racisme." La Revue du Cinema, No. 423 (January 1987): 60-65.

1701. Glaessner, Verina. "The Negro in the Contemporary Cinema." Film (Spring 1971): 12-16.

1702. Goldsmith, B. "No More Workin' for the Man, Black Films are Here to Stay." Harper's Bazaar (August 1972): 98-100.

1703. Green, Theophilus. "The Black Man as Movie Hero: New Films Offer a Different Male Image." Ebony (August 1972): 144-148.

1704. Greene, Laura. "A Bad Black Image in Film." Essence, Vol. 4 (May 1973): 70.

1705. Halliburton, Cecil D. "Hollywood Presents Us: The Movies and Racial Attitudes." Opportunity, Vol. 13 (October 1935): 296-297.

1706. Hardwick, Leon. "The Negro Looks at Hollywood." Hollywood Quarterly (Spring 1946).

1707. _____. "Negro Stereotypes on the Screen." Hollywood Quarterly, Vol. 1, No. 2 (January 1946): 234-236.

1708. _____. "Screen Stereotypes." Negro Digest, Vol. 4 (May 1946): 57-58.

1709. Harmon, Sidney. "How Hollywood is Smashing the Colour Bar." Films and Filming, Vol. 5, No. 6 (March 1959): 7+.

1710. Harrison, William. "The Negro in the Cinema." Sight and Sound (London), Vol. 9 (Spring 1939): 16-17.

1711. Hartung, Philip T. "Black, White and Technicolor." Commonweal (September 5 1969): 543-545.

1712. _____. "Guess Who's Coming to Lunch? Integration in Movies." Commonweal (August 23 1968): 571.

1713. Higgins, Chester, Sr. "Black Films: Boom or Bust?" Jet (June 8 1972): 52-59.

1714. "Hollywood and the Negro." New Republic (December 11 1961): 5.

1715. "Hollywood Phony on Negro Film." Negro History Bulletin (October 1960): 21.

1716. "Hollywood Report: Unchanging Attitude of Whites Towards the Negro." Phylon, Vol. 6 (Winter 1945): 13-16.

1717. Horowitz, Joy. "Hollywood's Dirty Little Secret." American Visions (August 1989): 16+. On racism in the motion picture industry.

1718. Hughes, Langston. "Is Hollywood Fair to Negroes in its Films?" Negro Digest, Vol. 1 (April 1943): 16-21.

1719. Hunter, Robert. "Hollywood and the Negro: the Slow Pace of Change." Negro Digest, Vol. 15 (May 1966): 37-41.

1720. "IATSE: No Negro Need Apply: Locals Stick to Exclusion." Variety (July 31 1963).

1721. "The Image Makers: Negro Stereotypes." Negro History Bulletin, Vol. 26 (December 1962): 127-128.

1722. Jabavu, Nuntando. "Hollywood's Celluloid Negro." Film Illustrated Monthly [London] (December 1946).

1723. Jefferson, Roland S. "Black Film Boom: Decerebrate, Dangerous and Declining." National Medical Association. Journal, Vol. 67 (January 1975): 11-15.

1724. Johnson, Albert. "Beige, Brown, or Black." Film Quarterly, Vol. 13, No. 1 (Fall 1959): 38-43.

1725. _____. "The Negro in American Films: Some Recent Works." Film Quarterly, Vol. 18, No. 4 (Summer 1965): 14-30.

1726. Jones, Juli, Jr. "Motion Pictures and Inside Facts." Half-Century Magazine (July 1919): 16, 19.

1727. _____. "The Moving Picture: Their Good to the General Public and to the Colored Race in Particular." Half-Century Magazine (June 1919): 9.

1728. Jones, Robert. "How Hollywood Feels About Negroes." Negro Digest, Vol. 5 (August 1947): 4-8.

1729. Kael, Pauline. "Notes on Black Movies." New Yorker (December 2 1972): 159-165.

1730. Kagan, Norman. "Black American Cinema: A Primer." Cinema, Vol. 6, No. 2 (Fall 1970): 2-7.

1731. Knight, Arthur. "Black Can Be Beautiful." Saturday Review (September 16 1972): 101+.

1732. _____. "The Negro in Films Today: Hollywood's New Cycle." Films in Review, Vol. 1 (February 1950): 14-19.

1733. Koppes, Clayton R., and Gregory D. Black. "Blacks, Loyalty, and Motion-Picture Propaganda in World War II." The Journal of American History, Vol. 73 (September 1986): 383-406.

1734. Kotlarz, Irene. "'The Birth of a Notion'." Screen, Vol. 24, No. 2 (March/April 1983): 21-29. On the representation of blacks in animated cartoons.

1735. Lardeau, Yann. "Cinema Noir Americain." Cahiers du Cinema, No. 340 (Octobre 1982): 48-52.

1736. "The Last 'Special Issue' on Race?" Screen (London), Vol. 29, No. 4 (Autumn 1988).

1737. Leab, Daniel J. "The Gamut from A to B: The Image of the Black in Pre-1915 Movies." Political Science Quarterly, Vol. 88 (March 1973): 553-570.

1738. Lee, Ernest, and Joan C. Russell. "Faces in the Crowd: A Historical Look at Black Films." Library Journal (May 15 1988): 37-42.

1739. "Lighting! Camera! Action!" Black Enterprise, Vol. 14 (December 1983): 48+.

1740. "Looking Back on Blacks in Films." Ebony (June 1973): 35-38+.

1741. Lubow, A. "Blacks in Hollywood: Where Have They All Gone?" People (May 17 1982): 30-35.

1742. McManus, John T., and Louis Kronenberger. "Motion Pictures, the Theatre, and Race Relations." The Annals of the American Academy of Political and Social Science, Vol. 244 (March 1946): 152-158. [Excerpted in Negro Digest (June 1946)].

1743. McMullin, Corinne. "Vers une Esthetique Specifique du Cinema Noir Americain." Cinema (Paris), No. 261 (September 1980): 50-55.

1744. "The Making of a Black Legacy in Film." Ebony, Vol. 40 (March 1985): 54+.

1745. Manners, Dorothy. "Negro Pictures." Motion Picture Classic (February 1929).

1746. Martin, Marcel. "Visages Noirs dans des Films Blancs." La Revue du Cinema, No. 423 (January 1987): 65-69.

1747. Martin, Michael T. "The Afro-American Image in Film and Television: The Legitimization of the Racial Divisions in the American Social Order." Presence Africaine, No. 124 (1982): 144-167.

1748. Masilela, Ntongela. "Interconnections: The African and Afro-American Cinema." The Independent, Vol. 11, No. 2 (January-February 1988): 14-17.

1749. Mason, B. J. "New Films: Culture or Con Game?" Ebony (December 1972): 60-62+. On the blaxploitation debate.

1750. Michener, Charles. "Black Movies: Renaissance or Ripoff?" Newsweek (October 23 1972): 74-82.

1751. Miller, Loren. "Hollywood's New Negro Films." The Crisis, Vol. 45 (January 1938): 8-9.

1752. _____. "Uncle Tom in Hollywood." The Crisis, Vol. 41 (November 1934): 329+.

1753. "Minorities Film Workshop." Sightlines, Vol. 4, No. 2 (November-December 1970): 24-26.

1754. Moore, Walter. "Needed: A Negro Film Movement." Negro Digest, Vol. 15 (January 1966): 45-48.

1755. Moss, Carlton. "The Negro in American Films." Freedomways, Vol. 3 (Spring 1963): 135-142. [Reprinted in # 1618]

1756. _____. "Your Future in Hollywood." Our World (May 1946): 9.

1757. Murray, James P. "Black Movies and Music in Harmony." Black Creation, Vol. 5, No. 1 (Fall 1973): 9-11.

1758. _____. "Black Movies/Black Theatre." The Drama Review, Vol. 16 (December 1972): 56-61.

1759. _____. "Lurid Boom Over, But Black Films Steady On." Variety (January 7 1976): 16+.

1760. _____. "The Subject is Money." Black Creation, Vol. 4 (Winter 1973): 26+.

1761. _____. "West Coast Gets the Shaft." Black Creation, Vol. 3, No. 4 (Summer 1972): 12-14. On Black film activity in New York.

1762. Myers, Arthur S. "The Black Man in Films." Film News, Vol. 26, No. 4 (September 1969): 6-9, 38.

1763. Napolitano, Antonio. "Cinema Negro: Il Linguaggio dell'Autentico." Filmcritica, No. 200 (September 1969): 284-288.

1764. Narine, Dalton. "Black America's Rich Film History; From Oscar Micheaux to Eddie Murphy." Ebony, Vol. 43 (February 1988): 132, 134, 136, 138.

1765. "The Negro and the Movies." Negro Digest, Vol. 1 (April 1943): 19-21.

1766. "The Negro in Film." Close-Up [London] (August 1929). Special issue.

1767. "New Look in Hollywood." Sepia, Vol. 7 (March 1959): 30-34.

1768. Newton, Edmund, and Udayan Gupta. "Fighting Black in Hollywood." Black Enterprise, Vol. 13 (September 1982): 35-39. On the struggles of Black actors, producers and directors in Hollywood.

1769. Noble, George. "The Negro in Hollywood." Sight and Sound, Vol. 8, No. 29 (Spring 1939): 14-17.

1770. Noble, Peter. "Colour Bar in Hollywood." Chelsea [London] (Spring 1948).

1771. _____. "Colour Bar on the Screen." World Review [London] (June 1944).

1772. _____. "The Negro in the American Film." Jazz Music [London] (October 1943).

1773. O'Neal, Mary. "Tricked by Flicks." Essence, Vol. 5 (October 1974): 17.   Discussion of blaxploitation films.

1774. Peavy, Charles D. "Cinema from the Slums." Cineaste, Vol. 3 (Fall 1969): 11-12.

1775. _____. "A Flood of Black Films." Essence, Vol. 3 (September 1972): 28.

1776. Pfaff, Francoise. "Negro Images in American Films from 1900 to 1960." Negro History Bulletin, Vol. 43 (October-December 1980): 92-94.

1777. Potamkin, Harry Alan. "The White Man's Negro." Liberator (March 28 1931).

1778. Poussaint, Alvin F. "Blaxploitation Movies: Cheap Thrills That Degrade Blacks." Psychology Today, Vol. 7 (February 1974): 22+.

1779. "Prejudicial Film: Progress and Stalemate (1915-1967)." Phylon, Vol. 31 (Summer 1970): 142-147.

1780. Pyros, John. "The Negro Film Image: Conference--Ferris State College." Filmmakers Newsletter, Vol. 2, No. 12 (October 1969): 42.

1781. Reddick, L. D. "Educational Programs for the Improvement of Race Relations: Motion Pictures, Radio, The Press, and Libraries." Journal of Negro Education (Summer 1944): 368-382. Includes a discussion of the Black image in film from The Birth of a Nation (1915) to The Negro Soldier (1944).

1782. Robb, David. "MGM-UA Signs with NAACP to Expand Overall Black Presence." Variety (December 29 1982): 3-4.

1783. Roffman, Peter, and Bev Simpson. "Black Images on White Screens." Cineaste, Vol. 13, No. 3 (June 1984): 14-21.

1784. Ronan, M. "Black Films: Values, Pro and Con." Senior Scholastic, No. 101 (December 11 1972): 8-10.

1785. Sankor, Shelby. "Hollywood Race Revolt." Flamingo [London] (January 1964): 44-45.

1786. Schickel, Richard. "Films for Blacks." _Life_ (June 9 1972): 20.

1787. Sharp, Saundra. "Hollywood Blacks Fighting Back." _The Black Collegian_, Vol. 11 (October-November 1980): 202-204.

1788. Smikle, Ken. "Inside Hollywood." _Black Enterprise_ (December 1986): 48-54.

1789. Smith, Jean Voltaire. "Our Need for More Films." _Half-Century Magazine_ (April 1922): 8.

1790. Stewart, Ted. "The Black Movie Boom." _Sepia_, Vol. 21 (April 1972): 44-52.

1791. Sugy, Catherine. "Black Men or Good Niggers? Race in the New Movies." _Take One_, Vol. 1, No. 8 (December 1967): 18-21. [Reprinted in # 1622]

1792. "Survol Noir Americain." _Cahiers du Cinema_, No. 308 (Janvier 1980): 4-19.

1793. Taylor, Clyde. "New U.S. Black Cinema." _Jump Cut_, No. 28 (April 1983): 46-48, 51.

1794. _____. "Why Not Stage a Film Festival? Black Films." _Essence_ (August 1978): 55-56+.

1795. _Theatre Arts_ (August 1942). Special issue on African Americans on stage and screen.

1796. _Theatre Arts_ (July 1935). Special issue on African Americans on stage and screen.

1797. Trumbo, Dalton. "Blackface, Hollywood Style." _Negro Digest_, Vol. 2 (February 1944): 37-39.

1798. Varlejs, J. "Cine-opsis: Searches for Roots." _Wilson Library Bulletin_ (November 1977): 258-259.

1799. Verrill, Addison. "Black Film Explosion." _Variety_ (January 9 1974): 30.

1800. Walsh, Moira. "More About Black Films." _America_ (November 25 1972): 459-460.

1801. _____. "One Vote for Black Films." _America_ (September 23 1972): 210-211.

1802. Wander, Brandon. "Black Dreams: The Fantasy and Ritual of Black Films." _Film Quarterly_, Vol. 29, No. 1 (Fall 1975): 2-11.

1803. Ward, Renee. "Black Films, White Profits." _Black Scholar_, Vol. 7 (May 1976): 13-25.

1804. Wesley, Richard. "Film/Opinion: Which Way the Black Film." _Encore_ (January 1973): 52-54.

1805. _____. "Toward a Viable Black Film Industry."
Black World, Vol. 22 (July 1973): 23-32.

1806. Westerbeck, C. L., Jr. "Black and White." Commonweal
(May 26 1972): 285-286.

1807. "White on Black." Film Comment, Vol. 20 (December
1984): 7+. Discussion of the Black image in American film.

1808. Wilkins, Roy. "Will Hollywood Change Its Tune?"
Headlines and Pictures (August 1946): 44.

1809. Williams, Grayling. "Black Image in Cinema and Theatre
in America." Ufahamu, Vol. 12, No. 2 (1983): 102-115.

1810. Williams, Robert. "Stereotypes of Negroes in Film."
Vision, Vol. 1, No. 2 (Summer 1962): 67-69.

1811. Yamada, George. "Old Stereotyped Pattern." The
Crisis, Vol. 60 (January 1953): 17-19.

1812. Yearwood, Gladstone L. "The Hero in Black Film: An
Analysis of the Film Industry and Problems in Black Cinema."
Wide Angle, Vol. 5, No. 2 (1982): 42-50.

1813. Young, A. S. "They Live on the Edge of Hollywood."
Sepia, Vol. 10 (November 1961): 29-32.

Newspaper Articles

1814. Adler, Renata. "The Negro that Movies Overlook." New
York Times (March 3 1968).

1815. Bart, Peter. "The Still Invisible Man." New York
Times (July 17 1966).

1816. Bernstein, Harry. "Hollywood Gives More Work, Roles to
Negro." Los Angeles Times (March 13 1966).

1817. "Black Movie Boom--Good or Bad?" New York Times
(December 17 1972): Sec. II.

1818. Bogle, Donald. "In Search of Cinema Verity." New York
Times/Supplement--A World of Difference (April 16 1989): 10-
11. Discussion of the Black presence in 1980s filmmaking.

1819. Burke, Vincent J. "US Plans to Prod Film Industry on
Job Discrimination Charges." Los Angeles Times (October 19
1969).

1820. Byron, Stuart. "Film: Bum Visions for Blaxploitation."
Village Voice (April 12 1973): 93.

1821. Champlin, Charles. "Re-evaluation Needed in Film
Industry." Los Angeles Times (April 9 1968).

1822. Crowther, Bosley. "The Negro in Films: Old Issue
Raised by New Screen Items." New York Times (October 6 1963).

1823. _____. "The Negro in Films: Poitier Points a
Dilemma Which The Cool World Helps Rebuff." New York Times
(August 26 1964).

1824. Davis, George. "Black Motion Pictures: The Past." New
York Amsterdam News (September 18 1971): D13-D14.

1825. DeAnda, Peter. "So Now I'm Back, and Black...and
Available." New York Times (October 10 1971).

1826. Gent, George. "Black Films Are In, So Are Profits."
New York Times (July 18 1972): 22.

1827. Glenn, Larry. "Hollywood Change." New York Times
(September 22 1963).

1828. Holly, Ellen. "Where Are the Films About Real Black
Men and Women." New York Times (June 2 1974): Sec. II.
[Reprinted in Freedomways (3rd Quarter, 1974)]

1829. "Is It Better to be Shaft than Uncle Tom?" New York
Times (August 26 1973): D11, D16. Excerpts from WOR radio
interview conducted by Heywood Hale Broun with critic Donald
Bogle and actress Rosalind Cash on black stereotypes in film.

1830. Keough, Peter. "Blacks in American Cinema. After 70
Years, Hollywood Still Relies on Stereotypes." Chicago
Sun-Times (June 7 1987).

1831. Knapp, Dan. "An Assessment of the Status of Hollywood
Blacks." Los Angeles Times (September 28 1969).

1832. _____. "Black Craftsmen's Talents Untapped on
Entertainment Scene." Los Angeles Times (October 5 1969).

1833. Miller, Henry. "Last Chance for a Black Cinema."
Village Voice (May 20-26 1981): 64.

1834. Milloy, Marilyn. "A Cinematic Schism in Black and
White." New York Newsday (September 28 1982).

1835. Morris, George. "Film: The Blaxploitation
Sweepstakes." Village Voice (July 18 1974): 69.

1836. Nicholson, David. "Why Can't We Give Black Cinema A
Chance?" Washington Post (August 30 1987): C1, C4.

1837. Nix, Crystal. "Changes in Black Films." New York
Times (October 25 1985): C8.

1838. Patterson, Lindsay. "Hollywood's Boy and Girl Next
Door--Color Them White." New York Times (June 16 1968): D9.

1839. Platt, David. "The Negro and the Hollywood Film."
Daily Worker (February 19-28, 1940). Seven-part series.

1840. Riley, Clayton. "Movies: 'Shaft Can Do Everything - I
Can Do Nothing'." New York Times (August 13 1972): D9.

1841. Wallace, Michele. "'I Don't Know Nothin' 'Bout
Birthin' No Babies!'" <u>Village Voice</u> (December 5 1989): 112.

1842. West, Hollie I. "Makers of Black Films Stand at
Crossroads." <u>Los Angeles Times</u> (January 28 1973).

1843. Wilford, Red. "Looking to the '80's: Blacks in the
Movies and Television." <u>St. Louis Argus</u> (April 24 1980).

1844. Wilkerson, Isabel. "Blacks Left Out of Movie Boom."
<u>Boston Globe</u> (August 29 1982).

1845. Winsten, Archer. "Movie Talk: The Negro Stereotype in
American Pictures." <u>New York Post</u> (April 7 1937).

Media Materials

1846. <u>Black Images from the Screen</u> (1978). Produced and
Directed by John Rier. 60 min. Narration by Barbara O with
performances by the black theater group, Bodacious
Buggerrilla. Documents a psychological survey that examines
the impact that Black media behavior models have on black
youth. [Available from the Black Filmmaker Foundation (80
Eighth Avenue, Suite 1704, New York, NY 10011. Tel. 212/
924-1198)].

1847. <u>Black Shadows on the Silver Screen</u> (1975). Post-
Newsweek Television. Ray Hubbard, executive producer;, Thomas
Cripps, writer, Ossie Davis, narrator. Hour-long television
compilation-film surveying the history of race movies from
1915 to 1950.

1848. <u>The Black Wave</u> (1970). Second German TV Net. 60 min.
TV documentary on blacks in American film. [See review--
"Problems of Blacks in U.S. Films Probed in German TV Series."
<u>Variety</u> (June 3 1970).]

1849. <u>Ethnic Notions</u> (1987). 58 min. Dir. Marlon Riggs.
Video documentary on the stereotyping of African Americans via
advertising, film and television. [Available from California
Newsreel, 149 9th St., Room 420-B, San Francisco, CA 94103.
Tel. 415/621-6196]

1850. <u>Minorities in Film</u>. Detroit: Wayne State University,
1975. 3-part television series detailing the history of
minority involvement in American film.

1851. <u>Representation and Blacks in American Cinema</u>. 70 min.
Includes excerpts from: The Littlest Rebel (1936), The Defiant
Ones (1958), Buck and the Preacher (1971), Cleopatra Jones
(1973), and Killer of Sheep (1977). [Available from the
British Film Institute, Education Department, 21 Stephen St.,
London W1P 1PL. Tel. 01-255 1444.]

1852. <u>Twenty-Five Years Later: Blacks in Society. 4, Blacks
in Hollywood</u> (Audiotape). 30 minutes. [Available from
National Public Radio, Cassette Publishing, 2025 M Street,
N.W., Washington, D.C. 20036. Cassette # HO-85-02-27.]

THE BLACK WOMAN IN AMERICAN FILM

1853. Gant, Lisbeth A. "Images of the Black Woman in Film."
In Film and Africana Politics. New Brunswick: Rutgers
University, 197?.

1854. Symposium on Black Images in Films, Stereotyping, and
Self-Perception as Viewed by Black Actresses, Boston
University, 1973. Boston: Afro-American Studies Program,
Boston University), 1974. 69p. (Occasional paper; No. 2)

Dissertations

1855. Donalson, Melvin Burke. "The Representation of
AfroAmerican Women in the Hollywood Feature Film, 1915-1949."
Dissertation (Ph.D.) Brown University, 1981. 171p.

Articles

1856. Burrell, Walter Price. "The Black Woman as a Sex Image
in Films." Black Stars (December 1972): 32-39.

1857. Del Guadio, S. "I'd Walk a Million Miles for one of
her Smiles." Jump Cut, No. 28 (April 1983): 23-25. On the
Mammy image in American film.

1858. Gant, Lisbeth. "Ain't Beulah Dead Yet?: Or Images of
Black Woman in Film." Essence, Vol. 4 (May 1973): 60-61,
72-75.

1859. Kisner, Ronald E. "What films are doing to image of
Black women." Jet (June 29 1972): 56-61.

1860. Mapp, Edward. "Black Women in Films." Black Scholar,
Vol. 4 (March-April 1973): 42-46; Also (Summer 1982): 36-40.

1861. Martin, Sharon Stockard. "Invisible Reflection: Images
and Self-Images of Black Women on Stage and Screen." Black
Collegian, Vol. 9 (May-June 1979): 74-75.

1862. Mealy, Rosemari. "Some Reflections on Black Women in
Film." Heresies, Issue 8 (1979?): 28-30.

1863. Mikell, C. A. "Hollywood and Black Women--The Way We
Were." Mademoiselle (November 1976): 62+.

1864. Sloan, Margaret. "Film: Keeping the Black Woman in Her
Place." Ms., Vol. 2 (January 1974): 30+.

1865. Stephens, Lenora C. "Black Women in Film." The
Southern Quarterly, Vol. 19, No. 3-4 (Spring-Summer 1981):
164-170.

1866. Taylor, Clyde. "Shooting the Black Woman." The Black
Collegian (May-June 1979): 94-96.

BLACK CAST AND RACE-THEME FILMS

1867. Cinema: Negro Features - Clippings [Billy Rose Theatre Collection]

1868. Kagan, Norman. "The Dark Horse Operas: A Film Article." Negro History Bulletin, Vol. 36 (January 1973): 13-14. Discussion of the black western genre of the all-black cast films of the 1920s and 1930s.

1869. _____. "Letters: All-Black Cast Sound Films 1930-1950." Films in Review (October 1972): 509-510. Letter listing the bulk of the Black cast features from 1930-1950.

1870. Leab, Daniel J. "'All-Colored'--But Not Much Different: Films Made for Negro Ghetto Audiences, 1913-1928." Phylon, Vol. 36 (September 1975): 321-339.

1871. _____. "A Pale Black Imitation: All-Colored Films: 1930-1960." Journal of Popular Film, Vol. 4, No. 1 (1975): 56-76.

1872. Sayre, Nora. "Racial Films of the 1940s: Safe Fearlessness." The Nation (February 4 1978): 117-119.

ANNA LUCASTA (1958)

1873. Bogle, Donald. Blacks in American Films and Television. New York: Garland Press, 1988, pp. 13-14.

Articles

1874. Anna Lucasta - Clippings [Billy Rose Theatre Collection]

1875. "Anna Lucasta." Variety (November 19 1958).

1876. "Anna Lucasta on Film." Newsweek (December 8 1958).

1877. Crowther, Bosley. "Trouble Enough. Anna Lucasta and an Old Problem in Films." New York Times (January 18 1959).

1878. McCarten, John. "The Current Cinema: Anna Again." New Yorker (January 24 1959): 111-112.

1879. Saturday Review (January 10 1959). [Review]

1880. Winsten, Archer. "Reviewing Stand: 'Anna Lucasta' Opens at Victoria." New York Post (January 15 1959).

1881. "Write-in Votes on 'Anna Lucasta'." New York Times (January 25 1959). Responses to Crowther review above (# 1876).

BIRTH OF A NATION (1915)

1882. Aitken, Roy E., as told to Al P. Nelson. The Birth of a Nation Story. Middleburg, VA: William A. Denlinger, 1965. 96p.

1883. Cuniberti, John. *The Birth of a Nation: a formal shot-by-shot analysis together with microfiche*. Woodbridge, CT: Research Publications, 1979. 232p. and 24 sheets of microfiche.

1884. Dixon, Thomas. *The Clansman, an historical romance of the Ku Klux Klan*. New York: Grosset & Dunlap, 1905. 374p. The novel upon which the film is based.

1885. *Fighting a Vicious Film: Protest Against 'The Birth of a Nation.'* Boston: Boston Branch of the National Association for the Advancement of Colored People, 1915. 47p.

1886. Grimke, Francis J. *The Birth of a Nation*. Washington, D.C.: the Author, 1915. 4p.

1887. Huff, Theodore. *A Shot Analysis of D. W. Griffith's "The Birth of a Nation."* New York: The Museum of Modern Art, 1961. 69p.

1888. Silva, Fred, ed. *Focus on The Birth of a Nation*. Englewood Cliffs, NJ: Prentice-Hall, 1971. 184p. Anthology of some of the most important writings on the Griffith film.

1889. Thomas, Isaac L. *The Birth of a Nation: A Hyperbole Versus A Negro's Plea for Fair Play*. Philadelphia: W. H. Watson, 1916. 64p.

Books with Sections on Birth of a Nation

1890. Bogle, Donald. *Blacks in American Films and Television*. New York: Garland, 1988, pp. 19-22.

1891. Christensen, Terry. *Reel Politics: American political movies from Birth of a Nation to Platoon*. New York: Blackwell, 1987, pp. 16-21.

1892. O'Dell, Paul, with the assistance of Anthony Slide. *Griffith and the Rise of Hollywood*. New York: A. S. Barnes, 1971, pp. 13-35.

Dissertations and Theses

1893. Fleener-Marzec, Nickieann. "D. W. Griffith's The Birth of a Nation: Controversy, Suppression, and the First Amendment as It Applies to Filmic Expression, 1915-1973." Dissertation (Ph.D.) University of Wisconsin-Madison, 1977. 577p.

1894. Hutchins, Charles L. "A Critical Evaluation of the Controversies Engendered by D. W. Griffith's The Birth of a Nation." Thesis (M.A.) University of Iowa, 1961.

Articles

1895. *L'Avant Scene [du] Cinema*, No. 193/194 (Octobre 1977). Special Birth of a Nation issue.

1896. Birth of a Nation - Scrapbook (Clippings, 1914-1935) (MFL n.c. 646 # 6). [Billy Rose Theatre Collection]

1897.   Birth of a Nation Scrapbooks.   12 vols.   [Held by the Museum of Modern Art Film Study Center/See # 6009]

1898.   Cinemages, Special Issue No. 1 (1955).   Special issue on Birth of a Nation written by Seymour Stern.

1899.   CinemaTexas Program Notes, Vol. 1, No. 3 (February 1 1972); Vol. 3, No. 4 (September 12 1972); Vol. 6, No. 7 (January 24 1974).

1900.   Cook, Raymond A.   "The Man Behind The Birth of a Nation."   North Carolina Historical Review, Vol. 29 (1962): 519-540.   Study of Thomas Dixon, Jr., author of The Clansman.

1901.   Film Culture, No. 36 (Spring/Summer 1965).   210p. Special issue on Birth of a Nation edited by Seymour Stern.

1902.   Fleener, Nickie.   "Answering film with film: the Hampton Epilogue, a positive alternative to the negative black stereotypes presented in The Birth of a Nation."   Journal of Popular Film and Television, Vol. 7, No. 4 (1980): 400-425.

1903.   Lowry, Ed.   "Birth of a Nation."   CinemaTexas Program Notes, Vol. 15, No. 1 (September 19 1978): 57-70.

1904.   Mackaye, Milton.   "The Birth of a Nation."   Scribner's Magazine (November 1937): 40-46, 69.

1905.   Merritt, Russell.   "Dixon, Griffith, and the Southern Legend."   Cinema Journal, Vol. 12, No. 1 (Fall 1972): 26-45.

1906.   Moving Pictures - Birth of a Nation (Microfiche) [Schomburg Center]

1907.   O'Dell, Paul.   "The Birth of a Nation."   The Silent Picture (Autumn 1969).

1908.   Simcovitch, Maxim.   "The Impact of Griffith's Birth of a Nation on the Modern Ku Klux Klan."   Journal of Popular Film, Vol. 1 (Winter 1972): 45-54.

1909.   Stern, Seymour.   "The Birth of a Nation in retrospect." International Photographer (April 1935): 4-5, 23-24.

1910.   Wohlforth, Robert.   "In and out of The Birth of a Nation."   Films in Review, Vol. 29, No. 8 (October 1978): 465-470.

CABIN IN THE SKY (1943)

1911.   Bogle, Donald.   Blacks in American Films and Television.   New York: Garland, 1988, pp. 43-45.

Articles

1912.   "Cabin in the Sky."   Time (April 12 1943).

1913.   "Cabin in the Sky."   Variety (February 10 1943).

1914. Cabin in the Sky - Pressbook (*ZAN-*T8, reel 104) [Billy Rose Theatre Collection]. Contains all materials used for MGM's "Cabin in the Sky" promotional campaign.

1915. Graham, Olive. "Cabin in the Sky." CinemaTexas Program Notes, Vol. 18, No. 3 (April 2 1980): 31-36.

1916. Hale, Wanda. "'Cabin in the Sky' is a musical honey." New York Daily News (May 28 1943).

1917. "It's a Sure 'Nuff Cabin in the Sky." PM (May 28 1943).

1918. Platt, David. "New MGM Film Caricatures Negro People." Daily Worker (June 5 1943).

CARMEN JONES (1954)

1919. Bogle, Donald. Blacks in American Films and Television. New York: Garland, 1988, pp. 50-51.

Articles

1920. Baldwin, James. "Life Straight In De Eye: Carmen Jones: Film Spectacular in Color." Commentary (January 1955): 74-77.

1921. Carmen Jones - Clippings [Billy Rose Theatre Collection]

1922. CinemaTexas Program Notes, Vol. 1, No. 10 (February 24 1972).

1923. Crowther, Bosley. "Negroes in a Film; "Carmen Jones" finds American types singing a foreign opera score." New York Times (October 3 1954).

1924. _____. "Screen in Review: 'Carmen Jones'." New York Times (October 29 1954).

1925. Marcel, Michael. "Interview: Otto Preminger on Black Movies." Encore, Vol. 2 (August 1973): 56-59. Discussion of Preminger's two black-cast films - Carmen Jones and Porgy & Bess - and his impressions of the black films of the 60s and 70s.

1926. "The New Pictures; Carmen Jones." Time (November 1 1954).

1927. Silverman, Stephen M. "That Black 'Carmen'." New York Post (July 16 1986): 42.

COLOR PURPLE (1985)

1928. Bogle, Donald. Blacks in American Films and Television. New York: Garland, 1988, pp. 58-62.

1929. Walker, Alice. The Color Purple. New York: Harcourt Brace Jovanovich, 1982. 245p.

Dissertations

1930.   Bobo, Jacqueline.   "Articulation and Hegemony: Black Women's Response to the Film 'The Color Purple.'" Dissertation (Ph.D.) University of Oregon, 1989.   273p.

Articles

1931.   Bobo, Jacqueline.   "Black Women's Responses."   Jump Cut, No. 33 (February 1988): 43-51.   On Black women's response to The Color Purple.

1932.   Bruning, Fred.   "When E.T. goes to Georgia."   Maclean's (March 24 1986): 9.

1933.   Chase, Donald.   "Spielberg Speaks Out."   Millimeter, Vol. 14, No. 2 (February 1986): 55-68.   Interview with Spielberg on "The Color Purple."

1934.   "'The Color Purple' brings new Black stars to screen in shocking story."   Jet (January 13 1986): 58+.

1935.   Color Purple - Clippings (MFL + n.c. 2895) [Billy Rose Theatre Collection]

1936.   "The Color Purple."   Films and Filming, No. 381 (June 1986): 26-27.

1937.   Dworkin, Susan.   "The making of 'The Color Purple.'" Ms. (December 1985): 66+.

1938.   Goldstein, William.   "Alice Walker on the set of The Color Purple."   Publishers Weekly (September 6 1985): 46+.

1939.   Guerrero, Ed.   "The Slavery Motif in Recent Popular Cinema."   Jump Cut, No. 33 (February 1988): 52-59.   Analysis of the slave theme in The Color Purple and Brother from Another Planet.

1940.   Stark, John.   "Seeing red over Purple."   People (March 10 1986): 102+.

1941.   "Steven Spielberg; the director says it's good-bye to spaceships and hello to relationships."   American Film (June 1988): 12+.   [Interview]

1942.   Wesley, Richard.   "'The Color Purple' debate; reading between the lines."   Ms. (September 1986): 62+.

1943.   Willimon, William H.   "Seeing red over The Color Purple."   The Christian Century (April 2 1986): 319.

Newspaper Articles

1944.   Collins, Glenn.   "New Departures for Two Major Directors; Spielberg films 'The Color Purple'."   New York Times (December 15 1985): Sec. 2, pp. 1, 23.

1945. Milloy, Marilyn. "The 'Color Purple' Debate." New York Newsday (February 24 1986): Pt. II, pp. 1+.

1946. Moving Pictures - Color Purple - Vertical File [Schomburg Center]

1947. Shipp, E. R. "Blacks in Heated Debate Over 'The Color Purple.'" New York Times (January 27 1986): 13.

1948. Wallace, Michele. "Blues for Mr. Spielberg." Village Voice (March 18 1986): 21-25.

Reviews

1949. Boyd, Herb. "Artist's Responsibility: Expose the Enemy; The Many Contrasting Shades of The Color Purple." New York Amsterdam News (January 4 1986).

1950. Canby, Vincent. "From a Palette of Cliches Comes 'The Color Purple'." New York Times (January 5 1986): Sec. 2, pp. 17, 30.

1951. Denby, David. "Purple People-Eater." New York (January 13 1986): 56-57.

1952. Hoberman, J. "Color Me Purple." Village Voice (December 24 1985): 76.

1953. Sinclair, Abiola. "Not Enough Balance of Purple Male Behavior." New York Amsterdam News (January 4 1986).

1954. White, Armond. "The Color Purple: A Rethinking of Archetypes." City Sun (January 18 1986).

GLORY (1989)

1955. Ansen, David. "Glory." Newsweek (December 18 1989): 73.

1956. Finkelman, Paul. "The Union Army's Fighting 54th; Black Men Banded Together in a Civil War Regiment to Prove their Might and Passion for Justice." American Visions (December 1989): 20-26. On the historical background to "Glory".

1957. Morrow, Lance. "Cinema: Manhood and the Power of Glory." Time (February 26 1990): 68. [Editorial]

1958. Southgate, Martha. "Guts and Glory: a forgotten civil war story comes to film." Essence (December 1989): 30.

1959. White, Armond. "Fighting Black." Film Comment (January/February 1990): 22-26. Interview with "Glory's" director, Edward Zwick.

Newspaper Articles

1960. Bernstein, Richard. "Heroes of 'Glory' Fought Bigotry Before All Else." New York Times (December 17 1989): Sec. 2, pp. 15, 22.

1961. Collins, Glenn. "'Glory' Resurrects Its Black Heroes; Filming in the South, it tells the forgotten story of a black Union Army regiment." New York Times (March 26 1989): Sec. 2, pp. 1, 16-17.

1962. Harris, Frank III. "Viewpoint: Some Thoughts on Glory." City Sun (February 28-March 6 1990): 33.

1963. Sterritt, David. "Hollywood focuses on civil rights." Christian Science Monitor (January 10 1990): 10. Discussion of "Glory" and "Driving Miss Daisy."

1964. Van Gelder, Lawrence. "Director of 'Glory'." New York Times (December 15 1989): C18. Profile of Edward Zwick.

Reviews

1965. Frechette, David. "Glory, A Tentative Step." Black Film Review, Vol. 5, No. 4 (Fall 1989?): 24.

1966. Giddins, Gary. "Why We Fight." Village Voice (December 19 1989): 98.

1967. Kauffmann, Stanley. "Glory." The New Republic (January 8 1990): 28-29.

1968. Ward, Geoffrey C. "Glory." Vogue (January 1990): 94.

1969. White, Armond. "Glory Elevates Hollywood's Historical Storytelling." City Sun (January 3-9 1990): 13.

GREEN PASTURES (1936)

See also # 3034

1970. Bogle, Donald. Blacks in American Films and Television. New York: Garland, 1988, pp. 99-100.

1971. Connelly, Marc. The Green Pastures. Edited with an introduction by Thomas Cripps. Madison: Published for the Wisconsin Center for Film and Theater Research by the University of Wisconsin Press, 1979. 206p. (Wisconsin/Warner Bros. screenplay series)

1972. _____. The Green Pastures: a fable. New York: Farrar & Rinehart, 1929. 173p. Hit play from which the film was adapted.

Articles

1973. Green Pastures - Clippings [Billy Rose Theatre Collection]

1974. Green Pastures - Pressbook (*ZAN-*T8, reel 40) [Billy Rose Theatre Collection]. Contains all materials used in Warner Bros. "Green Pastures" promotional campaign.

1975. Green Pastures - Scrapbook (MFL + n.c. 2178 #3) [Billy Rose Theatre Collection]. Clippings from the Wichita, Kansas premiere of "Green Pastures." Includes Warner Bros. press releases on the film and its star, Rex Ingram.

1976. "'The Green Pastures' Majestic Film." Literary Digest (May 16 1936).

1977. Levin, Meyer. "The Candid Cameraman; Watching the all-Negro cast of Green Pastures gives rise to odd reflections about realism." Esquire (September 1936): 98, 174.

1978. Willson, Dixie. "Making Heaven on Earth." Good Housekeeping (August 1936): 28-29, 163-166.

HALLELUJAH (1929)

See also # 3034

1979. Altman, Rick. The American Film Musical. Bloomington: Indiana University Press, 1987, pp. 291-296.

1980. Bogle, Donald. Blacks in American Films and Television. New York: Garland, 1988, pp. 102-103.

1981. Durgnat, Raymond, and Scott Simmon. King Vidor, American. Berkeley: University of California Press, 1988, pp. 96-113.

1982. Vidor, King. King Vidor: an American Film Institute Seminar on his work. Beverly Hills, Calif., 1977, pp. 28-29. (American Film Institute seminars, pt. 1, no. 180)

1983. _____. King Vidor Interviewed by Nancy Dowd and David Shepard. Metuchen, NJ: Scarecrow Press, 1988, pp. 98-108. (Directors Guild of America Oral History Series; no. 4)

1984. _____. A Tree is a Tree. New York: Harcourt, Brace and Co., 1953, pp. 175-187. Autobiographical account of the making of "Hallelujah" by the film's director.

Articles

1985. Baumgarten, Marjorie. "Hallelujah! (1929)." CinemaTexas Program Notes, Vol. 13, No. 2 (October 11 1977): 27-32.

1986. "'Dramatis Personae': Hallelujah!" The Crisis (October 1929): 342, 355-356.

1987. MacMahon, Henry. "Africa Invades Hollywood." Screen Secrets (April 1929): 68-69, 99.

1988. "Primitive emotions aflame in a Negro film." Literary Digest (October 5 1929): 42+.

1989. Vanity Fair (May 1929): 70-71.

Newspaper Articles

1990. "Another Negro Film; King Vidor realizes ambition by making 'Hallelujah,' an audible picture." New York Times (June 2 1929).

1991. Dougherty, Romeo L. "'Hallelujah' Film Continues to Draw." New York Amsterdam News (August 28 1929).

1992. "Finding Screen Negroes." New York Times (August 25 1929). On how King Vidor located the lead actors--Everett McGarrity, Daniel Haynes, Nina Mae McKinney, Harry Gray, Victoria Spivey, and Fannie Belle de Knight--for "Hallelujah."

1993. Hall, Mordaunt. "Hallelujah: A Negro Talking Picture." New York Times (August 21 1929).

1994. Hallelujah - Clippings (includes programs) [Billy Rose Theatre Collection]

1995. Hallelujah - Scrapbook (MFL + n.c. # 1476) [Billy Rose Theatre Collection]

1996. "Harlem First Night; A milestone in Negro culture." New York Amsterdam News (August 28 1929).

1997. Holt, Paul. "The Truth about 'Hallelujah'." New York Amsterdam News (February 12 1930).

HEARTS IN DIXIE (1929)

1998. Altman, Rick. The American Film Musical. Bloomington: Indiana University Press, 1987, pp. 290-291.

1999. Bogle, Donald. Blacks in American Films and Television. New York: Garland, 1988, pp. 104-105.

Articles

2000. Benchley, Robert. "Hearts in Dixie." Opportunity (April 1929): 122-123.

2001. Hall, Mordaunt. "Art in Negro Picture. 'Hearts in Dixie' is an outstanding achievement in dialogue and singing." New York Times (March 10 1929): Sec. X, p. 7.

2002. _____. "The Screen: Way Down Yonder." New York Times (February 28 1929): 30. [Review]

2003. Hearts in Dixie - Clippings [Billy Rose Theatre Collection]

2004. "Screen Negro Melodies." New York Times (February 24 1929): Sec. IX, p. 8.

HOME OF THE BRAVE (1949)

2005. Bogle, Donald. Blacks in American Films and Television. New York: Garland, 1988, pp. 109-111.

2006. Kramer, Stanley. <u>Stanley Kramer: an American Film Institute seminar on his work</u>. Beverly Hills, Calif., 1977, pp. 40-42. (American Film Institute seminars, pt. 1, no. 100)

2007. Spoto, Donald. "Filmmaking in Secrecy - Home of the Brave, 1949." In <u>Stanley Kramer, film maker</u>. New York: Putnam, 1978, pp. 43-53.

Articles

2008. Brown, John Mason. "Home of the Brave." <u>Saturday Review</u> (June 11 1949).

2009. "The Current Cinema: The Color Line." <u>New Yorker</u> (May 21 1949).

2010. "Home of the Brave. Hollywood independent makes first film on anti-Negro bias." <u>Ebony</u> (June 1949): 59. Discussion of the Stanley Kramer film "Home of the Brave."

2011. Miller, Warren. "Home of the Brave." <u>Masses and Mainstream</u> (July 1949): 79-82.

2012. "Movie of the Week: Home of the Brave; an outspoken film is first to break Hollywood's taboo against treating the Negro problem in America." <u>Life</u> (May 23 1949): 143-145.

2013. "Negro Films." <u>Sight and Sound</u>, Vol. 18 (January 1950): 27-30. Discussion of the late-40s race-theme films "Pinky", "Home of the Brave" and "Lost Boundaries".

2014. "New Films on View." <u>Cue</u> (May 14 1949).

2015. "The New Pictures; Home of the Brave." <u>Time</u> (May 9 1949).

2016. <u>Theatre Arts</u> (July 1949).

Newspaper Articles

2017. Crowther, Bosley. "Home of the Brave." <u>New York Times</u> (May 19 1949).

2018. Guernsey, Otis L., Jr. "Home of the Brave proves imagination, not cash, pays." <u>New York Herald-Tribune</u> (May 15 1949): Sec. 5, pp. 1+.

2019. "Home of the Brave." <u>Variety</u> (May 4 1949).

2020. Home of the Brave - Pressbook (MFL XXX 1056) [Billy Rose Theatre Collection]. Includes all materials used for United Artist's "Home of the Brave" promotional campaign.

2021. Melvin, Edwin F. "'Home of the Brave' in Film Form." <u>Christian Science Monitor</u> (June 10 1949).

2022. "Movies: Letter on 'Home of the Brave'." <u>Daily Worker</u> (May 24 1949): 13.

2023. Skolsky, Sidney. "Story of 'Secret' Filming." New York Post (April 1 1949): 62.

2024. Winsten, Archer. "Movies: 3 Negro Pictures Seen by a Negro." New York Post (November 2 1949): 58. Discussion of the late 1940s race-theme films "Pinky", "Home of the Brave" and "Lost Boundaries".

2025. Yglesias, Jose. "'Home of the Brave' film on Jim Crow." Daily Worker (June 5 1949).

IMITATION OF LIFE (1934)

2026. Bogle, Donald. Blacks in American Films and Television. New York: Garland, 1988, pp. 113-115.

Articles

2027. Butler, Jeremy G. "Imitation of Life (1934 and 1959): style and the domestic melodrama." Jump Cut, No. 32 (April 1986): 25-28.

2028. Caputi, Jane, and Helene Vann. "Questions of Race and Place: comparative racism in Imitation of Life and Places in the Heart." Cineaste, Vol. 15, No. 4 (August 1987): 16-21.

2029. "Imitation of Life." Literary Digest (December 8 1934). [Review]

INTRUDER IN THE DUST (1949)

2030. Bogle, Donald. Blacks in American Films and Television. New York: Garland, 1988, pp. 118-119.

Articles

2031. CinemaTexas Program Notes, Vol. 4, No. 18 (February 15 1973).

2032. "The Current Cinema: That Problem Again." New Yorker (November 29 1949).

2033. Degenfelder, E. Pauline. "The film adaptation of Faulkner's Intruder in the Dust." Literature/Film Quarterly, Vol. 1, No. 2 (April 1973): 138-148.

2034. "Intruder in the Dust." Life (December 12 1949): 149-150.

2035. Jones, Dorothy B. "William Faulkner: novel into film." Quarterly of Film, Radio and Television, Vol. 8, No. 1 (Fall 1953): 51-71.

2036. "Movie Review: Intruder in the Dust." Look (October 25 1949).

Newspaper Articles

2037. Crowther, Bosley. "A Great Film: Intruder in the Dust Commands High Praise." New York Times (November 27 1949).

2038. _____. "'Intruder in the Dust,' MGM's Drama of Lynching in the South, at the Mayfair." New York Times (November 23 1949).

2039. Guernsey, Otis L., Jr. "On the Screen." New York Herald Tribune (November 23 1949): 14.

2040. Winsten, Archer. "Reviewing Stand." New York Post (November 23 1949): 28.

2041. Yglesias, Jose. "Intruder in the Dust Another Evasive Film on the Negro." Daily Worker (November 23 1949).

LOST BOUNDARIES (1949)

2042. Bogle, Donald. Blacks in American Films and Television. New York: Garland, 1988, pp. 137-139.

2043. White, William L. Lost Boundaries. New York: Harcourt, Brace & Co., 1948. 91p.

2044. _____. ...Lost Boundaries, a drama of real life from the Reader's Digest. n.p., 1949. Shooting script for the film. [Held by the Schomburg Center]

Articles

2045. Brown, John Mason. "Seeing Things: Eyes That Blind." Saturday Review of Literature (September 10 1949): 32.

2046. "Cinema." New Yorker (July 9 1949).

2047. "Lost Boundaries." Cue (July 2 1949).

2048. "Lost Boundaries." Our World (July 1949): 30-32. Race-theme film of the 40s starring Bill Greaves, Canada Lee, and Bea Pearson.

2049. "Movie of the Week: Lost Boundaries; Film tells real-life story of Negroes "passing" as whites." Life (July 4 1949).

2050. Murdock, Clotye. "'Lost Boundaries' Family." Ebony (August 1952): 53-54.

2051. "Negro Films." Sight and Sound, Vol. 18 (January 1950): 27-30. Discussion of "Pinky", "Home of the Brave", and "Lost Boundaries".

2052. "The New Pictures: Lost Boundaries." Time (July 4 1949).

2053. "Superior Documentary." Newsweek (July 4 1949): 72.

Newspaper Articles

2054. Barnes, Howard. "'Lost Boundaries' Illustrates the Use of Understatement." New York Herald-Tribune (July 3 1949).

2055. Crowther, Bosley. "'Lost Boundaries', Racial Study with Mel Ferrer in Lead, New Feature at Astor." New York Times (July 1 1949).

2056. Lost Boundaries - Clippings [Billy Rose Theatre Collection]

2057. "Lost Boundaries." Variety (June 29 1949).

2058. "'Lost Boundaries' Banned in Atlanta; Censor finds film unfit for public showing." New York Herald Tribune (August 20 1949).

2059. "'Lost Boundaries' Faces Atlanta Ban." New York Times (August 21 1949).

2060. Pryor, Thomas M. "Censorship Issues: Atlanta Ban on 'Lost Boundaries' Goes Before Federal Court Tommorrow." New York Times (February 5 1950).

2061. _____. "Hoeing His Own Row; A Case History of Louis de Rochemont and His New Film, 'Lost Boundaries'." New York Times (June 26 1949).

2062. Sloper, L. A. "'Lost Boundaries' on the Screen; Racial Tolerance Film Presented at the Astor." Christian Science Monitor (July 16 1949).

2063. Winsten, Archer. "Movies: 3 Negro Pictures Seen by a Negro." New York Post (November 2 1949): 58. Discussion of the late 1940s race-theme films "Pinky", "Home of the Brave" and "Lost Boundaries".

2064. Yglesias, Jose. "Today's Films: 'Lost Boundaries' Shallow, Patronizing Film on Negro." Daily Worker (July 1 1949): 11.

NEGRO SOLDIER (1944)

2065. Cripps, Thomas R. "Casablanca, Tennessee Johnson and the Negro Soldier--Hollywood Liberals and World War II." In Feature Films as History, ed. K. R. M. Short. Knoxville: University of Tennessee Press, 1981, pp. 138-156.

2066. _____, and David H. Culbert. "The Negro Soldier (1944): Film Propaganda in Black and White." In Hollywood as Historian: American Film in a Cultural Context, ed. Peter C. Rollins. Lexington: University Press of Kentucky, 1983, pp. 109-133. [Reprint of # 2070]

2067. Warner, Virginia. "The Negro Soldier: A Challenge to Hollywood." In The Documentary Tradition: From Nanook to Woodstock, ed. Lewis Jacobs. New York: Hopkinson & Blake Publishers, 1971, pp. 224-225.

Dissertations

2068. Pounds, Michael Charles. "Details in Black: A Case Study Investigation and Analysis of the Content of the United States War Department Non-Fiction Motion Picture, The Negro Soldier" Dissertation (Ph.D.) New York University, 1982. 2 vols.

Articles

2069. "Court Rules for 'Negro Soldier.'" PM (May 10 1944).

2070. Cripps, Thomas R. "The Negro Soldier (1944): Film Propaganda in Black and White." American Quarterly, Vol. 31, No. 5 (1979): 616-640]. Analysis of film for which Frank Capra is credited as director and Carlton Moss as screenwriter, actor and consultant.

2071. Los Angeles Daily News (February 15 1944). [Review]

2072. McManus, John T. "McManus Speaking of Movies: The Boys from Syracuse Boost 'Negro Soldier.'" PM (April 30 1944).

2073. _____. "McManus Speaking of Movies: The Negro Soldier Fools the Experts." PM (July 12 1944): 20.

2074. Moving Pictures - Negro Soldier (Microfiche) [Schomburg Center]

2075. "'The Negro Soldier,' at four Broadway Theaters Today..." PM (April 21 1944).

2076. "'Negro Soldier' Documentary Makes Stirring Plea for Racial Tolerance." Variety (February 23 1944).

2077. "'Negro Soldier Superbly Done; Credit for Capra." The Hollywood Reporter (February 15 1944).

2078. Norman, Dorothy. "A World to Live In: 'The Negro Soldier.'" New York Post/Daily Magazine (March 6 1944): 26.

2079. "War Department Presents First Film on the American Negro." Daily Worker (February 2 1944).

PINKY (1949)

2080. Bogle, Donald. Blacks in American Films and Television. New York: Garland, 1988, pp. 164-166.

2081. Ciment, Michel. Kazan on Kazan. New York: Viking Press, 1974, pp. 59-62.

2082. Kazan, Elia. An American Odyssey. London: Bloomsbury, 1988, pp. 70-71.

2083. _____. Elia Kazan: a life. New York: Knopf, 1988, pp. 374-376. Brief autobiographical account of the making of "Pinky" by the film's director.

2084. Michaels, Lloyd. <u>Elia Kazan: a guide to references and resources</u>. Boston: G.K. Hall, 1985. See book's index for specific references to "Pinky".

2085. Pauly, Thomas H. <u>An American Odyssey: Elia Kazan and American Culture</u>. Philadelphia: Temple University Press, 1983, pp. 107-110.

Articles

2086. Campbell, Russell. "The Ideology of the Social Consciousness Movie: three films of Darryl F. Zanuck." <u>Quarterly Review of Film Studies</u>, Vol. 3, No. 1 (Winter 1978): 49-71.

2087. Jones, Christopher John. "Image and Ideology in Kazan's Pinky." <u>Literature/Film Quarterly</u>, Vol. 9, No. 2 (1981): 110-120.

2088. "Negro Films." <u>Sight and Sound</u>, Vol. 18 (January 1950): 27-30. Discussion of "Pinky", "Home of the Brave", and "Lost Boundaries".

2089. "Pinky." <u>Ebony</u> (September 1949): 23+. Discussion of film directed by Elia Kazan.

2090. "Pinky: Latest race-theme movie, "Pinky" marks another step forward for Hollywood." <u>Our World</u> (August 1949): 52-55.

2091. Pinky - Pressbook (*ZAN-*T8, reel 169) [Billy Rose Theatre Collection]. Contains all materials used for 20th Century Fox's "Pinky" promotional campaign.

Newspaper Articles

2092. Dunne, Philip. "Approach to Racism; Scenarist of Pinky explains how film will treat subject of Negro prejudice." <u>New York Times</u> (May 1 1949).

2093. "High Court Ends Another Film Ban; Cites 'Miracle' View in 'Pinky' Case." <u>New York Times</u> (June 3 1952).

2094. "Jeanne Crain in Pinky." <u>Christian Science Monitor</u> (October 22 1949).

2095. O'Neal, Frederick. "The Merits of 'Pinky.'" <u>New York Herald-Tribune</u> (November 6 1949): Sec. 2. Letter to the Editor.

2096. "'Pinky' Ban Upheld by Court in Texas; Censorship by City Ordinance to be Taken to Supreme Court, Johnston Hints." <u>New York Times</u> (July 31 1952).

2097. Pinky - Clippings [Billy Rose Theatre Collection]

2098. Platt, David. "Hollywood: Police Chief Bans Film, Says Inter-Racial Love is 'Obscene'." <u>Daily Worker</u> (February 7 1950): 11.

2099. Winsten, Archer. "Movies: 3 Negro Pictures Seen by a
Negro." New York Post (November 2 1949): 58. Discussion of
the late 1940s race-theme films "Pinky", "Home of the Brave",
and "Lost Boundaries".

Reviews

2100. Commonweal (October 14 1949): 15.
2101. Dramatics (December 1949): 18-19.
2102. Library Journal (February 1 1950): 180.
2103. Life (October 17 1949): 112-115.
2104. Look (November 22 1949).
2105. New Republic (October 3 1949): 23.
2106. New Yorker (October 1 1949): 50.
2107. Newsweek (October 10 1949): 89.
2108. Rotarian (February 1950): 38-39.
2109. Sequence (January 1 1950): 179-183.
2110. Time (October 10 1949): 96, 98.

Newspaper Reviews

2111. Brown, Lena. "'Pinky' Bares Greed, Prejudice; Fails to
Tell Story of Why She is 'White'." New York Amsterdam News
(October 1 1949).

2112. Crowther, Bosley. "Look Away, Dixieland; 'Pinky Scans
Anti-Negro Bias in the South." New York Times (October 9
1949).

2113. _____. "'Pinky', Zanuck's film study of anti-Negro
bias in deep South shown at Rivoli." New York Times
(September 30 1949).

2114. "Pinky." Variety (October 5 1949): 8.

2115. "'Pinky' at the Astor; Jeanne Crain in Title Role of
Film on Race Prejudice." Christian Science Monitor (October 8
1949).

2116. Yglesias, Jose. "On the Curious Reactions of the
Critics Toward 'Pinky'." Daily Worker (October 16 1949).

2117. _____. "Today's Films: 'Pinky' Sentimental,
Reactionary Film on Negro." Daily Worker (September 30 1949):
12.

PORGY AND BESS (1959)

2118. Bogle, Donald. Blacks in American Films and
Television. New York: Garland, 1988, pp. 166-169.

2119. Goldwyn (Samuel) Productions, Inc. The Samuel Goldwyn
motion picture production of Porgy and Bess. Edited by Ray
Freiman. New York: Random House, 1959. [36p].

Articles

2120. "American Classic Sings Anew." Life (June 15 1959).

2121.   "Boycott in Hollywood?" _Time_ (December 2 1957).
Report on the reluctance of Black actors to perform in film
version of Porgy and Bess.

2122.   Marcel, Michael.   "Interview: Otto Preminger on Black
Movies." _Encore_, Vol. 2 (August 1973): 56-59.   Discussion of
Preminger's two black-cast films - Carmen Jones and Porgy &
Bess - and his impressions of the black films of the 60s and
70s.

2123.   "Porgy and Bess is a Movie Now." _New York Times
Magazine_ (October 19 1958).

2124.   Wainwright, Loudon.   "The One-Man Gang is in Action
Again; At 76 Sam Goldwyn conquers crisis after crisis to
produce 'Porgy and Bess'." _Life_ (February 16 1959).

Reviews

2125.   Crowther, Bosley.   "Fitness of Folk Opera; A Rare Form
in Films is Exalted By Goldwyn's 'Porgy and Bess'." _New York
Times_ (June 28 1959).

2126.   _____.   "'Porgy and Bess' Again: Further Thoughts
on a Second Look at the Filmed Folk Opera." _New York Times_
(August 2 1959).

2127.   _____.   "Screen: Samuel Goldwyn's 'Porgy and Bess'
Has Premiere." _New York Times_ (June 25 1959).

2128.   Knight, Arthur.   "SR Goes to the Movies: Catfish Row in
Todd-AO." _Saturday Review_ (July 4 1959): 24.

2129.   McCarten, John.   "The Current Cinema: Gershwin with All
Stops Out." _New Yorker_ (July 4 1959).

2130.   "The New Pictures; Porgy and Bess." _Time_ (July 4 1959).

STORMY WEATHER (1943)

2131.   Bogle, Donald.   _Blacks in American Films and
Television_.   New York: Garland, 1988, pp. 205-207.

2132.   "It's 'Stormy' at the Roxy." _PM_ (July 22 1943).

2

The Black Filmmaker

GENERAL WORKS

2133. Black Visions '87: A Salute to the Black Filmmaker, February 1-28, 1987. Catalogue by James Briggs Murray. New York: Mayor's Office of Minority Affairs (New York, NY 10007), 1987. 32p. Includes brief interviews with St. Clair Bourne, Ayoka Chenzira, Kathleen Collins, William Greaves, Warrington Hudlin, Woodie King, Jr., Spike Lee, William Miles, Melvin Van Peebles.

2134. Cham, Mbye B., and Claire Andrade-Watkins, eds. Blackframes: Critical Perspectives on Black Independent Cinema. Cambridge: The MIT Press, 1988. 85p.

2135. Diakite, Madubuko. Film, Culture and the Black Filmmaker. New York: Ayer Company Publications, 1980. 184p.

2136. Independent Black American Cinema. New York: Third World Newsreel (335 W. 38th St., New York 10018), 1982. 30p.

2137. Yearwood, Gladstone L., ed. Black Cinema Aesthetics: Issues in Independent Black Filmmaking. Athens, OH: Center for Afro-American Studies, Ohio University, 1982. 120p.

Books with Sections on the Black Filmmaker

2138. Gerima, Haile. "Triangular Cinema: Community, Storyteller, Activist." In Questions of Third Cinema, eds. Jim Pines and Paul Willemen. London: BFI, 1989, pp. 65-70.

2139. Larkin, Alile Sharon. "Black Women Filmmakers Defining Ourselves: Feminism in Our Own Voice." In Female Spectators: Looking at Film and Television, ed. Diedre Pribram. London: Verso, 1988.

2140. Peavy, Charles D. "Through a Lens Darkly: America's Emerging Black Filmmakers." In Remus, Rastus, Revolution, ed. Marshall Fishwick. Bowling Green: Bowling Green University Popular Press, 1971(?), pp. 157-164. Analysis of Black filmmakers of the late Sixties with special emphasis on Richard Mason and Melvin Van Peebles.

2141. Quart, Barbara Koenig. "Sugarcane Alley and Other
Black Women's Cinema." In <u>Women Directors: The Emergence of a
New Cinema</u>. New York: Praeger, 1988, pp. 242-244. Very brief
assessment and dismissal of filmmaking by Black women.

Dissertations

2142. Birtha, Rachel Roxanne. "Pluralistic Perspectives on
the Black-Directed, Black-Oriented Feature Film: A Study of
Content, Intent and Audience Response." Dissertation (Ph.D.)
University of Minnesota, 1977. 628p.

2143. Gibson, Gloria J. "The Cultural Significance of Music
to the Black Independent Filmmaker." Dissertation (Ph.D.)
Indiana University, 1987. 324p.

2144. Reid, Mark Allen. "Black Oriented Film (1966-1977):
Film Form, Black Culture, Ideological Content." Dissertation
(Ph.D.) University of Iowa, 1988. 183p.

Articles

2145. "American Film Institute: Black Graduates Show Their
Stuff." <u>Ebony</u> (July 1985): 58+.

2146. "The Association of Black Motion Picture and Television
Producers Has Been Formed to Establish and Maintain Liaison
Between Credentialed Black Motion Picture and TV Producers and
the Telecommunications Industry." <u>Jet</u> (April 9 1981): 62.

2147. Bassan, Raphael, ed. "Le Cinema Independent Noir
Americain." <u>La Revue du Cinema</u>, No. 363 (Juillet-Aout 1981):
64-100.

2148. _____. "Vers la Legitimation du Cinema
Independant Noir Americain." <u>La Revue du Cinema</u>, No. 423
(janvier 1987): 70-74.

2149. "Black Directors: Though Few in Number They Have
Received Acclaim." <u>Ebony</u>, Vol. 42 (December 1986): 43+.

2150. "Blacks in the Director's Chair of Top-Rated TV Shows."
<u>Ebony</u> (July 1985): 58+.

2151. Brown, Dwight. "Black Filmmakers: The Trials and
Triumphs of of Bringing Our Culture into Focus." <u>Essence</u>,
Vol. 16 (April 1986): 54.

2152. Camp, Brian. "New Black Independent Films."
<u>Sightlines</u> (Summer 1980): 13.

2153. Campanella, Roy II. "Persistence of Vision: Surviving
in the Film World." <u>Ebony Man</u> (June 1987): 54-57, 70.
Discussion of Black independent filmmakers with profiles of
William Greaves (55), Kathleen Collins (56), Robert Townsend
(57), and Warrington Hudlin (70).

2154. "Coast to Coast Salute to Black Filmmakers." <u>Ebony</u>,
Vol. 41 (October 1986): 91+.

2155. Collier, Aldore. "The Year of the Black Male in Films." Ebony (August 1983): 168+.

2156. "Color Bars; In the days of segregation, Black filmmakers created Black films for Black audiences. Today - after years of knocking on Hollywood's doors - Black filmmakers are once more going their own way." American Film (April 1988): 37-42. Roundtable discussion with Charles Fuller, Richard Wesley, John Sayles and Reginald Hudlin.

2157. Davis, Zeinabu irene, and Clyde Taylor. "The Future of Black Film: The Debate Continues." Black Film Review, Vol. 5, No. 4 (Fall 1989?): 6-9, 26-28. Continuation of the debate on Black independent filmmaking begun by the Clyde Taylor (# 2179) and David Nicholson (# 2169) pieces below.

2158. Ferdinand, Val. "Making the Image Real: Black Producers of Theater, Film and Television." Black Collegian, Vol. 7 (March-April 1977): 54-58+.

2159. "A First - In Paris and in Film News." Film News (Fall 1980). Report on Paris's "Festival of Black Independent American Cinema 1920-1980."

2160. Harrell, Alfred D. "Film's Early Black Auteurs." Encore American and Worldwide News (May 8 1977): 36. Brief discussion of Noble Johnson, Oscar Micheaux and Spencer Williams.

2161. Harris, Valerie. "Location Shots; Black and Third World Women Who Want to Make Films Must Battle with Racism, Sexism and Money." Fuse (Toronto), Vol. V, No. 4-5 (May-June 1981): 166-169.

2162. Heijs, J. "Black Independents." Skrien (Amsterdam), No. 106 (April 1981): 6-7.

2163. Jackson, I. "Black Independents as Genre at BFF Criticism Conference." The Independent, Vol. 6 (December 1983): 8.

2164. Johnson, Pamela. "They've Gotta Have It. What Black independent filmmakers have is the talent to create smash hits. What they need is promotion and distribution clout." Black Enterprise (July 1989): 36-38, 40. Includes comments by Spike Lee, Robert Townsend, Keenen Ivory Wayans, Loretha Jones, Euzhan Palcy, William Greaves and Warrington Hudlin.

2165. Kruger, Barbara. "Recoding Blackness: The Visual Rhetoric of Black Independent Film." Art Forum, Vol. 24 (September 1985): 124-125.

2166. Lardeau, Yann. "Cineastes Noirs Americains a Paris; Out of the Ghetto." Cahiers du Cinema, No. 319 (janvier 1981): V-VI.

2167. Liggins, G. E. "Hollywood Blacks: Behind the Camera Jobs." New Lady (May 1971): 15-17. Brief sketches of Blacks in non-performance jobs: Stanley Robertson (producer), Harry Dolan (scriptwriter), William DuBois (cameraman), Walter Burrell (publicist), Joe Hartsfield (publicist), Kathi Fearn Banks (publicist), Luther James (director), Mark Warren (director), and Sid McCoy (director).

2168. McMullin, Corine. "Le Cinema des Noirs Americains." Cinema (Paris), No. 264 (decembre 1980): 55-62. Includes comments by William Greaves, Ben Caldwell, Charles Burnett and Larry Clark.

2169. Murray, James P. "The Independents: Hard Road for the Old and New." Black Creation, Vol. 3, No. 3 (Spring 1972): 8-11.

2170. Nicholson, David. "Which Way the Black Film Movement?" Black Film Review, Vol. 5, No. 2 (Spring 1989): 4-5, 16-17.

2171. Pines, Jim. "A Choice of Rambo or Sambo?" New Statesman (April 8 1988): 29-30. Includes discussion of "Hollywood Shuffle" and "She's Gotta Have It."

2172. Relich, Mario. "Black Movies." West Africa (March 1 1982): 563, 565-666. Survey of Black American independents.

2173. Sharky, Betsy. "Knocking on Hollywood's Door: Black filmmakers like Spike Lee struggle to see and be seen." American Film (July/August 1989): 22-27, 52, 54. [S. Lee/ R. Townsend/K. Wayans]

2174. Slater, Jack. "Hollywood's New Black Men." Essence, Vol. 15 (November 1984): 82-84+.

2175. Smith, Valerie. "Reconstituting the Image: The Emergent Black Woman Director." Callaloo, Vol. 11, No. 4 (Fall 1988): 709-719.

2176. Springer, Claudia. "Black Women Filmmakers." Jump Cut, No. 29 (February 1984): 34-37.

2177. Tajima, Renee E., and Tracey Willard. "Nothing Lights a Fire Like a Dream Deferred. Black Filmmakers in Los Angeles." The Independent, Vol. 7, No. 10 (November 1984): 18-21.

2178. Taylor, Clyde. "The L.A. Rebellion: New Spirit in American Film." Black Film Review, Vol. 2, No. 2 (1986): 11+.

2179. _____. "Next Wave: Women Film Artists at UCLA." Black Collegian, Vol. 35 (April/May 1980): 12, 16.

2180. _____. "The Paradox of Black Independent Cinema." Black Film Review, Vol. 4, No. 4 (Fall 1988): 2-3, 17-19.

2181. _____. "Screen: Visionary Black Cinema." Black Collegian, Vol. 35 (October/November 1980): 34-36.

2182. Waldron, Clarence. "Black Directors; Bosses Behind the
Camera Help Change Perception of Blacks on TV." Ebony Man
(May 1988): 56-59. Includes brief profiles of and comments
from television directors Kevin Hooks, Ted Lange, Gerren
Keith, Eric Laneuville, Roy Campanella, Oz Scott, Stan Lathan,
M. Neema Barnette, Helaine Head, Tony Singletary, Regge Life,
Chuck Rallen Vinson, Thomas Carter, Debbie Allen, Georg
Stanford Brown.

2183. Wali, Monona. "Los Angeles Black Filmmakers Thrive
Despite Hollywood's Monopoly." Black Film Review, Vol. 2, No.
2 (1986): 10+.

2184. Weaver, Harold D. "Black Filmmakers in Africa and
America." Sightlines (Spring 1976): 7-9, 12.

2185. White, Armond. "Black Filmmakers are Outside...Telling
It on the Mountain." Film Comment (October 1985): 39-41.

Newspaper Articles

2186. Beale, Lewis. "Black Directors Join Exclusive
Hollywood Club." Los Angeles Daily News (August 22 1986).

2187. Fraser, C. Gerald. "Black Women's Outlook in Whitney
Film Series." New York Times (December 28 1986). Review of
Whitney Museum's "The Black Woman Independent: Representing
Race and Gender" series.

2188. Greenberg, James. "In Hollywood, Black is In; Black
filmmakers are being welcomed as never before by studios that
recognize their moneymaking potential." New York Times (March
4 1990): Sec. 2, pp. 1, 22-23. Includes information on Spike
Lee, Charles Burnett, Wendell Harris Jr., Keenen Ivory Wayans,
Charles Lane, Bill Duke, Euzhan Palcy, Rolando Hudson,
Reginald and Warrington Hudlin.

2189. Jones, Patricia. "Some Declarations of Independents:
Black Filmmakers Reclaim their Roots." Village Voice
(September 2 1980): 42, 44.

2190. "Makers of Black Films Stand at Crossroads." Los
Angeles Times/Calendar (January 28 1973): 18.

2191. Mims, Sergio A. "Indie Black Filmmakers Spurred by
Renewed Interest from Public." Variety (November 18 1987):
80, 86.

2192. Murray, James P. "Now, A Boom in Black Directors."
New York Times (June 4 1972): 11.

2193. Rich, Frank. "Transcending Uncle Tom." New York Post
(March 20 1976): 14, 36. On Black independents.

2194. Rich, John. "About Negro Directors." New York Times
(December 24 1967). Letter to the Editor.

2195. Shepard, Thom. "Black Filmmakers Surviving the
Collapse." Soho Weekly News (August 12 1976): 26-27.

2196. Sterritt, David. "Black Women as Filmmakers."
Christian Science Monitor (January 14 1987): 24. Discussion
of Whitney series "The Black Woman Independent."

2197. Taubin, Amy. "Exile and Cunning." Village Voice
(January 13 1987): 68. Review of Whitney Museum series "The
Black Woman Independent."

2198. Thomas, Bob. "Job Outlook is Poor for Black
Directors." Staten Island Advance (August 17 1983).

INDIVIDUAL FILMMAKERS AND PRODUCERS

ALEXANDER, WILLIAM D. - Producer

2199. Johnson, Robert. "Top Black Movie Producer." Sepia
(January 1975): 25-30.

2200. "New Ideas Urged for Negro Movies." Los Angeles
Sentinel (April 4 1946): 11.

2201. "Producers to Make Dignified Pictures." Los Angeles
Sentinel (May 9 1946): 8.

ALLEN, DEBBIE - Director

See also # 2182

2202. "Allen a producer-director for 'A Different World'."
Jet (April 11 1988): 59.

2203. Stark, John. "It's A Different World for Dancer and
Choreographer Debbie Allen: She's moved to prime-time
directing." People (November 14 1988): 105-106.

AMOS, JOHN - Producer

2204. Salvo, Patrick. "John Amos: Will He Be First Black
Producer of Movies Glorifying Black Heroes of History?"
Sepia, Vol. 25 (March 1976): 24-33.

ANDERSON, MADELINE - Director

2205. "Profile: Madeline Anderson: Filmmaker." Columbia
Reports (October 1972).

I Am Somebody (1970)

See also # 6070

2206. Emmens, Carol. "I Am Somebody." Film Library
Quarterly, Vol. 4, No. 1 (Winter 1970-71): 45-47. [Review]

BALLENGER, MELVONNA - Director

2207. Campbell, Loretta. "Reinventing Our Image: Eleven
Black Women Filmmakers." Heresies, Issue 16 (1983): 58-62.

BARNETTE, M. NEEMA - Director

See also # 2182

2208. Witty, Susan. "Growing Up in Harlem." The Westsider
[New York] (March 16-22 1989): 22. [Profile]

BELAFONTE, HARRY - Producer

See also # 2829

2209. Shaw, Arnold. Belafonte: An Unauthorized Biography.
Philadelphia: Chilton, 1960. 338p.

Articles

2210. "Belafonte Becomes 'Big Business': Entertainer forms
million dollar corporation, branches into moviemaking."
Ebony, Vol. 13 (June 1958): 17-24.

2211. "Belafonte's 'Beat Street' Makes it Big." Jet (July 9
1984): 60+.

2212. "Movie Maker Belafonte: With His Second Picture, Folk
Balladeer Emerges as a Major Independent Producer." Ebony,
Vol. 14 (July 1959): 94-96.

2213. Young, A. S. "Harry Belafonte's Debut as a Hollywood
Producer." Sepia, Vol. 7 (July 1959): 34-39.

Newspaper Articles

2214. Cameron, Kate. "Singer, Actor, Now a Film Producer."
New York Sunday News (October 4 1959): Sec. 2, p. 1.

2215. Nason, Richard W. "Evaluating the 'Odds': Harry
Belafonte Tries Broad Racial Approach in Locally Made
Feature." New York Times (March 15 1959).

2216. Pryor, Thomas M. "Belafonte's Firm Plans First Film
Harbel to Produce 'End of World' with Sol Siegel." New York
Times (September 26 1957).

2217. Schumach, Murray. "Hollywood Patterns: Belafonte Hits
Studio Might--TV 'Buys'." New York Times (July 26 1959).

2218. Siskel, Gene. "Belafonte: he believes in 'Beat
Street'." New York Daily News (June 5 1984): 61.

BILLOPS, CAMILLE - Director

Suzanne, Suzanne (1982)

2219. Campbell, Loretta. "Hurting Women." Jump Cut, No. 34
(1989): 51-52. Discussion of Billop's documentary "Suzanne,
Suzanne."

BLUM, LYN - Director

2220. Campbell, Loretta. "Reinventing Our Image: Eleven Black Women Filmmakers." Heresies, Issue 16 (1983): 58-62.

BOND, JAMES III - Director

2221. Johnson, Pamela. "Reel Time." Essence (September 1988): 32.

2222. "Thesp James Bond 3d Makes Directing Debut on 'Temptation'." Variety (May 18 1988): 45.

BOONE, RONALD WAYNE - Director

2223. Boone, Ronald Wayne. "On Location: The Making of "Hayti, Mem Bagay." Black Film Review, Vol. 5, No. 1 (Winter 1988-89): 16-17, 20.

BOURNE, ST. CLAIR (1943-) - Director

See also # 2133

2224. Bourne, St. Clair. "Bright Moments: Black Filmmaking." Z Magazine (March 1989): 40-41.

2225. _____. "'Minority' Programming on PTV." PTR; Public Telecommunications Review (July-August 1980): 48.

2226. _____. "St. Clair Bourne: A Pioneer Looks Back at 20 Years in Film." Black Film Review, Vol. 4, No. 3 (Summer 1988): 13-17.

2227. Covert, Nadine. "Who's Who in Filmmaking: St. Clair Bourne." Sightlines, Vol. 8, No.3 (Spring 1975): 17-18, 31-32.

2228. Jones, Lisa. "Bourne Again: A Black Documentarian Looks Forward and Back." Village Voice (February 23 1988): 45.

2229. Mattox, Michael. "Film; St. Clair Bourne: Alternative Black Visions." Black Creation, Vol. 4, No. 3 (Summer 1973): 32-34.

2230. Mealy, Rosemary. "St. Clair Bourne: Becoming a Filmmaker." Black Film Review, Volume 4, No. 3 (Summer 1988): 8-12.

2231. Taylor, Clyde. "St. Clair Bourne: Capturing the Truth of the Black Experience." Black Film Review, Vol. 4, No. 3 (Summer 1988): 6-7, 17.

The Black and the Green

2232. Douglas, Pamela. "Going to the heart of Ireland's crisis." The National Leader (November 11 1982): 19-20.

2233.   Lacayo, Richard.   "Black Writers and Producers Are Widening Their Focus."   New York Times (May 29 1983): Sec. 2, p. 21.

Black Journal

2234.   Bourne, St. Clair.   "Bright Moments: The Black Journal Series."   The Independent (May 1988): 10-13.

In Motion: Amiri Baraka (1982)

2235.   Corry, John.   "TV: Documentary Film Examines Amiri Baraka."   New York Times (June 28 1983): C15.

Langston Hughes: The Dream Keeper (1986)

2236.   "Bourne Directs Hughes Film."   Black Film Review, Vol. 2, No. 1 (1985): 13.

Let the Church Say Amen! (1973)

2237.   Let the Church Say Amen - Clippings [Billy Rose Theatre Collection]

2238.   Sayre, Nora.   "Seminarian is the Hero of 'Let the Church Say Amen!'"   New York Times (November 14 1974): 58.

Making "Do the Right Thing" (1989)

See also # 2583

2239.   Bourne, St. Clair.   "Brothers Under the Skin."   Elle (August 1989): 100, 102.   Discussion by the filmmaker of his documentary on "Do the Right Thing."

2240.   Canby, Vincent.   "Double Bill Tracing Evolution of Spike Lee."   New York Times (November 3 1989).   [Review]

2241.   Carr, Jay.   "Behind the Scenes of 'Do the Right Thing.'"   Boston Globe (November 3 1989).

2242.   "Making 'Do the Right Thing'."   Variety (September 6-12 1989).

2243.   Nance, Larry.   "A Talk with St. Clair Bourne: African American Documentary Filmmaker on his latest film "Making 'Do the Right Thing.'"   Unity, Vol. 12, No. 12 (August 28 1989): 8.

On the Boulevard (1984)

2244.   White, Armond.   "Two Films That Make the Slice of Life Seem Real."   City Sun (July 31-August 6 1985): 15.

BROWN, GEORG STANFORD (1943-   ) - Producer

See also # 2182

2245.   "Brown Prod. Firm Links Up with Taft."   Variety (October 23 1985): 40.   On Brown's production company Nexus.

2246. Gardella, Kay. "Quality is Focus for Tyne and Georg."
New York Daily News (November 6 1987): 112.

BROWN, TONY - Producer

2247. Beauford, Fred. "Tony Brown." The Crisis
(August/September 1988): 18-23. [Interview]

2248. Brown, Tony (television producer) - Clippings [Billy
Rose Theatre Collection]

2249. Peterson, Franklynn. "Mr. Black Journal." Sepia
(March 1972): 51-58.

2250. "Tony Brown: a man for the people." Essence (October
1980): 22-23.

Black Journal

2251. Black Journal - Clippings [Billy Rose Theatre
Collection]

The White Girl

2252. "Arts Scene: Brown's New Movie Deal." American
Visions, Vol. 5, No. 1 (February 1990): 10. Notice on Brown's
anti-drug feature film "The White Girl."

2253. Sinclair, Abiola. "Media Watch: City Sun critic
attacks 'White Girl'." New York Amsterdam News (March 3
1990): 28. Attack on Armond White's negative review of "The
White Girl" (# 2257).

2254. "Tony Brown gets PG-13 rating for White Girl." Jet
(August 15 1988): 57.

2255. "Tony Brown Productions Charges WNYN-TV with Racism."
New York Amsterdam News (February 24 1990): 28. Report on the
refusal of a New York TV station to accept ads for Brown's
film.

2256. "Tony Brown rebukes R rating for White Girl." Jet
(July 18 1988): 39.

2257. White, Armond. "Just Say No to the White Girl." City
Sun (February 21-27 1990): 19, 28.

BULLARD, LARRY - Director

Dream is What You Wake Up From

2258. Bowser, Pearl. "Dream is What You Wake Up From."
Black Scholar, Vol. 4 (April 1980): 89-90. [Review]

BURNETT, CHARLES - Director

See also # 2168, 2188

2259. "Un Artisan du Quotidien: Charles Burnett." La Revue du Cinema, No. 363 (juillet/aout 1981): 92-94. [Profile]

2260. Burnett, Charles. "Inner City Blues." In Questions of Third Cinema, eds. Jim Pines and Paul Willemen. London: British Film Institute, 1989, pp. 223-226.

2261. "Charles Burnett; Propos Rompus." Cahiers du Cinema, No. 319 (Janvier 1981): V-VI.

Killer of Sheep (1977)

2262. Collins, Kathleen. "'A Place in Time' and 'Killer of Sheep': Two Radical Definitions of Adventure Minus Women." In In Color: 60 Years of Images of Minority Women in Film. New York: Third World Newsreel, 1982, pp. 5-7.

Articles

2263. Cros, Jean-Louis. "Killer of Sheep." La Revue du Cinema, No. 367 (Octobre 1982): 42-43. [Review]

2264. "Killer of Sheep." Variety (October 7 1981): 22. [Review]

2265. Maslin, Janet. "Screen: 'Killer of Sheep' is Shown at the Whitney." New York Times (November 14 1978): C10.

2266. Nacache, J. "Killer of Sheep." Cinema (Paris), No. 286 (Octobre 1982): 96-97. [Review]

My Brother's Wedding (1983)

2267. Hoberman, J. "Film: Mixed-Up Kids." Village Voice (April 3 1984): 54.

2268. Kehr, Dave. "My Brother's Wedding." Chicago (November 1983): 118.

2269. "My Brother's Wedding." Variety (September 21 1983): 18.

2270. "My Brother's Wedding" from Coast. New York Times (March 30 1984): C7.

2271. Taylor, P. "My Brother's Wedding." Monthly Film Bulletin, Vol. 52 (January 1985): 23-24.

To Sleep with Anger

2272. Hachem, Samir. "On Location: The House of Spirits." Village Voice (August 22 1989): 80. Report on Burnett's film-in-progress "To Sleep with Anger."

CAMPANELLA, ROY, JR. - Director

See also # 2182

2273. "Campanella signs program deal with Embassy group."
Jet (September 22 1986): 59.

2274. Chu, Dan. "Roy Campanella Jr. Begins a Hit Streak of
His Own as a Director of TV Films." People (May 19 1986):
141-142.

2275. George, Nelson. "Famous Son Makes Name as Filmmaker."
New York Amsterdam News (August 25 1979): 27.

2276. "Introducing: Roy Campanella Jr. Another Star Emerges
from the Campanella Family, but this one is a Hollywood TV and
Film Director." Ebony (September 1982): 69-70+.

CAREW, TOPPER - Producer

2277. Bunce, Alan. "Breaking Down the Color Barrier:
Producer Topper Carew Uses TV to Help Shape Values."
Christian Science Monitor (February 2 1988): 1, 28.

2278. "Carew Named WGBH's Program Manager." New York
Amsterdam News (November 27 1976): C8.

2279. Herbert, Solomon. "Carew 'Busts Loose'." Black
Enterprise (September 1987): 25.

2280. Lacayo, Richard. "Black Writers and Producers Are
Widening Their Focus." New York Times (May 29 1983): Sec. 2,
pp. 21-22.

2281. O'Connor, John J. "TV: This Producer Has a 'New Angle
of Vision.'" New York Times (May 18 1980): Sec. 2, p. 41.

2282. Testa, James. "TV: Topper Carew." The Aquarian (May
14-21 1980): 25.

CARTER, THOMAS - Director/Producer

See also # 2182

2283. Horowitz, Joy. "Why the 'Prince of Pilots' Turned
Producer." New York Times (February 11 1990): Sec. 2, pp. 33,
40.

CHEERS, MICHAEL - Director

2284. Johnson, Arthur J. "Film Clips: Notes on People,
Issues, and Events." Black Film Review, Vol. 3, No. 2 (Spring
1987): 4. Profile/interview with Michael Cheers on the
premiering of his documentary on Black opera star Lillian
Evanti.

CHENZIRA, AYOKA - Director

See also # 2133

2285. Campbell, Loretta. "Reinventing Our Image: Eleven
Black Women Filmmakers." Heresies, Issue 16 (1983): 58-62.

2286. Kafi-Akua, Afua. "Ayoka Chenzira, Filmmaker." <u>SAGE: A Scholarly Journal on Black Women</u>, Vol. IV, No. 1 (Spring 1987): 69-72.

Hairpiece: A Film for Nappy Headed People

2287. Maslin, Janet. "Screen: "Grotesques" and six others." <u>New York Times</u> (May 8 1985): C24. [Review]

CLARK, LARRY (1943-   ) - Director

See also # 2168

2288. "Un Cineaste Engage: Larry Clark." <u>La Revue du Cinema</u>, No. 363 (juillet/aout 1981): 95-97.

Passing Through (1977)

2289. Gibson, Gloria J. "Passing Through." <u>Ethnomusicology</u>, Vol. 28 (September 1984): 591. [Review]

2290. "Passing Through." <u>Variety</u> (August 31 1977): 30. [Review]

2291. Taylor, Clyde. "'Passing Through': An Underground Film About Black Music Underground." <u>The Black Collegian</u> (1980): 16-17.

COLLINS, KATHLEEN (1942-1988) - Director

See also # 2133, 2153

2292. Franklin, Oliver. "An Interview: Kathleen Collins." In <u>Independent Black American Cinema</u>. New York: Third World Newsreel, 1982, pp. 22-24.

Articles

2293. <u>Black Film Review</u>, Vol. 5, No. 1 (Winter 88/89). Memorial issue for Kathleen Collins with tributes by Peggy Dammond Preacely, Michelle Parkerson, and David Nicholson.

2294. Campbell, Loretta. "Reinventing Our Image: Eleven Black Women Filmmakers." <u>Heresies</u>, Issue 16 (1983): 58-62.

Obituaries

2295. Hudson, William. "Kathleen Collins, 1942-88." <u>Village Voice</u> (October 11 1988): 69.

2296. "Kathleen Collins." <u>Variety</u> (September 28 1988): 86-87.

2297. "Kathleen Collins, a Film Maker, Dies at 46." <u>New York Times</u> (September 24 1988): 33.

Losing Ground

2298. Nicholson, David. "Independent, and Liking It." American Visions (July/August 1986): 53-55. Profiles of filmmakers Kathleen Collins, Spike Lee, Michelle Parkerson, Billy Woodberry and their films.

CRAIN, WILLIAM - Director

Blacula (1972)

2299. Bogle, Donald. Blacks in American Films and Television. New York: Garland, 1988, pp. 27-28.

Articles

2300. "On Old Broadway." The New Yorker (September 9 1972): 29-30. Details some of the marketing strategies for "Blacula."

2301. Thomas, Bob. "Director Got 'Blacula' 'Because I Am Black.'" New York Post (February 21 1972): 17.

2302. Weaver, Richard. "Blacula." Films and Filming (November 1973): 49. [Review]

Dr. Black, Mr. Hyde (1976)

2303. Bogle, Donald. Blacks in American Films and Television. New York: Garland, 1988, p. 74.

Articles

2304. Bartholomew, D. "Dr. Black Mr. Hyde." Cinema Fantastique, Vol. 5, No. 2 (1976): 32.

2305. "Dr. Black Mr. Hyde." Variety (January 21 1976): 32.

2306. Munroe, D. "Dr. Black Mr. Hyde." Film Bulletin, Vol. 45 (February 1976): 39.

The Watts Monster

2307. "The Watts Monster." Variety (October 24 1979): 46.

CROUCH, WILLIAM - Director

2308. "How Movies Are Made." Ebony (March 1947): 40-43.

DASH, JULIE - Director

2309. Artist and Influence: Julie Dash (1989) (audiotape). Interview conducted by Valerie Smith. [Held by Hatch-Billops Collection (#6004)]

Articles

2310. Harris, Kwasi. "New Images: An Interview with Julie Dash and Alile Sharon Larkin." The Independent, Vol. 9 (December 1986): 16-20.

2311. Jackson, Lynne, with Karen Jaehne. "Eavesdropping on Female Voices: A Who's Who of Contemporary Women Filmmakers." Cineaste, Vol. 16, No. 1/2 (1987/88): 43.

2312. Tate, Greg. "Favorite Daughters: Julie Dash Films Gullah Country." Village Voice (April 12 1988): 27, 30-33.

DAVIS, OSSIE (1917-   ) - Director

See also # 1617, 3164-3165

2313. Peterson, Maurice. "Movies: Being About Ossie Davis." Essence, Vol. 3 (February 1973): 20.

Black Girl (1972)

2314. Bogle, Donald. Blacks in American Films and Television. New York: Garland, 1988, pp. 23-24.

Articles

2315. "Black Girl...A Movie About Real Black People!" Right On! (March 1973): 42-43.

2316. "Black Girl Film Review." Black Stars (March 1973): 64-67.

2317. Cocks, Jay. "Mother's Day." Time (December 4 1972).

2318. Dews, Angela. "Black Girl is Beautiful." Encore (January 1973): 50-51.

2319. Hurd, Laura E. "Director Ossie Davis Talks About Black Girl." Black Creation, No. 4 (Winter 1973): 38-39.

2320. Putterman, B. "Black Girl." Audience, Vol. 5 (February 1973): 1.

Cotton Comes to Harlem (1970)

2321. Bogle, Donald. Blacks in American Films and Television. New York: Garland, 1988, pp. 68-69.

Articles

2322. Chelminski, Rudolph. "'Cotton' Cashes In. All-black comedy is a box office bonanza." Life (August 28 1970).

2323. Doerfler, Joel. "A Minority of Multitudes." Boston After Dark (July 21 1970). [Review]

2324. Gold, Ronald. "Director Dared Use Race Humor; 'Soul' As Lure for 'Cotton's' B.O. Bale." Variety (September 30 1970): 1, 62.

2325. Kramer, Carol. "It's Soul Cinema - New Harlem Film a Black Version of James Bond." Chicago Tribune (August 3 1969): Sec. 5, p. 2.

2326. Milne, Emile. "A Black (Is Beautiful) Comedy." New York Post (May 14 1969). [Review]

2327. Patterson, Lindsay. "Movies: Cotton Comes to Harlem." Essence (September 1970): 75.

2328. _____. "Movies: In Harlem, a James Bond with Soul?" New York Times (June 15 1969).

2329. Silber, Irwin. "Film: Cotton Goes to Harlem." Guardian (July 11 1970).

Countdown at Kusini (1976)

2330. Bogle, Donald. Blacks in American Films and Television. New York: Garland, 1988, pp. 69-70.

Articles

2331. Baird, K. E. "Movie Review: 'Countdown at Kusini'." Freedomways, Vol. 16, No. 4 (1976): 251-252.

2332. Bottstein, D. "Countdown at Kusini." Film Bulletin, Vol. 45 (April 1976): E-F.

2333. "Countdown at Kusini." Ebony, Vol. 31 (April 1976): 90+.

2334. "Countdown at Kusini." Variety (April 7 1976): 22.

2335. Davis, Curt. "Countdown at Kusini--But No Blast Off." Encore, Vol. 5 (May 17 1976): 32-33.

2336. Perchaluk, E. "Countdown at Kusini." Independent Film Journal, Vol. 77 (April 14 1976): 9.

2337. Reed, Frankie A. "Countdown at Kusini." Black Scholar, Vol. 7 (May 1976): 52-53.

2338. Walker, A. "Black Sorority Bankrolls Action Film." Ms., Vol. 4 (June 1976): 45.

Gordon's War (1973)

2339. Bogle, Donald. Blacks in American Films and Television. New York: Garland, 1988, pp. 95-96.

Articles

2340. Braun, E. "Gordon's War." Variety (August 8 1973): 14.

2341. Burrell, Walter Price. "Ossie Davis Directs Anti-Drug Movie." Black Stars (June 1973): 64-69.

2342. Coleman, J. "Outlaws Incorporated." New Statesman (December 14 1973): 918.

2343. "Gordon's War." Variety (August 8 1973): 14.

2344. Hirsch, C. "Gordon's War." Millimeter, Vol. 2 (February 1974): 42.

2345. Mebane, M. E. "At Last - Brother Caring for Brother." New York Times (September 23 1973): Sec. 2, p. 13.

2346. Milne, T. "Gordon's War." Monthly Film Bulletin, Vol. 41 (February 1974): 28.

2347. Paul, W. "Certain Politics, Dubious Battle." Village Voice (February 14 1974): 73.

Kongi's Harvest (1970)

2348. Bennett, John. "First African Movie By and About Africans Made by Ossie Davis." Sepia (September 1971): 59-63. Discussion of Davis's production of Wole Soyinka's drama Kongi's Harvest.

2349. Davis, Ossie. "Movies: When is a Camera a Weapon?" New York Times (September 20 1970).

2350. "Kongi on Film." West Africa, No. 2775 (1970): 950.

2351. "Kongi's Harvest." Variety (May 5 1971): 16, 22.

2352. Lefkowitz, Bernard. "Film Review. Kongi's Harvest." Show Business (April 29 1971): 18.

DAVIS, ZEINABU IRENE - Director

See # 2157

DE PASSE, SUZANNE - Producer

2353. Allen, Bonnie. "Suzanne de Passe: Motown's $10-million Boss Lady." Essence (September 1981): 90-92, 141, 143-144.

DIXON, IVAN (1931-   ) - Director

2354. Film Information (October 1973).

2355. Hobson, Charles. "The Success of Ivan Dixon." Black Stars (October 1976): 6-9.

2356. Lucas, Bob. "Black TV Directors." Sepia (May 1971): 28-32. Profile of Mark Warren, Vantile Whitfield, Luther James, Sid McCoy and Ivan Dixon.

The Spook Who Sat by the Door

2357. Greenlee, Sam. The Spook Who Sat by the Door. New York: Bantam Books, 1970. 248p. Novel from which the film is adapted.

2358. Kantor, M. "This 'Spook' Has No Respect for Human Life." New York Times (November 11 1973): Sec. 2, p. 11.

2359. Piankhi, K. "The Spook Who Sat by the Door." The Blackstage Magazine (November 1973): 7, 47-48. Discussion of Dixon's film.

Trouble Man

2360. Bogle, Donald. Blacks in American Films and Television. New York: Garland, 1988, p. 222.

2361. Hirsch, C. "Trouble Man." Millimeter, Vol. 2 (February 1974): 42.

2362. James, Stuart. "Trouble Man." Films and Filming, Vol. 19 (June 1973): 52-53.

DUKE, BILL - Director

See also # 2188

2363. Cossou, Egon. "Film Clips." Black Film Review, Vol. 3, No. 4 (Fall 1987): 2. [Interview/Profile]

2364. Welsh, H. "Entretien avec Bill Duke et Elsa Rassbach." Jeune Cinema, No. 168 (July-August 1985): 13-16.

The Killing Floor

2365. Edelstein, David. "Film: Charnel House Blues." Village Voice (October 29 1985): 64.

2366. Kruger, Barbara. "The Killing Floor": Museum of Modern Art." Art Forum, Vol. 24 (April 1986): 113.

2367. Leahy, James. "The Killing Floor." Monthly Film Bulletin, No. 54 (April 1987): 115-116.

2368. Merigeau, P. "The Killing Floor." La Revue du Cinema, No. 407 (July-August 1985): 45.

2369. Nacache, J. "La Couleur de Sang." Cinema (Paris), No. 318 (June 1985): 30.

2370. Niogret, H. "The Killing Floor"/"The Colour of Blood." Positif, No. 293 (July-August 1985): 97.

EALEY, CYNTHIA - Director

2371. Campbell, Loretta. "Reinventing Our Image: Eleven Black Women Filmmakers." Heresies, Issue 16 (1983): 58-62.

FACEY, JEAN G. - Director

2372. Campbell, Loretta. "Reinventing Our Image: Eleven Black Women Filmmakers." Heresies, Issue 16 (1983): 58-62.

FALES, SUSAN - Producer

2373. "Susan Fales: in a different world; young producer makes leap from Harvard to top of television ratings." _Ebony_ (June 1989): 160, 162, 164.

FANAKA, JAMAA - Director

2374. McBride, Joseph. "Birth of a Black Director. Jamaa Fanaka Completes Two Features at 26; Master's Degree from UCLA." _Variety_ (September 8 1976): 6.

Penitentiary (1979)

2375. Auty, M. "Penitentiary." _Monthly Film Bulletin_, Vol. 48 (April 1981): 76-77.

2376. "Black Showmen Say 'Penitentiary' Needs to Play Good (White) Sites." _Variety_ (February 27 1980): 38.

2377. Canby, Vincent. "Screen: 'Penitentiary.'" _New York Times_ (April 4 1980): C6.

2378. "Jamaa Fanaka, Writer, Director, Producer of the Film "Penitentiary", Answers the NY Critics." _Harlem Weekly_ (April 16-22 1980): 1, 9.

2379. "Leon Kennedy steps out of wife Jayne's shadow with blockbuster movie." _Jet_ (April 3 1980): 58-60.

2380. "Penitentiary." _Variety_ (December 26 1979): 12.

2381. Perchaluk, E. "Penitentiary." _Film Journal_, Vol. 83 (May 1980): 13+.

Penitentiary II (1982)

2382. Brown, Dwight. "Penitentiary II." _Sepia_, Vol. 31 (July 1982): 18.

2383. Neuhauser, M. "Penitentiary II." _Film Journal_, Vol. 85 (March 22 1982): 19.

2384. "Penitentiary II." _Variety_ (April 7 1982): 14.

2385. Ross, P. "Le Defi du Tigre." _La Revue du Cinema_, No. 403 (Mars 1985): 29-30.

2386. Summers, J. "Penitentiary II." _Boxoffice_, No. 118 (May 1982): 58.

Penitentiary III

2387. "Fanaka Regains Enthusiasm with Third 'Penitentiary' Installment." _Variety_ (August 26 1987): 16.

FRANKLIN, WENDELL - Director

2388. "Breakthrough in Hollywood." Ebony (December 1963): 82-88.

2389. "Hollywood Hires a Negro Director." Sepia (April 1963): 35-38.

2390. Keats, Charles. "Wendell Franklin." Action! (The Magazine of the Directors Guild of America) (January-February 1972): 13-15.

2391. Schumach, Murray. "Negro Assistant Film Director Solves Problem of Protocol." New York Times (January 31 1963).

2392. "View from the Top. Wendell Franklin, director on the rise." Sepia (October 1966): 49-53.

2393. Wyatt, Hugh. "Black Films Hit the 'Tough' Life." New York Daily News (August 9 1974): 52.

The Bus is Coming (1971)

2394. "Black Director's 'Hopeful' Pic Gets Hissed by Blacks." Variety (October 20 1971): 1, 62.

2395. Village Voice (December 16 1971): 87. [Review]

Greatest Story Ever Told

2396. "Award Goes to Negro for Movie Work." Los Angeles Times (April 19 1965).

FRAZIER, JACQUELINE - Director

2397. Campbell, Loretta. "Reinventing Our Image: Eleven Black Women Filmmakers." Heresies, Issue 16 (1983): 58-62.

FREEMAN, MONICA - Director

2398. Andrews, Benny. "Female Filmmaker Freeman." Encore American and Worldwide News, Vol. 6 (September 12 1977): 40.

GARDNER, ROBERT (1957-   ) - Director

2399. Arnaud, C., and Yann Lardeau. "Robert Gardner." Les Deux Ecrans (Algiers), No. 50 (November 1982): 32-33.

2400. Rosen, Miriam. "Interview: Gardner and Akomfrah." Black Film Review, Vol. 5, No. 4 (Fall 1989?): 4-5, 30. Discussion with Black Audio Film Collective member John Akomfrah and African American independent Robert Gardner on the challenges facing Black filmmakers in the UK and USA.

Clarence and Angel (1979)

2401. "Clarence and Angel." Variety (August 20 1980): 1.

2402. Forbes, J. "Clarence and Angel." Monthly Film
Bulletin, Vol. 49 (May 1982): 81-82.

2403. George, Nelson. "Filmmaker Documents Urban Jargon."
New York Amsterdam News (September 29 1979): 34.

2404. Hoberman, J. "Wild in the 'Burbs." Village Voice
(December 16/22 1981): 92.

2405. Maslin, Janet. "Screen: 'Clarence and Angel,' 2 Harlem
Schoolboys." New York Times (December 9 1982).

King James Version (1987)

2406. "King James Version." Variety (April 6 1988): 13.

GARRETT, KENT - Director

A Time to Die

2407. O'Connor, John J. "TV Weekend: Coming Face to Face
with Death." New York Times (July 9 1982): C24.

2408. "A Time to Die." Variety (July 14 1982): 100.

GRAY, RONALD K. - Director

Transmagnifican Dambamutuality

2409. "Transmagnifican Dambamutuality: A Quiet Domestic
Drama." Young Viewers, Vol. 9, No. 2 (1986): 12. [Review]

GREAVES, WILLIAM (1926-   ) - Director/Producer

See also # 2133, 2136, 2153, 2164, 2168

2410. Black Writers: A Selection of Sketches from
Contemporary Authors. Detroit: Gale Research Inc., 1989, pp.
227-229.

Audiotapes

2411. Artist and Influence: William Greaves (1989)
(audiotape). Interview. [Held by the Hatch-Billops
Collection (# 6004)]

Articles

2412. Bourne, St. Clair. "The "Think Piece" Section. In
Dialogue with...." Chamba Notes (Spring 1979): 5-7.
[Interview]

2413. "A Concerned Filmmaker." Business Screen, Vol. 31
(September 1970); 22-23.

2414. "Film Producer Greaves, A Top Award Winner." Jet
(December 31 1970): 59.

2415. Greaves, William. "'100 Madison Avenues Will Be of No Help.'" New York Times (August 9 1970).

2416. _____. "Who's Who in Filmmaking." Sightlines, Vol. 3, No. 1 (September-October 1969): 6-9.

2417. Jimenez, Lillian. "Profile: William Greaves." The Independent, Vol. 3, No. 10 (1981): 8-11.

2418. Lee, Rohama. "The Whirlwind Career of William Greaves." American Cinematographer, Vol. 66 (August 1985): 68-72.

2419. M. M. "Portraits de Cineastes: La Carriere Exemplaire de William Greaves." La Revue du Cinema, No. 363 (juillet/ aout 1981): 89-91.

2420. Moore, Marie. "Producer William Greaves 'Bustin Loose' with Talent." New York Amsterdam News (June 13 1981): 27.

2421. Murray, James P. "Film; William Greaves: Creatively Independent." Black Creation, Vol. 4, No. 1 (Fall 1972): 10-11.

Ali, The Fighter

2422. Greaves, William. "Two Fighters on Film." Making Films in New York (February 1974): 13-14, 16, 41.

2423. Hamilton, Willie L. "Bill Greaves, The Talent Behind 'The Fighters.'" New York Amsterdam News (January 26 1974): D-5.

Black Journal

2424. Bourne, St. Clair. "Bright Moments." The Independent, Vol. 11, No. 4 (May 1988): 10-13. Detailed discussion of the early years of "Black Journal" by one of the series' directors.

2425. Greaves, William. "Black Journal: A Few Notes from the Executive Producer." Television Quarterly, Vol. VIII, No. 4 (Fall 1969): 66-72.

2426. Thomas, Dana L. The Media Moguls: From Joseph Pulitzer to William S. Paley. New York: G. P. Putnam's Sons, 1981, pp. 221-222. Brief discussion of "Black Journal."

From These Roots (1974)

2427. Millender, D. "From These Roots." Film News, Vol. 32 (May/June 1975): 12-13.

2428. Sumbi, J. "From These Roots." Film Library Quarterly, Vol. 8, No. 3-4 (1975): 42.

Ida B. Wells: A Passion for Justice (1989)

2429. Goodman, Walter. "Review/Television: Profile of an
Early Travler On the Road to Civil Rights." New York Times
(December 19 1989): C26. [Review]

In The Company of Men

2430. Greaves, William. "The Film Maker Speaks: Log: In the
Company of Men." Film Library Quarterly, Vol. 3, No. 1
(Winter 1969-70): 29-31, 34.

Marijuana Affair

2431. Alexander, J. B. "Can a Film About Grass Bring Green
Pastures." New York Post (September 26 1975). [Review]

GUNN, BILL (1934-1989) - Director

See also # 1617

2432. Black Writers: A Selection of Sketches from
Contemporary Authors. Detroit: Gale Research Inc., 1989, pp.
238-239.

2433. Leki, Ilona. "Bill Gunn." In Dictionary of Literary
Bibliography. Vol. 38: Afro-American Writers After 1955:
Dramatists and Prose Writers, eds. Thadious M. Davis and
Trudier Harris. Detroit: Gale Research, 1985, pp. 109-114.

Articles

2434. Adams, Janus Ingrid. "Interview: Bill Gunn." Encore
(June 1973): 54-57.

2435. Alexander, J. B. "Daily Closeup: 'The Only
Alternative.'" New York Post (January 17 1975): 37.
[Profile/Interview]

Obituaries

2436. "Bill Gunn." Variety (April 12 1989): 117.

2437. Bowser, Pearl. "Possibilities That Might Have Been..."
Black Film Review, Vol. 5, No. 2 (Spring 1989): 12, 17.

2438. Fraser, C. Gerald. "Bill Gunn, Playwright and Actor,
Dies at 59 on Eve of Play Premiere." New York Times (April 7
1989): D20.

2439. Tate, Greg. "Bill Gunn, 1934-89." Village Voice
(April 25 1989): 98, 153.

2440. Williams, John. "Bill Gunn: 1929-1989." The
Independent (July 1989): 10-11; Also Black Film Review (Spring
1989): 11-12.

Ganja and Hess (1973)

2441. Bogle, Donald. <u>Blacks in American Films and Television</u>. New York: Garland, 1988, pp. 87-88.

Articles

2442. Allombert, G. "Ganja and Hess." <u>La Revue du Cinema</u>, No. 276/277 (October 1973): 168-169.

2443. "Ganja and Hess." <u>Variety</u> (April 18 1973): 30+.

2444. Guerin, T. "Ganja and Hess." <u>Interview</u>, No. 32 (May 1973): 38.

2445. Gunn, Bill. "Letter to the Editor: 'To Be a Black Artist.'" <u>New York Times</u> (May 13 1973): Sec. 2, p. 7. Response to criticisms of Gunn's "Ganja and Hess."

2446. Monaco, James. "Blood and Blackness: An Untimely Death." <u>Village Voice</u> (March 14 1974): 75.

2447. Peterson, Maurice. "Movies: Bill Gunn." <u>Essence</u>, Vol. 4 (October 1973): 27, 96. [Interview]

Stop!

2448. Weiler, A. H. "Bill Gunn, Actor and Playwright, to Direct Film." <u>New York Times</u> (November 26 1969). On Gunn's directorial debut, "Stop!"

HARRIS, WENDELL JR. - Director

See # 2188

HEAD, HELAINE - Director

See # 2182

HOBSON, CHARLES - Director

From JumpStreet

2449. De Witt, Katherine. "History of Black Music is Traced in TV Series." <u>New York Times</u> (February 4 1980): C17.

HOOKS, KEVIN - Director

See # 2182

HUDLIN, REGINALD - Director

See also # 2156, 2188

2450. Boseman, K. "The BFR Interview: Reginald Hudlin Looks for Truth in Humor." <u>Black Film Review</u>, Vol. 2, No. 1 (1985): 3+.

2451. Caise, Yule. "The Distance Travelled." <u>Black Film Review</u>, Vol. 5, No. 4 (Fall 1989?): 16-20. [Interview]

2452. Tate, Greg. "Avant Pop 1986: Visual Hiphop." <u>Village Voice</u> (January 7 1986). [Profile]

House Party

2453. Emerson, Jim. "Cameos: Hyphenates the Hudlins." <u>Premiere</u> (January 1990): 44, 47. [Profile]

2454. Kennedy, Lisa. "Wack House: House Party Is Business as Usual." <u>Village Voice</u> (March 13 1990): 67. [Review]

2455. Rogers, Charles E. "Kid 'N' Play 'House Party'." New York <u>Amsterdam News</u> (March 3 1990): 26.

HUDLIN, WARRINGTON - Director

See also # 2133, 2153, 2164, 2188

2456. Caise, Yule. "The Distance Travelled." <u>Black Film Review</u>, Vol. 5, No. 4 (Fall 1989?): 16-20. [Interview]

2457. Daney, Serge, and Serge Le Peron. "Entretien avec Warrington Hudlin." <u>Cahiers du Cinema</u>, No. 308 (janvier 1980): 17-19. [Interview]

2458. Emerson, Jim. "Cameos: Hyphenates the Hudlins." <u>Premiere</u> (January 1990): 44, 47. [Profile]

2459. George, Nelson. "The Hudlin Brothers." <u>Essence</u>, Vol. 18 (September 1987): 32.

2460. Hesselink, A. "Interview met Warrington Hudlin." <u>Skrien</u> (Amsterdam), No. 106 (April 1981): 8-9.

Black at Yale: A Film Diary (1975)

2461. Canby, Vincent. "Film 2 about Youth." <u>New York Times</u> (February 22 1978): C22.

Color

2462. Lacayo, Richard. "Black Writers and Producers Are Widening Their Focus." <u>New York Times</u> (May 29 1983): Sec. 2, p. 21.

Street Corner Stories

2463. "Interview: Warrington Hudlin." <u>Chamba Notes</u> (Winter 1977-78).

HUDSON, ROLANDO - Director

See # 2188

JAMES, LUTHER - Director

See also # 2167

2464. Lucas, Bob. "Black TV Directors." Sepia (May 1971): 28-32. Profile of Mark Warren, Vantile Whitfield, Luther James, Sid McCoy and Ivan Dixon.

JOHNSON, DEMETRIUS - Producer

Disco 9000

2465. Young, A. S. Doc. "The First Disco Movie." Sepia (June 1977): 48-54.

JOHNSON, NOBLE - Director/Producer

See # 2160

JONES, LORETHA - Director

See # 2164

JONES, PHILIP MALLORY - Director

2466. Jackson, Elizabeth. "Interview." Black Film Review (Summer 1989): 4-5, 28-30. In-depth interview with video artist Philip Mallory Jones.

KEITH, GERREN - Director

See also # 2182

2467. Jenkins, Walter. "Gerren Keith: A Star Behind the Camera." Sepia (September 1978): 68-72.

KENNEDY, LEON - Producer

See also # 4505-4508

2468. "Kennedy's First Pic as Producer Wraps; 4 Others in Development." Variety (December 12 1984): 20+.

2469. "Leon Kennedy Denies his Films are Blaxploitation." Jet, Vol. 70 (May 26 1986): 57.

2470. Sanders, Charles L. "Ebony Interview with Jayne and Leon Kennedy. Did success break up their 10-year marriage?" Ebony (January 1982): 116+.

2471. Winters, Jason. "Jayne and Leon: Hollywood's Happiest Couple." Black Stars (July 1981): 41-43.

KING, WOODIE, JR. - Director

See also # 2133

The Long Night

2472. Davis, Curt. "The Long Night Wins the Day." Encore
American and Worldwide News (June 7 1976): 32-33.

2473. "Woodie King and Son: Talent Times Two." Encore
American and Worldwide News (June 21 1976): 31-32.

Torture of Mothers

2474. George, Nelson. "Woodie King Does Film on Harlem Six:
'Torture of Mothers.'" New York Amsterdam News (August 2
1980): 27.

LANE, CHARLES - Director

See also # 2188

2475. Arnaud, C., and Yann Lardeau. "Charles Lane." Les
Deux Ecrans, No. 50 (November 1982): 29-32.

2476. Leon, M. "Un Realisateur Subversif: Charles Lane." La
Revue du Cinema, No. 363 (juillet/aout 1981): 97-99.

A Place in Time (1976)

2477. Collins, Kathleen. "'A Place in Time' and 'Killer of
Sheep': Two Radical Definitions of Adventure Minus Women." In
In Color: Sixty Years of Images of Minority Women in Film.
New York: Third World Newsreel, 1982, pp. 5-7.

Sidewalk Stories (1989)

2478. Campanella, Roy II. "A Minute a Year." Black Film
Review, Vol. 5, No. 4 (Fall 1989?): 10-15. [Interview]

2479. Folk, Theodore. "New Kid on the Block: Charles Lane."
The Off-Hollywood Report, Vol. 5, No. 1 (January/February
1990): 18-20, 22. [Interview]

2480. Hoban, Phoebe. "Dim lights, sad city." New York
(November 6 1989): 36. [Profile]

2481. Mapp, Ben. "Off-Screen: Body and Soul." Village Voice
(November 7 1989): 67, 70. [Profile/interview]

2482. Ross, Michael E. "The serious ends of comedy." New
York Times (November 18 1989): 15. [Profile]

Reviews

2483. Hoberman, J. "Young, Gifted, Black." Village Voice
(November 7 1989): 67, 70. [Review]

2484. Kauffmann, Stanley. "Sidewalk Stories." The New
Republic (December 18 1989): 25.

2485. Maslin, Janet. "Review/Film: Chaplinesque Artist and Waif among the Homeless." New York Times (November 3 1989): C14.

2486. Salamon, Julie. "Sidewalk Stories." Wall Street Journal (November 2 1989): A16.

2487. "Sidewalk Stories." Variety (October 4 1989): 34.

Though Shalt Not Miscegenate

2488. Jones, Patricia. Discussion of a preview showing of Lane's "Thou Shalt Not Miscegenate" at the Black Filmmakers Foundation. Village Voice (August 27 1980): 44.

LANEUVILLE, ERIC (1952-   ) - Director

See also # 2182

2489. Rothenberg, Fred. "New Directions." New York Post (October 28 1987): 87, 89.

LANGE, TED - Director

See also # 2182

LARKIN, ALILE SHARON - Director

2490. Campbell, Loretta. "Reinventing Our Image: Eleven Black Women Filmmakers." Heresies, Issue 16 (1983): 58-62.

2491. Harris, Kwasi. "New Images: An Interview with Julie Dash and Alile Sharon Larkin." The Independent, Vol. 9 (December 1986): 16-20.

2492. Jackson, Lynne, with Karen Jaehne.   "Eavesdropping on Female Voices: A Who's Who of Contemporary Women Filmmakers." Cineaste, Vol. 16, No. 1/2 (1987-88): 43.

LATHAN, STAN (c.1944-   ) - Director

See also # 2182

2493. Douglas, Pamela. "Stan Lathan: The TV Director as an Artist." Black Creation, Vol. 5, No. 1 (Fall 1973): 35-36.

2494. Peterson, Maurice. "On the Aisle: Focus on Stan Lathan." Essence, Vol. 5 (February 1975): 17.

Almos' A Man (1977)

2495. Goldstein, Richard. "Almos' A Man." Film News, Vol. 35 (Summer 1978): 23.

Amazing Grace (1974)

2496. "Amazing Grace." Independent Film Journal, Vol. 74 (August 7 1974): 8.

2497. "Amazing Grace." Variety (July 17 1974): 18.

2498. Cocks, Jay. "Bigots and Bromides; Black Power; A Star is Born." Time (December 16 1974): 6+.

2499. Crist, Judith. "Movies: And a Little Child Shall Lead Us." New York (November 11 1974): 106+.

Beat Street

2500. "Beat Street." Variety (May 23 1984): 26.

2501. Canby, Vincent. "Beat Street." New York Times (June 8 1984): C10.

2502. Grubb, K. "Hip-hoppin' in the South Bronx: Lester Wilson's "Beat Street." Dance Magazine (April 1984): 76-78.

2503. Hoberman, J. "Their Big Break." Village Voice (June 19 1984): 53+.

2504. Marlow, Curtis. "Beat Street Breaks Out!" Right On! (August 1984): 10-12.

2505. Maslin, Janet. "At the Movies: Capturing the Hip-Hop Culture." New York Times (June 8 1984): C12. [Interview]

2506. Verniere, James. "Electrifying!" The Aquarian (June 13 1984): 6-7.

Go Tell It on the Mountain

2507. "Go Tell It on the Mountain." Variety (August 1 1984): 14.

A House Divided: Denmark Vesey's Rebellion (1982)

2508. Shepard, Richard F. "TV: A Forgotten Rebellion of Slaves." New York Times (February 17 1982): C23.

Save the Children (1973)

2509. "Save the Children." Ebony, Vol. 28 (October 1973): 48-50+.

2510. "Save the Children." Variety (September 19 1973): 16.

The Sky is Gray

2511. Carrico, J. P. "The American Short Story: The Sky is Gray." Film News (Fall 1980): 26.

2512. O'Connor, John J. "TV: Sky is Gray, Short Story by Ernest Gaines." New York Times (April 7 1980): C18.

A Tribute to Martin Luther King Jr.: A Celebration of Life

2513. "A Tribute to Martin Luther King Jr.: A Celebration of Life." Variety (January 18 1984): 70.

Uncle Tom's Cabin

2514. Farber, Stephen. "Cable Service Dusts Off 'Uncle Tom's Cabin' for TV." New York Times (June 13 1987): 50.

LAWRENCE, CAROL MUNDAY - Director

2515. Beals, Melba. "Essence Women: Carol Munday Lawrence." Essence (March 1980): 38, 41.

LEE, SPIKE [Shelton Jackson Lee] (1957-   ) - Director

See also # 2133, 2164, 2173, 2188

2516. Stone, Les. "Lee, Spike." Black Writers: A Selection of Sketches from Contemporary Authors. Detroit: Gale Research Inc., 1989, pp. 352-355.

Articles

2517. "Black youth need new value system: Spike Lee." Jet (September 11 1989): 24.

2518. Brathwaite, F. "Spike Lee." Interview, Vol. 17 (March 1987): 74-75.

2519. Collier, Aldore. "Spike Lee Playing Hollywood Hardball." Ebony Man (November 1989): 79-80, 82.

2520. Dickey, Christopher. "That's the truth, Ruth." Newsweek (July 3 1989): 66.

2521. Frechette, David. "Spike Lee's Declaration of Independence." Black Enterprise, Vol. 17 (December 1986): 56-59.

2522. Glicksman, Marlaine. "Lee Way." Film Comment, Vol. 22, No. 5 (SeptemberOctober 1986): 46-49. [Interview]

2523. "'He's Gotta Have It': Director Spike Lee Reaches for Fame as a 'Great Filmmaker.'" Ebony (January 1987): 42+.

2524. Johnson, Pamela. "Showstopper Spike Lee." Essence, Vol. 17 (September 1986): 29.

2525. Kimble, Sonya R. "Spike Lee...Making Waves." Right On! (August 1989): 75-76; (September 1989): 28-29, 68.

2526. "Lee, Spike." Current Biography 1989.

2527. Little, B. "Brooklyn's Baby Mogul, Spike Lee, Finds the Freedom He's Gotta Have." People (October 13 1986): 67-68.

2528. McDowell, Jeanne. "He's got to have it his way; angry over racial inequities and stereotypes, filmmaker Spike Lee combines his message and his own pop image into a provocative media voice." Time (July 17 1989): 92-94.

2529. Margolin, Francois. "Spike Lee en 15 Questions."
Cahiers du Cinema, No. 385 (juin 1986): VI.

2530. Norment, Lynn. "Spike Lee: The Man Behind the Movies
and the Controversy." Ebony (October 1989): 140, 142-145.

2531. Parra, D. "Entretien avec Spike Lee." La Revue du
Cinema, No. 423 (janvier 1987): 24-25. [Interview]

2532. Relin, David Oliver, and Tom Beller. "Uplifting His
Race." Scholastic Update (April 7 1989): 27.

2533. "Spike Lee." Stills, No. 29 (February 1987): 72.
[Profile/Interview]

2534. "Spike Lee Challenges Black Show Biz Figures." Jet
(March 6 1989): 57.

2535. Tate, Greg. "Spike Lee." American Film, Vol. 11
(September 1986): 48-49.

2536. Warren, Larkin. "Spike Lee: filmmaker." Esquire
(December 1989): 102.

Newspaper Articles

2537. Cooper, Carol. "Homeboy Hopeful." Village Voice
(January 8 1985).

2538. Goldstein, Patrick. "A Jazzy Director Who's Got It."
Los Angeles Times/Calendar (August 25 1986): 1, 3.

2539. Kempley, Rita. "Spike Lee, Training His Lens on Life."
Washington Post (October 22 1986): C1, C8-9.

2540. Mieher, Stuart. "Spike Lee's Gotta Have It." New York
Times Magazine (August 9 1987): 26-29, 39, 41.

2541. Newton, Edmund. "Spike Gets His Shot." New York Daily
News Sunday Magazine (August 10 1986): 17-18.

2542. "Spike Lee Sparks NYU 'Future Filmmakers'." New York
Amsterdam News (April 8 1989): 21.

2543. Thomas, Keith L. "Filmmaking is a Longtime Goal Spike
Lee's Just Gotta Go For." Atlanta Journal and Constitution
(September 12 1986): 1P-2P.

Do the Right Thing

2544. Lee, Spike, with Lisa Jones. Do the Right Thing. New
York: Fireside Books, 1989. 297p.

Articles

2545. Bourne, St. Clair. "Brothers Under the Skin: In 'Do
the Right Thing,' Spike Lee Assails Racial Discord." Elle
(August 1989): 100, 102.

2546. Corliss, Richard. "Hot Time in Bed-Stuy Tonight."
Time (July 3 1989): 62.

2547. Glicksman, Marlaine. "Spike Lee's Bed-Stuy BBQ." _Film
Comment_ (July-August 1989): 12-16. [Interview]

2548. Gold, Richard. "Spike Lee's latest does the lucrative
thing; Brooklyn filmer fighting off controversy." _Variety_
(July 5 1989): 5.

2549. Hentoff, Nat. "Doing the Wrong Thing." _Present Tense_
(November-December 1989): 54+.

2550. "Insight to Riot." _Rolling Stone_ (July 13 1989): 104+.

2551. Johnson, Arthur J.   "White Man, Listen: Spike and the
Critics." _Black Film Review_, Vol. 5, No. 2 (Spring 1989): 14-
15.

2552. Jones, Jacquie. "Spike Lee's Look at the Realities of
Racism." _Black Film Review_, Vol. 5, No. 2 (Spring 1989): 13-
14.

2553. Katsahnias, Iannis, and Nicolas Saada. "A Propos de
'Do the Right Thing': Entretien avec Spike Lee." _Cahiers du
Cinema_ (Juin 1989): 9-11.

2554. Kunen, James S. "Spike Lee inflames the critics with a
film he swears is The Right Thing." _People_ (July 10 1989):
67-68.

2555. Lee, Spike. "Spike to Spike." _Essence_ (July 1989):
55-56. Lee interviews himself re: "Do the Right Thing".

2556. McLane, Daisann. "Known for his stylish satire, Spike
Lee takes on darker issues of violence and racism in his new
film, Do the Right Thing." _Vogue_ (July 1989): 76-78.

2557. Moore, Trudy S. "EM Interview: Spike Lee; Doing the
'Right Thing' in Film." _Ebony Man_ (July 1989): 17-19.

2558. Morrison, Micah. "The World According to Spike Lee."
National Review (August 4 1989): 24-25. Right wing analysis
of "Do the Right Thing."

2559. Orenstein, Peggy. "Spike's Riot." _Mother Jones_
(September 1989): 32+.

2560. Saada, Nicolas. "'Do the Right Thing' de Spike Lee:
Black is Back." _Cahiers du Cinema_ (Juin 1989): 6-8.

2561. White, Armond. "Scene on the Street: Black cinema from
Catfish Row to Stuyvesant Ave." _Mother Jones_ (September
1989): 35-36.

Newspaper Articles

2562. Canby, Vincent. "Film View: Spike Lee Raises the Movies' Black Voice." <u>New York Times</u> (May 28 1989): Sec. 2, pp. 11, 14. Discussion of Cannes reaction to "Do the Right Thing."

2563. Davis, Thulani, et al. "We've Gotta Have It." <u>Village Voice</u> (June 20 1989): 67-75. Special section on "Do the Right Thing" with interviews with the film's stars, Danny Aiello, Ossie Davis, Ruby Dee, Bill Nunn, and Rosie Perez, and critiques by Thulani Davis (pro) and Stanley Crouch (con).

2564. Do the Right Thing - Clippings [Billy Rose Theatre Collection]

2565. "'Do the Right Thing': Issues and Images." <u>New York Times</u> (July 9 1989): Sec. 2, pp. 1, 23. Round-table discussion of "Do the Right Thing" with Dr. Mary Schmidt Campbell, NYC Commissioner of Cultural Affairs; Henry Louis Gates Jr.; Nathan Glazer; Dr. Alvin F. Poussaint; Burton B. Roberts, Bronx judge; filmmaker Paul Schrader; Dr. Betty Shabazz, widow of Malcolm X, and editors of the Arts and Leisure section.

2566. Kaufman, Michael T. "In a New Film, Spike Lee Tries To Do the Right Thing." <u>New York Times</u> (June 25 1989): Sec. 2, pp. 1, 20. [Interview]

2567. Marriott, Michel. "Brooklyn's Reactions to a Film on Racism: Spike Lee's Movie Inspires Debate Where It Was Made." <u>New York Times</u> (July 3 1989): 21.

2568. Staples, Brent. "Spike Lee's Blacks: Are They Real People?; Do the simplistic characters of 'Do the Right Thing' foster racial stereotyping?" <u>New York Times</u> (July 2 1989): Sec. 2, pp. 9, 26.

2569. Taubin, Amy. "Shooting Script: When You're Hot." <u>Village Voice</u> (August 30 1988): 57, 71. Progress report on the making of "Do the Right Thing".

2570. Wood, Joe. "Yes, and I Read the Book..." <u>Village Voice</u> (August 22 1989): 59, 61. Commentary on the film and Lee's book on the film.

Reviews

2571. Ansen, David. "Do the Right Thing." <u>Newsweek</u> (July 3 1989): 65-66.

2572. Denicolo, David. "Do the Right Thing." <u>Glamour</u> (August 1989): 168.

2573. Dyson, Michael Eric. "Do the Right Thing." <u>Tikkun</u> (September-October 1989): 75+.

2574. Harvey, Ken. "Do the Right Thing." <u>Unity</u> (July 24 1989): 8.

2575. Hoberman, J. "Pass/Fail." Village Voice (July 11 1989): 59-62.

2576. Kauffmann, Stanley. "Do the Right Thing." The New Republic (July 3 1989): 24-26.

2577. Kroll, Jack. "Do the Right Thing." Newsweek (July 3 1989): 64-65.

2578. Novak, Ralph. "Do the Right Thing." People (July 3 1989): 13-14.

2579. Rafferty, Terrence. "Do the Right Thing." New Yorker (July 24 1989): 78+.

2580. Szamuely, George. "Do the Right Thing." Insight (July 10 1989): 56.

2581. Travers, Peter. "Do the Right Thing." Rolling Stone (June 29 1989): 27-28.

2582. Williamson, Bruce. "Do the Right Thing." Playboy (August 1989): 20.

Media Materials

2583. Making "Do The Right Thing" (1989). Director, St. Clair Bourne. 58 min. Film and video formats. Documentary on the making of the Spike Lee film. [Distributed by First Run/Icarus Films, 153 Waverly Place, New York, NY 10014. Tel. 212-727-1711]

Joe's Bed-Stuy Barbershop: We Cut Heads

See also # 6070

2584. "Joe's Bed-Stuy Barbershop: We Cut Heads." Variety (March 30 1983): 15.

2585. Maslin, Janet. "Screen: "Barbershop" and Italian "Truuuuth." New York Times (March 23 1983): 55.

2586. "NYU Grad Filmmaker Wins H'wood 'Oscar.'" New York Amsterdam News (July 2 1983): 20.

School Daze

2587. Lee, Spike. Uplift the Race; the Construction of School Daze. New York: Fireside Books, 1988. 352p.

Articles

2588. Allen, Bonnie. "The Making of School Daze: Talking with Spike." Essence, Vol. 18 (February 1988): 50, 130.

2589. Cheers, D. Michael. "Spike Lee: He's Gotta Have More; and New School Daze Film Promises to Give it to Him." Ebony Man (March 1988): 30-31.

2590. Conant, Jennet. "A Question of Class and Color; Spike Lee takes a hard look at black college life." Newsweek (February 15 1988): 62.

2591. Duvall, Henry. "The Golden Spike: Nationwide Debate Over 'School Daze'." about...time (April 1988): 22-23.

2592. Frechette, David. "Interview: Rappin' with Spike Lee." Black Film Review, Vol. 4, No. 1 (Winter 1987/88): 6-7, 20-21. See also reviews of School Daze by Janet Singleton (p.8) and Daniel Garrett (p.9) in this same issue.

2593. Goldberg, Michael. "America gets behind a new dance: Spike Lee's film 'School Daze' launches 'Da Butt'." Rolling Stone (June 30 1988): 21.

2594. "In defense of 'Da Butt.'" Harper's Magazine (July 1988): 28+. Letter from Marcus Miller and Spike Lee.

2595. "Island Drops Lee's 'Daze' Musical Pic; Col's Holding a Net." Variety (February 4 1987): 6.

2596. Johnson, Pamela. "The Making of School Daze: Behind the Scenes." Essence, Vol. 18 (February 1988): 51-52, 130, 132.

2597. Lee, Spike. "Class Act." American Film (January-February 1988): 57-58.

2598. Moore, Trudy S. "Spike Lee's "School Daze" Takes Comic Look at Life on Black College Campus." Jet (February 22 1988): 28-31.

2599. Nash, Dawn. "'School Daze' didn't have it: studio support spiked." Black Enterprise (May 1988): 39.

2600. "Spike Lee Filming Banned at Alma Mater in Atlanta." Jet (May 11 1987): 55.

2601. "Spike Lee Returns with Another Major Film: School Daze." Ebony (February 1988): 172+.

2602. Weinstein, Wendy. "Spike Lee pioneers new black film image. College years recalled in fierce and funny School Daze." Film Journal (February/March 1988): 24, 124.

2603. Wofford, Willie, Jr. "Spike Lee's movie starts new dance craze: 'Da Butt.'" Jet (June 13 1988): 58+.

Newspaper Articles

2604. "Daze of Our Lives; Did Spike Lee Get It With 'School Daze'?" Village Voice (March 22 1988): 35-39. Interview with Lee by Thulani Davis along with comments by black critics Dalton Narine, Vernon Reid, Lisa Kennedy, Hilton Als, Ben Mapp, Greg Tate, Toni Chin, Donald Suggs, and Harry Allen on Lee's "School Daze."

2605. Lee, Spike. "Letter to the Editor: 'School Daze'
Days." New York Times (March 6 1988). Angry response to
critical reviews in the New York Times and elsewhere.

2606. "The New York Newsday Interview with Spike Lee; He
Points a Critical Lens at His Own." New York Newsday
(September 23 1987).

2607. Poulson-Bryant, Scott. "Daze of Heaven." Village
Voice (February 16 1988). Review of Lee's "School Daze"
(# 2587) and "She's Gotta Have It" (# 2617) books.

Reviews

2608. Denby, David. "A Color Line." New York (February 29
1988): 117.

2609. Fuller, Richard. "School Daze." Philadelphia Magazine
(April 1988): 78.

2610. Hoberman, J. "Hoodoo You Love?" Village Voice
(February 16 1988): 78. [Review]

2611. Moore, Suzanne. "School Daze." New Statesman &
Society (July 29 1988): 52.

2612. "School Daze." Variety (February 17 1988): 22.

2613. Shindler, Merrill. "School Daze." Los Angeles
Magazine (March 1988): 185.

2614. Wallace, Michelle. "School Daze." The Nation (June 4
1988): 800+.

2615. Williamson, Bruce. "School Daze." Playboy (May 1988):
18.

She's Gotta Have It (1986)

See also # 2171

2616. Bogle, Donald. Blacks in American Films and
Television. New York: Garland, 1988, pp. 187-189.

2617. Lee, Spike. Spike Lee's She's Gotta Have It: Inside
Guerilla Filmmaking. New York: Fireside Books, 1987. 448p.

Articles

2618. Bollag, Brenda. "NY independent cinema at Cannes: Jim
Jarmusch's Down by Law and Spike Lee's She's Gotta Have It."
Film Quarterly (Winter 1986): 11-13.

2619. Gold, Richard. "Lee sez MPAA 'rigid, unfair' regarding
cut of 'Gotta Have It.'" Variety (August 13 1986): 7-8.

2620. "Interview with Spike Lee: Shooting A Low-Budget
Feature Film." Black Filmmaker Foundation Newsletter, Vol. 2,
No. 3 (Fall 1985): 3.

2621. Moore, Trudy S. "Spike Lee: Producer, Director, Star Discusses Making of Film 'She's Gotta Have It'." Jet (November 10 1986): 54-56.

2622. Nicholson, David. "Independent, and Liking It." American Visions (July/August 1986): 53-55. Profiles filmmakers Kathleen Collins, Spike Lee, Michelle Parkerson, Billy Woodberry and their films.

2623. Van Poznak, Elissa. "She's Got It." The Face, No. 82 (February 1987): 46-48. [Interview]

Newspaper Articles

2624. Barth, Jack. "Spike Lee on Deck." Village Voice (August 12 1986): 56. [Profile]

2625. Poulson-Bryant, Scott. "Daze of Heaven." Village Voice (February 16 1988). Review of Lee's "She's Gotta Have It" (# 2617) and "School Daze" (# 2587) books.

2626. Rohter, Larry. "Spike Lee Makes His Movie." New York Times (August 10 1986): Sec. II, pp. 14, 18.

2627. Sinclair, Abiola. "Media Watch: New Film by Spike Lee Premiers in New York." New York Amsterdam News (August 2 1986): 24, 28.

Reviews

2628. Ansen, David. "She's Gotta Have It." Newsweek (September 8 1986): 65.

2629. Denby, David. "She's Gotta Have It." New York (August 18 1986): 59.

2630. Edelstein, David. "Birth of a Salesman." Village Voice (August 12 1986): 54.

2631. Heath, Leila. "Three Women; black sexuality comes to the silver screen." The Canadian Forum, Vol. 66, No. 767 (March 1987): 32-34.

2632. Kael, Pauline. "She's Gotta Have It." The New Yorker (October 6 1986): 128+.

2633. Kauffmann, Stanley. "She's Gotta Have It." The New Republic (September 15 1986): 30.

2634. McHenry, Susan. "She's Gotta Have It." Ms. (October 1986): 14-15.

2635. Radin, Victoria. "She's Gotta Have It." New Statesman (October 24 1986): 27.

2636. Rosenbaum, Ron. "She's Gotta Have It." Mademoiselle (January 1987): 168.

2637. "She's Gotta Have It." <u>New Statesman</u> (March 6 1987): 32.

2638. "She's Gotta Have It." <u>Time</u> (October 6 1986): 94.

2639. "She's Gotta Have It." <u>Variety</u> (April 2 1986): 20-21.

2640. Travers, Peter. "She's Gotta Have It." <u>People</u> (October 20 1986): 10.

2641. Wallace, Michelle. "She's Gotta Have It." <u>The Nation</u> (June 4 1988): 800+.

2642. Williamson, Bruce. "She's Gotta Have It." <u>Playboy</u> (October 1986): 26.

Variations on the Mo' Better Blues
(former title: Love Supreme)

2643. Gold, Richard. "Lee's 'Love Supreme' next; 'Dreamgirls' adaptation for Geffen Co. could follow." <u>Variety</u> (August 30 1989): 16.

2644. Marshall, Victoria. "Film Clips: Love Supreme Becomes Mo Better." <u>Black Film Review</u>, Vol. 5, No. 4 (Fall 1989?): 3.

2645. Van Gelder, Lawrence. "At the Movies: Spike Lee's Latest." <u>New York Times</u> (November 24 1989): C10.

LIFE, REGGE - Director

See also # 2182

2646. "Regge Life Directs New 'Cosby Show' Episodes." <u>Jet</u>, (August 31 1987): 38.

2647. Seaton, Charles. "Life Has Been Reel Good to Life." New York <u>Daily News</u> (January 6 1983): 74.

LYNCH, EDIE - Director

2648. Campbell, Loretta. "Reinventing Our Image: Eleven Black Women Filmmakers." <u>Heresies</u>, Issue 16 (1983): 58-62.

2649. Riley, Clayton. "Who's Who in Filmmaking: Edie Lynch." <u>Sightlines</u> (Spring 1976): 21-24.

MCCOY, SID - Director

See also # 2167

2650. <u>CBMR Digest</u>, Vol. 2, No. 2 (Fall 1989): 9-10. [Profile]

2651. Lucas, Bob. "Black TV Directors." <u>Sepia</u> (May 1971): 28-32. Profile of directors Mark Warren, Vantile Whitfield, Luther James, Sid McCoy and Ivan Dixon.

MANNAS, JIMMIE - Director

2652. Mannas, Jimmie - Clippings [Billy Rose Theatre Collection]

MARTIN, D'URVILLE (1939-1984) - Producer

2653. "Candid Comments......D'Urville Martin." <u>Right On</u>! (April 1973): 42-43.

2654. Collins, Lisa. "D'Urville Martin...Still Hustling." <u>Black Stars</u> (April 1975): 26-32.

2655. Moore, Bob. "D'Urville Martin: Actor, Producer, Angry Black Man." <u>Sepia</u>, Vol. 22 (October 1973): 69-80.

2656. Newton, Edmund. "The Blaxploitation Movies and Their Place in the Sun." <u>New York Post</u> (March 12 1975): 52. [Profile]

2657. Smith, Angela E. "Producer of 'Boss Nigger' Just That." New York <u>Amsterdam News</u> (March 1 1975): D-17.

Obituaries

2658. "D'Urville Martin." <u>Variety</u> (June 6 1984): 93.

2659. <u>Jet</u> (June 11 1984): 14.

2660. <u>Jet</u> (Dec. 31 1984/Jan. 7 1985): 23.

MASON, RICHARD - Director

See also # 2140

2661. Peavy, Charles D. "The Films of Richard Mason." <u>Cineaste</u>, Vol. II, No. 4 (Spring 1969): 4-5, 31.

MICHEAUX, OSCAR (1884-1951) - Director

See also # 2160

2662. Bogle, Donald. <u>Blacks in American Films and Television</u>. New York: Garland, 1988, pp. 422-425.

2663. Edelman, Rob. "Micheaux, Oscar." In <u>The International Dictionary of Films and Filmmakers. Vol. II: Directors/ Filmmakers</u>, ed. Christopher Lyon. Chicago: St. James Press, 1984, pp. 369-370.

2664. Fontenot, Chester J., Jr. "Oscar Micheaux, Black Novelist and Film Maker." In <u>Vision and Refuge: Essays on the Literature of the Great Plains</u>, eds. Virginia Faulkner and Frederick C. Luebke. Lincoln: University of Nebraska Press, 1982, pp. 109-125.

2665. Hoover, Dwight W. "Micheaux, Oscar." In <u>Dictionary of American Biography</u>, Supplement 5, pp. 490-491.

2666. "Micheaux, Oscar." In World Film Directors. Vol. 1: 1890-1945, ed. John Wakeman. New York: H.W. Wilson, 1987, pp. 765-770.

2667. Porter, Kenneth Wiggens. "Micheaux, Oscar." In Dictionary of American Negro Biography, eds. Rayford W. Logan and Michael R. Winston. New York: W.W. Norton, 1982, pp. 433-434.

2668. Woodland, J. Randal. "Oscar Micheaux." In Dictionary of Literary Biography. Vol. 50: Afro-American Writers Before the Harlem Renaissance. Detroit: Gale Research, 1986, pp. 218-225.

Articles

2669. Allen, Carole Ward. "Remembrance of Things Past: The First Black Filmmaker." Encore American and Worldwide News, Vol. 4 (November 24 1975): 2.

2670. Bogle, Donald. "No Business Like Micheaux Business: "B"...for Black." Film Comment, Vol. 21, No. 5 (September/ October 1985): 31-34.

2671. Bowser, Pearl. "Oscar Micheaux: Pioneer Filmmaker." Chamba Notes (Winter 1979): 5.

2672. "Director Oscar Micheaux Gets 'Walk of Fame' Star." Jet (February 23 1987): 54.

2673. Herbert, Janis. "Oscar Micheaux: A Black Pioneer." South Dakota Review, Vol. 11 (Winter 1973): 62-69.

2674. Hoberman, J. "Bad Movies." Film Comment, Vol. 16 (July/August 1980): 11-12.

2675. "Hollywood in the Bronx." Time (January 29 1940): 67-68. Brief report on Oscar Micheaux and his Bronx film company.

2676. Micheaux, Oscar. "The Negro and the Photo-Play." The Half-Century Magazine (May 1919): 9, 11.

2677. Peterson, Bernard L. "Films of Oscar Micheaux: America's First Fabulous Black Filmmaker." The Crisis (April 1979): 136-141; (December 1980): 555.

2678. Phelps, Howard A. "In the Limelight: Oscar Micheaux." The Half-Century Magazine (April 1919): 12. [Profile]

2679. Reid, Marc A. "Pioneer Black Filmmaker: The Achievement of Oscar Micheaux." Black Film Review, Vol. 4, No. 2 (Spring 1988): 6-7.

Newspaper Articles

2680. Cox, Clinton. "We Were Stars in Those Days." New York Sunday News Magazine (March 9 1975): 15-16, 18, 26-27. Interview with former stars of Oscar Micheaux's films.

2681. Friendly, David T. "An Overdue Honor for Film
Pioneer." <u>Los Angeles Times</u> (May 17 1986): 1, 4. On
Micheaux's posthumous reception of a Directors Guild of
America award.

2682. Hoberman, Jim. "A Forgotten Black Cinema Surfaces."
<u>Village Voice</u> (November 17 1975): 85-86.

The Betrayal (1948)

2683. "The Betrayal." <u>Variety</u> (June 30 1948). [Review]

Body and Soul (1924)

2684. Bogle, Donald. <u>Blacks in American Films and
Television</u>. New York: Garland, 1988, pp. 32-33.

2685. Hoberman, J. "Film: Blankety-Blank." <u>Village Voice</u>
(May 29 1984): 58.

The Exile

2686. Clark, W. E. "The Exile at Lafayette Theatre." <u>New
York Age</u> (May 23 1931).

2687. "'The Exile'. Lafayette Patrons Give it 'O.K.'"
<u>Pittsburgh Courier</u> (May 23 1931).

God's Step Children (1938)

2688. "Black Film: God's Step Children." <u>New Yorker</u> (April
18 1970): 34-35.

2689. Bogle, Donald. <u>Blacks in American Films and
Television</u>. New York: Garland, 1988, pp. 91-92.

2690. Graham, Olive. "God's Step Children." <u>CinemaTexas
Program Notes</u>, Vol. 15, No. 2 (November 13 1978): 117-122.

The Homesteader (1919)

See also # 2676, 2678

2691. "The Negro on the Stage." <u>The Half-Century Magazine</u>
(April 1919): 9. Mention of "The Homesteader" along with
photos of its two stars, Evelyn Preer and Trevy Woods.

2692. Phelps, Howard A. "Negro Life in Chicago." <u>The Half-
Century Magazine</u> (May 1919): 14. Brief comment on Micheaux's
Chicago studio and his popular film "The Homesteader."

Swing

2693. Hoberman, J. "Film: White Boys." <u>Village Voice</u> (June
5 1984): 64.

Underworld

2694. Hoberman, J. "Film: American Fairy Tales." Village Voice (June 12 1984): 48.

MILES, WILLIAM (1931-) - Director

See also # 2133

2695. Willis-Thomas, Deborah. "Documentary Artist; William Miles: Award-Winning Filmmaker." The Schomburg Center Journal, Vol. 2, No. 4 (Fall 1983): 2-3.

The Different Drummer

2696. Fraser, C. Gerald. "Television Week: Blacks in the Military." New York Times (May 15 1983).

2697. O'Connor, John J. "TV: Three-Part Series on Blacks in the Military." New York Times (May 18 1983).

I Remember Harlem

2698. De Witt, Karen. "A Memory of Harlem." American Film, Vol. 4, No. 2 (November 1978): 18-27.

2699. Garisto, Leslie. "Some Positive Thinking About Harlem." New York Times (February 1 1981): Sec. 2, p. 29.

2700. George, Nelson. "Wanted: Harlem Film Documentary Angel." New York Amsterdam News (August 4 1979): 28.

2701. _____. "William Miles Films Harlem." New York Amsterdam News (October 7 1978): D-3.

2702. Tapley, Mel. "Bill Miles and Baruch Professor Make TV Documentary on Harlem." New York Amsterdam News (January 24 1981): 33.

Men of Bronze

2703. Canby, Vincent. "Two Documentaries Depict Erosion of Ideals by Time." New York Times (September 24 1977): 15.

2704. Drane, Francesca. "'Harlem Hellfighter', 94, Looks Back on a Rich Life." New York News World (February 22 1978): 1A, 6A.

2705. _____. "'Men of Bronze' Reflect on Glory." New York News World (February 21 1978): 1A, 6A.

2706. _____. "One Man's Quest to Immortalize 'Men of Bronze.'" New York News World (February 23 1978): 1A, 6A. Final part of a 3-part newspaper story on the making of and the individuals profiled in 'Men of Bronze.'

2707. Gross, Kenneth. "A Belated Accounting for the Old 15th." Newsday (November 13 1977).

2708. Howard, J. R. "Men of Bronze." Film Library Quarterly, Vol. 12, No. 4 (1979): 44-46.

2709. "Men of Bronze." Variety (September 28 1977): 22+. [Review]

2710. Millender, D. H., and William Greaves. "Men of Bronze." Film News, Vol. 37 (Spring 1980): 36.

2711. Newton, Edmund. "Photographs, Old Records Inspire Film of Harlem Unit Fighting in France." New York Post (November 2 1977): 53.

2712. York, Max. "Film Captures Regiment's History." The Tennessean (June 10 1977).

MUMFORD, THAD - Producer

2713. Lacayo, Richard. "Black Writers and Producers Are Widening Their Focus." New York Times (May 29 1983): Sec. 2, pp. 21-22.

MUNGEN, DONNA - Director

2714. Mungen, Donna. "On Location: Filmmaking in Greece." Black Film Review, Vol. 5, No. 1 (Winter 88/89): 18-20.

NELSON, STANLEY - Director

Two Dollars and a Dream

2715. "Two Dollars and a Dream." Variety (December 2 1987): 32+. [Review] [For distribution information see # 6069]

NICHOLAS, DENISE - Producer

See # 3155-3156

NOBLE, GIL - Producer

See also # 3230, 3232

2716. Noble, Gil. Black is the Color of My TV Tube. Secaucus, NJ: Lyle Stuart Inc., 1981. 190p.

Articles

2717. Cunningham, Barry. "Gil Noble: It's All in the Telling." New York Post (November 9 1968): 33.

2718. Ernest, E. "Media's Warrior: Gil Noble." Encore American and Worldwide News (October 1981): 20-23.

2719. "Gil Noble, two others, honored by Urban League." New York Amsterdam News (March 3 1979): 56.

2720. Hazziezah. "Harlemite Gil Noble: award-winning TV editor." New York Amsterdam News (October 8 1977): D-7, D-10.

2721. "Profile: Gil Noble Tells It Like It Is." New York
Amsterdam News (January 27 1979): 49.

2722. Tapley, Mel. "Gil Noble, Bob Teague handle heat on
television." New York Amsterdam News (December 11 1982): 29.

Like It Is

2723. Fraser, C. Gerald. "'Like It Is,' Black-Oriented Show
Celebrates Its 10th Birthday." New York Times (February 12
1978): 55.

2724. Gupta, Udayan. "For 'Like It Is,' amid landmark
achievements, the struggle continues." New York Amsterdam
News (May 13 1978): D-17.

2725. Hazziezah. "'Like It Is' Goal: Freeing America's
Mind." New York Amsterdam News (October 8 1977): D8-9.

2726. Like It Is (tele) - Clippings [Billy Rose Theatre
Collection]

PARKERSON, MICHELLE - Director

2727. Gibson, Gloria J. "Moving Pictures to Move People:
Michelle Parkerson is the Eye of the Storm." Black Film
Review, Vol. 3, No. 3 (Summer 1987): 16-17; Also published as
"Michelle Parkerson Interview." Black Camera; The Newsletter
of The Black Film Center/Archive (Bloomington, IN), Vol. 3,
No. 1 (Winter 1988): 5-6, 8.

2728. Nicholson, David. "Independent, and Liking It."
American Visions (July/August 1986): 53-55. Profiles of
filmmakers Kathleen Collins, Spike Lee, Michelle Parkerson,
Billy Woodberry and their films.

2729. Parkerson, Michelle. "Answering the Void." The
Independent, Vol. 10, No. 3 (April 1987): 12-13.

But Then, She's Betty Carter

2730. "But Then, She's Betty Carter." Variety (April 22
1981): 24. [Review]

PARKS, GORDON, Jr. (1935-1979) - Director

2731. Bogle, Donald. Blacks in American Films and
Television. New York: Garland, 1988, pp. 437-438.

2732. Clark, Bob. "Interview: Gordon Parks, Jr. Hooked on
Photography." Encore (January 1973): 56-58.

2733. Moore, Deedee. "Shooting Straight: the many worlds of
Gordon Parks." Smithsonian (April 1989): 66-77.

2734. Winsten, Archer. "Rages and Outrages." New York Post
(August 28 1972): 21. [Profile]

Obituaries

2735. Cine Revue, Vol. 59 (April 19 1979): 61.
2736. Cinema (Paris), No. 247/248 (July-August 1979): 197.
2737. Ecran, No. 80 (May 15 1979): 81.
2738. Jet (April 19 1979): 60.
2739. New York Times (Aprill 4 1979): B-8.
2740. Time (April 16 1979): 99.
2741. Variety (April 4 1979): 127.

Aaron Loves Angela (1975)

2742. "Aaron Loves Angela." Variety (December 24 1975): 16.

2743. Allen, T. "Aaron Loves Angela." Village Voice
(February 16 1976): 147+.

2744. Davis, Curt. "Aaron Loves Angela is Less Than
Lovable." Encore American and Worldwide News (February 2
1976): 34-35.

2745. Perchaluk, E. "Aaron Loves Angela." Independent Film
Journal, Vol. 77 (January 7 1976): 6.

2746. Veihdeffer. "Aaron Loves Angela." Film Bulletin, Vol.
45 (January 1976): 26.

Super Fly (1972)

2747. Bogle, Donald. Blacks in American Films and
Television. New York: Garland, 1988, pp. 208-209.

2748. Ward, Francis. Super Fly: A Political and Cultural
Condemnation by the Kuumba Workshop. Chicago: Institute of
Positive Education, 1972. 18p.

Articles

2749. Berry, W. E. "How 'Super Fly' Film is Changing
Behavior of Blacks." Jet (December 28 1972): 54-58.

2750. Cocks, Jay. "Racial Slur." Time (September 11 1972).
[Review]

2751. "Criticism Mounts Over Superfly." Jet (September 28
1972): 55.

2752. Mannberg, C. "Superfly." Chaplin, No. 120 (1973): 11.

2753. Murray, James P. "How Fly is Your High." Encore
(October 1972): 57. [Review]

2754. Stuart, Alex. "Superfly." Films and Filming (April
1973): 52-53. [Review]

2755. Verrill, Addison. "'Super Fly' A Blackbuster Phenom;
Gross Already Tops $5,000,000 in Limited Dates; How About an
Oscar?" Variety (October 4 1972): 3, 26.

2756. _____. "'Superfly's' Happy Harlem Stay; Crew Black and Hispanic; Financing Script, Director, P.R. All Black." Variety (April 12 1972): 3, 24.

2757. Ward, Francis. "Super Fly: The Black Film Rip Off." Black Position, No. 2 (July 2 1972): 37-42.

Thomasine and Bushrod (1974)

2758. Bogle, Donald. Blacks in American Films and Television. New York: Garland, 1988, pp. 215-216.

Articles

2759. Cocks, Jay. "Grand Tour; Gang Fight; Quick Cuts." Time (May 6 1974): 90-91.

2760. Crist, Judith. "Available in All Colors." New York, Vol. 7 (April 22 1974): 90-91.

2761. Haskell, Molly. "Between the Super-Genteel and Super Cop." Village Voice (April 25 1974): 79.

2762. Landau, Jon. "Thomasine and Bushrod." Rolling Stone, No. 164 (July 4 1974): 82.

2763. Millar, S. "Thomasine and Bushrod." Monthly Film Bulletin, Vol. 42 (February 1975): 40.

2764. Putterman, B. "Father and Son: A Sort of Celebration." Audience, Vol. 6 (June 1974): 13-15.

2765. "Thomasine and Bushrod." Independent Film Journal, Vol. 73 (April 15 1974): 10-11.

2766. "Thomasine and Bushrod." Variety (April 10 1974): 20.

Three the Hard Way

2767. Combs, R. "Three the Hard Way." Monthly Film Bulletin, Vol. 45 (May 1978): 98-99.

2768. Lucas, Bob. "The Ego 'Trip' That Was Canceled." Black Stars (June 1974): 66-69.

2769. "Three the Hard Way." Independent Film Journal, Vol. 74 (July 10 1974): 15.

2770. "Three the Hard Way." Variety (June 26 1974): 18.

PARKS, GORDON, Sr. (1912-) - Director

See also # 1617

2771. Harnan, Terry. Gordon Parks: Black Photographer and Film Maker. Champaign, IL: Garrard Publishing Co., 1972. 96p.

2772. Parks, Gordon. A Choice of Weapons. New York: Harper
& Row, 1966. 274p. [Autobiography]

2773. _____. To Smile in Autumn, A Memoir. New York:
Norton, 1979. 249p. Autobiography dealing with the years
1944-1979.

Books with Sections on Gordon Parks

2774. Ball, Jane. "Gordon Parks." In Dictionary of Literary
Biography. Vol. 33: Afro-American Fiction Writers After 1955.
Detroit: Gale Research Co., 1984, pp. 203-208.

2775. Bogle, Donald. "Gordon Parks, Sr." In Blacks in
American Films and Television. New York: Garland, 1988, pp.
438-439.

2776. Gaiownik, Melissa. "Parks, Gordon." In Black Writers:
A Selection of Sketches from Contemporary Authors. Detroit:
Gale Research Inc., 1989, pp. 447-449.

2777. Shepard, Thom. "Gordon Parks." In Cineaste
Interviews: On the Art and Politics of the Cinema, eds. Dan
Georgakas and Lenny Rubenstein. Chicago: Lake View Press,
1983, pp. 173-180.

2778. Toppin, Edgar A. "Parks, Gordon." In A Biographical
History of Blacks in America since 1528. New York: David
McKay, 1971, pp. 381-384.

Articles

2779. Bosworth, Patricia. "'How Could I Forget What I Am?'"
New York Times (August 17 1969).

2780. "Gordon Parks Releases Second Movie." The Crisis (July
1971): 162.

2781. Melves, Barbara. "'I Don't Make Black Exploitation
Films.'" Village Voice (May 10 1976): 149-150.

2782. Myers, Walter Dean. "Gordon Parks: John Henry with a
Camera." Black Scholar (January-February 1976): 27-30.

2783. "Parks, Gordon." Current Biography 1968.

2784. Peterson, Maurice. "Gordon Parks." Essence, Vol. 3
(October 1972): 62+. [Interview]

2785. Thomas, Bob. "A Talk with Gordon Parks." Action!
(July-August 1972): 15-18.

Charlotte Forten's Mission: Experiment in Freedom

2786. Lawson, S. "An Unsung Civil War Heroine Lives Again on
the Home Screen." New York Times (February 24 1985): Sec. 2,
p. 33.

Leadbelly (1976)

2787. Bogle, Donald. <u>Blacks in American Films and Television</u>. New York: Garland, 1988, pp. 130-131.

Articles

2788. Burns, Ben. "The Creative Wizardry of Gordon Parks." <u>Sepia</u>, Vol. 25 (April 1976): 36-40, 44, 46.

2789. Campanella, Roy, Jr. "Gordon Parks Interview." <u>Millimeter</u>, Vol. IV, No. 4 (April 1976): 30-35, 48-51.

2790. "Daughter's Restraint Suit on Ledbetter Par Pic a Failure." <u>Variety</u> (July 23 1975): 6.

2791. Davis, Curt. "Film: "Leadbelly's" Rhythms Are Off." <u>Encore American and Worldwide News</u> (April 19 1976): 34.

2792. Parks, Gordon. "A Last Visit to Leadbelly." <u>New York</u> (May 10 1976): 66-68.

2793. Verrill, Addison. "Par Rebuts Parks' "Diller Bias" Crack." <u>Variety</u> (April 28 1976): 5, 30. Parks asserts that the new administration at Paramount Pictures refused to adequately distribute or advertise his film.

Newspaper Articles

2794. Canby, Vincent. "The Screen: Park's Elegiacal 'Leadbelly.'" <u>New York Times</u> (May 29 1976).

2795. Hand, Judson. "Where'd That Leadbelly Movie Go?" New York <u>Sunday News</u> (May 2 1976).

2796. Hunter, Charlayne. "Film: 'Leadbelly Speaks for Every Black Who's Catching Hell.'" <u>New York Times</u> (July 4 1976): Sec. 2, pp. 11, 16.

2797. Kevles, Barbara. "Gordon Parks Fights Paramount: 'I Don't Make Black Exploitation Films'." <u>Village Voice</u> (May 10 1976): 149-150.

2798. Tapley, Mel. "Gordon's War to Save Leadbelly." New York <u>Amsterdam News</u> (April 24 1976): D8-D9.

2799. Taylor, Frances. "Movie Review: 'Leadbelly' is the Finest Black Film Made So Far." <u>Long Island Press</u> (May 29 1976).

The Learning Tree (1969)

2800. Parks, Gordon. <u>The Learning Tree</u>. New York: Harper & Row, 1963. 303p.

Articles

2801. Arnold, Gary. "Film: Family 'Tree'." <u>Washington Post</u> (September 27 1969): C8.

2802. David, Gunter. "Directs Film from Own Book." Newark Sunday News (September 14 1969): Sec. 6, p. E16.

2803. Fowler, Giles M. "With Camera and Script, Parks Goes Home Again." The Kansas City Star (October 6 1968): 1D-2D.

2804. "Gordon Parks: The Learning Tree." Sepia, Vol. 19 (April 1970): 50-54.

2805. "The Learning Tree." Variety (June 25 1969).

2806. Lindsay, Michael. "The Learning Tree." Cinema, Vol. 5, No. 1 (1969): 14-19.

2807. Moore, Gerald. "Suddenly, Doors Open Up." Life (November 15 1968): 116-117.

2808. Rice, Susan. "The Learning Tree." Take One, Vol. 2, No. 3 (January-February 1969): 22-25.

Shaft (1971)

2809. Bogle, Donald. Blacks in American Films and Television. New York: Garland, 1988, pp. 185-186.

2810. Tidyman, Ernest. Shaft. New York: Macmillan, 1970. 188p. Novel from which the film is adapted.

Articles

2811. B. A. B. "Book into Movie: What's Happening to Ernest Tidyman's "Shaft" on the Way to the Screen." Publishers' Weekly (April 19 1971): 22-23.

2812. "Black-Owned Ad Agency On 'Shaft' Credited for B.O. Boom, 80% Black." Variety (July 28 1971).

2813. "Blacks vs. Shaft: Formation of Coalition Against Blaxploitation." Newsweek (August 28 1972): 88.

2814. Combs, Richard. "Shaft." Films and Filming (April 1972). [Review]

2815. Lucas, Bob. "The Shaft Business." Sepia (July 1972): 36-44.

2816. Murray, James P. "Do We Really Have Time for a 'Shaft'?" Black Creation, Vol. 3, No. 2 (Winter 1972): 12-14.

2817. Riley, Clayton. "A Black Critic's View of 'Shaft': A Black Movie for White Audiences?" New York Times (July 25 1971): D-13.

2818. "Shaft." Essence (August 1971): 76.

2819. Village Voice (July 8 1971): 58. [Review]

Shaft's Big Score (1972)

2820. Bogle, Donald. Blacks in American Films and Television. New York: Garland, 1988, pp. 186-187.

Articles

2821. Greenspun, Roger. "Film: Something's Happened on the Way to the Sequel." New York Times (June 22 1972).

2822. Kramer, Carol. "Movies: The Great Chase for the Black Market." Chicago Tribune (April 2 1972): Sec. 11, pp. 3-4.

2823. Robinson, Hubbell. "Shaft's Big Score." Films in Review (October 1972). [Review]

Solomon Northup's Odyssey

2824. Bennetts, Leslie. "TV Film by Parks Looks at Slavery." New York Times (February 11 1985): C18.

2825. Sinclair, Abiola. "Media Watch: 'Solomon Northup's Odyssey' on PBS; Parks Directs." New York Amsterdam News (December 1 1984): 29.

POITIER, SIDNEY - Director/Producer

Buck and the Preacher (1972)

2826. Bogle, Donald. Blacks in American Films and Television. New York: Garland, 1988, pp. 40-41.

Articles

2827. Burrell, Walter Price. "Movies: Buck and the Preacher." Black Stars (February 1972): 58-60.

2828. Giovanni, Nikki. "Film: Buck Wore Two Guns!" Encore (Summer 1972): 59.

2829. Goodman, George. "Durango: Poitier meets Belafonte. Two Wary Rivals Patch Up a Fight to Make a Movie, Together." Look (August 24 1971): 56-61.

2830. Gow, G. "Buck and the Preacher." Films and Filming, Vol. XVIII, No. 9 (June 1972): 54. [Review]

2831. Hale, Wanda. "Movies: Sidney Poitier - A Star's Director." New York Sunday News (March 26 1972): S7.

2832. "Soul Reels: Black Stars in Motion." Right On! (May 1972): 22-23.

2833. "U.S. Black Settlers of Wild West Pic 'Had to be Directed by Poitier.'" Variety (March 17 1971): 6.

Uptown Saturday Night (1974)

2834. Bogle, Donald. Blacks in American Films and Television. New York: Garland, 1988, pp. 224-226.

2835. _____. "Uptown Saturday Night: A Look at its Place in Black Film History." Freedomways, Vol. 14, No. 4 (1974): 320-330.

2836. "Uptown Saturday Night; Hilarious comedy features largest black all-star cast in movie history." Ebony (July 1974): 52+.

RIGGS, MARLON - Director

2837. Simmons, Ron. "Other Notions." Black Film Review (Summer 1989): 20-22. [Interview]

Ethnic Notions

See also # 1849

2838. Grant, Nancy. "Ethnic Notions." Journal of American History (December 1987): 1107. [Review]

2839. Trojan, Judith. "Ethnic Notions." Wilson Library Bulletin (May 1988): 82. [Review]

ROBERTSON, HUGH A. (1932-1988) - Director/Editor

2840. "Movie Film Editor." Ebony (October 1960): 7.

Obituaries

2841. "Hugh A. Robertson." New York Times (January 14 1988): B-8.

2842. "Hugh A. Robertson." Variety (February 3 1988): 158-159.

2843. Williams, John. "Hugh Robertson, 1932-1988." The Independent (May 1988): 7.

Bim

2844. "Bim." Variety (March 31 1976): 14. [Review]

Melinda

2845. Jenkins, Flora. "Rappin' on the Set of Melinda." Right On! (August 1972): 46-47. Interview with the two leads in "Melinda" - Vonetta McGee and Calvin Lockhart.

2846. Murray, James P. "Melinda, Oh Melinda." Encore (October 1972): 56-57.

ROBERTSON, STAN - Producer

See also # 2167

2847. Copage, Eric. "A Conversation with...Stan Robertson, a Man Who Knows about Blacks in Film." _Essence_ (June 1985): 40.

ST. JACQUES, RAYMOND (1930-   ) - Director/Producer

Book of Numbers (1973)

2848. Bogle, Donald. _Blacks in American Films and Television_. New York: Garland, 1988, p. 34.

Articles

2849. "Document Life Style of Blacks." New York _Sunday News_ (July 2 1972): 11. Report on the making of Book of Numbers, Raymond St. Jacques directorial debut.

2850. Ebert, Roger. "Black Box-Office is Beautiful." _Saturday Review_ (September 12 1972): 67-69.

2851. "Movie Review: Book of Numbers." _Black Stars_ (June 1973): 60-61.

2852. Peterson, Maurice. "He's Making a Big 'Numbers' Racket." _New York Times_ (May 13 1973): Sect. 2, pp. 13, 15.

2853. "St. Jacques Played Money Game to Get Book of Numbers on Film." New York _Amsterdam News_ (September 2 1972): D-1. Discussion of difficulties faced by St. Jacques in trying to find black backers for Book of Numbers.

2854. "U.S. Black Money Not Easy for Pix: Ray St. Jacques." _Variety_ (August 16 1972): 1, 62.

ST. JOHN, CHRISTOPHER - Director

2855. St. John, Christopher. "First Feature: Top of the Heap." _Action; The Magazine of the Directors Guild of America_ (July-August 1973): 30-32.

SANDLER, KATHE - Director

2856. Campbell, Loretta. "Reinventing Our Image: Eleven Black Women Filmmakers." _Heresies_, Issue 16 (1983): 58-62.

A Question of Color (1990)

2857. "Director Euzhan Palcy hosts fundraiser for Sandler Film." _The City Sun_ (March 17 1990): 23.

SCHAPIRO, SUE - Producer

2858. "Sue Schapiro, Lady Movie Producer." _Sepia_, Vol. 19 (August 1970): 32-36.

SCHULTZ, MICHAEL (1940-   ) - Director

See also # 1617

2859. Bogle, Donald. <u>Blacks in American Films and</u>
<u>Television</u>. New York: Garland, 1988, pp. 462-463.

Articles

2860. Ferdinand, Val. "Communicator: Michael Schultz.."
<u>Black Collegian</u> (September-October 1976): 44+.

2861. Flatley, G. "At the Movies." <u>New York Times</u> (July 29
1977): C6. [Interview]

2862. Lloyd, Llana. "Hollywood's 'Hottest' New Black Movie
Director." <u>Sepia</u>, Vol. 25 (November 1976): 26-34.

2863. "Michael Schultz: An Artist for the People!" <u>Right On</u>!
(January 1980): 49.

2864. Newton, Edmund. "A Conversation with ... Michael
Schultz." <u>Essence</u> (April 1984)): 12-13.

2865. Robinson, Louie. "Michael Schultz: A Rising Star
Behind the Camera." <u>Ebony</u>, Vol. 33 (September 1978): 94-96+.

2866. "Schultz' Crystalite Gameplant: 3 Low-Budget Features
Plus TV." <u>Variety</u> (April 20 1983): 10, 26.

2867. Silverman, Marie Saxon. "Schultz Forms Own Prod. Co.;
Three Features in Development." <u>Variety</u> (July 23 1986): 9.

2868. Tallmer, Jerry. "At Home with Lauren Jones and Michael
Schultz." <u>New York Post</u> (January 22 1972): 35.

Car Wash (1976)

2869. Bogle, Donald. <u>Blacks in American Films and</u>
<u>Television</u>. New York: Garland, 1988, pp. 45-49.

Articles

2870. Canby, Vincent. "'Car Wash' Frothy Pop Film." <u>New</u>
<u>York Times</u> (October 16 1976).

2871. Silber, Irwin. "Resistance and Reaction at the Car
Wash." <u>Jump Cut</u>, No. 15 (July 1977): 16.

2872. Winsten, Archer. "'Car Wash' Sparkles with Humor."
<u>New York Post</u> (October 16 1976).

Cooley High (1975)

2873. Bogle, Donald. <u>Blacks in American Films and</u>
<u>Television</u>. New York: Garland, 1988, pp. 64-65.

Articles

2874. Murphy, Frederick D. "Cooley High: The Way We Really Were." _Encore_, Vol. 4 (September 22 1975): 30.

2875. Slater, Jack. "'Cooley High' - More Than Just a Black 'Graffiti.'" _New York Times_ (August 10 1975): D13.

2876. Van Gelder, Lawrence. "Screen: 'Cooley High.'" _New York Times_ (June 26 1975). [Review]

2877. Wolcott, James. "Takes." _Village Voice_ (July 21 1975): 70.

Last Dragon

2878. Wilmington, Michael. "Movie Review: 'Last Dragon': It's Fun But its Dumb." _Los Angles Times_ (March 22 1985): Sec. VI, p. 6.

Sgt. Pepper's Lonely Hearts Club Band

2879. Grant, Lee. "'Sgt. Pepper's' Lone Black Director." _Washington Post_ (August 20 1978): K-3.

Which Way is Up? (1977)

2880. Which Way is Up? - Clippings [Billy Rose Theatre Collection]

SCOTT, OZ - Director

See also # 2182

2881. "Oz Scott's Standing Broad Jump from Off-B'way 'To Film for U.'" _Variety_ (May 13 1981): 12, 380.

2882. Winsten, Archer. "On the Town: Director 'Oz' Scott Bustin' Out." _New York Post_ (June 27 1981): 15.

SHANNON, JOY - Director

Until the Last Stroke

2883. "Until the Last Stroke." _Young Viewers_, Vol. 9, No. 2 (1986): 13. [Review]

SHEARER, JACKIE - Director

A Minor Altercation

2884. Conrad, Randall. "A Minor Altercation." _Cineaste_, Vol. 8, No. 2 (Fall 1977): 50-51. [Review]

2885. George, Nelson. 'Minor Altercation': Boston's School Problems. New York _Amsterdam News_ (December 3 1977): D-3.

SINGLETARY, TONY - Director

See # 2182

TOWNSEND, ROBERT (c.1956-   ) - Director

See also # 2153, 2164, 2173

2886. Allen, Bonnie. "Spotlight: Robert Townsend." Essence, Vol. 18 (September 1987): 88-90+. [Interview]

2887. "Class Clowns; Woody Allen and Robert Townsend." Film Comment, Vol. 23 (April 1987): 11+.

2888. Donoloe, Darlene. "In Hollywood Shuffle Comic Actor Robert Townsend Wields His Wit Against Movie Industry Racism." People (May 18 1987): 61-62.

2889. Ellis, Trey. "Robert Townsend." Interview, Vol. 17 (May 1987): 42-46.

2890. Hirshey, Gerri. "The Black Pack." Vanity Fair (July 1988): 58-63, 118-120, 123. Profiles of Townsend, Eddie Murphy, Keenen Ivory Wayans, Arsenio Hall and Paul Mooney.

2891. Horner, Cynthia. "Shufflin' to Success: Robert Townsend shows that movies made on a shoestring can rack up dollars." Right On! (September 1987): 76-77, 71.

2892. Marshall, Marilyn. "Robert Townsend: Hollywood 'Shuffling' to the Top." Ebony, Vol. 42 (July 1987): 54D+.

2893. Rochlin, M. "Close-Up: Robert Townsend." American Film, Vol. 12, No. 6 (April 1987): 62-63.

2894. Singleton, Janet. "Interview: Robert Townsend on the real Hollywood Shuffle." Black Film Review, Vol. 3, No. 2 (Spring 1987): 6-7.

2895. Townsend, Robert. "Eddie, the Black Pack and Me." American Film, Vol. 13, No. 3 (December 1987): 28-31.

Newspaper Articles

2896. Brown, Dwight. "Close-Up: Robert Townsend A Career on Credit." New York Daily News (March 22 1987): 6.

2897. "Comic-Cum-Director Townsend on a Roll Following 'Hollywood'." Variety (December 10 1986): 23.

2898. Tate, Greg. "Off-Screen: Hollywood Shuffle's Fancy Dancer." Village Voice (March 31, 1987). [Interview]

2899. White, Armond. "Actor-Comedian Makes a Movie, Much to his Credit." The City Sun (March 18-24 1987): 11, 14.

Hollywood Shuffle (1987)

See also # 2171

2900. Bogle, Donald. Blacks in American Films and Television. New York: Garland, 1988, pp. 108-109.

Articles

2901. Als, Hilton. "Hollywood Shuffle." Essence (May 1987): 28.

2902. Ansen, David. "Hollywood Shuffle." Newsweek (April 6 1987): 64+.

2903. Benson, Sheila. "Hollywood Shuffle." Whole Earth Review (Summer 1987): 119.

2904. Brown, Geoff. "Hollywood Shuffle." Monthly Film Bulletin (April 1988): 99.

2905. Corliss, Richard. "Hollywood Shuffle." Time (April 27 1987): 79.

2906. Denby, David. "The Visible Man." New York (April 6 1987): 90-91.

2907. "Hollywood Shuffle." Variety (March 18 1987): 16.

2908. Kauffmann, Stanley. "Hollywood Shuffle." The New Republic (May 4 1987): 26.

2909. Lally, K. "Doing the 'Shuffle' Hustle." Film Journal (April 1987): 20-21.

2910. O'Toole, Lawrence. "Hollywood Shuffle." Maclean's (June 1 1987): 55.

2911. Pines, Jim. "Hollywood Shuffle." New Statesman (April 8 1988): 29-30.

2912. Shindler, Merrill. "Hollywood Shuffle." Los Angeles Magazine (April 1987): 240-241.

2913. Slate, L. "Declarations of Independence: Financing Films Outside the Studio System." American Premiere, Vol. 8, No. 2 (1987): 10+.

2914. Stockler, B. "Close-Ups: Robert Townsend." Millimeter, Vol. 15 (May 1987): 227.

2915. Waldron, Clarence. "Robert Townsend Explains Why he Produced Hit Comedy Film, 'Hollywood Shuffle.'" Jet (June 1 1987): 58-60.

2916. Williamson, Bruce. "Hollywood Shuffle." Playboy (May 1987): 34.

2917. Wolcott, James. "Hollywood Shuffle." _Texas Monthly_ (May 1987): 156-157.

Newspaper Articles

2918. Fein, Esther B. "Robert Townsend Has Fun at Hollywood's Expense." _New York Times_ (April 19, 1987): Sec. II, pp. 18, 35.

2919. Harrington, Richard. "Stepping Into the 'Shuffle'. Robert Townsend's 2 12-Year Struggle to Bring His Hollywood Satire to the Screen." _Washington Post_ (March 17 1987): C1, C4.

2920. Johnson, Charles A., and David Pecchia. "For Some, It's the Same Old Shuffle." _Los Angeles Times/Calendar_ (May 31 1987). A look at the careers of some of "Hollywood Shuffle's" actors.

2921. Maslin, Janet. "Film: 'Hollywood Shuffle,' Satire by Townsend." _New York Times_ (March 20 1987): C8.

2922. Salamon, Julie. "Film: 'Hollywood Shuffle', Satire by Townsend." _New York Times_ (March 20 1987): C8.

2923. Suggs, Donald. "Pas de Duh." _Village Voice_ (March 31, 1987). [Review]

VAN PEEBLES, MELVIN (1932-   ) - Director/Producer

See also # 1617, 2133

2924. Abdul, Raoul. "Melvin Van Peebles." In _Famous Black Entertainers of Today_. New York: Dodd, Mead & Co., 1974, pp. 125-131.

2925. _Black Writers: A Selection of Sketches from Contemporary Authors_. Detroit: Gale Research Inc., 1989, pp. 563-566.

2926. Bogle, Donald. _Blacks in American Films and Television_. New York: Garland, 1988, pp. 474-477.

2927. Edelman, Rob. "Van Peebles, Melvin." In _The International Dictionary of Films and Filmmakers. Vol. II: Directors/Filmmakers_, ed. Christopher Lyon. Chicago: St. James Press, 1984, pp. 548-549.

Articles

2928. Abeke. "Van Peebles on the Inside." _Essence_ (June 1973): 36-37, 62, 75.

2929. Brown, Geoff. "From Baadasssss to Blaxploitation." _Black Music and Jazz Review_, Vol. 3, No. 9 (January 1981): 20-23.

2930. Coffin, H. A. "Melvin Van Peebles." _Biographical News_ (May 1975): 677.

2931. Coleman, Horace W. "Melvin Van Peebles." Journal of
Popular Culture, Vol. 5 (Fall 1971): 368-384.

2932. Euvrard, Janine. "Entretien avec Melvin van Peebles."
La Revue du Cinema, No. 347 (fevrier 1980): 139-141.

2933. _____. Interview. Image et Son [Paris] (fevrier
1980).

2934. Le Peron, Serge. "Entretien avec Melvin van Peebles."
Cahiers du Cinema, No. 308 (janvier 1980): 14-16.

2935. Murphy, Frederick D. "Melvin van Peebles Sings His
BaadAsssss Song." Black Stars (September 1974): 52-58.

2936. "On the Scene: Melvin van Peebles." Playboy (September
1970).

2937. Rubine, M. "The Decolonizer of the Black Mind." Show
(July 1971).

Newspaper Articles

2938. Cohn, Lawrence. "Van Peebles Returns to Filmmaking
After Decade-Long Sabbatical." Variety (February 8 1989): 11.

2939. Murray, James P. "Cover Story: Where is Sweetback
Today?" New York Amsterdam News (January 12 1974): D10-D11.

2940. Van Peebles, Melvin. "A Stork Flew Over the Zero
Fence..." New York Sunday News (October 3 1971): 53.

Just an Old Sweet Song (1976)

2941. O'Connor, John J. "Van Peebles Sings a New 'Sweet
Song.'" New York Times (September 12 1976). TV film.

Sophisticated Gents (1981)

2942. Crouch, Stanley. "Up with Characters, Down with
Message." Village Voice (October 14-20 1981): 38.

2943. O'Connor, John. "TV: Blacks on Way Up In
'Sophisticated Gents.'" New York Times (September 29 1981):
C10.

2944. Sharp, Christopher. "Melvin Van Peebles Sings His
Streetwise Song Again." Women's Wear Daily (September 23
1981): 16.

2945. "The Sophisticated Gents." Variety (October 7 1981):
172.

Story of a 3 Day Pass (1968)

See also # 2140

2946. Bogle, Donald. Blacks in American Films and
Television. New York: Garland, 1988, pp. 207-208.

Articles

2947. Alpert, Hollis. "The Van Peebles Story." <u>Saturday Review</u>, Vol. 51 (August 3 1968): 35.

2948. Crist, Judith. "Black on Black." <u>New York</u> (July 15 1968): 62-63.

2949. Gilliatt, Penelope. "The Current Cinema. Telling It Like It Isn't." <u>New Yorker</u> (July 20 1968).

2950. Hartung, Philip T. "The Screen: Guess Who's Coming to Lunch?" <u>Commonweal</u> (August 23 1968): 571.

2951. Kauffmann, Stanley. "Stanley Kauffman on Films." <u>New Republic</u> (August 10 1968): 23.

2952. Peavy, Charles D. "An Afro-American In Paris: The Films of Melvin Van Peebles." <u>Cineaste</u>, Vol. 3, No. 1 (Summer 1969): 2-3.

2953. "The Story of a Three-Day Pass: French Film Pushes Melvin van Peebles into Ranks of Award-Winning Directors." <u>Ebony</u> (September 1968): 54-56. Analysis and background history of the Van Peebles film.

2954. Wolf, William. "Never a Whole Week." <u>Cue</u> (July 13 1968).

Newspaper Articles

2955. Adler, Renata. "Screen: A Black G.I. and a French Girl." <u>New York Times</u> (July 9 1968).

2956. Blume, Mary. "Self-Proclaimed Genius - Could Be Right." <u>International Herald Tribune</u> (April 13-14 1968).

2957. Sarris, Andrew. "Films." <u>Village Voice</u> (August 29 1968).

2958. Stone, Judy. "An American Who Went to Paris." <u>New York Times</u> (November 12 1967): D19.

2959. Winsten, Archer. "Rages and Outrages." <u>New York Post</u> (July 29 1968): 22.

Sweet Sweetback's Badasssss Song (1971)

2960. Bogle, Donald. <u>Blacks in American Films and Television</u>. New York: Garland, 1988, pp. 210-212.

2961. Van Peebles, Melvin. <u>Sweet Sweetback's Baadasssss Song</u>. New York: Lancer Books, 1971. 192p.

Articles

2962. Bennett, Lerone, Jr. "The Emancipation Orgasm: Sweetback in Wonderland." <u>Ebony</u>, Vol. 26 (September 1971): 106-108.

2963. Darrach, Brad. "Sweet Melvin's Very Hot, Very Cool Black Movie." Life (August 13 1971).

2964. Higgins, Chester. "Meet the Man Behind the 'Sweetback' Movie." Jet (July 1 1971): 54-58.

2965. Jones, Norma R. "Sweet Sweetback's Badasssss Song." CLA Journal, Vol. 19 (June 1976): 559-565.

2966. Lee, Don L. "The Bittersweet of Sweetback/Or Shake Yo Money Maker." Black World (November 1971): 43-48.

2967. Monaco, James. "Sweet Sweetback..." Take One, Vol. 3, No. 1 (September-October 1970): 29-32.

2968. Murray, James P. "Film: Running with Sweetback." Black Creation, Vol. 3, No. 1 (Fall 1971): 10-12.

2969. Newton, Huey P. "Sweet Sweetback." The Black Panther, Vol. 6 (June 19 1971): A-L. Entire issue devoted to analysis of the Van Peebles film.

2970. "Power to the Peebles." Time (August 16 1971): 47.

2971. "Stud on the Run." Newsweek (May 10 1971).

2972. "Sweet Song of Success." Newsweek (June 21 1971): 89.

Newspaper Articles

2973. Arnold, Gary. "'Sweetback': The Ego is Willing but the Aptitude is Weak." Washington Post (May 30 1971): E3.

2974. Canby, Vincent. "'Sweetback': Does It Exploit Injustice?" New York Times (May 9 1971): Sec. 2, pp. 1, 18.

2975. Gussow, Mel. "Baadasssss Success of Melvin Van Peebles." New York Times Magazine (August 20 1972): 15+.

2976. Mandell, Nancy. "Mr. Van Peebles for the Prosecution." Boston After Dark (June 8 1971): 21. On the trial against Van Peebles' distributor for cutting out 7 min. of the film without prior permission.

2977. Riley, Clayton. "What Makes Sweetback Run?" New York Times (May 9 1971).

2978. Sheahan. "Eye Too." Women's Wear Daily (June 1 1971): 12. On Van Peebles' complaint over lack of serious recognition from the white filmmaking establishment even as Sweetback plays as the No. 1 film in America!

2979. Village Voice (May 13 1971): 68.

Watermelon Man (1970)

2980. Bogle, Donald. Blacks in American Films and Television. New York: Garland, 1988, p. 227.

Dissertations

2981. Scott, Ronald Brunson. "Interracial Relationships in Films: A Descriptive and Critical Analysis of 'Guess Who's Coming to Dinner?' and 'Watermelon Man.'" Dissertation (Ph.D.) University of Utah, 1984. 443p.

Articles

2982. Francis, John. "Watermelon Man." Films and Filming (September 1970): 63, 65.

2983. "Godfrey Cambridge Turns White." Look (December 20 1969): 57+.

2984. Goldstein, Norman. "Enter the Black Director." Louisville Courier-Journal and Times (April 19 1970): 1-2.

2985. J.M. "Off-Color Joke." Newsweek (May 25 1970).

2986. Village Voice (July 16 1970): 50.

VINSON, CHUCK RALLEN - Director

See also # 2182

2987. "Stage manager Chuck Vinson directs 'Cosby Show' episode." Jet (February 1 1988): 57.

WARREN, MARK (1931-   ) - Director

See also # 2167

2988. Black Stars (January 1973): 68-71.

2989. Lucas, Bob. "Black TV Directors." Sepia (May 1971): 28-32. Profile of Mark Warren, Vantile Whitfield, Luther James, Sid McCoy and Ivan Dixon.

2990. "TV's Black Skyrocket. Youthful Mark Warren directs top-rated Laugh-In." Ebony (April 1970): 113-120.

Come Back, Charleston Blue

2991. Bogle, Donald. Blacks in American Films and Television. New York: Garland, 1988, p. 62.

Articles

2992. Carroll, Kathleen. "Hollywood is Bullish on Black Movie Sequels." New York Sunday News (June 11 1972): 7E.

2993. Gates, Tudor. "Come Back Charleston Blue." Films and Filming (November 1973).

2994. Gold, Ronald. "Talks Underway on Job-Training." Variety (March 22 1972): 1, 26. On protests in Harlem over the underrepresentation of Blacks in "Come Back, Charleston Blue's" behind the camera staff.

2995. Kramer, Carol. "Movies: The Great Chase for the Black Market." Chicago Tribune (April 2 1972): Sec. 11, pp. 3-4.

2996. Murray, James P. "First Round Rages in Harlem v. Hollywood Bout." New York Amsterdam News (April 29 1972): D-1, D-6.

2997. "Ossie Davis Quits 'Cotton' Sequel; Mark Warren Takes Over." Jet (February 3 1972): 6.

2998. Warren, Mark. "Come Back, Charleston Blue." Action!, Vol. 8, No. 2 (March-April 1973): 24-27. [Interview]

WATT, REUBEN - Director

2999. "Operation Bastrap. Asst. Director Reuben Watt rides to fame on Batman's cape." Sepia (October 1966): 44-48.

WAYANS, KEENEN IVORY - Director

See also # 2164, 2173, 2188

3000. Feldman, Jill. "Keenen Wayan's Sucker Punch." Rolling Stone (November 3 1988): 34.

3001. Hirshey, Gerri. "The Black Pack." Vanity Fair (July 1988): 58-63, 118-120, 123. Profiles of Wayans, Robert Townsend, Eddie Murphy, Arsenio Hall and Paul Mooney.

3002. Sessums, Kevin, and Amy Etra. "The Black-Pack Attack." Interview (December 1988): 56.

I'm Gonna Git You Sucka'

3003. "Don't Mess with Eddie Murphy's pal Keenan Ivory Wayans--he's making his own move, Sucka." People (December 12 1988): 185.

3004. "'I'm Gonna Get You Sucka' scores hit as funny black film." Jet (January 16 1989): 28-30.

3005. Kauffmann, Stanley. "I'm Gonna Git You Sucka." The New Republic (March 6 1989): 24-25.

3006. Klawans, Stuart. "I'm Gonna Git You Sucka." The Nation (February 13 1989: 208.

3007. Salamon, Julie. "Film: 'blaxploitation' alums poke fun at themselves." Wall Street Journal (January 31 1989): A16.

3008. Suggs, Donald. "Giving Sucka an Even Break." Village Voice (January 17 1989): 69. [Review]

3009. Travers, Peter. "I'm Gonna Get You Sucka." People (January 23 1989): 16-17.

3010. "Wayans spoofs '70s films in 'Gonna Git You Sucka'." Jet (December 26 1988): 52.

WHITE, IVERSON - Director

3011. Ward, Arvli. "Iverson White Continues Independent Black Cinema Tradition." CAAS Newsletter (UCLA Center for Afro-American Studies), Vol. 9, No. (1986): 3, 12-13.

WHITFIELD, VANTILE - Director

3012. Lucas, Bob. "Black TV Directors." Sepia (May 1971): 28-32. Profile of Mark Warren, Vantile Whitfield, Luther James, Sid McCoy and Ivan Dixon.

WILLIAMS, MARCO - Director

From Harlem to Harvard

3013. Bailey, R. "From Harlem to Harvard." Film Library Quarterly, Vol. 17, No. 2-4 (1984): 86-87. [Review]

WILLIAMS, OSCAR - Director

3014. Pasquariello, Nicholas. "A Talk with Oscar Williams." Action!, Vol. 9, No. 5 (September-October 1974): 18-21.

Five on the Black Hand Side (1973)

3015. Bogle, Donald. Blacks in American Films and Television. New York: Garland, 1988, p. 83.

Articles

3016. "Five on the Black Hand Side; Warm Comedy Focuses on Problems of a Black Middle-Class Family." Ebony (May 1974): 96-98+.

3017. Guarino, Ann. "Warm Comedy Shows Black Middle Class." New York Daily News (October 26 1973).

3018. Hunter, Vicky. "Movie Review/Five on the Black Hand Side." The Black American (July 20-27, 1973).

3019. James, H. "Five on the Black Hand Side." Films in Review, Vol. 24 (December 1973): 623-624.

3020. "Movie Review: Five on the Black Hand Side." Black Stars (February 1974): 68-73.

3021. Paul, W. "Certain Politics, Dubious Battle." Village Voice (February 14 1974): 73.

3022. Peterson, Maurice. "Film Reviews: Five on the Black Hand Side." Essence (January 1974): 87.

3023. Purdy, J. "Five on the Black Hand Side." Movietone News, No. 32 (May-June 1974): 36.

3024. "United Artists' 'Black Hand Side' Draws Big Promotional Budget, Some 'Hip' Black Mags 'Bored'?" Variety (February 6 1974): 5+.

3025. Verrill, Addison. "Five on the Black Hand Side."
Variety (October 24 1973): 16.

3026. Winsten, Archer. "'Five on the Black Hand Side' Bows."
New York Post (October 26 1973): 32.

3027. Yvonne. "Well, We Have to Start Somewhere." Ms., Vol.
2 (March 1974): 40.

Hot Potato (1976)

3028. "Hot Potato." Variety (April 7 1976): 30.

3029. "'Hot Potato' Scoring High in 286 Opening Dates."
Boxoffice (May 17 1976): 10.

3030. Perchaluk, E. "Hot Potato." Independent Film Journal,
Vol. 77 (April 14 1976): 9.

WILLIAMS, SPENCER (1893-1969) - Director

See also # 2160

3031. Bogle, Donald. Blacks in American Films and
Television. New York: Garland, 1988, pp. 484-485.

3032. Cripps, Thomas R. "The Films of Spencer Williams."
Black American Literature Forum, Vol. 12, No. 4 (Winter 1978):
128-134.

3033. Tate, Greg. "Smiley the Redeemer." Village Voice
(January 10 1989): 61. Review of Spencer Williams
retrospective at New York's Whitney Museum.

The Blood of Jesus

3034. Seward, Adrienne Lanier. "Early Black Film and Folk
Tradition: An Interpretive Analysis of the Use of Folklore in
Selected All-Black Cast Feature Films." Dissertation (Ph.D.)
Indiana University, 1985. 303p. [Hallelujah, The Green
Pastures, The Blood of Jesus]

3035. _____. "A Film Portrait of Ritual Expression: The
Blood of Jesus." In Expressively Black: The Cultural Basis of
Ethnic Identity, eds. Geneva Gay and Willie L. Baber. New
York: Greenwood Press, 1987.

WILLIAMSON, FRED - Producer

See # 3160-2162

WINFREY, OPRAH - Producer

3036. Colander, Pat. "Oprah Winfrey's Odyssey: Talk-Show
Host to Mogul." New York Times (March 12 1989): Sec. 2, pp.
31, 37. Discussion of Winfrey's production company - Harpo
Productions.

Women of Brewster Place

3037.   Naylor, Gloria. The Women of Brewster Place. New
York: Viking Press, 1982. 192p. Novel from which the TV
drama is adapted.

Articles

3038.   Herbert, Solomon. "The Women of Brewster Place."
Essence (November 1988): 39.

3039.   Kaufman, Joanne. "Oprah goes Hollywood." People (June
13 1988): 40-43.

3040.   Kort, Michele. "Lights, camera, affirmative action."
Ms. (November 1988): 55.

3041.   Leonard, John. "The Women of Brewster Place." New
York (March 20 1989): 76-77.

3042.   O'Connor, John J. "TV View: 'Brewster Place,' Women
Lead the Way." New York Times (March 19 1989): Sec. 2, p. 31.

3043.   Stark, John. "The Women of Brewster Place." People
(March 20 1989): 15-16.

3044.   Tarbell, Marta. "Oprah Winfrey: 'This is a magical,
spiritual story.'" Redbook (December 1988): 44.

3045.   Warren, Elaine. "'The Women of Brewster Place.'
There's Oprah, Jackee, Robin Givens--and a Break Men May Not
Deserve." TV Guide (March 18 1989): 4-5, 8.

3046.   "The Women of Brewster Place." Ebony (March 1989):
122+.

3047.   "Women of Brewster Place." Jet (March 20 1989): 58-60.

3048.   "The Women of Brewster Place." Variety (March 29
1989): 51-52.

WOODBERRY, BILLY - Director

Bless Their Little Hearts (1984)

3049.   Bogle, Donald. Blacks in American Films and
Television. New York: Garland, 1988, pp. 29-30.

Articles

3050.   Bassan, Raphael. "Bluesy Dream." La Revue du Cinema,
No. 429 (July-August 1987): 28.

3051.   "Bless Their Little Hearts." Variety (March 7 1984):
368-369.

3052.   Canby, Vincent. "Screen: 'Little Hearts', Drama of
Life in Watts." New York Times (December 12 1984): C25.

3053. Chevrier, M. "Bless Their Little Hearts" de Billy Woodberry. Cahiers du Cinema, No. 360/361 (Summer 1984): 74.

3054. Ciment, Michel. "Bless Their Little Hearts." Positif, No. 281/282 (July-August 1984): 86.

3055. Dowell, P. "Independents: Blues for Mr. Charlie." American Film, Vol. 10 (December 1984): 16.

3056. Edelstein, David. "Film: All in the Family." Village Voice (December 18 1984): 82, 84.

3057. Magny, J. "Bless Their Little Hearts." Cinema (Paris), No. 306 (June 1984): 28.

3058. Nicholson, David. "Independent, and Liking It." American Visions (July/August 1986): 53-55. Profiles of filmmakers Kathleen Collins, Spike Lee, Michelle Parkerson, Billy Woodberry and their films.

3059. Parra, D. "Bless Their Little Hearts." La Revue du Cinema, No. 396 (July-August 1984): 45.

3060. Strauss, Frederic. "The Sad and the Beautiful." Cahiers du Cinema, No. 398 (July-August 1987): 47-48.

WOODS, FRONZA - Director

3061. Campbell, Loretta. "Reinventing Our Image: Eleven Black Women Filmmakers." Heresies, Issue 16 (1983): 58-62.

FILM TECHNICIANS

3062. Directory of Black Film/TV Technicians & Artists, West Coast. Los Angeles, CA: Togetherness Productions, 1980. 310p.

DICKERSON, ERNEST - Cameraman

3063. Trefz, Linda. "The Brother from Another Planet." American Cinematographer (December 1984): 43-46, 48. Profile of cinematographer Ernest Dickerson.

DUBOIS, WILLIAM - Cameraman

See # 2167

HOWARD, HARRY - Film Editor

3064. "Black Film Company Enters New York Field." New York Amsterdam News (January 8 1977): D-16. Profile of Howard's production company Double HH Productions.

3065. Natale, Richard. "Cut Up." Women's Wear Daily (December 21 1971). [Profile]

3066. Winsten, Archer. "Rages and Outrages." New York Post (July 3 1972): 16. [Profile]

MAPLE, JESSIE - Camerawoman/Director

3067. Maple, Jessie. How to Become a Union Camerawoman: Film-Videotape. New York: LJ Film Productions, 1977. 85p.

Articles

3068. "A Lady Behind the Lens: Jessie Maple Cracks Tough Cinematographers Union in New York." Ebony (February 1976): 44+.

3069. Maple, Jessie - Clippings [Billy Rose Theatre Collection]

3070. "New York Has its First Black Camerawoman." New York Amsterdam News (July 16 1975): D20.

3071. Perry, Jean. "Lights, Action, Camera, Women!" New York Daily News (March 9 1976).

PINN, PEGGY

3072. Berg, Beatrice. "Pinning Their Hopes on Peggy." New York Times (July 4 1971): Sec. 2, pp. 15, 23.

3073. "Mrs. Mastermind of TV's Black Tech School. Peggy Pinn pushes hard to put much-needed soul behind cameras." Ebony (May 1972): 103-104, 106-107.

WALTON, JOHN - Film Editor

3074. Harvey, Almena Ruth. "Post Production Editing." Right On! (January 1981): 56-57. [Interview]

SCREENWRITERS

3075. "Blacks Find Jobs Scarce for Writers in Hollywood." Jet (March 23 1987): 25.

3076. Murray, James P. "A Young Woman Executive Says: Hollywood's Looking for Black Scripts." New York Amsterdam News (January 5 1974): D-15.

3077. Narine, Dalton. "The Write Stuff: Black TV and Movie Scriptwriters." Ebony, Vol. 43 (March 1988): 92+.

3078. "Writers Query on How Many Blacks Are Writing Scripts." Variety (December 31 1975): 2+.

DOLAN, HARRY E. (c.1928-1981)

See also # 2167

3079. Dolan, Harry - Clippings [Billy Rose Theatre Collection]

3080. Dolan, Harry. "Television: Can an Angry Black Man Write of Love and Laughter?" New York Times (August 31 1969): D13.

3081. Gent, George. "From Watts, a New Writer." New York Times (February 19 1967): D17.

3082. _____. "Playwright from Watts Sells TV Script to NBC." New York Times (October 19 1966).

3083. Gould, Jack. "TV: Experiment in Watts. Play by Ex-Janitor from Los Angeles Slum Begins New N.B.C. Series." New York Times (February 20 1967).

3084. Gross, Ben. "TV: Both Defects and Promise in Experimental Drama." New York Daily News (February 21 1967).

Obituaries

3085. "Harry Dolan." Variety (September 23 1981): 95.

DOUGLAS, PAMELA

3086. Douglas, Pamela. "Personal Experiences." Essence (December 1978): 64, 87-88, 112, 116. Personal notes from a Black film and television screenwriter.

3087. _____. "Reflections...an artist reflects on a decade in media." Neworld, No. 3 (1978): 26-30, 42.

ELDER, LONNE III (1931-   )

3088. Millichap, Joseph. "Lonne Elder III." In Dictionary of Literary Biography 44: American Screenwriters (Second Series). Detroit: Gale Research, 1986, pp. 120-123.

Articles

3089. Burrell, Walter Price. "Lonne Elder, III. Hollywood's Biggest Black Screenwriter." Black Stars (March 1973): 68-70, 72-73.

3090. Elder, Lonne III. "Movie Mailbag: 'As the Screenwriter of 'Sounder', I Was Shocked'." New York Times (November 26 1972). Screenwriter Elder's response to Times reviews of "Sounder" by Clive Barnes and Lindsay Patterson.

3091. "The Life of Lonne Elder III: 'Sounder's' Master Craftsman." New York Amsterdam News (September 23 1972).

3092. Reed, Rochelle. "Lonne Elder III on Sounder." Dialogue on Film, Vol. 2, No. 7 (May 1973): 2-12.

FULLER, CHARLES

See also # 2156

3093. "'I Have Written an American Story!' Pulitzer Prize-winning playwright Charles Fuller has a hit movie on his hands." Right On! (February 1985): 56, 55. [A Soldier's Story]

HUNKINS, LEE

3094. Adams, Val. "Television: A don't-miss drama on Harlem blacks." New York Daily News (June 22 1979): 62.

3095. Anderson, David. "Lee Hunkins' 'Hollow Image.'" New York Amsterdam News (July 14 1979): 27-28.

3096. "Hollow Image." Variety (June 27 1979): 50.

3097. Unger, Arthur. "'Much-needed black' drama is superb TV." Christian Science Monitor (June 21 1979): 19.

3098. Webster, Ivan. "ABC-TV's "Hollow Image": The We Nobody Showed 'Til Now." Encore American and Worldwide News (June 4 1979): 30-32, 34-36.

MASON, JUDI ANN

3099. Mason, Judi Ann. "I Wrote for the Soaps." Essence (August 1988): 59-60, 115-116.

MAYFIELD, JULIAN (1928-1984)

3100. Branch, William B. "Obituaries--Julian Mayfield (1928-1984)." In Dictionary of Literary Biography Yearbook: 1984. Detroit: Gale Research Inc., 1984, pp. 181-185.

3101. Malinowski, Sharon. "Mayfield, Julian." In Black Writers: A Selection of Sketches from Contemporary Authors. Detroit: Gale Research Inc., 1989, pp. 390-392.

3102. Taylor, Estelle W. "Julian Mayfield." In Dictionary of Literary Biography 33: Afro-American Fiction Writers After 1955. Detroit: Gale Research Inc., 1984, pp. 174-178.

MEDINA, HAZEL

3103. Jenkins, Walter. "Hazel Medina--A Talent for Every Occasion." Black Stars (August 1976): 62-68.

MOSS, CARLTON (1910-   )

See also # 2065-2079

3104. Norman, Dorothy. "A World to Live In: The Strange Case of Carlton Moss." New York Post (May 8 1944).

WESLEY, RICHARD

See also # 2156

3105. Duckett, Alfred. "The Birth of a Screenwriter." Sepia (January 1977): 62-70.

WILLIAMS, LEON

3106. Roberts, Steven V. "My Whole Family Said, 'Leon, You is Lazy.'" New York Times (March 26 1967). Profile of the screenwriter for Richard Mason's film "You Dig It."

WILLIAMS, SAMM-ART (1946-   )

3107. Lacayo, Richard. "Black Writers and Producers Are Widening Their Focus." New York Times (May 29 1983): Sec. 2, pp. 21-22.

3108. Lawson, Steve. "An Unsung Civil War Heroine Lives Again on the Home Screen." New York Times (February 24 1985): Sec. 2, p. 33. [Charlotte Forten's Mission]

3109. O'Connor, John J. "'Cagney and Lacey' on Racism." New York Times (September 28 1987). Discussion of a special episode of 'Cagney and Lacey' on racism written by Williams.

CRITICS

3110. Buchanan, Singer A. "A Study of the Attitudes of the Writers of the Negro Press Toward the Depiction of the Negro in Plays and Films, 1930-1965." Dissertation (Ph.D.) University of Michigan, 1968. 319p.

Articles

3111. Ammons, Linda. "Film: A Talk with Critic Donald Bogle." Encore American and Worldwide News (August 1980): 38-39.

3112. Murray, James P. "Clayton Riley on the Film Critic." Black Creation, Vol. 3, No. 4 (Summer 1972): 15-16.

3113. Parker, M. "Blacks in the Cinema: An Interview with Donald Bogle." Media Montage, Vol. 1, No. 1 (1976): 30-31.

3114. Riley, Clayton. "The Black Critic--Theatre and Film." New York Amsterdam News (Black Academy of Arts and Letters Supplement) (September 18 1971): D-18.

3115. Rosen, Miriam. "Interview: Raphael Bassan Discusses Black American Cinema in France." Black Film Review, Vol. 3, No. 4 (Fall 1987): 4-6. Discussion with France's leading writer on black film, Raphael Bassan, on the history of black independent films and their reception in France.

FILM PRODUCTION COMPANIES

3116. Golden, Herb. "Negro and Yiddish Film Boom." Variety (January 3 1940). Discussion of the leading Black cast film production companies and their films.

3117. "Negro Hollywood: Films and Their Makers." Headlines and Pictures (August 1946): 15-18. Profile of the big five Black cast film companies--Astor Pictures, Hollywood Pictures, Toddy Pictures, Associated Producers of Negro Pictures, and Hollywood Studios and Sack Amusement Enterprises.

3118. "The Sepia Screen." Newsweek (July 8 1946): 85-86. Profile of the top six makers of all-black features in the 1940s--Hollywood Pictures (NY), Astor Pictures (NY), Quigley and Leonard (NY), Toddy Pictures (NY), Harlemwood Pictures (Dallas), and All American News (Chicago).

ALL AMERICAN NEWS (Chicago)

See # 3118

ASSOCIATED PRODUCERS OF NEGRO PICTURES (New York)

See # 3117

ASTOR PICTURES (New York)

See also # 3117-3118

3119. "Robert M. Savini." Variety (May 2 1956). [Obituary]

3120. "Robert M. Savini, Film Distributor." New York Times (April 30 1956). Obituary for the president of one of the leading Black-cast film producton companies of the 1930s and 40s.

BIRTH OF A RACE COMPANY

3121. "Archival Finds." American Film (November 1980): 76. On the discovery of a new print of "Birth of a Race", the Birth of a Race Company's cinematic response to D. W. Griffith's "Birth of a Nation." Indicates that it has now been restored by the American Film Institute and is held by the Library of Congress in its national film archive.

3122. Cripps, Thomas R. "The Birth of a Race Company: An Early Stride Toward a Black Cinema." Journal of Negro History, Vol. 59 (January 1974): 28-37.

3123. _____. "The Lincoln Motion Picture Company and the Birth of a Race Company: Two Early Strides Toward a Black Aesthetic." In Film and Africana Politics. New Brunswick, Rutgers University, 1973.

BLACKSIDE, INC.

3124. "Henry Hampton's Blackside, Inc., Boston, Mass., Has Been in Operation Since June 1968 and Has Made Over 40 Film Productions." Black Enterprise (June 1980): 72.

Eyes on the Prize

3125. Baskin, Jeff. "PBS debuts civil rights series; it's as good as television gets." Variety (January 21 1987): 47.

3126. Jarvis, Jeff. "Eyes on the Prize." People (January 26 1987): 13.

3127. Little, Monroe H., Jr. "Eyes on the Prize: the American civil rights struggle, 1954-1965; changing of the guard." Journal of American History (December 1986): 837-838.

3128. Lord, Lewis J., and Jeannye Thornton. "A Journey to Another Time and, to Many, Another World." U.S. News & World Report (March 9 1987): 58-59.

3129. Powledge, Fred. "Eyes on the Prize: America's civil rights years, 1954-1965." The Nation (January 31 1987): 120-122.

3130. Rosen, Jay. "Eyes on the Prize: no hype was necessary to make this six-part history of America's civil-rights movement one of the most powerfully dramatic programs TV has aired in many a season." Channels (October 1987): 48-50.

3131. Schine, Cathleen. "Eyes on the Prize: America's civil rights years, 1954-1965." Vogue (January 1987): 46-47.

3132. Thelwell, Michael. "Eyes on the Prize: America's civil rights years, 1954-65." Mother Jones (February-March 1987): 58-59.

Newspaper Articles

3133. Butterfield, Fox. "Black Film Makers Retrace the Civil-Rights Struggle." New York Times (January 26 1986): Sec. II, pp. 29, 38.

3134. Darnton, Nina. "At the Movies: Summoning the Ghosts of Protests Past." New York Times (November 28 1986): C8.

3135. Davis, Thulani. "Rebirth of a Nation." Village Voice (November 25 1986): 60. [Review]

Eyes on the Prize II

3136. Barol, Bill. "A Struggle for the Prize; documenting the last 20 years of civil rights." Newsweek (August 22 1988): 63.

3137. Chavis, Benjamin F., Jr. "Eyes on the Prize: Part Two." New York Amsterdam News (January 6 1990): 13, 30.

3138. Davis, Thulani. "Eyes on the Prize II: A Sequel Due North." Village Voice (January 30 1990): 57.

3139. DeMarco, Darcy. "Keep Your Eyes on Henry Hampton; Creator Readies 'Eyes on the Prize II'." Black Film Review, Vol. 3, No. 3 (Summer 1987): 14-15.

3140. Hays, Constance L. "Overcoming Obstacles to a Civil-Rights Chronicle." New York Times (January 14 1990): Sec. 2, pp. 30-31.

3141. King, Sharon R. "Eyes on the Money." Black Enterprise (November 1988): 25. On Blackside Inc.'s difficulties in raising funds for Eyes on the Prize II.

COLORED PLAYERS FILM CORPORATION (c.1925-1929) (Phila., PA)

Scar of Shame (1927)

3142. Bogle, Donald. Blacks in American Films and Television. New York: Garland, 1988, p. 184.

3143. Cripps, Thomas R. "'Race Movies' as Voices of the Black Bourgeoisie: The Scar of Shame." In American History/American Film: Interpreting the Hollywood Image, eds. John E. O'Connor and Martin A. Jackson. New York: Ungar, 1979, pp. 39-55.

Articles

3144. Canby, Vincent. "'Scar of Shame,' a Pioneer Black Film, at Whitney." New York Times (March 18 1976).

3145. Gaines, Jane. "'The Scar of Shame': Skin Color and Caste in Black Silent Melodrama." Cinema Journal, Vol. 26, No. 4 (1987): 3-21.

3146. Graham, Olive. "Scar of Shame." CinemaTexas Program Notes, Vol. 15, No. 2 (November 13 1978): 115-117.

3147. Kalinak, Kathryn. "Kathryn Kalinak responds to Jane Gaine's "Scar of Shame": Skin color and caste in black silent melodrama." Cinema Journal, Vol. 27, No. 2 (1988): 54-59.

HARBEL PRODUCTIONS

See # 2209-2218

HARLEMWOOD PICTURES (Dallas, TX)

See # 3118

HARPO PRODUCTIONS

See # 3036

HOLLYWOOD PICTURES (New York)

See # 3117-3118

HOLLYWOOD STUDIOS AND SACK AMUSEMENT ENTERPRISES (Dallas, TX)

See # 3117

INDIGO PRODUCTIONS

3148. "Charley Smiley named head of Pryor's Indigo Productions Company." Jet (March 12 1984): 64.

3149. "Coast NAACP angered over failure of Indigo to produce any films." Variety (June 18 1986): 4, 36.

3150. "Hollywood NAACP calls for parley with Columbia exec. to discuss Brown's firing." Jet (January 16 1984): 58.

3151. Indigo Productions - Clippings [Billy Rose Theatre Collection]

3152. "Pryor announces revamp of Indigo Productions; he'll take lighter load." Jet (November 26 1984): 64.

3153. "Pryor fires Brown as head of his company." Jet (January 2 1984): 58-59.

LINCOLN MOTION PICTURE COMPANY (1916-1923) (Los Angeles, CA)

3154. Cripps, Thomas R. "The Lincoln Motion Picture Company and the Birth of a Race Company: Two Early Strides Toward a Black Aesthetic." In Film and Africana Politics, ed. Harold Weaver. New Brunswick: Rutgers University, 1973.

MASAI PRODUCTIONS

3155. "Denise Nicholas Tries a New Life Behind the Cameras." Sepia (January 1981): 26-31, 70-71.

3156. White, Joyce. "Professional Switch: Denise Nicholas." Essence (April 1976): 28, 30, 38.

NORMAN MOTION PICTURE MANUFACTURING COMPANY

3157. A collection of films and company records from this maker of all-black-cast films is held by Indiana University's Black Film Center/Archive (# 6005).

OSCAR MICHEAUX PRODUCTIONS (1918-1948)

See # 2662-2694

PAST AMERICA INC.

3158. "The Making of a Black Legacy in Film." Ebony, Vol. 40 (March 1985): 54+.

PIONEER FILMS INC.

3159. "Movie Making on a Dime." Our World (May 1948): 18-19. On the Black production company behind the film version of "Anna Lucasta".

PO' BOY PRODUCTIONS

3160. "Fred Williamson Finds Success as a Filmmaker." Jet (April 8 1976): 58-62.

3161. "Fred Williamson Moves Film Works to Canada." Jet (May 15 1980): 22-23.

3162. "One more for the Po' Boys." Black Enterprise
(September 1982): 38-39.

QUIGLEY AND LEONARD (New York)

See # 3118

SPECTRUM ARTS, INC.

3163. "A Strange Love Story; Negro movie company starts its
invasion of the film industry with red hot story on color
prejudice among Negroes themselves." Our World (March 1954):
26-28.

THIRD WORLD CINEMA PRODUCTIONS

3164. "Black Market." Time (April 10 1972): 53. Discussion
of Ossie Davis's Third World Cinema film company.

3165. "Davis Heads Minority-Controlled Motion Picture
Corporation." Jet (March 11 1971): 59. Profile of Ossie
Davis.

3166. Oestreicher, David. "Third World People in Film World
Jobs." New York Daily News (September 9 1973): Leisure-1.

Claudine (1974)

3167. Bogle, Donald. Blacks in American Films and
Television. New York: Garland, 1988, pp. 54-56.

Articles

3168. Carpenter, Sandra. "TWC - The Movie Company Behind
'Claudine'." Encore American and Worldwide News (June 9
1975): 40-41, 45.

3169. "Claudine: A Movie that Blacks Can Relate to." Jet
(July 4 1974): 56-59.

3170. Gilliatt, Penelope. "The Current Cinema. Bouncing
Back." The New Yorker (April 29 1974): 115-116.

3171. Moving Pictures - Claudine - Vertical File (includes
Production Information Guide) [Schomburg Center]

3172. Tolbert, Jane C. "Misplaced Laughter." Encore (August
1974): 45.

Newspaper Articles

3173. Campbell, Barbara. "Third World Pins Movie Hopes on
'Claudine' Run." New York Times (June 5 1975): 49.

3174. Canby, Vincent. "Cheers for Claudine." New York Times
(May 5 1974): Sec. 2, pp. 1, 8.

3175. Newton, Edmund. "Picture Brightens for Blacks in
Movies." New York Post (October 1 1973): 41.

3176. Sterritt, David. "'Claudine': New Kind of Black Film from Minority Producers." Christian Science Monitor (May 22 1974): F1.

3177. Torres, Jose. "Movie-makers." New York Post (June 15 1974): 26.

TODDY PICTURES (New York)

See # 3117-3118

TRANS OCEAN PRODUCTIONS

3178. Pantovic, Stan. "The Making of a Black Movie." Sepia (December 1973): 54-62. [The Legend of Toby Kingdom]

V

BLACKS IN AMERICAN TELEVISION AND VIDEO

3179. Barcus, F. Earle. Images of Life on Children's Television: Sex Roles, Minorities, and Families. New York: Praeger, 1983. 217p.

3180. Berry, Gordon L., ed. Television and the Socialization of the Minority Child. New York: Academic Press, 1982. 289p.

3181. Gerbner, George, and Nancy Signorielli. Women and Minorities in Television Drama, 1969-1978: A Research Report. Philadelphia: University of Pennsylvania, Annenberg School of Communications, 1979. 16p.

3182. Hill, George. Coloring the Soaps: Blacks on Television and Radio Soap Operas - A History and Bibliography. Carson, CA: Daystar Publishing Co., 1987. 50p.

3183. _____. Wee TV - Black Children and Television, Prime Time and Day Time: A History and Bibliography. Carson, CA: Daystar Publishing Co., 1986. 60p.

3184. _____, ed. Afro American Media: Challenges and History. Carson, CA: Daystar Publishing Co., 1987. 56p.

3185. _____, ed. Ebony Images: Black Americans and Television. Carson, CA: Daystar Publishing Co., 1985. 152p.

3186. _____, ed. From Claire and Weezie to Julia and Buelah: Black Women on TV: Historical Perspective and Bibliography. Carson, CA: Daystar Publishing Co., 1987. 72p.

3187. MacDonald, J. Fred. Black and White TV: Afro-Americans in Television since 1948. Chicago: Nelson-Hall, 1983. 288p.

3188. United States Commission on Civil Rights. Window Dressing on the Set: Women and Minorities in Television; A Report of the United States Commission on Civil Rights. Washington: The Commission, 1977. 181p.

3189. United States Commission on Civil Rights. <u>Window
Dressing on the Set, An Update: A Report of the United States
Commission on Civil Rights</u>. Washington, D.C.: The Commission,
1979. 97p.

Books with Sections on Afro-Americans in Television

3190. Archer, Leonard C. "Blacks in Radio and Television."
In <u>Black Images in the America Theatre: NAACP Protest
Campaigns -Stage, Screen, Radio and Television</u>. Brooklyn:
Pageant-Poseidon, Ltd., 1973, pp. 225-262.

3191. Bogle, Donald. "Television." In <u>Black Arts Annual
1987/88</u>. New York: Garland, 1989, pp. 185-209.

3192. Bond, Jean Carey. "The Media Image of Black Women."
In <u>A Freedomways Reader: Afro-America in the Seventies</u>, ed.
Ernest Kaiser. New York: International Publishers, 1977, pp.
230-234.

3193. Collier, Eugenia. "'Black' Shows for White Viewers."
In <u>A Freedomways Reader: Afro-America in the Seventies</u>, ed.
Ernest Kaiser. New York: International Publishers, 1977, pp.
235-245.

3194. Warren, Nagueyalti. "From Uncle Tom to Cliff Huxtable,
Aunt Jemima to Aunt Nell: Images of Blacks in Film and the
Television Industry." In <u>Images of Blacks in American
Culture: A Reference Guide to Information Sources</u>, ed. Jessie
Carney Smith. Westport, CT: Greenwood Press, 1988, pp. 51-
117. Includes extensive filmographies and an excellent
bibliography.

Dissertations and Theses

3195. Donaldson, Edward Lawrence. "Does Commercial
Television Abet Racism: the effects of television programming
upon human behavior." Thesis (M.A.) Colorado State
University, 1979. 52p.

3196. Jackson, Harold. "From "Amos 'N' Andy" to "I Spy:
Chronology of Blacks in Prime Time Network Television
Programming, 1950-1964." Dissertation (Ph.D.) University of
Michigan, 1982. 132p.

Articles

3197. "Black TV: Its Problems and Promises." <u>Ebony</u>, Vol. 24
(September 1969): 88-90, 92-94.

3198. "Blacks at the top in TV." <u>Ebony</u> (April 1987): 82+.
On Black executives at U.S. television stations.

3199. "Blacks on TV: Tuning in to the new season." <u>Ebony</u>
(October 1985): 68+.

3200. Brown, Les. "Television's Comedy Ghetto." <u>Channels of
Communications</u> (November 1986): 16.

3201. "Can TV Crack America's Color Line?" Ebony, Vol. 6
(May 1951): 58-65.

3202. Cripps, Thomas. "The Noble Black Savage: A Problem in
the Politics of Television Art." Journal of Popular Culture,
Vol. 8 (Spring 1975): 687-695.

3203. Cummings, Melbourne S. "The Changing Image of the
Black Family on Television." Journal of Popular Culture (Fall
1988): 75+.

3204. Douglas, Pamela. "Black Television: Avenue of Power."
Black Scholar, Vol. 5, No. 1 (September 1973): 23-31.

3205. Ellison, Mary. "The Manipulating Eye: Black Images in
Non-Documentary TV." Journal of Popular Culture, Vol. 18
(Spring 1985): 73-79.

3206. Gibbons, R. Arnold. "Minority Programming on American
Commercial Television Networks." Black Academy Review, Vol.
1, No. 1 (Spring 1970): 48-51, 65.

3207. Gitlin, Todd. "Prime-Time Whitewash." American Film
(November 1983): 36-38. On the lack of minorities in
television.

3208. "Is TV Hurting the Negro? NAACP and Talmadge Raise TV
Objections." Color (April 1952): 12-16.

3209. Johnson, Herschel. "Blacks on the soaps: things are
getting better on daytime TV." Ebony (November 1982): 123+.

3210. Jones, Kenneth M. "Essay: The Black and White of
Television." Ebony Man (October 1986): 62.

3211. Kalter, Joanmarie. "Yes, there are more Blacks on TV -
but mostly to make viewers laugh." TV Guide (August 13 1988):
26+.

3212. Marshall, Marilyn. "Texas TV pioneer; Clara McLaughlin
is first Black women to own stations." Ebony (March 1987):
78+.

3213. Matabane, Paula W. "Television and the Black Audience:
Cultivating Moderate Perspectives on Racial Integration."
Journal of Communication (Autumn 1982): 21+.

3214. Mills, John II. "Blackness in Televisionland."
Essence, Vol. 6 (April 1976): 15.

3215. Narine, Dalton. "Blacks on Soaps: From Domestics to
Interracial Lovers." Ebony (November 1988): 92+.

3216. "The Negro and TV." Our World (February 1954): 17-23.

3217. Robinson, Gene. "What is Madison Avenue Really
Selling." Black Film Review, Vol. 5, No. 4 (Fall 1989?): 21,
28. Analysis of TV commercials.

3218. Robinson, Louie. "TV Discovers the Black Man. Afro-Americans make mass debut on network shows." Ebony (February 1969): 27+.

3219. Roth, Morry. "Black inroads on broadcasting: dramatic change in U.S. TV audience and viewing." Variety (January 30 1985): 1+.

3220. Sampson, Claudia A. "Television: The Black Image: The more it remains the same." Encore American and Worldwide News (May 1980): 40-42.

3221. Sanders, Charles L. "Has TV Written Off Blacks? With many shows cancelled, new season looks bleak." Ebony (September 1981): 114+.

3222. Sanoff, Alvin P. "TV's Disappearing Color Line." U.S. News & World Report (July 13 1987): 56-57.

3223. Slater, Jack. "Does TV Have a Special Formula for Blacks? Buffoonery continues as key ingredient of Black series." Ebony (January 1980): 106+.

Newspaper Articles

3224. Brown, Roscoe C., Jr. "Let's Uproot TV's Image of Blacks." New York Times (February 18 1979): Sec. 2, p. 35.

3225. Gates, Henry Louis, Jr. "TV's Black World Turns - But Stays Unreal." New York Times (November 12 1989): Sec. 2, pp. 1, 40.

3226. Holly, Ellen. "How Black Do You Have To Be?" New York Times (September 15 1968).

3227. _____. "Living a White Life--For a While." New York Times (August 10 1969).

3228. "Letters: TV's Black World." New York Times (December 3 1989): 3, 43. Responses to # 3211.

3229. O'Connor, John J. "Cosby Leads the Way, but TV Still Stumbles in Depicting Blacks." New York Times (March 30 1986): Sec. 2, pp. 1, 27.

Media Materials

3230. Positively Black: The Role of Minorities in Television [Part one] [videorecording]. New York: WNBC-TV, 1979. 28 min. Summary: Three panelists, WABC producer/host Gil Noble, Screen Actors Guild officer/actor David Connell, and NBC vice president of station relations J. Tabor Bolden, answer audience questions about the role of minorities in television including: why there aren't more minority producers and directors, how minorities can get into the business, what roles minorities play and why. Also discussed is the role the public can play in pressuring station management and the need for more minorities in the higher administrative positions. [Held by the Schomburg Center - Sc Visual VRB-172]

3231. <u>Positively Black: The Role of Minorities in Television</u>
[Part two] [Videorecording]. New York: WNBC-TV, 1979. 28
min. Summary: Three network executives answer questions on
the relationship of the network to local stations, the options
available to network affiliates, the ways minorities can
become a more integral part of programming and the
opportunities for minorities in the television industry.
[Held by the Schomburg Center - Sc Visual VRB-173]

3232. <u>Straight Talk: Blacks in Television</u> [videorecording].
New York: WOR-TV, 1981. 55 min. Summary: This episode is
made up of three segments. First, TV producer Gil Noble talks
about himself and his work. Noble comments on the lack of
blacks in decision making positions in the broadcast industry
and the impact this has on television broadcasting. Secondly,
Noble is joined by Mel Watkins of the New York Times and they
discuss the portrayal of blacks on television. Third, a
discussion on the need for a directory of minority performers
with Lorrie Davis, actress and president of the Minority
Performers Guide Inc., musician Neal Tate and actor Joey
Ginza. [Held by the Schomburg Center - Sc Visual VRB-283]

Black Entertainment Television

3233. Arlen, Gary. "A Good BET." <u>American Film</u> (July-August
1980): 12+.

3234. Beck, Kirsten. "BET faces music, comes up with talk;
BET survived nine years with lots of paid programming and
music videos. Now they're serious about original shows."
<u>Channels: The Business of Communications</u> (June 1989): 58-60.

3235. "Black Cable Network Prospers in 500 Systems." <u>Jet</u>
(December 2 1985): 34.

3236. Black Entertainment Television - Clippings [Billy Rose
Theatre Collection]

3237. Osborne, Karen. "BET: tuning into viewers." <u>Black
Enterprise</u> (April 1989): 24.

3238. Smikle, Ken, and Udayan Gupta. "The Best Bet in Cable;
lucrative partnerships and improved programming signal
continued growth for Bob Johnson's cable network." <u>Black
Enterprise</u> (November 1985): 60-64.

3239. Trescott, Jacqueline. "This BET hasn't paid off -
yet." <u>TV Guide</u> (October 12 1985): 53-55. Discussion of the
Black Entertainment Television company.

3240. Williams, Christopher C. "A Black Network Makes Its
Move: Cable's BET puts plenty of ambition into its fall
schedule." <u>New York Times</u> (September 17 1989): Sec. 3, p. 4.

Community Television Network

3241. "Black-Owned Network to Link TV in 14 Cities." <u>New
York Times</u> (September 16 1980): C16.

3242. "First black-owned TV network planned." _Jet_ (October 2 1980): 16.

Black Cast or Race-Theme TV Series and Specials

AMEN (1986-)

3243. Bogle, Donald. _Blacks in American Films and Television_. New York: Garland Pub., 1988, pp. 249-250.

Articles

3244. Amen - Clippings [Billy Rose Theatre Collection]

3245. "Amen." _Variety_ (October 8 1986): 136, 138.

3246. Gardella, Kay. "Gospel Truth: 'Amen' is Funny." New York _Daily News_ (September 26 1986): 67.

3247. Jones, Debra. "Black Clergy Fair Game for Sitcoms?" New York _Amsterdam News_ (October 18 1986): 26.

3248. Merrill, Don. "Review: Amen." _TV Guide_ (December 27 1986): 1.

AMOS 'N' ANDY (1951-1953)

3249. Andrews, Bart, and Ahrgus Juilliard. _Holy Mackerel!: the Amos 'n' Andy Story_. New York: E.P. Dutton, 1986. 188p.

3250. Bogle, Donald. _Blacks in American Films and Television_. New York: Garland Pub., 1988, pp. 250-254.

Articles

3251. "Amos 'n' Andy on Television." _Ebony_ (May 1951): 21-22, 24.

3252. "'Amos 'n' Andy' revival urged by BET viewers." _Television-Radio Age_ (February 16 1987): 28.

3253. Bohn, William E. "The Home Front: 'Amos 'n' Andy' and the NAACP." _The New Leader_ (August 13 1951): 5.

3254. Clayton, Edward T. "The Tragedy of Amos 'n' Andy. Show made originators rich, Negro actors got little." _Ebony_ (October 1961): 66-68, 70, 72-73.

3255. Henry, William A. III. "Buried Treasure." _Channels of Communications_ (July-August 1986): 63. Production history and criticism of 'Amos 'n' Andy'.

3256. "NAACP still opposing "Amos 'n' Andy" show." _Jet_ (May 30 1983): 55.

3257. Slater, Jack. "History." _Emmy_, Vol. 7, No. 1 (January/ February 1985): 46-49. History of 'Amos 'n' Andy'.

3258.   Temple, Mary.   "Amos 'n' Andy in Search of Themselves."
Radio Nostalgia, No. 4 (1973?): 35-37.

3259.   Washington, Chester L.   "Amos 'n' Andy TV show has
brilliant all-Negro Talent..."   Color (June 1951): 42-43.

Newspaper Articles

3260.   "Amos 'n' Andy Set to Begin on Video; CBS network will
carry show starting in June - All-Negro Cast Already Chosen."
New York Times (January 31 1951).

3261.   Amos 'n' Andy (tele) - Clippings [Billy Rose Theatre
Collection]

3262.   Brown, Harold.   "Television: Five-Year Hunt Finds New
Amos 'n' Andy."   New York Herald Tribune (June 24 1951): Sec.
4, p. 7.   On the search for the television cast of Amos 'n'
Andy.

3263.   "Fed. Judge Blacks CBS In 'Amos 'n' Andy' Suit."
Variety (August 12 1987): 101.

3264.   Gerard, Jeremy.   "TV Notes: 'Amos 'n' Andy': for CBS, a
continuing albatross."   New York Times (February 9 1989): C24.

3265.   Giddins, Gary.   (On the announcement of the successful
legal battle of Stephen M. Silverman to win the rights to
adapt TV's Amos 'n' Andy as a Broadway musical).   Village
Voice (March 7 1989).

3266.   Hinckley, David.   "Amos 'n' Andy return and with them,
the debate about their portrayal of blacks."   New York Daily
News (August 7 1986): 55.

3267.   "It's not the last laugh for 'Amos 'n' Andy."
Christian Science Monitor (November 29 1989): 13.

3268.   Margolick, David.   "Writer Sues to Make 'Amos 'n' Andy'
a Musical."   New York Times (September 5 1985): C17.

3269.   "Negro Thesps Score NAACP on A & A Stand; Set 'Positive
Action' Council."   Variety (August 8 1951).   On a Black actors
group set up to defend the Amos 'n' Andy show against the
anti-Amos 'n' Andy stand taken by the NAACP.

3270.   "No Stage for 'Amos 'n' Andy."   New York Newsday
(August 5 1987): Sec. 2, p. 10.

3271.   "Notes on TV: Video's 'Amos 'n' Andy' Inferior to Radio
Version."   Cue (July 14 1951): 22.

3272.   "Split Decision in Amos 'n' Andy Suit."   Variety (April
23 1986).

3273.   Squiers, Deborah.   "Amos 'n' Andy Trademarks
Invalidated."   New York Law Journal (February 8 1989): 1-2.

Media Materials

3274. Amos 'n' Andy: Anatomy of a Controversy (1983) [video].
55 min. Documentary produced by Michael R. Avery.

3275. "'Amos 'n' Andy' Comedy Spec Gets Reborn as a Docu."
Variety (March 23 1983): 48. [Review]

AUTOBIOGRAPHY OF MISS JANE PITTMAN (1974)

3276. Bogle, Donald. Blacks in American Films and
Television. New York: Garland Pub., 1988, pp. 315-317.

3277. Gaines, Ernest J. The Autobiography of Miss Jane
Pittman. New York: Dial Press, 1971. 245p.

3278. Wynn, Tracy Keenan. The Autobiography of Miss Jane
Pittman: screenplay; from the novel by Ernest Gaines. Los
Angeles: Barbara's Place, 1973. 135p. Typescript. [Held by
the Billy Rose Theatre Collection - NCOI+ 88-2096]

Articles

3279. Autobiography of Miss Jane Pittman - Clippings [Billy
Rose Theatre Collection]

3280. Crist, Judith. "To Set the Tube Aglow." New York
(January 28 1974): 58-59.

3281. Giovanni, Nikki. "'Jane Pittman' Fulfilled My Deepest
Expectations." New York Times (March 3 1974): Sec. 2, p. 17.
Response to Harrington article below (# 3282).

3282. Harrington, Stephanie. "Did 'Jane Pittman' Really Show
Us Black History?" New York Times (February 10 1974): Sec. 2,
p. 17.

3283. Hunter, Charlayne. "'Jane' Show: Tale of Hope and
Efforts." New York Times (January 31 1974): 68.

3284. Kael, Pauline. "The Current Cinema: Cicely Tyson Goes
to the Fountain." New Yorker (January 28 1974): 73-75.

3285. O'Connor, John. "TV: Splendid 'Jane Pittman' Relates
Black History." New York Times (January 31 1974): 67.

3286. "Two Opionions on 'Jane Pittman'." New York Amsterdam
News (February 9 1974): D-11. Pro (Angela E. Smith) and Con
(Wesley Brown).

3287. Unger, Arthur. "110-year walk to a fountain."
Christian Science Monitor (January 30 1974): F6.

3288. Wilkins, Roy. "Cheers for 'Miss Jane'." New York Post
(February 16 1974): 33.

GENERATIONS (1989-   )

3289. Bianculli, David. "Soap's a Spoof." <u>New York Post</u> (March 28 1989): 81.

3290. Birnbaum, Jesse. "A Soap Goes Black and White; NBC unveils an interracial daytime serial, Generations." <u>Time</u> (March 27 1989): 85.

3291. Gardella, Kay. "More Than Black and White; New NBC soap opera will look at 'Generations'." New York <u>Daily News</u> (March 14 1989): 92.

3292. Kitman, Marvin. "Soap Opera Whys." New York <u>Newsday</u> (April 3 1989): Sec. II, pp. 7, 11.

3293. Mackenzie, Robert. "Review: Generations." <u>TV Guide</u> (May 27 1989): 29.

3294. O'Connor, John J. "Review/Television: A New Ingredient, Race, Spices a Formula." <u>New York Times</u> (April 3 1989): C22.

3295. Torchin, Mimi. "Black Family Shares Spotlight in a New Soap Opera." <u>New York Times</u> (March 26 1989): Sec. 2, p. 27, 31. Discussion of the new integrated soap "Generations" and the economic realities behind its entry into the TV lineup.

GOOD TIMES (1974-1979)

3296. Bogle, Donald. <u>Blacks in American Films and Television</u>. New York: Garland Pub., 1988, pp. 275-277.

Articles

3297. "Bad Times on the 'Good Times' Set." <u>Ebony</u> (September 1975).

3298. Good Times - Clippings [Billy Rose Theatre Collection]

3299. Hazziezah. "Good Times: the making of a positive black comedy or fun at any cost." New York <u>Amsterdam News</u> (December 4 1976): D10-D11.

THE JEFFERSONS (1975-1985)

3300. Bogle, Donald. <u>Blacks in American Films and Television</u>. New York: Garland Pub., 1988, pp. 282-284.

Articles

3301. "'The Jeffersons' Becomes No. 1 TV Show." <u>Jet</u> (August 27 1981).

3302. The Jeffersons - Clippings [Billy Rose Theatre Collection]

3303. Katleman, Rita. "The Jeffersons: Up in the High-Rent (and High-Ratings) District." TV Showpeople (June 1975): 15-17.

3304. Robinson, Louie. "The Jeffersons: A look at life on black America's new 'Striver's Row'." Ebony (January 1976): 112+.

3305. Washington, Mary Helen. "As Their Blackness Disappears, So Does Their Character; the author says that with race becoming less and less of a factor on The Jeffersons, the series is losing its humor and vitality." TV Guide (July 30 1983): 4+.

ROOTS (1977)

3306. Bogle, Donald. Blacks in American Films and Television. New York: Garland Pub., 1988, pp. 337-343.

3307. Haley, Alex. Roots. Garden City, NY: Doubleday, 1976. 587p.

3308. Miami-Dade Community College. Instructional Guide for a Unique History Course Based on Roots. Miami: The College, 1976. 1 v. (various pagings).

Articles

3309. Hays, Scott. "Roots was a breakthrough, but look what happened to its stars; Almost 10 years after the miniseries made TV history, some of its performers find many Hollywood racial barriers still in place." TV Guide (November 29 1986): 10+.

3310. Journal of Broadcasting, Vol. 22, No. 3 (Summer 1978). Special issue on Roots.

3311. Marill, A. H. "Films on TV." Films in Review (June/July 1977): 359-362.

3312. Roots - Clippings (includes a teaching guide for the series) [Billy Rose Theatre Collection]

3313. Roots - Clippings (1977-1979) (MFL + n.c. 2636) (includes innumerable newspaper articles and reviews) [Billy Rose Theatre Collection]

3314. Roots - Scrapbook (MWEZ + n.c. 26, 071) [Billy Rose Theatre Collection]

3315. "Why 'Roots' Hit Home." Time (February 14 1977): 68-71.

3316. Zito, Stephen. "Out of Africa; Alex Haley's Roots, a search for black origins, is headed for twelve groundbreaking hours on network television." American Film (October 1976): 8+.

Media Materials

3317. <u>Black Journal: A Visit with Alex Haley</u> [videorecording].
New York: WNET/Educational Broadcasting Corp., 1977. 29 min.
Host: Tony Brown. Author Alex Haley talks about the
motivating factors and emotional experiences involved in
writing "Roots." He also tells of his experiences since the
broadcast of the TV mini-series based on his novel. [Held by
the Schomburg Center - Sc Visual VRB-11]

3318. <u>Roots - Myth or Reality</u>? (audiotape). New York:
Institute of Afro-American Affairs, 1977(?). 111 min. From a
panel discussion, held at New York University, concerning Alex
Haley's book Roots. Panelists include Elliott Skinner, Eric
Perkins, Eric Foner and Basil Patterson. A question and
answer period follows the presentation. [Held by the
Schomburg Center - Sc Audio C-234 (Sides 1 and 2) and Sc Audio
C-235 (Side 1, no. 1)]

ROOTS: THE NEXT GENERATIONS (1979)

3319. Bogle, Donald. <u>Blacks in American Films and
Television</u>. New York: Garland Pub., 1988, pp. 343-345.

Articles

3320. Davidson, Bill. "A Tough Act to Follow." <u>TV Guide</u>
(February 17 1979): 4+.

3321. Haddad, M. George. "Roots: The Next Generations."
<u>Black Stars</u> (March 1979): 71-74.

3322. Meyer, Karl E. "Television: TV's Little White Lies."
<u>Saturday Review</u> (June 23 1979): 32.

3323. Rich, Frank. "Television: A Super Sequel to Haley's
Comet." <u>Time</u> (February 19 1979): 84+.

3324. Waters, Harry F. "Back to 'Roots'." <u>Newsweek</u>
(February 19 1979): 85-87.

Newspaper Articles

3325. Fraser, C. Gerald. "Few Offers Accrue to Actors in
'Roots'." <u>New York Times</u> (March 18 1979): 46.

3326. Maslin, Janet. "TV: End of 'Roots II' Delineates
60's." <u>New York Times</u> (February 25 1979): 46.

3327. O'Connor, John J. "Strong 'Roots' Continues Black
Odyssey." <u>New York Times</u> (February 16 1979): C1, C27.

3328. Roots: The Next Generations - Clippings [Billy Rose
Theatre Collection]

3329. Roots: The Next Generations - Clippings (MWEZ + n.c.
26,072) [Billy Rose Theatre Collection]

3330. Wolcott, James. "Roots II: Provocative (Zzzzzzzz)."
<u>Village Voice</u> (February 19 1979): 54.

227 (1985-   )

3331. Bogle, Donald. <u>Blacks in American Films and
Television</u>. New York: Garland Pub., 1988, pp. 308-309.

3332. "Sex, sass and laughs keep "227" TV show a smash hit."
<u>Jet</u> (August 24 1987): 56+.

UP AND COMING (1981)

3333. "Black Family Breakthrough in Public TV. New series
portrayal of Blacks earns critical acclaim." <u>Ebony</u> (February
1981): 74+. Profile of TV show "Up and Coming."

WHAT'S HAPPENING!! (1976-1979)

3334. Bogle, Donald. <u>Blacks in American Films and
Television</u>. New York: Garland Pub., 1988, pp. 310-311.

3335. Lardine, Bob. "In TV, the 'in' color is black." New
York <u>Sunday News</u> (February 20 1977): Sec. 3, pp. 1, 12.

3336. "What's Happening!! ABC's popular teen-age sitcom
succeeds in spite of itself." <u>Ebony</u> (June 1978): 74+.

VI

THE BLACK PERFORMER

GENERAL WORKS

3337. "The Black Entertainer in the Performing Arts." In The Negro Almanac: A Reference Work on the Afro American, ed. Harry A. Ploski and James Williams. 4th ed. New York: John Wiley & Sons, 1983, pp. 1089-1126. Biographical sketches of a number of Black actors and entertainers.

3338. Bogle, Donald. "Author Fills History Gap of Black Actors." In Authors in the News, ed. Barbara Nykoruk. Detroit: Gale Research Co., 1976, Vol. 1, p. 51.

3339. _____. Brown Sugar: Eighty years of America's black female superstars. New York: Harmony Books, 1980. 208p.

3340. Hughes, Langston, and Milton Meltzer. Black Magic: A Pictorial History of the Negro in American Entertainment. Englewood Cliffs, NJ: Prentice-Hall, 1967. 375p.

3341. Null, Gary. Black Hollywood: The Negro in Motion Pictures. Secaucus, NJ: Citadel Press, 1984. 256p.

3342. Rhodes, Hari. The Hollow and the Human. New York: Vantage Press, 1976. 148p. Novel about Afro-American actors in Hollywood.

3343. Rollins, Charlemae Hill. Famous Negro Entertainers of Stage, Screen, and T.V. New York: Dodd, Mead, 1967. 122p.

3344. Rosenbaum, Ilene. Black Film Stars: A Picture Album. New York: Drake, 1973. 192p.

3345. Symposium on Black Images in Films, Stereotyping, and Self-Perception as Viewed by Black Actresses, Boston University, 1973. Boston: Afro-American Studies Program, Boston University), 1974. 69p. (Occasional paper; No. 2)

3346. Vance, Bobbye B. Black Starlet. Los Angeles: Holloway House Pub. Co., 1975. 215p. [Fiction]

Journals

3347. Black Hollywood. Hollywood, CA: Sonja Dunson
Productions, 1977-1979. Vol. 1, No. 1 (July 1977)--Vol. 2,
No. 11 (May 1979). "First Black casting magazine in America."

3348. Right On! 1971- . Monthly. Includes frequent
interviews and profiles of Black teen actors.

Articles

3349. "Actors Guild Offers Discount to Producers Who Hire
Minorities." Jet (September 3 1984): 17.

3350. Allen, Bonnie. "The Macho Men: Whatever Happened to
Them?" Essence (February 1979): 62-63, 90, 92, 95-96, 98-99.
Discussion of the male stars of blaxploitation films--Richard
Roundtree, Jim Kelly, Fred Williamson, Ron O'Neal and Calvin
Lockhart, and what has happened to them since the demise of
these films.

3351. Barrow, William. "A Gallery of Leading Men." Negro
Digest, Vol. 12 (October 1963): 45-48. Discussion of some of
the leading Black actors of the Sixties--Sidney Poitier, Harry
Belafonte, Ossie Davis, Brock Peters and William Marshall.

3352. "Black Actors Starred in Only 8 Films in '82." Jet
(January 3 1983): 58.

3353. "Black Stunt Men: Ex-athletes Organize to Gain Film
Roles." Ebony, Vol. 25 (December 1969): 114-122.

3354. "Black Stuntmen of Hollywood." Sepia (December 1971):
39-48. Includes a discussion of the Black Stuntmen's
Association along with interviews with several of its members
--Ernie Robinson, Peaches Jones, Eddie Smith, Henry Kingi,
Marie Louise Johnson, Evelyn Coffey, Rich Washington, Alonzo
Brown.

3355. "Blacks on 'Soaps'. Only a relative few land 'regular'
parts." Ebony (March 1978): 32+.

3356. Bourne, Stephen. "Star Equality." Films and Filming,
No. 351 (December 1983): 31-34; No. 352 (January 1984): 24-25.
On Black actresses.

3357. Burrell, Walter Price. "Reuben Cannon: Hollywood
Studios First Black Casting Director." Black Stars (April
1975): 48-54.

3358. Carmen. "A Letter from Hollywood." The Bronzeman
(193?-1932). Regular column detailing the activities of white
and Black actors in Hollywood during the early 1930s.

3359. Cieutat, Michel. "Actors Noirs: Les Nouveaux Acteurs
Noirs Americains ou la Poetique de l'Insolence." Positif, No.
313 (Mars 1987): 25-29.

3360. Collier, Aldore. "The Year of the Black Male in Films." Ebony, Vol. 38 (August 1983): 168+.

3361. Corliss, Richard. "Blues for Black Actors; America's Largest Minority Seeks Roles and Role Models." Time (October 1 1984): 75-76.

3362. Covington, Floyd C. "The Negro Invades Hollywood." Opportunity (April 1929): 111-113, 131. On the increase in opportunities for African American extras in Hollywood films. Includes statistics.

3363. Dee, Ruby. "The Tattered Queens." Negro Digest, Vol. 15 (April 1966): 32-36. Discusses status of the Black actress in Hollywood.

3364. Deleihbur, Don. "Stardom 'for Negroes Only'." Negro Digest, Vol. 3 (November 1944): 87-88.

3365. "Do Negroes Have a Future in Hollywood?" Ebony, Vol. 11 (December 1955): 24, 27-30.

3366. Gipson, Gertrude. "The ABC's of Movieland." Our World (September 1952): 60-64. On Black extras in Hollywood.

3367. Goodwin, Ruby B. "Negro Children in Hollywood." The Bronzeman (December 1931): 27-29. Discussion of child actors Sunshine Sammy (Ernie Morrison), Little Mango, Farina (Allen Hoskins), Eugene Jackson, Stymie (Mathew Beard), Doris and Haroldetta Garrison, Dorothy Morrison and Walter Tate.

3368. Green, Theophilus. "The Black Man as Movie Hero. New films offer a different male image." Ebony (August 1972): 144+.

3369. "Hollywood's Most Sought After Man. Reuben Cannon turns unknown into well-known." Ebony (July 1980): 62+. Profile of Hollywood's leading Black casting director.

3370. "Hollywood's New Black Beauties." Sepia, Vol. 22 (March 1973): 37-44. Profile of the leading Black actresses of the Seventies--Lola Falana, Brenda Sykes, Cicely Tyson, Diana Ross, Mae Mercer, Kathy Imrie, Paula Kelly, Rosalind Cash, Vonetta McGee, Freda Payne, Diana Sands, Lisa Moore, Denise Nicholas, Judy Pace, Margaret Ware.

3371. "Hollywood's New Breed. Negro actors are flatly refusing role of 'clown.'" Sepia (June 1963): 20-25.

3372. Horton, Luci. "The Battle among the Beauties. Black actresses vie for top movie roles." Ebony (November 1973): 144-146. Article on female film stars of the Black film boom --Vonetta McGee, Pam Grier, Gloria Hendry, and Tamara Dobson.

3373. "How to Survive in Hollywood Between Gigs." Ebony
(October 1978): 33-36+. Includes brief profiles of John Amos,
Jim Brown, Clifton Davis, Tamara Dobson, Gail Fisher, Pam
Grier, Jim Kelly, Yaphet Kotto, Vonetta McGee, Theresa
Merritt, Greg Morris, Nichelle Nichols, Brock Peters, Beah
Richards, Richard Roundtree, Raymond St. Jacques, Cicely
Tyson, and Fred Williamson.

3374. "Integration Showcase: Actors Equity Association
Performs for Producers, Urges More Roles for Negroes." Ebony,
Vol. 14 (August 1959): 71-74.

3375. "Is Hollywood Afraid to Star a Sexy Black Actress?"
Sepia, Vol. 18 (June 1969): 10-15.

3376. Locher, Mark. "Performers of Color: Breaking Through."
Screen Actor (Fall 1988): 12-15.

3377. Marsh, Antoinette. "Former TV Stars: Where Are They
Now?" Black Stars (March 1978): 48-51. Brief sketches of the
careers of Chelsea Brown, Le Var Burton, Marc Copage, Terry
Carter, Teresa Graves, Diahann Carroll, Lloyd Haynes, Whitman
Mayo, Nichelle Nichols, Adam Wade, Hal Williams, Flip Wilson,
Lisle Wilson.

3378. Marshall, Marilyn. "Hollywood's Hottest Hunks." Ebony
(November 1988): 33+.

3379. Mattox, Michael. "The Day Black Movie Stars Got
Militant." Black Creation, No. 4 (Winter 1973): 40-42.

3380. "NAACP vs. Hollywood. Hard-hitting organization waged
nation-wide campaign to get equal oppportunies for all in
movies and TV." Sepia (March 1964): 66-71.

3381. "Negro Actors in Dramatic Roles." America, Vol. 115
(September 17 1966): 298-300.

3382. "The New Wave of Black Starlets." Ebony (March 1989):
29+. Profiles of Dawnn Lewis, Olivia Brown, Holly Robinson,
Jasmine Guy, Cat, Vanessa Bell Calloway, Shari Headley, Tracy
Camila Johns, Tisha Campbell, Kimberly Russell and Tatiana
Thumbtzen.

3383. Robb, David. "Growing number of lead roles going to
Black actresses, SAG reports." Variety (April 19 1989): 18.

3384. _____. "Minority Actors Are Still Slighted Says a
Report by SAG-AFTRA." Variety (June 4 1986): 2-4.

3385. Robinson, Louie. "Have Blacks Really Made It In
Hollywood? New films increase job prospects but most stars
still have problems." Ebony (June 1975): 33-36, 38, 40, 42.

3386. _____. "The Jeffersons. TV show tells of life on
Black America's new 'Strivers Row'." Ebony (January 1976):
112-115. Profiles of the show's stars - Zara Cully, Damon
Evans, Sherman Hemsley, Roxie Roker, Isabel Sanford, Berlinda
Tolbert.

3387. "'Roots' Dug Deep into the Lives of its Stars, and
Careers are Blossoming Out." People (February 21 1977): 26-
30. Includes brief biographical sketches of "Roots" stars
John Amos, LeVar Burton, Olivia Cole, Madge Sinclair and Ben
Vereen.

3388. Selznick, David O. "Negro Lobby in Hollywood." Negro
Digest, Vol. 4 (August 1946): 27-28.

3389. Slater, Jack. "Hollywood's New Black Men." Essence,
Vol. 15 (November 1984): 82-84+.

3390. _____. "The Real People Behind the Jeffersons.
Series stars offer glimpses into their off-screen lives."
Ebony (September 1980): 83+. Profiles Marla Gibbs, Sherman
Hemsley, Roxie Roker and Isabel Sanford.

3391. Welker, Robert H. "Rise of Negro Matinee Idol: New
Image of American Black." Variety (February 1961): 7.

Newspaper Articles

3392. Bernstein, Harry. "Hollywood Gives More Work, Roles to
Negro: Industry Program Also Seeks to End 'Servant' Stereotype
in Film Parts." Los Angeles Times (March 13 1966): A2.

3393. Cox, Clinton. "We Were Stars in Those Days." New York
Sunday News Magazine (March 9 1975): 15-16, 18, 26-27. On
early Black film actors and actresses.

3394. Handsaker, Gene. "Negro Employment Increases in
Films." Los Angeles Times (September 11 1967).

3395. Harmetz, Aljean. "Black Actors: 'Struggling for
Crumbs'?" New York Times (April 10 1980).

3396. "Hollywood Acts on Race Problem: Employment of Negro
Actors Shows Marked Rise." New York Times (September 21
1963): 82.

3397. McCabe, Bruce. "On and Off Camera, Blacks Get Few
Roles." The Boston Globe (April 18 1982).

3398. "The Negro Actor Asks Himself, 'Am I a Negro or Am I an
Actor?'" New York Times Magazine (October 15, 1967).

3399. "Rights Drive Spurs Casting of Negroes in Movies,
Television Shows: They Get 41 Roles in Warner's Film; NAACP
Seeks Bigger Parts, Theaters Boycott." Wall Street Journal
(September 24 1963).

Media Materials

3400. Passion and Memory (1985), dir. Roy Campanella, Jr.
Narration by Robert Guillaume. 60min. Documentary focusing
on five of the best known black actors and actresses of the
1930s-1970s - Stepin Fetchit, Hattie McDaniel, Bill Robinson,
Dorothy Dandridge and Sidney Poitier while touching on others
active during these years.

INDIVIDUAL ACTORS AND ACTRESSES

AALDA, MARIANN

3401. Hersch, Linda T. "Mariann Aalda Accentuates the
Positive." Soap Opera Digest (May 11 1982): 132-137.

3402. Marlow, Curtis. "Love in the Afternoon: Mariann Aalda,
'The Edge of Night.'" Right On! (August 1983): 40-42.

ADAMS, ROBERT (1906-   ) (Guyana/Great Britain)

3403. Films and Filming (December 1982): 44. Brief
biographical sketch of the British film actor, Robert Adams.

3404. "Two Negro Actors: Robert Adams...Orlando Martins."
Film Quarterly [London] (Spring 1947): 16-18.

AJAYE, FRANKLIN

3405. Ajaye, Franklin. "Hollywood: Fade to White?" Essence
(November 1981): 154. Personal statement by Ajaye.

3406. Burrell, Walter Price. "Franklin Ayaye: Comedy is No
Laughing Matter." Black Stars (June 1978): 60-65.

ALICE, MARY (1941-   )

3407. Basler, Barbara. "New Face: Mary Alice." New York
Times (August 10 1979).

3408. Collins, Lisa. "Mary Alice is Moving to Hollywood."
Black Stars (April 1976): 27-31.

3409. Hurley, Joseph. "Mary Alice, In Control of Her Life
and Work." New York Newsday (April 21 1987): Part II, p. 9.

3410. Shewey, Don. "Playing Around." Soho Weekly News
(December 17 1980): 34, 69. [Profile]

ALLEN, BYRON

3411. Ashley, Drew. "The Man's Real: Byron Allen Polishes
His Star." Right On! (February 1984): 68, 67.

3412. Chadwick, Bruce. "Byron Allen Does It All." New York
Daily News (March 13 1988): 22.

3413. "Lookout: Byron Allen." People (September 10 1979).

3414. Marsh, Antoinette. "Byron Allen: Black Stars Predicted
His Stardom." Black Stars (September 1980): 66-67.

3415. Slaton, Shell. "Byron Allen: The "Real People"
Person." Right On! (April 1980): 12-13.

3416. "Weekly 'Byron Allen Show' Joins Late Night Lineup."
Jet (January 30 1989): 60.

ALLEN, DEBBIE (1950-   )

3417. Bogle, Donald. Blacks in American Films and
Television. New York: Garland, 1988, pp. 353-354.

Articles

3418. "Allen, Debbie." Current Biography 1987.

3419. Banfield, Bever-Leigh. "Profile 3: A Closeup Look at
Today's Black Actress." Sepia (September 1981): 22-30.
[Debbie Allen/Tracy Reed/Vernee Watson]

3420. Eder, Bruce. "An Aquarian interview with Debbie Allen
Emmy winning star of 'Fame.'" The Aquarian (September 29-
October 6 1982): 32.

3421. Fee, Debi. "Fame's the Name of the Game!" Right On!
(May 1983): 26-27, 63.

3422. "For Debbie Allen, the price of 'Fame' is time without
her husband, CBS Exec Win Wilford." People (April 19 1982):
71-74.

3423. Hobson, Charles. "Deborah Allen: A Serious Young
Actress." Black Stars (September 1974): 32-35.

3424. Murphy, Frederick Douglas. "Debbie Allen: A Rising
Beautiful Star." Black Stars (June 1977): 22-28.

3425. _____. "Debbie Allen: A View from Within the Heart
of an Actress." Black Stars (April 1979): 6-9.

3426. Oliver, Stephanie Stokes. "Spotlight: Debbie Alen."
Essence (March 1984): 62.

3427. St. John, Michael. "Debbie Allen Swings on a Star."
Encore American and Worldwide News (October 2 1978): 26-29.

3428. "Sisters: Debbie Allen and Phylicia Rashad." McCall's
(July 1987): 90+.

ALLEN, JONELLE (1944-   )

3429. Davis, Curt. "Jonelle Allen Leaves "Verona" Behind."
Encore American and Worldwide News (October 6 1975): 35-36.

3430. Marsh, Antoinette. "Jonelle Allen: Broadway Actress
Tackles Tinseltown." Black Stars (September 1978): 20-25.

3431. Murray, James P. "Cover Story: A True Harlem
Personality." New York Amsterdam News (July 6 1974): D12-13.

AMOS, JOHN (1939-   )

See also # 3373, 3387

3432. Bogle, Donald. Blacks in American Films and
Television. New York: Garland, 1988, p. 354.

Articles

3433. Amos, John - Clippings [Billy Rose Theatre Collection]

3434. Berkow, Ira. "Even the Norfolk Neptunes Cut Him." TV Guide (August 17-23 1974): 15-16, 18.

3435. Charles, Roland M. "John Amos: A Man of Action." Black Stars (March 1975): 12-18.

3436. Jenkins, Walter. "Looking in on John Amos." Black Stars (July 1973): 56-61.

Newspaper Articles

3437. Guarino, Ann. "Filmland Touchdown." New York Daily News (November 5 1975): 42.

3438. Hale, Wanda. "Two for the Show: Wayne and a Walt Disney Film." New York Sunday News (February 4 1973): Sec. 3, p. 7. [Profile]

3439. "John Amos - A Very Private, Public Figure." New York Amsterdam News (October 22 1975): D-16.

3440. Williams, Bob. "Times Are Good for John Amos." New York Post (March 30 1977).

ANDERSON, EDDIE "ROCHESTER" (1906-1977)

3441. Bogle, Donald. Blacks in American Films and Television. New York: Garland, 1988, pp. 354-356.

Articles

3442. Anderson, Eddie - Clippings [Billy Rose Theatre Collection]

3443. "Benny and Rochester: TV's Hottest Team." Our World (August 1955): 51-55.

3444. Muir, Florabel. "What's That Boss?" Saturday Evening Post (June 19 1943): 15, 105-106.

3445. "Rochester in London." Our World (November 1950): 20-24.

Obituaries

3446. "Eddie Anderson, 71, Dies; Noted for His Role of Rochester." Variety (March 2 1977): 50.

3447. "Eddie (Rochester) Anderson dies at 72." New York Post (March 1 1977).

3448. "Remembrance of Things Past: Eddie Anderson--Radio's Raspy 'Rochester'." Encore American and Worldwide News (May 9 1977): 3.

3449. Tapley, Mel. "Eddie Rochester Dies in Los Angeles at 71." New York Amsterdam News (March 5 1977): A-3.

3450. Thomas, Robert McG. "Eddie Anderson, 71, Benny's Rochester." New York Times (March 1 1977).

ANDREWS, TINA

3451. Andrews, Tina - Clippings [Billy Rose Theatre Collection]

3452. Burrell, Walter Price. "'Conrack' Brings Stardom to Tina Andrews." Black Stars (June 1974): 20-26.

3453. Clay, Stanley. "Actor to Actor. Tina Andrews: She Means Business!!!" Right On! (March 1978): 36-37.

3454. Collins, Lisa. "Tina Andrews: Days of Her Life." Black Stars (January 1979): 20-23.

3455. Simms, Gregory. "Tina Andrews: A Star Glowing Ever Brighter." Black Stars (March 1977): 40-45.

ARCHEY, MARLON

3456. Paige, Anthony Carter. "From the Gridiron to TV." City Sun (February 14-20 1990): 35.

ATTAWAY, RUTH (c.1910-1987)

3457. Attaway, Ruth - Clippings [Billy Rose Theatre Collection]

3458. "Attaway Went Thataway." Sepia Record (March 1953): 16-19.

3459. "Ruth Attaway, Actress, Dies of Injuries in Apartment Fire." New York Times (September 24 1987).

AVERY, MARGARET

3460. Bogle, Donald. Blacks in American Films and Television. New York: Garland, 1988, p. 356.

Articles

3461. Collier, Aldore. "Margaret Avery says she 'couldn't buy a job' before 'The Color Purple'." Jet (March 10 1986): 58.

3462. "Margaret Avery: Anatomy of an Actress." Black Stars (April 1976): 68-73.

3463. Oliver, Stephanie Stokes. "Margaret 'Shug' Avery, Beyond 'The Color Purple.'" Essence (September 1986): 118-120, 140.

3464. "What a Sweet Role! The role of "Shug" in The Color
Purple brings Margaret Avery's illustrious career back to
life." Right On! (May 1986): 46-47.

BAILEY, PEARL (1918-   )

3465. Bailey, Pearl. Between You and Me. New York:
Doubleday, 1989. 270p.

3466. _____. Hurry Up, America, & Spit. New York:
Harcourt Brace Jovanovich, 1976. 106p.

3467. _____. The Raw Pearl. New York: Harcourt, Brace &
World, 1968. 206p.

3468. _____. Talking to Myself. New York: Harcourt
Brace Jovanovich, 1971. 233p.

3469. Bogle, Donald. Blacks in American Films and
Television. New York: Garland, 1988, pp. 356-357.

Articles

3470. "Bailey, Pearl." Current Biography 1969.

3471. Black, Doris. "The Pearl Bailey Nobody Knows." Sepia,
Vol. 20 (April 1971): 54-61.

3472. Davidson, Bill. "Pearl Bailey says 'Hello' to TV; a
backstage account of how the singer launched her Saturday
night show." TV Guide (March 27 1971): 40+. [Pearl Bailey
Show]

3473. "Hollywood Debut for Pearl Bailey." Ebony, Vol. 2
(April 1947): 38-39.

BAIRD, HARRY (c.1932-   ) (Guyana/Great Britain)

3474. "On the Threshold of Fame." Flamingo [London] (March
1964): 41-42.

BAKER, JOSEPHINE (1906-1975)

3475. Baker, Josephine. Les Memoires de Josephine Baker.
Recueillis et adaptes par Marcel Sauvage. Paris: Kra, 1927.
186p.

3476. _____, and Jo Bouillon. Josephine. Trans. from
the French by Mariana Fitzpatrick. New York: Harper & Row,
1977. 293p. (Orig. 1976).

3477. Haney, Lynn. Naked at the Feast: A Biography of
Josephine Baker. New York: Dodd, Mead, 1981. 338p.

3478. Haskins, Jim, and Kathleen Benson. "Baker, Josephine."
In Notable American Women: The Modern Period, eds. Barbara
Sicherman and Carol Hurd Green. Cambridge, MA: The Belknap
Press, 1980, pp. 40-41.

3479. Papich, Stephen. Remembering Josephine Baker.
Indianapolis: Bobbs-Merrill, 1976. 237p.

3480. Rose, Phyllis. Jazz Cleopatra: Josephine Baker in Her
Time. New York: Doubleday, 1989. 321p.

Articles

3481. "Baker, Josephine." Current Biography 1964.

3482. Gates, Henry Louis. "An Interview with Josephine Baker
and James Baldwin." The Southern Review, Vol. 21 (July 1985):
594-602.

3483. "Josephine Baker's Adopted Children Sell Her Last
Valuables at Public Auction." Jet (June 15 1987): 26-28.

3484. Taubin, Amy. Village Voice (February 14 1989). Review
of two Baker film features - "Princess Tam-Tam" (1934) and
"Zou-Zou" (1935).

Media Materials

3485. Josephine Baker: Chasing a Rainbow. British
documentary.

BANKOLE, ISAACH DE (Ivory Coast)

3486. Bourdain, G. S. "New Face: Isaach de Bankole; An
Actor's Road Taken to Cameroon of 'Chocolat.'" New York Times
(March 24 1989): C15. [Profile]

BASKETT, JAMES (1904-1948)

3487. "James Baskett." Variety (July 14 1948). [Obituary]

3488. "James Baskett, 44, Screen, Radio Actor." New York
Times (July 10 1948). [Obituary]

BASS, KIM

3489. "An American Export: young actor becomes TV star in
Japan: Kim Bass reaches the top and finds fame in Tokyo."
Ebony (September 1982): 48-50, 52.

BEARD, MATHEW "STYMIE" (1925-1981)

See also # 3367

3490. Bogle, Donald. Blacks in American Films and
Television. New York: Garland, 1988, pp. 357-358.

Articles

3491. Bann, Richard W. "Our Gang's Free Wheeling 'Stymie.'"
Blackhawk Film Digest (March 1979): 74.

3492. Jacques, Hal. "Our Gang's Stymie is Back in Movies
After Beating Drug Habit." National Enquirer (Marc 17 1974).

3493. "Mathew (Stymie) Beard." _Ebony_ (January 1975): 134.

Obituaries

3494. "Mathew Beard." _Variety_ (February 11 1981).

3495. "Mathew (Stymie) Beard." _Newsweek_ (January 19 1981): 63.

3496. _New York Times_ (January 9 1981): B6.

3497. "Rites held for 'Stymie' Beard of 'Our Gang'." _Jet_ (January 29 1981): 80.

3498. "'Stymie' Dies at 56." _New York Post_ (January 9 1981).

3499. Wilson, Alfred. "In Memoriam: Mathew 'Stymie' Beard." _Right On!_ (May 1981): 24-25.

BEAVERS, LOUISE (1902-1962)

3500. Bogle, Donald. _Blacks in American Films and Television_. New York: Garland, 1988, pp. 358-360.

Obituaries

3501. _New York Times_ (October 27 1962): 25.

3502. _Time_ (November 2 1962): 84.

3503. _Variety_ (October 31 1962).

BELAFONTE, HARRY (1927-   )

See also # 3351

3504. Bogle, Donald. _Blacks in American Films and Television_. New York: Garland, 1988, pp. 360-361.

3505. Shaw, Arnold. _Belafonte; an unauthorized biography_. Philadelphia: Chilton Book Co., 1960. 338p.

Articles

3506. Belafonte, Harry. "Belafonte: 'Look,' they tell me, 'don't rock the boat; play nice guy, play dead or maybe play a super-Negro who beats up communists'." _New York Times_ (April 21 1968).

3507. "Belafonte, Harry." _Current Biography 1956_.

3508. "Island in the Sun: Dandridge and Belafonte star in romantic interracial film." _Ebony_ (July 1957): 32-37.

3509. Morley, Sheridan. "Control and Conscience." _Films and Filming_ (September 1972): 26-27. [Interview]

3510. "See How They Run: New movie team, Dorothy Dandridge and Harry Belafonte, score in touching drama." _Our World_ (November 1952): 10, 12.

Newspaper Articles

3511. Belafonte, Harry - Clippings [Billy Rose Theatre Collection]

3512. Belafonte, Harry - Clippings (MWEZ + n.c. 17,914) [Billy Rose Theatre Collection]

3513. Belafonte, Harry - Clippings (MWEZ + n.c. 26,705) [Billy Rose Theatre Collection]

Media Materials

3514. <u>Dick Cavett Show. Harry Belafonte</u> (videorecording). New York: WNET/13, 1981. 58 min. [Held by the Schomburg Collection - Sc Visual VRB-51]

3515. <u>Like It Is: Harry Belafonte...Looking Back</u>. 2-parts. Original TV broadcast February 4 and 11, 1979.

BELL, JEANNE (c.1944-   )

3516. "Jeanne Bell: Pin-Up Model to Film Star." <u>Jet</u> (February 5 1976): 58-61.

BENJAMIN, PAUL

3517. Benjamin, Paul - Clippings [Billy Rose Theatre Collection]

BERNARD, ED (1939-   )

3518. Bernard, Ed - Clippings [Billy Rose Theatre Collection]

BERRINGS, HANK

3519. Rankin, Edwina L. "Hank Berrings: A Different Kind of Actor." <u>Black Stars</u> (May 1977): 66-69.

BERRY, FRED

3520. Martinez, Al and Joanne. "Instant Rerun; The producers of What's Happening!! were ready to cast a thin, white actor-until they met Fred Berry." <u>TV Guide</u> (April 2 1977): 8+.

BEST, WILLIE (1915-1962)

3521. Bogle, Donald. <u>Blacks in American Films and Television</u>. New York: Garland, 1988, pp. 361-362.

3522. "The Screen in Review: Out-Draggin Stepin." <u>Headlines and Pictures</u> (July 1946): 39.

3523. "Willie Best." <u>Variety</u> (March 7 1962). [Obituary]

BEYER, TROY

3524. Collier, Aldore. "'Dynasty's' Troy Beyer tells how fame helps and hurts." <u>Jet</u> (August 11 1986): 58+.

3525. Tapley, Mel. "Troy Beyer: Meet Diahann Carroll's 'Dynasty' Daughter." New York Amsterdam News (December 7 1985): 45.

3526. "Troy Beyer: More Than Meets the Eye." Ebony (December 1987): 102.

3527. Wallace, David. "Dynasty's Troy Beyer Credits Ex-Baby-Sitter Whoopi Goldberg for Giving Her a Leg Up on Success." People (March 24 1986).

BLACKMAN, DON (d.1977)

3528. "Black Samson. Bible-reading strongman, who once held world's wrestling championship, is promising actor." Our World (March 1954): 10, 12-13.

3529. "Don Blackman." Variety (September 21 1977): 111. [Obituary]

3530. "Don Blackman's Big Role in 'Santiago'. Ex-wrestler gives best performance of career in film on Cuban revolution." Color (August 1956): 7-9.

BLACQUE, TAUREAN

3531. Harvey, Almena Ruth. "Interview: Taurean Blacque Talks Back." Right On! (May 1981): 32-33.

3532. "Never Too Late To Become a Star." Right On! (June 1984): 59.

3533. Nolan, Tom. "He Pushed for the Toothpick and Beard--and That's All." TV Guide (February 14 1987): 39-42.

3534. Sanz, Cynthia, and Lois Armstrong. "Tube: With Two Houses and a Big Heart, Generations Star Taurean Blacque Becomes a Single Father to Nine." People (October 9 1989): 101-102, 104.

BLEDSOE, TEMPESTT

3535. Collier, Aldore. "Clifton Davis and Tempestt Bledsoe star in TV movie." Jet (October 16 1989): 22+. [Dream Date]

3536. "Growing Up on T.V.: Tempestt Bledsoe." Teen Magazine (November 1987): 64.

3537. Horner, Cynthia. "Chatting with Tempestt!" Right On! (February 1988): 16-18.

3538. Kimble, Sonya R. "A Tempestt in Cosby's Teacup!" Right On! (March 1986): 28-29.

3539. Polskin, Howard. "At 15 ... she had the clout to can the beer scene: Tempestt Bledsoe knows what's right for her and how to get it .. as she proved on location for 'Dream Date'." TV Guide (October 7 1989): 24-26.

BOND, JAMES III

3540. Marsh, Antoinette. "The Real James Bond, III."   Black Stars (May 1978): 66-67.

BONET, LISA

3541. Barol, Bill. "Lisa Bonet's Double Image." Newsweek (March 23 1987): 49.

3542. Ellis, Trey. "Lisa Bonet." Interview (April 1987): 42+.

3543. "Lisa Bonet." Harper's Bazaar (September 1986): 104.

3544. "Lisa Bonet finds new success in 'A Different World.'" Jet (October 26 1987): 54-55.

3545. "Lisa Bonet: The growing pains of a rising star." Ebony (December 1987): 150+.

3546. "Lisa Bonet: on her own." Ladies Home Journal (November 1987): 60-61.

3547. "Lisa Bonet: a very private person." Seventeen (April 1987): 79-81.

3548. Sinclair, Abiola. "Media Watch: Huxtable Daughter in Shameful Skin Flick." New York Amsterdam News (March 7 1987): 23, 31.

3549. _____. "Wedding Bells for Celebrity Kids." New York Amsterdam News (December 19 1987): 30.

BOWMAN, LAURA (1881-1957)

3550. Antoine, Le Roi. Achievement: The Life of Laura Bowman. New York: Pageant Press, 1961. 439p. [Biography]

3551. "Laura Bowman." Variety (April 3 1957). [Obituary]

3552. New York Times (March 31 1957): 89.

BRIDGES, TODD

3553. Ashley, Drew. "Todd's Best Friend Marcus Tells All!" Right On! (December 1983): 26-28.

3554. "Bail is set at $2 mil. for Bridges; Faces more charges." Jet (March 20 1989): 12. On charges facing Bridges after his shooting of a crack dealer.

3555. Brower, Montgomery. "Racial Harassment and Violence Shatter the Diff'rent Strokes World of Actor Todd Bridges." People (December 5 1983): 46+.

3556. Horner, Cynthia. "Tall, Tan and Tempting." Right On! (June 1983): 40-45.

3557.   Marsh, Antoinette.   "Gary Coleman and Todd Bridges: Little Kids with Big Minds."   Black Stars (March 1979): 40-45.

3558.   _____.   "Todd Bridges: Older is Better."   Black Stars (June 1979): 6-10.

3559.   Pitts, Leonard, Jr.   "What Will Happen to Todd Bridges? The Continuing Saga in the Perils of this Actor's Life." Right On! (May 1984): 30-31.

3560.   Samuels, Ashley, and Erik Sterling.   "Black Stars Visits Todd Bridges."   Black Stars (September 1980): 54-56.

3561.   "Todd Bridges: No Longer a Silent Partner."   Right On! (May 1980): 44-45.

3562.   "Todd Bridges: Trying to put his troubled past behind him."   Ebony (July 1987): 27+.

3563.   "Todd Bridges: a TV star too young to enjoy fame and money."   Jet (October 16 1980): 28+.

3564.   "Todd Bridges tells how Hollywood destroyed his life and how God is rebuilding it."   Jet (April 10 1989): 28-30.

BROOKS, AVERY

3565.   Cary, Lorene.   "'I Am No Tonto.'"   TV Guide (December 6 1986): 30-34.

3566.   Dennard, Darryl W.   "EM Interview: Avery Brooks." Ebony Man (June 1989): 17-19.

3567.   Southgate, Martha.   "Avery Brooks: Not Just Another Pretty Face."   Essence (April 1989): 74-76, 114.

3568.   White, Frank III.   "Avery Brooks/AKA Hawk: Costar of Spenser: For Hire is legitimate actor, professor and musician."   Ebony (April 1987): 62+.

BROOKS, HADDA

3569.   "Hadda Brooks; singer has new hit television program on West Coast."   Ebony (April 1951): 101-102.

3570.   Watrous, Peter.   "With Boogie-Woogie, Hadda Brooks is Back."   New York Times (July 26 1989): C17.

BROWN, ALONZO

See # 3354

BROWN, CHELSEA

See also # 3377

3571.   Brown, Chelsea - Clippings [Billy Rose Theatre Collection]

BROWN, GEORG STANFORD (1943-   )

3572. Armstrong, Lois. "Tyne Daly Gets Her Gun, Georg Brown
Finds His 'Roots,' and Their Marriage Prospers." People
(January 31 1977): 60-62.

3573. "At Home Visit: Georg Stanford Brown." Right On! (May
1973): 50-51.

3574. "A Closer Look at TV's Latest Black Cop!" Right On!
(February 1973): 59.

3575. Dunn, Lynn. "Georg Stanford Brown: Piecing Together a
Man." Black Stars (April 1973): 30-36.

BROWN, JIM (1935-   )

See also # 3373

3576. Bogle, Donald. Blacks in American Films and
Television. New York: Garland, 1988, pp. 362-364.

3577. Brown, Jim, with Steve Delsohn. Out of Bounds. New
York: Zebra, 1989. 248p. [Autobiography]

3578. Toback, James. Jim: the author's self-centered memoir
on the great Jim Brown. Garden City, NY: Doubleday, 1971.
133p.

Articles

3579. Banks, Lacy J. "Jim Brown Hungers for Home." Black
Stars (December 1974): 68-73.

3580. Jenkins, Walter. "A Chapter in the Life of Jim Brown."
Black Stars (October 1973): 70-73.

3581. "Jim Brown in Rio Conchos. Cleveland football star
makes his acting debut." Sepia (December 1964): 22-25.

3582. "Jim Brown Makes it Big in Hollywood." Sepia (October
1967): 64-68.

3583. Lucas, Bob. "Jim Brown: The Screen's No. 1 Black
Lover." Sepia (November 1972): 16-22.

3584. Sanders, Charles L. "Jim Brown. Film actor talks
about his marriage, women and career." Ebony (December 1968):
192+.

3585. Winters, Jason. "Jim Brown: The Man Behind the Image."
Black Stars (September 1977): 40-49.

3586. Young, A. S. Doc. "How Jim Brown Beats the 'Hollywood
System'." Sepia (February 1978): 26-31.

BROWN, JUANITA

3587. Jenkins, Walter. "Brainy Actress Tells How She Became A Star Overnight." Black Stars (September 1974): 60-65.

3588. Salvo, Patrick, and Barbara Salvo. "Juanita Brown: Phi Betta Kappa to Movie Prostitute." Sepia (June 1975): 45-51.

BROWN, OLIVIA

See also # 3382

3589. Horner, Cynthia. "Acting is Her Vice; Sexy Aries Olivia Brown is enjoying her new hit series, Miami Vice." Right On! (February 1985): 50-51.

3590. "Olivia Brown enjoys 'Miami Vice' role; a Black woman with street sense." Jet (January 18 1988): 56-58.

3591. "Philip Michael Thomas and Olivia Brown: how Blacks are influencing TV network shows." Jet (May 25 1987): 54-56.

3592. "Philip Michael Thomas and Olivia Brown sizzle in 'Miami Vice'." Jet (October 12 1987): 58-59.

3593. "Philip Thomas, Olivia Brown star in 'Miami Vice' TV series." Jet (October 29 1984): 58+.

BROWN, TIMOTHY (1937-   )

3594. Bacharach, Judy. "'That's Timmy Brown...He Once Was Dynamite'." Philadelphia Inquirer (June 17 1973): 4-6.

3595. Mathews, Les. "New Black Movie Star, Timmy Brown, Stars as CIA Agent in Film, 'Girls Are For Loving'." New York Amsterdam News (June 2 1973): D-4.

BROWN, ZARA CULLY (d.1978)

See also # 3386

3596. Collins, Lisa. "Darling Dozen...Zara Cully." Black Stars (October 1975): 20-25.

3597. "Zara Cully Brown." Variety (March 1 1978): 110. [Obituary]

3598. "Zara Cully Brown, 86, Actress; Was Mother Jefferson on TV." New York Times (March 1 1978): B2. [Obituary]

BROWNE, ROSCOE LEE (1925-   )

3599. Goudas, John N. "Roscoe Lee Browne adds weight to sitcom." Staten Island Advance (April 17 1979). [Miss Winslow and Son]

3600. "Roscoe Lee Browne: The Black Actor, The Black Man." Black Stars (March 1972): 68-69.

3601. Troupe, Quincy. "Roscoe Lee Browne: 'I Mimic No One'."
Essence, Vol. 7 (December 1976): 55, 57, 92-94, 112.

BUCHANAN, MORRIS

3602. "From 'Heartbreak Hotel' to Peyton Place. Years of
broken dreams have ended for actor Morris Buchanan." _Sepia_
(February 1967): 48-53.

BURGHARDT, ARTHUR

3603. Antonides, John. "The Criminal." _Encore_ (August
1974): 48-50.

3604. Burghardt, Arthur - Clippings [Billy Rose Theatre
Collection]

3605. Cox, Clinton. "On a Note of Freedom." New York _Sunday
News_ (September 25 1977): L-5, L-9.

3606. Douglas, Joanne. "Arthur Burghardt: Man with a
Mission!" _Soap Opera Digest_ (September 25 1979): 18-24.

BURTON, LEVAR (1957-   )

See also # 3377, 3387

3607. Buck, Jerry. "'Star Trek' Beams Up LeVar Burton."
Chicago Sun-Times (August 13 1987): 52.

3608. Cosby, Dennis. "Le Var Burton: Prince of the
Television Overnight Sensations." _Black Collegian_ (May-June
1977): 36-37.

3609. Grogan, D. "Star Trek's LeVar Burton Needs Space to
Escape His Roots." _People_ (March 7 1988): 65-66.

3610. "LeVar Burton Talks About Suffering Pain in Movie
Roles." _Jet_ (February 3 1986): 54-55.

3611. Robinson, Louie. "LeVar Burton. College drama student
uses Roots as springboard to success." _Ebony_ (October 1977):
146-148, 150.

3612. Roeder, B. "Newsmakers." _Newsweek_ (April 25 1977):
72.

3613. Warren, Elaine. "Meditation? Fire Walking? Yogic
Breathing? He's a Believer." _TV Guide_ (August 13 1988): 13-
15.

CAESAR, ADOLPH (1934-1986)

3614. Bogle, Donald. _Blacks in American Films and
Television_. New York: Garland, 1988, pp. 364-365.

Articles

3615. Bailey, A. Peter. "Introducing: Adolph Caesar." Ebony (December 1984): 60+.

3616. Brin, Douglas. "My Lunch with Adolph Caesar." New York Sunday News (March 24 1985): 6.

3617. Christon, Lawrence. "Caesar: An Actor's Story." Los Angeles Times (February 25 1985): 1, 3.

3618. Johnson, Herschel. "Behind the Scenes with Actor Adolph Caesar." Essence, Vol. 13 (December 1982): 12.

3619. Trescott, Jacqueline. "Adolph Caesar gets a break with 'Soldier'." Chicago Sun-Times (October 10 1984): 47.

3620. _____. "Adolph Caesar: A Seasoned Veteran's Big Movie Break." Washington Post (September 28 1984): C1, C6.

Obituaries

3621. "Adolph Caesar." Variety (March 12 1986): 166.

3622. "Adolph Caesar; Actor Was 52." New York Times (March 7 1986): A16.

3623. "Adolph Caesar. Fatal Heart Attack Fells Actor on Set." Los Angeles Times (March 7 1986).

3624. Kerr, Peter. "Adolph Caesar is Dead at 52; Acclaimed in 'Soldiers Story.'" New York Times (March 8 1986): 32.

3625. "Milestones: Adolph Caesar." Time (March 17 1986): 72.

3626. "Newsmakers: Transition: Adolph Caesar." Newsweek (March 17 1986): 84.

CALLOWAY, KIRK (1960-   )

3627. Burrell, Walter. "Kirk Calloway "Acts" Naturally at Age 13." New York Amsterdam News (February 23 1974): B-15.

3628. Calloway, Kirk - Clippings [Billy Rose Theatre Collection]

3629. Thomas, M. Martez. "Kirk Calloway: Child Actor is Now a Grown-Up Young Man!" Right On! (August 1977): 8-9.

CALLOWAY, NORTHERN J. (1948-1990)

3630. Walker, Jesse H. "'Sesame Street' actor dies from anti-seizure drug." The City Sun (February 17 1990): 47.

CALLOWAY, VANESSA BELL

See # 3382

CAMBRIDGE, GODFREY (1933-1976)

3631. Black, Doris. "Evolution of the Racial Joke." Sepia,
Vol. 21 (May 1972): 44-46.

3632. "Cambridge, Godfrey." Current Biography 1969.

3633. Dunbar, Ernest. "Godfrey Cambridge Turns White." Look
(December 30 1969): 57, 60.

3634. Ebert, Alan. "'God' Is Dead. Godfrey Cambridge is
alive and recasting." Essence (October 1975): 48-51, 79.

3635. "Godfrey Cambridge: Man of a Thousand Faces." Sepia,
Vol. 20 (March 1971): 34-37.

3636. Gussow, Mel. "Laugh at this Negro, But Darkly."
Esquire, Vol. 62 (November 1964): 94-95, 155-159.

3637. Higgins, Robert. "Godfrey Cambridge." TV Guide, Vol.
16 (May 11 1968): 18-20.

3638. "People." Time (July 21 1975): 39.

3639. Robinson, Louie. "Godfrey Cambridge wins 'battle of
bulges', loses 117 pounds." Ebony (October 1967): 160+.

3640. Russell, C. "Godfrey Cambridge." Biographical News,
Vol. 2 (May 1975): 502.

3641. Wolff, A. "Godfrey Cambridge's Open Door Policy."
Look, Vol. 33 (January 7 1969): 76-77.

Newspaper Articles

3642. Barthel, Joan. "The Black Power of Godfrey MacArthur
Cambridge." New York Times (November 20 1966): Sec. II, pp.
13, 18.

3643. Cambridge, Godfrey - Clippings [Billy Rose Theatre
Collection]

3644. Greene, Daniel. "Godfrey Cambridge, Comedian."
National Observer (March 28 1966): 1, 18.

3645. Herridge, Frances. "Actor Grows Beard to Play Woman."
New York Post (August 10 1961): 12. Discussion of Cambridge's
appearance in "The Blacks."

3646. Nachman, Gerald. "Godfrey Cambridge." New York Post
(June 21 1964): Sec. 3, p. 33.

Obituaries

3647. Boyer, Peter J. "Godfrey Cambridge Dies of Heart
Attack." New York Post (November 30 1976).

3648. Current Biography 1977, p. 460.

3649. "Godfrey Cambridge, 43, Dies on Set for Entebbe Movie in Hollywood." New York Times (December 1 1976): D-23.

3650. New York Times (November 30 1976): 1.

3651. Newsweek (December 13 1976): 57.

3652. Tapley, Mel. "Farewell to Godfrey." New York Amsterdam News (December 4 1976): D-2.

3653. Time (December 13 1976): 102.

3654. Variety (December 1 1976): 79.

CAMPBELL, TISHA

See also # 3382

3655. "Dazed, but not fazed." New York Post (April 13 1988): 33.

3656. Kimble, Sonya. "Movies: Tisha Campbell." Right On! (April 1989): 44-45.

3657. Tapley, Mel. "Tisha Campbell adds another dimension to 'School Daze.'" New York Amsterdam News (February 13 1988): 30.

CANTY, MARIETTA (1906-1986)

3658. Bogle, Donald. Blacks in American Films and Television. New York: Garland, 1988, p. 365.

Articles

3659. "Former Local Negro Plays on Broadway." Hartford Courant (February 28 1936): 6.

3660. "Marietta Canty." Variety (July 16 1986): 125. [Obituary]

3661. "This Canty is So-o-o Refined!" Sepia Record (May 1953): 32-35.

CAPERS, VIRGINIA (1925-   )

3662. Brown, Marcia L. "Onstage and Off...Talented Virginia Capers." Black Stars (August 1976): 6-10.

3663. Capers, Virginia - Clippings [Billy Rose Theatre Collection]

3664. Fields, Sidney. "Joy of Waking to a New Day." New York Daily News (October 11 1973): 101.

3665. Satterwhite, Sandra. "Daily Closeup: 'She's Just Mama.'" New York Post (November 20 1973): 39.

CARA, IRENE (1959-   )

3666. Collins, Lisa. "Irene Cara." Right On! (July 1977):
28-29.

3667. _____. "Irene Cara: A Star at 21." Sepia
(November 1980): 42-48, 76.

3668. _____. "Irene Cara...Teen-Aged Performer Enjoys
Sparkling Career." Right On! (February 1976): 28-29.

3669. "Irene Cara. A show biz veteran at age 22." Ebony
(July 1981): 88-90+.

3670. Merritt, J. "Irene Cara is Out on Her Own." Rolling
Stone (October 2 1980): 24.

3671. Miller, E. "Spotlight." Seventeen (August 1975): 110.

3672. "More Dazzling Than Ever." Right On! (March 1984): 22-
24.

3673. Sheff, D. "To the Top." People (November 10 1980):
125-128.

3674. Winters, Jason. "Irene Cara Talks About Her Career."
Black Stars (May 1980): 59-61.

CARROLL, DIAHANN (1935-   )

See also # 3377

3675. Bogle, Donald. Blacks in American Films and
Television. New York: Garland, 1988, pp. 365-366.

3676. Carroll, Diahann, with Ross Firestone. Diahann: An
Autobiography. Boston: Little, Brown, 1986. 247p.

Articles

3677. Burrell, Walter Price. "Diahann Carroll Talks About
Her Role in "Claudine"." Black Stars (November 1974): 46-49.

3678. Collier, Aldore. "Diahann & Billy Dee break taboo of
Blacks as lovers on the TV screen." Jet (January 28 1985):
58+.

3679. "Diahann Carroll: Talented Bombshell." Sepia (March
1962): 57-59.

3680. "Did Diahann Carroll Sell Out to TV?" Sepia (August
1970): 56-57.

3681. Haller, Scot. "Diahann Carroll dresses up 'Dynasty'."
People (May 14 1984): 125+.

3682. Newton, Edmund. "Diahann! As Dominique Deveraux,
Diahann Carroll, our diva of Dynasty, is wheelin' and dealin'
on prime time." Essence (October 1984): 80-82.

CARTER, BEN (1912-1946)

3683. "Ben Carter." Variety (December 18 1946). [Obituary]

3684. Robins, Sam. "Green Pastures, Indeed!" New York Times
(December 15 1940). [Profile]

CARTER, NELL (c.1949-   )

3685. Bogle, Donald. Blacks in American Films and
Television. New York: Garland, 1988, pp. 366-367.

Articles

3686. Adelson, S. "Tube." People (June 21 1982): 100-102.

3687. Banfield, Bever-Leigh. "Feeling Fit and Fabulous!"
Essence, Vol. 14 (January 1984): 72-74+.

3688. Bryes, M. "Sequel." People (November 14 1983):
81-82+.

3689. Nolan, Tom. "Says Nell Carter...there was a time when
I didn't like Nell." TV Guide (August 21-27 1982): 18-20+.

CARTER, RALPH (1962-   )

3690. Carter, Ralph - Clippings [Billy Rose Theatre
Collection]

3691. Carter, Ralph, as told to Stephen Wilding and Jason
Winters. "Ralph Carter: I Have Two Different Personalities."
Black Stars (March 1977): 60-65.

3692. Donnelly, Tom. "'Raisin' Star Ralph Carter is 12,
Going on Genius." Philadelphia Inquirer (July 8 1974): 6-8.

3693. Jenkins, Flo. "Closeup: Ralph Carter!" Right On!
(September 1976): 16-17.

CARTER, T. K.

3694. D'Agnese, Joe. "He's No Girl...He's T. K. Carter!"
Right On! (December 1987): 35-36.

3695. Ervolino, Bill. "This Role is Far from a Drag." New
York Post (September 10 1987): 36.

3696. Gardella, Kay. "'Just Our Luck' Needs Lots of It."
New York Daily News (September 10 1983): 65.

3697. Raso, Anne. "Show Biz is Just His Luck." Right On!
(March 1984): 20-21.

CARTER, TERRY

See also # 3377

3698.   Barber, Rowland. "He Who Gets Squelched on the Set...May prove unsquelchable off it: consider the case of Terry Carter." TV Guide (April 26-May 2 1975): 17-19.

3699. Carter, Terry - Clippings [Billy Rose Theatre Collection]

3700. Jenkins, Walter. "The Heavy World of Terry Carter." Sepia (May 1980): 74-77.

3701. Slaton, Shell. "Lights! Carter! Action! After 26 years in show biz Terry Carter tells it like it is!" Right On! (January 1978): 22-3.

CARTER, THOMAS

3702. Fee, Debi. "Thomas Carter: We Asked for It and We Got It!" Right On! (May 1979): 36-37. [The White Shadow]

CASEY, BERNIE (1939-   )

3703. "Bernie Casey on Art, Poetry and Soledad Brothers." New York Times (March 25 1977): C-6.

3704. Burrell, Walter Price. "Bernie Casey Defends Black Films." Black Stars (May 1973): 10-15.

3705. Casey, Bernie - Clippings [Billy Rose Theatre Collection]

3706. Davis, Curt. "Brother Bernie Casey." Encore American and Worldwide News (May 9 1977): 35-36.

3707. Liggins, G. E. "Bernie Casey Stars in Black Drama Series." Black Stars (August 1978): 20-25.

3708. Robles, Roland. "Bernie Casey." Essence (August 1977): 72, 99, 113.

CASH, ROSALIND (1938-   )

See also # 3370

3709. Cash, Rosalind - Clippings [Billy Rose Theatre Collection]

3710. Jenkins, Walter. "Rosalind Cash: Impressions of a Remarkable Lady." Black Stars (February 1976): 10-17.

3711. McLaurin-Allen, Irma. "Working: The Black Actress in the Twentieth Century." Contributions in Black Studies, No. 8 (1986-87): 67-76. [Interview]

3712. "Rosalind Cash, Black Star." Encore (January 1973): 51.

3713. Walters, Richard. "Rosalind Cash...A 'Star' in the True Sense of the Word!" Right On! (November 1975): 32-34.

Newspaper Articles

3714. Cash, Rosalind. "It Was Time to Get Back Home." New York Times (July 13 1969): Sec. II, pp. 1, 11.

3715. "Is It Better to Be Shaft Than Uncle Tom?" New York Times (August 26 1973): Sec. II, pp. 11, 16. Discussion between WOR radio host Heywood Broun, black film critic Donald Bogle and Rosalind Cash.

3716. "'Melinda' Role Perfect says Rosalind Cash." New York Amsterdam News (September 2 1972).

3717. Robinson, Major. "Rosalind Cash: Life Invested in Theatre." New York Amsterdam News (October 25 1980): 36.

3718. "Rosalind Cash Finds Hollywood Is Not Black People's Reality." New York Post (September 2 1972).

3719. Taylor, Nora E. "Rosalind Cash: Conversing with a New Star." Christian Science Monitor (August 21 1971).

CHAMBERLIN, LEE

3720. Anderson, Nancy. "Lee Chamberlin Enjoys Role in Weekly TV Series." New York News World (August 23 1979). TV show "Paris" with James Earl Jones.

3721. Davis, Curt. "Television: All's Fair for Lee Chamberlin." Encore American and Worldwide News (February 7 1977): 39.

CHASE, ANNAZETTE

3722. "Anazette Chase...Black Starlet on the Rise." Right On! (June 1973): 50-51.

3723. Jenkins, Walter. "Annazette Chase--The Serious World of the Lady and Her Profession." Black Stars (September 1977): 68-74.

3724. Slaton, Shell. "Meet Muhammad Ali's Movie Wife, Annazette Chase!" Right On! (July 1977): 14-15.

CHILDRESS, ALVIN (1908-1986)

3725. Bogle, Donald. Blacks in American Films and Television. New York: Garland, 1988, p. 369.

Articles

3726. Dawson, Cheryl. "An Inside Look at Alvin Childress." Black Stars (July 1975): 64-66.

3727. Sinclair, Abiola. "Film Tribute to Alvin Childress." New York Amsterdam News (August 9 1986): 24.

3728. "What happened to TV stars of 'Amos 'n' Andy'?" Jet (December 10 1981): 55-58.

3729. "Whatever Happened To...The 'Amos 'n Andy' Cast?"
Ebony (July 1973): 138.

Obituaries

3730. "Alvin Childress." Variety (April 30 1986): 182.

3731. "Alvin Childress Dead; Starred as TV's 'Amos'." New
York Times (April 22 1986): B8.

3732. "Childress of 'Amos N Andy' fame dies in Los Angeles."
Jet (May 5 1986): 8.

3733. Folkart, Burt A. "Alvin Childress, 78, of 'Amos 'n'
Andy' Series on TV, Dies." Los Angeles Times (April 22 1986):
1, 3.

CHONG, RAE DAWN

3734. Chong, Rae Dawn - Clippings [Billy Rose Theatre
Collection]

3735. Donahue, Deirdre. "With her young son at her side, Rae
Dawn Chong reaches for success and finds a Commando-size hit."
People (November 18 1985): 75+.

3736. Hackett, George. "Rae Dawn Chong in the hot seat."
Rolling Stone (November 21 1985): 60+.

3737. Johnson, Herschel. "Introducing: Rae Dawn Chong.
'Quest for Fire' fuels young actress' career." Ebony (June
1982): 126+.

3738. "Rae Dawn Chong." Playboy (April 1987): 132+.
[Interview]

3739. "Rae Dawn Chong: black actresses star in non-racial
movie roles." Jet (September 9 1985): 26-28.

3740. "Rae Dawn Chong gets Black filmmakers honors." Jet
(March 17 1986): 60. [Clarence Muse Youth Award]

3741. Rickey, Carrie. "Posture: Rae Dawn Chong." Film
Comment (March/April 1985): 36-37.

3742. Travers, Peter. "Tommy Chong's Daughter, Rae Dawn,
Launches a Fiery Quest for her own career." People (May 31
1982): 45-46, 51.

CHRISTIAN, ROBERT (1939-1983)

3743. Goldstein, Toby. "Robert Christian Is More Than the
Sum of His Parts." Soap Opera Digest (February 1 1983): 116-
121, 134.

3744. "Robert Christian." Variety (February 9 1983): 94.
[Obituary]

3745. "Robert Christian, 42; Actor Won An Obie In 'Blood Knot' Role." New York Times (January 29 1983): 9. [Obituary]

3746. Webster, Ivan. "Robert Christian: The Man Behind the Mascara." Encore American and Worldwide News (October 1979): 34-35.

CLANTON, RONY

3747. Lewis, Barbara. "Rony Clanton: Former youth worker finds career in films, stage." New York Amsterdam News (January 29 1983): 48.

CLARK, MARLENE

3748. Jenkins, Walter. "Lady from Slaughter." Black Stars (August 1973): 30-34.

CLAY, STANLEY

3749. Burrell, Walter Price. "Watch Out for Stanley Clay." Black Stars (June 1977): 10-15.

3750. Thomas, M. Martez. "Closeup...Stanley Clay!" Right On! (October 1976): 16-17.

CLEMMONS, FRANCOIS

3751. "Francois Clemmons: A Rare Treat for Millions." Black Stars (November 1973): 20-21.

COBBS, BILL

3752. Cobbs, Bill - Clippings [Billy Rose Theatre Collection]

3753. Lynch, Mark. "The Art of the Working Actor: A Conversation with Bill Cobbs." Jam Sessions (February 1989): 14.

COFFEY, EVELYN

See # 3354

COLE, OLIVIA (c.1942-   )

See also # 3387

3754. Lester, Peter. "At the White House, As in Her Own Life, Olivia Cole is a Quiet 'Backstairs' Sort of Woman." People (February 19 1979): 69-70.

3755. Lucas, Bob. "Olivia Cole: A Revealing Talk with a Talented TV Actress." Jet (July 19 1979): 44-47.

3756. Slaton, Shell. "Recalling Olivia Cole." Right On! (April 1978): 46-47.

COLEMAN, GARY (1968-   )

3757. Bogle, Donald. <u>Blacks in American Films and Television</u>. New York: Garland, 1988, pp. 370-372.

Articles

3758. Allis, T. "Fending off illness and family, Gary Coleman turns 21, an age he wasn't sure he would see." <u>People</u> (February 20 1989): 49+.

3759. "Coleman appears in court to fight for his millions." <u>Jet</u> (January 22 1990): 28.

3760. Coleman, Gary - Clippings [Billy Rose Theatre Collection]

3761. Collier, Aldore. "Gary Coleman, 19, and on his own." <u>Jet</u> (March 30 1987): 36-38.

3762. "Gary Coleman and mother battle over control of his $6 million fortune, income." <u>Jet</u> (December 25 1989): 22-24.

3763. "Gary Coleman, 'Diff'rent Strokes' star, sues his parents over earnings." <u>Jet</u> (February 27 1989): 60.

3764. "Gary Coleman's parents tell their side about his suit against them." <u>Jet</u> (April 17 1989): 56+.

3765. Littwin, Susan. "Goodbye, Cute Child Star - Hello, Troubled Young Man: at 21, Gary Coleman confronts a flagging career and chooses new friends his parents don't trust." <u>TV Guide</u> (April 1-7 1989): 18+.

3766. Marsh, Antoinette. "Gary Coleman and Todd Bridges: Little Kids with Big Minds." <u>Black Stars</u> (March 1979): 40-45.

3767. Robinson, Louie. "Diff'rent Strokes. Gary Coleman leaps from commercials to big time TV." <u>Ebony</u> (February 1979): 104+.

3768. _____. "Ebony Interview with Gary Coleman. Television star is a self-made millionaire at 12." <u>Ebony</u> (June 1980): 33+.

3769. Seligson, Marcia. "Small Wonder." <u>TV Guide</u> (March 3 1979): 26, 29-30.

CONNOR, EDRIC (d.1968)

3770. "Edric Connor." <u>Variety</u> (October 30 1968). [Obituary]

3771. "Edric Connor: Theatrical Genius." <u>Sepia</u> (December 1963): 52-55.

3772. "Movies: Moby Dick. Million dollar production of stirring classic has Negro in important role." <u>Our World</u> (June 1955): 62-64.

COOK, NATHAN (d.1988)

3773. Esterly, Glenn. "He Lives on the Edge Emotionally."
TV Guide (June 2 1984): 34-38.

3774. "Nathan Cook." Variety (July 15 1988): 79. [Obituary]

3775. "Nathan Cook, 'Hotel' star, 38, dies in L.A." Jet
(July 4 1988): 6.

COPAGE, MARC (1962-   )

See also # 3377

3776. Copage, Marc - Clippings [Billy Rose Theatre
Collection]

3777. "The Double Life of Marc Copage." Ebony (December
1969): 174-176, 178, 180, 182.

3778. Jenkins, Walter. "A Friendly Visit with Marc Copage."
Black Stars (June 1976): 28-33.

3779. "Marc Copage...Still Doin' It!" Right On! (January
1973): 52-53.

3780. "Marc Copage Today." Right On! (October 1971): 54-55.

3781. "Whatever Happened to Marc Copage." Ebony (September
1985): 122+.

3782. Whitney, Dwight. "Superchild Meets His Public." TV
Guide (June 28 1969): 10-13.

COSBY, BILL (1937-   )

3783. Bogle, Donald. Blacks in American Films and
Television. New York: Garland, 1988, pp. 372-374.

3784. Goldsworthy, Joan. "Cosby, William." In Black
Writers: A Selection of Sketches from Contemporary Authors.
Detroit: Gale Research Inc., 1989, pp. 119-122.

3785. Hill, George H. Bill Cosby: In Our Living Rooms for
Twenty Years: A Biobibliography. Los Angeles: Daystar
Publishing Co., 1986. 55p.

3786. Johnson, Robert. Bill Cosby: In Words and Pictures.
Chicago: Johnson Publishing Co., 1986.

3787. Smith, Ronald L. Cosby. New York: St. Martin, 1986.
218p.

Articles

3788. "Cosby beats Reagan, Pope as the most admired man."
Jet (October 27 1986): 54.

3789. Cosby, Bill - Clippings [Billy Rose Theatre Collection]

3790. Cosby, Bill - Clippings (MWEZ + n.c. 26,243) [Billy Rose Theatre Collection]

3791. "Cosby, Bill." Current Biography 1986.

3792. "Cosby, Bill." Current Biography 1967.

3793. "Cosby, Inc.: He has a hot TV series, a new book--and a booming comedy empire." Time (September 28 1987): 56-64.

3794. "Cosby's $84 million make him richest entertainer." Jet (September 28 1987): 52.

3795. Darrach, Brad. "Cosby! America's Funniest Father." Life (June 1985): 34-42.

3796. Davison, Muriel. "Bill Cosby: The Man, His Work, His World." Good Housekeeping (March 1970): 86-89, 212-214, 216, 218-219.

3797. Ebert, Alan. "Bill Cosby: A Piece of the Action." Essence (December 1977): 68-69, 140, 142, 144, 146.

3798. Haddad-Garcia, George. "Bill Cosby: Being a Daddy." Black Stars (February 1980): 22-26.

3799. Haley, Alex. "Talking with Cosby." Ladies' Home Journal (June 1985): 30, 32, 35-36, 107.

3800. Linderman, Lawrence. "Bill Cosby." Playboy (December 1985): 75+.

3801. Morgan, Thomas B. "I Am Two People, Man." Life (April 11 1969): 74+.

3802. "'Raceless' Bill Cosby; Comedian excludes 'color' reference from repertoire." Ebony (May 1964): 131-132, 134-136, 138, 140.

3803. Robinson, Louie. "Dr. Bill Cosby." Ebony (June 1977): 130-137.

3804. _____. "Man and Boy." Ebony (April 1971): 42+.

3805. _____. "Pleasures and Problems of Being Bill Cosby." Ebony (July 1969): 144+.

3806. Ryan, Cate. "The Man in Studio 41. He's Bill Cosby, and he has good reason to feel satisfied with himself these days." TV Guide (February 3-9 1972): 28-31.

3807. Sayre, John. "Bill Cosby Delivers." Pace (November 1969): 16-21.

3808. Stang, Joanna. "Private World of Bill Cosby." Good Housekeeping (June 1967): 26, 28, 32-33, 37.

3809. "TV's Bright-Spoken Bill Cosby Does the Vegas Bit." Look (May 30 1967): M16+.

Newspaper Articles

3810. Dudar, Helen. "Bill Cosby: Up from the Cellar." New York Post (February 23 1964): 31.

3811. Glenn, Larry. "Bill Cosby: the Clown as Straight Man." Tuesday Magazine [newspaper supplement] (October 1965): 26-28.

3812. Mee, Charles L., Jr. "That's the Truth, and other Cosby Stories." New York Times Magazine (March 14 1965): 96-97.

The Cosby Show

3813. Bogle, Donald. Blacks in American Films and Television. New York: Garland Pub., 1988, pp. 262-265.

Articles

3814. Bennetts, Leslie. "Bill Cosby Begins Taping NBC Series. Parenthood is focus of program." New York Times (August 6 1984): C20.

3815. "Cosby Lifts NBC-TV to No. 1; gets 51% of show valued at 400 million." Jet (May 5 1986): 54.

3816. The Cosby Show - Clippings [Billy Rose Theatre Collection]

3817. Hall, J. "Bill Cosby huffs and puffs on and off his hit sitcom, but his TV kids say father knows best." People (December 10 1984): 141+.

3818. Klein, T. "Bill Cosby: Prime Time's Favorite Father." Saturday Evening Post (April 1986): 42+.

3819. Norment, Lynn. "The Cosby Show: the real-life drama behind hit TV show about a black family." Ebony (April 1985): 27+.

3820. Whitman, Arthur. "The Spy Who Knocked 'em Cold." True: The Man's Magazine (January 1967): 55, 78-81.

I Spy

3821. Bogle, Donald. Blacks in American Films and Television. New York: Garland Pub., 1988, pp. 279-280.

Articles

3822. "Bill Cosby: Cool, Hip Spy." Sepia (July 1966): 22-27.

3823. "Color Him Funny." Newsweek (January 31 1966): 76.

3824. de Roos, Robert. "The Spy Who Came in for the Gold." TV Guide (October 23 1965): 14-17.

3825. Flagler, J. M. "Spy Off Duty." Look (May 30 1967): M16+.

3826. "I Spy." Ebony (September 1965): 65+.

3827. Karnow, S. "Bill Cosby: Variety is the Life of Spies."
Saturday Evening Post (September 25 1965): 86+.

3828. Peterson, F. "I Spy on Bill Cosby." Sepia (August
1969): 8-11.

3829. "Spy." Newsweek (December 14 1964): 51.

COUSAR, JAMES

3830. Dawson, Cheryl. "Meet the Handsome Star of
Blackenstein!!" Right On! (March 1973): 56-57.

CROSSE, RUPERT (1927-1973)

3831. Bogle, Donald. Blacks in American Films and
Television. New York: Garland, 1988, p. 374.

3832. "Rupert Crosse." Variety (March 28 1973). [Obituary]

CROTHERS, SCATMAN (1910-1986)

3833. "Scatman Crothers. After 50 years in show biz, an
'overnight success'." Ebony (July 1978): 62+.

3834. "Scat Man Crothers: Hollywood's forgotten man gets new
lease on life." Our World (June 1953): 21+.

3835. "'Scat Man' Finds Hollywood Gold! Stars in second
movie; Has own TV show on coast." Color (September 1953): 32.

3836. Winters, Jason. "Scat Man Crothers: A Star at Last!"
Black Stars (December 1977): 56-61.

Obituaries

3837. Classic Images, No. 139 (January 1987): 43.
3838. International Musician (September 1987): 18.
3839. Jet (December 15 1986): 62.
3840. New York Times (November 24 1986): D14.
3841. Newsweek (December 1 1986): 94.
3842. Time (December 1 1986): 70.
3843. Variety (November 26 1986): 150.

CULLY, ZARA

See Brown, Zara Cully

CUMBUKA, JI-TU

3844. "Without Hair, Ji-Tu Cumbuka Turns Heads." Black Stars
(February 1980): 69-70.

DANDRIDGE, DOROTHY (1924-1965)

See also # 3400

3845. Dandridge, Dorothy, and Earl Conrad. Everything and Nothing: the Dorothy Dandridge Tragedy. New York: Abelard, 1970. 215p.

3846. Mills, Earl. Dorothy Dandridge, a portrait in black. Los Angeles: Holloway House Pub. Co., 1970. 248p.

Books with Sections on Dorothy Dandridge

3847. Agan, Patrick. "Dorothy Dandridge." In The Decline and Fall of the Love Goddesses. New York: Pinnacle Books, 1980.

3848. Bogle, Donald. Blacks in American Films and Television. New York: Garland, 1988, pp. 375-377.

3849. _____. "Dandridge, Dorothy." In Dictionary of American Negro Biography, eds. Rayford W. Logan and Michael R. Winston. New York: W. W. Norton, 1982, pp. 157-158.

3850. Shout, John D. "Dandridge, Dorothy Jean." In Dictionary of American Biography, Supplement 7, pp. 162-163.

Articles

3851. Bogle, Donald. "The Dorothy Dandridge Story." Essence (December 1984): 100, 102, 146, 148.

3852. "Bright Road for Dorothy." Theatre Arts (May 1953): 12.

3853. "Can Dandridge Outshine Lena Horne?" Our World (June 1952): 28-32.

3854. Dandridge, Dorothy - Clippings [Billy Rose Theatre Collection]

3855. "Dandridge Gets Red Carpet Treatment." Ebony (August 1956): 24, 27-29.

3856. "Dandridge Marries: Simple Wedding is Movieland Wonder." Ebony (September 1959): 135-138.

3857. "The Decks Ran Red; In Her Eighth Movie, Dorothy Dandridge Displays Acting Skill." Ebony (November 1958): 60-62+.

3858. "Dorothy Dandridge: Hollywood's Tragic Enigma." Ebony (March 1966): 70-82.

3859. "Dorothy Dandridge Learns to Dance." Our World (December 1951): 50+.

3860. "Dorothy Dandridge's Greatest Triumph. She is first Negro nominated for a major Academy Award." Ebony (July 1955): 37-41.

3861. "Dorothy Dandridge's Hollywood Love Life." Tan (August 1957): 26-29.

3862. "Double Dynamite!" Negro Achievements (September 1952): 9.

3863. Fields, Sidney. "Dorothy Dandridge: Stardust for Carmen." New York Daily Mirror (October 29 1954): 28.

3864. "Hollywood's New Glamour Queen; with two new film roles, Dorothy Dandridge is groomed as No. 1 glamour girl of movies." Ebony (April 1951): 48-52.

3865. "Island in the Sun: Dandridge and Belafonte Star in Romantic Interracial Film." Ebony (July 1957): 32-37.

3866. Leavy, Walter. "The Real-Life Tragedy of Dorothy Dandridge." Ebony (September 1986): 136+.

3867. "Life Story in Song." Life (March 23 1953): 129+.

3868. "Movies: A New Beauty for Bizet." Life (November 1 1954): 87-90. [Cover story - Carmen Jones]

3869. "The Mystery of Dorothy Dandridge." Color (March 1956): 6-9.

3870. "A New Star is Born." Color (April 1953): 14-16.

3871. Parkerson, Michelle. "Diva Under Glass." Heresies, Issue 16 (1983): 11.

3872. _____. "The Tragedy of Dorothy Dandridge." Black Film Review, Vol. 4, No. 2 (Spring 1988): 10-11.

3873. Parsons, Louella. "Dorothy Dandridge Stars in a Great New Movie." Cosmopolitan (December 1954): 4-5.

3874. "Private World of Dorothy Dandridge." Ebony (June 1962): 116-121.

3875. "Remembrance of Things Past: Dorothy Dandridge, 1950s Screen Siren." Encore American and Worldwide News (February 21 1977): 3.

3876. Robertson, S. "Ill Fated Love Life of Dorothy Dandridge." Sepia (February 1963): 13-16.

3877. Robinson, Louie. "Dorothy Dandridge: Hollywood's Tragic Enigma." Ebony (March 1966): 70-72+.

3878. _____. "The Private World of Dorothy Dandridge." Ebony (June 1962): 116-121.

3879. "Screen Test: Dorothy Dandridge Wins Carmen Jones Title Role with Sizzling Performance." Ebony (September 1954): 37-42.

3880. "See How They Run: New movie team, Dorothy Dandridge and Harry Belafonte, score in touching drama." Our World (November 1952): 10, 12.

3881. Seeley, Nancy. "Closeup: The Road Ahead for 'Carmen'."
New York Post (November 7 1954). [Profile]

3882. "Tarzan's Perils. B-film scratches Hollyw'd "Keep Out"
sign to Negroes; Features Dorothy Dandridge." Our World
(April 1951): 9-10.

3883. "Two for the Show." Time (May 2 1955): 42.

3884. Wilson, Alfred. "Historical Feature: Dorothy
Dandridge--Screen Goddess." Right On! (April 1981): 20-23.

3885. Young, A. S. "Dorothy Dandridge Marries." Sepia, Vol.
7 (September 1959): 39-43.

3886. _____. "Life and Death of Dorothy Dandridge."
Sepia, Vol. 14 (December 1965): 8-12, 14-15.

Obituaries

3887. New York Post (September 9 1965).
3888. New York Times (September 9 1965): 41.
3889. Newsweek (September 20 1965): 66.
3890. Time (September 17 1965): 124.
3891. Variety (September 15 1965).

DANDRIDGE, RUBY (1904-1987)

3892. Bogle, Donald. Blacks in American Films and
Television. New York: Garland, 1988, pp. 377-378.

3893. "Dorothy Dandridge's mom dies in L.A. nursing home."
Jet (November 16 1987): 16.

3894. "Ruby Dandridge." Variety (October 28 1987): 110.
[Obituary]

DANELLE, JOHN

3895. Kowet, Don. "Both Married and Divorced. That's the
contradictory life 'All My Children' offers Lisa Wilkinson and
John Danelle." TV Guide (July 15 1978): 19-20.

DAVIS, CLIFTON (1945-   )

See also # 3373

3896. Baker, Essie. "Clifton Davis: 'I Can't Give Half'."
Encore American and Worldwide News (July 7 1975): 24-26.

3897. Buchalter, Gail. "Clifton Davis Believes, This Time,
Hollywood and Drugs Won't Do Him In. Amen!" TV Guide
(January 17 1987): 26-28.

3898. Burrell, Walter Price. "Clifton Davis: The Boy from
Patchogue, Long Island, Makes Good." Black Stars (May 1975):
28-35.

3899. "Clifton Davis in That's My Mama." Black Stars
(November 1974): 73.

3900. Collier, Aldore. "Clifton Davis and Tempestt Bledsoe
star in TV movie." Jet (October 16 1989): 22+. [Dream Date]

3901. _____. "Clifton Davis Finally Finds Peace,
Dedicates New Life to Serving God." Jet (June 18 1981): 36-
39.

3902. Cyclops. "TV Review: Toast to Melba, a Summer Peach.
Melba Moore-Clifton Davis Show." Life (July 14 1972): 17.

3903. Davis, Clifton - Clippings [Billy Rose Theatre
Collection]

3904. Fornay, Alfred. "Clifton Davis." Ebony Man (May
1987): 14.

3905. Hall, Jane. "A New Hit on TV, Ex-Addict Clifton Davis
Can Say Amen to His Past." People (December 15 1986): 84+.

3906. "Melba Moore-Clifton Davis Show." Variety (June 1
1972): 39.

3907. Moore, Trudy S. "Clifton Davis: How Marriage and
Ministry Changed Him." Jet (September 12 1983): 54-57.

3908. Norman, Shirley. "What's Next for Fallen Star Clifton
Davis?" Sepia (May 1976): 68-78.

3909. Peterson, Maurice. "On the Aisle: Spotlight on Clifton
Davis." Essence (July 1975): 19.

3910. Pikula, Joan. "Clifton Davis: Flying Over the
Mountain." After Dark (January 1976): 59-62.

3911. Taraborelli, J. Randy. "Handsome Screen Idol's Simply
an Ordinary Guy!!" Right On! (May 1977): 36-38.

3912. White, Frank III. "A Star is Reborn: Amen's Clifton
Davis Has a New Role on the Screen and in Life." Ebony
(February 1987): 104-108.

Newspaper Articles

3913. Campbell, Barbara. "Clifton Davis: Nothing Can Stop
Him Now." New York Times (June 4 1972): 17.

3914. Carter, Alan. "'Amen's' Clifton Davis has the Holy
Ghost and a hit series." New York Sunday News (March 29
1987): 23.

3915. Gardella, Kay. "Television: Clifton Davis: 'Young,
Gifted and Black.'" New York Sunday News (October 27 1974):
TV Sect., p. 1.

3916. Mishkin, Leo. "Clifton Davis More Than a Broadway
Star." New York Morning Telegram (January 18 1972): 3.

3917. O'Connor, John J. "TV: Refreshing Music-Variety Hour in Premiere. 'Melba Moore-Clifton Davis Show' on C.B.S." New York Times (June 9 1972).

3918. Wilson, Earl. "Clifton Davis' Rise: Is This Me?" New York Post (September 14 1974): 18.

DAVIS, GUY

3919. Roeser, Steve. "Interview: Guy Davis Rocks to the Beat." Right On! (December 1984): 28, 54. [Beat Street]

DAVIS, OSSIE (1917-)

See also # 3351

3920. Bogle, Donald. Blacks in American Films and Television. New York: Garland, 1988, pp. 378-379.

Articles

3921. Burgen, Michelle. "How We Made Our Marriage Last: Ruby Dee, Ossie Davis." Ebony (December 1979): 84-86, 88, 90.

3922. "The Cardinal. New movie casts Ossie Davis as bias fighting priest." Ebony (December 1963): 126+.

3923. "Davis, Ossie." Current Biography 1969.

3924. "Suddenly Ossie and Ruby Are Everywhere." Life (December 6 1963): 110-113.

3925. Wansley, Joyce. "Ossie Davis and Ruby Dee are Compared to the Lunts, but Hayden and Fonda also Apply." People (March 23 1981): 75+.

DAVIS, SAMMY, Jr. (1925-1990)

3926. Bogle, Donald. Blacks in American Films and Television. New York: Garland, 1988, pp. 379-381.

3927. Davis, Sammy, Jr. Hollywood in a Suitcase. New York: Morrow, 1980. 288p.

3928. _____, and Jane and Burt Boyar. Why Me?: the Sammy Davis, Jr. Story. New York: Farrar, Straus and Giroux, 1989. 373p.

3929. _____. Yes I Can: The Story of Sammy Davis, Jr. New York: Farrar, Straus and Giroux, 1965. 630p.

Articles

3930. Avins, Mimi. "Shot by Shot: creating a dance sequence with style and believability for 'Tap'." Premiere (March 1989): 72+.

3931. Davis, Sammy (Jr.) - Clippings (MWEZ + n.c. 26,645) [Billy Rose Theatre Collection]

3932. "Sammy Davis Jr. and Gregory Hines move to the beat in 'Tap'." Jet (February 13 1989): 58+.

3933. "TAP. Gregory Hines and Sammy Davis Jr. co-star in new film." Ebony (February 1989): 46+.

DAVIS, TODD

3934. "...A Bit About 'General Hospital's' Todd Davis." Soap Opera Digest (March 17 1981): 110.

3935. Douglas, Joanne. "An At-Home Visit with Todd Davis and wife Rosalind: 'We Feel Blessed'." Soap Opera Digest (August 4 1981): 34-40.

3936. "The Totally Impulsive Todd Davis." Right On! (June 1980): 52-53.

DAWN, MARPESSA (1935-   )

3937. "America's Dawn Comes Up in France." Life (March 14 1960): 57.

3938. "Girl on the Go in Paris. Triple threat Marpessa Dawn scores in Europe." Ebony (May 1965): 100, 102, 104-105.

3939. "Marpessa Dawn; American actress makes big splash in Europe." Ebony (November 1959): 85-88+.

DE ANDA, PETER (1938-   )

3940. De Anda, Peter - Clippings [Billy Rose Theatre Collection]

3941. De Anda, Peter. "'So Now I'm Back, and Black...And Available.'" New York Times (October 10 1971).

DEANE, PALMER

3942. Davis, Curt. "Palmer Deane's Dilemma." Encore American and Worldwide News (March 20 1978): 32-34.

DEE, RUBY (1923-)

3943. Bogle, Donald. Blacks in American Films and Television. New York: Garland, 1988, pp. 381-382.

3944. Fax, Elton C. Contemporary Black Leaders. New York: Dodd, Mead, 1970, pp. 220-236.

Articles

3945. Burgen, Michele. "How We Made Our Marriage Last: Ruby Dee, Ossie Davis." Ebony (December 1979): 84-86, 88, 90.

3946. "Dee, Ruby." Current Biography 1970.

3947. Ebert, Alan. "Ruby Dee: The Woman." Essence (June 1976): 58+.

3948.   Gary, Beverly. "For a Negro Actress, the Curtain
Raises All the Way." New York Post (April 13 1961): 56.

3949.   Leahy, Jack. "The Road is Open Now. But racial
barriers once blocked the way for actress Ruby Dee." New York
Sunday News Magazine (June 11 1961): 4, 15.

3950.   New Yorker (April 8 1961): 165. Review of the film
version of "A Raisin in the Sun", singling out Ruby Dee's
performance.

3951.   Wansley, Joyce. "Ossie Davis and Ruby Dee are Compared
to the Lunts, but Hayden and Fonda also Apply." People (March
23 1981): 75+.

DE KNIGHT, FANNIE BELLE

See # 1992

DE WINDT, SHEILA

3952.   "Sheila De Windt: BJ and the Bear star says beauty can
be handicap." Jet (August 6 1981): 54-56.

DILLARD, MIMI

3953.   "A Soaring Star Called Mimi." Sepia (April 1964): 42-
46.

DIXON, IVAN (1931-   )

3954.   Bogle, Donald. Blacks in American Films and
Television. New York: Garland, 1988, pp. 383-384.

Articles

3955.   Fessier, Michael, Jr. "A War Ivan Dixon is Winning."
New York Times (January 29 1967): D19.

3956.   Gratz, Roberta Brandes. "Ivan Dixon: A Choice of
Heroes." New York Post (June 17 1967): 35.

3957.   Hobson, Charles. "The Success of Ivan Dixon." Black
Stars (October 1976): 6-9.

3958.   "Ivan Dixon at Home." Sepia (February 1967): 38-41.

3959.   "The Many Faces of Ivan Dixon." Sepia (July 1965): 32-
36.

3960.   "The Sergeant's Hard Climb from the Ranks; How Ivan
Dixon Made It from Harlem to 'Hogan's Heroes'." TV Guide
(September 16 1967): 35-36.

DOBSON, TAMARA (1947-   )

See also # 3372-3373

3961. Bogle, Donald. <u>Blacks in American Films and Television</u>. New York: Garland, 1988, pp. 384-385.

Articles

3962. Banks, Lacy J. "Tamara Dobson Has all the Tools." <u>Black Stars</u> (February 1977): 50-57.

3963. "Cleopatra Jones. Tamara Dobson plays two-fisted crime buster in new black action flick." <u>Ebony</u> (July 1973): 48-50, 52, 54, 56.

3964. Haverstraw, Jack. "The Making of a Movie Star." <u>Sepia</u>, Vol. 24 (May 1975): 44-52.

3965. Jenkins, Flo. "Tamara Dobson...Bold, Black and Beautiful!!" <u>Right On</u>! (September 1973): 18-19.

3966. Kisner, Ronald E. "Tamara Dobson Takes on First Film Sex Role." <u>Jet</u> (December 23 1976): 58-61.

3967. Klemesrud, Judy. "Tamara Dobson - Not Super Fly but Super Woman." <u>New York Times</u> (August 19 1973): Sec. 2, p. 11.

3968. Lane, Bill. "Tamara Dobson Debuts in 'Cleopatra Jones'." <u>Black Stars</u> (July 1973): 10-17.

3969. Lucas, Bob. "Super Tall Super Sleuth in 'Cleopatra Jones'." <u>Sepia</u>, Vol. 22 (September 1973): 38-45.

3970. Murphy, Frederick Douglas. "Tamara Dobson Alias Cleopatra Jones." <u>Black Stars</u> (December 1975): 20-25.

3971. Murray, James P. "Cleopatra Jones is Something Else!" New York <u>Amsterdam News</u> (July 7 1973): D-5.

3972. "Newsmakers." <u>Newsweek</u> (August 27 1973): 49.

3973. Peterson, Maurice. "On the Aisle: Focus on Tamara Dobson." <u>Essence</u> (October 1976): 48.

3974. Sant'Angelo, Giorgio. "Tamara Dobson Yesterday, Today, and Tamara." <u>Interview</u> (October 1976): 30-31.

3975. Smilgis, Martha. "To the Top." <u>People</u>, Vol. 10 (December 18 1978): 82, 85.

3976. Thompson, M. Cordell. "Tamara Dobson: Tall, Tough, and Talented Actor." <u>Jet</u> (September 13 1973): 56-59.

DORN, MICHAEL

3977. Drennan, Kathryn. "Michael Dorn: Klingon Warrior." <u>Starlog</u> (January 1989): 37-40, 64.

3978. McNeil, Dee Dee. "Michael Dorn: Star of 'Chips' Cashes in on Success." <u>Black Stars</u> (May 1981): 21-23.

DOWNING, DAVID (1943-   )

3979. Downing, David - Clippings [Billy Rose Theatre Collection]

DRUMMOND, MALCOLM

3980. Fields, Sidney. "Man of Action." New York Daily News (February 1 1973): 58. Profile of stuntman Malcolm Drummond.

DU BOIS, JA'NET (aka Jeannette) (1938-   )

3981. Brown, Marcia L. "Ja'Net Du Bois Has It All Together!" Black Stars (August 1974): 24-26.

3982. "Jeannette Dubois: Actress of Many Faces." Sepia (May 1964): 68-71.

3983. Jenkins, Walter. "Are Ja'net Dubois 'Good Times' Days Numbered?" Black Stars (October 1978): 33-36.

3984. _____. "Ja'net Dubois--Tells Why They're Good Times on 'Good Times'." Black Stars (July 1977): 30-35.

3985. Norman, Shirley. "The Real Ja'net Du Bois." Sepia (March 1978): 19-24, 26.

3986. Ostroff, Roberta. "'I Keep Wondering if the World is Ready for Me'; a day with Ja'net DuBois and some very soulful friends in Malibu." TV Guide (July 19 1975): 10+.

3987. Seligsohn, Leo. "Off the Street and Onto a Stage." New York Newsday (August 26 1968): 32A, 30A.

3988. Slaton, Shell. "Ja'net Dubois: The Lady of Dreams, Flowers and Pearls." Right On! (March 1978): 54-56.

DUNHAM, KATHERINE

3989. "Casbah; Katherine Dunham has first acting role in new film." Ebony (March 1948): 36-38.

3990. "'Mambo': Katherine Dunham has Choice Acting, Dancing, Singing Role in New Italian Music Drama." Ebony (December 1954): 83-84, 86.

3991. "Miss Dunham Trains Dancers for New Film." Ebony (October 1958): 121-122+. [Green Mansions]

EDWARDS, ELLA

3992. Jenkins, Walter. "Ella Edwards Takes Care of Business." Black Stars (November 1973): 50-54.

EDWARDS, GLORIA (d.1988)

3993. "Black Stars Mourn Death of Gloria Edwards." Jet (March 21 1988): 18.

3994. "Gloria Edwards." Classic Images, No. 154 (April 1988): 61.

3995. "Gloria Edwards." Variety (March 2 1988): 117.

EDWARDS, JAMES (1916-1970)

3996. Bogle, Donald. Blacks in American Films and Television. New York: Garland, 1988, pp. 386-388.

Articles

3997. Edwards, James. "Hollywood: So What!" Our World (December 1953): 56-59.

3998. "Hollywood's Bronze Valentino: Catapulted to fame in "Home of the Brave", handsome Jimmy Edwards has started female hearts fluttering." Our World (February 1950): 26-29, 32.

3999. "Home of the Brave: Filmdom chucks Uncle Tom characterization for straight-forward movie about the Negro." Our World (June 1949): 33-36.

4000. "If You Married...Jimmie Edwards. What kind of a husband would the handsome young movie star make? He's a thoughtful, down-to-earth ex-CIO organizer." Tan Confessions (November 1950): 30-31.

4001. "Movie Debut: Ex-GI James Edwards Passes First Film Test with Star Robert Ryan's Advice." Ebony (April 1949): 25+.

4002. "Steel Helmet. James Edwards Has Excellent Role in Korean War Movie." Ebony (March 1951): 79+.

Obituaries

4003. New York Times (January 8 1970): 41.

4004. Newsweek (January 19 1970): 95.

4005. "The Sad, Semi-Secret Death of a Star." Sepia (March 1970): 72-77.

4006. Time (January 19 1970): 49.

4007. Variety (January 14 1970).

ELLIS, EVELYN (1894-1958)

4008. "Evelyn Ellis." Variety (June 11 1958). [Obituary]

EVANS, DAMON (1950-   )

See also # 3386

4009. "Damon Evans is a Serious Singer." New York Amsterdam News (October 15 1975): D-14.

4010. Davis, Curt. "Damon Evans--Giving What He's Got."
Encore American and Worldwide News (July 19 1977): 27-28.

4011. Evans, Damon - Clippings [Billy Rose Theatre
Collection]

4012. Maksian, George. "Damon Evans TV's New Lionel." New
York Daily News (July 14 1975): 66.

4013. Tapley, Mel. "The Jefferson's Son...Versatile Damon
Evans." New York Amsterdam News (May 8 1976): D8-D9.

EVANS, MIKE

4014. Benson, Sheila. "'Lionel' got the Bounce-Back Award.
Michael Evans finds it hard to talk about quitting 'The
Jeffersons' five years ago--but he's glad to be home." TV
Guide (August 9 1980): 36-40.

4015. Evans, Mike. "'I Performed to be Accepted.'" Black
Stars (November 1977): 45-49.

4016. Evans, Michael - Clippings [Billy Rose Theatre
Collection]

4017. Jenkins, Flo. "Mike Evans!...What's He Up to These
Days?" Right On! (July 1976): 38

4018. "Mike Evans...Candid Comments!" Right On! (November
1973): 42-43.

4019. "Mike Evans No Longer Member of The Jeffersons." Right
On! (August 1975): 60-61.

4020. Thomas, M. Martez. "Mike Evans...Actor Who Wants All
He Can Get Out of Life!" Right On! (October 1974): 48-50.

4021. Whitney, Dwight. "The Boy Next Door--to the Bunkers.
He's Michael Evans, who hopes All in the Family will help him
move into a better neighborhood." TV Guide (June 2-8 1973):
28-32.

FALANA, LOLA

See also # 3370

4022. Armstrong, Lois. "Whatever Lola Falana Wants, Lola's
Getting: She's Tigress of Her Own Spots and Specials." People
(March 29 1976): 63.

4023. "Dancers Go Dramatic. Newcomer Lola Falana, veteran
Fayard Nicholas try acting in new film." Ebony (September
1969): 38-40, 42, 46. [Liberation of Lord Byron Jones]

4024. Falana, Lola - Clippings [Billy Rose Theatre
Collection]

4025. Gardella, Kay. "Lola Gets What She Wants in Series of
TV Specials." New York Daily News (December 15 1975): 76.

4026. Thompson, M. Cordell. "Lola Falana: Whatever She
Wants, She Gets and Deserves." Black Stars (July 1976): 40-
46.

4027. Unger, Arthur. "ABC-TV 'Comes Up with a Winner'--Lola
Falana." Christian Science Monitor (December 17 1975): 10.

FARGAS, ANTONIO (c.1947-   )

4028. "Biography: Antonio Fargas." The Black American
(February 23 1978): 9.

4029. Collins, Lisa. "Antonio Fargas: Quite a Character."
Black Stars (February 1974): 62-65.

4030. Murray, James P. "You Know His Face, Folks, But Not
the Name." New York Amsterdam News (May 14 1975): D-14.

4031. Patman, Jean. "Fargas Is Young, Gifted, Black; At 22,
He's Already an Old Man." New York Post (August 9 1969).

FARINA

See Hoskins, Allen

FIELDS, KIM (1969-   )

4032. "Actress Kim Fields: Young and Sensitive Blooms." New
York Amsterdam News (July 26 1986): 28.

4033. Collier, Aldore. "Kim Fields: How She Copes with Life
in Hollywood." Jet (July 15 1985): 28-30.

4034. Fee, Debi. "It's Nice to Sign Autographs, But I'd
Rather Eat My Hamburger!" Right On! (February 1979): 38-40.

4035. Fields, Kim - Clippings [Billy Rose Theatre Collection]

4036. Grimes, Nikki. "Spotlight: Fields in Bloom." Essence
(August 1986): 84-86, 144.

4037. Horner, Cynthia. "Kim Fields: Up Close and Very
Personal." Right On! (August 1985): 40-42.

4038. "Kim Fields: what happened to child star after TV
fame?" Jet (January 23 1989): 56-59.

4039. Marsh, Antoinette. "Black Stars Interviews Kim
Fields." Black Stars (April 1980): 70-73.

4040. "Mother vs. Daughter: Kim and Chip Fields Keep Their
Rivalry in Perspective." Right On! (November 1983): 50-53,
65.

4041. Shaw, Ellen Torgerson. "Remember the Kid Who
Loooooovvvvved Mrs. Butterworth?" TV Guide (June 6 1981): 17-
18.

FISHBURNE, LARRY

4042. Collins, Lisa. "Laurence Fishburne III! Typical Teen-Ager...Talented Actor!" Right On! (June 1976): 22-24.

4043. Fishburn, Larry - Clippings [Billy Rose Theatre Collection]

FISHER, GAIL (c.1935-   )

See also # 3373

4044. Berkvist, Robert. "'Too Bad Liz Taylor's Already Beaten Me to Cleopatra.'" New York Times (April 9 1972): D19.

4045. Fisher, Gail - Clippings [Billy Rose Theatre Collection]

4046. Fisher, Gail, as told to Jason Winters. "Gail Fisher." Black Stars (September 1977): 50-55.

4047. "Gail Fisher--The Girl from Mannix." Ebony (October 1969): 140+.

4048. "Gail Fisher--Top Actress in TV Series." Jet (December 16 1971): 56-59.

4049. "Gail Fisher's Bid for Stardom." Sepia (October 1964): 48-51.

4050. Jenkins, Walter. "A Portrait of Gail Fisher." Sepia (March 1969): 34-37.

4051. Lucas, Bob. "Gail Fisher: TV's Top Black Actress." Black Stars (May 1973): 28-37.

FLUELLEN, JOEL (c.1909-1990)

4052. "Actor Joel Fluellen, 81, Dead of Apparent Suicide." Jet (February 26 1990): 11.

FOXX, REDD (1922-   )

4053. Bogle, Donald. Blacks in American Films and Television. New York: Garland, 1988, pp. 391-393.

4054. Price, Joe X., ed. Redd Foxx, B. S. (before Sanford). Chicago: Contemporary Books, 1979. 144p.

Articles

4055. Antoine, Roane. "Redd Foxx's New Television Show." Sepia (June 1980): 40-44.

4056. Bennett, Robert. "How Redd Fox Went from Blue Jokes to Black." Sepia (June 1972): 38-45.

4057. Leavy, Walter. "Eddie Murphy, Richard Pryor, Redd Foxx: three generations of Black comedy." Ebony (January 1990): 102+.

4058. Lyons, Douglas C. "Redd Foxx: Still Going Strong After 50 Years." Ebony (June 1988): 52+.

4059. Robinson, Louie. "Redd Foxx." Ebony (June 1974): 154+.

4060. Salvo, Patrick. "A Film First for Foxx." Sepia (October 1976): 60-65.

Media Materials

4061. Speak Easy: An Hour with Redd Foxx [videorecording]. Los Angeles: KCOP-TV, 1980. 47 min. Host, Marilyn Solomon. Summary: Redd Foxx discusses his philosophy of life, his career in show business and his plans for the future. Includes excerpts from Sanford and Son, and Foxx talks about the difficulties and people he worked with on that show. [Held by the Schomburg Center - Sc Visual VRB-210]

Sanford and Son

See also # 4061

4062. Bogle, Donald. Blacks in American Films and Television. New York: Garland Pub., 1988, pp. 301-304.

Articles

4063. Collier, Eugenia. "'Sanford and Son' is White to the Core." New York Times (June 17 1973): Sec. 2, pp. 1, 3.

4064. Cyclops. "TV Review: Black Sit-com, but Too Tame." Life (April 21 1972): 20.

4065. Gardner, Paul. "The Quick Redd Foxx Jumps Into a New Kettle of Fish." New York Times (February 6 1972): Sec. 2, p. 19.

4066. Robinson, Louie. "Sanford and Son. Redd Foxx, Demond Wilson wake up TV's jaded audience." Ebony (July 1972): 52+.

4067. Sanford and Son - Clippings [Billy Rose Theatre Collection]

4068. "TV Mailbag: Speaking Up for Sanford and Son." New York Times (July 8 1973): Sec. 2, pp. 1, 8, 15. Responses to # 4063.

FRANCIS, VERA

4069. Francis, Vera. "How I Crashed the Movies." Tan (January 1950): 28-29, 78-79.

4070. "From Vera to Viejah: Switching from her former role as a bundle of sex, Vera Francis storms Hollywood." Our World (April 1955): 14-15.

4071. Posner, George A. "Sexiest Gal in Movies. Former nurse now glamour queen." Color (April 1953): 11-13.

4072. "President's Lady: Vera Francis Gets Explosive Role in Movie Touching on Mixed Romance Theme." Ebony, Vol. 8 (February 1953): 71-75.

4073. "Vera Francis: Movies' New Sex Thrill." Our World, Vol. 8 (March 1953): 54-57.

FRANKLIN, CARL (c.1950-   )

4074. "Young Actor in New TV Series." New York Amsterdam News (March 29 1975): D-14.

FRAZIER, SHEILA (1948-   )

4075. Collins, Lisa. "Sheila Frazier: Sandwiched Between Pryor and Cosby...She's a Hit." Black Stars (February 1979): 65-67.

4076. "Flashback! Sheila Frazier!" Right On! (May 1979): 46-47.

4077. Frazier, Sheila - Clippings [Billy Rose Theatre Collection]

4078. Guarino, Ann. "Off Camera." New York Sunday News (June 30 1974): L28.

4079. Smith, Angela E. "She Wants to be a Movie Cleopatra." New York Amsterdam News (April 20 1974): B-12.

FREEMAN, AL, Jr. (1934-   )

4080. Bogle, Donald. Blacks in American Films and Television. New York: Garland, 1988, pp. 393-394.

Articles

4081. Berkvist, Robert. "'Why the Afro? You're Not that Kind of Guy.'" New York Times (January 18 1970): D19.

4082. Collins, Lisa. "The Checkered Career of Al Freeman, Jr." Black Stars (March 1976): 21-26.

4083. Freeman, Al, Jr. - Clippings [Billy Rose Theatre Collection]

4084. Johnson, Robert E. "Al Freeman Talks About TV Career and His 'Designing' Wife." Jet (August 13 1981): 60-63.

4085. Nencel, Debra. "Al Freeman, Jr. Give Him the Country Life." Soap Opera Digest (November 27 1979): 39-43.

FREEMAN, MORGAN (1937-   )

4086.   DeCurtis, Anthony. "Quiet Cool." Rolling Stone (May 5 1988): 27.

4087.   Levy, George Damon. "Morgan Freeman, behind the scenes." PC-Computing (September 1988): 180+.

4088.   Lombardi, John. "Morgan Freeman: in the role of his lifetime." Esquire (June 1988): 210-219.

4089.   Martin, A. R. "The Rise of Morgan Freeman." Connoisseur (September 1988): 84+.

4090.   Mieses, Stanley. "Street Smart." Premiere (December 1989): 122-123, 125-126. [Profile]

4091.   Toepfer, Susan. "Oscar hopeful Morgan Freeman knows better than anyone that sometimes genius isn't enough." People (April 4 1988): 89-90, 93.

4092.   Wetzsteon, Ross. "Morgan Freeman Takes Off: An Actor's Actor Becomes a Star." New York (March 14 1988): 54+.

4093.   Whitaker, Charles. "Is Morgan Freeman America's Greatest Actor?" Ebony (April 1990): 32-34.

4094.   "Zeke." New Yorker (July 3 1978): 19-22. [Profile]

Newspaper Articles

4095.   Berkvist, Robert. "New Face: Morgan Freeman." New York Times (April 21 1978): C-4. [Interview]

4096.   Dudar, Helen. "For Morgan Freeman, Stardom Wasn't Sudden." New York Times (December 10 1989): Sec. 2, pp. 15, 44.

4097.   Robertson, Nan. "Morgan Freeman Looks at Acting." New York Times (May 25 1987): 9.

Driving Miss Daisy

4098.   Alford, Henry, and Paula Bullwinkel. "Two for the Road." Interview (November 1989): 160-161. Interview with Freeman and his "Driving Miss Daisy" co-star, Jessica Tandy.

4099.   Frechette, David. "Freeman Avoids Lovable Servant Cliche in Daisy." Black Film Review, Vol. 5, No. 4 (Fall 1989?): 25.

4100.   Simpson, Janice C. "In the Driver's Seat: actor Morgan Freeman eases into high gear." Time (January 8 1990): 75.

Johnny Handsome

4101.   Seidenberg, Robert. "Johnny Handsome: Morgan Freeman does a flat-foot ground-pounder with authority." American Film (October 1989): 96-97.

Lean on Me

4102. Berlin, Joey. "Acting on Principal." <u>New York Post</u>
(March 1 1989): 27.

4103. Moore, Trudy S. "Morgan Freeman stars as tough
principal Joe Clark in hit movie, 'Lean on Me.'" <u>Jet</u> (March 6
1989): 24-26.

4104. Van Gelder, Lawrence. "At the Movies: Truth vs.
Fiction." <u>New York Times</u> (March 3 1989): C8.

GARRETT, SUSIE

4105. "Marla Gibbs ('The Jeffersons'), Susie Garrett ('Punky
Brewster'): two sisters star on TV." <u>Jet</u> (December 10 1984):
60+.

GARRISON, DORIS

See # 3367

GARRISON, HAROLDETTA

See # 3367

GENTRY, MINNIE (1915-   )

4106. Bogle, Donald. <u>Blacks in American Films and
Television</u>. New York: Garland, 1988, p. 394.

GIBBS, MARLA

See also # 3387

4107. Bogle, Donald. <u>Blacks in American Films and
Television</u>. New York: Garland, 1988, pp. 394-395.

Articles

4108. Buck, Jerry. "On the Jeffersons, Florence plays a role
naturally made from life." <u>New York Post</u> (January 3 1978):
49.

4109. Collier, Aldore. "227-Marla's Masterpiece: Star of The
Jeffersons develops own sitcom." <u>Ebony</u> (December 1986): 92+.

4110. Collins, Lisa. "And Then Came Marla Gibbs." <u>Black
Stars</u> (November 1977): 32-36.

4111. Hicks, Jack. "The Day Marla Gibbs Learned to Fight
Back." <u>TV Guide</u> (May 17 1986): 49-52, 54.

4112. Johnson, Pamela. "Spotlight: Marla Gibbs." <u>Essence</u>
(October 1988): 76+.

4113. Johnson, Robert E. "Marla Gibbs Makes Maid Role Pay
Off with Own TV Series." <u>Jet</u> (May 21 1981): 58-61.

4114. Kisner, Ronald E. "Marla Gibbs: TV Maid for the Jeffersons." Jet (April 6 1978): 20-23.

4115. "Marla Gibbs move up after 'The Jeffersons'." Jet (September 30 1985): 62-63.

4116. "Marla Gibbs sounds off on whites who write insensitive roles for Blacks." Jet (November 25 1985): 60-61.

4117. "Marla Gibbs ('The Jeffersons'), Susie Garrett ('Punky Brewster'): two sisters star on TV." Jet (December 10 1984): 60+.

4118. Reed, Claude, Jr. "A Conversation with Marla Gibbs." New York Amsterdam News (January 1 1983): 11-13.

4119. Sanders, Richard. "After Mopping Up as the Maid on The Jeffersons, Marla Gibbs Polishes Her Image as the Star of 227." People (November 25 1985).

4120. Torgerson, Ellen. "'I Don't Take Any Guff' Marla Gibbs of 'The Jeffersons' is no longer the shy daydreamer she was as a youngster." TV Guide (August 11 1979): 36-38.

4121. West, Stan. "Marla Gibbs--A Self-Maid Actress!" Right On! (February 1981): 66-68.

GILLIAM, STU (1943-   )

4122. "The Funny World of Stu Gilliam. A new star rises in the field of television comedy." Sepia (August 1969): 35-38.

4123. Gardella, Kay. "Roll Out a Barrell of Fun on a New Black Series." New York Daily News (July 12 1973): 95.

4124. Jenkins, Walter. "Stu Gilliam Keeps Rolling Along." Black Stars (February 1974): 12-18.

4125. Marsh, Antoinette. "Stu Gilliam: The Ambassador of Mirth." Black Stars (April 1979): 66-69.

GILYARD, CLARENCE, JR. (1959-   )

4126. "Not Just a Chip Off the Block." Right On! (June 1983): 24-26.

4127. "Right On! Talks To: Clarence Gilyard, Jr." Right On! (July 1983): 63.

GIMPEL, ERICA

4128. Fee, Debi. "Elusive Erica." Right On! (May 1983): 32.

4129. _____. "Playing the Fame Game." Right On! (July 1982): 32-33.

GIVENS, ROBIN

4130. Breslin, Kevin. "Claims to Fame: Robin Givens." New York Daily News (July 27 1986): People Section, p. 4.

4131. Givens, Robin - Clippings [Billy Rose Theatre Collection]

4132. Murphy, Mary. "Why Robin Givens Has Rolled with the Punches -and Still Loves Tyson." TV Guide (July 1 1989): 6-11.

GLASS, RON (c.1945-   )

4133. Fee, Debi. "Reflections Through Ron's Looking Glass." Right On! (February 1983): 22-23.

4134. Haddad-Garcia, George. "The Articulate Ron Glass." Black Stars (February 1980): 32-36.

4135. Jenkins, Walter. "Looking in on...Ron Glass." Black Stars (July 1976): 26-31.

4136. "Living in the Glass House." Right On! (March 1983): 26-33.

4137. Norman, Shirley. "Television's Top Black Detective." Sepia (May 1977): 54-60.

4138. Torgerson, Ellen. "Polished, Smooth, Vulnerable. That's 'Barney Miller's' Detective Harris and the actor who plays the part." TV Guide (September 23 1978): 36-38.

GLENN, ROY E. (1914-1971)

4139. New York Times (March 13 1971): 32. [Obituary]

4140. "Roy Glenn Sr." Variety (March 10 1971): 79. [Obituary]

GLOVER, DANNY

4141. Belkin, Lisa. "Fame and Controversy for Danny Glover." New York Times (January 26 1986): Sec. 2, pp. 21-22.

4142. Collier, Aldore. "Danny Glover: the Reluctant Movie Star." Ebony, Vol. 41 (March 1986): 82+.

4143. "Danny Glover stars in 'Mandela' movie that tugs at heart, shocks senses." Jet (October 5 1987): 58-60.

4144. Dennard, Darryl W. "EM Interview: Danny Glover." Ebony Man (May 1989): 17-19.

4145. Glover, Danny - Clippings [Billy Rose Theatre Collection]

4146. Krista, Charlene. "Danny Glover: an Interview." Films in Review, Vol. 36 (April 1985): 233-235.

4147. Moore, Trudy S. "Danny Glover: Villain in 'Color Purple' is a Kind Family Man." Jet (March 17 1986): 28-31.

GOLDBERG, WHOOPI [Caryn Jones] (c.1949-   )

4148. Bogle, Donald. Blacks in American Films and Television. New York: Garland, 1988, pp. 395-396.

Articles

4149. Collier, Aldore. "Whoopi Goldberg: Tough and tender in new film drama, 'Clara's Heart'." Jet (October 24 1988): 30-32.

4150. Ericson, Steve. "Whoopi Goldberg." Rolling Stone (May 8 1986): 39+.

4151. Goldberg, Whoopi - Clippings [Billy Rose Theatre Collection]

4152. "Goldberg, Whoopi." Current Biography 1985.

4153. Hite, Nancy. "Up Close: Whoopi Goldberg." Right On! (July 1986): 18-20.

4154. Kearney, Jill. "Whoopi Goldberg: Color Her Anything." American Film, Vol. 11 (December 1985): 25+. [Interview]

4155. Meeley, Darrah. "Close-Up: Whoopi Goldberg." Screen Actor (Fall 1988): 16-19.

4156. Rensin, David. "Whoopi Goldberg." Playboy (June 1987): 51+. [Interview]

4157. "Whoopi Goldberg." People (December 23 1985): 99+.

GOSSETT, LOUIS (1936-   )

4158. Bogle, Donald. Blacks in American Films and Television. New York: Garland, 1988, pp. 396-398.

Articles

4159. Broeske, P. H. "Louis Gossett, Jr." Films in Review, Vol. 35, No. 7 (August-September 1983): 431-435.

4160. "Close Up." Seventeen, Vol. 36 (January 1977): 54.

4161. Collins, Lisa. "Lou Gossett: Hollywood's Consummate Black Actor." Black Stars (June 1977): 30-35.

4162. Davis, Curt. "The Inner Voice of Louis Gossett." Encore American and Worldwide News (June 6 1977): 28-31.

4163. Gant, Liz. "A Peek at Louis Gossett, Jr." Essence, Vol. 8 (February 1978): 48+.

4164. Gossett, Louis - Clippings [Billy Rose Theatre Collection]

4165. Hofler, Robert. "Minority View: seeing white, being Black." Life (March 1989): 90. [Interview]

4166. Johnson, Robert E. "Lou Gossett Scores as Tough Marine Drill Sergeant." Jet (September 6 1982): 60-62.

4167. Long, M. "A Tree Did Not Grow in Brooklyn..." Gentleman's Quarterly (December 1988): 292-293.

4168. "Louis Gossett, Jr. Sizzles in Two Films: 'Enemy Mine', 'Iron Eagle.'" Jet, Vol. 69 (February 3 1986): 36-38.

4169. "The Many Faces of Lou Gossett." Jet (January 30 1984): 58-61.

4170. Norment, Lynn. "Lou Gossett: The Agony and the Ecstasy of Success." Ebony, Vol. 38 (December 1982): 142+.

4171. "An Officer and A Gentleman. Lou Gossett stars as tough drill sargeant at a naval flight school." Ebony (September 1982): 112+.

4172. Peterson, Maurice. "On the Aisle: Focus on Lou Gossett." Essence (June 1977): 16.

4173. Russell, D. "Finally Landing Some Big Ones." TV Guide, Vol. 26 (April 8 1978): 10-12.

4174. Salvo, Patrick William. "Lou Gossett: Rediscovered for the 8th Time." Sepia (September 1977): 42-46.

4175. Slater, Jack. "Television's New Primetime Black Man. Robert Guillaume, James E. Jones, Lou Gossett pioneer." Ebony (December 1979): 124+.

4176. Slaton, Shell. "Lou Gossett--From Fiddler to Fame!" Right On! (August 1977): 14-16.

4177. "Soul Reels: Black Stars in Motion." Right On! (April 1972): 26-27.

4178. Turan, Kenneth. "His Basic Training Continues." TV Guide, Vol. 31 (Oct 29-Nov 4 1983): 14-16+.

4179. Waldron, Clarence. "Behind the Scenes with Lou Gossett and Malcolm-Jamal Warner." Ebony Man (November 1987): 38-40, 42.

4180. Wiener, Thomas. "An Actor and a Gentleman." American Film, Vol. 8, No. 6 (April 1983): 48-52.

Newspaper Articles

4181. Archibald, Lewis. "An Aquarian Interview with Louis Gossett, Jr. Star of 'An Officer and A Gentleman.'" The Aquarian (August 25-September 1 1982): 24-25.

4182.   Collins, Glenn.   "Lou Gossett Jr. Battles the Hollywood Stereotype."   New York Times (February 19 1989): Sec. 2, pp. 33, 40.

4183.   Klemesrud, Judy.   "Earning Sergeant's Stripes for a Movie Role."   New York Times (July 25 1982): Sec. 2, pp. 1, 13.

4184.   Peck, Ira.   "'The Zulu' of Coney Island."   New York Times (February 20 1966).

4185.   Seligson, Tom.   "When Louis Gossett, Jr. Stopped Being Angry: An Interview."   New York Daily News/Parade (July 17 1988): 4-5, 7.

GRAVES, TERESA (c.1949-   )

See also # 3377

4186.   Gardella, Kay.   "Teresa Drops Bikini Roles to Don Costume of a Cop."   New York Daily News (July 10 1974): 43.

4187.   Graves, Teresa - Clippings [Billy Rose Theatre Collection]

4188.   Lardine, Bob.   "Teresa Graves--How They Got 'Christie Love.'"   New York Sunday News Magazine (August 10 1975): 11-12.

4189.   Lewis, Richard Warren.   "Teresa Graves of 'Get Christie Love.'"   TV Guide (November 30 1974): 20-23.

4190.   "Will the Real Teresa Graves Please Stand Up?   Star of "Get Christie Love" series is devout bible student."   Ebony (December 1974): 65+.

GRAY, HARRY

See # 1992

GREENE, LAURA

4191.   Carlson, Walter.   "Advertising: Just Don't Mention the Product.   Listerine employs a Negro student to advise students."   New York Times (July 24 1966).

4192.   Greene, Laura.   "Bring It Down Front: A Bad Black Image in Film."   Essence (May 1973): 70.

4193.   Hammond, Sally.   "It's Laura, Not Lena."   New York Post (July 18 1970): Sec. 3, p. 23.

4194.   "Laura Greene likes the commercials (that's where she stars)."   TV Guide (November 7 1964): 12-13.

4195.   "Laura Greene: Putting It All Together."   Sepia (March 1971): 60-63.

4196. "A Star is Born. Laura Greene finds frustration and hard work in struggle to stardom." Sepia (August 1964): 58-62.

4197. Taylor, Len. "Laura Greene." Essence (January 1971): 42-43.

GREENE, STANLEY N. (1911-1981)

4198. "Stanley Greene." Variety (July 8 1981): 79. [Obituary]

4199. "Stanley N. Greene, 70, An Actor and Producer." New York Times (July 11 1981): 16. [Obituary]

GRIER, DAVID ALAN

4200. Grier, David Alan - Clippings [Billy Rose Theatre Collection]

GRIER, PAM (c.1950-   )

See also # 3372-3373

4201. Bogle, Donald. Blacks in American Films and Television. New York: Garland, 1988, pp. 398-399.

Articles

4202. Ames, K., and S. Smith. "Queen of the B's." Newsweek, Vol. 87 (February 2 1976): 67.

4203. Collins, W. B. "Don't Mess Around with Pamela Grier." Biographical News, Vol. 1 (June 1974): 649.

4204. Ebert, Alan. "Pam Grier: Coming into Focus." Essence, Vol. 9 (January 1979): 43, 104, 107-108.

4205. Grier, Pam. "I'm Just a Human Being." Black Stars (November 1978): 28-30.

4206. Jacobson, Mark. "Sex Goddess of the Seventies." New York (May 19 1975): 43-46.

4207. Jenkins, Flo. "Pam Grier...Sexy, Successful, but Unspoiled!" Right On! (April 1974): 14-16.

4208. Johnson, Connie. "Pam Grier: The Lady Who Wants Everything!" Black Stars (November 1977): 56-63.

4209. Kincaid, Jamaica. "Pam Grier: the Mocha Mogul of Hollywood." Ms., Vol. 4 (August 1975): 49-53. [Interview]

4210. Kisner, Ronald. "Pam Grier's Sudden Rise to Stardom." Black Stars (April 1973): 38-42.

4211. Lucas, Bob. "Pam Grier is Big in Talent, Too." Jet (December 16 1976): 58-61.

4212. _____. "Pam Grier: Why Are Black Women Fading from Films?" Jet (November 6 1980): 58-61.

4213. Makel, Chris. "Movie Review: Pam Grier and Richard Pryor Co-Star in Greased Lightning." Black Stars (November 1977): 30-31.

4214. "Pam Grier Expands Her Film Career." Jet (April 17 1975): 56-60.

4215. "Pam Grier Finds Fame in Black Films." Jet (August 9 1973): 58-61.

4216. "Pam Grier: Growing Up Wasn't Always Fun!" Right On! (December 1976): 66-69.

4217. Rickey, Carrie. "Little Sheba's Comeback." Village Voice (March 4-10 1981): 42.

4218. Robinson, Louie. "Pam Grier: More Than Just a Sex Symbol." Ebony (June 1976): 33-36, 38, 40, 42. [Interview]

4219. Salvo, Patrick. "Pam Grier: The Movie Super-Sex Goddess Who's Fed Up with Sex and Violence." Sepia (February 1976): 48-56.

4220. "The Very Private Life of Pam Grier." Black Stars (January 1974): 20-22.

GUILLAUME, ROBERT (1927-   )

4221. Bogle, Donald. Blacks in American Films and Television. New York: Garland, 1988, p. 400.

Articles

4222. Collier, Aldore. "Robert Guillaume: Behind the Scenes with Benson." Ebony (November 1983): 133+.

4223. Davis, Curt. "Robert Guillaume: Winning the War if not the Battle." Encore American and Worldwide News (October 24 1977): 28-31.

4224. Guillaume, Robert - Clippings [Billy Rose Theatre Collection]

4225. Holmes, John. "Benson: From Butler to Budgetmeister." American Way (June 1984): 49-50, 53.

4226. Kiester, Edwin. "Prime Minister of Protests and Outbursts." TV Guide, Vol. 32 (October 6-12 1984): 35-36+.

4227. Lindsey, Robert. "Robert Guillaume - The Wise-Cracking Butler of 'Soap'." New York Times (December 18 1977): Sec. II, p. 37.

4228. Lucas, Bob. "Private Side of Benson TV Star." Jet (November 22 1979): 44-47.

4229. "Robert Guillaume Takes Benson from Butler to Lt. Governor." Jet, Vol. 70 (May 19 1986): 56-57.

4230. Salvo, Patrick William. "Interview with Robert Guillaume." Sepia, Vol. 28 (June 1979): 39-46, 80.

4231. Slater, Jack. "Television's New Primetime Black Man. Robert Guillaume, James E. Jones, Lou Gossett pioneer." Ebony (December 1979): 124+.

4232. Wahls, Robert. "Look Back Without Anger." New York Sunday News (January 7 1973): Sec. 3, p. 8

GUNN, BILL (1934-1989)

4233. Frederick, Robert B. "If Poitier Can't Do It They Rewrite For a White Actor: Bill Gunn's Beef." Variety (November 4 1964).

4234. Gunn, Bill - Clippings [Billy Rose Theatre Collection]

GUY, JASMINE

See also # 3382

4235. Bernstein, Fred. "After years of trying to fit in, actress Jasmine Guy at last finds happiness in A Different World." People (November 9 1987): 123-124.

4236. Duncan-Hall, Patricia. "The 'Different Worlds' of Jasmine Guy and Dawnn Lewis." Black Collegian (November/December 1988): 76+.

4237. "Jasmine Guy: Sexy snob on TV has different world at home." Jet (December 12 1988): 56+.

4238. Johnson, Robert E. "Jasmine Guy says making love to Eddie Murphy in 'Harlem Nights' is a 'different world'." Jet (December 18 1989): 60-62.

4239. McKinney, Rhoda E. "Introducing: Jasmine Guy of 'A Different World'." Ebony (June 1988): 68+.

4240. Ritz, David. "Spotlight: Jasmine Guy." Essence (August 1988): 46+.

HAIRSTON, JESTER (1901-   )

4241. Collier, Aldore. "Update: Jester Hairston." Ebony (March 1988): 126-130.

4242. Hairston, Jester - Clippings [Billy Rose Theatre Collection]

4243. Prince, Deirdre. "Jester Hairston, 'Mama' Co-star is Better Known as a Musician." Black Stars (October 1975): 52-56.

HALL, ALBERT

4244. Bennetts, Leslie. "New Faces Are Brightening Screen and Stage: Albert Hall." New York Times (August 24 1979): C1, C16.

4245. Collins, Lisa. "Albert Hall: The Next Brando?" Sepia (September 1980): 63-67.

4246. "People You Should Know: Albert Hall." Black Stars (April 1980): 14-15.

HALL, ARSENIO

4247. Allen, Bonnie. "All Hall is Breaking Loose!" Essence (July 1989): 50+.

4248. "Hall, Arsenio." Current Biography 1989.

4249. "New People: Arsenio Hall." Right On! (January 1981): 20.

4250. Pond, Steve. "Hotter than Hall." Playboy (December 1989): 144+.

Newspaper Articles

4251. Hall, Arceneo - Clippings [Billy Rose Theatre Collection]

4252. Jones, Lisa. "Arsenio Hall: Black by Popular Demand." Village Voice (December 15 1987): 120-121.

4253. Krier, Beth Ann. "Arsenio Hall: The Happiest Man in Show Biz." Los Angeles Times/Calendar (December 27 1987): 3, 86.

4254. _____. "TV: Hall: A Hot Property." New York Post (December 29 1987): 74.

Arsenio Hall Show

4255. "Arsenio Hall Makes It Big on Late Night TV Talk Show." Jet (November 9 1987): 58-59.

4256. "Arsenio Hall Show strong late night TV contender." Jet (January 23 1989): 55.

4257. "Arsenio Hall's TV talk show keeps fans awake with fun and famous faces." Jet (April 10 1989): 56.

4258. Collier, Aldore. "Arsenio Hall: Prince of Late Night TV." Jet (January 22 1990): 60-62.

4259. Leahy, Michael. "Arsenio Hall: getting hotter - but feeling the heat." TV Guide (September 30 1989): 16+.

4260. Morrison, Mark. "Midnight Rambler." The Cable Guide, Vol. 8, No. 96 (December 1989): 26-29.

4261. Waters, Harry F. "Arsenio Hall's late arrival; nighttime's first black talk-show host pulls himself up by pulling in young viewers." Newsweek (April 10 1989): 68-69.

4262. Zoglin, Richard. "'Let's Get Busy!!' Hip and Hot, talk host Arsenio Hall is grabbing the post-Carson generation." Time (November 13 1989): 92+.

Newspaper Articles

4263. Cooper, Barry Michael. "Move Over, David Letterman, The Night Belongs to Arsenio Hall." Village Voice (May 23 1989): 27-31.

4264. Mirabella, Alan. "Heeere's Arsenio! (Again). Can Hall Become the Johnny Carson of the '90s'?" New York Daily News (December 30 1988): 75.

4265. Norman, Michael. "TV's Arsenio Hall: Late-Night Cool." New York Times Magazine (October 1 1989): 28-31, 65-66, 92-93.

Coming to America

4266. "Arsenio Hall denies plagiarizing Buchwald script in making film." New York Times (December 19 1989): D20.

4267. Leavy, Walter. "Eddie Murphy and Arsenio Hall star in the new movie 'Coming to America'." Jet (July 18 1988): 36-38.

4268. Mirabella, Alan. "Movies: Having It Hall. The new Eddie Murphy vehicle, 'Coming to America,' is Arsenio Hall's ride to the big time." New York Sunday News (July 3 1988): 3.

HALL, JUANITA (1901-1968)

4269. "Juanita Hall, the Bloody Mary of 'South Pacific,' Dies at 66." New York Times (March 1 1968): 37.

4270. Newsweek (March 11 1968): 86. [Obituary]

4271. Time (March 8 1968): 92. [Obituary]

4272. Variety (March 6 1968). [Obituary]

HAMILTON, BERNIE

4273. "Bernie Hamilton: A Great Star in the Making." Sepia (August 1961): 59-63.

4274. Hamilton, Bernie - Clippings [Billy Rose Theatre Collection]

HAMILTON, KIM

4275. Jenkins, Walter. "Views and Comments on Kim Hamilton." Black Stars (March 1975): 6-11.

4276.   "No Longer Trying to Reach the Moon.   Kim Hamilton is finding other goals well within her reach."   *TV Guide* (September 7 1963): 27.

HAMILTON, LYNN

4277.   Jenkins, Walter.   "Lynn Hamilton Talks About Her Career."   *Black Stars* (October 1974): 70-74.

4278.   McNeil, Dee Dee.   "Lynn Hamilton: Her Sacrifices and Success."   *Black Stars* (April 1978): 64-69.

4279.   Marsh, Antoinette.   "Lynn Hamilton Fights Hollywood Racism."   *Black Stars* (July 1981): 52-55.

HARDEN, ERNEST, JR.

4280.   Slaton, Shell.   "Ernest Harden Jr. -- From the Silver Screen to the TV Screen."   *Right On!* (April 1978): 26-27.

HARDISON, KADEEEM

4281.   Warren, Elaine.   "Kadeem Hardison wants out of A Different World."   *TV Guide* (July 22 1989): 14-16.

HAREWOOD, DORIAN (c.1950-   )

4282.   Chadwick, Bruce.   "The Versatile Dorian Harewood." *Black Stars* (August 1979): 62-63.

4283.   Collier, Aldore.   "Dorian Harewood."   *Ebony Man* (April 1988): 80-82.

4284.   Davis, Curt.   "Cover Story: Picturing Dorian Harewood." *Encore American and Worldwide News* (April 17 1978): 24-26.

4285.   "Dorian Harewood: Versatile Actor Stars as Jesse Owens, Nat King Cole."   *Ebony* (July 1984): 55-56+.

4286.   Knutzen, Eirik.   "There is Life After Roots: Dorian Harewood Finds a Better Way."   *Right On!* (November 1983): 42-44.

4287.   Lane, Bill.   "Can Success Catch Up With Dorian Harewood?"   *Sepia*, Vol. 28 (July 1980): 39-43.

4288.   Murphy, Frederick Douglas.   "Dorian Harewood Brings Fresh Flair to Showbiz."   *Black Stars* (January 1977): 60-65.

4289.   Slaton, Shell.   "Dorian's Domain!"   *Right On!* (June 1979): 46-47, 65.

Newspaper Articles

4290.   Chase, Chris.   "The Audience Can Almost Hear Him Ticking."   *New York Times* (June 13 1976): D-5.

4291.   Fields, Sidney.   "Acting Actor and Singing Singer." New York *Daily News* (April 13 1978): 64.

4292. Scott, Vernon. "Bette Davis Helps Dorian Harewood."
New York News World (March 2 1982).

HARPER, ETHEL (d.1979)

4293. Campbell, Cathy. "A Battered Woman Rises: Aunt
Jemima's Corporate Makeover." Village Voice (November 7
1989): 45.

4294. "Ethel Harper." Variety (April 11 1979): 95.
[Obituary]

4295. "Ethel Harper, Actress Was Aunt Jemima In Ads for
Pancakes." New York Times (April 3 1979): C18. [Obituary]

HARRIS, AVENELLE

4296. Harris, Avenelle. "I Tried to Crash the Movies."
Ebony (August 1946): 5-10. Personal account of a Black
actress's attempt to make it in the film industry.

HARRIS, EDNA MAE

4297. The Bronzeman (May 1932): 9. [Photo]

4298. Stanton, Ali. "Harris Sisters Tell of Yesterday's
Black Theatre." New York Amsterdam News (February 10 1990):
25.

Media Materials

4299. Sirens, Sweethearts and Showgirls of the Stage and
Silver Screen (Audiotape). February 1990 interview with
Harris conducted by cultural historian Delilah Jackson. [Held
by the Hatch-Billops Collection (#6004)]

HARRIS, JULIUS W. (c.1924-   )

4300. Tallmer, Jerry. "Julius Harris: A Place to be
Somebody." New York Post (October 2 1971): Sec. 2, p. 15.

HARRY, JACKEE

4301. Buck, Jerry. "Jackee Harry of '227' Breaks from the
Soaps." Chicago Sun-Times (October 21 1986).

4302. Collier, Aldore. "Jackee reveals another side as she
debuts in own TV show." Jet (May 22 1989): 58-59.

4303. Hadley-Garcia, George. "Why is Jackee Harry TV's
Biggest Flirt?" Right On! (December 1987): 18-19, 75.

4304. "Jackee Out of Character." Ebony Man (October 1989):
46-47.

4305. "Jackee performs exciting dual role in TV movie 'Double
Your Pleasure.'" Jet (October 30 1989): 16-17.

4306. Whitaker, Charles. "Brassy, Sassy Jackee. With an
Emmy and a shorter name, sexy TV siren is making waves."
Ebony (January 1988): 60+.

HARTMAN, ENA

4307. "Ena Hartman: NBC's Cinderella Girl." Sepia (November
1963): 36-40.

4308. Jenkins, Walter. "Ena Hartman--Young Star on the Way
Up." New Lady (February 1970): 8-11.

HATCH, EDDIE EARL

4309. Marlow, Curtis. "Profile: The Eddie Earl Hatch Story."
Right On! (December 1984): 56-57.

HAUSER, FAY

4310. Jenkins, Walter. "Roots Brought New Meaning to Fay
Hauser." Black Stars (June 1979): 14-17.

HAYMAN, LILLIAN

4311. Hayman, Lillian - Clippings [Billy Rose Theatre
Collection]

HAYNES, DANIEL L. (1894-1954)

See also # 1992

4312. Haynes, Daniel L. - Clippings [Billy Rose Theatre
Collection]

4313. New York Times (July 30 1954): 17. [Obituary]

4314. Variety (August 4 1954). [Obituary]

HAYNES, HILDA (1912-1986)

4315. "Hilda Haynes." Variety (March 12 1986): 166.

HAYNES, LLOYD (1934-1987)

See also # 3377

4316. Haynes, Lloyd - Clippings [Billy Rose Theatre
Collection]

4317. Raddatz, Leslie. "His Message: Look Up! Lloyd Haynes
devotes his off-screen hours to educating hostile youth
through aviation." TV Guide (September 15 1973): 20-22.

4318. "'Room 222' stars in NBC-TV movie 'Born to Be Sold'."
New York Amsterdam News (October 31 1981): 32.

Obituaries

4319. "Actor Lloyd Haynes dies; star of TV's 'Room 222'."
Jet (January 19 1987): 18.

4320. "Lloyd Haynes." Variety (January 7 1987): 150.

4321. "Lloyd Haynes, 52, a TV actor and a Co-Star of 'Room
222'." New York Times (January 5 1987): B4.

HEADLEY, SHARI

See also # 3382

4322. Cadogan, Glenda. "Acting's Not All Fun and Kisses."
The City Sun (January 17-23 1990): 24.

4323. Denerstein, Robert. "She Really Liked Being Eddie's
Girl." New York Daily News (August 9 1988): 29.

4324. Horner, Cynthia. "Shari Headley." Right On! (April
1990): 64-65. [Interview]

4325. "Eddie Murphy's first love (but only, alas, on film),
model Shari Headley arrives in Coming to America." People
(July 25 1988): 94-95.

HEMPHILL, SHIRLEY

4326. Haddad, M. George. "The Real Shirley Hemphill." Black
Stars (July 1979): 34-36.

4327. "Shirley Hemphill: A Star is Born. Hefty comedienne
turns kingpin in TV's "One in a Million." Ebony (May 1980):
93+.

HEMSLEY, ESTELLE (1887-1968)

4328. Hemsley, Estelle - Clippings (includes brief
handwritten biography) [Billy Rose Theatre Collection]

4329. New York Times (November 8 1968): 47. [Obituary]

4330. Variety (November 13 1968). [Obituary]

HEMSLEY, SHERMAN (1938-   )

See also # 3386, 3390

4331. Bogle, Donald. Blacks in American Films and
Television. New York: Garland, 1988, pp. 400-401.

Articles

4332. Esterly, Glenn. "He Feared His Career Might Be Over.
Now a Hit on 'Amen', Sherman Hemsley Thought He Was So
Typecast He Would Never Land Another Role After 'The
Jeffersons' Was Canceled." TV Guide (August 29 1987): 8-10, 12.

4333. Haddad-Garcia, George. "The Real Sherman Hemsley."
Black Stars (March 1981): 26-31.

4334. Hobson, Dick. "Up from the Ghetto." TV Guide (June 21
1975): 20-22.

4335. Jenkins, Walter. "Sherman Hemsley: Call Him Cool,
Talented and Confident." Black Stars (February 1976): 58-65.

4336. "The Private World of Sherman Hemsley." Jet (April 2
1981): 58+.

4337. Unger, Arthur. "Meet 'George Jefferson'. Behind the
Role: a totally different person." Christian Science Monitor
(April 23 1975): 22.

4338. Whitney, Dwight. "Sherman Hemsley. Don't Ask How He
Lives or What He Believes In." TV Guide (February 6 1982):
30-32, 35.

HENDRY, GLORIA (1949-   )

See also # 3372

4339. Hendry, Gloria - Clippings [Billy Rose Theatre
Collection]

4340. Lucas, Bob. "The Black Girl Who Plays the Wife of
James 007 Bond." Sepia (May 1973): 35-42.

4341. Moore, Bob. "Another Side of Gloria Hendry." Black
Stars (July 1975): 20-27.

4342. Thompson, M. Cordell. "Gloria Hendry as 'Mrs. James
Bond.'" Black Stars (March 1973): 56+.

HERNANDEZ, JUANO (1896-1970)

4343. Bogle, Donald. Blacks in American Films and
Television. New York: Garland, 1988, pp. 401-402.

Articles

4344. "From Actor to College Prof: Movie Star Juano Hernandez
Returns to Native Puerto Rico for Teaching Job." Ebony
(November 1952): 122-126, 128.

4345. "Hollywood School for Actors. Professor Juano
Hernandez practices and teaches fundamentals in large field of
acting." Sepia (March 1960): 72-76.

4346. "Hollywood's 'Hottest' Negro Actor." Ebony (August
1950): 22-26.

4347. "Juano Hernandez in 'The Young Man.'" Sepia (March
1962): 16-18.

4348. "A Man from Puerto Rico: Busiest Negro actor in Hollywood today is Juano Hernandez, the guy who is putting Puerto Rico on the map." Our World (December 1949): 28-33.

4349. "Movies: The Breaking Point: Another Dignified, Outstanding Role for Juano Hernandez." Our World (August 1950): 51.

4350. "Trial: Cast as a Judge, Actor Juano Hernandez is Given Best Role of His Hollywood Career." Ebony (November 1955): 29-30, 32.

Obituaries

4351. "Juan G. Hernandez." Variety (July 20 1970).

4352. "Juan Hernandez, Actor, Dies at 74." New York Times (July 20 1970): 27. [Obituary]

HICKS, HILLY (1950-   )

4353. Gardella, Kay. "Roll Out a Barrell of Fun on a New Black Series." New York Daily News (July 12 1973): 95.

HINES, GREGORY (1946-   )

4354. Bogle, Donald. Blacks in American Films and Television. New York: Garland, 1988, pp. 402-404.

Articles

4355. Cartier, Jacqueline. "Gregory Hines: 'Je crois avoir su danser avant de savoir marcher!'" Cine-Tele-Revue, No. 33 (August 18 1988): 10-11. [Interview]

4356. "EM Interview: Gregory Hines." Ebony Man (September 1989): 17-19.

4357. Graustark, Barbara. "Tapped for Stardom." American Film, Vol. 10, No. 3 (December 1984): 28-34.

4358. "Gregory Hines." Playboy (September 1986): 108+. [Interview]

4359. Hadley-Garcia, George. "I've Got the Original Happy Feet!" Right On! (June 1983): 50-53.

4360. Hines, Gregory - Clippings [Billy Rose Theatre Collection]

4361. Jackson, Martin A. "For Gregory Hines, the Uncertainty is Over." Encore American and Worldwide News (November 1981): 28-31.

4362. Norment, Lynn. "Gregory Hines: Dancer Wins Stardom as Chicago Vice Cop." Ebony, Vol. 41 (October 1986): 100+.

4363. Singleton, Janet. "Gregory Hines: from dancing to acting." Black Film Review, Vol. 3, No. 2 (1987): 20.

4364. Vespa, Mary. "Far From Running Scared, Dancer Gregory Hines Takes His First Great Leap as a Leading Man." People (August 11 1986): 4-5.

Tap

4365. Avins, Mimi. "Shot by shot: creating a dance sequence with style and believability for 'Tap'." Premiere (March 1989): 72-75.

4366. "Sammy Davis Jr. and Gregory Hines move to the beat in 'Tap'." Jet (February 13 1989): 58+.

4367. Sommer, Sally. "Tap Happy: Hines on TAP." Dance Magazine (December 1988): 46-50.

4368. "TAP. Gregory Hines and Sammy Davis Jr. co-star in new film." Ebony (February 1989): 46+.

HOLLIDAY, KENE

4369. Whitney, Dwight. "Welcome to TV's 'Carter Country'...Where laughs are worth more than peanuts." TV Guide (March 11 1978): 24-27.

HOLLY, ELLEN (1931-   )

4370. Drake, Ross. "Black, but not Black Enough." TV Guide (March 18-24 1972): 38-40.

4371. Holly, Ellen. "Drama Mailbag: How Black Do You Have To Be?" New York Times (September 15 1968): Sec. 2, pp. 1, 5. Letter to the Editor.

4372. _____. "'Negro? Black? Colored?'" New York Times (August 10 1969): D13.

4373. Howell, Ronald O. "Ellen Holly: 'One Life to Live' star will have eight million guests at her TV wedding." Ebony (October 1979): 149-151.

4374. Payne, Andrea. "Ellen Holly and Her Grand Passions." Soap Opera Digest (December 6 1983): 132-135, 142.

4375. Ward, Candy. "Ellen Holly Yearns for Another World." Black Stars (March 1980): 7.

HOOKS, KEVIN (1958-   )

4376. Burrell, Walter Price. "Kevin Hooks: The 14-Year Old Movie Star." Black Stars (June 1973): 52-53.

4377. Harris, Ron. "Actors Robert and Kevin Hooks." Ebony (March 1980): 32+.

4378. Horner, Cynthia. "Kevin Hooks: He's the Mayor!" Right On! (April 1986): 40-41, 63.

4379. "Introducing...Kevin Hooks." Right On! (January 1973):
42-43.

4380. "Kevin Hooks: At 17, A New Look!" Black Stars (April
1976): 6-10.

4381. Slaton, Shell. "In Real Life Aaron Doesn't Really Love
Angela!!!" Right On! (May 1977): 46-48.

4382. Thomas, M. Martez. "Spotlight: Kevin Hooks. At 17-
years old, this young actor's future looks like a bright one!"
Right On! (July 1976): 29.

HOOKS, ROBERT (1937-   )

4383. Burrell, Walter Price. "Robert Hooks is Black Where it
Counts." Black Stars (March 1972): 46-51.

4384. Efron, Edith. "He Hasn't Forgotten the Rats." TV
Guide (February 10 1968): 22-24.

4385. Harris, Ron. "Actors Robert and Kevin Hooks: like
father, like son." Ebony (March 1980): 32-34+.

4386. Hooks, Robert - Clippings [Billy Rose Theatre
Collection]

4387. "Hooks, Robert." Current Biography 1970.

4388. Stasio, Marilyn. "Robert Hooks: Man Alive." Cue
(April 6 1968): 12.

Newspaper Articles

4389. Carmody, John. "Multi-Talented Robert Hooks Tries TV."
Washington Post (August 23 1967): B8. [N.Y.P.D.]

4390. Mason, Clifford. "Movies: For Hooks, the Sun Comes
Up." New York Post (April 9 1967): D13.

4391. Tallmer, Jerry. "Across the Footlights: A Little Trip
South." New York Post (August 29 1966): 24. [Hurry Sundown]

4392. _____. "Robert Hooks: More Than Skin Deep." New
York Post (December 9 1967): Sec. 3, p. 35.

HORNE, LENA (1917-   )

4393. Bogle, Donald. Blacks in American Films and
Television. New York: Garland, 1988, pp. 404-405.

4394. Buckley, Gail Lumet. The Hornes: An American Family.
New York: Knopf, 1986. 262p.

4395. Haskins, James, with Kathleen Benson. Lena: A Personal
and Professional Biography of Lena Horne. New York: Stein and
Day, 1984. 226p.

4396. Horne, Lena, and Richard Schickel. _Lena_. New York:
Limelight Editions, 1986. 300p. (Orig. 1965)

4397. Howard, Brett. _Lena_. Los Angeles: Holloway House
Pub., 1981. 218p.

Articles

4398. Crichton, Kyle. "Horne Solo." _Negro Digest_ (August
1943): 80-82.

4399. "Horne, Lena." _Current Biography 1985_.

4400. "Horne, Lena." _Current Biography 1941_.

4401. Horne, Lena. "My Life Story." _Negro Digest_ (July
1949): 3-13.

4402. "The Screen in Review: The New Lena Horne." _Headlines
and Pictures_ (September 1946): 28-29.

Media Materials

4403. _Destination Freedom: Negro Cinderella_ (Audiotape).
Chicago: WMAQ, 1949. 30 min. Script by Richard Durham.
Radio drama based on the early life of Lena Horne. [Held by
the Schomburg Center - Sc Audio C-324 (Side 2, no. 1)]

4404. _The Dick Cavett Show_. _Lena Horne_ [videorecording].
New York: WNET/13, 1981. 57 min. [Held by the Schomburg
Center - Sc Visual VRB-53]

HORSFORD, ANNA MARIA

4405. Buck, Jerry. "Anna Maria Horsford says 'Amen' to TV
Role as a Spinster Daughter." _Chicago Sun-Times_ (July 1
1988).

4406. Carter, Alan. "Well, Bless My Soul; This Actress'
Career Takes Off On a Wing and a Prayer." New York _Daily News_
(January 13 1987): Extra, p. 1.

4407. Kaufman, Joanne. "As Amen's vampy virgin-in-waiting,
Anna Maria Horsford keeps viewers congregating on Saturday
night." _People_ (May 2 1988): 71-72.

4408. "New People: Anna Maria Horsford." _Right On_!
(September 1981): 60.

4409. O'Hallaren, Bill. "If She's Not Partying with Swedish
Dentists, She's Meeting a Puerto Rican Ghost; The life of
Amen's Anna Maria Horsford seems like a series of grand
adventures." _TV Guide_ (June 27 1987): 27-29.

HOSKINS, ALLEN "FARINA" (1920-1980)

See also # 3367

4410. Bogle, Donald. <u>Blacks in American Films and Television</u>. New York: Garland, 1988, pp. 405-406.

Articles

4411. "Allen (Farina) Hoskins." <u>Variety</u> (July 30 1980): 95. [Obituary]

4412. "Farina." <u>Chicago Defender</u> (August 25 1928).

4413. "'Our Gang's 'Farina is Dead at 59. Allen C. Hoskins, Who Portrayed the Child Character in 300 Films." <u>New York Post</u> (July 28 1980): 9.

HUBBARD, DAVID

4414. "David Hubbard to Quit Show Biz?" <u>Right On</u>! (October 1979): 12.

4415. "NBC-TV's Hubbard: Hamburger to 'Ham'." New York <u>Amsterdam News</u> (October 29 1977): D-9.

HUDSON, ERNIE

4416. Berlin, Joey. "A 'Ghost of a Chance." <u>New York Post</u> (March 16 1989): 38.

4417. Burrell, Walter Price. "Ernie Hudson: More to Him than Meets the Eye." <u>Black Stars</u> (July 1981): 72-74.

4418. Kimble, Sonya. "Bustin' Ghosts." <u>Right On</u>! (October 1989): 62-63.

HYMAN, EARLE

4419. "Movies: I Was a Prisoner in Korea." <u>Our World</u> (July 1954): 34-35.

IMRIE, KATHY

See also # 3370

4420. Wyatt, Hugh. "Bares Nearly All for Her Acting Career." New York <u>Daily News</u> (December 23 1973): 18, 24.

INGRAM, REX (1895-1969)

See also # 1975

4421. Bogle, Donald. <u>Blacks in American Films and Television</u>. New York: Garland, 1988, pp. 406-407.

Articles

4422. "De Lawd' Cooks with Gas." <u>Negro Digest</u> (January 1944): 53-55.

4423. Gilbert, Douglas. "Ingram is Back After Playing 'de Lawd'." <u>New York World-Telegram</u> (May 21 1936).

4424. Ingram, Rex - Clippings [Billy Rose Theatre Collection]

4425. Ingram, Rex. "I Came Back from the Dead." Ebony, Vol. 10 (March 1955): 49-58.

4426. Maltin, Leonard. "Rex Ingram." Film Fan Monthly, No. 89 (November 1968): 3-7.

4427. "Moonrise. Rex Ingram's role called 'best ever written' for Negro in movies." Ebony (July 1948): 51+.

4428. Tazelaar, Marguerite. "'De Lawd' May Quit; No Bigger Parts." New York Herald Tribune (May 24 1936).

Obituaries

4429. Newsweek (September 29 1969): 98.

4430. "Rex Ingram, the Actor, Dies in Hollywood at 73." New York Times (September 20 1969): 29.

4431. Time (September 26 1969): 57.

4432. Variety (September 24 1969).

4433. "Veteran Black Film Actor Dies Suddenly of a Heart Attack at the Age of 73 in Los Angeles, Calif." Jet (October 2 1969): 56.

JACKSON, EUGENE

See # 3367

JACKSON, HORACE

4434. "Living Between Two Worlds - Horace Jackson had story to tell--and he told it." Sepia (February 1964): 62-66.

JACOBS, LAWRENCE-HILTON (1953-   )

4435. Collins, Lisa. "Lawrence-Hilton Jacobs: Cool 'n' Struttin'." Black Stars (April 1976): 14-18.

4436. English, Lori, and Jeffrey Rush. "A Conversation with Lawrence-Hilton Jacobs." Black Stars (May 1978): 32-36.

4437. Frechette, David. "Interview: Welcome Back, Larry." Right On! (May 1986): 60-61.

4438. Hollomon, Rickey. "Lawrence-Hilton Jacobs, Star of "Cooley High" Raps to Right On!" Right On! (November 1975): 22-25.

4439. Jenkins, Flo. "Lawrence-Hilton Jacobs Shares Thoughts on Ladies, Success and More!" Right On! (April 1976): 37-43; (May 1976): 42-46.

4440. "Lawrence-Hilton Jacobs! More Than Just a Teen Idol!" Right On! (October 1976): 24-25.

4441. "Lawrence-Hilton Jacobs! Photos of Days Gone By!"
Right On! (June 1976): 42-44.

4442. Manning, Steve. "Man to Man: Larry Jacobs Raps About
Life, Love, and His Future Plans!" Right On! (February 1977):
7-9.

4443. Torgerson, Ellen. "The Renaissance Sweathog." TV
Guide (August 19 1978): 25-29.

4444. Winters, Jason. "Lawrence-Hilton Jacobs: 'All of a
Sudden I'm a Sex Symbol'." Black Stars (August 1977): 52-56.

JEANNETTE, GERTRUDE (1918-   )

4445. Jeanette, Gertrude - Clippings (includes typescript
biography) [Billy Rose Theatre Collection]

JEFFRIES, HERB

See # 6035

JOHARI, AZIZI

4446. Johari, Azizi. "I Am...Azizi Johari." Black Stars
(December 1978): 6-8.

4447. Weston, Martin. "Azizi Johari: Hollywood Picks Up a
Rare Jewel." Black Stars (August 1976): 20-25.

JOHNS, TRACY CAMILA

See # 3382

JOHNSON, KYLE

4448. Sweeney, Louise. "Talk with the boy Gordon Parks
chose." Christian Science Monitor (August 20 1969).
Interview with the star of Gordon Parks's "The Learning Tree."

JOHNSON, MARIE LOUISE

See # 3354

JOHNSON, NOBLE (1881-c.1957)

4449. Everett, E. K. "Noble Johnson, the first black movie
star." Classic Film Collector, No. 52 (Fall 1976): 39.

4450. Leifert, D. "Portrait in Black: Noble Johnson." Gore
Creatures, No. 24 (October 1975): 27-29.

JOHNSON, RAFER (1935-   )

4451. "Athlete Rafer Johnson Becomes Top Hollywood Star."
Sepia (June 1962): 58-62.

4452. "Johnson, Rafer." Current Biography 1961.

4453.   "Rafer Johnson: Born to be a Star."   _Sepia_ (February 1970): 30-32.

JONES, DUANE (d.1988)

4454.   "Duane Jones."   _Variety_ (August 17 1988): 54-55. [Obituary]

4455.   Ferrante, Tim.   "A Farewell to Duane Jones."   _Fangoria_, No. 80 (February 1989): 14-18, 64.

4456.   Fraser, C. Gerald.   "Duane L. Jones, 51, Actor and Director of Stage Works, Dies."   _New York Times_ (July 28 1988): A24.

4457.   "Losing Ground."   _Black Film Review_ (Spring 1989): 10. [Obituary]

JONES, JAMES EARL (1931-   )

4458.   Abdul, Raoul.   _Famous Black Entertainers of Today_.   New York: Dodd, Mead & Co., 1974, pp. 80-86.

4459.   Bogle, Donald.   _Blacks in American Films and Television_.   New York: Garland, 1988, pp. 407-409.

4460.   Reed, Rex.   _Conversations in the Raw_.   New York: World, 1969, pp. 210-220.

Dissertations

4461.   Setrakian, Edward.   "The Acting of James Earl Jones." Dissertation (Ph.D.) New York University, 1976.   279p.

Articles

4462.   Antoine, Roane.   "Can James Earl Jones Win as a TV Cop? The show is good.   The cast is good.   The ratings are scary." _Sepia_ (January 1980): 39-42.

4463.   Black, Doris.   "James Earl Jones: Finest Serious Black Actor Confounded by His Success."   _Sepia_ (August 1976): 24-42.

4464.   Burg, Robert.   "Young Actor on the Way Up."   _Negro Digest_, Vol. 15 (April 1966): 26-31.

4465.   Cook, Bruce.   "James Earl Jones opens in PARIS." _American Film_ (October 1979): 73-77.

4466.   "Dynamo."   _Newsweek_, Vol. 62 (December 2 1963): 68.

4467.   Ferdinand, Val.   "James Earl Jones: A Great Black Hope."   _Black Collegian_ (January-February 1977): 32, 62-63.

4468.   Green, M.   "The Struggle to be James Earl Jones." _Saturday Review_, Vol. 9 (February 1982): 22-27.

4469.   "James Earl Jones."   _Negro Digest_ (October 1962): 43-44.

4470. "James Earl Jones--Actor Still Climbing." _Ebony_, Vol. 20 (April 1965): 98-106.

4471. "James Earl Jones' Goal is to Become Great Actor." _Sepia_, Vol. 13 (February 1964): 72-76.

4472. "James Earl Jones: Race is Still the Important Thing." _Sepia_, Vol. 20 (January 1971): 16-17.

4473. "Jones, James Earl." _Current Biography 1969_.

4474. Lewis, L. "James Earl Jones Speaks - and How! But He Didn't Stop Stuttering Until 15." _Biographical News_ (January 1975): 118.

4475. "People." _Time_ (February 21 1977): 50.

4476. "People Are Talking About..." _Vogue_ (November 1 1968): 166.

4477. Peterson, Maurice. "James Earl Jones: Committed to the Communication of Pain." _Essence_, Vol. 4 (April 1974): 32+.

4478. Slater, Jack. "Television's New Primetime Black Man. Robert Guillaume, James E. Jones, Lou Gossett pioneer." _Ebony_ (December 1979): 124+.

4479. "Sudden Stardom for James Earl Jones." _Sepia_, Vol. 18 (June 1969): 52-55.

4480. "We Talk To..." _Mademoiselle_ (August 1969): 344-345.

Newspaper Articles

4481. Blau, E. "James Earl Jones: How Does an Actor Make His Statement as an Artist?" _New York Times_ (December 10 1980): Sec. III, p. 23.

4482. Dudar, Helen. "James Earl Jones at Bat." _New York Times_ (March 22 1987): Sec. 2, pp. 1, 6.

4483. Dunning, Jennifer. "James Earl Jones Prepares to Map the Tormented Soul of 'Othello'." _New York Times_ (August 2 1981): Sec. 2, p. 1, 7.

4484. Nachman, Gerald. "James Earl Jones: What the Doctor Ordered." _New York Post_ (December 5 1965): 35. [As the World Turns]

4485. Richards, David. "James Earl Jones Gets the Classic Roles by Default." _Washington Star-News_ (March 2 1975).

4486. Tallmer, Jerry. "And in This Corner...James Earl Jones." _New York Post_ (February 8 1969): Sec. 3, p. 33.

Research Collections

4487. James Earl Jones Collection. Manuscript Collection - MS 227. [Held by the Schomburg Center]

JONES, PEACHES (d.1986)

See also # 3354

4488. Burrell, Walter P. "Hollywood Stunt Girl." _Ebony_ (December 1971): 147-148, 150, 152, 154. Profile of stuntwoman Peaches Jones.

4489. "Peaches Jones." _Variety_ (July 23 1986): 85-87. [Obituary]

JULIEN, MAX

4490. Bogle, Donald. _Blacks in American Films and Television_. New York: Garland, 1988, p. 409.

Articles

4491. Haynes, Howard. "Off-Screen Lovers United in Movie." _Sepia_ (April 1974): 40-44. Profile of Max Julien and Vonetta McGee on the set of "Thomasine and Bushrod."

4492. Julien, Max - Clippings (includes a 6 page typescript interview) [Billy Rose Theatre Collection]

4493. Lucas, Bob. "How Max Julien's Gamble in Rome Paid Off in Hollywood." _Black Stars_ (July 1973): 64-71.

KATON, ROSANNE

4494. Houghton, Jean Howard. "Success Story of a Movie Starlet." _Sepia_ (September 1976): 44-54.

KELLY, JIM

See also # 3350, 3373

4495. Burrell, Walter Price. "Jim Kelly Turns Karate into Movie Stardom." _Black Stars_ (October 1973): 50-57.

4496. Collins, Lisa. "An Intimate Chat with Jim Kelly." _Black Stars_ (November 1976): 30-36.

4497. Jenkins, Flo. "Jim Kelly...World Karate Champion Turns Actor!" _Right On_! (September 1973): 32-33.

4498. _____. "What's the Truth about Jim Kelly's Strange Disappearance?!" _Right On_! (October 1974): 22-23.

4499. Kelly, Jim - Clippings [Billy Rose Theatre Collection]

4500. Murray, James P. "Ex-Gridder Jim Kelly May Become Movie Star." New York _Amsterdam News_ (August 11 1973): D-4.

KELLY, PAULA (c.1944-   )

See also # 3370

4501. Kelly, Paula - Clippings [Billy Rose Theatre Collection]

4502. "Sweet Charity's Exciting Paula Kelly." Sepia (May 1967): 24-27.

4503. Swisher, Viola Hegyi. "The Dazzling Imperfections of Paula Kelly." After Dark (February 1973): 52-54.

4504. Watts, Sharryn E. "Paula Kelly Dances to Stardom." Right On! (May 1973): 48-49.

KENNEDY, LEON

See also # 2468-2471

4505. Fee, Debi. "Leon Kennedy: The Truth Behind the Breakup!" Right On! (March 1982): 16-17, 64.

4506. Horner, Cynthia. "Interview: The Making of a Movie--"Body and Soul." Right On! (July 1981): 24-25, 55.

4507. "The Next Screen Idol! Leon Kennedy." Right On! (June 1980): 36-37.

4508. Wright, Audrey. "In the Ring with Leon Kennedy." Right On! (April 1988): 70-71.

KILPATRICK, LINCOLN (c.1932-   )

4509. Jenkins, Walter. "The Serious Side of Lincoln Kilpatrick." Black Stars (May 1973): 62-67.

4510. Kilpatrick, Lincoln - Clippings [Billy Rose Theatre Collection]

KING, MABEL

4511. Burrell, Walter Price. "Mabel King Believes Fat is Beautiful." Black Stars (July 1976): 21-22, 24.

4512. Lyles, Donald R. "Mabel King Had to Find Success in Another Land." Black Stars (April 1980): 64-67.

4513. "Television: It's Happening for Mabel King." Encore American and Worldwide News (June 20 1977): 51-52.

KING, TONY (1944-   )

4514. Collins, Lisa. "The King is Here--Tony King That Is." Black Stars (July 1975): 28-35.

4515. King, Tony - Clippings [Billy Rose Theatre Collection]

KINGI, HENRY

See also # 3354

4516. Burrell, Walter Price. "Henry Kingi! Movie Stuntman." Black Stars (December 1975): 50-55.

KITZMILLER, JOHN (1913-1965)

4517. "John Kitzmiller." Variety (March 3 1965). [Obituary]

4518. Kitzmiller, John. "American Loves Acting in Italy." The Daily Compass [New York] (March 14 1950).

4519. "Star of Italian Movies; John Kitzmiller picked for movie role while playing poker, becomes steadiest-working actor." Ebony (November 1951): 71-73.

4520. "'Without Pity;' Italian film stars John Kitzmiller in Negro-white love story." Our World (May 1950): 37.

KOTTO, YAPHET (1937-   )

See also # 3373

4521. Bogle, Donald. Blacks in American Films and Television. New York: Garland, 1988, pp. 409-411.

4522. Kotto, Yaphet. Slow Dance in the Promised Land. Tacoma, WA: Ahimsa Publishers, 1987. 305p. [Autobiography]

Articles

4523. Armstrong, Lois. "Until He Found the Key in Meditation, Hollywood Was a Prison for 'Brubaker' Star Yaphet Kotto." People (July 21 1980): 106-107.

4524. Brack, Fred. "Mr. Kotto." The Dial [WNET/Thirteen] (February 1982): 44, 47.

4525. Kisner, Ronald E. "Seldom Seen Side of Yaphet Kotto - Filmland's Tough Dude." Jet (September 16 1976): 60-63.

4526. Kotto, Yaphet - Clippings [Billy Rose Theatre Collection]

4527. Marsh, Antoinette. "The Mysterious Yaphet Kotto." Black Stars (November 1980): 34-36.

4528. Trubo, Richard. "Black Star Who Won't Act in Black Movies." Sepia, Vol. 24 (September 1975): 32-39.

Newspaper Articles

4529. Bailey, Peter. "A New Black Hope for 'The Great White Hope.'" New York Times (October 26 1969): Sec. 2.

4530. "The Outlook Interview: Yaphet Kotto Talks to Desson Howe." Washington Post (July 21 1985): G3.

4531. Tapley, Mel. "Yaphet Kotto: Talent Has No Barrier!!" New York Amsterdam News (October 16 1976): D10-11.

LANEUVILLE, ERIC (1952-   )

4532. Collins, Lisa. "Eric Laneuville." Black Stars
(November 1975): 20-26.

4533. "Enterprising Eric Laneuville!" Right On! (December
1980): 18-19.

LANGE, GERRI

4534. Bates-Logan, Karen. "Television: Gerri Lange is a No-
Nonsense Lady." Encore American and Worldwide News (April 16
1979): 38-39. Profile of talk show host Gerri Lange.

4535. "No Time for Negatives." Woman's Day (April 24 1978):
21-22.

4536. Unger, Arthur. "PBS tackles female stereotypes.
'Turnabout' host Gerri Lange 'a nonabrasive revolutionary'."
Christian Science Monitor (February 1 1978): 14.

LANGE, TED (c.1947-   )

4537. Charles, Roland. "Ted Lange...Mr. Phenomenal." Black
Stars (September 1976): 24-29.

4538. Hicks, Jack. "He Watched His Weight--And Countless
Bartenders. Ted Lange prepared carefully for his 'Love Boat'
role." TV Guide (July 19 1980): 22+.

4539. Lane, Bill. "Ted Lange: "Love Boat's" Dream Boat."
Sepia (February 1979): 64-68.

4540. Lange, Ted - Clippings [Billy Rose Theatre Collection]

4541. "Love Boat's Ted Lange. Comic on hit television show
is really a serious actor." Ebony (March 1981): 66+.

4542. "'Ooooweee' Junior's doing his thing in "Friday Foster"
flick." New York Amsterdam News (December 13 1975): D-4.

4543. "Ted Lange inks major pact with Columbia Pictures TV."
Jet (September 22 1986): 59.

4544. "Ted Lange, TV's amiable bartender." New York
Amsterdam News (July 16 1983): 17.

LANGHART, JANET

4545. Adams, Val, and George Maksian. "TV Scene: Three
Strikes and She's Out." New York Daily News (September 3
1980): 10.

4546. Johnson, Wista. "WABC-TV's bold, beautiful newshound."
New York Amsterdam News (May 12 1979): 29-30.

4547. Langhart, Janet - Clippings [Billy Rose Theatre
Collection]

4548. Tapley, Mel. "Is Janet Langhart another TV Joan of Arc?" New York Amsterdam News (February 9 1980): 25.

4549. Webster, Ivan. "The Woman Worth a Thousand Pictures." Encore American and Worldwide News (October 15 1979): 32-34, 36-37. Profile of talk show host Janet Langhart.

LARKIN, JOHN (c.1873-1936)

4550. "John Larkin." Variety (March 25 1936). [Obituary]

LAWRENCE, MITTIE

4551. "Going Places with Mittie Lawrence." Sepia (November 1970): 16-19.

4552. "The Sexiest Hollywood Actress Since Lena Horne." Sepia (January 1963): 36-41.

LAWS, SAM

4553. Burrell, Walter Price. "Sam Laws is Great at Acting Mean." Black Stars (August 1976): 12-17.

LAWSON, RICHARD

4554. Collier, Aldore. "Richard Lawson; Focused on Career and Fatherhood." Ebony Man (June 1988): 80-82.

4555. Ketchum, Larry. "Poltergeist's Richard Lawson: Mixing Mediums." (Hollywood) Drama-Logue (June 10-16 1982): 16.

4556. Lawson, Richard - Clippings [Billy Rose Theatre Collection]

LEE, CANADA [Lee Cornelius Canegata] (1907-1952)

4557. Bogle, Donald. Blacks in American Films and Television. New York: Garland, 1988, pp. 411-413.

4558. Cruse, Harold W. "Lee, Canada." In Dictionary of American Biography, Supplement 5, pp. 418-420.

4559. Fletcher, Martin. "Canada Lee." In Our Great Americans: The Negro Contribution to American Progress. Chicago: Gamma Corporation, 1954, p. 34.

4560. Kanfer, Stefan. A Journal of the Plague Years. New York: Atheneum, 1973, pp. 178-181. Discussion of the effects of Hollywood blacklisting on Lee's film career.

4561. Kennedy, J. Scott. "Lee, Canada." In Dictionary of American Negro Biography, eds. Rayford W. Logan and Michael R. Winston. New York: W.W. Norton, 1982, pp. 390-391.

Audiotapes

4562. Destination Freedom: Do Something, Be Somebody (audiotape). Chicago: WMAQ, 1949. 30 min. Radio drama based on the early life of Canada Lee. [Held by the Schomburg Center--Sc Audio C-398 (Side 1)]

Articles

4563. Gill, Glenda E. "Careerist and Casualty: the Rise and Fall of Canada Lee." Freedomways, Vol. 21, No. 1 (1981): 14-27.

4564. "Lee, Canada." Current Biography 1944.

4565. Loubet, N. "Two of a Kind." Negro Digest, Vol. 8 (February 1950): 35-37.

4566. Marks, Robert W. "Canada Lee - Harlem Hamlet." Esquire (February 1948).

4567. "Memory Lingers On." Our World, Vol. 9 (September 1954): 46-49.

4568. "Nothing Too Big for 'Bigger.'" Negro Digest, Vol. 3 (February 1945): 77-80.

4569. "Our Part in Body and Soul." Opportunity (January 1948): 21.

4570. Rudd, Irving. "Programs for Pugilism." Negro Digest, Vol. 4 (April 1946): 47-50.

Newspaper Articles

4571. Guernsey, Otis L., Jr. "The Playbill: Canada Lee, Negroes and the War." New York Herald Tribune (December 26 1943): Sec. IV, p. 1. Includes comments by Lee on his appearance in Alfred Hitchcock's "Lifeboat".

4572. Lee, Canada - Vertical File [Schomburg Center]

4573. Thirer, Irene. "Screen Views: Canada Lee - 'Beloved Country' Star." New York Post (January 27 1952).

Obituaries

4574. "Canada Lee, 45, is Dead; Stage and Film Star." New York Herald-Tribune (May 11 1952).

4575. "Lee, Canada." Current Biography 1952.

4576. New York Times (May 10 1952).

4577. Variety (May 14 1952).

Research Collections

4578. Canada Lee Papers. Manuscript Collection - MS 238.
[Held by the Schomburg Center]

LEE, CARL (d.1986)

4579. "Carl Lee." Variety (May 28 1986): 99. [Obituary]

4580. Lee, Carl - Clippings [Billy Rose Theatre Collection]

4581. Mathews, Les. "Canada Lee's Son Finds His Niche
Playing in Super Fly." New York Amsterdam News (January 20
1973): D-2.

LEE, IRVING

4582. Harvey, Almena Ruth. "A Day at the Edge of Night!
Irving Allen Lee Tells How Things Are Done at a Who-Done-It."
Right On! (December 1981): 18-19.

4583. McNair, Richard O. "'Edge of Night' detective in heart
of Harlem." New York Amsterdam News (November 20 1982): 70.

LESTER, KETTY (1938-   )

4584. Jenkins, Walter. "The Acting Bug Bites Ketty Lester."
Sepia (May 1970): 65-67.

4585. _____. "Ketty Lester Talks About Her Role as an
Actress." Black Stars (December 1973): 64-68.

4586. Lester, Ketty - Clippings (includes 4p. typescript bio)
[Billy Rose Theatre Collection]

LEWIS, DAWNN (c.1962-   )

See also # 3382

4587. Brennan, Patricia. "Television: A Different World for
Dawnn Lewis." Washington Post/TV Week (April 24-30 1988): 5, 9.

4588. D'Agnese, Joe. "Up Close: Meet Dawnn Lewis! She won a
role on The Cosby Show spinoff and found it's A Different
World." Right On! (December 1987): 76-77, 75.

4589. Duncan-Hall, Patricia. "The 'Different Worlds' of
Jasmine Guy and Dawnn Lewis." Black Collegian (November/
December 1988): 76+.

4590. Kimble, Sonya. "Dawnn Lewis: She's Taking the World by
Storm." Right On! (April 1990): 52-53.

LEWIS, EMMANUEL

4591. "Emmanuel Lewis: TV's Newest Star." Ebony (February
1984): 35+.

4592. Esterly, Glenn. "Emmanuel Lewis, 15: Kidd Boss." <u>TV Guide</u> (June 14 1986): 35+.

4593. Flanagan, Sylvia P. "Emmanuel Lewis: Busiest Little Man in Hollywood." <u>Ebony</u> (February 1985): 136+.

4594. Lewis, Emmanuel - Clippings [Billy Rose Theatre Collection]

4595. Turan, Kenneth. "Emmanuel Lewis remains a down-to-earth 12-year-old despite his instant success as the star of Webster." <u>TV Guide</u> (January 14 1984): 28-30.

Webster

4596. Bogle, Donald. <u>Blacks in American Films and Television</u>. New York: Garland Pub., 1988, pp. 309-310.

4597. Hall, Jane. "Emmanuel Lewis got a boost from Michael Jackson, but as Webster he stands on his own." <u>People</u> (April 9 1984): 75, 77-78.

4598. Moore, Trudy S. "Emmanuel Lewis: star of TV commercials to debut in TV series." <u>Jet</u> (August 22 1983): 60+.

4599. "'Webster'--An Overnight Sensation." <u>Right On</u>! (January 1984): 50-51.

LEWIS, SANDY

4600. "Hollywood Opens Its Doors to Two New Stars." <u>Sepia</u> (August 1963): 59-62.

4601. "Sandy Lewis Fights for Stardom." <u>Sepia</u> (June 1965): 68-73.

LINCOLN, ABBEY (1930-   )

4602. "Aminata Moseka (Abbey Lincoln) and Her New Career." <u>Black Stars</u> (July 1975): 30-35.

4603. "For Love of Ivy. Abbey Lincoln joins Sidney Poitier in romantic comedy film." <u>Ebony</u> (October 1968): 52+.

4604. Hentoff, Nat. "Movies: 'How Wonderful to Be a Black Woman'." <u>New York Times</u> (January 14 1968): D11.

4605. Smith, Bill. "Abbey Lincoln talks with Bill Smith." <u>Coda</u>, No. 170 (December 1979): 12-16.

LITTLE, CLEAVON (1939-   )

4606. "Chatting with Cleavon Little." <u>Right On</u>! (February 1973): 30-31.

4607. Jenkins, Walter. "Cleavon Little: Call Him--Mr. Talent." <u>Black Stars</u> (August 1978): 35-37.

4608. Klemesrud, Judy. "Black is Beautiful Actor Named Cleavon Little." New York Times (October 5 1969).

4609. Little, Cleavon - Clippings [Billy Rose Theatre Collection]

4610. Peterson, Maurice. "On the Aisle: Spotlight on Cleavon Little." Essence (June 1975): 9.

4611. Thompson, M. Cordell. "The Serious Side of Cleavon Little." Black Stars (September 1974): 68-74.

4612. Weiss, Hedy. "The Big Talent of Cleavon Little." Chicago Sun Times (May 3 1987): 1, 4.

LITTLE MANGO

See # 3367

LOCKHART, CALVIN (1934-   )

See also # 3350

4613. Bogle, Donald. Blacks in American Films and Television. New York: Garland, 1988, pp. 413-414.

Articles

4614. Allen, Bonnie. "Calvin Lockhart: The Second Time Around." Essence, Vol. 9 (February 1979): 96+.

4615. "Calvin Lockhart! The Actor with 'Style'!" Right On! (January 1976): 29-30.

4616. Clark, Bob. "Calvin Lockhart: He Never Stops Trying To Win." Essence (September 1970): 28, 74, 76-77.

4617. Craft, Mona. "The Super Talented Calvin Lockhart." Black Stars (September 1974): 24-30.

4618. Haverstraw, Jack. "Calvin Lockhart: Hollywood's Reluctant Black 'Sex Symbol'." Sepia (April 1976): 24-26.

4619. Klemesrud, Judy. "Calvin: Champagne, Yes, Coca-Cola, No." New York Times (April 19 1970): Sec 2, pp. 1, 26.

4620. Marsh, Antoinette. "The New Calvin Lockhart." Black Stars (October 1978): 12-17.

4621. Mills, B. "He's Found His Real World in Ghana." Biographical News, Vol. 1 (January 1974): 65.

4622. Schulberg, Budd. "The Real Anger Was Backstage." Life (August 21 1970): 50-52. On behind-the-scenes conflicts between male lead Lockhart and director Paul Bogart on the set of Halls of Anger.

LONG, AVON (1910-1984)

4623. "Avon Long." <u>Variety</u> (February 22 1984): 110.
[Obituary]

4624. Fraser, C. Gerald. "Avon Long, Actor and Singer in
Theater and Film 50 Years." <u>New York Times</u> (February 17
1984): B4.

LOVE, VICTOR

4625. Allen, Bonnie. "Spotlight: Victor Love." <u>Essence</u>
(April 1987): 41-42, 110.

4626. Everette, Cheryl. "Love's Launch to Stardom." New
York <u>Sunday News</u> (December 7 1986): 6.

LOWE, JAMES B. (d.1963)

4627. "James B. Lowe." <u>Variety</u> (May 29 1963). [Obituary]

MCBROOM, MARCIA (1947-   )

4628. Anekwe, Simon. "Marcia McBroom: Actress and Sunday
School Teacher." New York <u>Amsterdam News</u> (November 13 1976):
D-2.

4629. McDonald, Denise. "Marcia McBroom." <u>Essence</u> (December
1970): 56.

MCDANIEL, HATTIE (1895-1952)

See also # 3400

4630. Jackson, Carlton. <u>Hattie: The Life of Hattie McDaniel</u>.
Lanham, MD: Madison Books, 1989. 220p.

Biographical Dictionaries

4631. Bogle, Donald. <u>Blacks in American Films and
Television</u>. New York: Garland, 1988, pp. 415-418.

4632. "McDaniel, Hattie." In <u>The Penguin Encyclopedia of
Popular Music</u>, ed. Donald Clarke. New York: Viking, 1989.

4633. Skerrett, Joseph T. "McDaniel, Hattie." In <u>Notable
American Women: The Modern Period</u>, eds. Barbara Sicherman and
Carol Hurd Green. Cambridge, MA: The Belknap Press, 1980, pp.
445-446.

4634. Traylor, Eleanor W. "McDaniel, Hattie." In <u>Dictionary
of American Negro Biography</u>, eds. Rayford W. Logan and Michael
R. Winston. New York: W.W. Norton, 1982, pp. 414-415.

Articles

4635. Leff, L. J. "The Search for Hattie McDaniel." <u>New
Orleans Review</u>, Vol. 10, No. 2/3 (1983): 91-98.

4636. "McDaniel, Hattie." Current Biography 1940.

4637. "Mammy Goes to Town." Photoplay (June 1940): 80.

4638. "The Passing of Beulah: Hattie McDaniel's death may mark the end of the kitchen comedy era." Our World (February 1953): 12-15.

4639. Wilson, Alfred. "Historical Feature: Hattie McDaniel-- Queen of the Character Actresses!" Right On! (June 1981): 26-27.

Obituaries

4640. Current Biography 1952.
4641. New York Amsterdam News (November 1 1952).
4642. New York Herald-Tribune (October 27 1952).
4643. New York Times (October 27 1952).
4644. New York Times (November 2 1952).
4645. New York Times (November 5 1952).
4646. Our World (February 19 1952).
4647. Variety (October 29 1952).

Collections

4648. Hattie McDaniel Collection. [Held by the Black American Film History Collection (# 5994)]

MCEACHIN, JAMES (1930-   )

4649. McEachin, James - Clippings [Billy Rose Theatre Collection]

MCGARRITY, EVERETT

See # 1992

MCGEE, VONETTA (c.1950-   )

See also # 3370, 3372-3373

4650. Bogle, Donald. Blacks in American Films and Television. New York: Garland, 1988, p. 418.

Articles

4651. Berry, William Earl. "Vonetta McGee: Simple, Soulful and Sexy." Black Stars (September 1973): 22-26.

4652. Brown, Marcia L. "Intimate Rap Session with Vonetta McGhee!!" Right On! (November 1973): 26-27; (December 1973): 22-23.

4653. Burrell, Walter Price. "Vonetta McGee: The Ugly Duckling Got the Prince." Black Stars (December 1974): 58-61.

4654. "Flashback: Vonetta McGee." Right On! (February 1977): 52-53.

4655. Haynes, Howard. "Off-Screen Lovers United in Movie." Sepia (April 1974): 40-44. Profile of McGee and Max Julien on the set of "Thomasine and Bushrod."

4656. "Jimmie Walker, Vonetta McGee Star in TV's 'Bustin Loose'." Jet (November 2 1987): 58-60.

4657. Lucas, Bob. "Here Comes Vonetta McGee!" Black Stars (February 1973): 44-46, 48-49.

4658. McGee, Vonetta. "I'm Worth a Kingdom." Black Stars (December 1978): 16-18.

4659. Singleton, Janet. "Portrait of a Survivor: Vonetta McGee's Career Continues." Black Film Review, Vol. 4, No. 2 (Spring 1988): 12-13.

4660. "Vonetta McGee's Own Story: Hollywood's Daring Mixed Romance Movie." Sepia (March 1975): 28-38. [Eiger Sanction]

MCKEE, LONETTE (c.1956-   )

4661. Bogle, Donald. Blacks in American Films and Television. New York: Garland, 1988, p. 419.

Articles

4662. Cantwell, M. "Up Close: Lonette McKee." Mademoisselle, Vol. 83 (April 1977): 198-199+.

4663. Collins, Lisa. "Lonette McKee: Looking Back All the Way." Black Stars (August 1977): 60-65.

4664. _____. "Lonette McKee: A Struggling Actress is 'On the Way Up'!" Right On! (August 1977): 20-21.

4665. Lane, Bill. "Sexiest New Star in Movies." Sepia, Vol. 26 (May 1977): 28-36.

4666. "Lonette McKee...Sparkling Her Way to Stardom!" Right On! (October 1976): 32.

4667. Mitchell, Elvis. "Detroit Diva: Lonette McKee." Film Comment, Vol. 21 (March/April 1985): 40-41.

4668. "The Rising Stars!" Harper's Bazaar, Vol. 118 (February 1985): 138-147.

4669. Rubenstein, Hal. "Lonette McKee." Interview (December 1987): 151-152.

Newspaper Articles

4670. Fraser, C. Gerald. "New Face: Lonette McKee." New York Times (January 20 1978): Sec. III, p. 11. [Interview]

4671. Robertson, Nan. "Voyage to Broadway." New York Times (May 12 1983): C17.

4672. Shipp, E. R. "Lonette McKee On Becoming Lady Day."
New York Times (February 22 1986): Sec. II, p. 6, 31.
Profile/interview with McKee on her film and stage career.

MCKINNEY, NINA MAE (1913-1967)

See also # 1992

4673. Bogle, Donald. Blacks in American Films and
Television. New York: Garland, 1988, pp. 419-420.

4674. Southern, Eileen. Biographical Dictionary of Afro-
American and African Musicians. Westport, CT: Greenwood
Press, 1982, p. 260.

Articles

4675. Bourne, Stephen. "Hallelujah Chorus Girl." Wire
Magazine (April 1989): 25-27.

4676. New York Amsterdam News (May 13 1967). [Obituary]

4677. Snelson, Floyd G. "Harlem Limited Broadway Bound. No.
10: Nina Mae McKinney." Pittsburgh Courier (December 30
1930).

4678. Tazelaar, Marguerite. "Let Miss Nina Mae McKinney Tell
You About Her First Film." New York Herald Tribune (August 18
1929): 3, 5.

4679. Watts, Richard, Jr. "Sight and Sound." New York
Herald Tribune (June 17 1934). [Profile]

4680. Williams, Francis. "Nina Mae McKinney. 'The Black
Garbo.'" Cinema (Beverly Hills), No. 35 (1976): 18-19.

MACLACHLAN, JANET

4681. "How Janet MacLachlan Overcame Her Shyness." Sepia
(March 1979): 52-58.

4682. "Janet MacLachlan Grabs Hollywood's Brass Ring." Sepia
(March 1970): 54-58.

4683. Jenkins, Walter. "Glancing at the Interesting World of
Janet MacLachlan." Black Stars (October 1973): 42-47.

4684. Moore, Bob. "Janet MacLachlan: Talented, Beautiful and
Lucky." Black Stars (August 1979): 48-50.

MCNAIR, BARBARA (1939-   )

4685. "Barbara McNair: The Acting Debut of a Singer." Sepia
(April 1964): 74-78.

4686. "McNair, Barbara." Current Biography 1971.

MCQUEEN, BUTTERFLY (1911-   )

4687. Bogle, Donald. <u>Blacks in American Films and
Television</u>. New York: Garland, 1988, pp. 420-422.

Articles

4688. Black, Doris. "Yesterday's Hitmakers: Butterfly
McQueen." <u>Sepia</u> (February 1977): 80.

4689. Davis, Curt. "McQueen is Floating Like a Butterfly."
<u>Encore American and Worldwide News</u> (September 5 1978): 24-25.

4690. Haddad, M. George. "Butterfly McQueen: 'I'm Not Mammy
Anymore.'" <u>Black Stars</u> (April 1979): 60-64.

4691. McQueen, Butterfly - Clippings [Billy Rose Theatre
Collection]

4692. Neuhaus, Cable. "Prissy Proves that What Floats Like a
Butterfly May Sting Like a McQueen." <u>People</u> (January 28
1980): 36.

4693. Tinkerbelle. "Butterfly McQueen: McQueen for a Day."
<u>Interview</u>, Vol. IV, No. 11 (November 1974): 18-19.

Newspaper Articles

4694. Hammond, Sally. "Butterfly McQueen: Never Really
Gone." <u>New York Post</u> (June 1 1968): Sec. 3, p. 33.

4695. Hancock, Carla. "Actress Still Remembered as
'Prissy.'" <u>Christian Science Monitor</u> (October 4 1965): 15.

4696. Hunter, Charlayne. "Butterfly McQueen Has a Family
Now." <u>New York Times</u> (July 28 1970): 20.

4697. Wahls, Robert. "Once a Butterfly, Always..." New York
<u>Daily News</u> (July 7 1968): 2S.

MARRIOTT, JOHN (1893-1977)

4698. Calta, Louis. "John Marriott, Actor, Dead at 83;
Appeared on Stage." <u>New York Times</u> (April 8 1977): A-25.

4699. "John Marriott." <u>Variety</u> (April 13 1977). [Obituary]

MARSHALL, WILLIAM (1924-   )

See also # 3351

4700. Bogle, Donald. <u>Blacks in American Films and
Television</u>. New York: Garland, 1988, pp. 414.

Articles

4701. Beaupre, Lee. "Black Actor William Marshall Gives
Pedagogs Lowdown on 'Coon' Age." <u>Variety</u> (August 15 1973): 2,
47.

4702. "Bill Marshall: Matinee Idol." Our World (February 1954): 38-41.

4703. Chrisman, Robert. "The Black Scholar interviews William Marshall." The Black Scholar (July/August 1985): 48-53.

4704. "Demetrius and the Gladiators; William Marshall has Choice Role in 3-D Film." Ebony (November 1953): 91-94, 96. Review of film with a biographical sketch of the actor.

4705. "Haiti Goes to the Movies: 20th century stages junket to show off 'Lydia Bailey'." Our World (August 1952): 46-53.

4706. "Lydia Bailey. William Marshall Stars in Movie Glorifying History of Haiti." Ebony (January 1952): 39+.

4707. Marshall, William. "What I Want in a Wife." Tan (October 1952): 28-31, 68.

4708. "Movie Review: William Marshall Stars in 'Lydia Bailey'." Color (July 1952): 45-47.

4709. "Movies: The Gladiators; Rising Negro actor has brilliant role in stirring Biblical drama." Our World (October 1953): 8, 10-11.

4710. Robertson, Nick. "Blacula Without the Fangs." Sepia, Vol. 23 (February 1974): 28-32.

4711. "William Marshall; De Lawd's Gift to Hollywood." Our World, Vol. 6 (December 1951): 12-14.

Newspaper Articles

4712. Bird, Robert S. "New 'Lawd' on Broadway. William Marshall, 27, Began in Steel Mill, Came to His Big Role the Hard Way." New York Herald-Tribune (March 18 1951): 1.

4713. Marshall, William - Clippings [Billy Rose Theatre Collection]

4714. Sheaffer, Louis. "Curtain Time." Brooklyn Eagle (March 28 1951): 12.

MARTIN, D'URVILLE (1939-1984)

See # 2653-2657

MARTIN, HELEN

4715. Bogle, Donald. Blacks in American Films and Television. New York: Garland, 1988, pp. 414-415.

4716. Collier, Aldore. "Helen Martin: Veteran actress continues to make her mark." Ebony (June 1988): 36+.

MARTINS, ORLANDO (1899-   ) (Nigeria)

4717. Folami, Takiu. <u>Orlando Martins, the Legend: An Intimate Biography of the First World Acclaimed African Film Actor</u>. Lagos: Executive Publishers, 1983.   122p.

4718. "Man of Two Worlds." <u>Drum</u> [Johannesburg] (February 1952): 36+.   Profile of Nigerian film actor Orlando Martins.

4719. "Two Negro Actors: Robert Adams...Orlando Martins." <u>Film Quarterly</u> [London] (Spring 1947): 18-20.

MAXWELL, DAPHNE

See Reid, Daphne Maxwell

MAYFIELD, JULIAN (1928-1984)

See also # 3100-3102

4720. MacArthur, Harry.   "Actor in Spite of Himself." Washington, D.C. <u>Evening Star</u> (December 5 1968): B-13.

4721. Mayfield, Julian.   "'Explore Black Experience.'"   <u>New York Times</u> (February 2 1969).

4722. Mayfield, Julian - Clippings [Billy Rose Theatre Collection]

4723. "Up Tight! Film that aims to tell it like it is stars a Black "anti-hero"." <u>Ebony</u> (November 1968): 47-48, 52-54.

Obituaries

4724. "Actor-Author Julian Mayfield dies in Maryland hospital." New York <u>Amsterdam News</u> (October 27 1984): 21.

4725. Brooke, James. "Julian Mayfield, 56, an Actor and Writer on Black Themes." <u>New York Times</u> (October 23 1984): 30.

4726. "Julian Mayfield." <u>Variety</u> (October 31 1984): 109.

MAYO, WHITMAN (1930-   )

See also # 3377

4727. Collins, Lisa. "Whitman Mayo--'Shady Grady'." <u>Black Stars</u> (July 1974): 24-30.

4728. Dawson, Cheryl. "Grady's New Life as a Grandfather." <u>Black Stars</u> (March 1976): 14-18.

4729. Lucas, Bob. "Whitman Mayo: Don't Let 'Grady' Fool You!" <u>Black Stars</u> (September 1975): 59-63.

4730. Salvo, Patrick. "Whitman Mayo: From Stand In to Star." <u>Sepia</u> (February 1976): 26-33.

4731. Mayo, Whitman - Clippings [Billy Rose Theatre Collection]

MERCER, MAE

See also # 3370

4732. Mercer, Mae - Clippings [Billy Rose Theatre Collection]

MERRITT, THERESA (1922-   )

See also # 3373

4733. Merritt, Theresa - Clippings [Billy Rose Theatre Collection]

4734. Raddatz, Leslie. "Mama: The Role Suits Theresa Merritt; being called a stereotype does not." TV Guide (January 18 1975): 20-22.

4735. Smith, Angela E. "Mama Becomes Wicked Witch of the West?" New York Amsterdam News (May 8 1976): D-5.

MILES, ROSALIND

4736. Fields, Sidney. "No More Long Spaces." New York Daily News (March 8 1972).

4737. Jenkins, Walter. "Looking in on Rosalind Miles." Black Stars (April 1973): 68-73.

4738. Johnson, Connie. "Rosalind Miles Talks About Her Experiences in Hollywood." Black Stars (March 1978): 6-9.

MILLS, ALISON

4739. "Alison Mills: Image of Hollywood's New Breed." Sepia (July 1970): 14-17.

MINOR, BOB

4740. Martinez, Al. "Breakthrough for a Stunt Man." New York Post (April 28 1977): 45. Profile of stunt man Bob Minor.

4741. Steinberg, Jay, and Pat Salvo. "The Incredible Hollywood Stuntman." Sepia (November 1978): 56-64.

MITCHELL, SCOEY

4742. Jenkins, Walter. "Scoey Mitchell--The New Master of Comedy." New Lady (March 1970): 20-23.

4743. Mitchell, Scoey - Clippings [Billy Rose Theatre Collection]

MOGOTLANE, THOMAS (South Africa)

4744. Maslin, Janet. "Mapantsula." <u>New York Times</u> (December 3 1989): 89. Review of film for which Mogotlane both wrote the script and starred.

4745. Phillips, Julie. "Negative Space." <u>Village Voice</u> (December 12 1989). Review of "Mapantsula."

MOODY, LYNNE

4746. Banfield, Bever-Leigh. "A Cozy Candlelight Conversation with Lynne Moody." <u>Right On</u>! (August 1981): 14-16.

4747. Collins, Lisa. "Is Hollywood Really Spoiling Lynne Moody." <u>Black Stars</u> (May 1977): 60-65.

4748. Jenkins, Walter. "A Revealing Glance at Lynne Moody." <u>Black Stars</u> (September 1975): 6-11.

4749. Mills, John II. "Checkin' Out Lynne Moody! What's This Foxy Lady Like?" <u>Right On</u>! (April 1977): 36-37.

MOORE, ARCHIE (1913-   )

4750. Moore, Archie. <u>The Archie Moore Story</u>. New York: McGraw-Hill, 1960. 240p.

Articles

4751. "Moore, Archie." <u>Current Biography 1960</u>.

4752. Moore, Archie. "Why I Played Jim, The Slave." <u>Ebony</u> (September 1960): 43+.

4753. Skolsky, Sidney. "Tintyped: Archie Moore." <u>New York Post</u> (January 24 1960): M3. Includes comments by Moore's mother in which she corrects the widely cited birthdate of Moore from 1916 to 1913.

4754. Zunser, Jesse. "Archie Lands a Movie 'K.O.' World light-heavyweight champion Archie Moore is instant hit in second career as movie actor." <u>Cue</u> (June 4 1960): 12.

MOORE, HARRY R. [TIM] (1888-1958)

4755. Bogle, Donald. <u>Blacks in American Films and Television</u>. New York: Garland, 1988, pp. 425-426.

Articles

4756. Adams, Val. "Another Show Set By 'Amos 'n' Andy'." <u>New York Times</u> (December 20 1954). On the creation of an Amos 'n' Andy spinoff - The Adventures of the Kingfish - which was to star Tim Moore.

4757. Moore, Harry - Clippings [Billy Rose Theatre Collection]

4758. "Requiem for the Kingfish. Tim Moore was one of the world's funniest men." Ebony (July 1959): 57-58, 60-62, 64.

4759. "What happened to TV stars of 'Amos 'n' Andy'?" Jet (December 10 1981): 55-58.

Obituaries

4760. New York Times (December 14 1958): 5.

4761. Variety (December 17 1958).

MOORE, JUANITA (1922-   )

4762. Bogle, Donald. Blacks in American Films and Television. New York: Garland, 1988, p. 425.

4763. "Imitation of Life; Juanita Moore stars in new version of film." Ebony (April 1959): 70-73.

4764. Moore, Juanita - Clippings (Includes a 4p. typed interview) [Billy Rose Theatre Collection]

MOORE, LISA

See also # 3370

4765. Jenkins, Walter. "Speaking Seriously About Lisa Moore." Black Stars (September 1975): 66-71.

MORELAND, MANTAN (1902-1973)

4766. Bogle, Donald. Blacks in American Films and Television. New York: Garland, 1988, pp. 427-428.

Articles

4767. "Mantan Moreland." Variety (October 3 1973). [Obituary]

4768. "Mantan Moreland, Who Played in Chan Films and 'Godot,' Dies." New York Times (September 29 1973): 34.

4769. Moreland, Mantan - Clippings [Billy Rose Theatre Collection]

MORGAN, DEBBI

4770. "Debbi Morgan Resigns From 'All My Children.'" Jet (February 26 1990): 37.

4771. Jenkins, Walter. "Debbi Morgan: Hollywood Wasn't Really That Hard to Crack." Black Stars (June 1977): 60-65.

4772. Jones, Debra. "Debbi Morgan Went Out and Tackled Prince Charming." New York Amsterdam News (March 3 1984): 28.

4773. Marsh, Antoinette. "Debbie Morgan: Looking Beyond Roots." Black Stars (September 1979): 6-9.

4774. Sinclair, Abiola. "Debbi Morgan to leave 'All My Children'." New York <u>Amsterdam News</u> (February 24 1990): 32.

4775. Townley, Roderick. "Debbi Morgan's Made a Career of <u>Not</u> Heeding Her Mother." <u>TV Guide</u> (January 26 1985): 37-39.

4776. Trescott, Jacqueline. "The Roots of Stardom: Debbi Morgan Gets the Big Break." <u>Washington Post</u> (January 11 1979): B1, B7.

MORRIS, GARRETT (1937-   )

4777. Haddad-Garcia, George. "Garrett Morris: Never on Saturday." <u>Black Stars</u> (October 1980): 6-9.

4778. Smith, Y. "Garrett Morris: Comic Exploration or Exploitation?" <u>Essence</u>, Vol. 10 (November 1979): 12-13+.

MORRIS, GREG (1933-   )

See also # 3373

4779. Bogle, Donald. <u>Blacks in American Films and Television</u>. New York: Garland, 1988, p. 428.

Articles

4780. Anderson, Nancy. "'Vega$' Star Greg Morris Gives Credit Where It's Due." New York <u>News World</u> (March 28 1979).

4781. Burrell, Walter Price. "Greg Morris: Mission Accomplished." <u>Black Stars</u> (February 1972): 38-45.

4782. Davis, Bruce C. "Take Time Out with Greg Morris: The Man from Mission Impossible." <u>Essence</u>, Vol. 3 (January 1973): 40-41+.

4783. "Greg Morris Family Beats Old Show Business 'Jinx.' Happily married 25 years, couple are proud parents of three." <u>Ebony</u> (May 1981): 33+.

4784. Klemesrud, Judy. "He Was a Man, and Knew It." <u>New York Times</u> (May 11 1969): D19.

4785. "Mission Impossible's Greg Morris." <u>Ebony</u> (December 1967): 99-104.

4786. Salvo, Patrick, and Barbara Salvo. "Greg Morris Speaks Out on Blackness and Movies." <u>Sepia</u> (December 1973): 46-52.

4787. Slaton, Shell. "At Home with Actor Greg Morris!" <u>Right On</u>! (February 1977): 75-77.

4788. Staudacher, Carol P. "What Manner of Man is Gregg (sic) Morris?" <u>New Lady</u> (November 1969): 16-19.

4789. "TV's Greg Morris Talks About His Family and Future." <u>Jet</u> (January 12 1978): 20-24.

4790. Young, A. S. Doc. "Greg Morris: World's Most Famous Black Actor." Black Stars (November 1977): 22-28.

MORRIS, PHILLIP

4791. Marlow, Curtis. "Phillip Morris: He's Young and Restless." Right On! (June 1985): 56-57. [Interview]

4792. "Mission Possible: Phil Morris takes over dad's role in suspense TV series." Ebony (June 1989): 70, 72, 74.

MORRISON, DOROTHY

See # 3367

MORRISON, ERNIE (d.1989)

See also # 3367

4793. "Ernie Morrison." Variety (August 2 1989): 83. Obituary for "Our Gang" series star Ernie Morrison [Sunshine Sammy].

MORTON, JOE (1947-   )

4794. Morton, Joe - Clippings [Billy Rose Theatre Collection]

4795. Musto, Michael. "Joe Morton: Silent Running." Village Voice (September 18 1984): 59.

4796. Silberg, Jon. "Close-Up: Joe Morton." American Film (April 1988): 72.

MOSLEY, ROGER

4797. Armstrong, Lois. "Unknown Roger Mosley Scores in 'Leadbelly', But He's Got the Blues over its Distribution." People (June 7 1976): 81-82.

4798. Collier, Aldore. "Roger E. Mosley: An Actor with a Conscience." Ebony (November 1982): 79+.

4799. _____. "Roger Mosley and Tom Selleck: Black TV Star Rose from Ghetto to Fame." Jet (October 4 1982): 62-64.

4800. Goodwin, Betty. "One Foot in the Ghetto, One in His Rolls Royce." TV Guide (August 28 1982): 20, 22, 24.

4801. "It's Better to Be Looked Over, Than Overlooked!" Right On! (April 1983): 18-20.

4802. "Roger Mosley: An Actor with a Conscience, 'Magnum P.I.', Star Tries to Set an Example for Youth Who Watch Him." Ebony (November 1982): 79-80+.

4803. Sternberg, Robert. "A Conversation with Roger Mosley." Black Stars (December 1976): 48-53.

MOTEN, ETTA (1901-   )

See # 6035

MURPHY, EDDIE (1961-   )

4804. Bogle, Donald. <u>Blacks in American Films and Television</u>. New York: Garland, 1988, pp. 428-431.

4805. Ruth, Marianne. <u>Eddie: Eddie Murphy from A to Z</u>. Los Angeles: Holloway House Publishing Co., 1985. 192p.

Articles

4806. Allen, Bonnie. "Eddie Murphy: Black Humor with an Edge." <u>Essence</u> (January 1983): 12.

4807. _____. "Spotlight: Eddie Murphy, Serious Business." <u>Essence</u> (December 1988): 44-46, 108, 110, 112.

4808. Collier, Aldore. "The Ebony Interview with Eddie Murphy, Hollywood's Hottest Property." <u>Ebony</u> (July 1985): 40+.

4809. _____. "Eddie Murphy; In Search of Love." <u>Ebony Man</u> (November 1988): 78-80, 82.

4810. _____. "Eddie Murphy's interview reveals..." <u>Jet</u> (March 18 1985): 60-64.

4811. Corliss, Richard. "The Good Little Bad Little Boy; At 22, Comedian Eddie Murphy has Become a Multimedia Star." <u>Time</u> (July 11 1983): 64-67.

4812. Dalton, Joseph, and David Hirshey. "Eddie Murphy: The Prince of Comedy." <u>Rolling Stone</u> (July 7 1983): 10+.

4813. "Eddie; the unauthorized, unexpurgated, and unsolicited biography." <u>Esquire</u> (December 1985): 335-338.

4814. "Eddie Murphy: It's No Joke: He Makes Folks Mad, but He's Got It Made." <u>People</u> (December 26 1983-January 2 1984): 52.

4815. "Eddie Murphy: makes switch from TV comedy to films." <u>Jet</u> (January 16 1984): 60-63.

4816. Grenier, R. "Eddie Murphy, American." <u>Commentary</u> (March 1985): 63-67.

4817. Hadley-Garcia, George. "All About Eddie." <u>Right On!</u> (September 1983): 30-33.

4818. _____. "Golden Eddie Murphy." <u>Right On!</u> (January 1987): 18-19.

4819. Hirshey, Gerri. "The Black Pack." <u>Vanity Fair</u> (July 1988): 58-63, 118-120, 123.

4820. Horner, Cynthia. "Eddie Murphy Talks to Right On."
Right On! (February 1990); (March 1990): 60-63; (April 1990):
54-56.

4821. Jackson, Gary. "Saturday Night at the Movies." Right
On! (April 1985): 44-47, 65. [Profile]

4822. Jarvis, Jeff. "Pryor and Murphy." People (July 11
1983): 86+.

4823. Leavy, Walter. "Eddie Murphy; An incredible leap to
superstardom." Ebony (October 1983): 35-36, 38, 40, 42.

4824. _____. "Eddie Murphy; Will movie hit create
problems for controversial comic?" Ebony (April 1983): 88,
90, 92, 94.

4825. Lyons, Gene. "Crazy Eddie." Newsweek (January 7
1985): 48-55.

4826. _____. "Laughing with Eddie." Newsweek (January 3
1983): 46-48.

4827. "Murphy, Eddie." Current Biography 1983.

4828. Murphy, Eddie - Clippings (MFL + n.c. 2723) [Billy Rose
Theatre Collection]

4829. Pitts, Leonard, Jr. "He's Wicked. He's Not Only Live
on Saturday Night." Right On! (February 1983): 20-21.

4830. "The Prince of Paramount: Eddie Murphy." Interview
(September 1987): 60+.

4831. Zehme, Bill. "Eddie Murphy: The Rolling Stone
Interview." Rolling Stone (August 24 1989): 50+.

Beverly Hills Cop (1984)

4832. Bogle, Donald. Blacks in American Films and
Television. New York: Garland, 1988, pp. 16-18.

4833. Collier, Aldore. "Eddie Murphy: Race and wit make cop
movie a box-office hit." Jet (January 21 1985): 56-59.

4834. Ellis, Trey. "The Gay Subtext in Beverly Hills Cop:
Did Hollywood Set Out to Undo Eddie Murphy?" Black Film
Review, Vol. 3, No. 2 (Spring 1987): 15-17.

Beverly Hills Cop II (1987)

4835. "Eddie Murphy scores again with 'Beverly Hills Cop
II.'" Jet (June 15 1987): 56-58.

Coming to America

4836. Bernard, Jami. "Eddie Murphy's troubled route to
America." Video Magazine (June 1989): 16-17.

4837. "Eddie Murphy's testimony disputes Buchwald's suit."
Jet (January 15 1990): 54-55.

4838. Leavy, Walter. "Eddie Murphy and Arsenio Hall star in
the new movie 'Coming to America'." _Jet_ (July 18 1988): 36-
38.

4839. _____. "Eddie Murphy's Princely Role." _Ebony_
(July 1988): 31+.

4840. McBride, James. "Eddie Murphy comes clean; does Coming
to America reflect Murphy's own difficulties in life and love?
Yes, says the star in a rare interview." _People_ (August 8
1988): 76+.

4841. "Murphy hits out at Black critics 'Coming to America'
criticism." _Variety_ (August 3 1988): 8.

4842. "Murphy's 'America' earns $28.4 mil. in six days; star
hit with lawsuit." _Jet_ (July 25 1988): 55.

4843. "Paramount loses 'Coming to America' suit; Judge
absolves Eddie Murphy." _Jet_ (January 22 1990): 57.

48 Hours

4844. Bogle, Donald. _Blacks in American Films and
Television_. New York: Garland, 1988, pp. 85-86.

4845. Flippo, Chet. "Muscling in on movies with 48 Hours,
Eddie Murphy may take Richard Pryor's crown." _People_ (January
31 1983): 42-44.

Harlem Nights

4846. Ansen, David. Harlem Nights. _Newsweek_ (November 27
1989): 92. [Review]

4847. Canby, Vincent. "Harlem Nights." _New York Times_
(November 17 1989): C19. [Review]

4848. Collier, Aldore. "Eddie Murphy; Getting the last laugh
on critics." _Ebony Man_ (February 1990): 79-80, 82.

4849. "Eddie laughs all way to bank as critics bash 'Harlem
Nights'." _Jet_ (December 11 1989): 56+.

4850. Frechette, David. "Reviews: Harlem Nights." _Black
Film Review_, Vol. 5, No. 4 (Fall 1989?): 24.

4851. Johnson, Robert E. "Eddie says he cast Richard in
'Harlem Nights' because 'he is my idol'." _Jet_ (November 20
1989): 56+.

4852. Leavy, Walter. "Eddie Murphy, Richard Pryor, Redd
Foxx: three generations of Black comedy." _Ebony_ (January
1990): 102+.

4853. Schickel, Richard. Harlem Nights. _Time_ (November 27 1989): 88. [Review]

Saturday Night Live

4854. Flippo, Chet. "Eddie Murphy Live." _New York_ (October 11 1982): 57+.

4855. Rein, Richard K. "Heard of Eddie Murphy's Law? If anything can survive on 'Saturday Night', he will." _People_ (January 25 1982): 87+.

4856. Ribowsky, Mark. "'Hey, This is Happening Too Fast'. At 21, 'Saturday Night' live wire Eddie Murphy is a fast-rising comic genius, harried by success and haunted by Freddie Prinze." _TV Guide_ (July 3 1982): 18-21.

4857. Schwartz, Tony. "How an Amiable Youth Became a TV Star at 20." _New York Times_ (October 26 1981).

4858. Shore, Michael. "Eddie Murphy Re-Ignites Black Comedy." _Soho Weekly News_ (February 2 1982): 12, 14.

4859. Young, Charles M. "Head and Shoulders Above the Rest: Saturday Night Live's Eddie Murphy." _New York Sunday News Magazine_ (January 31 1982): 8-9, 19.

Trading Places

4860. Bogle, Donald. _Blacks in American Films and Television_. New York: Garland, 1988, pp. 220-221.

4861. Hadley-Garcia, George. "All About Eddie." _Right On!_ (September 1983): 30-33.

MUSE, CLARENCE (1889-1979)

4862. Bogle, Donald. _Blacks in American Films and Television_. New York: Garland, 1988, pp. 431-433.

4863. Southern, Eileen. _Biographical Dictionary of Afro-American and African Musicians_. Westport, CT: Greenwood Press, 1982, p. 284.

Articles

4864. Black, Doris. "Yesterday's Hitmakers: Clarence Muse." _Sepia_ (October 1976): 80.

4865. Lewis, Barbara. "Spry Talk from Clarence Muse." _Encore American and Worldwide News_ (April 18 1977): 33-34.

4866. Lucas, Bob. "Hollywood Champion: 218 Movie Roles in Half a Century." _Black Stars_ (January 1977): 28-31.

4867. Mason, B. J. "The Grand Old Man of Good Hope Valley. Actor Clarence Muse talks about his life and his work." _Ebony_ (September 1972): 50+.

4868. Patterson, Lindsay. "On the Aisle: Focus on Clarence Muse." Essence (April 1976): 17, 103.

4869. Theatre Arts (August 1942): 510.

Newspaper Articles

4870. "Clarence Muse as Seen in 'The Count of Monte Cristo'." New York Amsterdam News (October 6 1934).

4871. "Hollywood Hails Clarence Muse as Gentleman and Artist." Baltimore Afro-American (September 12 1931).

4872. White, Alvin E. "The Talented Muse, Ahead of His Time." (Worcester, Mass.) Evening Gazette (February 12 1980): 1E-2E.

Obituaries

4873. Black Perspective in Music, Vol. 8, No. 2 (Fall 1980): 264.

4874. "Clarence Muse." Variety (October 24 1979): 119.

4875. Fraser, C. Gerald. "Clarence Muse, 89; Acted in 219 Films." New York Times (October 17 1979): D-23.

Media Materials

4876. Black Star of the Silver Screen: The Story of Clarence Muse (video). 30 min. [Available from Media Unlimited Productions, P.O. Box 4242, Stanford, CA 94305. Tel. 415/324-8277.]

MYERS, PAULINE

4877. Myers, Pauline - Clippings [Billy Rose Theatre Collection]

NELSON, HAYWOOD

4878. "Hey, Hey, Hey, Hey, Hey.....It's Haywood! Nelson-That Is!" Right On! (December 1976): 4-5.

4879. "Interview: What's Haywood Nelson Been Up to Lately?" Right On! (January 1986): 16-18, 65.

4880. Russell, Liz. "Closeup with Haywood Nelson." Right On! (May 1976): 22-24.

NICHOLAS BROTHERS [(Fayard (1917-   )/Harold (1924-   )]

4881. Bogle, Donald. Blacks in American Films and Television. New York: Garland, 1988, pp. 434-435.

Articles

4882. Collier, Aldore. "Whatever Happened to the Nicholas Brothers?" Ebony, Vol. 38 (May 1983): 103-104+.

4883. "Dancers Go Dramatic. Newcomer Lola Falana, veteran Fayard Nicholas try acting in new film." Ebony (September 1969): 38-40, 42, 46.

4884. Francis, Robert. "Lives of Nicholas Brothers Run As Parallel as Their Dance Steps." Brooklyn Daily Eagle (April 28 1946).

4885. "How We Dance: The Nicholas Brothers spill the beans." Our World (October 1946): 24-25.

4886. "Nicholas Brothers Biggest Split; Harold, Fayard are 7,000 Miles Apart." Ebony, Vol. 15 (May 1960): 77-80+.

4887. Nicholas Brothers - Clippings [Billy Rose Theatre Collection]

4888. Nicholas Brothers. "Our 3 Gravy Years in Europe." Our World, Vol. 8 (January 1952): 24-27.

4889. "Nicholas Brothers Steppin' High with 50 Years of Success." Jet (June 25 1981): 56-57+.

4890. "The Nicholas Brothers Still A Team in 'St. Louis Woman'." Brooklyn Daily Eagle (March 24 1946).

4891. Nicholas, Harold - Clippings [Billy Rose Theatre Collection]

4892. "The Pirate. Nicholas Brothers cavort with Gene Kelly in new film." Ebony (February 1948): 32-34.

4893. "What Became of...the Nicholas Brothers, Amazing Young Dancers?" Sepia, Vol. 7 (July 1959): 57.

NICHOLAS, DENISE (c.1944-   )

See also # 3155-3156, 3370

4894. Bogle, Donald. Blacks in American Films and Television. New York: Garland, 1988, p. 434.

Articles

4895. "Denise Nicholas: Star in Room 222." Sepia (June 1970): 48-52.

4896. Dupree, Adolph. "Stargazing: A Celestial Conversation with Denise Nicholas." about time, Vol. 13, No. 12 (December 1985): 14-16.

4897. Gershman, Michael. "What Ever Happened to Denise Nicholas?" Right On! (April 1979): 45.

4898. Mills, Jon II. "Exclusive: Denise Nicholas--Looking Straight Ahead with the World Looking Back!!!" Right On! (December 1976): 30-33.

4899. Salvo, Patrick, and Barbara Salvo. "It Takes a Hell of a Man to Put Up with Me." Sepia, Vol. 24 (February 1975): 36-40+.

4900. Wasserman, John L. "The Girl in 'Room 222.'" TV Guide (September 20 1969): 24-27.

4901. Winters, Jason. "Denise Nicholas: Beauty Isn't Everything." Black Stars (June 197?): 59-61.

4902. Womble, Candace. "Denise Nicholas is Doing It Again." Encore American and Worldwide News (January 19 1976): 30-31.

NICHOLS, NICHELLE (c.1936-   )

See also # 3373, 3377

4903. Asherman, Allan. The Star Trek Interview Book. New York: Pocket Books, 1988, pp. 64-75.

Articles

4904. "At the Salute Nichelle Nichols." Starlog (November 1986): 54-55, 88.

4905. Collins, Lisa. "As Quiet as its Kept, Nichelle Nichols is an Actress." Black Stars (February 1975): 62-65.

4906. George, Nelson. "Nichelle Nichols Travels Far on Star Trek." New York Amsterdam News (March 1 1980): 52.

4907. Lowry, Brian. "Nichelle Nichols - The Songs of Uhura." Starlog (March 1987): 28-31.

4908. Moore, Marie. "Nichelle Nichols zooms thru space on Star Trek II." New York Amsterdam News (June 19 1982): 27, 30.

4909. Mourges-Rudolph, Denise. "Nichelle Nichols: Woman on the Go." Sepia (May 1978): 47-51.

4910. Murphy, Frederick Douglas. "Nichelle Nichols and the Uhura Connection." Black Stars (January 1980): 28-32.

4911. "New Star in the TV Heavens. Nichelle Nichols plays spaceship crew woman in Star Trek." Ebony (January 1967): 71+.

4912. "Nichelle Nichols and the Possible Dream." Encore American and Worldwide News (January 15 1979): 23-24.

4913. Nichols, Nichelle - Clippings [Billy Rose Theatre Collection]

4914. "Space Stars: Nichelle Nichols, Billy Dee Williams play futurist roles." Ebony (August 1985): 150+.

4915. Willson, Karen E. "Starlog Interview: Nichelle Nichols Opens All Hailing Frequencies." Starlog (July 1980): 24-28.

NORMAN, MAIDIE (1912-   )

4916. Bogle, Donald. Blacks in American Films and
Television. New York: Garland, 1988, p. 436.

O'NEAL, RON (1937-   )

See also # 3350

4917. Abdul, Raoul. Famous Black Entertainers of Today. New
York: Dodd, Mead & Co., 1974, pp. 102-108.

4918. Bogle, Donald. Blacks in American Films and
Television. New York: Garland, 1988, pp. 436-437.

Articles

4919. Films and Filming (April 1978): 46. Biographical
sketch.

4920. Fremont, V., J. Jade, and R. Cutrone. "Ron O'Neal's
Superfly." Inter/View, Vol. 28 (December 1972): 6-8, 41.

4921. Horner, Cynthia. "Is Super Fly Dead? Ask Ron O'Neal."
Right On! (October 1977): 22-23.

4922. Jenkins, Flo. "Ron O'Neal!...From Super Fly to
Shakespeare's Macbeth!" Right On! (December 1974): 22-24.

4923. Manning, Steve J. "Ron O'Neal...Super Fly at Last!"
Right On! (April 1973): 24-25.

4924. "Ron O'Neal Raps!" Right On! (June 1973): 54-55.

Newspaper Articles

4925. Murray, James P. "Ron O' Neal Finds Movie Business...A
Sociologist's Hunting Ground." New York Amsterdam News (May
18 1974): B10-11.

4926. _____. "Whatever Happened To...Ron O'Neal of
'Super Fly' Fame?" New York Amsterdam News (May 7 1975): A-9.

4927. Tallmer, Jerry. "Ron O'Neal Super Fly II." New York
Post (June 16 1973).

4928. Wahls, Robert. "The Real Ron." New York Sunday News
(June 15 1975): L-8.

4929. White, Joyce. "'Super' Actor Flies Off the Handle."
New York Sunday News (March 25 1973).

OVERTON, BILL (c.1947-   )

4930. Murray, James P. "A Pretty Actor: Check Out My
Talent." New York Amsterdam News (August 31 1974): D-8.

PACE, JUDY (1946-   )

See also # 3370

4931. Barnard, Ken. "No Questions Asked: Nudity a Now Thing." Detroit News (May 24 1970): 1-H, 2-H. Interview focusing on Pace's nude scene in "Cotton Comes to Harlem."

4932. Dawson, Cheryl. "The Two Worlds of Judy Pace." Black Stars (October 1973): 16-23.

4933. Jenkins, Flo. "Don Mitchell and Judy Pace. Behind the beautiful face." Black Stars (June 1978): 21-24.

4934. "Judy Pace: Bad Black Beauty of 'Peyton Place'." Sepia (April 1969): 45-48.

4935. "Judy Pace--The Thinking Man's Star." Ebony (March 1971): 112+.

4936. Pace, Judy - Clippings [Billy Rose Theatre Collection]

PAGE, LA WANDA (1920-   )

4937. Johnston, Ernie, Jr. "Aunt Esther, a big hit in the Bronx." New York Amsterdam News (December 30 1978): B-5.

4938. Lucas, Bob. "La Wanda Page: Everybody's Got an Esther." Black Stars (April 1974): 45-49.

4939. Page, La Wanda - Clippings [Billy Rose Theatre Collection]

4940. Winters, Jason. "La Wanda Page: A Cinderella Story." Black Stars (December 1977): 28-33.

PALEY, PETRONIA

4941. Goldstein, Toby. "10 Questions for Petronia Paley." Soap Opera Digest (December 6 1983).

4942. Townley, Rod. "Petronia Paley says she was a priest in ancient Egypt; There's certainly an air of mystery about this star from Another World." TV Guide (February 4 1984): 57-58.

PAYNE, FREDA (c.1944-   )

See also # 3370

4943. Allen, Zita. "Freda Payne: A Star is Reborn." Essence (March 1982): 72-74, 154.

4944. Johnson, Robert E. "Freda Payne: sweet TV success follows marriage that turned sour." Jet (January 21 1982): 60+.

4945. Lucas, Bob. "Why I Decided to 'Go Nude' in Movies - Freda Payne." Sepia (December 1972): 36-44.

PENDLETON, DAVID (1937-   )

4946. Pendleton, David - Clippings [Billy Rose Theatre Collection]

PERRY, FELTON

4947. Buck, Jerry. "TV: Felton Perry Builds an Arresting Career." New York Post (June 10 1988): 98.

4948. Jenkins, Walter. "Felton Perry Tells What Acting Has Done For Him." Black Stars (August 1973): 22-29.

4949. Perry, Felton - Clippings [Billy Rose Theatre Collection]

4950. "Up-Front: Felton Perry Investigating New Success on 'Hooperman'." Ebony Man (October 1988): 6.

PERRY, LINCOLN [Stepin Fetchit] (1892-1985)

See also # 3400

4951. Bogle, Donald. Blacks in American Films and Television. New York: Garland, 1988, pp. 388-391.

Articles

4952. Cobb, Delmarie, and Antoinette Marsh. "Stepin Fetchit: The Father of Black Movie Stars." Black Stars (December 1978): 32-36.

4953. "Do You Remember Stepin' Fetchit?" Negro Digest, Vol. 9 (November 1950): 42-43.

4954. "'I'm No Derogatory Black Image': Stepin' Fetchit." Jet (May 3 1973): 61.

4955. McBride, Joseph. "Stepin Fetchit Talks Back: Interview." Film Quarterly, Vol. 24 (Summer 1971): 20-26.

4956. Perry, Lincoln - Clippings [Billy Rose Theatre Collection]

4957. "Stepin Fetchit Calls His Film Image Progressive." New York Times (July 24 1968).

4958. "Stepin Fetchit Comes Back." Ebony (February 1952): 64-67.

4959. "$3 Million 'Fetchit' Suit Goes to Trial Sept. 18." Jet (August 24 1972): 54.

4960. "Whatever Happened to Lincoln Stepin Fetchit Perry?" Ebony, Vol. 26 (November 1971): 202.

Obituaries

4961. "Actor Stepin Fetchit, 83, dies in L.A. hospital." _Jet_ (December 9 1985): 53.

4962. "Film Actor Stepin Fetchit dies at 83 in California." _Atlanta Constitution_ (November 20 1985).

4963. "Lincoln Theodore Perry." _Newsweek_ (December 2 1985): 104.

4964. "Lincoln Theodore Perry." _Time_ (December 2 1985): 104.

4965. _New York Times_ (November 20 1985): D31; (November 21 1985): B-22.

4966. "Stepin Fetchit, 83, Dies; Pioneer Black Film Actor." _Washington Post_ (November 21 1985).

4967. _Variety_ (November 27 1985): 4, 36.

PETERS, BROCK (1927-   )

See also # 3351, 3373

4968. Bogle, Donald. _Blacks in American Films and Television_. New York: Garland, 1988, pp. 439-440.

4969. Southern, Eileen. _Biographical Dictionary of Afro-American and African Musicians_. Westport, CT: Greenwood Press, 1982, p. 304.

Articles

4970. Beaupre, Lee.   "Brock Peters on Negro Skepticism: One Colored Star Hardly a Trend." _Variety_ (December 20 1967).

4971. "Brock Peters." _Ebony_, Vol. 18 (June 1963): 106+.

4972. "Brock Peters: Veteran Actor-Singer Reaps Rewards of Hard Work and Persistence." _Ebony_ (November 1987): 92-101.

4973. "The Long Distance Runners: Brock Peters." _Ebony_ (November 1987): 92+.

PETERS, EDITH

4974. "American in Italian Movies." _Ebony_, Vol. 15 (June 1960): 85-86+.

POITIER, SIDNEY (1927-   )

See also # 3351, 3400

4975. Ewers, Carolyn H. _The Long Journey; a biography of Sidney Poitier_. New York: New American Library, 1969. 126p.

4976. Hoffman, William. _Sidney_. New York: L. Stuart, 1971. 175p.

4977.   Kelley, Samuel L.   The Evolution of Character Portrayals in the Films of Sidney Poitier, 1950-1978.   New York: Garland, 1983.   279p.

4978.   Keyser, Lester J., and Andre H. Ruszkowski.   The Cinema of Sidney Poitier: The Black Man's Changing Role on the American Screen.   San Diego: A. S. Barnes, 1980.   192p.

4979.   Marill, Alvin H.   The Films of Sidney Poitier. Secaucus, NJ: Citadel Press, 1978.   222p.

4980.   Paige, David.   Sidney Poitier.   Mankato, MN: Creative Education, 1976.   31p.

4981.   Poitier, Sidney.   This Life.   New York: Knopf, 1980. 374p.   [Autobiography]

4982.   Sidney Poitier: An American Film Institute Seminar on his Work.   Beverly Hills, CA, 1977.   61p.

Books with Sections on Sidney Poitier

4983.   Black Writers: A Selection of Sketches from Contemporary Authors.   Detroit: Gale Research Inc., 1989, pp. 458-461.

4984.   Bogle, Donald.   Blacks in American Films and Television.   New York: Garland, 1988, pp. 440-446.

4985.   Hernton, Calvin C.   "And You, Too, Sidney Poitier!"   In White Papers for White Americans, ed. Calvin C. Hernton.   New York: Doubleday, 1966, pp. 53-70.

Dissertations

4986.   Kelley, Samuel Lawrence.   "The Evolution of Character Portrayals in the Films of Sidney Poitier: 1950-1978." Dissertation (Ph.D.) University of Michigan, 1980.   287p.

Articles

4987.   Ansen, David.   "A Superstar Returns to the Screen." Newsweek (February 22 1988): 73.

4988.   Baldwin, James.   "Sidney Poitier."   Look (July 23 1968): 50-54.

4989.   Bennett, Lerone, Jr.   "Hollywood's First Negro Movie Star: Sidney Poitier breaks film barrier to become screen idol."   Ebony, Vol. 14 (May 1959): 100-103, 106-108.

4990.   Black, Doris.   "A Quarter Century in Movies for Sidney Poitier."   Sepia, Vol. 23 (August 1974): 36-42.

4991.   "Blackboard Jungle: Sidney Poitier Has Key Role in Brutal Film About Teacher, Juvenile Delinquents."   Ebony (May 1955): 87-93.

4992. Elliston, Maxine Hall. "Two Sidney Poitier Films."
Film Comment, Vol. 5 (Winter 1969): 26-33.

4993. "For Love of Ivy. Abbey Lincoln joins Sidney Poitier
in romantic comedy film." *Ebony* (October 1968): 52+.

4994. Goodman, George. "Durango: Poitier meets Belafonte."
Look (August 24 1971): 56+.

4995. Greenfeld, J. "What's the Secret of Sidney Poitier's
Zooming Appeal?" *Good Housekeeping* (May 1968): 92+.

4996. "Guess Who's Coming to Dinner. Poitier, Hepburn and
Tracey team in daring Kramer film." *Ebony* (January 1968):
56+.

4997. Hirsch, Foster. "Uncle Tom is Becoming a Superhero."
Readers and Writers (November 1968): 12-14.

4998. "How Sidney Poitier Won an Oscar." *Sepia* (June 1964):
14-17.

4999. "Lilies of the Field. Sidney Poitier stars in unique
low-budget movie." *Ebony* (October 1963): 55+.

5000. Makel, Chris W. "The Organization." *Black Stars*
(March 1972): 52-53. Review of a Poitier feature.

5001. Morton, F. "Audacity of Sidney Poitier." *Holiday*
(June 1962): 103+.

5002. Nipson, Herbert. "Sidney Poitier is Back. Film star
resumes his brilliant acting career." *Ebony* (May 1988): 31+.

5003. Poirier, N. "Sidney Poitier's Long Journey." *Saturday
Evening Post* (June 20 1964): 26+.

5004. "Poitier, Sidney." *Current Biography 1959*.

5005. Poitier, Sidney. "How to be an Actor." *Flamingo*
[London] (February 1965): 22-24.

5006. _____. "Why I Became An Actor." *Negro Digest*,
Vol. 11 (March 1962): 80-97.

5007. "Poitier's New Film Makes Black Beautiful." *Jet* (May 3
1973): 56-60.

5008. Robinson, Louie. "The Expanding World of Sidney
Poitier: Superstar, Director, Producer Eyes Future." *Ebony*,
Vol. 27 (November 1971): 100-113.

5009. _____. "Sidney Poitier Tells How To Stay on Top in
Hollywood. Star of 38 films succeeds as director-producer."
Ebony, Vol. 33 (November 1977): 53-62.

5010. Sanders, Charles L. "Sidney Poitier: The Man Behind
the Superstar." *Ebony*, Vol. 23 (April 1968): 172-182.

5011. "Sidney Poitier: Hollywood's Angry Young Man." <u>Tan</u> (December 1960): 12-14, 74.

5012. "Sidney Poitier, 60, Begins His 42nd Film." <u>Jet</u> (March 23 1987): 56.

5013. "Sidney Poitier's Fight with a Nazi." <u>Sepia</u> (September 1962): 40-44. Profile of Poitier's role in "Pressure Point."

5014. "Sidney Poitier's 10 most significant movies." <u>Black Stars</u> (February 1972): 18-28.

5015. "To Sir, With Love." <u>Ebony</u> (April 1967): 68+.

5016. "Top Actor of the Year: Poitier Maintains Stardom with Succesive Film Hits." <u>Ebony</u>, Vol. 19 (March 1964): 123-129.

5017. "Wailing for them All." <u>Time</u> (April 24 1964): 52+.

5018. Webster, Ivan. "Sidney Poitier: Playing the Hollywood Game to Win." <u>Encore American and Worldwide News</u> (August 1980): 34-37.

Newspaper Articles

5019. Canby, Vincent. "Milestones Can Be Millstones." <u>New York Times</u> (July 19 1970).

5020. Champlin, Charles. "Sidney Poitier: The Burden of Power." <u>New York Post</u> (February 3 1969).

5021. Crowther, Bosley. "The Significance of Sidney." <u>New York Times</u> (August 6 1967).

5022. Flatley, Guy. "Sidney Poitier as Black Militant." <u>New York Times</u> (November 10 1968).

5023. Harmetz, Aljean. "After a Decade, Poitier Returns as an Actor to a Changing Hollywood." <u>NYT Biographical Service</u> (May 1987): 407-408.

5024. Mason, Clifford. "Why Does White America Love Sidney Poitier So?" <u>New York Times</u> (September 10 1976).

5025. "Poitier to Play Porgy After All." <u>New York Times</u> (December 11 1957): 42.

5026. Ross, Michael E. "Sidney Poitier on 40 years of change." <u>New York Times</u> (February 28 1989): C18.

5027. "To Sidney, Mostly With Love." <u>New York Times</u> (October 1 1976). Letters in response to # 5008.

POLK, OSCAR

5028. Bogle, Donald. <u>Blacks in American Films and Television</u>. New York: Garland, 1988.

Articles

5029. Evelove, Alex. "Gabriel: 6 Feet 4 of Duskiness, Every Inch the Baptist Deacon." New York Herald-Tribune (July 5 1936).

5030. "Oscar Polk's Pulpit Ambitions Faded at First Sight of Stage." New York Herald-Tribune (May 23 1943).

5031. "Oscar Polk's a Tap Dancer, but he Never Gets a Chance to Dance." New York Evening Post (April 8 1933).

5032. Polk, Oscar - Clippings [Billy Rose Theatre Collection]

POUNDER, C. C. H.

5033. Sinclair, Abiola. "TV Update." New York Amsterdam News (March 8 1986): 25. [Profile]

POWERS, BEN

5034. Davis, Curt. "Times are good and busy for Powers." New York Post (July 11 1979): 35.

PREER, EVELYN (d.1932)

See also # 2691

5035. "Evelyn Preer." Variety (November 22 1932).

5036. "Hollywood Mourns Passing of First Lady of the Silver Screen. Evelyn Preer, Noted Movie Actress, Dead." Baltimore Afro-American (November 26 1932).

5037. "Stage Mourns Evelyn Preer. Thousands Grieve as Noted Actress is Laid to Rest." Chicago Defender (November 26 1932).

PRINGLE, JOAN

5038. Collins, Lisa. "Joan Pringle...One for Tomorrow." Black Stars (February 1976): 52-56.

5039. Haddad-Garcia, George. "Joan Pringle and the White Shadow." Black Stars (April 1980): 22-25.

5040. Hollomon, Rickey. "Joan Pringle! The New Lady on 'That's My Mama'." Right On! (November 1975): 30.

5041. Jares, Sue Ellen. "Joan Pringle's Twins Make Her Schoolmarm Role on TV's 'White Shadow' a Family Affair." People (September 15 1980).

5042. "Joan Pringle: Close-Up." Right On! (September 1981): 28-29.

5043. Russell, Dick. "For Joan Pringle, They Toe the Line. 'The White Shadow's' vice principal brings a natural authority to her role." TV Guide (November 3 1979): 44-46.

PRYOR, RICHARD (1940-   )

See also # 3148-3153

5044. Bogle, Donald. <u>Blacks in American Films and Television</u>. New York: Garland, 1988, pp. 446-450.

5045. Haskins, Jim. <u>Richard Pryor, A Man and His Madness: A Biography</u>. New York: Beaufort Books, 1984. 227p.

5046. Nazel, Joseph. <u>Richard Pryor: The Man Behind the Laughter</u>. Los Angeles: Holloway House Pub., 1981. 205p.

5047. Robbins, Fred, and David Ragan. <u>Richard Pryor: This Cat's Got 9 Lives</u>! New York: Delilah Books, 1982. 159p.

Articles

5048. "Beyond Laughter." <u>Ebony</u> (September 1967): 86-88, 90, 92, 94.

5049. Brashler, William. "Berserk Angel." <u>Playboy</u> (December 1979).

5050. Cassese, Sid. "Spotlight: Richard Pryor: No Laughing Matter." <u>Essence</u> (March 1986): 78-80, 83, 113.

5051. Collins, Lisa. "Time Out For Richard Pryor." <u>Black Stars</u> (June 1976): 40-45.

5052. Corliss, Richard. "Pryor's back - twice as funny." <u>Time</u> (March 29 1982): 62-63.

5053. Davis, Curt. "Subsequent Thoughts on Richard Pryor." <u>Encore American and Worldwide News</u> (March 20 1978): 36-37.

5054. "Ebony Interview: Richard Pryor." <u>Ebony</u> (October 1980): 33-36, 38, 40, 42.

5055. Egan, Nona. "This Time He's Winning." <u>Right On</u>! (August 1983): 16-20.

5056. Felton, David. "Pryor's Inferno." <u>Rolling Stone</u> (July 24 1980): 11+.

5057. Haddad-Garcia, George. "Richard Pryor, Survivor." <u>Black Stars</u> (February 1981): 40-44.

5058. Jacobson, Mark. "Richard Pryor is the Blackest Comic of Them All." <u>New West</u> (August 30 1976): 56+.

5059. Jarvis, Jeff. "Pryor and Murphy." <u>People</u> (July 11 1983): 86+.

5060. Lane, Bill. "Richard Pryor...He's Movin' On Up." <u>Sepia</u> (August 1977): 32-33.

5061. Lee, Jennifer. "Trouble Man." <u>Spin</u> (May 1988): 46-49, 61.

5062. Murphy, Frederick D. "Cover Story: Richard Pryor: Teetering on Jest, Living by His Wit." Encore American and Worldwide News (November 24 1975): 26-29.

5063. "A New Black Superstar." Time (August 22 1977): 66-67.

5064. Orth, Maureen. "The Perils of Pryor." Newsweek (October 3 1977): 60-63.

5065. Patton, Robert. "The Private/Public World of Richard Pryor." Black Stars (August 1973): 68-74.

5066. Reilly, Sue. "Richard Pryor's Ordeal." People (March 13 1978): 44+.

5067. "Richard Pryor." Interview (March 1986): 44+.

5068. Robinson, Louie. "Richard Pryor Talks." Ebony (January 1978): 116+.

5069. Rosenbaum, Jonathan. "The Man in the Great Flammable Suit." Film Comment (July/August 1982): 17-20.

5070. Sanders, Charles L. "Richard Pryor: Is he the biggest, richest black movie star ever?" Ebony (December 1981): 141+.

5071. Weston, Martin. "Richard Pryor Close-Up. It's been a tough ascent to movie stardom." Ebony (September 1976): 55+.

Newspaper Articles

5072. Farber, Stephen. "Success Holds No Laughter for Richard Pryor." New York Times (June 12 1983): Sec. 2, pp. 1, 19.

5073. McPherson, James. "The New Comic Style of Richard Pryor." New York Times Magazine (April 27 1975): 20+.

5074. Maynard, Joyce. "Richard Pryor, King of the Scene-Stealers." New York Times (January 9 1977): D-11.

5075. Pryor, Richard - Clippings [Billy Rose Theatre Collection]

5076. Pryor, Richard - Clippings (MWEZ + n.c. 26,244) [Billy Rose Theatre Collection]

Blue Collar (1978)

5077. "Blue Collar." Sepia (May 1978): 76-80. Discussion of the film of the same name.

5078. Bogle, Donald. Blacks in American Films and Television. New York: Garland, 1988, pp. 30-31.

Brewsters Millions (1985)

5079. Bogle, Donald. Blacks in American Films and Television. New York: Garland, 1988, pp. 35-36.

5080.   Canby, Vincent.   "Film View: Richard Pryor in Search of His Comic Genius."   New York Times (June 2 1985): Sec. 2, pp. 19-20.

Bustin' Loose (1981)

5081.   Bogle, Donald.   Blacks in American Films and Television.   New York: Garland, 1988, pp. 42-43.

Articles

5082.   Armstrong, Lois.   "Healthy and No Longer 'Ba-ad,' Richard Pryor is Bustin' Loose."   People (June 29 1981): 74-78.

5083.   Kroll, Jack.   "Richard Pryor, Bustin Loose."   Newsweek (May 3 1982): 48+.

5084.   Wright, Frankie.   "Bustin' Loose.   Richard Pryor's sensational follow-up to 'Stir Crazy.'"   Sepia (June 1981): 58-62.

Greased Lightning (1977)

5085.   Bogle, Donald.   Blacks in American Films and Television.   New York: Garland, 1988, pp. 96-97.

5086.   Makel, Chris W.   "Movie Review: Pam Grier and Richard Pryor Co-Star in Greased Lightning."   Black Stars (November 1977): 30-31.

Harlem Nights

5087.   Leavy, Walter.   "Eddie Murphy, Richard Pryor, Redd Foxx: three generations of Black comedy."   Ebony (January 1990): 102+.

JoJo Dancer (1986)

5088.   Bogle, Donald.   Blacks in American Films and Television.   New York: Garland, 1988, p. 122.

5089.   Lee, Jennifer.   "Richard Pryor, Now Your Ex-Wife is Calling."   People (June 16 1986): 53-54.   Article by Pryor's ex-wife asserting that Pryor's portrait of himself in "JoJo Dancer" is false.

5090.   Whitaker, Charles.   "Richard Pryor Changes Direction: With JoJo Dancer he opens movie jobs for blacks."   Ebony (July 1986): 132+.

See No Evil, Hear No Evil (1989)

5091.   "Richard Pryor, Gene Wilder: together again in a new movie comedy."   Jet (June 5 1989): 36-38.

Silver Streak (1976)

5092. Bogle, Donald. Blacks in American Films and
Television. New York: Garland, 1988, pp. 190-191.

5093. Makel, Chris W. "Richard Pryor Broadens Constituency
in 'Silver Streak'." Black Stars (April 1977): 21.

Stir Crazy

5094. Bogle, Donald. Blacks in American Films and
Television. New York: Garland, 1988, pp. 204-205.

5095. Gardner, Bob. "'Stir Crazy': Richard Pryor's Clowning
Glory." Sepia (January 1981): 39-45, 67-69.

PULLIAM, KEISHA KNIGHT

5096. Littwin, Susan. "This Star Wants to Be a Doctor...a
Pilot..and, Oh Yes, an Actress." TV Guide (December 19 1987):
10-12.

5097. Marshall, Marilyn. "Keisha Knight Pulliam: coping with
success at 7." Ebony (December 1986): 27+.

RALPH, SHERYL LEE

5098. Chadwick, Bruce. "Sheryl Ralph: Young Actress on the
Move." Black Stars (May 1978): 70-74.

5099. Donahue, Deirdre. "With a New Song and TV Series,
Sheryl Lee Ralph is a Dreamgirl with the Moxie to Make It."
People (April 8 1985): 107+.

5100. Majette, Winston. "Sheryl Lee Ralph: 'Right Place at
Right Time.'" New York Amsterdam News (May 25 1985): 30.

5101. Wright, Audrey. "Codename: Maggie." Right On! (July
1985): 46-47.

RANDOLPH, AMANDA (1902-1967)

5102. Bogle, Donald. Blacks in American Films and
Television. New York: Garland, 1988, pp. 450-451.

Obituaries

5103. "Amanda Randolph." Variety (August 30 1967).

5104. "Amanda Randolph, Actress in 'Amos 'n Andy,' Was 65."
New York Times (August 25 1967).

RANDOLPH, LILLIAN (1915-1980)

5105. Bogle, Donald. Blacks in American Films and
Television. New York: Garland, 1988, pp. 451-452.

Obituaries

5106. "Lillian Randolph." Variety (September 17 1980): 95.

5107. "Lillian Randolph, 65; Movie and TV Actress." New York
Times (September 17 1980).

RASHAD, PHYLICIA (nee Ayers-Allen) (c.1948-   )

5108. Bogle, Donald. Blacks in American Films and
Television. New York: Garland, 1988, p. 452.

Articles

5109. Norman, Lynn. "Phylicia and Ahmad Rashad: TV's super
couple juggle careers and family." Ebony (May 1987): 148+.

5110. "Phylicia Rashad." Harpers Bazaar (September 1988):
188+.

5111. "Sisters: Debbie Allen and Phylicia Rashad." McCall's
(July 1987): 90+.

5112. Townley, Roderick. "Phylicia Ayers-Allen. She'll show
you the serenity but not the strife." TV Guide (September 7
1985): 27-29.

RASULALA, THALMUS (1939-   )

5113. Page, Clarence. "Black Revolution and the Big Rip
Off." Chicago Tribune (April 2 1972): Sec. 11, p. 3.

RAY, GENE ANTHONY (1962-   )

5114. Cubas, Carlos R. "From Harlem to Hollywood." Right
On! (May 1983): 28-29.

5115. Manning, Steve. "Gene Anthony Ray: Can He Handle the
Fame?" Right On! (December 1980): 34-35, 61.

5116. Ray, Gene Anthony - Clippings [Billy Rose Theatre
Collection]

REED, ALAINA (1946-   )

5117. Connelly, Sherryl. "Say? Aren't You...?" New York
Daily News (April 20 1986): 20.

5118. Reed, Alaina - Clippings [Billy Rose Theatre
Collection]

REED, ALBERT

5119. Dawson, Cheryl. "Albert Reed Talks About His Most
Difficult Role." Black Stars (September 1975): 50-55.

REED, TRACY (c.1949-   )

5120. Banfield, Bever-Leigh. "Profile 3: A Closeup Look at Today's Black Actress." Sepia (September 1981): 22-30. [Tracy Reed/ Vernee Watson/Debbie Allen]

5121. Jenkins, Walter. "Sharing Points of Interest with Tracey Reed." Black Stars (November 1976): 22-26.

5122. Reed, Tracy - Clippings [Billy Rose Theatre Collection]

REID, DAPHNE MAXWELL

5123. Collier, Aldore. "Tim and Daphne Reid: A Close Look at Hollywood's Hottest Couple." Ebony (January 1988): 70+.

5124. Johnson, Robert E. "Tim Reid and Daphne Maxwell talk about marriage, careers, live-in love and jealousy." Jet (March 15 1982): 58+.

5125. Key, D. D. "Meet a Star on the Rise, Daphne Maxwell." Right On! (June 1985): 44-45.

5126. O'Hallaren, Bill. "She Snoops to Conquer: Daphne Maxwell Reid of Snoops." TV Guide (October 28 1989): 10-12.

5127. "Tim Reid and Daphne Maxwell: 'Simon & Simon' stars husband and wife." Jet (December 3 1984): 58+.

5128. "Tim Reid and Daphne Maxwell Reid return in new TV series 'Snoops'." Jet (September 18 1989): 58+.

5129. Vespa, Mary. "Tim Reid and wife Daphne Maxwell top the Menu at Frank's Place." People (April 18 1988): 71+.

REID, TIM

5130. Collier, Aldore. "Tim and Daphne Reid: A Close Look at Hollywood's Hottest Couple." Ebony (January 1988): 70+.

5131. Johnson, Robert E. "Tim Reid and Daphne Maxwell talk about marriage, careers, live-in love and jealousy." Jet (March 15 1982): 58+.

5132. "The Making of a Comic! Tim Reid." Right On! (May 1980): 30.

5133. Rense, Rip. "Tim's Place: The Executive Suite (Until he got an ulcer)." TV Guide (April 16 1988): 34-39.

5134. Samuels, Ashley. "Tim Reid: Why He's A Ladies Man." Black Stars (July 1980): 59-60.

5135. "Tim Reid and Daphne Maxwell: 'Simon & Simon' stars husband and wife." Jet (December 3 1984): 58+.

5136. "Tim Reid Parlays Quick Wit Into TV Stardom." Right On! (February 1984): 20-22.

5137. Wilson, John M. "'I'm Definitely not the Sheepish
Type.' Simon and Simon's Tim Reid has faced the Ku Klux Klan
and fought stereotyped roles - but his biggest battle has been
to control his temper." TV Guide (June 23 1984): 12-14.

Frank's Place

5138. Bayles, Martha. "'Frank's Place': A New Recipe for
TV." Wall Street Journal (December 28 1987): 11.

5139. "'Frank's Place' axed by CBS, Tim Reid 'wounded'." Jet
(October 24 1988): 62.

5140. Frank's Place - Clippings [Billy Rose Theatre
Collection]

5141. Garfinkel, Perry. "'Frank's Place: The Restaurant as
Life's Stage." New York Times (February 17 1988): C1, C14.

5142. Jones, Debra. "Frank's Place and Tim Reid entertain
with daring." New York Amsterdam News (December 19 1987): 34.

5143. Vespa, Mary. "Tim Reid and wife Daphne Maxwell top the
Menu at Frank's Place." People (April 18 1988): 71+.

Snoops

5144. Collier, Aldore. "Tim Reid: TV Snoop Uncovers Great
New Role." Ebony Man (December 1989): 79-80, 82.

5145. Mitchell, Elvis. "He Snoops to Conquer." Village
Voice (December 5 1989): 69-70.

5146. O'Connor, John J. "Snoops." New York Times (October
25 1989): C22.

5147. Powers, Ron. "Tim Reid has a dream." Gentlemen's
Quarterly (November 1989): 151-153.

5148. Sinclair, Abiola. "CBS Cancels 'Snoops'." New York
Amsterdam News (February 10 1990): 36.

5149. "Tim Reid advises others after his 'Snoops' is axed."
Jet (January 22 1990): 29.

5150. "Tim Reid and Daphne Maxwell Reid return in new TV
series 'Snoops'." Jet (September 18 1989): 58+.

RENARD, KEN

5151. Renard, Ken - Clippings [Billy Rose Theatre Collection]

REYNOLDS, JAMES

5152. Fee, Debi. "Only on the Soaps! Spotlight: James
Reynolds from 'Days of Our Lives'." Right On! (September
1982): 50-51.

5153. Hersch, Linda T. "James Reynolds is Going Places."
Soap Opera Digest (December 21 1982): 128-132.

RHODES, HARI (1932-   )

5154. Hobson, Dick. "On Maneuvers with Hari Rhodes. An ex-
Marine, author and actor has carried his life-long war into
TV." TV Guide (April 20 1968): 18-19.

5155. Rhodes, Hari - Clippings [Billy Rose Theatre
Collection]

RICH, RON (1938-   )

5156. Hendrick, Kimmis. "Ron Rich: 'Maybe Six' Negroes
Star." Christian Science Monitor (February 3 1967).

5157. "What Makes Ron Rich Run?" Sepia (July 1966): 44+.

RICHARDS, BEAH

See also # 3373

5158. Bogle, Donald. Blacks in American Films and
Television. New York: Garland, 1988, pp. 453-454.

Articles

5159. Hendrick, Kimmis. "Beah Richards on Acting and Two
Lives." Christian Science Monitor (October 18 1968).

5160. "The Long Distance Runner. Veteran actress Beah
Richards has persevered." Ebony (October 1987): 61-66.

5161. Richards, Beah - Clippings [Billy Rose Theatre
Collection]

5162. Richards, Beah, as told to Stephen Wilding. "I'm
Achieving A Skinless View of Life." Black Stars (March 1980):
26-27.

RILEY, LARRY

5163. Ballard, Gary. "Larry Riley: From 'Dream' Play to
'Soldier' Film." (Hollywood) Drama-Logue (July 14-20 1983):
17.

5164. Riley, Larry - Clippings [Billy Rose Theatre
Collection]

RIPPY, RODNEY ALLEN (1968-   )

5165. Jenkins, Flo. "We've Got Rodney!!! Everybody is in
Love with Him!" Right On! (December 1973): 24-27.

5166. Rippy, Rodney Allen - Clippings [Billy Rose Theatre
Collection]

5167. "Whatever Happened to...Rodney Allen Rippy." Ebony
(March 1979): 72-73.

ROBERTS, DAVIS (1917-   )

5168. "The man everybody has seen but nobody knows. Actor
Davis Roberts survives 35 years in hollywood." Ebony
(September 1981): 48+.

5169. Roberts, Davis - Clippings [Billy Rose Theatre
Collection]

ROBESON, PAUL (1898-1976)

5170. Bogle, Donald. Blacks in American Films and
Television. New York: Garland, 1988, pp. 454-457.

5171. Davis, Lenwood G. A Paul Robeson Research Guide: A
Selected Annotated Bibliography. Westport, CT: Greenwood
Press, 1982. 879p.

5172. Duberman, Martin B. Paul Robeson. New York: Knopf,
1989. 804p.

ROBINSON, BILL "BOJANGLES" (1878-1949)

See also # 3400

5173. Haskins, Jim, and N. R. Mitang. Mr. Bo Jangles: The
Biography of Bill Robinson. New York: Morrow, 1988. 320p.

Books with Sections on Bill Robinson

5174. Bogle, Donald. Blacks in American Films and
Television. New York: Garland, 1988, p. 457.

5175. _____. "Robinson, Luther [Bill "Bojangles"]." In
Dictionary of American Negro Biography, eds. Rayford W. Logan
and Michael R. Winston. New York: W.W. Norton, 1982, pp.
528-529.

5176. Fletcher, Martin, ed. Our Great Americans: The Negro
Contribution to American Progress. Chicago: Gamma
Corporation, 1954, p. 33.

Articles

5177. "Bill Robinson - The Unforgettable Bojangles Who
Invented 'Copasetic.'" Color (May 1950): 8.

5178. "Bits about Bojangles." Negro Digest, Vol. 8 (May
1950): 97-98.

5179. McKelway, St. Clair. "Profiles - Bojangles." New
Yorker (October 6 1934): 26-28; (October 13 1934): 30-34.

5180. Mitang, N. R. "Remembrance of Things Past: I Knew the
Man Bojangles." Encore American and Worldwide News (May 17
1976): 2-3.

5181. "Robinson, Bill." Current Biography 1941.

5182. Robinson, Fannie. "I Remember Bojangles." Ebony, Vol. 8 (February 1953): 49-50+.

5183. "This Week in Black History: Bill 'Bojangles' Robinson." Jet (May 30 1983): 24.

5184. Thompson, E. B. "Bill Robinson as she knew Him." Negro Digest, Vol. 8 (June 1950): 56-61. Reminiscences of Bill Robinson by his wife Fannie.

Newspaper Articles

5185. "Bill Robinson's Estate. Dancer Left $2,534 and Debts of $68,990, Mostly Taxes." New York Times (June 19 1953).

5186. Keir, Alissa. "Snapshots." New York Daily News (December 22 1931).

5187. "The Mikado, Himself." New York Times (April 9 1939): Sec. X, p. 2.

5188. Mok, Michael. "Portrait of a Swell Guy; Bill Robinson has danced from dark obscurity into the hearts of the White people." New York Post (December 12 1936).

5189. Robinson, Bill - Clippings (MWEZ + n.c. 26,119) [Billy Rose Theatre Collection]

5190. Robinson, Bill, 1878-1949 - Clippings [Dance Collection - Lincoln Center]

5191. Stewart, Walter. "Beloved Ebony. Bill Robinson, with the world at his feet, remains an unpretentious soul." New York World-Telegram (February 6 1937).

5192. Strouse, Richard. "At 70, Still Head Hoofer." New York Times Magazine (May 23 1948): 17, 48-52.

5193. Sullivan, Robert. "The Indestructible; Bill Robinson's Magic Feet Tap Out His 60th Year as a Performer." New York Sunday News (April 28 1946): 66-67.

5194. Woolf, S. J. "Bill Robinson, 60, Taps Out the Joy of Living." New York Times Magazine (May 22 1938): 4+.

Obituaries

5195. "Bill (Bojangles) Robinson Dies; 'King of the Tap Dancers' Was 71." New York Times (November 26 1949).

5196. "Bill Robinson Dies Broke." Dance News (January 1950).

5197. "Bill Robinson is Dead at 71. Noted Dancer, Whose Nimble Feet Carried Him to Fame, Is Victim of Heart Disease." New York Sun (November 26 1949).

5198.   "Bill Robinson, Tap Dancer, Died at 71; an Entertainer 63 Years." New York Herald Tribune (November 26 1949).

5199.   "Celebrities and 8 Miles of Crowds Pay Last Tribute to Bill Robinson." New York Times (November 29 1949).

5200.   "Goodbye to Bojangles. Forty-five thousand file by casket of Bill Robinson." Life (December 12 1949): 56.

5201.   Laurie, Joe Jr. "Bill 'Bojangles' Robinson." Variety (November 30 1949).

5202.   Livingston, DD. "Taps for Bill Robinson." Dance Magazine (January 1950).

5203.   New York Times (November 28, 1949): 1+.

5204.   Newsweek (December 5 1949): 61.

5205.   "O'Dwyer to Speak at Robinson Rites. Cortege from Harlem Church to Palace Theatre to Mark the Funeral Tommorrow. Schools There to Close." New York Times (November 27 1949).

5206.   "Robinson, Bill." Current Biography 1950.

5207.   Time (December 5 1949): 98.

ROBINSON, ERNIE

See # 3354

ROBINSON, HOLLY

See also # 3382

5208.   Davidson, Bill. "This rookie cop shoots a mean water pistol, sings rock and speaks four languages." TV Guide (August 20 1988): 37+.

5209.   "A feisty straight-shooter, Holly Robinson puts the jump in TV's 21 Jump Street." People (September 21 1987): 75-77.

5210.   Horner, Cynthia. "On the Street with Holly Robinson." Right On! (June 1988): 20-21.

ROBINSON, ROGER (1941-   )

5211.   Canham, Cleve. "Actor on the Verge." Audience, No. 41 (November 1971): 5+.

5212.   Murphy, Frederick Douglas. "Kojak's Roger Robinson Looks Ahead." Black Stars (June 1976): 50-55.

RODRIGUEZ, PERCY (1924-   )

5213.   Rodriguez, Percy - Clippings [Billy Rose Theatre Collection]

ROKER, ROXIE

See also # 3386, 3390

5214. Collins, Lisa. "Introducing Miss Roxie Roker." Black Stars (July 1975): 46-51.

5215. Davis, Curt. "Cover Story/Entertainment: Roxie Roker and the Possible Dream." Encore American and Worldwide News (November 22 1976): 26, 28-30.

5216. Norman, Shirley. "Television's First Mixed Marriage." Sepia (December 1976): 66-78.

5217. Roker, Roxie - Clippings [Billy Rose Theatre Collection]

5218. Shaw, Ellen Torgerson. "We Haven't Begun to See the Other Side of Black Life." TV Guide (April 4 1981): 12-14. [Interview]

ROLLE, ESTHER (1922-   )

5219. Bogle, Donald. Blacks in American Films and Television. New York: Garland, 1988, p. 458.

Articles

5220. Fields, Sidney. "Rolle Hits the Big Role." New York Daily News (May 24 1972): 70.

5221. Klemesrud, Judy. "Florida Finds Good Times in Chicago." New York Times (May 5 1974): Sec. 2, p. 12.

5222. Lewis, Shawn. "Esther Rolle: Down from Her Television Pinnacle but Far from Out." Ebony (May 1978): 91-92, 94, 96.

5223. Mills, Jon. "Esther Rolle: A Television Mother Speaks Out!" Right On! (December 1979): 44-45.

5224. Richards, David. "The Latest Stage of Esther Rolle." Washington Post (November 11 1986): B1, B9.

5225. Winters, Jason. "Esther Rolle: The Black Velvet Lady." Black Stars (August 1977): 32-37.

Media Materials

5226. Like It Is. 60 min. Broadcast date: April 13, 1980. Television interview conducted by Gil Noble.

ROLLINS, HOWARD E. (1951-   )

5227. Bogle, Donald. Blacks in American Films and Television. New York: Garland, 1988, p. 458.

Articles

5228. Bennetts, Leslie. "'Soldier's Story' Star, Four Years of Waiting." New York Times (September 22 1984): 33.

5229. Eady, Brenda. "Howard Rollins' Stalled Career Marches on with A Soldier's Story." People (October 1 1984): 143-145.

5230. "Howard Rollins lands first TV role in 'Wildside' western." Jet (April 29 1985): 54-55.

5231. McMurran, Kristin. "Handsome Howard Rollins goes from Ragtime to the big time - at last." People (March 29 1982): 88-89.

5232. Norment, Lynn. "Ragtime Star is Rich in Talent. Howard Rollins steals the show in new movie." Ebony (February 1982): 115+.

5233. Quindlen, Anna. "Will He Go from 'Ragtime' to Riches." New York Times (November 15 1981): Sec. 2, pp. 1, 23.

5234. Rhodes, Crystal V. "From Ragtime to Realtime: A Profile of Howard Rollins." Black Collegian (September-October 1983): 134+.

5235. Roffman, Peter, and Bev Simpson. "A Soldier's Story: An Interview with Howard E. Rollins, Jr." Cineaste, Vol. 14, No. 1 (1985): 43.

5236. Williams, Charles L. "'Ragtime's' Howard E. Rollins defies racism in movie you've got to see." Sepia (March 1982): 40-45.

ROSS, DIANA (1944-   )

See also # 3370

5237. Bogle, Donald. Blacks in American Films and Television. New York: Garland, 1988, p. 459.

5238. Taraborelli, J. Randy. Call Her Miss Ross: An Unauthorized Biography of Diana Ross. New York: Birch Lane Press, 1989. 488p.

5239. _____, with Reginald Wilson and Darryl Minger. Diana. Garden City, NY: Doubleday, 1985. 245p.

Articles

5240. "Mahogany. Diana Ross stars as high fashion model in new movie." Ebony (October 1975): 144+.

5241. "Ross, Diana." Current Biography 1973.

ROUNDTREE, RICHARD (1942-   )

See also # 3350, 3373

5242. Bogle, Donald. <u>Blacks in American Films and Television</u>. New York: Garland, 1988, pp. 459-460.

Articles

5243. Berry, William Earl. "Richard Roundtree Stars on 'Shaft in Africa'." <u>Black Stars</u> (August 1973): 38-44.

5244. Brown, K. "Richard Roundtree." <u>Films in Review</u>, Vol. XXXIV, No. 5 (May 1983): 257.

5245. Chelminski, Rudolph. "Richard Roundtree's Big Score." <u>Life</u>, Vol. 73 (September 1 1972): 51-52.

5246. Ebert, Alan. "Roundtree." <u>Essence</u> (March 1974): 64-65, 70, 81.

5247. Harrington, Cliff. "'Shaft is Dead,' says Richard Roundtree." <u>Black Stars</u> (January 1976): 6-12.

5248. Jenkins, Flo. "Soul Reels: At Last! A Meeting with Richard Roundtree." <u>Right On</u>! (September 1972): 38-40.

5249. Klemesrud, Judy. "Shaft - 'A Black Man Who is For Once a Winner." <u>New York Times</u> (March 12 1972): Sec. 2, p. 13.

5250. Lucas, Bob. "Actor Finds Success without 'Shaft' Image." <u>Jet</u> (December 18 1975): 58-61.

5251. _____. "The Shaft Business." <u>Sepia</u> (July 1972): 36-44.

5252. Martin, Ken. "'Shaft' Star Scores Again." New York <u>Sunday News</u> (May 7 1972).

5253. Miller, Don Lee. "Whatever Happened to Richard Roundtree." <u>Right On</u>! (July 1981): 28-29.

5254. Murphy, Frederick D. "Roundtree, from Model to Movie Star." <u>Essence</u>, Vol. 2 (June 1971): 54-5+.

5255. Roundtree, Richard. "There's More to Me Than Shaft." <u>Black Stars</u> (February 1979): 12-17.

5256. Roundtree, Richard - Clippings [Billy Rose Theatre Collection]

5257. "The Unforgettable Shaft. Take a stroll back in time to share some intimate moments and thoughts with this character and the man who played him!" <u>Right On</u>! (February 1980): 46-47.

RUSSELL, KIMBERLY

See also # 3382

5258. D'Agnese, Joe. "Profile: Kim's Classy Act." <u>Right On</u>! (November 1987): 54-56.

5259.   "Kimberly Russell." Teen Magazine (June 1987): 66.

5260.   Littwin, Susan. "Head of the Class Yearbook: meet the 10 young stars who are passing the stern test of prime-time survival." TV Guide (January 9 1988): 26+.

ST. JACQUES, RAYMOND (1930-   )

See also # 3373

5261.   Bogle, Donald. Blacks in American Films and Television. New York: Garland, 1988, pp. 466-467.

Articles

5262.   "Black Playboy of Hollywood." Sepia, Vol. 20 (July 1971): 64-71.

5263.   Black Stars (January 1972): 22-27.

5264.   Johnson, Connie. "Interview: Raymond St. Jacques." Newworld, No. 5 (1979): 22-24.

5265.   Kisner, Ron. "The Money Problems of the Stars." Ebony (May 1977): 144-145.

5266.   "Raymond St. Jacques: A New Meaning for 'Superstar.'" Sepia, Vol. 19 (August 1970): 62-65.

5267.   Sanders, Charles L. "Raymond Saint-Jacques: New 'Bad Guy' of the Movies." Ebony (June 1967): 171+.

5268.   _____. "Raymond the Magnificent: 'Man, It's a Ball Being a Star!'" Ebony (November 1969): 175-178.

5269.   Stoop, Norma McLain. "Raymond St. Jacques: "If I Had Been White..." After Dark (January 1974): 47-48.

Newspaper Articles

5270.   Barnard, Ken. "No Questions Asked." Detroit News (May 24 1970): 1-H.

5271.   Gardella, Kay. "Negro Role in the West Gets Some TV Recognition." New York Daily News (August 26 1965).

5272.   Klemesrud, Judy. "St. Jacques: Our Next Black Matinee Idol?" New York Times (December 8 1968): D19.

5273.   Molloy, Paul. "St. Jacques of B'way Breaks Color Line Among TV Cowboys." New York Post (July 23 1965).

5274.   Roth, Daniel. "St. Jacques States Case as TV Judge." Chicago Sun-Times (August 31 1988).

ST. JOHN, KRISTOFF

5275.   "Profile: Who is Kristoff St. John?" Right On! (December 1985): 41.

SANDS, DIANA (1934-1973)

See also # 3370

5276. Bogle, Donald. Blacks in American Films and Television. New York: Garland, 1988, pp. 460-461.

Articles

5277. Bradley, B. "Making of a Broadway Star." Sepia, Vol. 8 (July 1960): 58-60.

5278. Castan, S. "Diana Sands: Notes on a Broadway Pussycat." Look, Vol. 29 (February 9 1965): 38-39+.

5279. Coombs, Orde. "Lunching with Diana Sands." Essence (August 1970): 56-57, 82.

5280. "Diana Sands: Collecting Acting Prizes is her Hobby." Sepia, Vol. 15 (May 1966): 60-63.

5281. "Diana Sands, First Tan Cleopatra." Sepia, Vol. 16 (August 1967): 18-20.

5282. "Diana Sands in Death Struggle with Cancer." Jet (October 4 1973): 92.

5283. "Final Rites Held for Diana Sands." Jet (October 11 1973): 90-92.

5284. Gussow, Mel. "And Now, Diana at the Stake." New York Times (December 31 1967).

5285. "Mime; to speed up her progress on the stage, Diana Sands turned to Pantomime." Our World, Vol. 10 (July 1955): 25-27.

5286. Peterson, Maurice. "Diana, Diana." Essence, Vol. 3 (June 1972): 34-35, 72.

5287. Sands, Diana - Clippings [Billy Rose Theatre Collection]

5288. Stang, Joanna. "The Carpenter's Daughter. Diana Sands, Praised for Her Performance in Baldwin Drama Discusses Her Past and the Future." New York Times (May 10 1964).

5289. Wolff, A. "The Passion of Diana Sands." Look, Vol. 32 (January 9 1968): 70-73.

Obituaries

5290. Davis, Ossie. "Diana Sands: 1934-1973." New York Times (September 30 1973): Sec. 2, p. 3.

5291. "Diana Sands 1934-1973." Ms. (December 1973).

5292. "Diana Sands, 39, Dies of Cancer; Acclaimed for 'Raisin in the Sun.'" New York Times (September 23 1973): 65.

5293. Newsweek (October 1 1973): 61.

5294. Slater, Jack. "Death of Diana Sands." Ebony, Vol. 29 (January 1974): 115-121.

5295. Time (October 1 1973): 79.

5296. Variety (September 26 1973).

SANFORD, ISABEL (1917-   )

See also # 3386, 3390

5297. Bogle, Donald. Blacks in American Films and Television. New York: Garland, 1988, pp. 461-462.

Articles

5298. Adelson, Suzanne. "Her TV Family is More Loyal Than Royal, But Isabel Sanford is a Queen on 'The Jeffersons.'" People (June 16 1980).

5299. Barber, Rowland. "Movin' On Up." TV Guide (October 30 1976): 20-23.

5300. Davis, Curt. "Television: Isabel is a Belly Laugh." Encore American and Worldwide News (June 6 1977): 32-33.

5301. Dawson, Cheryl. "Isabel Sanford Mixes Career with Creole Cookery." Black Stars (July 1975): 59-63.

SAULSBERRY, RODNEY

5302. Horner, Kim. "I've Finally Made It! I'm in Right On!" Right On! (March 1983): 4-5, 67.

SAVAGE, ARCHIE

5303. "'Vera Cruz'. In this story of a Mexican revolt, Archie Savage displays both his acting and dancing talent." Our World (March 1955): 36-37.

SCOTT, HAZEL (1920-1981)

5304. Bogle, Donald. Blacks in American Films and Television. New York: Garland, 1988, pp. 463-464.

5305. "Hazel Crashes TV: Glamorous pianists' sensational TV debut crashes race barrier." Our World (June 1950): 60-61.

5306. Pool, Marquita. "Hazel Scott: Mighty Like the Blues." Encore (October 1972): 46-51. [Interview]

Obituaries

5307. "Hazel Scott." Variety (October 7 1981): 48.

5308. Ledbetter, Les. "Hazel Scott, 61, Jazz Pianist, Acted in Films, on Broadway." New York Times (October 3 1981): 33.

5309. Marques, Stuart. "Jazz Great Hazel Scott dies of cancer at 61." New York Daily News (October 3 1981): 4.

5310. Stanton, Ali. "Hazel Scott, 61, cancer victim." New York Amsterdam News (October 10 1981): 53.

Media Materials

5311. Hazel Scott Remembers [videorecording]. Host, Orde Coombs. New York: WPIX-TV, 1980. 21 min. Interview with Hazel Scott. Scott talks about her Hollywood career, her marriage to Adam Clayton Powell, Jr. and her life in Paris in the early 1960's. [Held by the Schomburg Collection - Sc Visual VRB-223]

SCOTT, LARRY B.

5312. Clay, Stanley. "Actor to Actor. Larry Scott: A Hero of Talent and Direction!" Right On! (April 1978): 36-37.

5313. Klemesrud, Judy. "New Face: Larry B. Scott, Centered Young Hero." New York Times (February 24 1978): C14.

5314. Robles, Roland. "The star who still does dishes." New York Daily News (March 3 1978): 5.

SCOTT, SERET

5315. Scott, Seret - Clippings [Billy Rose Theatre Collection]

SEKKA, JOHNNY (1939-   ) (The Gambia/G. Britain)

5316. "African Movie Star, Johhny Sekka on Tap for New VA Movie." New York Amsterdam News (May 26 1973): D-3.

5317. Peters, Dennis Alaba. "Meet Johnny Sekka." Flamingo [London] (August 1964): 38-40.

5318. Sekka, Johnny - Clippings [Billy Rose Theatre Collection]

5319. Thomas, Bob. "The Actor Who Beat Out Ali." New York Post (March 15 1977): 25.

SHARP, SAUNDRA (c.1943-   )

5320. Jenkins, Walter. "A Look at Saundra Sharp." Black Stars (January 1977): 32-35.

SHAW, STAN

5321. "Cover Story: Stan Shaw: Negotiating from Strength." Encore American and Worldwide News (February 6 1978): 26-28.

5322. George, Nelson. "An Actor Whose Time Has Come." New York Amsterdam News (February 11 1978): B-4.

SIDNEY, P. JAY

5323. Anderson, David. "Producers Favor More Negro Roles."
New York Times (October 31 1962).

5324. Sidney, P. Jay - Clippings [Billy Rose Theatre
Collection]

SILVERA, FRANK (1914-1970)

5325. Bogle, Donald. Blacks in American Films and
Television. New York: Garland, 1988, pp. 464-465.

Articles

5326. Barrow, William. "The Many Faces of Frank Silvera."
Negro Digest, Vol. 12 (September 1963): 40-43.

5327. "Frank Silvera; famous Negro character actor portrays
many nationalities and races but seldom his own." Ebony, Vol.
7 (March 1952): 51-55.

5328. Silvera, Frank - Clippings [Billy Rose Theatre
Collection]

Obituaries

5329. "Frank Silvera, Actor-Director, Electrocuted in Coast
Mishap." New York Times (June 12 1970): 27.

5330. Newsweek (June 22 1970): 61.

5331. Variety (June 17 1970).

SIMMS, HILDA (1920-   )

5332. "Here is Marva: Search for movie Marva in Joe Louis
Story ends when Hilda Simms quits Europe for role." Our World
(July 1953): 12-13.

5333. Simms, Hilda - Clippings [Billy Rose Theatre
Collection]

SINCLAIR, MADGE (1940-   )

See also # 3387

5334. Bogle, Donald. Blacks in American Films and
Television. New York: Garland, 1988, pp. 465-466.

Articles

5335. Davis, Curt. "Seven in the Spotlight." Encore
American and Worldwide News (May 17 1976): 27.

5336. Peterson, Maurice. "On the Aisle: Focus on Madge
Sinclair." Essence (January 1977): 23.

5337. Sako, Tsuyoko. "The Talented Madge Sinclair." Black Stars (July 1981): 14-17.

5338. Shaw, Ellen Torgerson. "Fine Actress, Great Cheekbones, Sexpot with a Sense of Humor..." TV Guide (April 17 1982): 24-26, 28.

5339. Tusher, Will. "Madge Sinclair Running Ahead of Changing World." Daily Variety Forty-Eighth Anniversary Issue (1981): 252, 266.

5340. Webster, Ivan. "The Case of the Overqualified Actress." Encore American and Worldwide News (December 3 1978): 40-41.

SMITH, DWAN

5341. McNeil, Dee Dee. "Dwan Smith is Ready for Success!" Right On! (January 1976): 32-34.

SMITH, EDDIE

See # 3354

SMITH, TOUKIE

5342. Stark, John. "The worst of times are over for 227's red-hot Toukie Smith." People (December 18 1989): 135-136.

SOMMERFIELD, DIANE

5343. Fee, Debi. "Only in the Soaps: Spotlight: Diane Sommerfield." Right On! (November 1982): 46-47.

SPEED, CAROL

5344. Speed, Carol. Inside Black Hollywood. Los Angeles: Holloway, 1980. 256p. Actress Carol Speed's first novel.

Articles

5345. "Carol Speed: A Star on the Move." Black Stars (December 1972): 68-71.

5346. Jenkins, Walter. "Carol Speed...Nearing Her Finest Hour." Black Stars (April 1975): 20-25.

5347. _____. "Carol Speed Taking New Lease on Acting Career." Black Stars (June 1980): 14-17.

5348. _____. "Carol Speed Talks About Life-Love and Her Career." Black Stars (September 1973): 36-40.

5349. Tucker, Dimple. "Carol Speed: Pretty Star of The Mack! Raps." Right On! (September 1973): 48-49.

5350. "Whatever Happened to: Carol Speed!" Right On! (June 1980): 57.

SPIVEY, VICTORIA (1906-1976)

See # 1992

STANIS, BERNADETTE

5351. Black, Stu. "'No one tried to help me.'" TV Guide (December 12 1981): 12+.

5352. Stanis, Bernadette - Clippings [Billy Rose Theatre Collection]

5353. Tapley, Mel. "Cover Story: BernNadette Stanis Looks at Positive Image ... of Young Black Women!" New York Amsterdam News (February 21 1976): D10-D11.

5354. "When Does the Next Pumpkin Leave? BernNadette Stanis proves that there's still room for Cinderella stories in show business." TV Guide (July 31 1976): 12-13.

STEPIN FETCHIT

See Perry, Lincoln

STERMAN, OTTO (1913-   )

5355. "Otto Sterman, the Man of a Hundred Faces: A Negro actor is one of Holland's biggest stars." Our World (February 1955): 17-23.

STEWART, BYRON

5356. "'Coolridge is Cool!' Byron Stewart, the tall handsome sharpshooter on The White Shadow, is a righteous actor who believes in realism." Right On! (November 1979): 31-33.

STEWART, MEL

5357. Stewart, Melvin - Clippings [Billy Rose Theatre Collection]

STEWART, NICK

5358. "One Man's Poison." Emmy Magazine (January/February 1985): 48. Interview with a former star of the "Amos 'n' Andy" show.

5359. "What happened to TV stars of 'Amos 'n' Andy'?" Jet (December 10 1981): 55-58.

STICKNEY, PHYLLIS

5360. Brown, Wesley. "Showstopper Phyllis Stickney." Essence, Vol. 17 (July 1986): 33.

5361. George, Nelson. "Phyllis Stickney: Concrete Comedy." Village Voice (March 24 1987): 15-17.

5362. "Phyllis Stickney Stopped Seeing Herself as an Outcast When She Found It's a Different World." People (July 13 1987): 111.

STOKER, AUSTIN

5363. Stoker, Austin - Clippings [Billy Rose Theatre Collection]

STRODE, WOODY (1914-   )

5364. Bogle, Donald. Blacks in American Films and Television. New York: Garland, 1988, pp. 467-468.

Articles

5365. "Black Actor Woody Strode Is Another Yank Who Got His Break in Italo Pix." Variety (December 8 1971): 2, 47.

5366. Burrell, Walter Rico. "Whatever Happened to Woody Strode? Macho actor is still going strong at age 68." Ebony (June 1982): 140+.

5367. Hunter, Charlayne. "Woody Strode? 'He Wasn't the Star But He Stole the Movie.'" New York Times (September 19 1971): D5.

5368. "Just A Hardworking, Action Actor." Variety (February 17 1971): 34.

5369. "Lion Man. Woody Strode plays comic beast in movie Androcles and the Lion." Ebony (August 1952): 39-42, 44.

5370. "Mandrake the Magician. Muscular Woody Strode gets Lothar role in new TV series." Ebony (December 1954): 103+.

5371. "Sgt. Rutledge. Woody Strode stars in cavalry drama." Ebony (July 1960): 75+.

5372. "Strode is Brilliant as 'Black Jesus.'" Jet (October 7 1971): 53.

5373. "Strode Muscles In. Rugged, ex-All-American football end plays African prince in new "Mandrake the Magician" TV film." Our World (December 1954-January 1955): 34-37.

5374. "Woody Strode Does It Again." Sepia (August 1965): 18-21.

STYLES, ROVENIA

5375. Styles, Rovenia. "An Extra is Born." Essence (March 1978): 54, 60.

STYMIE

See Beard, Mathew

SUL-TE-WAN, MADAME [Nellie Conley] (1873-1959)

5376. "Madame Sul-Te-Wan: At 80, Hollywood's oldest Negro actress is still a spry rug-cutter." Our World (February 1954): 80-82.

5377. "Sul Te Wan (Nellie Conley)." Variety (February 11 1959). [Obituary]

SUNSHINE SAMMY

See Morrison, Ernie

SYKES, BRENDA (c.1949-   )

See also # 3370

5378. "Brenda Sykes: Successful Career...Disastrous Love Life!" Right On! (March 1973): 26-27.

5379. Dawson, Cheryl. "Brenda Sykes: Talented, Quiet, and Conservative." Black Stars (November 1973): 60-65.

5380. "How Brenda Sykes Keeps It All Together!" Right On! (May 1974): 26-27.

5381. "99 Pounds of Surprises. Her Name's Brenda Sykes." TV Guide (April 10 1971): 21.

5382. "Soul Reels: Brenda Sykes: Not Just Another Pretty Face!" Right On! (October 1972): 46-47.

5383. Stewart, Ted. "Hollywood's Prettiest Black Star." Sepia (January 1975): 36-44.

5384. Sykes, Brenda - Clippings [Billy Rose Theatre Collection]

SYLVESTER, HAROLD

5385. Sylvester, Harold - Clippings [Billy Rose Theatre Collection]

5386. Tapley, Mel. "Sounder II has new cast." New York Amsterdam News (October 23 1976): D-6.

MR. T [Lawrence Tureaud] (1952-   )

5387. Bogle, Donald. Blacks in American Films and Television. New York: Garland, 1988, pp. 468-469.

5388. Mr. T. Mr. T: The Man with the Gold. New York: St. Martin's Press, 1984. 276p.

Articles

5389. Banks, Lacy J. "Mr. T Can Be One Rude Dude." Black Stars (February 1981): 32-35.

5390. Eisenberg, L. "Drink to me only with thy $23,000 goblet." TV Guide (April 22-28 1989): 24-25.

5391. Fee, Debi. "The Other Side of Mr. T." Right On! (May 1983): 40-43.

5392. Mills, Barbara Kleban. "Would you fight this man? Sly Stallone did, and now Mr. T is a winner in Rocky III." People (July 12 1982): 72-73.

5393. "Mr. T among stars in hottest new TV show." Jet (March 28 1983): 54-56.

5394. Pitts, Leonard, Jr. "The Real T." Right On! (March 1984): 16-19, 67.

TAMU

5395. People (May 6 1974): 44. [Profile]

TATE, WALTER

See # 3367

TAYLOR, CLARICE

5396. "Clarice Taylor calls Cosby her son on TV, but finds sassier fun as Moms Mabley." People (October 26 1987): 79-80.

5397. Nash, Dawn. "Cosby's TV Mom Clarice Taylor: From NEC to NBC." New York Daily News (November 23 1986): 5.

5398. Taylor, Clarice - Clippings [Billy Rose Theatre Collection]

5399. Thompson, M. Cordell. "Clarice Taylor Says She Knows Mrs. Brooks Very Well." Black Stars (April 1974): 70-73.

TAYLOR, MESHACH

5400. Rudolph, Ileane. "Why Meshach Taylor is Laughing All the Way to the Bank." TV Guide (November 11 1989): 23.

5401. Weston, Martin. "Meshach Taylor makes a name for himself." Chicago (January 1978): 22, 24.

THOMAS, BILLIE "BUCKWHEAT" (1931-1980)

5402. Bogle, Donald. Blacks in American Films and Television. New York: Garland, 1988, p. 470.

Articles

5403. "Billy Thomas, 49, of 'Our Gang.'" New York Times (October 12 1980): 44. [Obituary]

5404. Miles, Patrice A. "Buckwheat Thomas Discovered in Manhattan." New York Amsterdam News (March 17 1979): 19.

5405. Variety (October 22 1980). [Obituary]

5406. Wilson, Alfred. "In Memoriam: Billie "Buckwheat" Thomas." Right On! (February 1981): 52-53.

THOMAS, ERNEST

5407. Burrell, Walter Price. "Ernest Thomas is 'What's Happening'." Black Stars (August 1977): 12-16.

5408. Lardine, Bob. "In TV, the 'in' color is Black." New York Sunday News (February 20 1977): L1, L12.

5409. Torgerson, Ellen. "'I Don't Want to be Scraping Grits Out of Pans'. To Ernie Thomas of 'What's Happening!!', that kind of realism is no recipe for a hit series." TV Guide (March 18-24 1978): 29-32.

THOMAS, PHILIP MICHAEL (1949-   )

5410. Bogle, Donald. Blacks in American Films and Television. New York: Garland, 1988, p. 471.

Articles

5411. Brown, Marcia L. "Philip Thomas...Handsome?!...There's More to Him Than Meets the Eye!" Right On! (August 1973): 26-27.

5412. Brown-Rowe, Marsallay. "You Can't Stop Greatness! Philip Thomas." Black Stars (September 1976): 32-36.

5413. Collier, Aldore. "Phylicia and Philip are lovers and lawyers in thriller, 'False Witness.'" Jet (October 30 1989): 60+.

5414. Laughlin, Meg. "Philip Michael Thomas: is he in career arrest - or is there life after Miami Vice?." TV Guide (October 21 1989): 18-21.

5415. Moore, Trudy S. "'Miami Vice' star is TV's newest sex symbol: Philip Michael Thomas." Jet (May 20 1985): 60+.

5416. _____. "Philip Michael Thomas." Ebony Man (October 1987): 31-33.

5417. _____. "Philip Michael Thomas: The hot and handsome star of TV's Miami Vice." Ebony (September 1985): 92+.

5418. "Philip Michael Thomas and Olivia Brown: how Blacks are influencing TV network shows." Jet (May 25 1987): 54-56.

5419. "Philip Michael Thomas and Olivia Brown sizzle in 'Miami Vice'." Jet (October 12 1987): 58-59.

5420. "Philip Michael Thomas' career 'like a coin - head is 'Miami Vice' and tail is music.'" Jet (September 26 1988): 60-62.

5421. "Philip Thomas!" <u>Right On</u>! (October 1976): 57-59.

5422. "Philip Thomas: Newest Black Matinee Idol." <u>Black Stars</u> (May 1973): 16-18.

5423. "Philip Thomas, Olivia Brown star in 'Miami Vice' TV series." <u>Jet</u> (October 29 1984): 58+.

5424. Randolph, Laura B. "The Philip Michael Thomas Even 'Miami Vice' Fans Don't Know." <u>Ebony</u> (April 1988): 52+.

5425. _____. "Spotlight: The Spice of Vice." <u>Essence</u> (November 1985): 64+.

5426. "TV Series for Talented Philip Thomas." <u>Right On</u>! (April 1976): 35.

5427. Wallace, Carol. "The Ego Has Landed." <u>People</u> (December 9 1985): 131-132, 137-138.

THUMBTZEN, TATIANA

See # 3382

TODD, BEVERLY (1946-   )

5428. "People: Beverly Todd." <u>Essence</u> (September 1970): 62, 70, 79.

5429. Todd, Beverly - Clippings [Billy Rose Theatre Collection]

5430. Todd, Beverly. "Security Is What I Want." <u>Black Stars</u> (December 1978): 20-23.

TOLBERT, BERLINDA

See also # 3386

5431. Collins, Lisa. "Berlinda Tolbert: Fresh Out of the Sticks." <u>Black Stars</u> (November 1975): 14-18.

5432. Jenkins, Walter. "Berlinda Tolbert: I'm Still Discovering Myself!" <u>Black Stars</u> (March 1979): 6-10.

5433. Swertlow, Frank. "I Am the American Dream." <u>TV Guide</u> (October 16 1982): 26-28.

5434. Tolbert, Berlinda - Clippings [Billy Rose Theatre Collection]

TOWNSEND, ROBERT

See also # 2153, 2164, 2173, 2886-2923

5435. O'Connell, Nancy. "If You See a Chance Take It...He's an actor and comedian but in the game of life Robert Townsend is a real gambler." <u>Right On</u>! (August 1986): 52-53, 65.

TRAVIS, ALICE

5436. "ABC-TV fires AM New York's Alice Travis." New York Amsterdam News (August 20 1975): A-3.

5437. "...Black Woman' TV Series." New York Amsterdam News (May 21 1977): D-15. Brief notice on Travis's "For You, Black Woman" talk show.

5438. Davis, Curt. "Television: Alice Travis Presents the Permanent Stone--The Black Woman." Encore American and Worldwide News (July 18 1977): 33-34. TV talk show host.

5439. Fraser, C. Gerald. "Ali 'spars' with woman in a TV interview." New York Times (January 22 1978): 40.

TUCKER, LORENZO (1907-1986)

5440. Bogle, Donald. Blacks in American Films and Television. New York: Garland, 1988, pp. 471-472.

5441. Gruppenhoff, Richard. Black Valentino: The Stage and Screen Career of Lorenzo Tucker. Metuchen, NJ: Scarecrow Press, 1988. 202p.

Dissertations

5442. Gruppenhoff, Richard. "Whatever the Occasion Demands: The Stage and Screen Career of Lorenzo Tucker, "The Colored Valentino." Dissertation (Ph.D.) Ohio State University, 1986. 210p.

Articles

5443. Gruppenhoff, Richard. "Lorenzo Tucker: The Black Valentino." Black Film Review, Vol. 4, No. 2 (Spring 1988): 3-5. [Interview]

5444. Sun, Douglas. "Lorenzo Tucker - 'The Black Valentino.'" Los Angeles Times/Calendar (January 20 1985): 19, 32.

Obituaries

5445. Classic Images, No. 136 (October 1986): 33.
5446. Jet (September 15 1986): 51.
5447. New York Times (August 30 1986): 30.
5448. Variety (August 27 1986): 110-111.

Research Collections

5449. Lorenzo Tucker Papers. Manuscript Collection - 2nd Tier. [Held by the Schomburg Collection]

TURMAN, GLYNN (c.1946-   )

5450. Clay, Stanley. "Stanley Clay interviews Glynn Turman!" Right On! (November 1977): 20-22.

5451. Davis, Curt. "Glynn Turman Nears Stardom." Encore American and Worldwide News (September 22 1975): 37-38, 40.

5452. Jenkins, Flo. "Glynn Turman! Searching for the Poetry of My Life." Right On! (July 1976): 30-31.

5453. _____. "Glynn Turman!!! Young Actor Who's a Billion-to-One Shot!" Right On! (May 1974): 30-31.

5454. Sanders, Charles L. "Aretha and Glynn." Ebony (July 1978): 104+.

TYSON, CICELY (1939-   )

See also # 3370, 3373

5455. Abdul, Raoul. "Cicely Tyson." In Famous Black Entertainers of Today. New York: Dodd, Mead & Co., 1974, pp. 118-124.

5456. Bogle, Donald. Blacks in American Films and Television. New York: Garland, 1988, pp. 472-473.

Articles

5457. Angelou, Maya. "Cicely Tyson: Reflections on a Lone Black Rose." Ladies Home Journal (February 1977): 40-41, 44, 46.

5458. Berry, William Earl. "Cicely Tyson Makes It Big--At Last." Jet (March 15 1973): 58-62.

5459. Bright, Daniel. "An Emmy Award for Cicely?" Sepia, Vol. 23 (April 1974): 16-20.

5460. Cassidy, Robert. "'She Does it All With Love.' Cicely Tyson learns the secret of the legendary ghetto teacher she's portraying this week." TV Guide (November 28 1981): 15+. [The Marva Collins Story]

5461. "Cicely Tyson." Time, Vol. 100 (October 9 1972): 58+.

5462. Considine, Shaun. "Ciceley Tyson: A Rare Avis Who Never Wings It." After Dark (July 1976): 56-58.

5463. "Creative Woman: Success Requires Talent and Drive." Ebony, Vol. 32 (August 1977): 138.

5464. Davidson, Muriel. "What Makes Miss Tyson Run..." TV Guide (January 26-February 1 1974): 14-16.

5465. Dreyfuss, Joel. "A Woman Called Cicely." Redbook, Vol. 153 (October 1979): 31, 97-98, 103.

5466. Ebert, Alan. "Inside Cecily." Essence (February 1973): 40-41, 74, 80.

5467. Ferdinand, Val. "Cicely Tyson: A Communicator of Pride." Black Collegian, Vol. 8 (November-December 1978): 52-54+.

5468. Garland, Phyl. "Cicely Tyson: Her Mother Made Her a Star." Good Housekeeping, Vol. 179 (October 1974): 37-40+.

5469. Hepburn, Dave. "Cicely Tyson: Versatile Dynamo." Flamingo (April 1962): 23-27.

5470. Jenkins, Flo. "Cicely Tyson! A True Star Who Hasn't 'Gone Hollywood'!" Right On! (July 1976): 36-37.

5471. "Keep Your Eyes On: Cicely Tyson." Harpers Bazaar, Vol. 115 (December 1981): 160-161+.

5472. Norment, Lynn. "The Ebony Interview with Cicely Tyson." Ebony, Vol. 36 (February 1981): 124-126+.

5473. Robinson, Louie. "Cicely Tyson: A Very Unlikely Movie Star." Ebony, Vol. 29 (May 1974): 33+.

5474. Sanders, Charles L. "Cicely Tyson: She Can Smile Again After a Three-Year Ordeal." Ebony (January 1979): 27-36.

5475. Simor, G. "Destination: Stardom." Sepia, Vol. 16 (March 1967): 26-29.

5476. "Tyson, Cicely." Current Biography 1975, pp. 422-425.

5477. Tyson, Cicely - Clippings (MWEZ + n.c. 28,059) [Billy Rose Theatre Collection]

5478. Webster, Ivan. "A Woman Called Tyson." Encore American and Worldwide News (November 6 1978): 24-27; Profile followed by an interview with Ida Lewis, pp. 28-29.

5479. Yvonne. "The Importance of Cicely Tyson." Ms. (August 1974): 45-47+.

Newspaper Articles

5480. Bennetts, Leslie. "How Cicely Tyson Got to Teach in Wales." New York Times (August 22 1983).

5481. "Cover Story: Cicely Tyson Enjoys Another Historic Role." New York Amsterdam News (January 5 1974): D-11.

5482. Gardella, Kay. "Cicely Tyson: Actress by Accident, Star by Design." New York Sunday News (January 6 1974): Sec. 3, p. 1.

5483. Klemesrud, Judy. "Cicely, the Looker from 'Sounder.'" New York Times (October 1 1972): Sec. 2, pp. 13, 35.

5484. O'Connor, John J. "TV: 'A Woman Called Moses' with Cicely Tyson." New York Times (December 11 1978): C20.

5485. Reed, Rex. "Cicely Tyson: Actress with Standards,
Courage, Talent." New York Daily News (January 18 1974): 51.

5486. Sweeney, Louise. "Sounding Out 'Sounder' Star Cicely
Tyson." Christian Science Monitor (December 21 1972): 15.

5487. Unger, Arthur. "'Integrity is the Word for Cicely
Tyson'-'Pittman' star." Christian Science Monitor (January 30
1974): 6.

5488. Weingrad, Jeff. "Tyson: Work is the Message." New
York Post (December 11 1978).

Media Materials

5489. For You Black Woman; An Interview with Cicely Tyson
[video]. New York: Gerber/Carter Communications, 1978.   23
min. Cicely Tyson discusses her acting career and why, at the
risk of never working again, she chose not to work in
"blaxploitation" films of the late 1960's, early 70's. Tyson
goes on to talk about her roles in Sounder, The Autobiography
of Miss Jane Pittman and Roots. [Held by the Schomburg Center
- Sc Visual VRB-107]

UGGAMS, LESLIE (1943-   )

5490. Bogle, Donald. Blacks in American Films and
Television. New York: Garland, 1988, pp. 473-474.

5491. Uggams, Leslie - Clippings (MFL + n.c. 2957) [Billy
Rose Theatre Collection]

5492. "Uggams, Leslie." Current Biography 1967.

UNDERWOOD, BLAIR

5493. "Blair Underwood Adds Spice to TV's 'L.A. Law.'" Jet
(February 8 1988): 58-59.

5494. Collier, Aldore. "Blair Underwood; Laying Down the
Law." Ebony Man (March 1988): 80-82.

5495. Dunn, Marcia. "'L.A. Law' Star Courts Success in a big
way." Chicago Sun-Times (July 7 1988).

5496. Horner, Cynthia. "Hanging Out with Blair Underwood."
Right On! (January 1987): 27-29.

5497. Johnson, Pamela. "Spotlight: Blair Underwood."
Essence (June 1988): 52+.

5498. Marshall, Marilyn. "Blair Underwood: Riding High on
'L.A. Law'." Ebony (March 1989): 96+.

VAN PEEBLES, MARIO

5499. D'Agnese, Joe. "Make Room for Sonny Spoon!: Mario Van
Peebles comes to the screen in an historic TV series!" Right
On! (June 1988): 24-25, 72.

5500. Fornay, Alfred. "Mario Van Peebles." Ebony Man (June 1987): 49.

5501. Gardella, Kay. "Mario's in Series Business. Van Peebles dishes the comedy in 'Sonny Spoon.'" New York Daily News (February 12 1988): 111.

5502. Horner, Cynthia. "Mario Van Peebles Lays Down the Law!" Right On! (May 1987): 44-47.

5503. "Mario, Baby!" Right On! (November 1987): 62-63.

5504. "Mario Van Peebles makes it big in 'Jaws the Revenge'." Jet (July 27 1987): 28-30.

5505. Stark, John. "You've Met Dad Van Peebles, Now Here's the Son." People (March 23 1987): 91-92.

5506. White, Frank III. "Introducing: Mario Van Peebles." Ebony (May 1987): 80+.

VEREEN, BEN (1946-   )

See also # 3387

5507. Curreri, Joseph. "Ben Vereen: Running with the Mantle." Sepia (March 1979): 36-37.

5508. Purvis, C. "Ben Vereen: Backstage with Claude Purvis." Interview, Vol. IV, No. 3 (March 1974): 18.

5509. Ribowsky, Mark. "Is Ben Vereen Finally Ready to Become a Superstar?" Sepia (April 1977): 46-54.

5510. "Vereen, Ben." Current Biography 1978.

VITTE, RAY (1949-1983)

5511. Collins, Lisa. "Ray Vitte: Stardom is His Reward." Black Stars (September 1978): 6-10.

5512. George, Nelson. "Vitte Thanks God All Right-His Career is Moving Right Along." New York Amsterdam News (July 1 1978): D-12.

Obituaries

5513. "Actor Dies After Arrest." New York Daily News (February 22 1983): 4.

5514. "Raymond Vitte, 33, an actor, Dies After Scuffle with Police." New York Times (February 22 1983): B6.

5515. "TV Star Dies in Patrol Car After Battle with Police." New York Post (February 22 1983): 8.

5516. Variety (March 2 1983).

WADE, ADAM (1935-   )

See also # 3377

5517. Maksian, George. "Adam Wade - First Black to Host Game
Series." New York Sunday News (June 15 1975): Sec. 3, p. 2.

5518. "Profile of a Professional." New York Amsterdam News
(January 10 1976): D-2.

WADE, ERNESTINE

5519. "Profile: The Star Who Was Sapphire." Encore American
and Worldwide News (January 5 1976): 28-29.

5520. "What happened to TV stars of 'Amos 'n' Andy'?" Jet
(December 10 1981): 55-58.

5521. "Whatever Happened To...The 'Amos 'n Andy' Cast?"
Ebony (July 1973): 138.

WALKER, BILL

5522. "Jamaica Sea: Veteran actor Bill Walker gets meaty role
in movie on tropical intrigue." Our World (December 1952):
60-61.

WALKER, JIMMIE (1949-   )

5523. Bogle, Donald. Blacks in American Films and
Television. New York: Garland, 1988, pp. 477-478.

Articles

5524. Barber, Rowland. "'No Time for Jivin'." TV Guide
(December 14 1974): 28+.

5525. Haverstraw, Jack. "Jimmie Walker: The Women in My
Life." Sepia (October 1975): 34-46.

5526. Jenkins, Flo. "Jimmie Walker!...Dy-No-Mite!!" Right
On! (February 1975): 20-22.

5527. Jenkins, Walter. "Jimmie Walker's Dyn-o-mite Business
Venture." Black Stars (April 1976): 58-66.

5528. Lardine, Bob. "Jimmie Walker: the hottest skinny in
comedy." New York Sunday News Magazine (February 22 1976):
16+.

5529. Lucas, Bob. "Jimmie Walker: A Real Funny Dude." Black
Stars (September 1974): 18-23.

5530. Robinson, Louie. "Bad Times on the 'Good Times' Set.
Cast seeks changes in program, more depth in characters."
Ebony (September 1975): 33+.

5531. _____. "J.J. in Search of Jimmy Walker. Good Times TV show comic strives for own identity." Ebony (April 1975): 136+.

5532. Walker, Jimmy - Clippings [Billy Rose Theatre Collection]

5533. Waters, Harry F. "Kid Dyn-o-mite." Newsweek (October 13 1975): 63.

5534. Williams, Bob. "Jimmy Walker Defends J.J." New York Post (November 1 1977): 46.

WARD, RICHARD (1915-1979)

5535. "Richard Ward, 64, Actor, Was TV's 'Grandpa Evans.'" Newsday (July 5 1979). [Obituary]

5536. Treaster, Joseph B. "Richard Ward Dies; Stage & TV Actor. Played in 'Ceremonies in Dark Old Men' and 'Anna Lucasta' -- 'Good Times' Grandpa." New York Times (July 4 1979).

5537. Variety (July 11 1979). [Obituary]

WARE, MARGARET

See # 3370

WARFIELD, MARSHA

5538. Davidson, Bill. "Her Message to Night Court: Ripping a Deck of Cards in Half." TV Guide (July 9 1988): 12-15.

5539. "Introducing: Actress/Comedienne Marsha Warfield." Ebony (May 1988): 92, 94, 98.

WARNER, MALCOLM-JAMAL

5540. Warner, Malcolm-Jamal, and Daniel Paisner. Theo and Me: Growing Up Okay. New York: Dutton, 1988. 208p.

Articles

5541. Deeb, Gary. "TV: Cosby No. 1 son gets by acting naturally." New York Post (April 15 1987): 70.

5542. Fornay, Alfred. "Malcolm-Jamal Warner." Ebony Man (August 1986): 18.

5543. Kogan, Rick. "Malcolm-Jamal Warner at 17-'I'm Not a Role Model'." TV Guide (December 12 1987): 49+.

5544. Moore, Trudy S. "Malcolm-Jamal Warner; Looking Beyond the Cosby Show." Ebony Man (August 1989): 79-80, 82.

5545. Rogers, Charles E. "Malcolm-Jamal Warner Has His Feet on Solid Ground." Black Collegian (September-October 1986): 17-23.

5546. Waldron, Clarence. "Behind the Scenes with Lou Gossett and Malcolm-Jamal Warner." Ebony Man (November 1987): 38-40, 42.

WARREN, MICHAEL

5547. Buck, Jerry. "A Former 'Hill Street' Cop Plays New Role for His Kids." Chicago Sun-Times (July 13 1988).

5548. Goodwin, Betty. "Michael Warren Doesn't Want to be the Perfect Cop." TV Guide (January 18 1984): 10+.

5549. Hill, Michael E. "Unless Viewers Tune In, He Won't Be 'Home Free'." Washington Post/TV Week (July 10-16 1988).

5550. Horner, Cynthia. "Michael Warren: Darling or Daring?" Right On! (May 1982): 30-33, 67.

5551. Marsh, Antoinette. "Michael Warren Tells What's Wrong with TV." Black Stars (June 1981): 62-63.

5552. Marshall, Marilyn. "Prime Time for Michael Warren. Actor is riding high on TV's award-winning Hill Street Blues." Ebony (April 1982): 48+.

5553. Wieder, Judy. "Hill Street's Michael Warren." Sepia (November 1981): 38-40.

WASHINGTON, DENZEL

5554. Burns, Khephra. "Denzel." Essence (November 1986): 56, 131-132.

5555. Collier, Aldore. "Denzel Washington, Taking His Career Seriously." Ebony Man (November 1987): 29-32.

5556. Deforrest, Deborah. "Son of a Preacherman." Right On! (March 1984): 40-43.

5557. "Denzel." Essence (November 1986): 54+.

5558. "Denzel Washington." Ebony Man (July 1989): 79-80, 82. [Profile]

5559. "Denzel Washington." Interview (September 1985).

5560. Miller, Edwin. "Denzel Washington--An Actor with Talent, Charm, and a Philosophy That Works." Seventeen (June 1985): 118+.

5561. Shah, D. K. "Soldier, Healer, Seller of Rye." Gentleman's Quarterly (October 1988): B12+.

5562. Van Gelder, Lawrence. "At the Movies: Denzel Washington." New York Times (February 24 1989): C14. On actor's latest movie projects.

5563. Washington, Denzel - Clippings [Billy Rose Theatre Collection]

Cry Freedom

5564. Denby, David. "Movies: Denzel Washington brings Steven Biko back to life in 'Cry Freedom.'" New York (September 21 1987): 54-55.

5565. Haynes, Kevin. "Denzel Washington bringing Biko back to life." Women's Wear Daily (November 4 1987): 21.

5566. Mifflin, Margot. "Biko." Vogue (November 1987): 82.

5567. Stern, Gary. "A black Gandhi; Attenborough's new political film about two men - one black, one white - and their cry for freedom in apartheid-ruled South Africa." Horizon (November 1987): 37-38.

5568. Trucco, Terry. "Re-creating Steve Biko's life." New York Times (December 26 1987): 15.

5569. Van Gelder, Lawrence. "At the Movies: Preparing to become Steve Biko." New York Times (August 1 1986): C8.

5570. "Washington set for Attenborough's 'Biko'." Variety (July 9 1986): 4-5.

For Queen and Country

5571. Kerrigan, Marybeth. "A Movie Targets London Slums." New York Times (March 6 1988): Sec. 2, pp. 19, 38.

5572. Turan, Kenneth. "A British Outsider Examines the Rules of the Club." New York Times (May 14 1989): Sec. 2, p. 19.

Glory

5573. Collins, Glenn. "In 'Glory,' Denzel Washington takes a break from the clean--cut roles." New York Times (December 28 1989): C13.

Mighty Quinn

5574. "Black stars shine in murder mystery 'The Mighty Quinn'." Jet (February 20 1989): 46-48.

Variations on the Mo' Better Blues

5575. "Denzel Washington to star in Spike Lee's next movie." Jet (September 18 1989): 55.

St. Elsewhere

5576. "Denzel Washington likes his 'St. Elsewhere' role, hopes 'good' drama lasts." Jet (April 11 1983): 65.

5577. Ryan, Michael. "Denzel Washington of TV's "St. Elsewhere": A Profile." New York Daily News/Parade (April 12 1987): 4-5.

WASHINGTON, FREDI (1903-   )

5578. Bogle, Donald. Blacks in American Films and
Television. New York: Garland, 1988, pp. 478-479.

Articles

5579. Darden, Norma Jean. "Oh, Sister! Fredi and Isabel
Washington Relive '30s Razzmatazz." Essence (September 1978):
98+.

5580. Films and Filming (July 1983): 7. Biographical sketch.
5581. Washington, Fredi - Clippings [Billy Rose Theatre
Collection]

Research Collections

5582. Papers of Fredi Washington. [Held by the Amistad
Research Center (# 5997)]

WASHINGTON, RICH

See # 3354

WASHINGTON, SHIRLEY

5583. Jenkins, Walter. "Shirley Washington Tells How She
Cracked Hollywood." Black Stars (June 1975): 32-35.

WATERS, ETHEL (1896-1977)

5584. Bogle, Donald. Blacks in American Films and
Television. New York: Garland, 1988, pp. 479-481.

5585. DeKorte, Juliann. Ethel Waters: Finally Home. Old
Tappan, NJ: F. H. Revell Co., 1978. 128p.

5586. Knaack, Twila. Ethel Waters, I Touched a Sparrow.
Waco, TX: Word Books, 1978. 128p.

5587. Waters, Ethel. To Me It's Wonderful. New York: Harper
& Row, 1972. 162p. [Autobiography]

5588. _____, with Charles Samuels. His Eye Is On The
Sparrow: an autobiography. New York: Harcourt, Brace,
Jovanovich, 1951. 278p.

Articles

5589. Giddins, Gary. "Ethel Waters: Mother of Us All."
Village Voice (October 10 1977): 63, 92.

5590. Waters, Ethel. "The Men in My Life." Ebony (January
1952): 24-32, 34-36, 38.

5591. Waters, Ethel - Clippings [Billy Rose Theatre
Collection]

WATSON, VERNEE

5592. Banfield, Bever-Leigh. "Profile 3: A Closeup Look at Today's Black Actress." Sepia (September 1981): 22-30. [Vernee Watson/Tracy Reed/Debbie Allen]

5593. Collins, Lisa. "Vernee Watson: Portrait of Success." Black Stars (October 1976): 68-73.

5594. Slaton, Shell. "Vernee Watson." Right On! (December 1976): 40.

5595. _____. "The Wonder of Vernee Watson." Right On! (August 1978): 26-27.

5596. Watson, Vernee. "Fame Has Its Problems." Black Stars (April 1979): 20-23.

WAYANS, KEENEN IVORY

See also # 2164, 2173, 2188, 3000-3010

5597. Williams, Gregory. "Keenen Wayans: Cleared for Take-Off." Right On! (December 1983): 68-70.

WEATHERS, CARL

5598. Collier, Aldore. "Carl Weathers." Ebony Man (July 1988): 79-82.

5599. Salvo, Patrick. "Carl Weathers' War Against the Giants." Sepia (December 1979): 48-54.

5600. Slaton, Shell. "Rocky Star's Career is Weather-Proof." Right On! (November 1978): 38-40.

WELCH, ELISABETH (1909-)

5601. Slide, Anthony. "Elisabeth Welch." Films in Review (October 1987): 480-483.

WHIPPER, LEIGH (1876-1975)

5602. Papers (1861-1963). 1 box. Includes family papers (1861-1943); Correspondence (1926-1961); Contracts (1940-1942); Writings and Typescripts (1927, n.d.); Playscripts (n.d.); Programs (1924-1963) and a scrapbook. [Held by the Schomburg Center -- Sc Rare Mss-47 & Sc Micro R-3807]

Articles

5603. Adamson, Jimmy. "Hollywoodism." The Bronze Tattler, Vol. III, No. 1 (September 29 1941): 5.

5604. "Paramount Pictures Speaks of Leigh Whipper." The Bronze Tattler, Vol. III, No. 2 (October 25 1941): 1, 7.

Obituaries

5605. Jet (September 4 1975): 44-45.

5606. "Leigh Whipper, 98, Character Actor." New York Times (July 27 1975).

5607. Variety (July 30 1975).

WHITAKER, FOREST

5608. "Forest Whitaker: actor." Esquire (December 1988): 118.

5609. McKinney, Rhoda E. "Forest Whitaker: Bird reborn; through the award-winning actor, the legendary jazz musician Charlie (Yardbird) Parker has gained new life." Ebony (November 1988): 84+.

5610. _____. "Up-Front: Forest Whitaker makes his mark in "Bird" land." Ebony Man (October 1988): 10.

5611. Ransom, Lou. "Forest Whitaker takes to the air as 'Bird' Parker." Jet (November 7 1988): 56-57.

5612. Wheaton, Robert, and Martha Southgate. "Forest Whitaker." Essence Magazine (October 1988): 32.

Newspaper Articles

5613. Bloom, Steve. "The Passion and the Pain: for Forest Whitaker, star of 'Bird', jazz legend Charlie Parker's synergy with sound was the saxman's refuge from a life of addictions." New York Newsday (October 4 1988): Pt. II, p. 3. [Interview]

5614. Lindsey, Robert. "Young Man with a Sax." New York Times Magazine (September 11 1988).

5615. O'Haire, Patricia. "'Bird' Man; Forest Whitaker has traded in his 'Good Morning, Vietnam' fatigues for Charlie Parker's sax." New York Daily News (September 29 1988): 49, 60.

5616. Van Gelder, Lawrence. "The 'Bird' Man." New York Times (October 7 1988): C8. [Profile]

WHITE, JANE (1925-   )

5617. Peterson, Maurice. "On the Aisle: Spotlight on Jane White." Essence (April 1975): 7.

5618. Sullivan, Dan. "Determined Jane White Gets Off Racist Treadmill." New York Times (March 25 1968).

WHITMAN, ERNEST (1893-1954)

5619. "Educated for a Lawyer Whitman Went on Stage." Boston Globe (November 28 1926).

Obituaries

5620. New York Times (August 10 1954): 19.
5621. Variety (August 11 1954).
5622. Variety (August 18 1954).

WILKINSON, LISA

5623. Kowet, Don. "Both Married and Divorced. That's the contradictory life 'All My Children' offers Lisa Wilkinson and John Danelle." TV Guide (July 15 1978): 19-20.

5624. "Lisa Wilkinson, actress with multifacet talents." New York Amsterdam News (February 26 1983): 19, 21.

5625. Marlow, Curtis. "A Truly Afternoon Delight." Right On! (September 1983): 44-47.

WILLIAMS, BILLY DEE (1937-   )

5626. Bogle, Donald. Blacks in Americans Film and Television. New York: Garland, 1988, pp. 481-484.

Articles

5627. Bernikow, Louise. "Billy Dee Williams Strikes Back." Mademoiselle (June 1983): 32+.

5628. "The Black Gable." Time (August 23 1976): 64.

5629. Burrell, Walter Price. "Billy Dee Williams: An In-Depth Personal View." Black Stars (December 1973): 20-28.

5630. Campbell, Bebe Moore. "Spotlight: Billy Dee Williams." Essence (July 1985): 60-61, 107.

5631. Collier, Aldore. "Billy Dee Williams." Ebony Man (August 1988): 79-82.

5632. _____. "Billy Dee Williams tells how mother and twin sister helped career." Jet (May 15 1989): 28-30.

5633. Horner, Betty. "Billy Dee Williams: Up Close and Very Personal." Right On! (July 1985): 50-53.

5634. Jones-Miller, Alice. "The Love Man." Essence (February 1981): 52-53, 72, 75.

5635. Mercer, M. "New Clark Gable?" McCall's (February 1977).

5636. Murphy, Frederick Douglas. "The World of Billy Dee Williams." Black Stars (September 1978): 40-45.

5637. Neimark, Paul. "Billy Dee Williams: Top Black Movie Lover." Sepia (June 1976): 34-41.

5638. Norment, Lynn. "Billy Dee Williams." Encore American and Worldwide News, Vol. 36 (January 1981): 31-34+.

5639. _____. "Ebony Interview with Billy Dee Williams."
Ebony (January 1981): 31+.

5640. Pierce, Ponchita. "The Private Life of Billy Dee
Williams." Ebony (April 1974): 54-56+.

5641. Pile, S., E. Walsh, and J. Moran. "Mr. Lady Sings the
Blues Talks." Inter/View, Vol. 32 (May 1973): 8-11, 40.

5642. Plutzik, Roberta. "Billy Bounces Back." After Dark,
Vol. 13 (June 1980): 52-55.

5643. Robles, Roland. "Cover Story: Billy Dee Williams Wants
the 'Whole Trip.'" Encore American and Worldwide News
(October 20 1975): 26-29.

5644. Sanders, Charles L. "Serious Side of a Sex Symbol."
Ebony, Vol. 38 (June 1983): 126-128+. [Interview]

5645. "Space Stars: Nichelle Nichols, Billy Dee Williams play
futurist roles." Ebony (August 1985): 150+.

5646. "Williams, Billy Dee." Current Biography 1984.

5647. Wilson, Reggie. "He's Not Singing the Blues." Right
On! (July 1983): 38-48.

Newspaper Articles

5648. Carter, Claire. "We Were Always in His Corner: There
Was Pain in Billy Dee Williams Childhood, but Love Prevailed."
New York Sunday News/Parade (January 15 1989): 4-7.

5649. "Cover Story: Singer Billy Dee Williams." New York
Amsterdam News (November 26 1975): D10-D11.

5650. Klemesrud, Judy. "Billy Dee Williams--'The Black Clark
Gable' Branches Out." New York Times (September 19 1976):
Sec. 2, p. 3.

5651. Kogan, Rick. "Balancing Integrity and Stardom: A
Successful Billy Dee Williams still wrestles with an ugly side
of Hollywood." Newsday (June 7 1983): Pt II, pp. 22-23.

5652. Lardine, Bob. "Just a Simple Person Who always Wanted
a Mercedes." New York Sunday News Magazine (September 26
1976): 13, 39-40.

5653. Newton, Edmund. "Billy Dee Williams: Travelling All-
Star." New York Post (July 31 1976): Sec. 2, p. 1

5654. West, Hollie I. "A Man at Ease with Stardom, Traveling
a Legendary Road." Washington Post (December 27 1975): A9-
A10.

5655. Williams, Billy Dee - Clippings (MWEZ + n.c. 25,828)
[Billy Rose Theatre Collection]

Dynasty

5656. Bogle, Donald. <u>Blacks in American Films and Television</u>. New York: Garland Pub., 1988, pp. 268-270.

5657. Collier, Aldore. "Diahann & Billy Dee break taboo of Blacks as lovers on the TV screen." <u>Jet</u> (January 28 1985): 58+.

5658. Sanders, Charles L. "Diahann Carroll, Billy Dee Williams: Newest Sassy, Sexy Couple on Dynasty." <u>Ebony</u> (October 1984): 155+.

The Empire Strikes Back (1980)

5659. Armstrong, Lois. "Billy Dee Williams Wins the Latest Battle of 'Star Wars' - Integrating Outer Space." <u>People</u> (July 7 1980): 82+.

5660. Benson, Chris. "Billy Dee Williams Introduces New Character in "Star Wars" Sequel." <u>Black Stars</u> (August 1980): 40-45.

5661. _____. "Billy Dee Williams: a thrilling force in "Star Wars" sequel." <u>Jet</u> (June 5 1980): 44+.

The Last Angry Man (1959)

5662. "The Last Angry Man. Young actor Billy Dee Williams got movie role without test." <u>Ebony</u> (January 1960): 42-44.

5663. "Rebel with a Cause. The story of Billy Dee Williams, young star of Columbia's hit, "The Last Angry Man." <u>Sepia</u> (March 1960): 37-41.

Nighthawks

5664. Stewart, Phyllis. "No More Mr. Sidekick. Billy Dee Williams, now in 'Nighthawks', turns varied roles into stardom." New York <u>Newsday</u> (April 26 1981): Sec. II, p. 3, 6.

WILLLIAMS, CLARENCE III (1939-   )

5665. "Right On! Close Up: Clarence Williams III." <u>Right On!</u> (March 1972): 28-29.

5666. Riley, John. "Clarence Williams III on 'How I Feel About Being Black and Playing a Cop and blah, blah, blah.'" <u>TV Guide</u> (February 28 1970): 20-21.

5667. Robinson, Louie. "Star Couple. Clarence Williams III and wife Gloria Foster combine marriage with brilliant acting careers." <u>Ebony</u> (March 1970): 142-144, 146-148, 150.

5668. Tallmer, Jerry. "Closeup: Actor from Harlem." <u>New York Post</u> (December 29 1964).

5669. Williams, Clarence - Clippings [Billy Rose Theatre Collection]

WILLIAMS, DARNELL

5670. Brown, Meredith. "Darnell Williams: Brings Street Life to the Soaps!" Soap Opera Digest (January 5 1982): 118-123.

5671. Marshall, Marilyn. "Darnell Williams: Gaining Fame and Fans on the Soaps." Ebony (February 1984): 61+.

5672. Mirabella, Alan. "Darnell Williams." New York Sunday News (April 13 1986): 4.

5673. Payne, Andrea. "From Street Hood to Upstanding Citizen: Jesse's Metamorphosis." Soap Opera Digest (January 4 1983): 28+.

5674. Richardson, Djane, and Steve Manning. "Only on the Soaps! Darnell Williams." Right On! (October 1982): 26-27.

WILLIAMS, DICK (1938-   )

5675. Dawson, Cheryl. "Dick Williams Takes Care of Business." Black Stars (December 1973): 32-37.

5676. Peterson, Maurice. "On the Aisle: Spotlight on Dick Anthony Williams." Essence (May 1976): 42.

WILLIAMS, HAL

See also # 3377

5677. Cole, Deborah. "Hal Williams Talks About His Career." Black Stars (February 1977): 11-15.

5678. Ketchum, Larry. "Hal Williams." (Hollywood) Drama-Logue (May 21-27, 1981): 13.

5679. O'Hallaren, Bill. "Hal Williams and the 227 Ladies." TV Guide (May 30 1987): 10-12.

WILLIAMS, SPENCER (1893-1969)

See also # 3031-3033

5680. "Spencer Williams." Variety (December 24 1969). [Obituary]

5681. "Spencer Williams Jr., Andy in 'Amos 'n' Andy' TV Series." New York Times (December 24 1969): 25. [Obituary]

5682. "What happened to TV stars of 'Amos 'n' Andy'?" Jet (December 10 1981): 55-58.

WILLIAMSON, FRED (1938-   )

See also # 3350, 3373

5683. Bogle, Donald. Blacks in American Films and Television. New York: Garland, 1988, pp. 485-486.

Articles

5684. "At Home, Fred's A Nice, Nice Guy." Ebony (January 1975): 50-54+.

5685. Black, Doris. "Hollywood's New King of Ego." Sepia, Vol. 22 (August 1973): 37-43.

5686. Burrell, Walter Price. "Fred Williamson is the Greatest." Black Stars (March 1972): 16-20.

5687. Chisholm, Earle. "The Legend of the 'Bad Nigger'." Sepia (July 1972): 54-62. Profile of Williamson in "Nigger Charley."

5688. Ebert, Alan. "It's A Bird, It's A Plane, It's Fred (Williamson), Baby!" Essence (November 1973): 46-47, 97.

5689. _____. "Will the Real Fred Williamson Please Stand Up." Essence, Vol. 6 (February 1976): 46-7+.

5690. "Fred Williamson...Is He Just a Big 'Put-On'?!" Right On! (October 1976): 42-45, 47.

5691. Hoffman, L. "Super Fred T.N.T." Show, Vol. 3 (October 1973): 52-56.

5692. Rapp, Elaine, and Oscar Williams. "Soul Reels: Black Stars in Motion." Right On! (June 1972): 26-27.

5693. St. John, Michael. "Fred is Williamson's Only Business." Encore American and Worldwide News (July 19 1976): 31, 33.

5694. Slaton, Shell. "The Fred Williamson Experience!" Right On! (December 1979): 52-54.

5695. Williamson, Fred - Clippings [Billy Rose Theatre Collection]

5696. Winters, Jason. "Fred Williamson: The Sexy Superman!" Black Stars (February 1978): 20-24.

5697. Wyse, Chris. "Fred Williamson...A Special Brand of Man." Black Stars (December 1973): 52-61.

Newspaper Articles

5698. "Fred Williamson: More Than Macho Moviemaker." New York Amsterdam News (November 8 1980): 34.

5699. Klemesrud, Judy. "Fred - 'Don't Compare Me with Sidney.'" New York Times (March 18 1973): Sec. 2, pp. 1, 32.

5700. Newton, Edmund. "The Hammer Nails Hollywood." New York Sunday News/Magazine (November 20 1983): 17, 62-27.

WILSON, DEMOND (1946-   )

5701. Bogle, Donald. Blacks in American Films and
Television. New York: Garland, 1988, p. 486.

Articles

5702. Moses, Gavin. "Sanford's Son, Demond Wilson, Leaves
His Demons Behind to Become A Full-Time Evangelist." People
(April 15 1985).

5703. Tucker, Dimple. "What's It Like Being Close to Demond
Wilson?!!" Right On! (July 1973): 24-25.

5704. Unger, Norma O. "Demond Wilson: Black and Proud of His
Image." Black Stars (November 1979): 28-30.

5705. Walters, Richard. "Demond Wilson...A Snob or a Shy
Guy?" Right On! (May 1976): 28-29.

WILSON, DOOLEY (1894-1953)

5706. Bogle, Donald. Blacks in American Films and
Television. New York: Garland, 1988, p. 487.

Articles

5707. "Dooley Wilson." Variety (June 10 1953). [Obituary]

5708. Francis, Robert. "Dooley Wilson, Another Good Reason
Why 'Cabin in the Sky' Plays to Standees." Brooklyn Daily
Eagle (November 24 1940).

5709. Paneth, Donald. "Once a Singing Drummer." New York
Times (December 16 1945).

5710. Wilson, Dooley - Clippings [Billy Rose Theatre
Collection]

WILSON, EDITH (1896-1981)

5711. Black Perspective in Music, Vol. 9, No. 2 (Fall 1981):
242. [Obituary]

5712. Macleans (April 13 1981): 4. [Obituary]

5713. New York Times (April 1 1981): D22. [Obituary]

5714. Variety (April 1 1981). [Obituary]

WILSON, FLIP [Clerow Wilson] (1933-   )

See also # 3377

5715. Bogle, Donald. Blacks in American Films and
Television. New York: Garland, 1988, p. 487-489.

5716. Hudson, James A. Flip Wilson Close-Up. New York: Avon
Books, 1971. 128p.

Articles

5717. Brown, Joseph E. "The Flip Side of Flip Wilson." SAGA
(December 1972): 38-41, 90, 92, 94.

5718. Burke, Tom. "It Pays to Be Flip." New York Times
(October 13 1968).

5719. Davidson, Bill. "Likability." TV Guide (January 23
1971): 20-23.

5720. _____. "Many Faces of Flip Wilson." Good
Housekeeping (April 1971): 15+.

5721. Pierce, P. "All Flip Over Flip." Ebony (April 1968):
64+.

5722. "Wilson, Flip." Current Biography 1969.

Flip Wilson Show

5723. Bogle, Donald. Blacks in American Films and
Television. New York: Garland Pub., 1988, pp. 272-273.

Articles

5724. "Flip Scores Big in New Television Season." Jet
(November 25 1971): 56-58.

5725. "Flip Wilson, Host of TV's Hottest New Show." Jet
(January 14 1971): 60-63.

5726. "Flip Wilson: Something New for His TV Season." Jet
(October 25 1973): 88-91.

5727. Higgins, Robert. "Flip Wilson, the Gentle Spoofer."
TV Guide (January 17 1970): 35-40.

5728. Johnson, Robert. "Flip, He's Now No. 1 on TV." Sepia
(May 1971): 40-49.

5729. Leonard, John. "TV Review: Funny, Funky and, ah,
Flip." Life (January 22 1971): 12.

5730. Robinson, Louie. "Evolution of Geraldine." Ebony
(December 1970): 176+.

5731. "TV's First Black Superstar: Comedian Flip Wilson."
Time (January 31 1972): 56-60.

5732. Whitney, Dwight. "'I'm on the Case'. Which is what
Flip Wilson has to be to avoid being 'spotty with the funny.'"
TV Guide (January 8 1972): 20-25.

Newspaper Articles

5733. Beaufort, John. "Viewing Things: Wilsonian Flip."
Christian Science Monitor (February 6 1971).

5734. Brome, George O. "Geraldine? She Isn't So Flip." New York Times (September 3 1972): D11.

5735. Greenfeld, Josh. "Flip Wilson: 'My Life is My Own'." New York Times (November 14 1971): D17.

5736. Lardine, Bob. "The Stars Smile on Flip Wilson." New York Sunday News Magazine (December 5 1971): 6-8.

5737. Wilson, Flip - Clippings [Billy Rose Theatre Collection]

WILSON, FRANK H. (1886-1956)

5738. "Frank H. Wilson." Variety (February 22 1956). [Obituary]

5739. "Frank H. Wilson, Actor, 70, Is Dead." New York Times (February 17 1956).

WILSON, LISLE

See also # 3377

5740. Collins, Lisa. "Lisle Wilson: What's Next for Leonard?" Black Stars (May 1976): 12-17.

WILSON, THEODORE "TEDDY"

5741. Wilson, Theodore - Clippings [Billy Rose Theatre Collection]

WINFIELD, PAUL (1941-   )

5742. Bogle, Donald. Blacks in American Films and Television. New York: Garland, 1988, pp. 489-490.

Articles

5743. Armstrong, Lois. "From Out of Watts, Paul Winfield is the Man Who Would be 'King'." People (February 13 1978): 107-109.

5744. Davis, Curt. "Paul Winfield Nears the Mountaintop." Encore American and Worldwide News (October 10 1977): 22+.

5745. Dorsey, Helen. "Paul Winfield. His Impossible Dream Has Led Him to Stardom." New York Sunday News (August 26 1973): 5.

5746. Ebert, Alan. "Paul Winfield: A Man Unto Himself." Essence (June 1973): 26, 67, 76, 79.

5747. Leahy, Michael. "Paul Winfield: 227." TV Guide (September 23 1989): 16.

5748. "Paul Winfield joins cast of '227' sitcom." Jet (August 21 1989): 64.

5749. Peterson, Maurice. "On the Aisle: Focus on Paul Winfield." Essence (March 1975): 11.

5750. Salvo, Patrick William. "Paul Winfield: An Exclusive Interview." Sepia, Vol. 27 (August 1978): 74-77.

5751. Tallmer, Jerry. "Paul Winfield - In Heady Company." New York Post (September 1 1973).

5752. Winfield, Paul - Clippings [Billy Rose Theatre Collection]

WINFREY, OPRAH (1954-   )

See also # 3036-3048

5753. Bogle, Donald. Blacks in American Films and Television. New York: Garland, 1988, pp. 490-491.

5754. King, Norman. Everybody Loves Oprah!: her remarkable life story. New York: Morrow, 1987. 222p.

5755. Waldron, Robert. Oprah! New York: St. Martin's Press, 1987. 201p.

Articles

5756. Edwards, Audrey. "Spotlight: Oprah Winfrey: Stealing the Show." Essence (October 1986): 50+.

5757. Fury, Kathleen. "Oprah! Why She's Got America Talking." TV Guide (March 5 1988): 27-32.

5758. Harrison, Barbara Grizzuti. "The Importance of Being Oprah." New York Times Magazine (June 11 1989): 28-30, 46, 54, 130, 134, 136.

5759. "Here Comes Oprah! From the "The Color Purple" to TV Talk Queen." Ms. (August 1986): 46+.

5760. "Here's Oprah." Women's Day (October 1 1986): 48+.

5761. Markey, Judy. "Opionionated Oprah." Women's Day (October 4 1988): 60+.

5762. Noel, Pamela. "Oprah Winfrey: Zigzagging Her Way to TV Fame." Ebony (April 1985): 100+.

5763. "Oprah Winfrey: Wonder Woman." Ladies Home Journal (December 1988): 40+.

5764. Rautbord, Sugar. "Oprah Winfrey." Interview (March 1986): 62-64.

5765. Richman, Alan. "Cover: Oprah." People (January 12 1987).

5766. Sanders, Richard, and Barbara Kleban Mills. "TV Host Oprah Winfrey, Chicago's Biggest Kick, Boots Up for a Star-Making Role in The Color Purple." People (December 16 1985): 161+.

5767. "Simply...Oprah!" Cosmopolitan (February 1989): 212+.

5768. Waters, Harry F. "Chicago's Grand New Oprah." Newsweek (December 31 1984): 51.

5769. Whitaker, Charles. "TV's New Daytime Darling." Saturday Evening Post (July/August 1987): 42+.

5770. _____. "Oprah Winfrey: The Most Talked-About TV Talk Show Host." Ebony (March 1987): 38+.

5771. "Winfrey, Oprah." Current Biography 1987.

5772. Winfrey, Oprah - Clippings (MFL + n.c. 2296) [Billy Rose Theatre Collection]

5773. Zoglin, Richard. "People Sense the Realness; look out, Phil Donahue; here comes Oprah Winfrey." Time (September 15 1986): 99.

5774. _____. "Profile: Lady with a Calling." Time (August 8 1988): 62-64.

WOODARD, ALFRE (1953-   )

5775. Bogle, Donald. Blacks in American Films and Television. New York: Garland, 1988, pp. 491-492.

5776. Hardy, Karen, and Kevin J. Koffler. The New Breed: Actors Coming of Age. New York: Holt & Co., 1988, pp. 85-88.

Articles

5777. "Alfre Woodard portrays Thomas' mom in NBC film." Jet (October 9 1989): 50.

5778. Clancy, Frank. "From St. Elsewhere to South Africa: a profile of actress Alfre Woodard." Mother Jones (October 1987): 34+.

5779. Dougherty, Margot. "Playing South African activist Winnie Mandela, Alfre Woodard captures the soul of a nation." People (September 28 1987): 103+.

5780. Green, Tom. "Talented, inspiring Alfre Woodard." Cosmopolitan (March 1989): 168.

5781. Hirschberg, Lynn. "Oscar Wild; the fifty-two days of Alfre Woodard." Esquire (September 1984): 267+.

5782. Johnson, Pamela. "Spotlight: Alfre Woodard, Power Player." Essence (April 1988): 56+.

5783. Krista, Charlene. Interview. <u>Films in Review</u>, Vol. 35, No. 1 (January 1984): 14-17.

5784. "Maid role again boosts only Black Oscar nominee." <u>Jet</u> (March 5 1984): 55.

5785. Vallely, Jean. "The Alfre nobody knows." <u>Ms</u>. (April 1989): 68+.

WOODARD, CHARLAINE

5786. "Television: The Cinderella Girl." <u>Encore American and Worldwide News</u> (March 6 1978): 30-31

YANCY, EMILY (1939-   )

5787. Wahls, Robert. "Girl, You've Arrived. Emily Yancy, Newest Star on Broadway's Horizon." New York <u>Sunday News</u> (November 26 1967).

YOUNG, OTIS (1932-   )

5788. Hobson, Dick. "The Odyssey of a Black Man in 'White Man's Television.'" <u>TV Guide</u> (March 1-7 1969): 18-22.

5789. "Otis Young's Film Debut in 'The Last Detail.'" New York <u>Amsterdam News</u> (December 8 1973): D-16.

5790. Ware, Cade. "Otis Young: Sleeping at the Movies, Sleeping in the Hall." <u>Black Stars</u> (January 1974): 28-35.

Appendix I
Reference Works

GENERAL WORKS

5791. Books in Print 1989-1990
5792. British Books in Print 1988
5793. International Books in Print 1989
5794. International Literary Market Place 1989-90

Computer Databases/CD ROMs

5795. Academic Index (1986-Feb. 1990)
5796. General Periodicals Index (1986-Feb. 1990)
5797. Magazine Index [May 1982-Feb. 1990]
5798. MLA International Bibliography (1981-Sept. 1989)
5799. National Newspaper Index (Sept. 1983-Feb. 1990)
5800. RLIN (Research Libraries Information Network)
5801. UMI Newspaper Abstracts Ondisc (Jan 1988-June 1989)

Dictionary Catalogues

5802. CATNYP - Computer catalogue of the research libraries of the New York Public Library (1972-Jan. 1990).

5803. New York Public Library. Schomburg Center for Research in Black Culture. Dictionary Catalog of the Schomburg Collection of Negro Literature and History. Boston: G.K. Hall, 1962. 9 vols.; First and Second Supplements (1969-1972). 6 vols. Continued by annual supplements under the title Bibliographic Guide to Black Studies.

Book, Newspaper and Periodical Indexes

Note: Dates in parentheses indicate years viewed by the author.

5804. Daniel, Walter C. Black Journals of the United States. Westport, CT: Greenwood Press, 1982. 432p.

5805. Essay and General Literature Index [1900-1988]
5806. A Guide to Negro Periodical Literature [1941-1943]
5807. Humanities Index [1973-Sept. 1989]
5808. Index to Black Periodicals [1984-1988]

5809. Index to Periodical Articles by and About Blacks [1950-1983]
5810. International Index [1907-1965]
5811. MLA International Bibliography [1957-1981]
5812. Reader's Guide to Periodical Literature [1890-1988]

Journals

5813. American Visions [1986-April 1990]
5814. Black Creation [1970-1974/75]
5815. Black Stars [1972-1981]. Continues Tan.
5816. Color [1945-1957]
5817. Ebony [1945-March 1990]
5818. Ebony Man [1986-Feb 1990]
5819. Encore American and Worldwide News [1972-1982]
5820. Essence [1970-Feb 1990]
5821. First World [1977-1980]
5822. Half-Century Magazine [1916-1923]
5823. Headlines and Pictures [1944-1946]
5824. Negro Achievements. Continued by Sepia.
5825. New Lady [1969-1971]
5826. Our World [1946-1955]
5827. Right On! [1971-Nov 1989]
5828. Sepia [1952-53/1959-1981]
5829. Sepia Record. Continued by Sepia.
5830. Tan [1950-Oct 1961]. Continued by Black Stars.
5831. Village Voice [1959-1989]

Biographical Indexes

5832. Biography Index (1961-Feb. 1990)

5833. The New York Times Obituaries Index 1858-1968. New York: New York Times/Arno Press, 1970.

5834. The New York Times Obituaries Index 1969-1978. New York: New York Times, 1980.

5835. Perry, Jeb H. Variety Obits: An Index to Obituaries in Variety, 1905-1978. Metuchen, NJ: Scarecrow Press, 1980.

5836. Spradling, Mary Mace. In Black and White. 3rd ed. Detroit: Gale, 1980. 2 vols. Bibliographic index to more than 15,000 Black individuals and groups.

5837. _____. In Black and White: Supplement. Detroit: Gale, 1985. 628p. Supplement to the above with information on some 6,700 additional individuals and groups.

5838. Variety Obituaries, 1905-1986. New York: Garland Pub., 1986. 11 vols.

Dissertation and Theses Indexes

5839. ASLIB; Index to Theses accepted for higher degrees by the Universities of Great Britain and Ireland and the Council for National Academic Awards [1950-1987].

5840. Comprehensive Dissertations Index [1861-1988].

5841. <u>Dissertations Abstracts International</u> [1986-Jan. 1990]

5842. <u>Masters Abstracts</u> [1962-Summer 1989].

5843. <u>Master's Theses in the Arts and Social Sciences</u>,
No. 1-12 [1976-1988].

GENERAL REFERENCE WORKS - AFRICA

5844. <u>African Book Publishing Record</u> [1975-No. 3/1989].

5845. Zell, Hans. <u>African Books in Print</u>. 3rd ed. London:
Mansell Information Pub., Ltd., 1984. 2 vols.

5846. _____, and Carol Bundy, eds. <u>The African Book
World & Press: A Directory</u>. New York: K.G. Saur, 1988. 340p.

Bibliographies and Indexes

5847. <u>Africa Bibliography</u> [1984-1987], ed. Hector Blackhurst.
Manchester: Manchester University Press, 1985-1988.

5848. <u>Africa Index to Continental Periodical Literature</u>.
No. 1 (1976) - No. 6 (1981).

5849. Cooperative Africana Microform Project and The Center
for Research Libraries. <u>CAMP Catalog; 1985 Cumulative
Edition</u>. Catalog of the microform collection at Chicago's
Center for Research Libraries which consists of Africana
microforms from the collections of the New York Public Library
- General Research Division; The Schomburg Center for Research
in Black Culture; Columbia University; Yale University; Boston
University; Harvard University - Widener Library; University
of Pennsylvania; Howard University; Library of Congress;
Michigan State University; University of Wisconsin; University
of Chicago - Joseph Regenstein Library; Northwestern
University - Melville J. Herskovits Library; University of
Texas at Austin; UCLA - Graduate Research Library; California
Institute of Technology - Munger Africana Library.

5850. <u>A Current Bibliography on African Affairs</u>
[1962-No. 4/1989].

5851. <u>International African Bibliography</u> [1971-No. 4/1989].
Continues the quarterly bibliographies previously published in
<u>Africa: Journal of the International African Institute</u>.

5852. <u>International African Bibliography, 1973-1978: Books,
articles and papers in African Studies</u>, ed. J. D. Pearson.
London: Mansell, 1982. 343p. Cumulative record of literature
collected between 1973 and 1978 in the bibliographic journal
<u>International African Bibliography</u> with additional citations
not previously cited. Supercedes the quarterly issues for
this period.

5853. Ojo-Ade, Femi. <u>Analytic Index of Presence Africaine,
1947-1972</u>. Washington, D.C.: Three Continents Press, 1977.
181p. Index to the influential journal <u>Presence Africaine</u>.

5854. United Kingdom Publications and Theses on Africa.
Cambridge: W. Heffer [1963-1967/68]. Bibliographic index of
British books, periodical articles and theses on Africa.

5855. Western, Dominique Coulet. A Bibliography of the Arts
of Africa. Waltham, MA: African Studies Association, Brandeis
University, 1975. 128p.

Dissertation and Theses Indexes

5856. Lauer, Joseph J., Gregory V. Larkin, and Alfred Kagan,
comps. American and Canadian Doctoral Dissertations and
Master's Theses on Africa, 1974-1987. Atlanta, GA: Crossroads
Press, 1989. 377p.

5857. McIlwaine, J. H. St. J. Theses on Africa, 1963-1975,
accepted by universities in the United Kingdom and Ireland.
London: Mansell, 1978. 123p.

5858. "Recent Doctoral Dissertations." ASA News [1985-mid '89]

5859. Repertoire des Theses Africanistes Francaises
[1977-1984/85].

5860. Sims, Michael, and Alfred Kagan, comps. American and
Canadian Doctoral Dissertations and Masters Theses on Africa,
1886-1974. 2nd ed. Los Angeles: African Studies Association,
1976. 365p.

Periodicals

5861. Blake, David, and Carole Travis. Periodicals from
Africa: A Bibliography and Union List of Periodicals Published
in Africa. First Supplement. Boston: G.K. Hall, 1984. 217p.

5862. Travis, Carole, and Miriam Alman. Periodicals from
Africa: A Bibliography and Union List of Periodicals Published
in Africa. Boston: G.K. Hall, 1977. 619p.

REGIONAL STUDIES

West Africa

5863. West Africa (1978-Jan 28 1990). Weekly journal
containing frequent reports on film activity in Africa.

CAMEROON

5864. Baratte-Eno Belinga, Therese. Ecrivains, Cineastes et
Artistes Camerounais: Bio-Bibliographie. Yaounde: C.E.P.E.R.,
1978. 217p.

GHANA

5865. Aguolu, Christian C. Ghana in the Humanities and
Social Sciences, 1900-1971: A Bibliography. Metuchen, NJ:
Scarecrow Press, 1973. 469p.

5866. Amedekey, E. Y. The Culture of Ghana: A Bibliography.
Accra: Ghana Universities Press, 1970. 215p.

5867. Dua-Agyeman, H., comp. Legon Theses: A Checklist of
Theses and Dissertations Accepted for Higher Degrees by the
University of Ghana, Legon, 1964-1977. Legon: The Balme
Library, University of Ghana, 1978. 35p.

5868. Ghana: A Current Bibliography [1967-May/June 1979].

5869. Ghana National Bibliography [1965-1977].

5870. Kafe, Joseph Kofi. Ghana: An Annotated Bibliography of
Academic Theses, 1920-1970 in The Commonwealth, the Republic
of Ireland and the United States of America. Boston: G.K.
Hall, 1973. 219p.

5871. Smit, Hettie M. Ghana in non-Ghanaian Serials and
Collective Works, 1974-1977: A Bibliography. Legon: Balme
Library, University of Ghana, 1981. 90p.

IVORY COAST

5872. Bibliographie de la Cote d'Ivoire [1969-1975].

5873. Janvier, Genevieve. Bibliographie de la Cote-d'Ivoire.
Vol. 2 (Sciences de l'Homme). Abidjan: Universite d'Abidjan,
1973. 431p.

MALI

5874. Brasseur, Paule. Bibliographie Generale du Mali
(Anciens Soudan Francais et Haut-Senegal-Niger). Dakar: IFAN,
1964. 461p.

5875. _____. Bibliographie Generale du Mali (1961-1970).
Dakar: Les Nouvelles Editions Africaines, 1976. 284p.

NIGERIA

5876. Aguolu, Christian. Nigeria: A Comprehensive
Bibliography in the Humanities and Social Sciences, 1900-1971.
Metuchen: Scarecrow Press, 1973. 620p.

5877. Baum, Edward. A Comprehensive Periodical Bibliography
of Nigeria, 1960-1970. Athens: Ohio University, Center for
International Studies, 1975. 249p.

5878. The National Bibliography of Nigeria [1973-1984].
Continues Nigerian Publications [1950-1972].

Dissertation and Theses Indexes

5879. Amoso, Margaret. Nigerian Theses: A List of Theses on
Nigerian Subjects and of Theses by Nigerians. Ibadan: Ibadan
University Press, 1965. 36p.

5880. Ezeji, Joe, comp. Ahmadu Bello University Thesis and Dissertation Abstracts 1962-1978. Zaria, Nigeria: Kashim Ibrahim Library, 1985. 313p.

5881. Theses and Dissertations Accepted in Nigerian Universities [1968-1977]

5882. Toye, B. O., and S. O. Oderinde, comps. Abstracts of Ibadan University Theses and Dissertations, 1964-1975. Ibadan: Ibadan University Library, 1979. 605p.

5883. University of Ife. A Catalogue of the Ife University Higher Degree Theses Deposited in the University Library, 1962-1978. Ile-Ife, Nigeria, May 1978.

SENEGAMBIA

5884. Bibliographie du Senegal (1972-). Continues Archives Nationales du Senegal.

5885. National Bibliography of the Gambia [1978-Dec. 1984].

5886. Porges, Laurence. Bibliographie des Regions du Senegal. Dakar: Ministere du Plan et du Developpment, 1967. 705p.

SIERRA LEONE

5887. Sierra Leone Publications [1962-1978].

5888. Thompson, J. S. T. Sierra Leonean Theses: A List of Doctoral and Masters' Theses by Sierra Leoneans and non-Sierra Leoneans writing on Sierra Leone. Freetown, Sierra Leone: the Author, 1978. 78p.

5889. Zell, Hans M. A Bibliography of non-Periodical Literature on Sierra Leone, 1925-1966 (excluding Sierra Leone government publications). Freetown: Fourah Bay College Bookshop, 1966. 44p.

Central Africa and Southern Africa

5890. Pollak, Oliver B., and Karen Pollak. Theses and Dissertations on Southern Africa: An International Bibliography. Boston: G.K. Hall, 1976. 236p.

BOTSWANA

5891. National Bibliography of Botswana [1969-1985].

LESOTHO

5892. Lesothana (1982-). National bibliography.

5893. Willet, Shelagh M., and David P. Ambrose. Lesotho, A Comprehensive Bibliography. Oxford: Clio Press, 1980. 496p.

RWANDA

5894. Levesque, Albert. Contribution to the National
Bibliography of Rwanda, 1965-1970. Boston: G. K. Hall, 1979.
541p.

SOUTH AFRICA

5895. South African National Bibliography (1959-).

ZAMBIA

5896. The National Bibliography of Zambia [1970/71-1981
and 1985].

ZIMBABWE

5897. Pollak, Oliver B., and Karen Pollak. Rhodesia/Zimbabwe:
An International Bibliography. Boston: G. K. Hall, 1977. 621p.

5898. Rhodesia National Bibliography [1967-1978]. Continues
List of Publications... [1961-1966].

5899. Zimbabwe National Bibliography [1979-1985].

East Africa

5900. Accessions List, Eastern Africa. United States,
Library of Congress, Nairobi Office, 1968- .

KENYA

5901. Kenya National Bibliography [1980-1983].

MALAWI

5902. Malawi National Bibliography (Zomba, Malawi).

TANZANIA

5903. Tanzania National Bibliography [1974/75-1983].
Continues Printed in Tanzania [1969-1973].

UGANDA

5904. Library Bulletin and Accessions List. Makerere
University. Library. Kampala, July 1960- .

GENERAL REFERENCE WORKS - AFRICAN DIASPORA

Bibliographies

5905. Black Latin America: A Bibliography. Los Angeles:
Latin American Studies Center, California State University,
1977. 73p.

5906. <u>Caribbean Orientations: a bibliography of resource</u>
<u>materials on the Caribbean experience in Canada</u>, ed. W. W.
Anderson.   Toronto: OCCI and Williams-Wallace Publishers,
1985.   238p.

5907. Fowler, Carolyn.   <u>Black Arts and Black Aesthetics: a</u>
<u>bibliography</u>. 2nd ed. Atlanta: First World Foundation, 1981.
211p.

5908. Hall-Alleyne, Beverley, Garth White, and Michael Cooke,
comps. <u>Towards a Bibliography of African-Caribbean Studies,</u>
<u>1970-1980</u>. Kingston, Jamaica: African-Caribbean Institute of
Jamaica, 1982. 37p. Excellent survey of the literature on
the life and culture of the Black Diaspora.

5909. Nodal, Roberto. <u>Black Culture in Latin America: An</u>
<u>Updated Bibliography</u>. Milwaukee: Dept. of Afro-American
Studies, University of Wisconsin-Wilwaukee, February 1977.
31p.

·5910. _____. <u>A Preliminary Bibliography on African</u>
<u>Cultures and Black Peoples of the Caribbean and Latin America</u>.
Milwaukee: Dept. of Afro-American Studies, University of
Wisconsin-Wilwaukee, February 1972. 48p.

Bibliographic Indexes

5911. <u>Bibliographic Guide to Latin American Studies</u> [1978-
1987]. Annual supplement to the University of Texas at
Austin's <u>Catalogue of the Latin American Collection</u> compiled
in collaboration with the Library of Congress. Covers all
aspects of Latin America and the Caribbean.

5912. <u>Dictionary Catalog of the History of the Americas</u>.
Boston: G.K. Hall, 1961. 28 vols. First supplement (1973).
9 vols. Dictionary catalog of the Americas Division of the
New York Public Library.

5913. <u>Hispanic American Periodicals Index</u> [1970-1987]. Los
Angeles: UCLA Latin American Center Publications. Annual
index which complements the University of Texas' <u>Bibliographic</u>
<u>Guide to Latin American Studies</u> and the Organization of
American States' <u>Index to Latin American Periodical Literature</u>.

5914. <u>Index to Latin American Periodical Literature, 1929-</u>
<u>1960</u>. Boston: G.K. Hall, 1962. 8 vols.; <u>First Supplement,</u>
<u>1961-1965</u> [1968]. 2 vols.; <u>Second Supplement, 1966-1970</u>
[1980]. 2 vols. Indexed catalog of the Organization of
American States (aka Pan American Union) library collection.
Important record of the periodical literature on Latin America
from 1929-1970.

REGIONAL STUDIES

The Caribbean and Latin America

5915. Brathwaite, Edward, comp. Our Ancestral Heritage: A Bibliography of the English-speaking Caribbean, designed to record and celebrate the several origins of our structural, material and creative culture and to indicate how this is being used by us to mek ah-we. Kingston, Jamaica: Savacou, 1977. 194p. (Reprint of 1976 ed.)

5916. The CARICOM Bibliography [1977-1985]. Georgetown, Guyana, Caribbean Community Secretariat Library. Picking up where its predecessor, Current Caribbean Bibliography, left off, this work offers the most complete coverage of regionally published Caribbean materials now available.

5917. Chang, Henry C. A Selected, Annotated Bibliography of Caribbean Bibliographies in English. St. Thomas: Caribbean Research Institute, College of the Virgin Islands, 1975. 54p.

5918. Comitas, Lambros. The Complete Caribbeana, 1900-1975: A Bibliographic Guide to the Scholarly Literature. Millwood, NY: Kraus-Thompson Press, 1977. 4 vols.

5919. Current Caribbean Bibliography [1951-1973]. When this work was first published its intention was to provide a timely and comprehensive guide to Caribbean-based publications. However it has now fallen hopelessly out of date and, due to its poor organization, is of limited use.

5920. Evelyn, Shirley. West Indian Social Sciences Index. An Index to Moko, New World Quarterly, Savacou, Tapia, 1963-1972. St. Augustine, Trinidad, 1974. 117p. Index to four important West Indian newspapers and journals.

5921. Jordan, Alma, and Barbara Comissiong. The English-speaking Caribbean: A Bibliography of Bibliographies. Boston: G.K. Hall, 1984. 411p.

5922. University of the West Indies. Theses Accepted for Higher Degrees [August 1963-July 1977].

Dictionary Catalogues

5923. Institute of Jamaica, Kingston. West India Reference Library. The Catalogue of the West India Reference Library. Millwood, NY: Kraus International Publications, 1980. 6 vols.

5924. University of Miami. Catalog of the Cuban and Caribbean Library, University of Miami, Coral Gables, Florida. Boston: G.K. Hall, 1977. 6 vols.

Bibliographic Journals

5925. Bibliography of the English-Speaking Caribbean [Vol. 3, No. 2 (1981)-Vol. 6, No. 1 (1984)]. Ceased publication.

5926. Notes Bibliographiques Caraibes [1979-1987]. Regional bibliography of the French-speaking Antilles--Dominica, Guadeloupe, Guyane, Haiti, Martinique and St. Barthelemy.

BARBADOS

5927. National Bibliography of Barbados [1976-1979].

BRAZIL

5928. Alves, Henrique L. Bibliografia Afro-Brasileira: Estudos Sobre o Negro. 2nd ed. rev. e ampliada. Rio de Janeiro: Livraria Editora Catedra, 1979. 179p.

5929. Bibliografia Brasileira [1983-No. 1/1988]. Continues Boletim Bibliographico da Bibliotheca Nacional [1951-1967 and 1973-1982]. National bibliography.

5930. Porter, Dorothy B. Afro-Braziliana: A Working Bibliography. Boston: G.K. Hall, 1978. 294p.

GUYANA

5931. Guyanese National Bibliography (Georgetown, Guyana).

HAITI

5932. Bissainthe, Max. Dictionnaire de Bibliographie Haitienne. Washington, D.C.: Scarecrow Press, 1951. 1052p.

5933. _____. Dictionnaire de Bibliographie Haitienne. Premier Supplement (1950-1970). Metuchen, NJ: Scarecrow Press, 1973. 269p.

5934. Laguerre, Michel. The Complete Haitiana: A Bibliographic Guide to the Scholarly Literature, 1900 to 1980. New York: Kraus International, 1982. 2 vols.

JAMAICA

5935. Institute of Jamaica, Kingston. The Jamaican National Bibliography, 1964-1974. Millwood, NY: Kraus International Publications, 1981. 439p. This cumulative work is continued by the quarterly issues of Jamaican National Bibliography [1975-July/Sept. 1985].

TRINIDAD AND TOBAGO

5936. Trinidad and Tobago National Bibliography [1975-1982].

VENEZUELA

5937. Pollak-Eltz, Angelina. Bibliografia Afrovenozolana. Caracas: Universidad Catolica Andres Bello, Instituto de Investigaciones Historicas, 1976. 25p.

5938. _____. Nuevos Aportes a la Bibliografia Afro-Venezolana; Datos recolectados desde la publicacion de la BIBLIOGRAFIA AFROVENEZOLANA en la Revista MONTALBAN, Caracas, No. 5, 1976. Caracas: Centro de Religiones Comparadas, Universidad Catolica Andres Bello, 1983. 16p.

5939. Ramos Guedez, Jose Marcial. Bibliografia Afrovenozolana. Caracas: Instituto Autonomo Biblioteca Nacional y de Servicios de Bibliotecas, 1980. 125p.

5940. _____. El Negro en Venezuela; aporte bibliografico. 2a ed., rev., corregida y aum. Caracas: Instituto Autonomo Biblioteca Nacional y Servicios de Bibliotecas, 1985. 279p.

GENERAL FILM REFERENCE WORKS

5941. Brady, Anna, comp. Union List of Film Periodicals: holdings of selected American Collections. Westport, CT: Greenwood Press, 1984. 316p.

5942. Slide, Anthony. International Film, Radio, and Television Journals. Westport, CT: Greenwood Press, 1985. 428p.

Film Periodical Indexes

5943. Alvarez, Max Joseph. Index to Motion Pictures Reviewed by Variety, 1907-1980. Metuchen, NJ: Scarecrow Press, 1982. 510p.

5944. Film Literature Index [1973-No. 3/1988]

5945. International Index to Film Periodicals [1972-1987]

5946. New York Times Encyclopedia of Film, 1896-1979. New York: Times Books, 1984. 13 vols.

5947. Retrospective Index to Film Periodicals [1930-1971]

Filmographies

5948. Educational Film/Video Locator of the Consortium of University Film Centers and R.R. Bowker. 4th ed. New York: R.R. Bowker, 1990. 2 vols.

5949. Film and Video Finder. 2nd ed. Medford, NJ: Plexus Publishing, 1989. 3 vols. Compiled by the National Information Center for Educational Media.

5950. Limbacher, James L., ed. Feature Films on 8mm, 16mm and Videotape: A Directory of Feature Films Available for Rental, Sale, and Lease in the United States and Canada. 8th ed. New York: Bowker, 1985. 481p.

FILM BIBLIOGRAPHIES AND FILMOGRAPHIES - AFRICA

Bibliographies

5951. Schmidt, Nancy J. African Films and Filmmakers: A
Preliminary Bibliography. Bloomington: African Studies
Program, Indiana University, 1986. 111p.

5952. _____, Sub-Saharan African Films and Filmmakers:
an Annotated Bibliography. New York/London: Zell, 1988.
401p. Includes nearly 4,000 entries on African film and
filmmakers with a strong emphasis on materials from African
newspapers and journals.

Filmographies

5953. Africa: a handbook of film and video resources:
supplementary list, May 1987. London: British Universities
Film & Video Council, 1987. 23p. Supplement to Ballantyne
work below.

5954. Ballantyne, James, and Andrew Roberts. Africa: a
handbook of film and video resources. London: British
Universities Film & Video Council, 1986. 120p.

5955. Cyr, Helen W. A Filmography of the Third World,
1976-1983: An Annotated List of 16mm Films. Metuchen, NJ:
Scarecrow Press, 1985. 285p.

5956. _____. A Filmography of the Third World: An
Annotated List of 16mm Films. Metuchen, NJ: Scarecrow Press,
1976. 319p.

5957. France. Ministere des Affaires Etrangeres.
Cinematheque. Catalogue de Films Afrique Noire, Ocean Indien,
Afrique Noire: films 16mm son optique. Paris: The Library,
between 1973 and 1978. 91p.

5958. Martin, Janet, et al. Africa Projected: A Critical
Filmography. Waltham, MA: African Studies Association, 1972.
28p.

5959. Ohrn, Stephen, and Rebecca Riley, eds. Africa from
Real to Reel: An African Filmography. Los Angeles: African
Studies Association, 1976. 144p.

5960. Premier Catalogue Selectif International de Films
Ethnographiques sur l'Afrique Noire. Paris: UNESCO, 1967.
408p.

5961. Stephens, Warren D. African Film Bibliography, 1965.
Bloomington, IN: African Studies Association, 1966. 31p.
(Occasional Papers; 1). In spite of it's misleading title
this work is an ethnographic filmography, not a bibliography.

5962. Wiley, David S., et al. Africa on Film and Videotape
1960-1981: A Compendium of Reviews. East Lansing, MI: African
Studies Center, Michigan State University, 1982. 551p.

Articles

5963. Boughedir, Ferid. "Petit Guide des Cineastes
Africains." Cinema Quebec, Vol. III, No. 9-10 (August 1974):
44-45.

5964. Morgenthau, Henry. "Guides to African Films." Africa
Report, Vol. XIII, No. 5 (May 1968): 52-54.

BIOGRAPHICAL DICTIONARIES, FILM BIBLIOGRAPHIES
AND FILMOGRAPHIES - AFRICAN DIASPORA

Biographical Dictionaries

5965. Bogle, Donald. Blacks in American Films and
Television: An Encyclopedia. New York: Garland Publishing,
1988. 510p.

5966. Mapp, Edward. Directory of Blacks in the Performing
Arts. 2nd ed. Metuchen, NJ: Scarecrow Press, 1990. 612p.
(Orig. 1978)

Bibliographies

5967. Black & Third Cinema: a film & television bibliography.
London: BFI Education, 1989. 200p.

5968. Hyatt, Marshall, ed. The Afro-American Cinematic
Experience: An Annotated Bibliography and Filmography.
Wilmington, Del.: Scholarly Research Inc., 1983. 260p.

5969. Powers, Anne. Blacks in American Movies: A Selected
Bibliography. Metuchen, NJ: Scarecrow Press, 1974. 157p.

5970. Woll, Allen L., and Randall M. Miller. "Afro-Americans."
In Ethnic and Racial Images in American Film and Television:
Historical Essays and Bibliography. New York: Garland
Publishing, 1987, pp. 39-177. The first part of this section
is an essay on the black image in film (pp. 39-120) and the
second an unnannotated bibliography (pp. 121-177).

Articles

5971. Fielding, Raymond. "Sixth Bibliographic Survey of
Theses and Dissertations on the Subject of Film Filed at U.S.
Universities, 1916-1981." Journal of the University Film and
Video Association, Vol. 34, No. 1 (Winter 1982): 41-54.

5972. Kaiser, Ernest. "Blacks in the Mass Media: A
Bibliography." Freedomways, Vol. 22, No. 3 (1982). Includes
sections on TV, Film and Theatre.

5973. Kennedy, James H. "The Images of Blacks in Lusophone
Literatures and Cinema: A Research Bibliography." A Current
Bibliography on African Affairs, Vol. 20, No. 1 (1987-88):
5-16. [Brazil]

5974. Leab, Daniel J.   "The Black in Films: An Annotated Bibliography." Journal of Popular Film, Vol. 4, No. 4 (1975): 345-356.

Filmographies and Directories

5975. "The Black in Films." In The Negro Almanac, eds. Harry A. Ploski and James Williams. 4th ed. New York: John Wiley & Sons, 1983, pp. 1185-1210. A brief survey of blacks in American film precedes this extensive filmography.

5976. Black Video Directory: An Authoritative Guide to Black Films and Performance on Video. New York: R.R. Bowker, Jan. 1990. 250p.

5977. The Black Video Guide: your complete home video reference directory. 1985-1986 ed. St. Louis, MO: Video Publications, 1985. 200p.

5978. Black Videos and Films: A Directory. New York: R. R. Bowker, Nov. 1989.

5979. Bogle, Donald. Black Entertainers in Film and Television: An Encyclopedia. New York: Garland, 1988. 510p. Almost two-thirds of this work is given over to synopses of film and television shows in which Blacks either starred or were the sole cast members.

5980. Klotman, Phyllis R. Frame by Frame: A Black Filmography. Bloomington: Indiana University Press, 1979. 720p.

5981. Limbacher, James L. "Blacks on Film: A Selected List..." Journal of Popular Film, Vol. 4 (1975): 358-378.

5982. Noble, Peter, comp. The Cinema and the Negro 1905-1948. London: Sight and Sound, 1948. 21p. (Special Supplement to Sight and Sound. Index Series. No. 14)

5983. Oshana, Maryann. Women of Color: A Filmography of Minority and Third World Women. New York: Garland Publishing, 1985. 338p.

5984. Parish, James Robert, and George H. Hill. Black Action Films: Plots, Critiques, Casts and Credits for More Than 225 Theatrical and Made-for-Television Releases. Jefferson, NC: McFarland & Co., 1989. 385p.

5985. Sharp, Saundra. Black History Film List: 150 Films and Where to Find Them. Los Angeles, CA: Poets Pay Rent Too (P.O. Box 75796, Sanford Station, Los Angeles 90075), 1989. 44p.

5986. Sprecher, Daniel. Guide to Films (16 mm) About Negroes. Alexandria, VA: Serina Press, 1970. 87p.

5987. Weaver, Harold D., Jr. "Black Politics Projected: A Selected Critical Filmography." In Film and Africana Politics. New Brunswick: Rutgers University, between 1972 and 1977. 20p.

TELEVISION/VIDEO BIBLIOGRAPHIES - AFRO-AMERICA

5988. Hill, George. TV Guide on the Black Side: A
Bibliography. Carson, CA: Daystar Publishing Co., 1986.   55p.

5989. _____, and Sylvia Hill. Blacks on Television: A
Selectively Annotated Bibliography. Metuchen, NJ: Scarecrow
Press, 1985. 237p.

5990. _____, and Lorraine Raglin. The African American
Television Experience: A Researcher's Bibliography of
Scholarly Writings. Carson, CA: Daystar Publishing Co., 1986.
55p.

5991. _____. Afro American Video Experience: A
Researcher's Bibliography of Scholarly Writings. Carson, CA:
Daystar Publishing Co., 1986. 40p.

5992. Lam, Errol R., and Kalman S. Szekely. "Blacks in
Television: A Selective, Annotated Bibliography." Journal of
Popular Film and Television, Vol. 14, No. 4 (Winter 1987):
176-183.

Appendix II
Film Resources

ARCHIVES AND RESEARCH CENTERS

5993. Allen, Nancy. <u>Film Study Collections: A Guide to Their</u>
<u>Development and Use</u>. New York: Frederick Ungar Pub., 1979.
194p.

5994. ACADEMY OF MOTION PICTURE ARTS AND SCIENCES - MARGARET
HERRICK LIBRARY - Black American Film History Collection (8949
Wilshire Blvd., Beverly Hills, CA 90211. Tel. 213/278-4313).

5995. New York <u>Amsterdam News</u> (July 23 1977): D3, D5.
Profile of the Black American Film History Collection.

5996. AMERICAN FILM INSTITUTE CENTER FOR ADVANCED FILM
STUDIES - Charles K. Feldman Library (501 Doheny Road, Beverly
Hills, CA 90210. Tel. 213/278-8777).

5997. AMISTAD RESEARCH CENTER (Tilton Hall, Tulane
University, 6823 St. Charles Ave., New Orleans, LA 70118.
Tel. 504/865-5535).

5998. Nielsen, Barbara. "Spotlight: The Amistad Research
Center." <u>American Visions</u> (August 1987): 62-63.

5999. AUDIO-VISUAL INSTITUTE, MINISTRY OF INFORMATION AND
BROADCASTING - National Film Library (P.O. Box 9310, Dar es
Salaam, Tanzania. Tel. 68635/8).

6000. BLACK AMERICAN CINEMA SOCIETY (Western States Black
Research Center, 3617 Montclair St., Los Angeles, CA 90018.
Tel. 213/737-3292). Director: Mayme Clayton. Film archives
of the Western States Black Research Center which maintains
one of the largest collections of vintage black films in the
U.S. Founded 1976.

6001. Williford, Stanley O. "Spotlight: The Western States
Black Research Center." <u>American Visions</u> (April 1987): 62,
64.

6002. BLACK ARTS RESEARCH CENTER (30 Marion St., Nyack, NY
10960. Tel. 914/358-2089). Director: John Gray. Archival
resource center dedicated to the documentation, preservation
and dissemination of the African cultural legacy. Resources
include approx. 500 books and journals, 250 clipping files and
a Black Arts Database consisting of some 30,000 bibliographic
entries. Provides personalized computer searches. Founded
1989.

6003. BRITISH FILM INSTITUTE - National Film Archive (81 Dean
Street, London WIV 6AA. Tel. 01/437 4355).

6004. HATCH-BILLOPS COLLECTION - Archives of Black American
Cultural History (491 Broadway, 7th Fl., New York, NY 10012.
Tel. 212/966-3231). Contains a number of oral history
interviews with African American directors and performers.

6005. INDIANA UNIVERSITY - Black Film Center/Archive (Dept.
of Afro-American Studies, Memorial East M 37, Indiana
University, Bloomington, IN 47405). Director: Phyllis
Klotman. Founded 1983.

6006. "This New Old World of Black Cinema is a Film Buff's
Delight." Black Enterprise, Vol. 16 (August 1985): 124.

6007. LIBRARY OF CONGRESS - Motion Picture, Broadcasting and
Recorded Sound Division (Rm. 236, Madison Building,
Washington, DC 20540. Tel. 202/426-5840). Holdings include
the American Film Institute Collection of Black Films.

6008. Edelman, Rob. "AFI's Black Films." American Film,
Vol. 12 (June 1987): 38-39. Profile of the American Film
Institute's collection of all-black cast feature films held by
the Library of Congress.

6009. MUSEUM OF MODERN ART - Film Study Center (11 West 53rd
St., New York, NY 10019. Tel. 212/956-4212).

6010. NEW YORK PUBLIC LIBRARY - PERFORMING ARTS RESEARCH
CENTER AT LINCOLN CENTER - Billy Rose Theatre Collection (111
Amsterdam Ave., New York, NY 10023. Tel. 212/799-2200). The
particular strength of this collection lies in its thousands
of clipping files.

6011. NEW YORK PUBLIC LIBRARY - SCHOMBURG CENTER FOR RESEARCH
IN BLACK CULTURE - Moving Image and Recorded Sound Division
(515 Lenox Ave., New York, NY 10037. Tel. 212/283-4949).
Curator: James Briggs Murray.

6012. Scrapbooks - Moving Pictures. 4 vols. Collection of
clippings from the Black press covering Black activity in film
from the 1930s to the late 1950s. [Located in Schomburg's
Reference Division, Reading Room 2]

6013. RESEARCH CENTER OF LOS ANGELES - Black Cinema Library

6014. "Black Cinema Expo., '72: Black Cinema Library Research
Center." Ebony (May 1972): 151-154.

6015. SOUTHERN METHODIST UNIVERSITY - SOUTHWESTERN FILM/VIDEO
ARCHIVES - Tyler, Texas Black Film Collection (Dallas, TX
75275(?). Tel. 214/373-3665). Curator: G. William Jones.
14 of the films from this collection have been restored and
are now available for rental from Phoenix Films & Video (468
Park Avenue South, New York, NY 10016. Tel. 212/684-5910).

6016. Carstarphen, Meta G. "Rare Films: The Tyler, Texas
Treasure Trove." American Visions (June 1989): 36-38.

6017. "Early Black Film Collections Found in Texas
Warehouse." Jet (February 27 1984): 24.

6018. Schickel, Richard. "Artifacts of a Lost Culture: A
Texas find quickens interest in black film history." Time
(February 27 1984): 102-103.

6019. "This New Old World of Black Cinema is a Film Buff's
Delight." Black Enterprise, Vol. 16 (August 1985): 124.

6020. UNIVERSITY OF CALIFORNIA, LOS ANGELES - POWELL LIBRARY
- DEPT. OF SPECIAL COLLECTIONS - George P. Johnson Negro Film
Collection. Manuscripts, scrapbooks, and other personal
mementoes of George P. Johnson.

6021. UNIVERSITY OF CALIFORNIA, LOS ANGELES - UCLA Film
Archive (Melnitz Hall, Rm. 1438, Los Angeles, CA 90024. Tel.
213/825-4142).

6022. UNIVERSITY OF SOUTHERN CALIFORNIA - Archives of
Performing Arts (Los Angeles, CA 90007. Tel. 213/743-6058).

FILM SOCIETIES AND ASSOCIATIONS

6023. ASSOCIATION OF BLACK CINEMA (77 Route de la Folie, Fort
de France, Martinique).

6024. ASSOCIATION OF BLACK FILM AND VIDEO WORKSHOPS (Unit
215, 22 Highbury Grove, London N5 2EA. Tel. 01-359 0302).

6025. ASSOCIATION OF BLACK MOTION PICTURE AND TELEVISION
PRODUCERS (c/o Leroy Robinson, Chocolate Chip Productions,
6515 Sunset Blvd., Suite 206, Los Angeles, CA 90028).

6026. ATLANTA AFRICAN FILM SOCIETY (P.O. Box 50319, Atlanta,
GA 30302. Tel. 404/525-1136 or 758-9410).

6027. BLACK AND HISPANIC IMAGES (11-45 47th Ave., Suite 201,
Long Island City, NY 11101. Tel. 718/729-3232). Support
organization. Provides training and equipment for minority
film and video makers.

6028. "New York Black/Latino Media group established."
Independent (April 1988): 8.

6029. BLACK AUDIO FILM COLLECTIVE (89 Ripley Road, London E8
2NH. Tel. 01 254-9536). Members: John Akomfrah, Reece
Auguiste, Eddie George, Lina Goupaul, Avril Johnson and Trevor
Mathison.

6030. BLACK FILM INSTITUTE (University of the District of Columbia, Carnegie Building, 8th St. and Mt. Vernon Pl., NW, Washington, DC 20001). Director: Tony Gittens. Founded 1976.

6031. BLACK FILMMAKERS HALL OF FAME (477-15th St., Suite 200, Oakland, CA 94612. Tel. 415/465-0804). Founded 1974.

6032. Assagai, Mel. "Lights, Camera, Action for Black Moviemakers." Encore American and Worldwide News (April 2 1979): 35-36.

6033. Hillinger, Charles. "Black Film Makers Get Special Place in Oakland." Staten Island Advance [New York] (November 2 1983).

6034. Nicholson, David. "Glitz and Glitter is Only Part of Oakland Hall of Fame Purpose." Black Film Review, Vol. 2, No. 2 (1986): 7-8.

Media Materials

6035. All Together Now: Black Filmmakers Hall of Fame [videorecording]. San Francisco: KPIX-TV, 1979. 25 min. Host, Belva Davis. A look at the sixth annual Oscar Micheaux Awards at the Black Filmmakers Hall of Fame. Includes interviews with Etta Moten and Herb Jeffries who discuss their film careers; an interview with animators Floyd Norman and Leo Sullivan; and statements from actors and actresses attending the event. [Held by the Schomburg Center - Sc Visual VRB-147]

6036. BLACK PRESERVATION FILM COMMITTEE (c/o Paul Robeson Theatre, 40 Green Ave., Brooklyn, NY 11238).

6037. Friedman, Dan. "Preserving and Building: The Black Preservation Film Committee." The National Alliance (July 27 1984): 13.

6038. CEDDO FILM AND VIDEO WORKSHOP (South Tottenham Education and Training Center, Braemer Road, N15 London).

6039. CINEMATECA NACIONAL DE ANGOLA (Caixa Postal 3512, Largo Luther King 4, Luanda, Angola).

6040. EDUCATIONAL VIDEO CENTER (87 Lafayette Street, New York, NY 10013. Tel. 212/219-8129). Multi-racial video workshop for students and youth programs.

6041. Murdock, David. "Younger Views." New York Times/ Supplement--A World of Difference (April 16 1989): 19.

6042. INSTITUTE OF NEW CINEMA ARTISTS (505 Eighth Ave., New York, NY). Director: Cliff Frazier. Devoted to developing young minority talents in film.

6043. Fields, Sidney. "Making Film Makers." New York Daily News (May 28 1970).

6044. Fraser, C. Gerald. "Minority Youths Find Gold in Film, TV and Discs." New York Times (November 28 1979): C19.

6045.   Tapley, Mel.   "Cliff Frazier: Producer of Black Theatre Opportunities."   New York Amsterdam News (August 18 1984): 23.

6046.   INSTITUTO CUBANO DEL ARTE E INDUSTRIA CINEMATOGRAFICOS (ICAIC) (Calle 23 No. 1155 Vedado, Havana, Cuba).

6047.   Salaam, Kalamu ya.   "Film: Cinema as Revolutionary Art."   First World, Vol. 2, No. 2 (1979): 43-46.

6048.   NATIONAL BLACK PROGRAMMING CONSORTIUM (929 Harrison Ave., Suite 104, Columbus, OH 43215.   Tel. 614/299-5355). Executive Director, Mable Haddock.

6049.   OFFICE CINEMATOGRAPHIQUE NATIONAL DU MALI (P.O. Box 197, Bamako, Mali).

6050.   PICTURE THIS (766 1/2 Hayes St., San Francisco, CA 94102.   Tel. 415/864-2941).

6051.   Amato, Mia.   "Media Clips: Black Cinema Group Forms in Bay Area."   The Independent, Vol. 10, No. 2 (March 1987): 2.

6052.   SANKOFA FILM/VIDEO COLLECTIVE (Unit K, 32-34 Gordon House Rd., London NW5 16P.   Tel. 01 485-0848).   Members: Martina Attille, Maureen Blackwood, Isaac Julien, Nadine Marsh-Edwards.

6053.   SOCIETE NATIONALE DE CINEMATOGRAPHIE (104, Rue Carnot, BP 1388, Dakar, Senegal).

6054.   SOCIETE NATIONALE VOLTAIQUE DE CINEMA (B.P. 206, Ouagoudougou, Burkina Faso).

FILM PRODUCTION COMPANIES

6055.   CALPENNY - NIGERIA FILMS LTD. (PO Box 1815, Lagos, Nigeria).   Nigerian production company of Francis Oladele.

6056.   Bekele, Solomon.   "Zur Lage des Films in Nigeria: Interview mit Francis Oladele, Produzent von 'Kongis Ernte' und Direktor der Calpenny Nigeria Films Ltd."   Afrika Heute, Vol. 11 (April 1973): 45.

6057.   Hunter, Frederic.   "Trials and Tribulation. Calpenny's Nigerian Filmmaking."   Christian Science Monitor (October 20 1971): 12.

6058.   CHAMBA ORGANIZATION (230 West 105th St. (2A), New York, NY 10025.   212/864-7350).   Production company of independent filmmaker St. Clair Bourne.

6059.   EYE OF THE STORM PRODUCTIONS (1716 Florida Ave., NW (#2), Washington, D.C. 20009).   Production company of independent filmmaker Michelle Parkerson.

6060.   FILM TWO PRODUCTIONS (736 West End Ave., Suite 1B, New York, NY 10025.   Tel. 212/864-4343).   Production company of independent filmmaker Kathe Sandler.

6061. FORTY ACRES & A MULE FILMWORKS (124 Dekalb Ave., Brooklyn, NY 11217. Tel. 718/624-3703). Spike Lee's production homebase.

6062. Davis, Thulani. "Local Hero. Workin' 40 Acres and a Mule in Brooklyn." American Film (July/August 1989): 26-27.

6063. WILLIAM GREAVES PRODUCTIONS (80 8th Ave., New York, NY 10011. Tel. 212/206-1213).

FILM DISTRIBUTORS

6064. ALTERNATIVE VIDEOS (P.O. Box 270797, Dallas, TX 75227. Tel. 1-800 888-0263). Specializes in Black videos - Classics, Children, Documentaries, Health, Literary Adaptations, Music, Action.

6065. BLACK FILMMAKER FOUNDATION (80 Eighth Ave., Suite 1704, New York, NY 10011. Tel. 212/924-1198). Serves as both an information resource center and distributor for the films of African American independents. Write for catalogue.

6066. Fraser, C. Gerald. "Group celebrates a decade of distributing black films." New York Times (June 7 1989): C20.

6067. Oliver, Denise. "BFF Finds Europe Easy to Please." The Independent (July-August 1982): 15-18.

6068. CINEMA GUILD (1697 Broadway, Rm. 802, New York, NY 10019. Tel. 212/246-5522). Distributes Jackie Shearer's "A Minor Altercation", Sergio Giral's "Bounty Hunter" and "Maluala", and several documentaries by Haiti-Films.

6069. FILMMAKERS LIBRARY (124 E. 40th Street, Suite 901, New York, NY 10016. Tel. 212/808-4980). Distributes Stanley Nelson's documentary "Two Dollars and a Dream" on Black millionairess and entrepreneur Madame C. J. Walker.

6070. FIRST RUN/ICARUS FILMS (153 Waverly Place, 6th Fl., New York, NY 10014. Tel. 212/727-1711 or 800/876-1710). Distributes Madeline Anderson's documentary "I Am Somebody", Spike Lee's "Joe's Bed-Stuy Barbershop" and St. Clair Bourne's "Making 'Do the Right Thing'".

6071. HAITI-FILMS (1398 Flatbush Ave., Brooklyn, NY 11210. Tel. 718/434-8100). Distributes several documentaries on Haiti including the widely acclaimed "Bitter Cane."

6072. MYPHEDUH FILMS (48 Q Street, NE, Washington, DC 20002. Tel. 202/529-0220). Major distributor of African and African American films. Write for catalogue.

6073. NEW YORKER FILMS (16 W. 61st, New York, NY 10023. Tel. 212/247-6110). Leading distributor of African and Caribbean feature films including works by Ousmane Sembene, Ababacar Samb, Desire Ecare, Mahama Johnson Traore, Sarah Maldoror, Euzhan Palcy, Sergio Giral and Sara Gomez as well as one Spike Lee work - "She's Gotta Have It".

6074.   PROUD TO BE... (41 Bowdoin, Cambridge, MA 02138.   Tel.
617/868-8965).   Mail order source for black videos.   Also
sponsors a Black Video Collectors Society.

6075.   Kimmel, Dan.   "Boston Mail-Order Firm Features Vids for
Blacks; 100 tapes in catalog."   _Variety_ (February 8 1989): 47.

6076.   THIRD WORLD NEWSREEL (335 W. 38th Street, 5th Floor,
New York, NY 10018.   Tel. 212/947-9277).   Distributes a large
number of African, Black British, and African American feature
and documentary films.   Write for catalogue.

6077.   WOMEN MAKE MOVIES (Suite 212, 225 Lafayette St., New
York, NY 10012.   Tel. 212/925-0606).   Distributes numerous
films by Black women independents.   Write for catalogue.

BLACK FILM FESTIVALS

6078.   BLACKLIGHT FILM FESTIVAL (10 E. Ontario, Suite 2202,
Chicago, IL 60611.   Tel. 312/988-7091 / FAX 312/988-7092).

6079.   NEWARK BLACK FILM FESTIVAL (c/o The Newark Museum, P.O.
Box 540, Newark, NJ 07101.   Tel. 201/733-6600).

Artist Index

Title Index

Subject Index

Author Index

A

Abdul, Raoul
2924, 4458, 4917, 5455
Abeke
2929
Abo, Klevor
520
Abraham, Arthur
118
Abrantes, Jose Mena
655
Ackermann, Jean Marie
224
Adam, Hussein M.
230
Adams, Janus Ingrid
2434
Adams, Val
3094, 4545, 4756
Adamson, Jimmy
5603
Adelson, Suzanne
3686, 5298
Adler, Renata
1814, 2955
Afum, Ata
791
Agan, Patrick
3847
Agbe-Davies, A. A.
243
Aguolu, Christian C.
5865, 5876
Ahmed, Saleh
964
Ahrold, Kyle
629
Ahua, B.
468, 775, 881-882

Aig-Imoukhuede, Frank
611
Aithnard, K. M.
119
Aitken, Roy E.
1882
Aizicovici, Francine
1130
Ajaga, Mikaila Ishola
607
Ajaye, Franklin
1645, 3405
Ajayi-Bembe, Alex
109
Akinsemoyin, 'Kunle
601
Akudinobi, Jude G.
244
Akue, Miwonvi
651
Alain, Yves
421, 1166, 1362, 1366
Ales, D.
1052
Alexander, Francis W.
1646
Alexander, J. B.
2431, 2435
Alfaro, Hugo R.
1583
Alford, Henry
4098
Ali, Z. S.
110
Allen, Bonnie
1647, 2353, 2588, 2886,
3350, 4247, 4614, 4625,
4806-4807
Allen, Carole Ward
2669
Allen, Harry
2604
Allen, Nancy
5993
Allen, Tom
1242, 2743
Allen, Zita
4943
Allis, T.
3758
Allombert, G.
2442
Allones, F. R. d'
1120
Allou
1295
Alman, Miriam
5862
Almeida, Ayi-Francisco
337
Alpert, Hollis
2947

Bhely-Quenum, Olympe
1329
Bianculli, David
3289
Binet, Jacques
305, 340-343, 864, 872
Bird, Robert S.
4712
Birnbaum, Jesse
3290
Birtha, Rachel Roxanne
2142
Biskind, P.
1461
Bissainthe, Max
5932-5933
Black, Doris
3471, 3631, 4463, 4688,
4864, 4990, 5685
Black, Gregory D.
1733
Black, Stu
5351
Blake, David
5861
Blatchford, R.
1485
Blau, E.
4481
Blauner, Robert
203-204
Bloom, Samuel William
1629
Bloom, Steve
5613
Blume, Mary
2956
Bobo, Jacqueline
1930-1931
Bogle, Donald
1587-1588, 1607, 1662-1666,
1818, 1829, 2670, 2835,
3191, 3338-3339, 3849,
3851, 5175, 5965, 5979
Bohn, William E.
3253
Bollag, Brenda
2618
Bond, Jean Carey
3192
Bondroit, A.
675
Bonds, Frederick W.
1608
Bonneau, Richard
571
Bonner, Lesley
1153

Bonnet, Jean-Claude
1225, 1252
Boone, Ronald Wayne
2223
Borsten, Joan
509
Boseman, K.
2450
Bosseno, Christian
344, 471-472, 928, 1056,
1074, 1253
Bosworth, Patricia
2779
Botombele Ekanga Bokkoga
129, 676
Bottstein, D.
2332
Boughedir, Ferid
226, 305-306, 345-348, 398,
400, 497-498, 533, 553,
575, 585, 595, 633-635,
664, 783, 803, 941, 1003,
1100, 1339, 5963
Bouillon, Jo
3476
Bourdain, G. S.
3486
Bourne, St. Clair
2224-2226, 2239, 2412,
2424, 2545, 2583
Bourne, Stephen
3356, 4675
Bowser, Pearl
1667, 2258, 2437, 2671
Boyar, Burt
3928-3929
Boyar, Jane
3928-3929
Boyd, Herb
1949
Boyer, Peter J.
3647
Brack, Fred
4524
Bradley, B.
5277
Brady, Anna
5941
Brahimi, M.
853
Branch, William B.
3100
Brashler, William
5049
Brasseur, Paule
5874-5875
Brathwaite, Edward
5915

Robinson, Louie (cont.)
3877-3878, 4059, 4066,
4218, 5008-5009, 5473,
5530-5531, 5667, 5730
Robinson, Major
3717
Robles, Roland
3708, 5314, 5643
Rochlin, M.
2893
Roddick, N.
1578
Roeder, B.
3612
Roeser, Steve
3919
Roffman, Peter
1783, 5235
Rogers, Charles E.
2455, 5545
Rohter, Larry
2626
Rollins, Charlemae Hill
3343
Rolot, Christian
384, 661, 667, 670
Ronan, M.
1784
Ropars-Wuilleumier, M. C.
1294
Rose, Phyllis
3480
Rosen, Jay
3130
Rosen, Marjorie
1504
Rosen, Miriam
1184, 1405, 1455, 2400,
3115
Rosenbaum, Ilene
3344
Rosenbaum, Jonathan
5069
Rosenbaum, Ron
2636
Ross, Jacob
185
Ross, Michael E.
2482, 5026
Ross, P.
2385
Rotberg, Robert I.
153
Roth, Daniel
5274
Roth, Morry
3219
Rothenberg, Fred
2489

Rouch, Jean
328-329, 1169
Roundtree, Richard
5255
Rout, Leslie B.
158
Roy, Andre
869
Rubenstein, Hal
4669
Rubine, M.
2937
Rudd, Irving
4570
Rudolph, Ileane
5400
Ruelle, Catherine
318, 465, 830, 854, 891,
936
Rugg, Akua
1492, 1559
Rush, Jeffrey
4436
Rushdie, Salman
1421
Russell, C.
3640
Russell, Charlie L.
217
Russell, Dick
4173, 5043
Russell, Joan C.
1738
Russell, Liz
4880
Ruszkowski, Andre H.
4978
Ruth, Marianne
4805
Ryan, Cate
3806
Ryan, Michael
5577

S

Saada, Nicolas
2553, 2560
Sachs, Albie
142, 735
Safford, T.
974
Said, Abdulkadir N.
79
St. John, Christopher
2855
St. John, Michael
3427, 5693

About the Compiler

JOHN GRAY is a cultural historian specializing in Black culture. He is Director of the Black Arts Research Center, an archival resource center dedicated to the documentation, preservation, and dissemination of the African cultural legacy. His previous publications include *Blacks in Classical Music* (1988), *Àshe, Traditional Religion and Healing in Sub-Saharan Africa and the Diaspora* (1989), and *Black Theatre and Performance: A Pan-African Bibliography* (1990), all published by Greenwood Press.

UNIVERSITY OF RHODE ISLAND LIBRARY

3 1222 00484 543 7

NO LONGER THE PROPERTY
OF THE
UNIVERSITY OF R. I. LIBRARY